# JUMP AT HOME

## MATH WORKSHEETS FOR THE ELEMENTARY CURRICULUM

JOHN MIGHTON

ANANSI

Published in 2004 by
House of Anansi Press Inc.
110 Spadina Avenue, Suite 801
Toronto, ON, M5V 2K4
Tel. 416-363-4343
Fax 416-363-1017
www.anansi.ca

Distributed in Canada by
Publishers Group Canada
250A Carlton Street
Toronto, ON, M5A 2L1
Tel. 416-934-9900
Toll free order numbers:
Tel. 800-663-5714
Fax 800-565-3770

08 07 06 05 04 1 2 3 4 5

Some of the material in this book has previously been published by JUMP.

**Author's Acknowledgements**

In writing the worksheets for this volume, I received an enormous amount of help from JUMP staff and volunteers.

Contributing Authors — Katie Baldwin, James Bambury, Dana Born, Kate Green, Allison Hall, Margaret McClintock, Laura Miggiani, Raegan Mighton, Ravi Negi, and Sudha Shrestha.

Layout Team — Katie Baldwin, James Bambury, Dana Born, Kate Green, Mahbuba Haq, Laura Miggiani, Ravi Negi, Sudha Shrestha, Linda Thai, and Laura Visentin.

Proofing and Editing Team — Katie Baldwin, James Bambury, Nandita Biswas-Mellamphy, the team at Capital One (particularly Andrew Cowan, Geoff Thiessen, Sebastian Grobys, and Yuanhui Lang), Stephen Hong, Imogen Jenkins, Paul Mates, Margaret McClintock, Laura Miggiani, Chloe Mighton, Alex Oehlert, Sindi Sabourin, Jeremy Sills, Oliver Stock, Sayaka Yajima, and Hyun Youk.

Answer Key Team — Katie Baldwin, James Bambury, Dana Born, the team at Capital One (particularly Andrew Cowan, Geoff Thiessen, Sebastian Grobys, and Yuanhui Lang), Stephen Hong, John Lim, Laura Miggiani, Alex Oehlert, Sindi Sabourin, and Hyun Youk.

Support Team — Jon Alexander, Krisztina Benczik, the Fields Institute, Laura Gass, Midori Hyndman, the JUMP Board, Jonathan Kassian, Richard Michael, Lynne Patterson, Philip Spencer, and the teachers, administrators, and support staff at our partner schools.

The following people gave us helpful suggestions and advice — Nicki Boycott, Liam Carmichael, Helen Garland, Ken Scott, and Isaac Stein.

This book, like the JUMP program itself, is made possible by the efforts of the volunteers and staff of JUMP.



**Library and Archives Canada Cataloguing in Publication Data**

Mighton, John, 1957–
JUMP at home — grade 4 : math worksheets for the elementary curriculum / John Mighton.

(JUMP at home workbooks)
ISBN 0-88784-720-X

1. Mathematics — Problems, exercises, etc. — Juvenile literature.
I. Title. II. Series: Mighton, John, 1957– JUMP at home workbooks.

QA139.M554 2004 j510'.76 C2004-906602-1

Cover design: The Bang    Cover photograph: Getty Images    Printed and bound in Canada

Canada Council for the Arts    Conseil des Arts du Canada

*We acknowledge for their financial support of our publishing program the Canada Council for the Arts, the Ontario Arts Council, and the Government of Canada through the Book Publishing Industry Development Program (BPIDP).*

# Contents

## INTRODUCTION

Based on my work with hundreds of elementary students, spanning fifteen years, I am convinced that all children can be led to think mathematically. Even if I am wrong, the results of JUMP suggest that it is worth suspending judgment in individual cases. A parent or teacher who expects a child to fail is almost certain to produce a failure. The method of teaching outlined in this book (or any method, for that matter) is more likely to succeed if it is applied with patience and an open mind.

If you are a parent and you believe that your child is not capable of leaning math, I recommend that you read *The Myth of Ability: Nurturing Mathematical Talent in Every Child*, and consult the JUMP website (at www.jumptutoring.org) for testimonials from teachers who have tried the program and for a report on current research on the program.

You are more likely to help your child if you teach with the following principles in mind:

1) *If a child doesn't understand your explanation, assume there is something lacking in your explanation, not in your child.*

   When a teacher leaves a student behind, it is almost always because they have not taken responsibility for examining the way they teach. I often make mistakes in my lessons: sometimes I will go too fast for a student or skip steps inadvertently. I don't consider myself a natural teacher. I know many teachers who are more charismatic or faster on their feet than I am. But I have had enormous success with students who were thought to be unteachable because if I happen to leave a student behind I always ask myself: What did I do wrong in that lesson? (And I usually find that my mistake is neglecting one of the principles listed below.)

2) *In mathematics, it is always possible to make a step easier.*

   A hundred years ago, researchers in logic discovered that virtually all of the concepts used by working mathematicians could be reduced to one of two extremely basic operations, namely, the operation of counting or the operation of grouping objects into sets. Most people are able to perform both of these operations before they enter kindergarten. It is surprising, therefore, that schools have managed to make mathematics a mystery to so many students.

   A tutor once told me that one of her students, a girl in Grade 4, had refused to let her teach her how to divide. The girl said that the concept of division was much too hard for her and she would never consent to learn it. I suggested the tutor teach division as a kind of counting game. In the next lesson, without telling the girl she was about to learn how to divide, the tutor wrote in succession the numbers 15 and 5. Then she asked the child to count on her fingers by multiples of the second number, until she'd reached the first. After the child had repeated this operation with several other pairs of numbers, the tutor asked her to write down, in each case, the number of fingers she had raised when she stopped counting. For instance,

   15 5 3

   As soon as the student could find the answer to any such question quickly, the tutor wrote, in each example, a division sign between the first and second number, and an equal sign between the second and third.

   $15 \div 5 = 3$

   The student was surprised to find she had learned to divide in 10 minutes. (Of course, the tutor later explained to the student that 15 divided by five is three because you can add 5 three times to get 15: that's what you see when you count on your fingers.)

   In the exercises in the JUMP Workbook we have made an effort to break concepts and skills into steps that children will find easy to master. But the workbooks are far from perfect. Fitting the full curriculum into 300 pages was not an easy task. Some pages are more cramped than we would have liked and some pages do not provide enough practice or preparation. The worksheets are intended as models for parents to improve upon: we hope you will take responsibility for providing your child with warm-up questions and bonus questions (see below for a discussion of how to create these questions), and for filling in any gaps our materials wherever you find them. We have made a serious effort to introduce skills and concepts in small steps and in a coherent order, so a committed parent should have no trouble seeing where they need to create extra questions for practice or where they need to fill in a missing step in the development of an idea.

3) *With a weaker student, the second piece of information almost always drives out the first.*

   When a teacher introduces several pieces of information at the same time, students will often, in trying to comprehend the final item, lose all memory and understanding of the material that came before (even though they may have appeared to understand this material completely as it was being explained). With weaker students, it is always more efficient to introduce one piece of information at a time.

I once observed an intern from teachers college who was trying to teach a boy in a Grade 7 remedial class how to draw mixed fractions. The boy was getting very frustrated as the intern kept asking him to carry out several steps at the same time.

I asked the boy to simply draw a picture showing the number of whole pies in the fraction 2 ½. He drew and shaded two whole pies. I then asked him to draw the number of whole pies in 3 ½, 4 ½ and 5 ½ pies. He was very excited when he completed the work I had assigned him, and I could see that he was making more of an effort to concentrate. I asked him to draw the whole number of pies in 2 ¼, 2 ¾, 3 ¼, 4 ¼, then in 2 ⅓, 2 ⅔, 3 ⅓ pies and so on. (I started with quarters rather than thirds because they are easier to draw.) When the boy could draw the whole number of pies in any mixed fraction, I showed him how to draw the fractional part. Within a few minutes he was able to draw any mixed fraction. If I hadn't broken the skill into two steps (i.e., drawing the number of whole pies then drawing the fractional part) and allowed him to practice each step separately, he might never have learned the concept

As your child or student learns to concentrate and approach the work with real excitement (which generally happens after several months if the early JUMP units are taught properly), you can begin to skip steps when teaching new material, or even challenge your child or student to figure out the steps themselves. But if your child or student ever begins to struggle with this approach, it is best to go back to teaching in small steps.

4) *Before you assign work, verify that your student has the skills needed to complete the work.*

In our school system it is assumed that some students will always be left behind in mathematics. If a teacher is careful to break skills and concepts into steps that every student can understand, this needn't happen. (JUMP has demonstrated this in dozens of classrooms.)

Before you assign a question from one of the JUMP workbooks you should verify that your child or student is prepared to answer the question without your help (or with minimal help). On most worksheets, only one or two new concepts or skills are introduced, so you should find it easy to verify that your child or student can answer the question. The worksheets are intended as final tests that you can give when you are certain your child or student understands the material.

Always give a short diagnostic quiz before you allow your child or student to work on a worksheet. In general, a quiz should consist of four or five questions similar to the ones on the worksheet. The quizzes will help you identify whether your child or student needs an extra review before you move on.

5) *Raise the bar incrementally.*

Any successes I have had with weaker students are almost entirely due to a technique I use which is, as a teacher once said about the JUMP method, "not exactly rocket science." When a student has mastered a skill or concept, I simply raise the bar slightly by challenging them to answer a question that is only incrementally more difficult or complex than the questions I had previously assigned. I always make sure, when the student succeeds in meeting my challenge, that they know I am impressed. Sometimes I will even pretend I'm about to faint (students always laugh at this) or I will say "You got that question but you'll never get the next one." Students become very excited when they succeed in meeting a series of graduated challenges. And their excitement allows them to focus their attention enough to make the leaps I have described in *The Myth of Ability*. As I am not a psychologist I can't say exactly why the method of teaching used in JUMP has such a remarkable effect on children who have trouble learning. But I am certain that the thrill of success and the intense mental effort required to remember complex rules and carry out long chains of computation and inference helps open new pathways in their brains.

In designing the JUMP workbooks, I have made an effort to introduce only one or two skills per page, so you should find it easy to create bonus questions: just change the numbers in an existing question or add an extra element to a problem on a worksheet. For instance, if your child has just learned how to add a pair of three-digit numbers, you might ask your child to add a pair of four- or five-digit numbers. If you become excited when you assign more challenging questions, you will find that even a child who previously had trouble focusing will race to finish their work so they can answer a bonus question.

6) *Repetition and practice are essential.*

Even mathematicians need constant practice to consolidate and remember skills and concepts. I discuss this point in more detail below.

7) *Praise is essential.*

We've found the JUMP program works best when teachers give their students a great deal of encouragement. Because the lessons are laid out in steps that any student can master, you'll find that you won't be giving false encouragement. (This is one of the reasons kids love the program so much: for many, it's a thrill to be doing well at math.)

We haven't observed a student yet – even among scores of remedial students – who couldn't learn math. When it is taught in steps, math is actually the subject in which children with attention deficits and learning disabilities can most easily succeed, and thereby develop the confidence and cognitive abilities they need to do well in other subjects. Rather than being the hardest subject, math can be the engine of learning for delayed students. This is one of JUMP's cornerstone beliefs. If you disagree with this tenet, please reconsider your decision to use JUMP. Our program will only be fully effective if you embrace the philosophy.

## JUMP and Current Philosophies of Education

Perhaps the most exciting development in JUMP this year has been the growth of our partnerships with dedicated educators. A number of teachers and administrators in Canada and the United States have demonstrated that schools can easily implement JUMP in classrooms or in after-school programs, without stretching their resources. (See our website for information about our partnerships.)

While JUMP has found many advocates among teachers, principals and parents, the program has met with skepticism or outright resistance from many educational theorists and administrators at boards and ministries of education. Some educators, who are not aware of the full scope of the program, seem to think that JUMP is a throw back to the kind of rote learning of mathematics that schools have tried to move away from. *The Myth of Ability* may have reinforced this opinion, as it advocates that students be led in small, rigorously laid out steps in the early part of a math program. In *The Myth of Ability*, I focused almost exclusively on the more mechanical side of JUMP program because I believe that teachers must be trained to break skills and concepts into the most basic atoms of perception and understanding. But I was also careful to stress that students are expected to work more independently and to discover and explain concepts on their own as they progress through the JUMP program. (Our new, grade-specific workbooks show the scope of the program more fully: our enriched units, which are still in development, will complete the program by introducing young children to deeper mathematical investigations.)

I believe the educational debates that have raged for so many years in our schools have been so divisive and unfruitful because the basic terms of the debate have never been properly established. In particular, the word "conceptual" has come to be defined too narrowly in math education, in a way that does not fully reflect the actual practice of mathematics or the way children (particularly children with learning disabilities) acquire concepts.

In my opinion, every side in the "math wars" has something of value to contribute to the debate. I have learned a great deal from educational philosophies that are different from my own, and I have tried to incorporate a variety of styles and approaches in new JUMP materials. But the various parties in the wars will never have a fruitful debate about best practices in math education, until educators examine the nature of mathematical concepts more carefully (after all, who wouldn't want to teach math "conceptually?").

I will examine four leading ideas about what it means to teach mathematics "conceptually." These ideas have been adopted by many educators in North America and in some school boards have attained the status of dogmas. Each of the dogmas is based on a reasonable idea. The ideas only become dogmas when they are held up as the only way to teach mathematics. When educators try to block JUMP in schools or claim that the program represents a return to rote learning, it is usually because they are not aware or the full scope of the program or because they have adopted one of the dogmas uncritically in an extreme way.

## Four Dogmas of Contemporary Education

### The First Dogma

A teacher who neglects to use concrete materials (such as pattern-blocks or fraction-strips) whenever they introduce a mathematical idea is not teaching "conceptually."

Pattern blocks, base-10 materials, and fraction strips, as well as three-dimensional shapes such as prisms and pyramids, are very useful tools for teaching mathematics. These materials (or diagrams representing these materials) are used extensively in the JUMP workbooks. There are topics in elementary mathematics, such as the classification of three-dimensional solids, which are hard to teach without a physical model. But many topics in elementary mathematics can also be taught more abstractly, even at the same time as they are introduced with concrete materials. Young children, as early as Grade 1 or 2, can be taught to appreciate math as an algebraic or symbolic game that they can play sitting at their desks with no other tools than a pencil and a piece of paper. Dozens of JUMP implementations have shown that children enjoy and benefit from playing with mathematical rules and operations, even when those rules and operations are taught with scarcely any reference to a physical model (see *The Myth of Ability* and the JUMP website for details of research on this topic).

The idea that mathematical concepts must always be introduced with blocks and rods and pies, and that there is never any point in allowing children to play with mathematical symbols without having spent years playing with the things those symbols represent, is widespread in our schools. The idea is based on a serious misunderstanding of the nature of mathematical concepts and of the way mathematics connects to the world. The idea is also based on dubious assumptions about the way children acquire mathematical concepts.

Mathematics was invented for practical purposes: for counting sheep and measuring fields. In the modern world, through its applications in science and industry, mathematics is the source of virtually all of our material comforts. But mathematics became effective as a material tool primarily by becoming an abstract language in its own right. Over the centuries, mathematicians have more often made discoveries by seeking to understand the logic or internal structure of that language, than by following their intuitions about the physical world. The nineteenth century mathematicians who discovered the laws of curved space did not intend to launch a revolution in the physical sciences, as happened when Einstein applied their ideas in the twentieth century. They simply wanted to make the axioms of geometry a little more concise. Richard Feynman, one of the great physicists of last century, once said: "I find it quite amazing that it is possible to predict what will happen by mathematics, which is simply following rules which really have nothing to do with the original thing."

Einstein's famous equation $E = mc^2$ is clearly an abstract or symbolic representation of a physical law. But the floor plan of a house is also a symbolic representation: the floor plan is a set of lines drawn on flat paper that bears little resemblance to the three dimensional house it represents. Similarly, the calculation a carpenter makes to determine how many nails are needed to build the house is entirely different from the act of counting out the nails. This is something we have lost sight of in our schools: mathematics, even in its most practical applications, in carpentry or finance or computer science, is fundamentally a game of inventing and manipulating symbols. And mathematical symbols, and the operations by which they are combined, are very different from the things they represent.

To understand this point, it helps to consider the operation of adding fractions. The operation is based on two rules:

i) If the denominators of a pair of fractions are the same, you add the fractions by adding the numerators (keeping the denominator the same).

ii) To make the denominators of a pair of fractions the same, you may multiply or divide the denominator of either fraction by any number as long as you do the same thing to the numerator.

These two rules have various physical representations: you can show children how the rules work by cutting up pieces of pie or by lining up fraction strips. But you can also teach children to add fractions without ever showing them a physical model of a fraction.

Of course I don't advocate that children be taught mathematics without concrete materials. The JUMP workbooks are filled with exercises that show students how mathematical rules are embodied in physical models. But it is important to notice that the rules listed above don't make any mention of pies or blocks or fraction strips. Everything you need to know to perform the operation of adding fractions is given in the rules. And the rules are simple enough that virtually any eight year old can learn to apply them flawlessly in a matter of weeks (this has been demonstrated conclusively in dozens of JUMP pilots). By focusing exclusively on models we have lost sight of how utterly easy it is for children to learn the individual steps of an operation (such as the addition of fractions) when those steps are isolated and taught one at a time.

An employee of a board of education once told me that research has proven that children should not be taught any operations with fractions until Grade 7. I'm not sure how research proved this, but I suspect that the research was based on fairly narrow assumptions about what children are capable of learning and on a limited understanding of the nature of mathematical concepts.

Contrary to current "research," I believe that we should introduce kids to the symbolic game of mathematics at an early age. I can think of six reasons for doing so, which I give below.

NOTE: The Fractions Unit is the only unit I have developed to date that is designed solely to introduce kids to math as a symbolic or algebraic game. The JUMP Workbooks (3 to 6) were developed for other purposes: they cover the regular elementary curriculum, so they introduce mathematical concepts in a fairly standard way, usually with concrete materials, although some sections provide enriched exercises or extra practice in following mathematical rules and operations. Eventually JUMP will develop enriched units that will allow kids explore the symbolic side of math in more depth.)

1) We underestimate children by assuming that they will only enjoy learning concepts that have obvious physical models or applications. While I wouldn't discourage a teacher from serving pieces of pie or pizza to their class to illustrate a point about fractions, this is not the only way to get kids interested in math. Children will happily play a game with numbers or mathematical symbols, even if it has no obvious connection to the everyday world, as long as the game presents a series of interesting challenges, has clear rules and outcomes, and the person playing the game has a good chance of winning. Children are born to solve puzzles: in my experience, they are completely happy at school if they are allowed to exercise their minds and to show off to a caring adult. What children hate most is failure. They generally find mathematical rules and operations boring only because those things are often poorly taught, without passion, in a manner that produces very few winners.

2) Children acquire new languages more readily than adults. Mathematics itself is a kind of language, with its own rules and grammatical structures. Why not let them children become fluent in the language of mathematics at an age when they are most ready to learn it? (Several JUMP instructors have noticed that Grade 1 and 2 students often learn the JUMP Fractions Unit as quickly as or more quickly than children who are much older).

3) Many fundamental mathematical concepts are not embodied in any concrete model. As early as Grade 7 students encounter concepts and operations that have no physical interpretation.

   Operations with negative numbers were first introduced in mathematics as a means for solving equations. For centuries, mathematicians multiplied negative numbers without knowing how to make sense of the operation. Leonard Euler, the greatest mathematician of the 1700s, said that negative multiplication shouldn't be allowed because it was senseless.

   It's easy to see why a negative number times a positive number is a negative number. For instance, negative three times positive two is negative six: if you have a debt of three dollars and you double your debt, you end up with a debt of six dollars. But why should a negative times a negative equal positive? As it turns out, there is no physical model or explanation for this rule.

   If the rule "A negative times a negative is a positive" has no physical interpretation, then why should we accept it as a rule of mathematics? And how is it that a rule with no physical interpretation has proven to be so useful in physics and in other sciences? Mathematicians only found the answer to the first question in the 1800s. The second question remains a mystery.

   To understand why a negative times a negative is a positive, it helps to look at the axioms of mathematics that govern the addition and multiplication of positive numbers. If you add the numbers three and five and then multiply the sum by two, the result is sixteen. But you get exactly the same result if you multiply three by two and five by two and then add the products:

$$(3 + 5) \times 2 = 3 \times 2 + 5 \times 2$$

   Sums and products of positive numbers always satisfy this simple equivalence (which is called the law of distribution). In the 1800s, mathematicians realized that if the law of distribution is to hold for negative numbers, then a negative times a negative must be a defined as a positive: otherwise the law produces nonsense (i.e., if you define a negative times a negative as a negative you can easily prove, using the distributive law, that the sum of any two negative numbers is zero).

   This is an example of what I meant when I said that mathematicians are more often led by the internal logic of mathematics than by physical intuition. Because negative numbers had proven to be so useful for solving problems, mathematicians decided to extend the distributive law (that holds for positive numbers) to negative numbers. But then they were forced to define negative multiplication in a particular way. The rule for negative multiplication has found countless applications in the physical world, even though there is no physical reason why it should work! This is one of the great mysteries of mathematics: how do rules that have no straightforward connection to the world (and that are arrived at by following the internal logic of mathematics) end up having such unreasonable effectiveness?

   I always thought that I was a bit of an idiot in high school for not understanding negative multiplication (and even worse, the multiplication of complex or imaginary numbers). My teachers often implied that the rules for these operations had models or explanations, but I was never able to understand those explanations. If my teachers had told me that math is a powerful symbolic language in its own right, and that the world of our everyday experience is described by a tiny fragment of that language (as I later learned in university) I believe

I would have found math somewhat easier and more interesting. The results of JUMP we have shown that young children have no fear of the symbolic side of mathematics: they are much more open minded, and more fascinated by patterns and puzzles then most adults. If children were taught to excel at the symbolic game of math at an earlier age they wouldn't encounter the problems that most students face in high school.

4) For some time now educators have advocated that we move away from the rote learning of rules and operations. This is a very positive development in education. Students should understand why rules work and how they are connected to the world. But unfortunately, in arguing against rote learning, some educators have set up a false dichotomy between mathematical rules and operations on the one hand and concepts and models on the other.

Not all concepts in mathematics are concrete (as the case of negative multiplication illustrates). And if a rule is taught without reference to a model, it is not necessarily taught in a rote way. Whenever a child sees a pattern in a rule, or applies a rule to a case they have never encountered, they are doing math conceptually, even if they haven't consulted a model in their work (and even if they haven't discovered the rule themselves). The fact that children should also be taught to see the connection between the rule and the model doesn't take away from my point.

I read in an educational journal recently that when a child uses a rule to find an answer to a problem, the child isn't thinking. I was surprised to learn this, as most of the work I did as a graduate student consisted in following rules. Many of the rules I learned in graduate school were so deep I doubt I could have discovered their applications on my own (especially not in the five and a half years it took me to get my masters and doctorate). But I was always proud of myself whenever I managed to use one of those rules to solve a problem that wasn't exactly like the examples my professors had worked out on the board. Every time I used a rule to solve a problem I hadn't seen before, I had the distinct impression that I was thinking. I find it hard to believe now that this was all an illusion!

Many teachers and educators have trouble recognizing that there is thought involved in following rules, because they are convinced that students must discover mathematical concepts in order to understand them (I will discuss this point below ) and because they believe that "conceptual" always means "having a model" or "being taught from a model." I recently showed an influential educator the results of a JUMP pilot that I was very proud of: after a month of instruction, an entire Grade 3 class that I taught (including several slow learners) had scored over 90% on a Grade 7 test on operations with fractions. On seeing the tests the educator said they made her blood boil. I explained that many children had shown remarkable improvements in confidence and concentration after completing the unit. I also pointed out that the regular JUMP workbooks also teach the connection between the operation and the model: the Fractions Unit is just a brief excursion into the symbolic world of math. But I don't think she heard anything I said. I expect she was so upset because I wasn't supposed to be teaching fractions without models in Grade 3. This episode (and many other recent encounters) showed me the extent to which educators have come to associate mathematical concepts with concrete materials.

I recently came across the following question on a Grade 7 entrance exam for a school for gifted children:

If $a \lozenge b = a \times b + 3$, what does $4 \lozenge 5$ equal?

Most educators would probably say that this is a very good "conceptual" question for Grade 7 students. To solve the problem a student must see which symbols change and which ones remain the same on either side of the equal sign in the left hand equation. The letters a and b appear on both sides of the equal sign, but on the left hand side they are multiplied (then added to the number 3): once a student notices this they can see that the solution to the problem is $4 \times 5 + 3 = 23$. The ability to see patterns of this sort in an equation and to see what changes and what stays the same on either side of an equal sign are essential skills in algebra.

When I teach the JUMP Fractions Unit, I start by showing students how to add a pairs of fractions with the same denominators: you add the numerators of the fractions while keeping the denominator the same. But then, without further explanation, I ask students how they would add three fractions with the same denominator: in other words, I ask:

If $\frac{1}{4} + \frac{1}{4} = \frac{2}{4}$, what does $\frac{1}{4} + \frac{1}{4} + \frac{1}{4}$ equal?

The logical structure of this question is very similar to the question from the enriched entrance exam: to find the answer, students have to notice that the number 4 remains unchanged in the denominators of the fractions and the numbers in the numerators are combined by addition. In my opinion, the question is "conceptual" in much that same that the way the question on the entrance exam is conceptual. Yet the educator whose blood boiled when she saw the Fractions Unit undoubtedly assumed that, because I hadn't used manipulatives in teaching the unit, I was teaching in a rote way.

The exercises in the JUMP Fractions Unit contain a good deal of subtle conceptual work of the sort found in the example above: in virtually every question, students are required to see what changes and what stays the same in an equation, to recognize and generalize patterns, to follow chains of inference and to extend rules to new cases (for many students, it is the first time they have ever been motivated to direct their attention to these sorts of things at school). But because the questions in the Fractions Unit are not generally formulated in terms of pie diagrams and fraction strips, many educators have had trouble seeing any value in the Fractions Unit.

5) It can take a great deal of time (relative to the amount of learning that takes place) to conduct a lesson with manipulatives. While it is important that students receive some lessons with manipulatives, students often learn as much mathematics from drawing a simple picture as they do from playing with a manipulative. In mathematics, the ability to draw a picture or create a model in which only the essential features of a problem are represented is an essential skill.

Lessons with manipulatives must be very carefully designed to ensure that every student is engaged and none are left behind. In some of the inner city classes I have observed, I have seen children spend more time arguing over who had what colour of block or who had more blocks than they spent concentrating on the lesson. Students need to be confident, focused and motivated to do effective work with manipulatives. In JUMP we begin with the Fractions Unit (in which students are expected to work independently with pencil and paper) to allow students to develop the confidence and focus required for work with manipulatives.

If a teacher aims to engage all of the students (not just the ones who are more advanced than their peers), and if children must be confident and attentive to learn, then it seems obvious that the teacher must start a math program by assigning work that every student can complete without the help of their peers. When students work in groups with manipulatives, it is often hard to verify that every student has understood the lesson. The JUMP Fractions Unit is designed to allow teachers to identify and help students who need remediation immediately, so that every student gains the confidence they need to do more independent work.

6) Concrete materials do not, as is widely believed, display their interpretations on their surface. You can't simply hand out a set of manipulatives to a group of children and expect the majority to use them to derive efficient rules and operations. Children usually need a great deal of guidance in order to deduce anything significant from playing with concrete materials.

The mathematical "opaqueness" of concrete materials was demonstrated quite strikingly by a recent anthropological discovery. Scientists found a tribe that has been catching and sharing great quantities of fish since prehistoric times, but the members of the tribe can't say exactly how many fish they've caught when there are more than two fish in a net. This shows quite clearly that mathematical concepts don't suddenly spring into a person's mind when you slap a concrete material (like a fish) in their hands. Efficient rules and operations often take civilizations centuries to develop. So it's not surprising that children need lots of practice with rules and operations, even if they have spent an enormous amount of time playing with blocks and rods.

The line between abstract and concrete thought is often rather fuzzy: even the simplest manipulatives and models do not provide transparent representations of mathematical concepts. I once saw kids in a remedial class reduced to tears when their teacher tried to introduce the operation of addition using base-10 materials. When I showed the children how to add (and how to subtract, multiply and divide) by counting up on their fingers, they were able to perform the operations instantly. In my experience the hand is the most effective (and cheapest) manipulative for students who have serious learning difficulties. When children perform operations by counting or skip counting on their fingers, they get a sense of the positions of the numbers in their body. I've yet to meet a child, even as early as Grade 1, who couldn't do all of the operations required for the Grade 7 Fractions Unit on their fingers.

(Of course children should eventually be weaned off of using their fingers: the JUMP manuals contain a number mental math tricks to help children learn their number facts. And base-10 materials are very useful tools for teaching arithmetical operations to students who are confident and focused enough to use the materials. But in the early phases of a math program, I would recommend teaching weaker students who need to catch up to perform basic operations on their fingers.)

I believe students would cover far more material in a year if we could find a better balance between symbolic and concrete work in our curriculum. Finding this balance may prove difficult, however, as schools are being pushed by educational experts to include more manipulatives in their mathematics programs. And increasingly, the research that "proves" that manipulatives are effective is being funded (directly or indirectly) by companies that sell textbooks and manipulatives. This is a rather alarming trend in education, particularly as research in math education is not scientific and is sometimes based on poor experimental designs and on rather startling leaps of logic.

### The Second Dogma

A student who only partially understands a mathematical rule or concept, and who can't always apply the concept or extend it to new cases consistently, understands nothing.

In the days when students were taught operations almost entirely by rote, the majority only partially understood the operations. Some educators who observed this state of affairs concluded that partial knowledge in mathematics is, in itself, always a bad thing. Rather than simply advocating that people be taught why operations work as well as how they are performed, these educators took the position that if you teach a student how to perform an operation without first teaching all of the concepts underlying the operation (or allowing the student to discover the operation) then you will prevent the student from ever learning those concepts properly in the future. This conclusion, however, is not supported by the actual practice of mathematics. Far from being bad, partial knowledge is the daily bread of every practising mathematician.

Mathematicians usually start their research by trying to master a small or artificially restricted area of knowledge. Often they will play with simplified systems of rules and operations, even before they have devised a physical model for the rules. Ideas seldom arrive full blown in mathematics: even after a mathematician discovers a new rule or operation, it can take generations before the rule is fully understood. And often it is the relentless practice with the rule, more than any physical intuition, that allows for the emergence of complete understanding. As one of the great mathematicians of the twentieth century, John von Neumann, said, understanding mathematics is largely a matter of getting used to things.

If we applied the standards and methods that are now used to teach children in elementary schools to graduate students in universities, very few students would ever complete their degrees. Children need to be given more practice using rules (so that they can "get used to" and gain a complete understanding of the rules) and they need more guidance when they fail to discover rules by themselves. Rules and concepts are often hard to separate: even in cases where the distinction is clear, the mastery of rules can help induce the understanding of concepts as much as the understanding of concepts supports the mastery of rules.

For a more complete discussion of this point, we need to look at a dogma that is a close cousin to the idea that partial knowledge is always bad, namely . . .

### The Third Dogma

Children have definite stages of cognitive development in mathematics that can be precisely defined and accurately diagnosed and that must always be taken account of in introducing concepts. A child who can't explain a concept fully or extend the concept to new cases is not developmentally ready to be introduced to the concept. Any effort to introduce a child to a concept before they are ready understand the concept in its entirety (or to discover the concept by themselves) is a violation of a child's right to be taught at their developmental level.

This dogma has done inestimable damage in remedial classes and to weaker students in general. I have worked with many Grade 6 and 7 students who were held back at a Grade 1 or 2 level in math because their teachers didn't think they were cognitively or developmentally ready to learn more advanced material.

Having worked with hundreds of students who have struggled in math, I am convinced that the mind is more plastic than most psychologists and educators would allow (even after the first six years, which is when scientists have shown the brain is extremely plastic). I have seen dramatic changes in attitude and ability in very challenged students even after several weeks of work on the Fractions Unit (see *The Myth of Ability* and the JUMP website for details). In a recent survey, all of the teachers who used the fractions unit for the first time acknowledged afterward that they had underestimated (and in many cases greatly underestimated) the abilities of their weaker students in ten categories, including enthusiasm, willingness to ask for harder work, ability to keep up with faster students, and ability to remember number facts.

Not long ago, in the 1960s, mathematicians and scientists began to notice a property of natural systems that had been overlooked since the dawn of science: namely that tiny changes of condition, even in stable systems, can have dramatic and often unpredictable effects. From stock markets to storm fronts, systems of any significant degree of complexity exhibit non-linear or chaotic behaviour. If one adds a reagent, one drop at a time, to a chemical solution, nothing may happen at all until, with the addition of a single drop, the whole mixture changes colour. And if, as a saying made current by chaos theory goes, a butterfly flaps its wings over the ocean, it can change the weather over New York.

As the brain is an immensely complicated organ, made up of billions of neurons, it would be surprising if it did not exhibit chaotic behaviour, even in its higher mental functions. Based on my work with children, I am convinced that new abilities can emerge suddenly and dramatically from a series of small conceptual advances, like the chemical solution that changes colour after one last drop of reagent. I have witnessed the same progression in dozens of students: a surprising leap forward, followed by a period where the student appears to have reached the limits of their abilities; then another tiny advance that precipitates another leap. One of my students, who was in a remedial Grade 5 class when he started JUMP, progressed so quickly that by Grade 7 he received a mark of 91% in a regular class (and his teacher told his mother he was now the smartest kid in the class). Another student, who couldn't count by 2s in Grade 6, now regularly teaches herself new material from a difficult academic Grade 9 text.

A teacher will never induce the leaps I have described if they are unwilling to start adding the small drops of knowledge that will cause a student's brain to reorganize itself. If the teacher waits, year after year, until the student is "developmentally ready" to discover or comprehend a concept in its entirety, the student will inevitably become bored and discouraged at being left behind, and the teacher will miss an opportunity to harness the enormous non-linear potential of the brain. This is what happens in far too many remedial classes. And this is why, in JUMP, we teach even the most challenged students to multiply on their fingers by 2s, 3s, and 5s and then launch them into a Grade 7 unit with fractions whose denominators divide by those numbers. Students who complete the unit don't know how to add and subtract every type of fraction, nor do they understand fractions in great depth, but the effect of allowing them to completely master a small domain of knowledge is striking.

If a teacher only teaches concepts that students are ready to understand or explain in their entirety, then the teacher will not be able to use the method of "raising the bar incrementally" that I described earlier and that is the key to JUMP's success with weaker students. In Ontario, students in Grade 3 are not expected to add pairs of numbers with more than three digits: I suppose this is because they are not developmentally ready to add larger numbers and because they haven't spent enough time playing with concrete models of large numbers. But I have seen children in Grade 3 classes jump out of their seats with excitement when I've challenged them to extend the method for adding three-digit numbers to ten-digit numbers.

Whenever I challenge a class to add larger numbers, I start by teaching students who don't know their addition facts how to add one-digit numbers by counting up on their fingers. I make sure that the digits of the numbers I write on the board are relatively small, so that every student has a chance of answering. As I write longer and longer numbers on the board, even the weakest students invariably start waving their hands and shouting "Oh, oh." When they succeed in finding the sum of a pair of ten-digit numbers, they think they've conquered Mt. Everest.

When Grade 3 students use a rule they have learned for adding three-digit numbers to add ten-digit numbers, they are behaving exactly like mathematicians: they see a pattern in a rule and they guess how the rule might work in more complex cases. Children needn't wait until their teacher has purchased the right set of manipulatives or until they are developmentally ready before they can explore their hypotheses.

I still remember the impression left by a lesson my Grade 7 math teacher gave on Fermat's Last Theorem. At the time I barely understood the concept of squares, let alone higher exponents. But I remember feeling that Fermat's Theorem was very deep and mysterious and I remained fascinated with the theorem for the rest of my life.

By insisting that partial knowledge is always bad and that kids must always be taught according to their developmental level, educators risk removing any sense of enchantment from learning. Children would undoubtedly find mathematics and science more interesting if they were introduced to the deepest and most beautiful ideas in those fields at an early age. There are countless fascinating topics in pure and applied mathematics that only require elementary math, and that we needn't wait until high school or university to teach.

To spark children's imaginations, I have given several different lessons on theoretical computer science to students as early as Grade 3 (for details see *The Myth of Ability*). The students were able to complete the tasks I assigned them and they often asked me to extend the lessons. (JUMP is now developing enriched lessons on logic, problem solving, graph theory and topology and on applications of mathematics in biology, chemistry, physics, magic tricks, games, sports, and art.)

I start one of my lessons on computer science by showing students how to draw a picture of a theoretical model of a computer (called a finite state automata). Students then try to figure out what kind of patterns their "computer" will recognize by moving a penny around on their sketch like a counter on a board game. Following a suggestion of my daughter, I once gave kids in a Grade 3 class paper clips to hold their drawings in place on a cardboard folder. Rather than using a penny as a counter, the kids put pairs of fridge magnets on their drawings (one on the front and one on the back) and they used the back magnet to pull the front one around like a cursor. Many of the children mentioned this lesson in their thank you letters to JUMP: even though they only had a partial understanding of finite state automata, in their minds they had made real computers.

Representatives of a school board in Eastern Canada recently observed a JUMP lesson on how computers read binary codes. The lesson culminated in a mind reading trick that kids love. Afterward the teacher was barred from using JUMP in the class because the lesson hadn't been taught "developmentally."

NOTE: While partial knowledge isn't necessarily bad, partial success is. Even when I introduce kids to ideas that they may only partially understand, I make sure that they are able to complete the exercises I give them. (However, if students are more motivated and confident, I will sometimes let them struggle more with an exercise: students eventually need to learn that it's natural to fail on occasion and that solving problems often takes a great deal of trial and error.)

### The Fourth Dogma

If a student is taught how to perform a mathematical operation, rather than discovering the method on their own, they are unlikely to ever understand the concepts underlying the operation.

I recently read a research paper in math education that found that many adults don't know how to multiply or divide large numbers very well and many don't understand the algorithms they were taught for performing those operations. Considering the way math was taught when I went to school, this news didn't surprise me. But the conclusion the authors drew from their observations did. Rather than recommending that schools do a better job teaching operations, the authors claimed their data showed that standard methods for operations should not be emphasized in schools: instead children should be encouraged to develop their own methods of computation.

I certainly agreed with the authors that children should be encouraged to develop various non-standard tricks and "mental math" strategies for computation (and if they fail to discover these strategies they should be taught them). But it's important to bear in mind that entire civilizations failed to discover the idea of zero as a place holder for division. If the Romans were incapable of developing an effective method of division over the course of eight centuries (just try dividing large numbers with Roman Numerals!) it seems a little unrealistic to expect a child to discover their own method in the course of a morning.

The idea that children have to discover an operation to understand it, like many ideas I have encountered in math education, is based on a reasonable idea that has simply been stretched too far. As a teacher I always encourage my students to make discoveries and extend their knowledge to new situations by themselves. But as a mathematician I have a realistic idea what discovery means. I know, from my work as a student and as a researcher, that discoveries in mathematics are almost always made in tiny, painstaking steps.

My best teacher in high-school always had my classmates and me on the edge of our seats during his chemistry lessons. He led the class in steps, always giving us enough guidance to deduce the next step by ourselves. We always felt like we were on the verge of recreating the discoveries of the great chemists. But he didn't expect us to discover the entire periodic table by ourselves. (Of course, if a class is ready to discover the periodic table, then by all means let them discover it: the goal of JUMP is to raise the level of students to the point where they can make interesting discoveries. Also, I would not discourage a teacher from sometimes assigning more difficult, open-ended exercises – as long as students who fail to make discoveries during the exercise are guided through the material afterwards.)

In the present educational climate, teachers will seldom verify that all of their students can perform an operation before they assign work that involves the operation. And students are rarely given enough practice or repetition to learn an operation properly. Students can easily reach Grade 9 now without anyone noticing that they have failed to discover even the most basic facts about numbers.

Educators seem to assume that if a child discovers an operation or a concept they will always find it easy to apply the concept in new situations, and they will be able to recall the concept immediately, even if they haven't had any opportunity to think about it for a year. This certainly does not reflect my experience as a mathematician. I have discovered original (and rather elementary) algorithms in knot theory that I only mastered after months of practice. And if you were to ask me how one of those algorithms works now, I would have to spend several weeks (of hard work) to remember the answer.

(Repetition and practice don't have to be boring. If students are encouraged to discover and extend steps by themselves, if they are made to feel like they are meeting a series of challenges and if they are allowed to apply their knowledge to solve interesting problems, they will happily learn even the most challenging operations.)

JUMP has shown that children in Grade 2 can learn to perform operations with fractions flawlessly in less than a month and that children in Grade 3 will beg to stay for recess for lessons on theoretical computer science. Rather than compelling children to spend so much time attempting to discover rather mundane standard algorithms (or discover inferior versions of their own), why not guide children through the curriculum as quickly and efficiently as possible, and then allow them use the tools they have acquired to explore more substantial and more beautiful mathematics?

JUMP is a fledgling program with very limited resources. It may take years before we find the right balance between concrete and symbolic work, or between guided and independent work. But I think we have demonstrated one fact beyond a shadow of a doubt: it is possible to teach mathematics without leaving children behind. The results of JUMP have shown that we need to reassess current research in math education: in order to be called a "best practice" a new program must do far more than show that, on average, children in the program do a little better in math. No one would ever say, "It was a great day at school today, only one child starved." Any program that claims to be a best practice must now demonstrate that it can take care of every child.

## The Fractions Unit

To prepare your child or student to use this book, you should set aside 40 to 50 minutes a day for three weeks to teach them the material in the JUMP Fractions Unit. You may print individual copies of the unit from the JUMP website at no charge The Fractions Unit has proven to be a remarkably effective tool for instilling a sense of confidence and enthusiasm about mathematics in students. The unit has helped many teachers discover a potential in their students that they might not otherwise have seen. In a recent survey, all of the teachers who used the Fractions Unit for the first time acknowledged afterwards that they had underestimated the abilities of some of their students. (For details of this study, see the JUMP website at www.jumptutoring.org.)

**Note**: Questions that introduce new concepts or skills are marked by a stop sign in the left margin of a worksheet. Take time to teach the new skill or concept before you assign the question.

**Name of month** ______

| Sunday | Monday | Tuesday | Wednesday | Thursday | Friday | Saturday |
|---|---|---|---|---|---|---|
| | | | | | | |
| | | | | | | |
| | | | | | | |
| | | | | | | |
| | | | | | | |

**Name of month** ______

| Sunday | Monday | Tuesday | Wednesday | Thursday | Friday | Saturday |
|---|---|---|---|---|---|---|
| | | | | | | |
| | | | | | | |
| | | | | | | |
| | | | | | | |
| | | | | | | |

**Name of month** ______

| Sunday | Monday | Tuesday | Wednesday | Thursday | Friday | Saturday |
|---|---|---|---|---|---|---|
| | | | | | | |
| | | | | | | |
| | | | | | | |
| | | | | | | |
| | | | | | | |

| 1 | 2 | 3 | 4 | 5 | 6 | 7 | 8 | 9 | 10 |
|---|---|---|---|---|---|---|---|---|---|
| 11 | 12 | 13 | 14 | 15 | 16 | 17 | 18 | 19 | 20 |
| 21 | 22 | 23 | 24 | 25 | 26 | 27 | 28 | 29 | 30 |
| 31 | 32 | 33 | 34 | 35 | 36 | 37 | 38 | 39 | 40 |
| 41 | 42 | 43 | 44 | 45 | 46 | 47 | 48 | 49 | 50 |
| 51 | 52 | 53 | 54 | 55 | 56 | 57 | 58 | 59 | 60 |
| 61 | 62 | 63 | 64 | 65 | 66 | 67 | 68 | 69 | 70 |
| 71 | 72 | 73 | 74 | 75 | 76 | 77 | 78 | 79 | 80 |
| 81 | 82 | 83 | 84 | 85 | 86 | 87 | 88 | 89 | 90 |
| 91 | 92 | 93 | 94 | 95 | 96 | 97 | 98 | 99 | 100 |

| 1 | 2 | 3 | 4 | 5 | 6 | 7 | 8 | 9 | 10 |
|---|---|---|---|---|---|---|---|---|---|
| 11 | 12 | 13 | 14 | 15 | 16 | 17 | 18 | 19 | 20 |
| 21 | 22 | 23 | 24 | 25 | 26 | 27 | 28 | 29 | 30 |
| 31 | 32 | 33 | 34 | 35 | 36 | 37 | 38 | 39 | 40 |
| 41 | 42 | 43 | 44 | 45 | 46 | 47 | 48 | 49 | 50 |
| 51 | 52 | 53 | 54 | 55 | 56 | 57 | 58 | 59 | 60 |
| 61 | 62 | 63 | 64 | 65 | 66 | 67 | 68 | 69 | 70 |
| 71 | 72 | 73 | 74 | 75 | 76 | 77 | 78 | 79 | 80 |
| 81 | 82 | 83 | 84 | 85 | 86 | 87 | 88 | 89 | 90 |
| 91 | 92 | 93 | 94 | 95 | 96 | 97 | 98 | 99 | 100 |

| 1 | 2 | 3 | 4 | 5 | 6 | 7 | 8 | 9 | 10 |
|---|---|---|---|---|---|---|---|---|---|
| 11 | 12 | 13 | 14 | 15 | 16 | 17 | 18 | 19 | 20 |
| 21 | 22 | 23 | 24 | 25 | 26 | 27 | 28 | 29 | 30 |
| 31 | 32 | 33 | 34 | 35 | 36 | 37 | 38 | 39 | 40 |
| 41 | 42 | 43 | 44 | 45 | 46 | 47 | 48 | 49 | 50 |
| 51 | 52 | 53 | 54 | 55 | 56 | 57 | 58 | 59 | 60 |
| 61 | 62 | 63 | 64 | 65 | 66 | 67 | 68 | 69 | 70 |
| 71 | 72 | 73 | 74 | 75 | 76 | 77 | 78 | 79 | 80 |
| 81 | 82 | 83 | 84 | 85 | 86 | 87 | 88 | 89 | 90 |
| 91 | 92 | 93 | 94 | 95 | 96 | 97 | 98 | 99 | 100 |

| 1 | 2 | 3 | 4 | 5 | 6 | 7 | 8 | 9 | 10 |
|---|---|---|---|---|---|---|---|---|---|
| 11 | 12 | 13 | 14 | 15 | 16 | 17 | 18 | 19 | 20 |
| 21 | 22 | 23 | 24 | 25 | 26 | 27 | 28 | 29 | 30 |
| 31 | 32 | 33 | 34 | 35 | 36 | 37 | 38 | 39 | 40 |
| 41 | 42 | 43 | 44 | 45 | 46 | 47 | 48 | 49 | 50 |
| 51 | 52 | 53 | 54 | 55 | 56 | 57 | 58 | 59 | 60 |
| 61 | 62 | 63 | 64 | 65 | 66 | 67 | 68 | 69 | 70 |
| 71 | 72 | 73 | 74 | 75 | 76 | 77 | 78 | 79 | 80 |
| 81 | 82 | 83 | 84 | 85 | 86 | 87 | 88 | 89 | 90 |
| 91 | 92 | 93 | 94 | 95 | 96 | 97 | 98 | 99 | 100 |

PARENT:
Trying to do math without knowing your times tables is like trying to play the piano without knowing the location of the notes on the keyboard. Your students will have difficulty seeing patterns in sequences and charts, solving proportions, finding equivalent fractions, decimals and percents, solving problems etc. if they don't know their tables.

Using the method below, you can teach your students their tables in a week or so. (If you set aside five or ten minutes a day to work with students who need extra help, the pay-off will be enormous.) There is really no reason for your students not to know their tables!

### DAY 1: Counting by 2s, 3s, 4s, and 5s

If you have completed the JUMP Fractions unit you should already know how to count and multiply by 2s, 3s, 4s, and 5s. If you do not know how to count by these numbers you should memorize the hands:

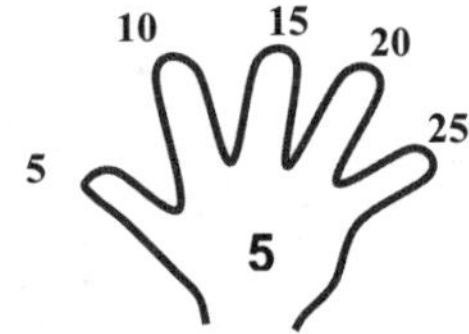


If you know how to count by 2s, 3s, 4s, and 5s, then you can multiply by any combination of these numbers. For instance, to find the product of 3 × 2, count by 2s until you have raised 3 fingers:

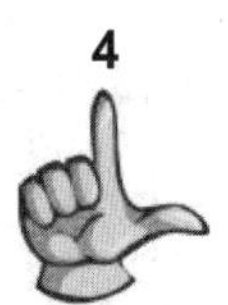

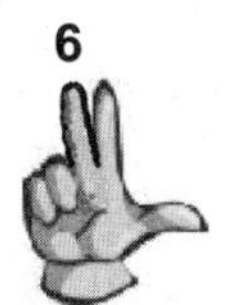


**3 × 2 = 6**

### DAY 2: The 9 Times Table

The numbers you say when you count by 9s are called the **multiples** of 9 (0 is also a multiple of 9). The first ten multiples of 9 (after 0) are 9, 18, 27, 36, 45, 54, 63, 72, 81, and 90. What happens when you add the digits of any of these multiples of 9 (such as 1 + 8 or 6 + 3)? The sum is always 9!

Here is another useful fact about the 9 times table: Multiply 9 by any number between 1 and 10 and look at the tens digit of the product. The tens digit is always one less than the number you multiplied by:

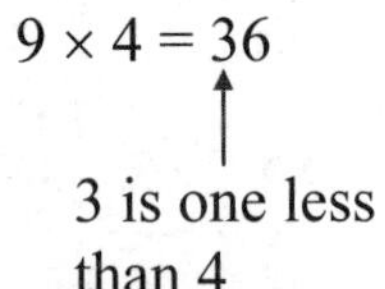

$9 \times 4 = 36$ — 3 is one less than 4

$9 \times 8 = 72$ — 7 is one less than 8

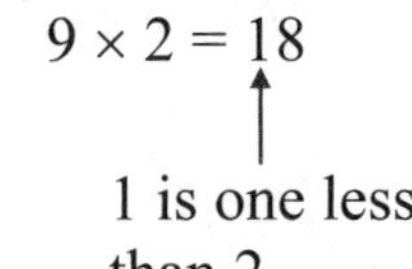

$9 \times 2 = 18$ — 1 is one less than 2

You can find the product of 9 and any number by using the two facts given above. For example, to find 9 × 7, follow these steps:

Step 1: $9 \times 7 =$ __ __

Subtract 1 from the number you are multiplying by 9: **7 – 1 = 6**

$9 \times 7 =$ 6 __

Now you know the tens digit of the product.

Step 2: $9 \times 7 = \underline{6}\ \underline{\ \ }$

These two digits add to 9.

$9 \times 7 = \underline{6}\ \underline{3}$

So the missing digit is 9 – 6 = **3**.

(You can do the subtraction on your fingers if necessary.)

Practise these two steps for all of the products of 9: 9 × 2, 9 × 3, 9 × 4, and so on.

**DAY 3: The 8 Times Table**

There are two patterns in the digits of the 8 times table. Knowing these patterns will help you remember how to count by 8s.

Step 1: You can find the ones digit of the first five multiples of 8, by starting at 8 and counting backwards by 2s.

8
6
4
2
0

Step 2: You can find the tens digit of the first five multiples of 8, by starting at 0 and counting up by 1s.

08
16
24
32
40

(Of course you do not need to write the 0 in front of the 8 for the product 1 × 8.)

Step 3: You can find the ones digit of the next five multiples of 8 by repeating step 1.

8
6
4
2
0

Step 4: You can find the remaining tens digits by starting at 4 and counting by 1s.

48
56
64
72
80

Practise writing the multiples of 8 (up to 80) until you have memorized the complete list. Knowing the patterns in the digits of the multiples of 8 will help you memorize the list very quickly. Then you will know how to multiply by 8.

$8 \times 6 = 48$

Count by 8 until you have 6 fingers up: 8, 16, 24, 32, 40, 48.

### DAY 4: The 6 Times Table

If you have learned the 8 and 9 times tables, then you already know $6 \times 9$ and $6 \times 8$.

And if you know how to multiply by 5 up to $5 \times 5$, then you also know how to multiply by 6 up to $6 \times 5$! That is because you can always calculate 6 times a number by calculating 5 times the number and then adding the number itself to the result. The pictures below show how this works for $6 \times 4$:

6 × 4 — 5 × 4 — plus one more 4

5 fours — plus one more 4

$$6 \times 4 = \overbrace{4 + 4 + 4 + 4 + 4}^{\text{5 fours}} + 4$$

$$\mathbf{6} \times 4 = \mathbf{5} \times 4 + 4 = 20 + 4 = 24$$

Similarly: $\mathbf{6} \times 2 = \mathbf{5} \times 2 + 2$; $\mathbf{6} \times 3 = \mathbf{5} \times 3 + 3$; $\mathbf{6} \times 5 = \mathbf{5} \times 5 + 5$.

Knowing this, you only need to memorize 2 facts:

$\mathbf{6 \times 6 = 36}$ $\mathbf{6 \times 7 = 42}$

Or, if you know $6 \times 5$, you can find $6 \times 6$ by calculating $6 \times 5 + 6$.

### DAY 5: The 7 Times Table

If you have learned the 6, 8, and 9 times tables, then you already know $6 \times 7$, $8 \times 7$, and $9 \times 7$.

And since you also already know $1 \times 7 = 7$, you only need to memorize 5 facts:

$\mathbf{2 \times 7 = 14}$ $\mathbf{3 \times 7 = 21}$ $\mathbf{4 \times 7 = 28}$ $\mathbf{5 \times 7 = 35}$ $\mathbf{7 \times 7 = 49}$

If you are able to memorize your own phone number, then you can easily memorize these 5 facts!

NOTE: You can use doubling to help you learn the facts above: 4 is double 2, so $4 \times 7$ (28) is double $2 \times 7$ (14); 6 is double 3, so $6 \times 7$ (42) is double $3 \times 7$ (21).

---

Try this test every day until you have learned your times tables.

| | | | |
|---|---|---|---|
| 1. $3 \times 5 =$ _____ | 2. $8 \times 4 =$ _____ | 3. $9 \times 3 =$ _____ | 4. $4 \times 5 =$ _____ |
| 5. $2 \times 3 =$ _____ | 6. $4 \times 2 =$ _____ | 7. $8 \times 1 =$ _____ | 8. $6 \times 6 =$ _____ |
| 9. $9 \times 7 =$ _____ | 10. $7 \times 7 =$ _____ | 11. $5 \times 8 =$ _____ | 12. $2 \times 6 =$ _____ |
| 13. $6 \times 4 =$ _____ | 14. $7 \times 3 =$ _____ | 15. $4 \times 9 =$ _____ | 16. $2 \times 9 =$ _____ |
| 17. $9 \times 9 =$ _____ | 18. $3 \times 4 =$ _____ | 19. $6 \times 8 =$ _____ | 20. $7 \times 5 =$ _____ |
| 21. $9 \times 5 =$ _____ | 22. $5 \times 6 =$ _____ | 23. $6 \times 3 =$ _____ | 24. $7 \times 1 =$ _____ |
| 25. $8 \times 3 =$ _____ | 26. $9 \times 6 =$ _____ | 27. $4 \times 7 =$ _____ | 28. $3 \times 3 =$ _____ |
| 29. $8 \times 7 =$ _____ | 30. $1 \times 5 =$ _____ | 31. $7 \times 6 =$ _____ | 32. $2 \times 8 =$ _____ |

# Tangram

A **tangram** is an ancient Chinese puzzle. The tangram is a square cut into seven pieces called tans.

Make a copy of the tangram square and, very carefully, cut along the edges:

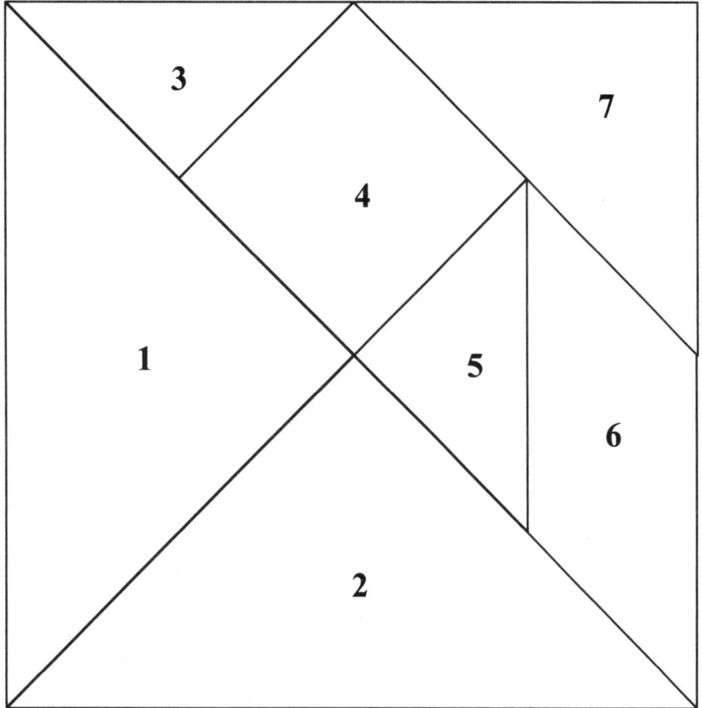


REMEMBER: A shape with 5 sides is a **pentagon** and a shape with 6 sides is a **hexagon**.

# Pattern Blocks

Triangles

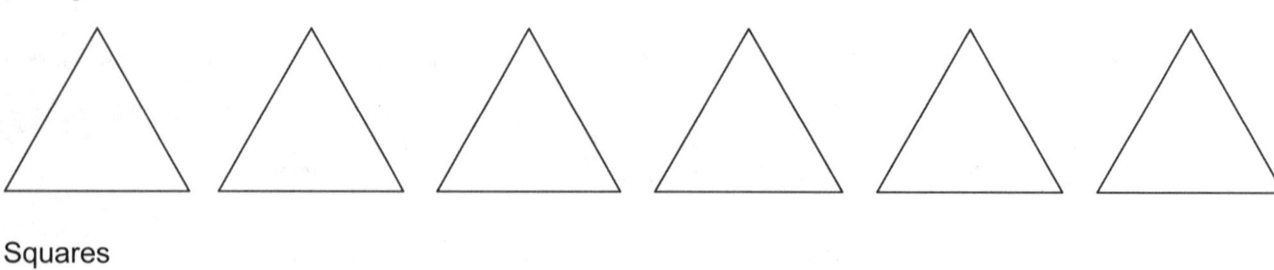

Squares

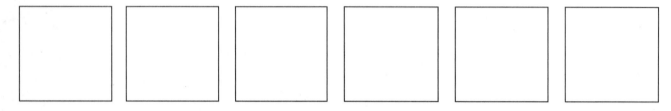

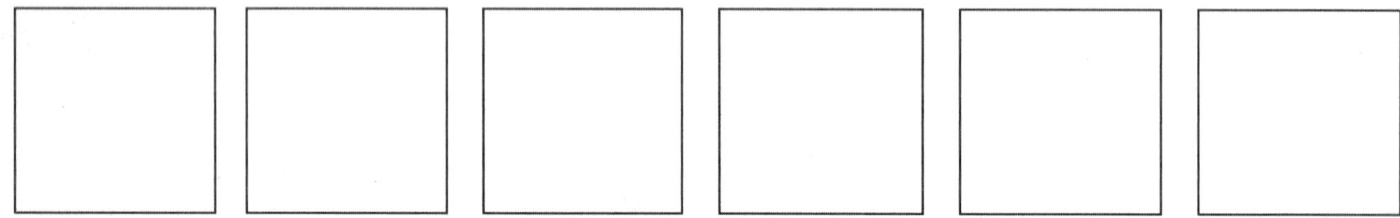

Rhombuses

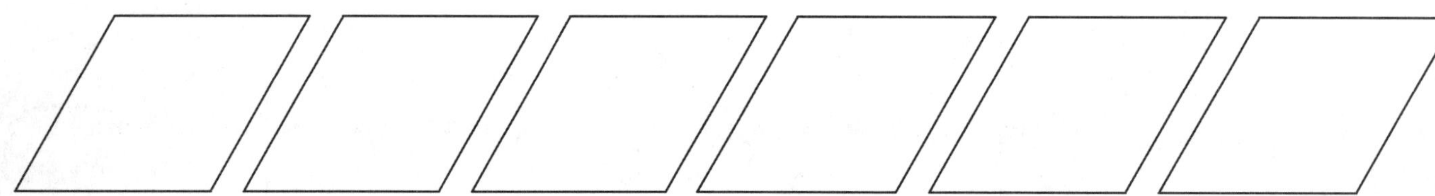

Trapezoids

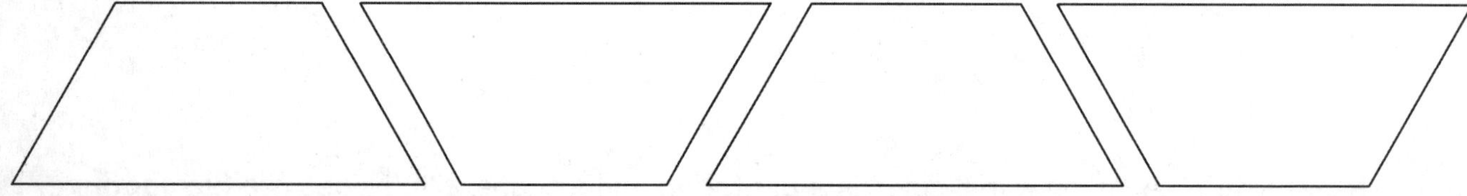

Hexagons

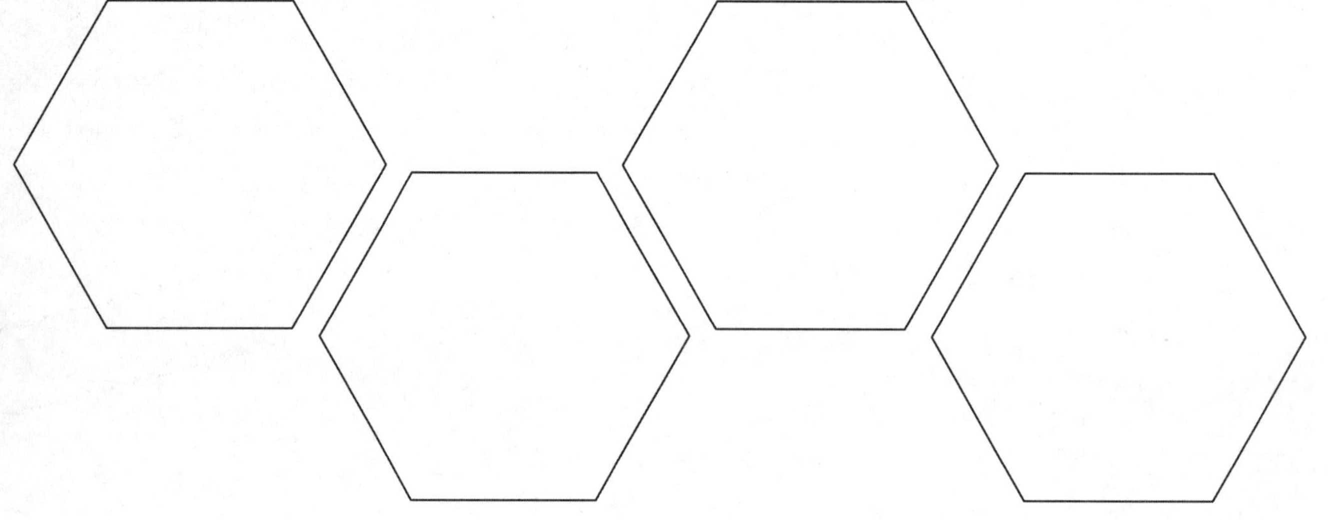

# Pyramid Nets



Use these nets to make your own solid shapes. Trace, cut, fold, and glue these nets for **pyramids**.

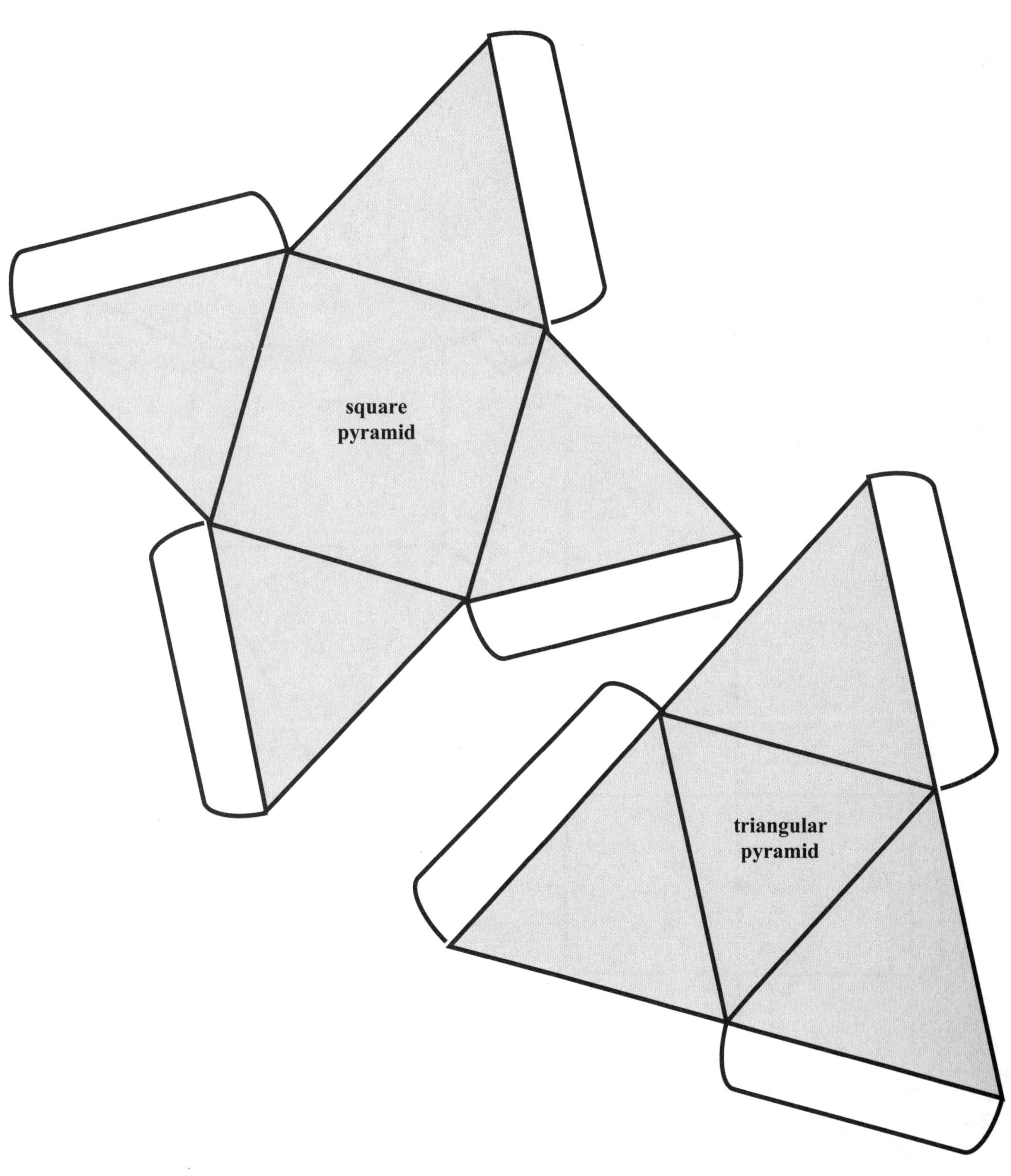

## Prism Nets

Use these nets to make your own solid shapes. Trace, cut, fold, and glue these nets to make **prisms**.

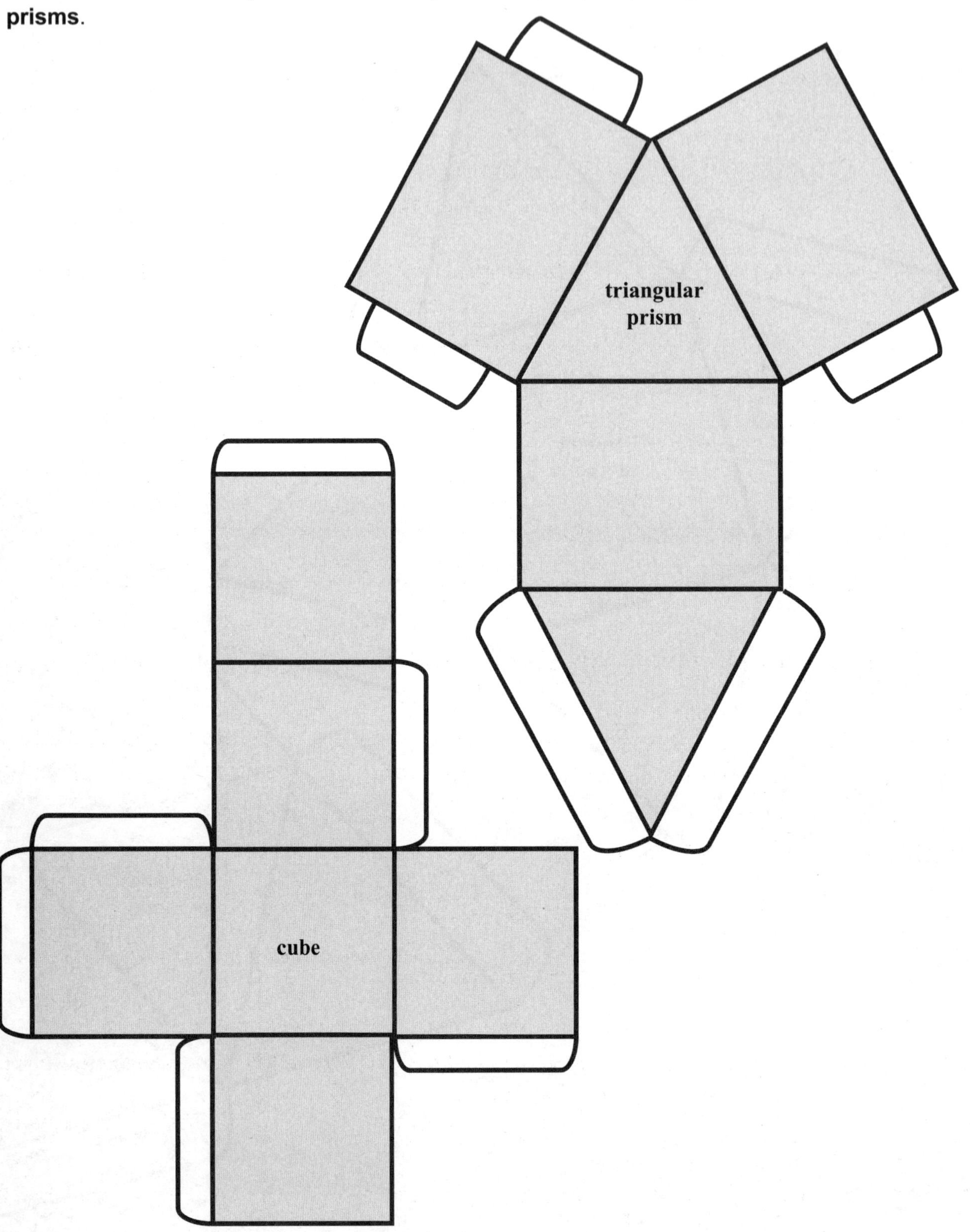

# PA4-1: Counting

What number added to 6 gives 9? $6 + \boxed{?} = 9$

Anne finds the answer using a **number line**. She puts her finger on 6 and counts the number of spaces between 6 and 9:

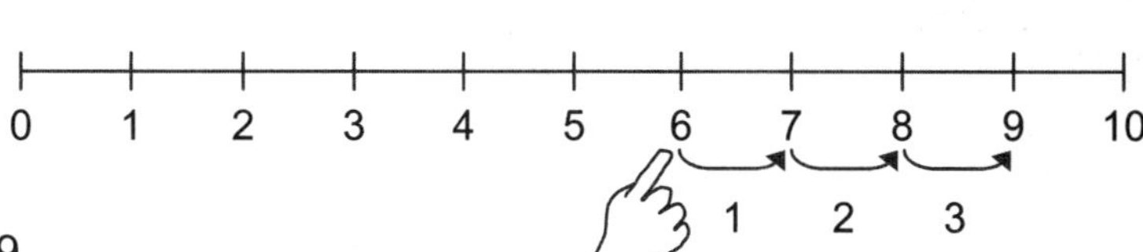


She counts 3 spaces, so: $6 + \boxed{3} = 9$

and: 9 is 3 **more than** 6

and: 3 is called the **difference** between 9 and 6

---

1. Use the following number line to find the **difference** between the two numbers. Write your answer in each box.

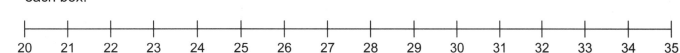

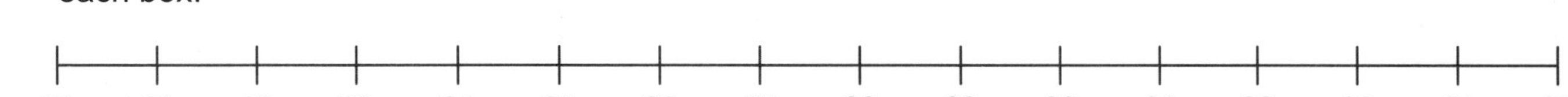


a) $23 + \square = 25$ b) $22 + \square = 26$ c) $24 + \square = 27$

d) $\square + 22 = 24$ e) $23 + \square = 30$ f) $\square + 28 = 31$

g) $\square + 23 = 32$ h) $21 + \square = 29$ i) $22 + \square = 32$

2. Use the following number line to find the **difference** between the two numbers. Write your answer in each circle.

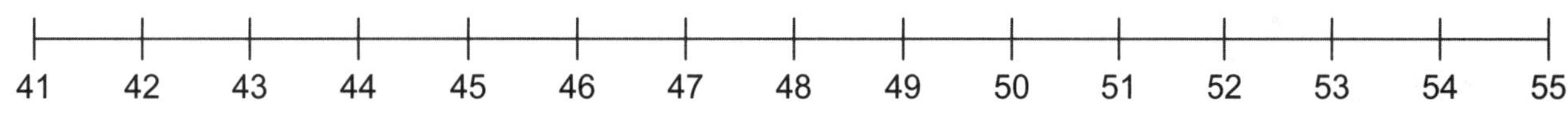


a) 42 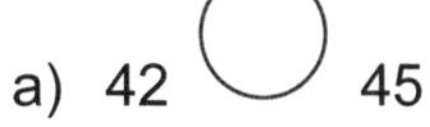 45 b) 43  47 c) 51 ◯ 54 d) 44 ◯ 51

e) 42 ◯ 44 f) 49 ◯ 53 g) 47 ◯ 48 h) 45 ◯ 49

3. Fill in the missing numbers. (HINT: Use the number lines to find the **difference** between the smaller and the larger number.)

a) 25 is __2__ more than 23 b) 30 is __3__ more than 27 c) 53 is __7__ more than 46

d) 32 is _____ more than 29 e) 28 is _____ more than 25 f) 26 is __1__ more than 25

g) 50 is _____ more than 49 h) 47 is _____ more than 43 i) 53 is _____ more than 48

Helen finds the **difference** between 15 and 12 by counting on her fingers. She says "12" with her fist closed, then counts to 15, raising one finger at a time:

13

When she says "15," she has raised 3 fingers. So the difference or "gap" between 12 and 15 is 3.

---

4. Count the gap between the numbers. Write your answer in the circle (if you know your subtraction facts, you may find the answer without counting).

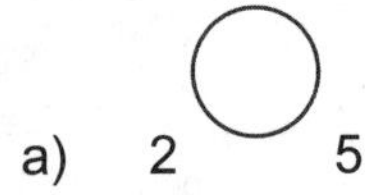

| | | | |
|---|---|---|---|
| a) 2 ◯ 5 | b) 3 ◯ 8 | c) 6 ◯ 8 | d) 4 ◯ 9 |
| e) 12 ◯ 16 | f) 13 ◯ 17 | g) 21 ◯ 26 | h) 37 ◯ 39 |
| i) 26 ◯ 29 | j) 32 ◯ 37 | k) 24 ◯ 29 | l) 44 ◯ 47 |
| m) 51 ◯ 55 | n) 46 ◯ 49 | o) 28 ◯ 32 | p) 34 ◯ 39 |
| q) 89 ◯ 91 | r) 62 ◯ 71 | s) 87 ◯ 89 | t) 59 ◯ 63 |

BONUS:

| | | | |
|---|---|---|---|
| u) 96 ◯ 101 | v) 79 ◯ 83 | w) 98 ◯ 104 | x) 117 ◯ 122 |
| y) 219 ◯ 223 | z) 146 ◯ 151 | aa) 99 ◯ 108 | bb) 99 ◯ 107 |

ACTIVITY:

5. On a separate piece of paper, draw a picture to show how you can use a number line to find the difference between two numbers.

# PA4-2: Preparation for Increasing Sequences

What number is 4 **more than** 16? (Or, what is 16 + 4?)

Alissa finds the answer by counting on her fingers. She says "16" with her fist closed, then counts up from 16 until she has raised 4 fingers:

16 17 18 19 20

The number 20 is 4 **more than** 16.

---

1. Add the number in the circle to the number beside it. Write your answer in each blank.

a) 5 (4) ______ b) 8 (2) ______ c) 7 (3) ______ d) 3 (4) ______

e) 17 (5) ______ f) 18 (4) ______ g) 14 (8) ______ h) 19 (6) ______

i) 30 (8) ______ j) 27 (9) ______ k) 34 (7) ______ l) 32 (5) ______

BONUS:

m) 67 (2) ______ n) 85 (5) ______ o) 42 (3) ______ p) 68 (4) ______

q) 54 (6) ______ r) 63 (5) ______ s) 98 (4) ______ t) 93 (8) ______

2. Fill in the missing numbers.

a) ______ is 4 more than 6 b) ______ is 6 more than 5 c) ______ is 5 more than 7

d) ______ is 1 more than 19 e) ______ is 6 more than 34 f) ______ is 5 more than 18

g) ______ is 8 more than 29 h) ______ is 7 more than 24 i) ______ is 8 more than 37

ACTIVITY:

3. On a separate piece of paper, draw a picture to show how you could use a number line to find what number is 5 more than 8.

# PA4-3: Increasing Sequences

Angel wants to continue the number pattern: 6 , 8 , 10 , 12 , ?
She finds the **difference** between the first two numbers by counting on her fingers. She says "6" with her fist closed and counts until she reaches 8:

She has raised 2 fingers so the difference between 6 and 8 is 2.

(2) 6 , 8 , 10 , 12 , ?

By counting on her fingers, Angel finds that the difference between the other numbers in the pattern is also 2. So, the pattern was made by adding 2.

(2) (2) (2) 6 , 8 , 10 , 12 , ?

To continue the pattern, Angel adds 2 to the last number in the sequence. She says "12" with her fist closed and counts until she has raised 2 fingers:

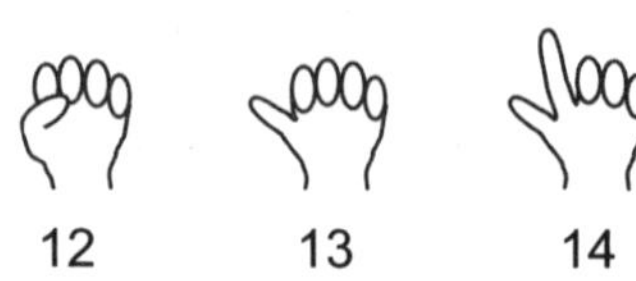


(2) (2) (2) (2) 6 , 8 , 10 , 12 , 14

---

1. Extend the following patterns. NOTE: It is important to start by finding the gap between the numbers.

a) 1 ◯ 3 ◯ 5 ◯ ___ ◯ ___ ◯ ___

b) 0 ◯ 2 ◯ 4 ◯ ___ ◯ ___ ◯ ___

c) 3 ◯ 7 ◯ 11 ◯ ___ ◯ ___ ◯ ___

d) 2 ◯ 6 ◯ 10 ◯ ___ ◯ ___ ◯ ___

e) 1 ◯ 4 ◯ 7 , ___ , ___ , ___

f) 5 ◯ 9 ◯ 13 , ___ , ___ , ___

BONUS:

2. Extend the patterns.

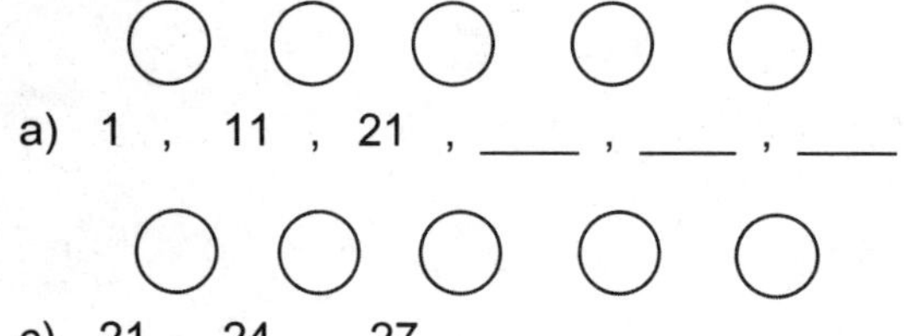

a) 1 , 11 , 21 , ___ , ___ , ___

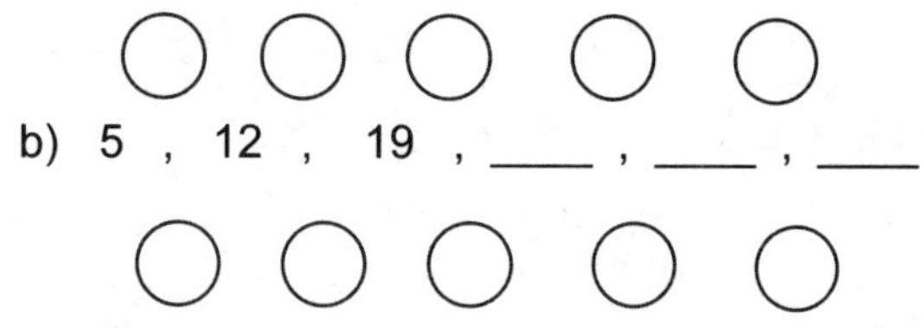

b) 5 , 12 , 19 , ___ , ___ , ___

◯ ◯ ◯ ◯ ◯

c) 21 , 24 , 27 , ___ , ___ , ___

◯ ◯ ◯ ◯ ◯

d) 86 , 88 , 90 , ___ , ___ , ___

Use increasing sequences to solve these problems.

3. Mary reads 5 pages of her book each night. Last night she was on page 72. What page will she reach tonight? tomorrow night?

4. Jane is training for the track meet. She runs 12 blocks on Monday. Each day she runs 4 blocks further than the day before. How far does she run on Tuesday? on Wednesday?

   On what day of the week will she run 28 blocks?

# PA4-4: Counting Backwards



What number **subtracted** from 8 gives 5? $8 - \boxed{?} = 5$

Mary finds the answer using a **number line**.

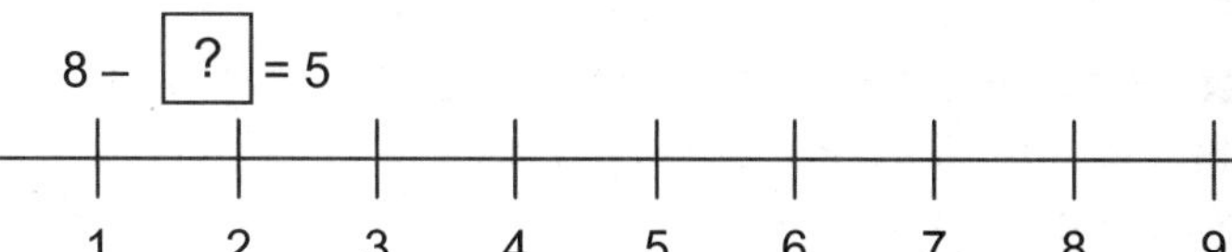


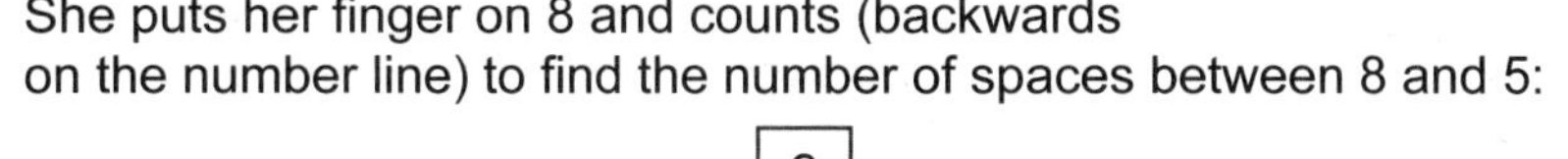

She puts her finger on 8 and counts (backwards on the number line) to find the number of spaces between 8 and 5:

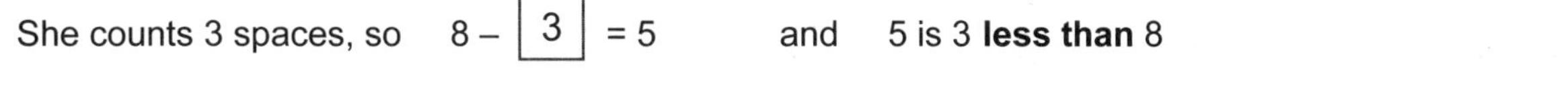

She counts 3 spaces, so $8 - \boxed{3} = 5$ and 5 is 3 **less than** 8

1. Use the number line to find the **difference** between the two numbers. Write your answer in the box.

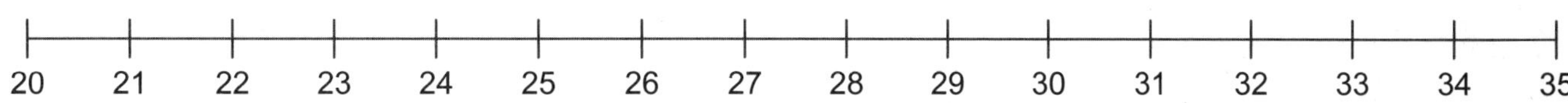


a) 27 – ☐ = 24 b) 26 – ☐ = 23 c) 29 – ☐ = 27

d) 25 – ☐ = 21 e) 28 – ☐ = 24 f) 30 – ☐ = 25

g) 32 – ☐ = 29 h) 35 – ☐ = 34 i) 30 – ☐ = 24

2. What number must you **subtract** from the bigger number to get the smaller number? Write your answer in each circle (with a minus sign, as shown in the first question).

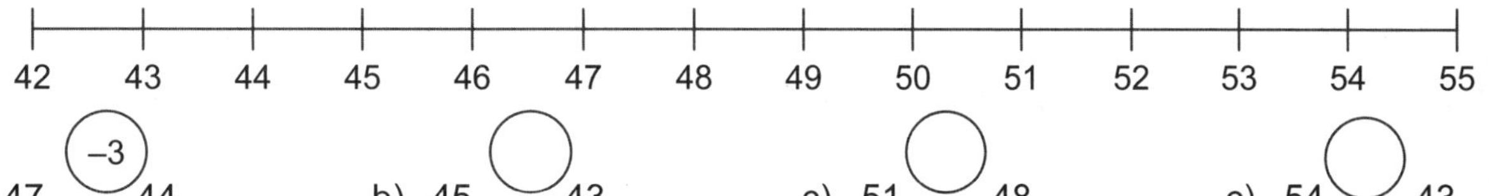


a) 47 (–3) 44 b) 45 ◯ 43 c) 51 ◯ 48 c) 54 ◯ 43

d) 48 ◯ 41 e) 49 ◯ 44 f) 54 ◯ 47 g) 52 ◯ 43

BONUS:

3. Fill in the missing numbers.

a) 47 is ____ less than 50 b) 51 is ____ less than 55 c) 46 is ____ less than 51

d) 49 is ____ less than 51 e) 48 is ____ less than 54 f) 45 is ____ less than 52

g) 44 is ____ less than 49 h) 43 is ____ less than 51 i) 52 is ____ less than 55

What number must you **subtract** from 22 to get 18?

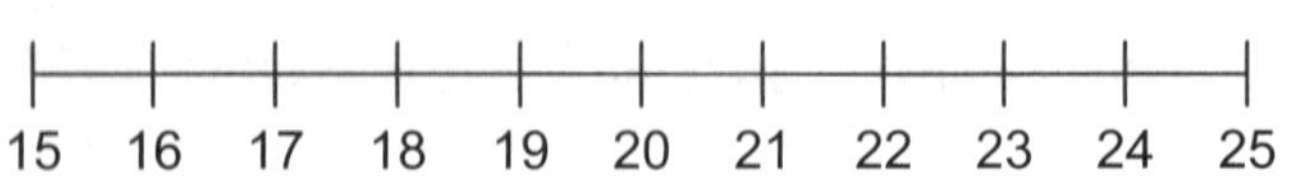


Dana finds the answer by counting backwards on her fingers.
She uses the number line to help.
Dana has raised 4 fingers. So, 4 subtracted from 22 gives 18.

If you do not know how to count backwards from 25 to 15, practise using the number line. Then cover up the number line and answer the questions below by counting backwards on your fingers.

---

4. What number must you **subtract** from the greater number to get the lesser number? REMEMBER: Find the answer by counting backwards on your fingers. If you know your subtraction facts, you can write the answer directly.

a) 23 (−3) 20 b) 24 ◯ 19 c) 21 ◯ 16 d) 22 ◯ 15

e) 24 ◯ 17 f) 19 ◯ 16 g) 23 ◯ 17 h) 25 ◯ 19

5. Practise counting backwards from 45 to 35 using the number line. Then, cover up the number line and find the gap between the numbers by counting backwards on your fingers.

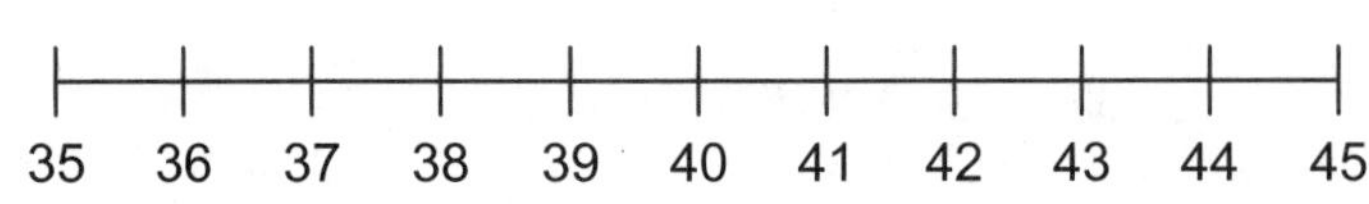


a) 42 (−4) 38 b) 41 ◯ 39 c) 42 ◯ 37 d) 38 ◯ 37

e) 41 ◯ 37 f) 40 ◯ 36 g) 42 ◯ 35 h) 43 ◯ 35

6. Find the gap between the numbers by counting backwards on your fingers (or by using your subtraction facts).

a) 86 ◯ 81 b) 58 ◯ 52 c) 50 ◯ 48 d) 80 ◯ 78

e) 52 ◯ 47 f) 67 ◯ 63 g) 45 ◯ 36 h) 62 ◯ 56

i) 58 ◯ 51 j) 101 ◯ 97 k) 82 ◯ 76 l) 97 ◯ 89

NOTE:
Do not move on until you can find the gap between pairs of numbers by subtracting or counting backwards. You will not be able to extend or describe patterns if you cannot find the gap between pairs of numbers.

# PA4-5: Decreasing Sequences

What number is 3 less than 9? (Or, what is 9 – 3?)
Keitha finds the answer by counting on her fingers. She says 9 with her fist closed and counts backwards until she has raised 3 fingers:
The number 6 is 3 **less than** 9.

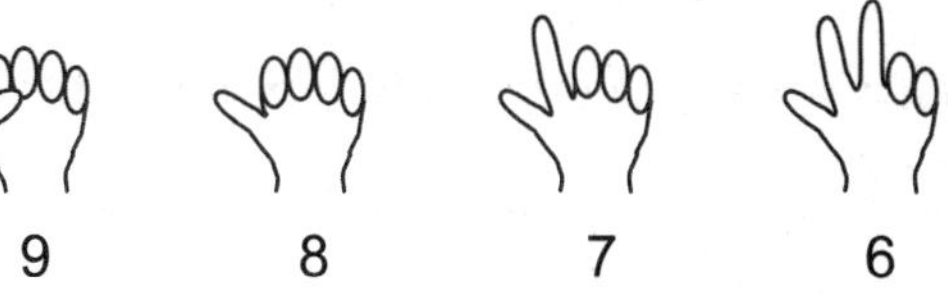


---

1. Subtract the number in the circle from the number beside it. Write your answer in each blank.

a) 3 (−2) _____ b) 12 (−3) _____ c) 8 (−4) _____ d) 9 (−1) _____

e) 8 (−5) _____ f) 10 (−4) _____ g) 5 (−1) _____ h) 9 (−2) _____

BONUS:

i) 28 (−4) _____ j) 35 (−6) _____ k) 57 (−8) _____ l) 62 (−4) _____

2. Fill in the missing numbers.

a) _____ is 4 less than 7 b) _____ is 2 less than 9 c) _____ is 3 less than 8

d) _____ is 5 less than 17 e) _____ is 4 less than 20 f) _____ is 6 less than 25

g) _____ is 7 less than 28 h) _____ is 4 less than 32 i) _____ is 5 less than 40

3. Extend the following **decreasing** patterns. NOTE: It is important to start by finding the gap between the numbers.

Example:

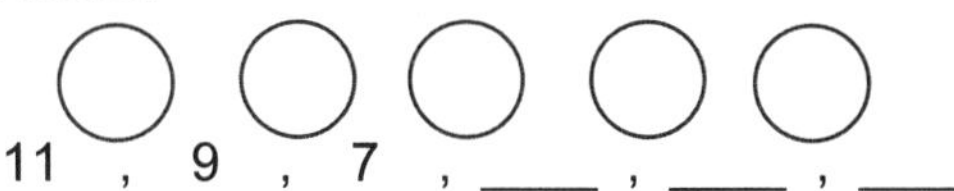

11 , 9 , 7 , _____ , _____ , _____

Step 1:

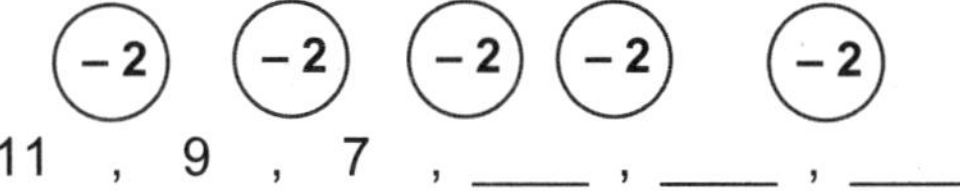


11 , 9 , 7 , _____ , _____ , _____

Step 2:

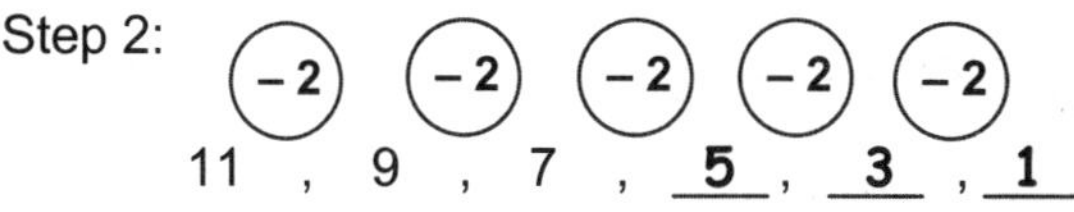


11 , 9 , 7 , **5** , **3** , **1**

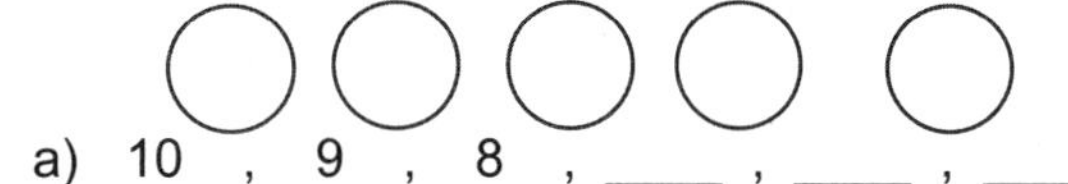

a) 10 , 9 , 8 , _____ , _____ , _____

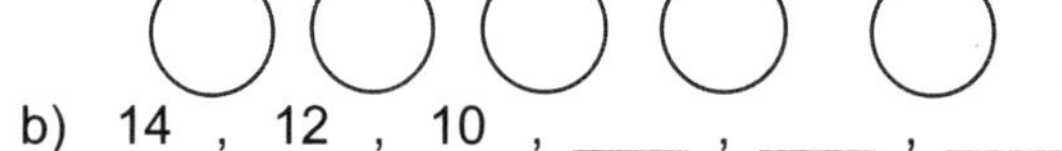

b) 14 , 12 , 10 , _____ , _____ , _____

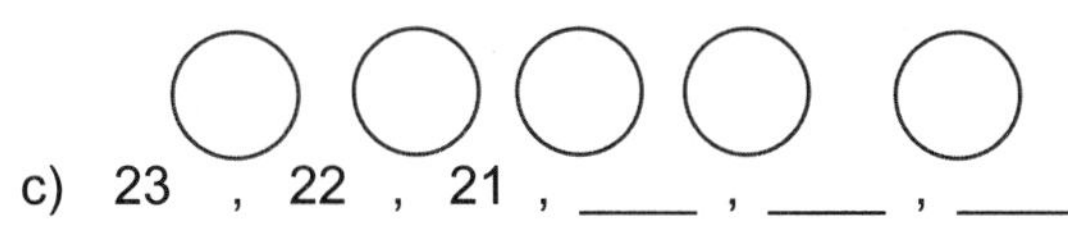

c) 23 , 22 , 21 , _____ , _____ , _____

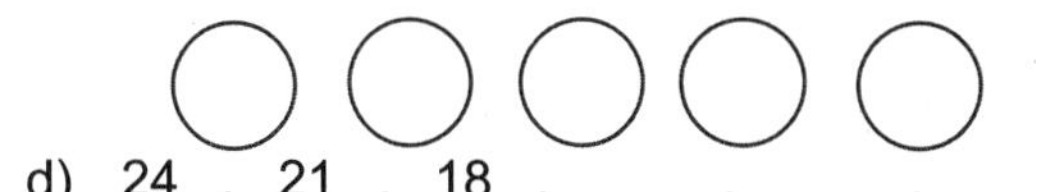

d) 24 , 21 , 18 , _____ , _____ , _____

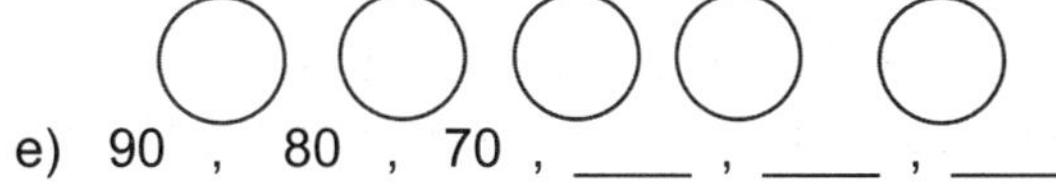

e) 90 , 80 , 70 , _____ , _____ , _____

f) 45 , 40 , 35 , _____ , _____ , _____

1. Extend the patterns, using the "gap" provided.

Example 1:

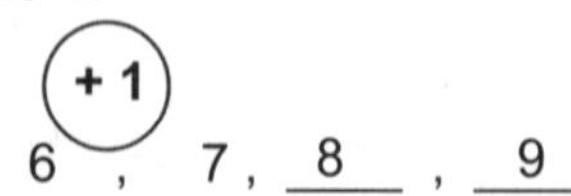

6 (+1) , 7 , 8 , 9

Example 2:

8 (−2) , 6 , 4 , 2

a) 5 (+5) , 10 , ____ , ____ , ____

b) 1 (+3) , 4 , ____ , ____ , ____

c) 3 (+3) , 6 , ____ , ____ , ____

d) 6 (+2) , 8 , ____ , ____ , ____

e) 12 (+2) , 14 , ____ , ____ , ____

f) 10 (+5) , 15 , ____ , ____ , ____

g) 14 (−1) , 13 , ____ , ____ , ____

h) 16 (−2) , 14 , ____ , ____ , ____

2. Extend the following patterns by first finding the "gap." NOTE: You should first check that the gap is the same between each pair of numbers.

Example:

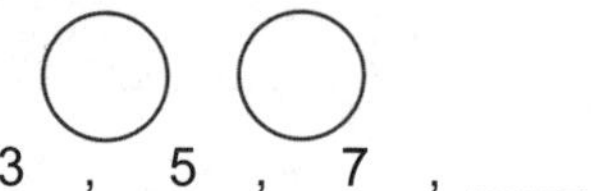

3 , 5 , 7 , ____

Step 1:

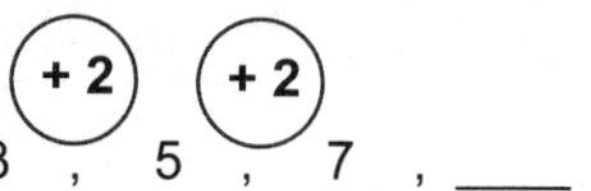

3 (+2) , 5 (+2) , 7 , ____

Step 2:

3 (+2) , 5 (+2) , 7 , 9

a) 5 , 8 , 11 , ____ , ____

b) 2 , 4 , 6 , ____ , ____

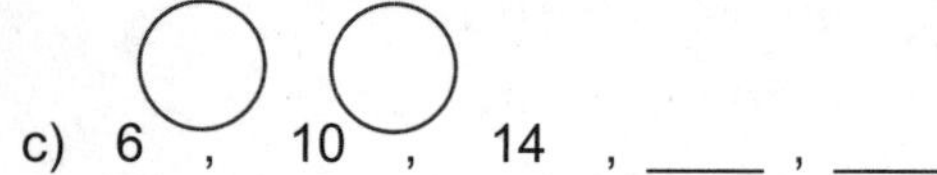

c) 6 , 10 , 14 , ____ , ____

d) 1 , 3 , 5 , ____ , ____

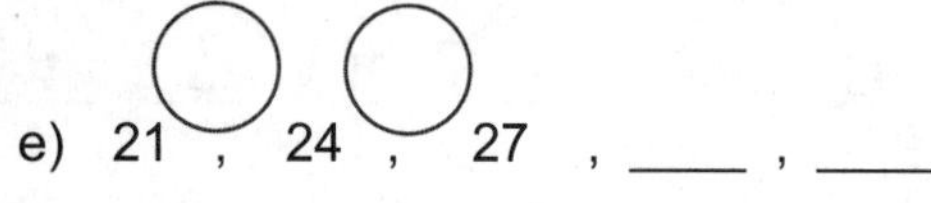

e) 21 , 24 , 27 , ____ , ____

f) 12 , 17 , 22 , ____ , ____

g) 25 , 23 , 21 , ____ , ____

h) 59 , 54 , 49 , ____ , ____

Show your work for these questions on a separate piece of paper.

BONUS:

3. Rachel has a box of 24 chocolates. She eats 3 each day for 5 days. How many are left?

4. Emi has saved $17. She saves $4 each day. How much money has she saved after 4 days?

# PA4-7: Repeating Patterns

Marco makes a **repeating** pattern using blocks:

This is the core of Marco's pattern.

The **core** of a pattern is the part that repeats.

---

1. On a separate piece of paper (or using blocks), make several repeating patterns of your own. Have a friend guess the core of your pattern.

2. Circle the core of the each pattern. The first one is done for you.

a) 

b) 

c) 

d) 

e) 

f) 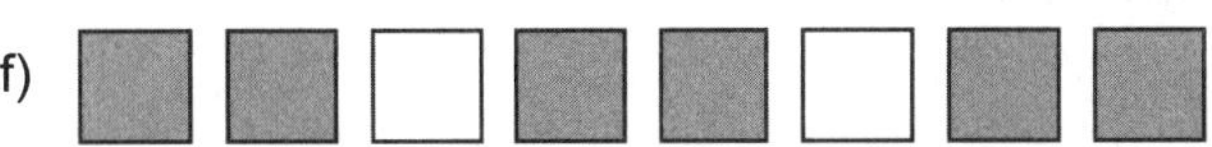

g) 

h) 

i) C B B C B B C B B

j) 1 2 4 1 2 4 1 2 4

k) 1 2 3 4 8 1 2 3 4 8

l) 9 8 7 8 9 8 7 8 9 8

m) 

n) X Y Z X Y Z X Y Z

3. Circle the core of the pattern, then continue the pattern.

a) 

b) 

c) A B C A B C A ____ ____ ____ ____ ____

d) 2 8 9 6 2 8 9 6 ____ ____ ____ ____ ____

e) 3 0 0 4 3 0 0 4 ____ ____ ____ ____

f) 1 8 1 1 8 1 1 8 1 ____ ____ ____ ____

# PA4-8: Attributes

Cathy is making patterns. She uses 4 different 2-D **shapes**:

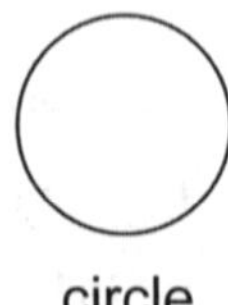
circle

triangle

square

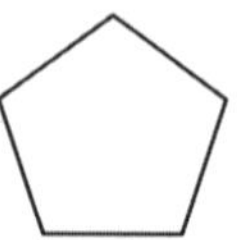
pentagon

She uses 3 **colours**: red = R
yellow = Y
blue = B

She uses 2 different **sizes**:

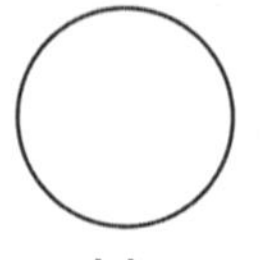
big small

**Shape**, **colour**, and **size** are referred to as the shapes' **attributes**.

NOTE:
Make sure you understand that while the two circles above are different sizes, they are still the same shape. This means that they are **similar** (see GE4-10).

---

1. Circle the **one** attribute that changes in each pattern (HINT: Check each attribute one at a time. First ask, "Does the **shape** change?" Then ask, "Does the **colour** change?" Then ask, "Does the **size** change?")

a) 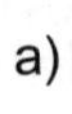 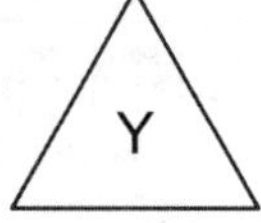  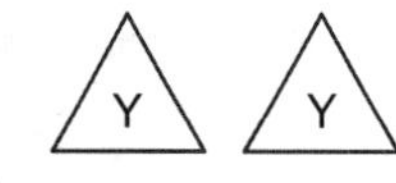

shape colour size

b) 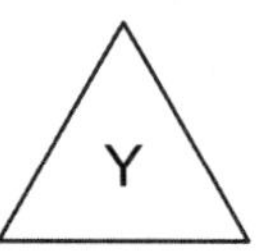  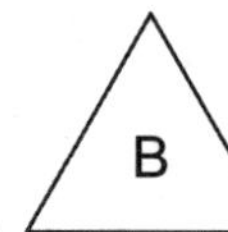 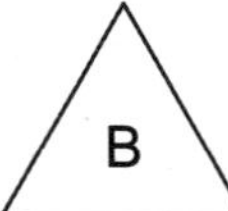

shape colour size

c) 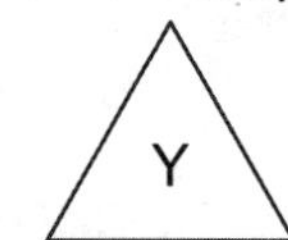  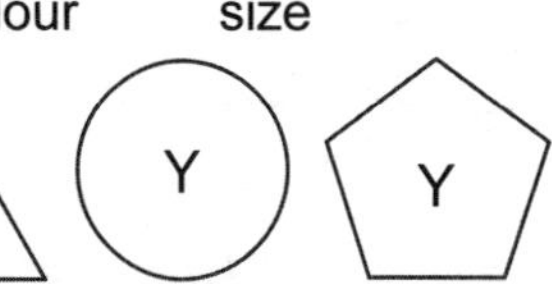 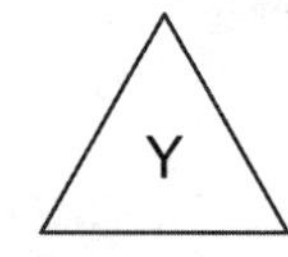

shape colour size

d) 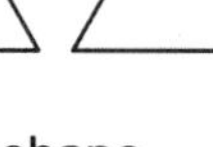

shape colour size

e) 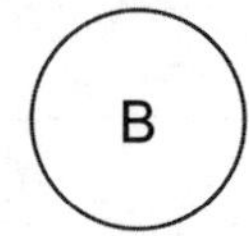 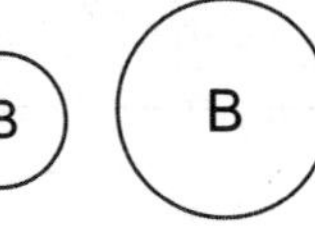

shape colour size

f) 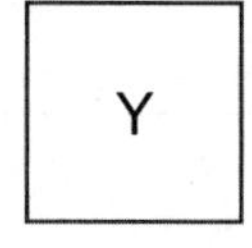 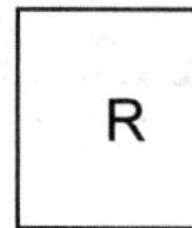 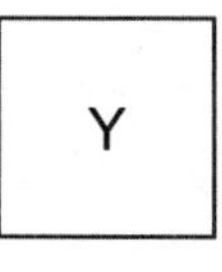

shape colour size

2. Write the **one** attribute that changes in each pattern.

a) 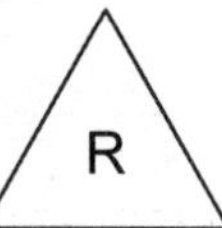 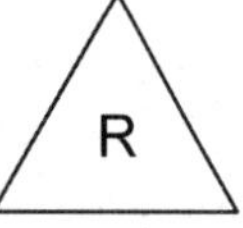

______________________

b) 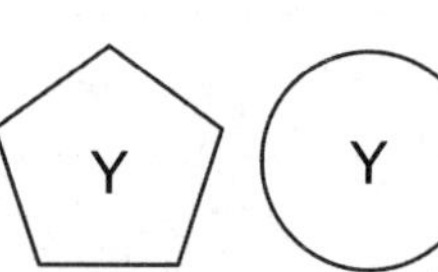 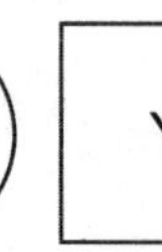 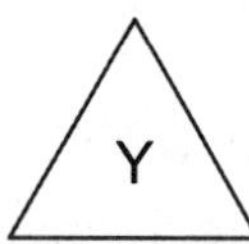

______________________

c) 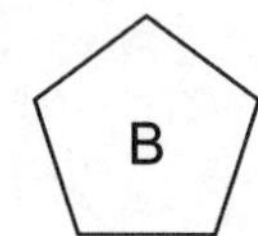 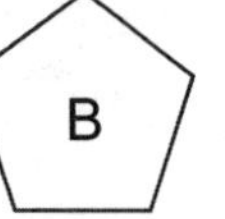

______________________

d) 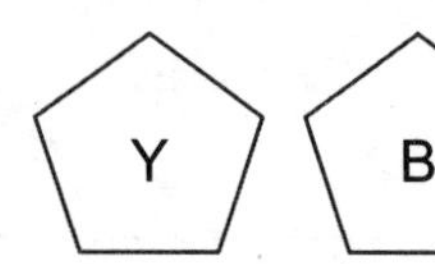 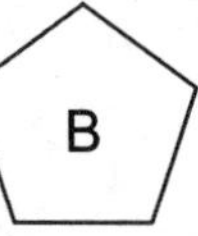 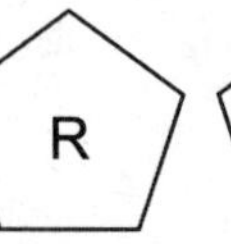 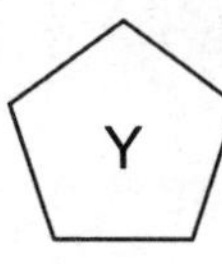

______________________

3. Circle the **two** attributes that change in each sequence.

a) 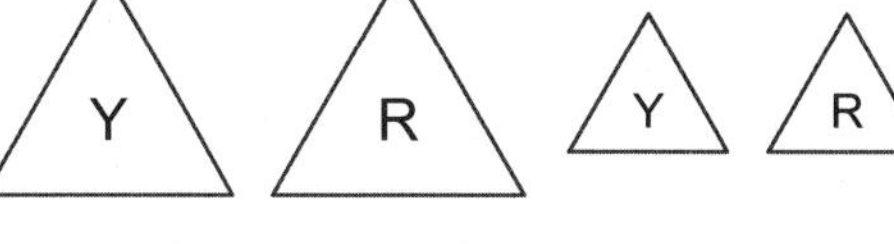

shape size colour

b)

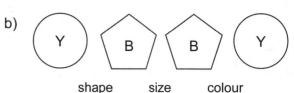

shape size colour

c)

shape size colour

d) 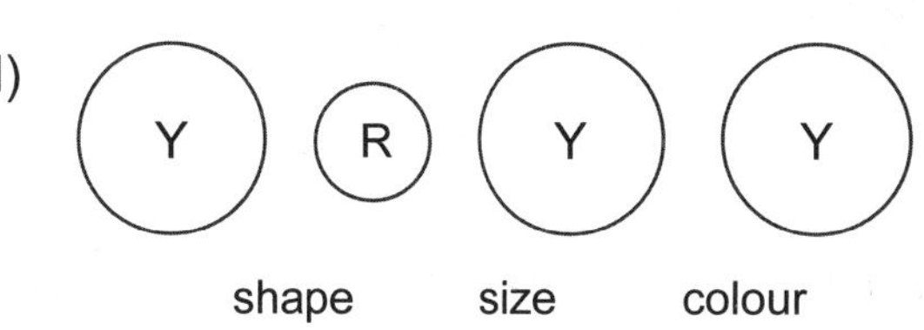

shape size colour

4. Write the **two** attributes that change in each pattern.

a) 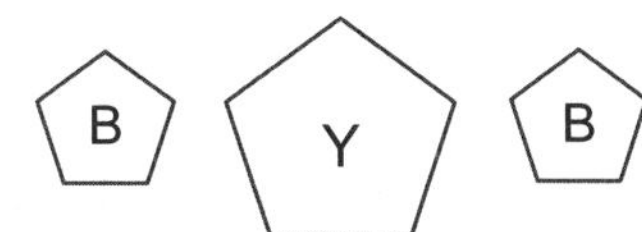

______________________

b) 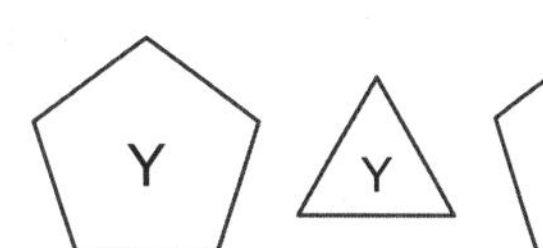 

______________________

c)  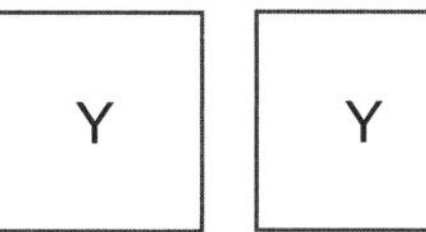

______________________

d) 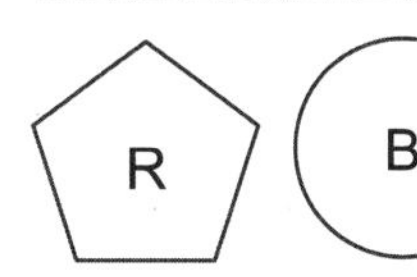  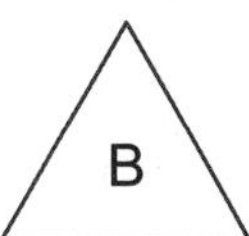

______________________

5. Write the **one**, **two**, or **three** attributes that change in each sequence.

a) 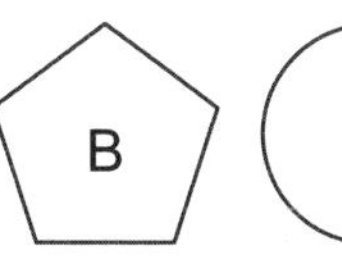 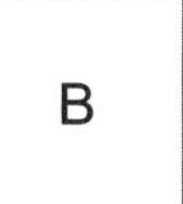 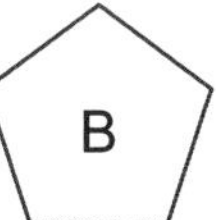

______________________

b) 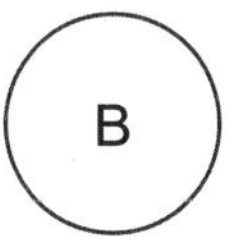 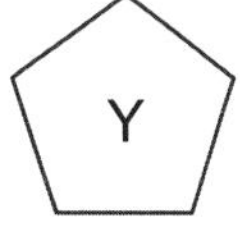  

______________________

c) 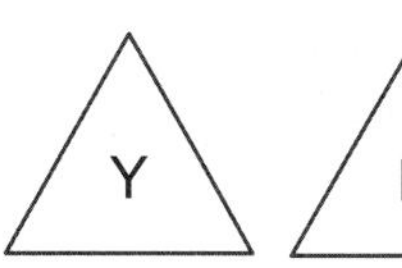 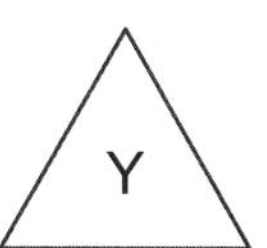 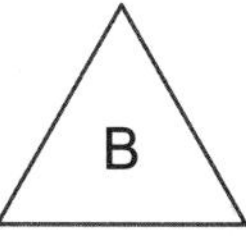

______________________

d) 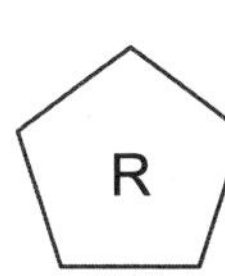 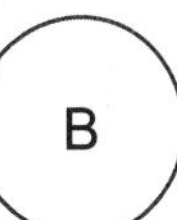 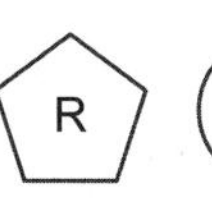

______________________

6. Each day, Asad drinks a small glass of juice at breakfast, a small glass of milk at lunch, and a large glass of water at dinner. Draw a pattern to show the sequence of drinks. Write the two attributes that change in the sequence.

Hyun makes a pattern with 2-D shapes:

He describes his pattern by saying how each attribute changes.

**shape**: circle, pentagon, triangle, then repeat
**colour**: yellow, yellow, blue, blue, then repeat
**size**: stays the same

1. Colour the shapes (R = red; B = blue; Y = yellow). On a separate piece of paper, describe how each attribute (shape, colour, size) changes.

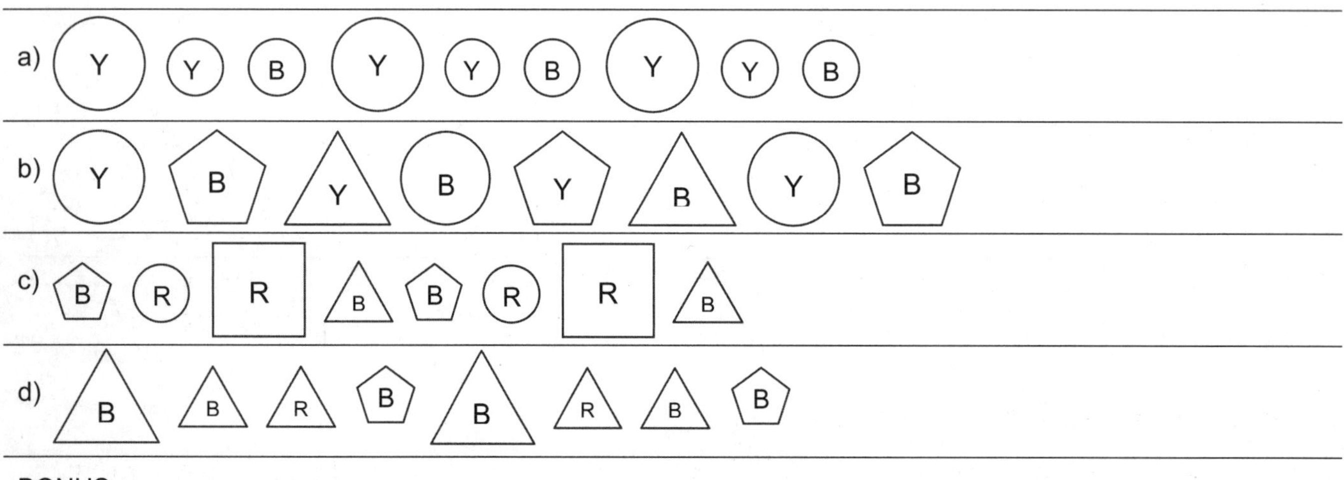


EXTRA CHALLENGE:
Find the length of the period of the pattern for each attribute. (For the example at the top of the page, the period for shape has length 3, while the period for colour has length 4.)

2. Sarah makes a pattern using beads. On a separate piece of paper, describe how the pattern changes by describing colour and size, as well as shape. Use the words "cone" – ; "cylinder" – ; "ball" – and "cube" – .

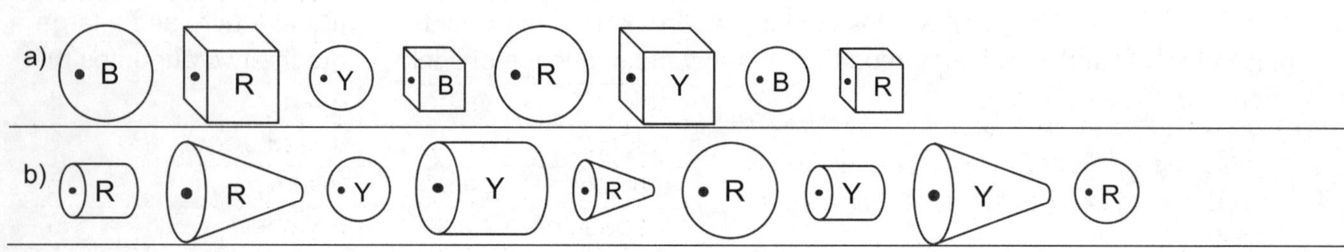

# PA4-10: Making Patterns

To make a pattern, you can change the **colour**, **shape**, **size**, or **position** of a figure, or you can change the **number** of times a figure occurs.

1. Circle the word that tells you which attribute of a figure or figures changes in the pattern.

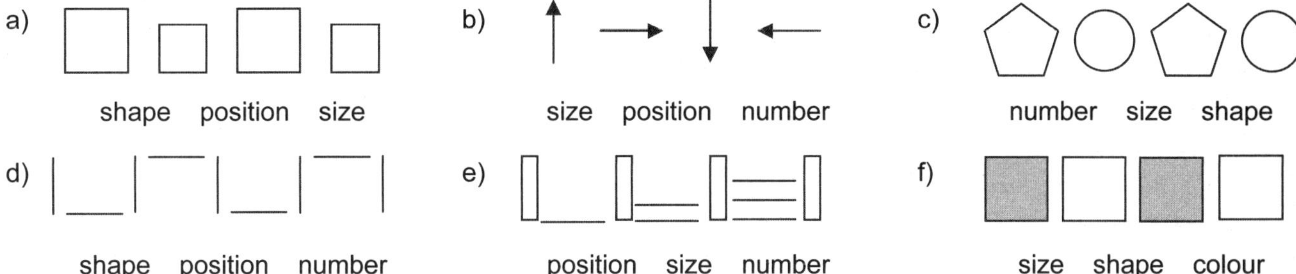


2. Circle the **two** words that tell you which attributes of a figure or figures changes in the pattern.

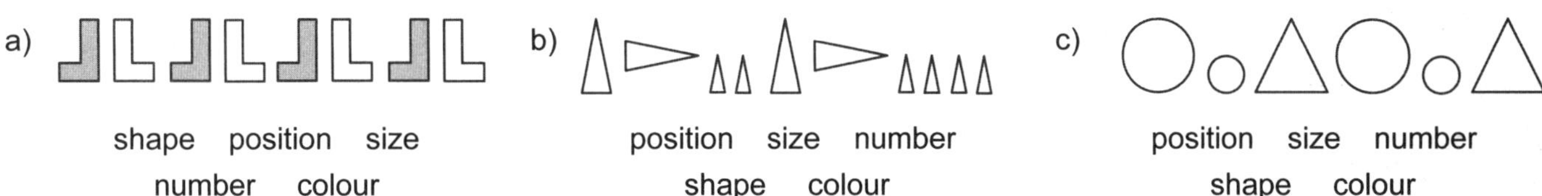


Answer the remaining questions on a separate piece of paper.

3. Make a pattern of your own with blocks or beads, changing at least two attributes. Explain which attributes you used in making your pattern, and how the attributes changed. Draw your pattern.

4. Rocks and minerals are rated on a scale of hardness from 1 to 10. Geologists test unknown rocks by scratching them with a rock whose hardness is known. For instance, quartz has a hardness of 7. If you scratch quartz against rock and it leaves a mark, you know that the mystery rock is softer than quartz. Rocks can be opaque (you cannot see through them) or transparent (you can see through them).

   Andrea made this chart of information about some rocks in her collection:

   a) Make a pattern using some or all of Andrea's rocks.
      Example:
      calcite, gypsum, jade, calcite, gypsum, jade . . .

   b) Describe how your pattern changes by saying how each attribute changes.

   c) Show a friend your description of how the attributes in your pattern change. See if your friend can guess the rocks in your pattern.

| Rock | Colour | Transparency | Hardness |
|---|---|---|---|
| calcite | white | transparent | 3 |
| gypsum | white | opaque | 2 |
| jade | green | transparent | 6 |
| fluorite | purple | transparent | 4 |
| halite | purple | transparent | 2 |
| gold | yellow | opaque | 3 |
| sulphur | yellow | transparent | 2 |
| malachite | green | opaque | 4 |
| magnetite | black | opaque | 6 |

# PA4-11: Extending a Pattern Using a Rule

1. Continue the sequences by **adding** the number given.

   a) (add 3) 31, 34, ____, ____, ____
   b) (add 5) 70, 75, ____, ____, ____
   c) (add 2) 24, 26, ____, ____, ____
   d) (add 10) 50, 60, ____, ____, ____

2. Continue the sequences, by **subtracting** the number given.

   a) (subtract 2) 14, 12, ___, ___, ___
   b) (subtract 3) 15, 12, ___, ___, ___
   c) (subtract 5) 75, 70, ___, ___, ___
   d) (subtract 3) 66, 63, ___, ___, ___

3. Continue the sequences by **adding** the number given.

   a) (add 4) 31, 35, ____, ____, ____
   b) (add 9) 11, 20, ____, ____, ____
   c) (add 6) 10, 16, ____, ____, ____
   d) (add 7) 70, 77, ____, ____, ____

4. Continue the sequences by **subtracting** the number given.

   a) (subtract 4) 46, 42, ___, ___, ___
   b) (subtract 7) 49, 42, ___, ___, ___
   c) (subtract 3) 91, 88, ___, ___, ___
   d) (subtract 11) 131, 120, ____, ____, ____

BONUS:

5. Create a pattern of your own. After writing down the pattern in the blanks, give the rule you used.

   ______, ______, ______, ______, ______ My rule: ________________________

6. Which one of the following sequences was made by adding 3? Circle it. (HINT: Check all the numbers in the sequence.)

   a) 3, 5, 9, 12 b) 3, 6, 8, 12 c) 3, 6, 9, 12

7. **2, 6, 10, 14 . . .**

   Christian says the above pattern was made by adding 4 each time. Is he right? Explain how you know on a separate piece of paper.

8. **72, 64, 56, 48, 40 . . .**

   Zannat says the sequence was made by subtracting 7 each time. Faruq says it was made by subtracting 8. Who is right? Explain how you found the answer on a separate piece of paper.

# PA4-12: Identifying Pattern Rules

1. The following sequences were made by **adding** a number repeatedly. In each case, write the number that was added.

   a) 2, 5, 8, 11 add ____
   b) 3, 6, 9, 12 add ____
   c) 15, 17, 19, 21 add ____
   d) 44, 46, 48, 50 add ____
   e) 41, 46, 51, 56 add ____
   f) 19, 22, 25, 28 add ____
   g) 243, 245, 247, 249 add ____
   h) 21, 27, 33, 39 add ____
   i) 15, 18, 21, 24 add ____
   j) 41, 45, 49, 53 add ____

2. The following sequences were made by **subtracting** a number repeatedly. In each case, write the number that was subtracted.

   a) 18, 16, 14, 12 subtract ____
   b) 35, 30, 25, 20 subtract ____
   c) 100, 99, 98, 97 subtract ____
   d) 41, 38, 35, 32 subtract ____
   e) 17, 14, 11, 8 subtract ____
   f) 99, 97, 95, 93 subtract ____
   g) 180, 170, 160, 150 subtract ____
   h) 100, 95, 90, 85 subtract ____
   i) 27, 25, 23, 21 subtract ____
   j) 90, 84, 78, 72 subtract ____
   k) 81, 76, 71, 66 subtract ____
   l) 220, 200, 180, 160 subtract ____

3. State the rule for each pattern.

   a) 119, 112, 105, 98, 91 subtract ____
   b) 1, 9, 17, 25, 33, 41 add ____
   c) 101, 105, 109, 113 __________
   d) 110, 99, 88, 77, __________

BONUS:

4. For the following pattern, use the first three numbers to find the rule. Then continue the pattern by filling in the blanks.

   12, 17, 22, _____, _____, _____ Rule: ____________________

5. **5, 8, 11, 14, 17 . . .**

   Keith says the pattern rule is "Start at 5 and subtract 3 each time." Jane says the rule is "Add 4 each time." Molly says the rule is "Start at 5 and add 3 each time."

   a) Whose rule is correct? Explain why on a separate piece of paper.

   b) What mistakes did the others make?

# PA4-13: Introduction to T-Tables



Abdul makes a **growing pattern** with blocks. He records the number of blocks in each figure in a chart or T-table. He also records the number of blocks he adds each time he makes a new figure:

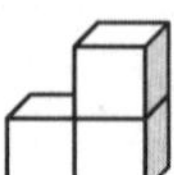
Figure 1

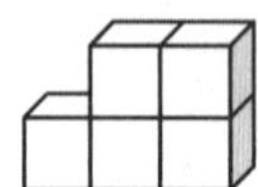
Figure 2

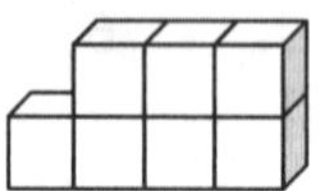
Figure 3

| Figure | Number of blocks | |
|---|---|---|
| 1 | 3 | |
| | | (2) ← number of blocks **added** each time |
| 2 | 5 | |
| | | (2) ← |
| 3 | 7 | |

The number of blocks in the figures are 3, 5, 7, . . .

Abdul writes a rule for this number pattern:

**RULE: Start at 3 and add 2 each time.**

---

1. Abdul makes another **growing pattern** with blocks. How many blocks does he add to make each new figure? Write your answer in the circles provided. Then write a rule for the pattern.

a)

| Figure | Number of blocks |
|---|---|
| 1 | 3 |
| 2 | 7 |
| 3 | 11 |

Rule:

b)

| Figure | Number of blocks |
|---|---|
| 1 | 2 |
| 2 | 6 |
| 3 | 10 |

Rule:

c)

| Figure | Number of blocks |
|---|---|
| 1 | 2 |
| 2 | 4 |
| 3 | 6 |

Rule:

d)

| Figure | Number of blocks |
|---|---|
| 1 | 1 |
| 2 | 6 |
| 3 | 11 |

Rule:

e)

| Figure | Number of blocks |
|---|---|
| 1 | 5 |
| 2 | 9 |
| 3 | 13 |

Rule:

f)

| Figure | Number of blocks |
|---|---|
| 1 | 12 |
| 2 | 18 |
| 3 | 24 |

Rule:

g)

| Figure | Number of blocks |
|---|---|
| 1 | 2 |
| 2 | 10 |
| 3 | 18 |

Rule:

h)

| Figure | Number of blocks |
|---|---|
| 1 | 3 |
| 2 | 6 |
| 3 | 9 |

Rule:

i)

| Figure | Number of blocks |
|---|---|
| 1 | 6 |
| 2 | 13 |
| 3 | 20 |

Rule:

BONUS:

2. Extend the number pattern. How many blocks would be used in Figure 6?

a)

| Figure | Number of blocks |
|---|---|
| 1 | 2 |
| 2 | 7 |
| 3 | 12 |
| | |
| | |
| | |

b)

| Figure | Number of blocks |
|---|---|
| 1 | 3 |
| 2 | 6 |
| 3 | 9 |
| | |
| | |
| | |

c)

| Figure | Number of blocks |
|---|---|
| 1 | 3 |
| 2 | 8 |
| 3 | 13 |
| | |
| | |
| | |

3. Amy makes a growing pattern with blocks. After making Figure 3, she has only 14 blocks left. Does she have enough blocks to complete Figure 4?

a)

| Figure | Number of blocks |
|---|---|
| 1 | 3 |
| 2 | 7 |
| 3 | 11 |
| | |

YES NO

b)

| Figure | Number of blocks |
|---|---|
| 1 | 7 |
| 2 | 10 |
| 3 | 13 |
| | |

YES NO

c)

| Figure | Number of blocks |
|---|---|
| 1 | 1 |
| 2 | 5 |
| 3 | 9 |
| | |

YES NO

4. On a separate piece of paper, make a T-table to show how many squares are needed to make the fifth figure in each pattern.

a)

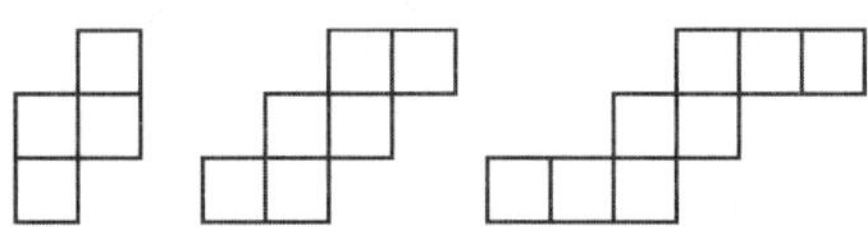

b)

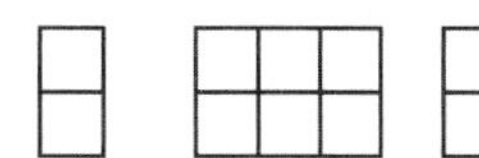

# PA4-14: T-Tables



1. Count the number of line segments in each set of figures by marking each line segment as you count as shown in the example. (HINT: Count around the outside of the figure first.)

Example:

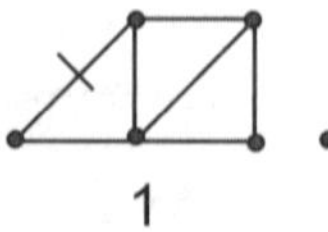
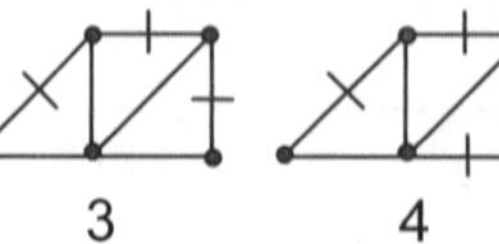
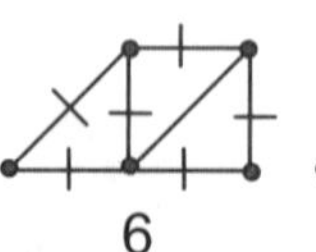
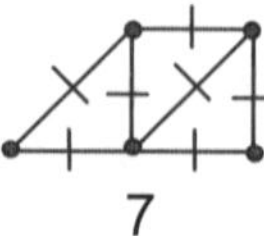

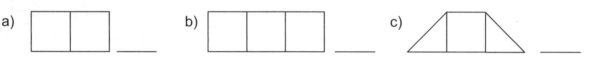

1 2 3 4 5 6 7

a)  ____

b) ____

c) ____

d) ____

e)  ____

f) 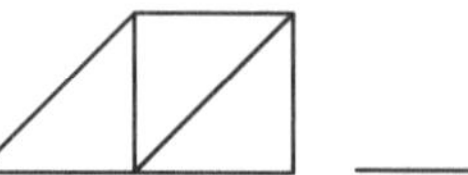 ____

2. Continue the pattern below, then complete the chart.

Figure 1

Figure 2

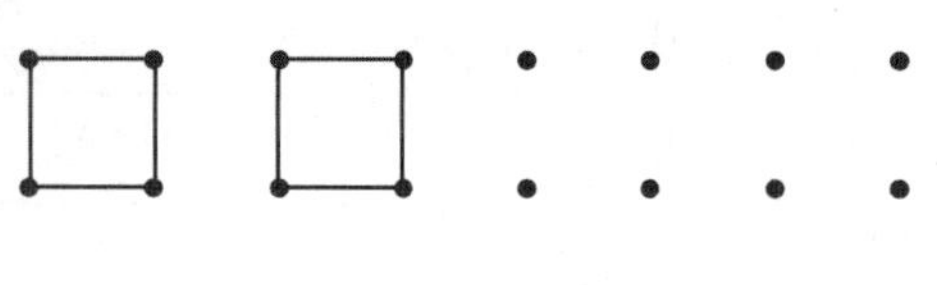

Figure 3

Figure 4

| Figure | Number of line segments |
|---|---|
| 1 | 4 |
| 2 | 8 |
| 3 | |
| 4 | |

a) How many line segments would Figure 5 have? ________________

b) How did you find your answer for part a)?

3. Continue the pattern below, then complete the chart.

Figure 1

Figure 2

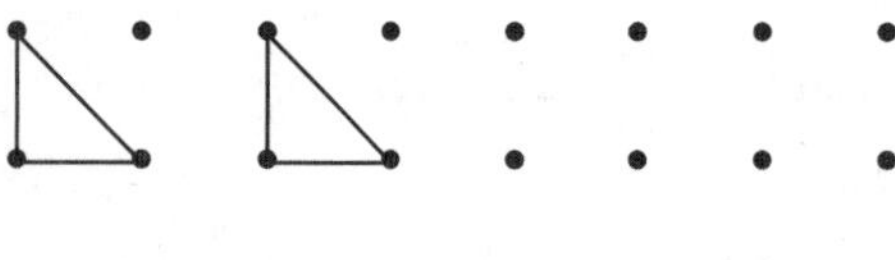

Figure 3

Figure 4

| Figure | Number of line segments |
|---|---|
| 1 | |
| 2 | |
| 3 | |
| 4 | |

How many line segments would Figure 5 have? ________________

## PA4-14: T-Tables *(continued)*

4. Continue the pattern below, then complete the chart.

Figure 1

Figure 2

Figure 3

Figure 4

| Figure | Number of line segments |
|---|---|
| 1 | |
| 2 | |
| 3 | |
| 4 | |

a) How many line segments would Figure 5 have? _______________

b) How many line segments would Figure 6 have? _______________

c) How many line segments would Figure 8 have? _______________

5. Continue the pattern below, then complete the chart.

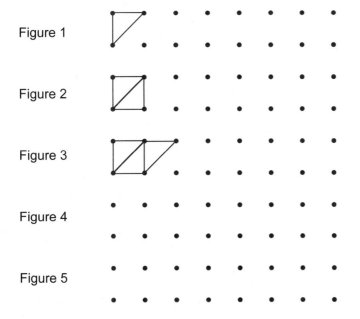

Figure 1

Figure 2

Figure 3

Figure 4

Figure 5

| Figure | Number of line segments |
|---|---|
| 1 | |
| 2 | |
| 3 | |
| 4 | |
| 5 | |

a) How many line segments would Figure 6 have? _______________

b) How many line segments would Figure 7 have? _______________

c) How many line segments would Figure 8 have? _______________

6. Extend the chart. How many young would five animals have?

a)

| Arctic fox | Number of cubs |
|---|---|
| 1 | 5 |
| 2 | 10 |
| | |
| | |
| | |

b)

| Wood-chuck | Number of pups |
|---|---|
| 1 | 4 |
| 2 | 8 |
| | |
| | |
| | |

c)

| Osprey | Number of eggs |
|---|---|
| 1 | 3 |
| 2 | 6 |
| | |
| | |
| | |

d)

| White tailed deer | Number of fawns |
|---|---|
| 1 | 2 |
| 2 | 4 |
| | |
| | |
| | |

Show your work for the remaining questions on a separate piece of paper.

7. How much money would Claude earn for four hours of work?

a)

| Hours worked | Dollars earned in an hour |
|---|---|
| 1 | $14 |
| | |
| | |
| | |

b)

| Hours worked | Dollars earned in an hour |
|---|---|
| 1 | $12 |
| | |
| | |
| | |

c)

| Hours worked | Dollars earned in an hour |
|---|---|
| 1 | $15 |
| | |
| | |
| | |

8. 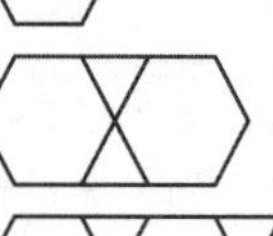

Hanna makes a Christmas ornament using a trapezoid (the shaded shape) and 3 triangles. She has 5 trapezoids. How many triangles will she need if she plans to use all 5 trapezoids to make ornaments?

9. Step 1: 

Step 2:

Step 3: 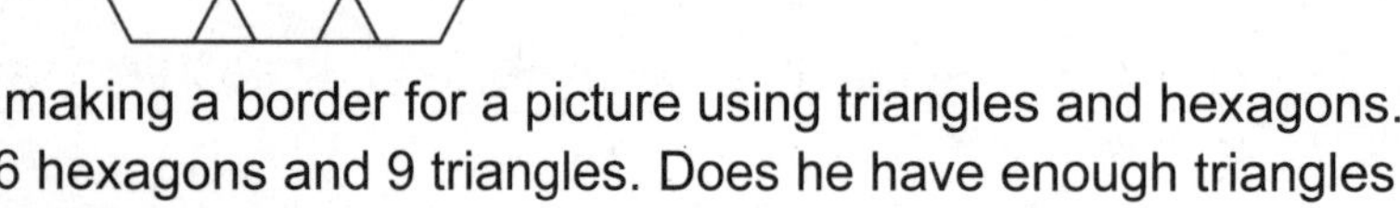

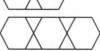

Peter is making a border for a picture using triangles and hexagons. He has 6 hexagons and 9 triangles. Does he have enough triangles to use all 6 hexagons?

| Hexagons | Triangles |
|---|---|
| | |
| | |
| | |
| | |
| | |
| | |

10. A marina rents canoes at $7 for the first hour and $4 for every hour after that. How much would it cost to rent a canoe for 6 hours?

11. A bookstore has a special sale. The first book you buy costs $10. Each book after that costs $5. Claude has $25. Does he have enough to buy 5 books? (How did you solve the problem? Did you use a T-table? a model? a calculation?)

# PA4-15: Patterns Involving Time



For the exercises on this page you will need to know . . .

the days of the week: **Monday, Tuesday, Wednesday, Thursday, Friday, Saturday, Sunday**

the months of the year: **January, February, March, April, May, June, July, August, September, October, November, December**

1. Harry starts work on Tuesday morning. He repairs 4 bikes each day. How many bikes has he repaired by Friday evening?

| Day | Total number of bikes repaired |
|---|---|
| Tuesday | 4 |
| | |
| | |
| | |

2. Meryl saves $20 in July. She saves $10 each month after that. How much has she saved by the end of October?

| Month | Spent |
|---|---|
| July | $20 |
| | |
| | |
| | |

3. During a snow storm, 5 cm of snow had fallen by 6 p.m. Every hour after that, 3 cm of snow fell. How deep was the snow at 9 p.m.?

| Hour | Depth of snow |
|---|---|
| 6 p.m. | 5 cm |
| | |
| | |
| | |

4. Adria's maple sapling grows 3 cm in May. It grows 6 cm each month after that. How high is the sapling by the end of August?

| Month | Height of sapling |
|---|---|
| May | |
| | |
| | |
| | |

On a separate piece of paper, make a chart to solve the following problems:

5. Karen writes 14 pages of her book in February. She writes 8 pages every month after that. How many pages has she written by the end of June?

6. Mario starts work on Wednesday morning. He plants 5 trees each day. How many trees has he planted by Friday evening?

7. The snow is 19 cm deep at 3 p.m. Every hour, 5 cm of snow falls. How deep is the snow at 7 p.m.?

BONUS:

8. Jennifer takes 8 cans of food to the food bank every month. She starts donating cans at the beginning of October. How many cans has she donated at the end of March?

9. Sandhu's candle is 30 cm long when he lights it at 6 p.m. It is 27 cm long at 7 p.m. and 24 cm long at 8 p.m.

   a) How many centimetres does the candle burn down every hour? (Write your answer with a minus sign in the circles provided.)

   b) How long is the candle at 11 p.m.?

| Hour | Length of the candle |
|---|---|
| 7 p.m. | 30 cm |
| 8 p.m. | 27 cm |
| 9 p.m. | 24 cm |
| 10 p.m. | |
| 11 p.m. | |

10. Abdullah has $35 in his savings account at the end of March. He spends $7 each month. How much does he have in his account at the end of June?

| Month | Savings |
|---|---|
| March | $35 |
| | |
| | |
| | |

11. Allishah has $38 in her savings account at the end of October. She spends $7 each month. How much does she have at the end of January?

| Month | Savings |
|---|---|
| | |
| | |
| | |
| | |

BONUS:
To solve each of the problems you will have to make two charts and compare your answers.

12. Jacob saves $30 in July. He saves $4 each month after that. Amanda saves $22 in July. She saves $6 each month after that. Who has saved the most money by the end of January?

13. Edith's maple sapling grows 5 cm in July. It grows 7 cm each month after that. Ron's sapling grows 7 cm in July. It grows 3 cm each month after that. Whose sapling is higher by the end of September?

14. Chloe's candle is 28 cm high when she lights it at 5 p.m. It burns down 4 cm every hour. Dora's candle is 21 cm high when she lights it at 5 p.m. It burns down 3 cm every hour. Whose candle is taller at 10 p.m.?

# PA4-16: Calendars

PARENT:
For the exercises on this page your child will need two copies of page xvi: Calendars from the Introduction.

NOTE: To answer these questions, you will need to know the number of days in each month.

Months with 31 days: **January, March, May, July, August, October, December**

Months with 30 days: **April, June, September, November**

Months with 28 days: **February (during a leap year, February has 29 days)**

---

1. a) Write the title "December" on a blank calendar. Write the numbers of the days so that December 1$^{st}$ is a Wednesday.

   b) Rona has guitar lessons every **fourth** day of the month starting on December 4$^{th}$. Mark the days when she has a guitar lesson with an "X."

For the following questions, start by filling in the numbers for the days of the week on a blank calendar:

2. April 1$^{st}$ is a Sunday. Huyan receives an allowance of $5 every Tuesday. How much money has he received by the end of the month?

3. August 1$^{st}$ is a Monday. Paula buys a plant on August 4$^{th}$. She waters her plant every 4$^{th}$ day after she buys it and gives it plant food every 6$^{th}$ day after she buys it. On which dates does she give it both water and food?

4. The first day of October is a Tuesday. Alex has piano lessons every 6$^{th}$ day of the month starting on October 6$^{th}$. Dan has lessons every Friday. On which dates do they have lessons on the same day?

5. Fill in a calendar for any month you choose. (You will have to pick a day of the week to be the first day of the month).

   a) Shade the numbers along any column of your calendar. What pattern do you see? Write a rule for the pattern. Look at any other column. How do you explain what you see?

   b) Shade any diagonal of your calendar as shown. What pattern do you see in the numbers you shaded? (Shade a diagonal in the other direction. What pattern do you see?)

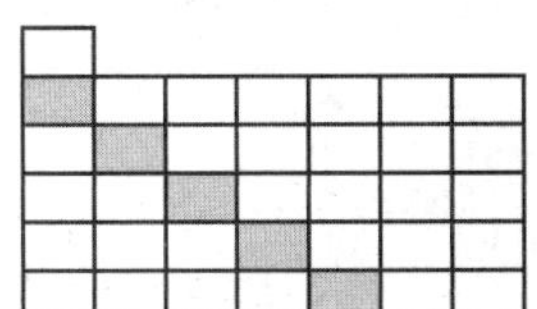

BONUS:

6. Fill in a blank calendar, using any month and any day for the first day of the month. Draw a square around any 4 numbers. Add the pair of numbers on the diagonal. Then add the pair of numbers on the other diagonal. What do you notice about the sum? Will this always happen?

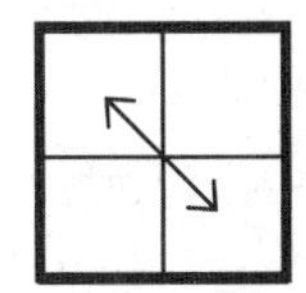

1. Karen makes a repeating pattern using red (R) and yellow (Y) blocks. The box shows the core of her pattern. Continue the patterns by writing Rs and Ys in the correct order.

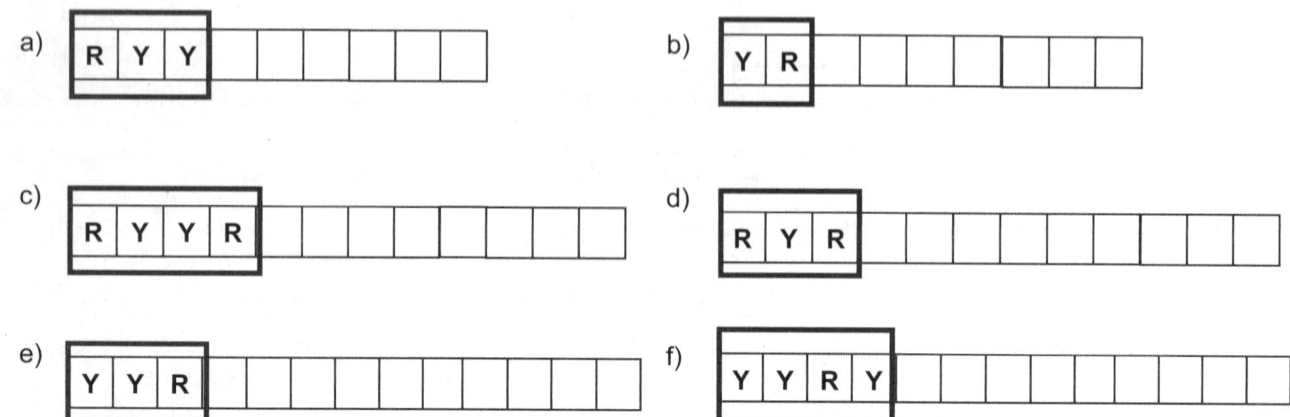


2. Rachel designed a core for a **repeating** pattern. Stan tried to continue the pattern. Did he continue the pattern correctly? Shade the reds (R) as in parts a) and b) if it helps.

NOTE: You should draw rectangles around successive groups of letters. Each rectangle should contain as many letters as the core. If the sequence of letters in any rectangle is different from those in the core, Stan has copied the pattern incorrectly.

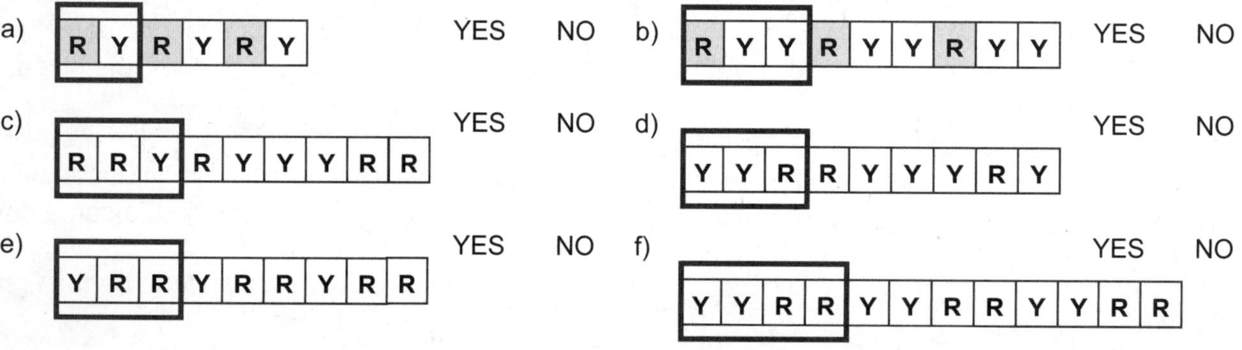


3. For each pattern, say whether the blocks in the rectangle are the **core** of the pattern. If the blocks **do not** show the core, circle NO and put your own rectangle around the correct core.

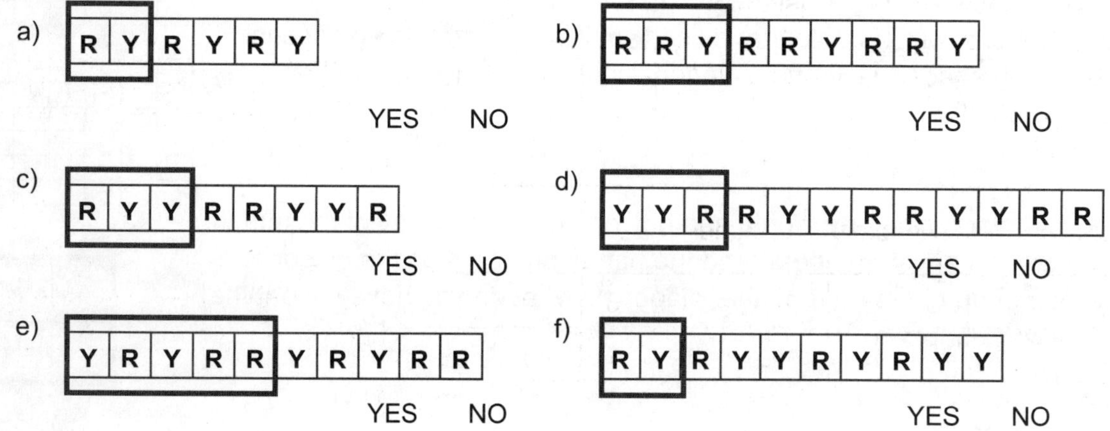

Sally makes a repeating pattern using red and yellow blocks:

| R | R | Y | R | R | Y | R | R | Y |
|---|---|---|---|---|---|---|---|---|

She wants to predict the colour of the 17th block in her pattern. First she finds the core of the pattern:

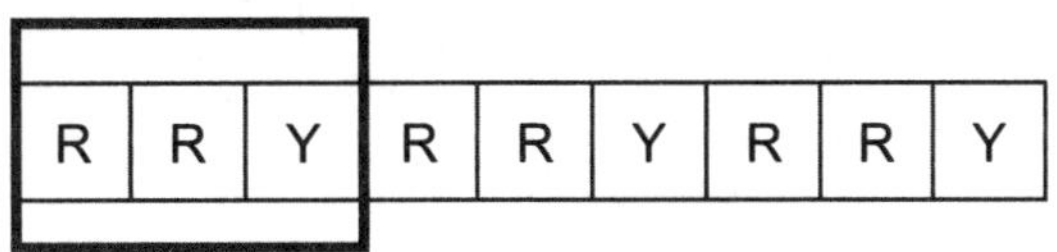


The third block is the last block in the core. Sally marks every third number on a hundreds chart (she starts at 3 and counts on by 3s). Each "X" shows the position of a block where the core ends:

| 1 | 2 | ~~3~~ | 4 | 5 | ~~6~~ | 7 | 8 | ~~9~~ | 10 |
|---|---|---|---|---|---|---|---|---|---|
| 11 | ~~12~~ | 13 | 14 | ~~15~~ | 16 R | 17 R | 18 Y | 19 | 20 |

The core ends on the 15th block and starts again on the 16th block. Sally writes the letters of the core on the chart, starting at 16. The 17th block is red.

---

4. In the patterns, put a rectangle around the blocks that make up the core.

a)

| Y | R | R | Y | R | R | Y | R | R |
|---|---|---|---|---|---|---|---|---|

b)

| R | R | R | Y | R | R | R | Y |
|---|---|---|---|---|---|---|---|

c)

| Y | Y | R | R | Y | Y | R | R | Y | Y | R | R |
|---|---|---|---|---|---|---|---|---|---|---|---|

d)

| Y | R | R | Y | Y | R | R | Y |
|---|---|---|---|---|---|---|---|

e)

| R | Y | R | Y | Y | Y | R | Y | R | Y | Y | Y |
|---|---|---|---|---|---|---|---|---|---|---|---|

f)

| R | Y | R | Y | R | Y | R | Y |
|---|---|---|---|---|---|---|---|

5. Predict the colour of the 18th block using the chart.
NOTE: Start by finding the core of the pattern.

| R | Y | Y | Y | R | Y | Y | Y |
|---|---|---|---|---|---|---|---|

| 1 | 2 | 3 | 4 | 5 | 6 | 7 | 8 | 9 | 10 |
|---|---|---|---|---|---|---|---|---|---|
| 11 | 12 | 13 | 14 | 15 | 16 | 17 | 18 | 19 | 20 |

6. Predict the colour of the 19th block using the chart.

| 1 | 2 | 3 | 4 | 5 | 6 | 7 | 8 | 9 | 10 |
|---|---|---|---|---|---|---|---|---|---|
| 11 | 12 | 13 | 14 | 15 | 16 | 17 | 18 | 19 | 20 |

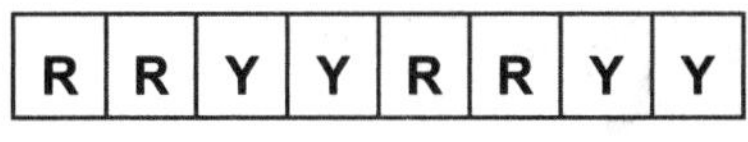


7. Predict the colour of the 17th block using the chart.

| 1 | 2 | 3 | 4 | 5 | 6 | 7 | 8 | 9 | 10 |
|---|---|---|---|---|---|---|---|---|---|
| 11 | 12 | 13 | 14 | 15 | 16 | 17 | 18 | 19 | 20 |

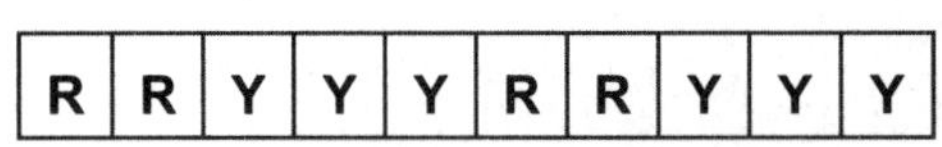

8. Draw a box around the core of the pattern and predict the colour of the $35^{th}$ block using the chart.

| 1 | 2 | 3 | 4 | 5 | 6 | 7 | 8 | 9 | 10 |
|---|---|---|---|---|---|---|---|---|---|
| 11 | 12 | 13 | 14 | 15 | 16 | 17 | 18 | 19 | 20 |
| 21 | 22 | 23 | 24 | 25 | 26 | 27 | 28 | 29 | 30 |
| 31 | 32 | 33 | 34 | 35 | 36 | 37 | 38 | 39 | 40 |

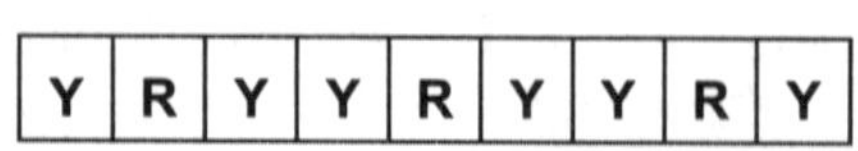


PARENT: Your child will need a copy of page xvii: Hundreds Charts from the Introduction.

Answer the remaining questions on a separate piece of paper.

9. Carl makes a pattern with red, white, and blue beads:

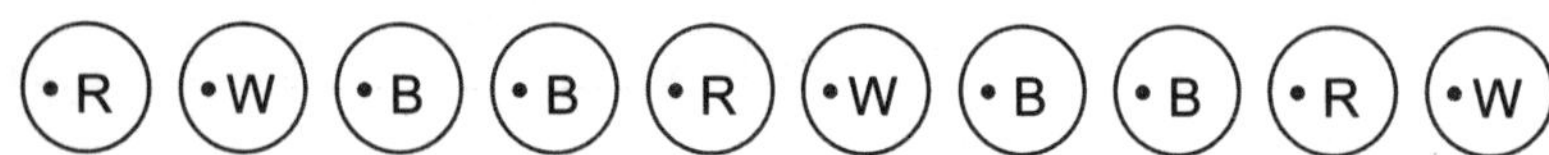


What colour will the $41^{st}$ bead be?

10. Angie makes a pattern with triangles:
Will the $22^{nd}$ triangle in her pattern point up or down?

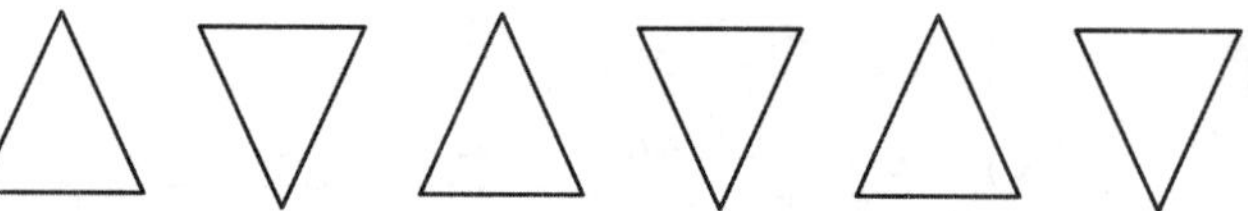

How do you know?

11. Explain how you could find the colour of the $46^{th}$ block in this pattern without using a hundreds chart.
(HINT: How could skip counting help?)

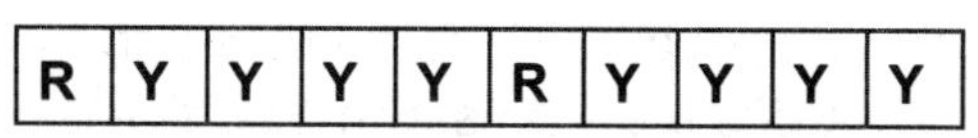


12.      

a) What is the $19^{th}$ coin in this pattern? Explain how you know.

b) What is the $91^{st}$ coin in this pattern?

13.

a) What is the $15^{th}$ coin in this pattern? Explain how you know.

BONUS:

b) What is the total value of the first 15 coins? (HINT: Try grouping coins together rather than adding one coin at a time.)

# NS4-1: Counting by 10s, 100s, and 1000s

1. Count by 10s to continue the pattern.

   a) 30, 40, 50, ______, ______, ______
   b) 10, 20, 30, ______, ______, ______
   c) 50, 60, 70, ______, ______, ______
   d) 100, 110, 120, 1____, 1____, 1____
   e) 140, 150, 160, ______, ______, ______
   f) 210, 220, 230, ______, ______, ______

2. Lara estimates that there are approximately 10 fish in each fish tank at a pet store.

   a) About how many fish are in 3 fish tanks? ____________________
   b) About how many fish are in 5 fish tanks? ____________________

3. Count by 10s to complete the pattern. The first one is done for you. NOTE: The ones digit stays the same, and the tens digit increases by 1.

   a) 23, 33, 43, 53, 63
   b) 1, 11, 21, ______, ______
   c) 27, 37, 47, ______, ______, ______
   d) 15, 25, 35, ______, ______, ______
   e) 49, 59, 69, ______, ______, ______
   f) 68, 78, 88, ______, ______, ______

4. Count by 100s to continue the pattern.

   a) 100, 200, 300, ______, ______, ______
   b) 600, 700, 800, ______, ______, ______
   c) 300, 400, 500, ______, ______, ______
   d) 1000, 1100, 1200, ______, ______, ______

5. There are 200 jelly beans in a jar. How many jelly beans would there be in . . .

   a) 2 bags? ________
   b) 4 bags? ________
   c) 5 bags? ________

6. Count by 100s to complete the pattern. The first one is done for you. NOTE: The ones and tens digits stay the same, and the hundreds digit increases by 1.

   a) 101, 201, 301, 401, 501
   b) 110, 210, 310, ______, ______
   c) 227, 327, 427, ______, ______, ______
   d) 399, 499, 599, ______, ______, ______
   e) 45, 145, 245, ______, ______, ______
   f) 525, 625, 725, ______, ______, ______

7. Count by 1000s to continue the pattern.

   a) 1000, 2000, ______, ______, ______
   b) 6000, 7000, ______, ______, ______

8. There are 1000 nails in a bag. How many nails would there be in . . .

   a) 3 bags? ________
   b) 4 bags? ________
   c) 5 bags? ________

BONUS:

9. Count backwards by 100s.

   a) 700, 600, 500, ______, ______, ______
   b) 1000, 900, 800, ______, ______, ______

10. Count backwards by 1000s.

   a) 9000, 8000, 7000, ______, ______
   b) 5000, 4000, ______, ______, ______

# NS4-2: Place Value—Ones, Tens, Hundreds, and Thousands

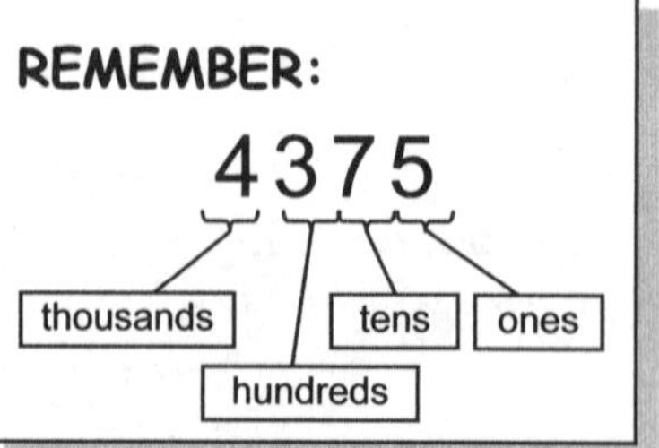


1. Beside each number, write the place value of the underlined digit. The first one is done for you.

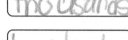

a) 35<u>6</u>4  tens

b) 1<u>3</u>36 

c) 25<u>6</u> 

d) <u>1</u>230 

e) <u>3</u>859 

f) 5<u>7</u>45 

g) 2<u>3</u>8 

h) 6<u>2</u>14 

i) 8<u>7</u> 

j) <u>9</u>430 

2. Give the place value of the number 5 in each of the numbers below. (HINT: First underline the number 5 in each question.)

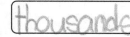

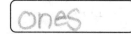

a) 15 640 thousands

b) 547 

c) 451 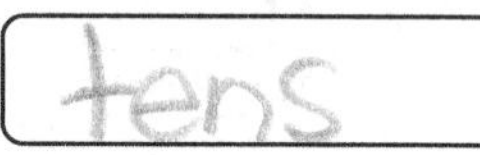


d) 2415 ones

e) 1257 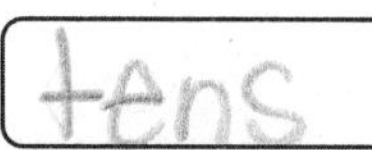


f) 5643 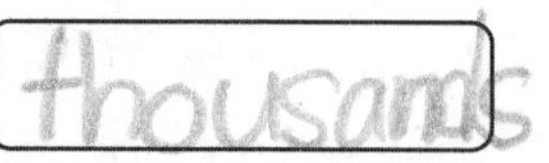


3. You can also write numbers using a place value chart.

Example:

In a place value chart, the number 3264 is

| Thousands | Hundreds | Tens | Ones |
|---|---|---|---|
| 3 | 2 | 6 | 4 |

Write the following numbers into the place value chart. The first one is done for you.

| | Thousands | Hundreds | Tens | Ones |
|---|---|---|---|---|
| a) 5231 | 5 | 2 | 3 | 1 |
| b) 8053 | 8 | 0 | 5 | 3 |
| c) 489 | 0 | 4 | 8 | 9 |
| d) 27 | 0 | 0 | 2 | 7 |
| e) 9104 | 9 | 1 | 0 | 4 |
| f) 4687 | 4 | 6 | 8 | 7 |

4. Write numerals for each number word.

a) two thousand, five hundred and fifty-six 2556

b) five thousand, three hundred and ninety-one 5391

c) six thousand, eight hundred and seventy 6870

d) eight thousand, four hundred and nine 8409

e) nine thousand, two hundred and seventeen 9217

f) nine thousand, one hundred and ten 9110

5. On a separate piece of paper, write number words for the following numerals (for example, the number word for 3724 is "three thousand, seven hundred and twenty-four").

a) 1235 b) 5205 c) 1649 d) 2080 e) 9701 f) 2234 g) 5605

# NS4-3: Representation with Base-10 Materials

1. For each question, give the number represented by the picture. Write each number in expanded word form first.

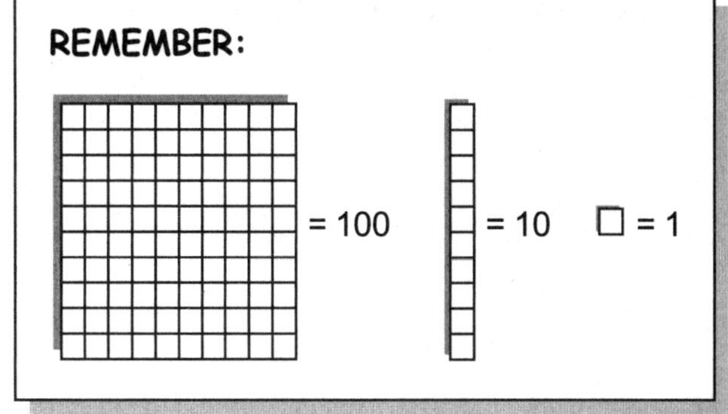


Example: 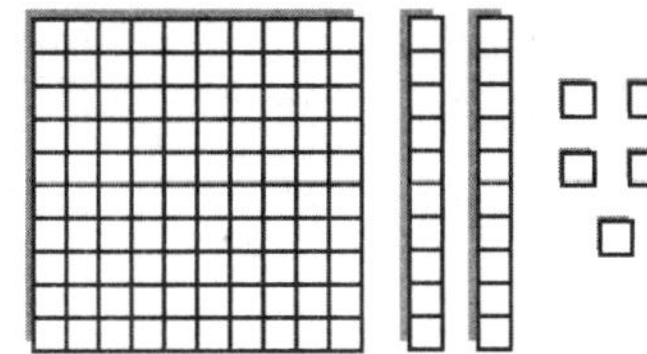

1 hundreds + 2 tens + 5 ones = 125

a)

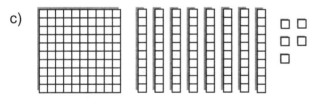

2 hundreds + 5 tens + 2 ones = 252

b) 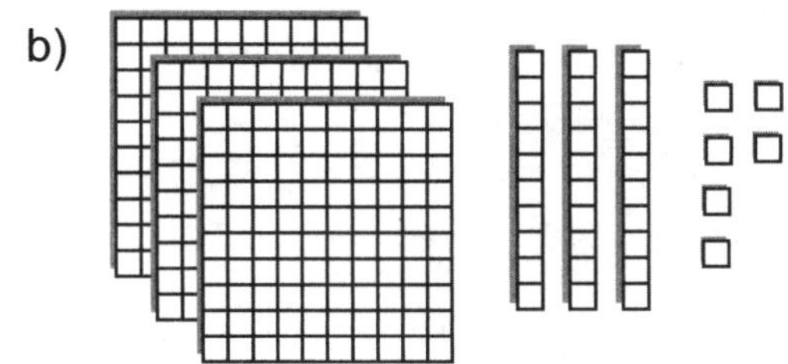

3 hundreds + 3 tens + 6 ones = 336

c)

1 hundred + 8 tens + 5 ones = 185

d) 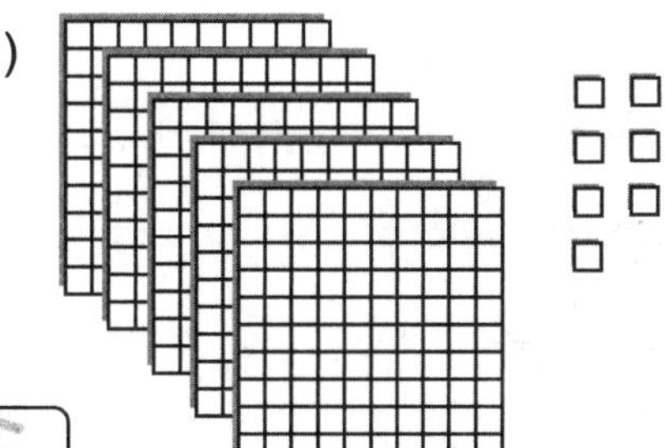

5 hundred + 0 tens + 7 ones = 507

3. Using the chart paper, draw the base-10 model for the following numbers:

a) 123

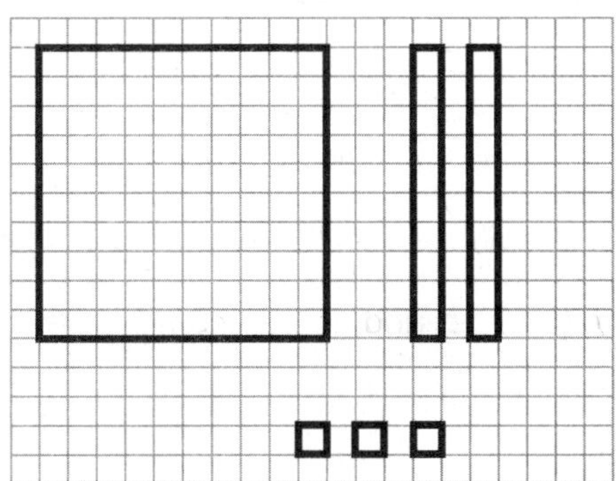

b) 87

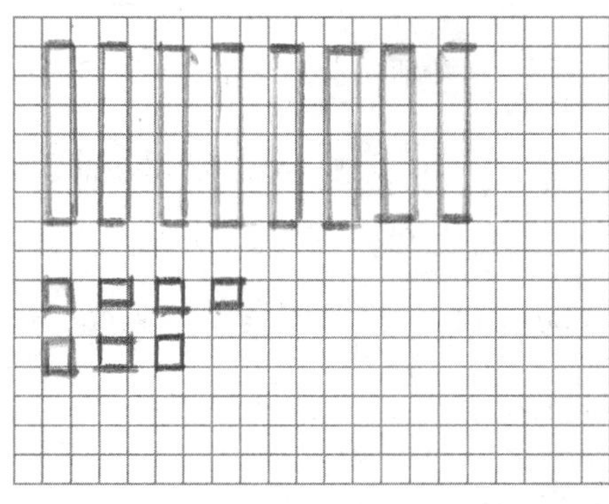

4. On separate grid paper, draw base-10 models for . . . a) 68 b) 350 c) 249

5. For each question, give the number represented by the picture. Write each number in expanded form (numerals and words) first.

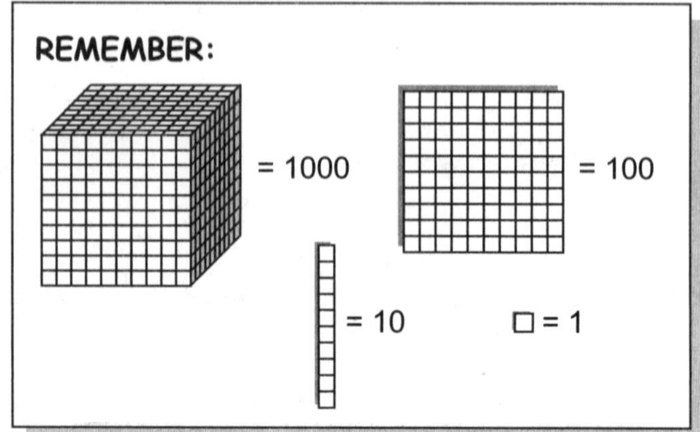


Example:

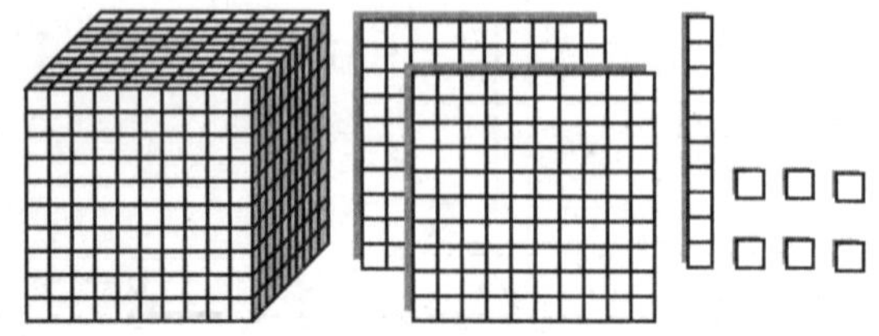

1 thousands + 2 hundreds + 1 tens + 6 ones = 1216

a)

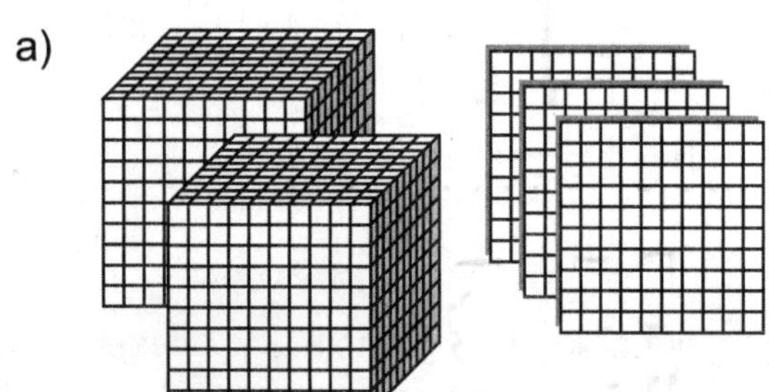

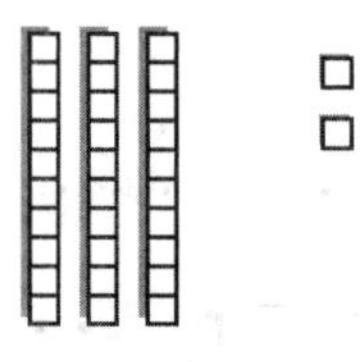

2 thousands + 3 hundreds + 3 tens + 2 ones = 2332

b)

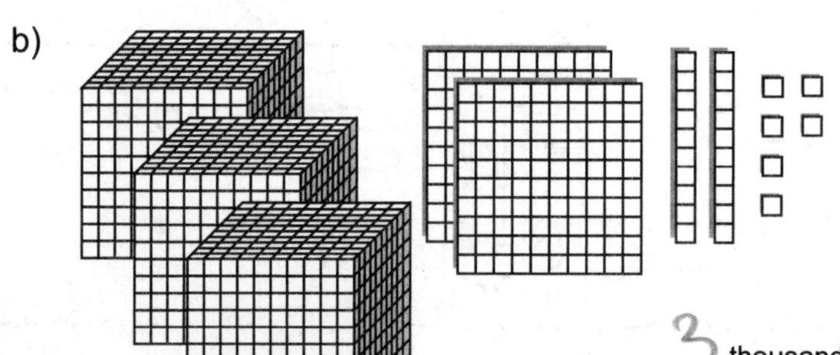

3 thousands + 2 hundreds + 2 tens + 6 ones = 3226

c)

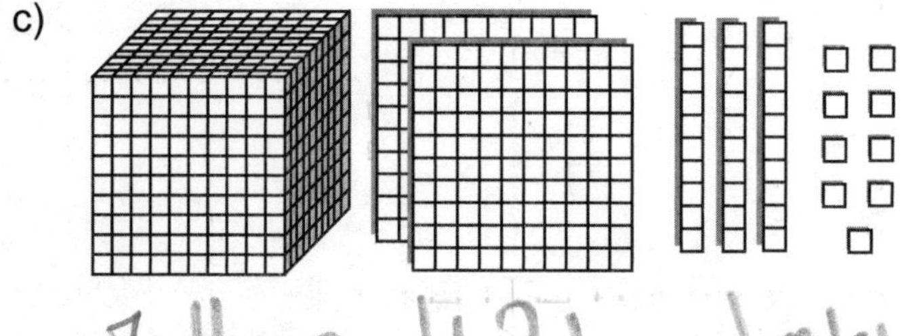

1 thousand + 2 hundreds + 3 tens + 9 ones. = 1239

BONUS:

6. Make you own model of a number using base-10 materials. Write your number in expanded form.

# NS4-3: Representation with Base-10 Materials *(continued)*

Steps for drawing a thousands cube:

Step 1:
Draw a square.

Step 2:
Draw lines from its 3 vertices.

Step 3:
Join the lines.

7. Represent the given numbers with the base-10 materials in the place value chart. The first one is started for you.

| | Number | Thousands | Hundreds | Tens | Ones |
|---|---|---|---|---|---|
| a) | 2314 | | | | |
| b) | 1245 | | | | |
| c) | 3143 | | | | |

8. Write the numbers for the given base-10 materials.

| | Thousands | Hundreds | Tens | Ones | Number |
|---|---|---|---|---|---|
| a) | | | | | 2234 |
| b) | | | | | 1368 |

# NS4-4: Expanded Form

1. For each number below, draw the base-10 model. Write each number in expanded form first (as shown in the example).

Example: 1213 = 1000 + 200 + 10 + 3

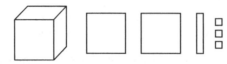

a) 2317 = 2000 + 300 + 10 + 7

b) 1446 = 1000 + 400 + 40 + 6

2. Expand the following numbers using **numerals** and **words**. The first one is done for you.

a) 2427 = 2 thousands + 4 hundreds + 2 tens + 7 ones

b) 4569 = 4 thousands + 5 hundreds + 6 tens + 9 ones

c) 3875 = 3 thousands + 8 hundreds + 7 tens + 5 ones.

d) 7210 = 7 thousands + 2 hundreds + 1 ten + 0 ones.

e) 623 = 0 thousands + 6 hundreds + 2 tens + 3 ones.

f) 9542 = 9 thousands + 5 hundreds + 4 tens + 2 ones.

3. Write the number in expanded form (using **numerals**). The first one is done for you. Use a separate piece of paper for the questions after part c).

a) 2613 = 2000 + 600 + 10 + 3 b) 27 = 20 + 7 c) 48 = 40 + 8

d) 1232= e) 6103 f) 3570 g) 598 h) 2901 i) 8112

j) 4213 k) 26 l) 6486 m) 1789 n) 3657 o) 9412

BONUS: Write 10, 100, or 1000 in the box to make each equation true.

a) 2316 + 100 = 2416 b) 5723 + 1000 = 6723 c) 4021 + 100 = 4121

d) 9188 + 10 = 9198 e) 3617 + 1000 = 4617 f) 7928 + 1000 = 8028

# NS4-5: Representing Numbers

Eugene makes a **model** of the number 342 using base-10 materials. He writes the number in **expanded form** in two ways, using **numerals and words**, and using **numerals alone**:

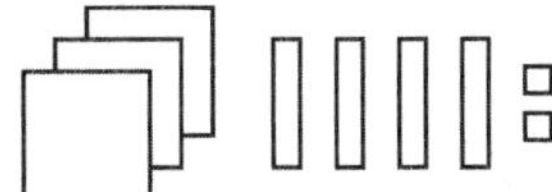

342 = 3 hundreds + 4 tens + 2 ones    expanded form (using numerals and words)

342 = 300 + 40 + 2    expanded form (using numerals)

---

1. Make a model of each number using base-10 materials. Sketch your model. Write the number in expanded form using numerals and words **and** using numerals. The first one is done for you.

a) 125

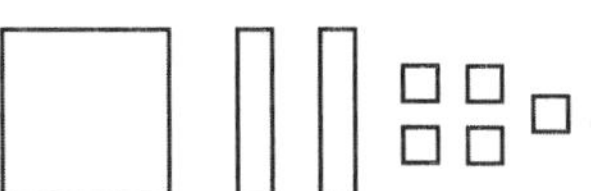

125 = 1 hundred + 2 tens + 5 ones

125 = 100 + 20 + 5

b) 238

238 = 2 hundred+3 tens+ 8 ones.

238 = 200+30+8.

c) 517

517 = 5 hundred +1 tens+ 7 ones

517 = 500+10+7.

d) 164

164 = 1 hundred + 6 tens + 4 ones.

164 = 100+60+4.

e) 307

307 = 3 hundreds + 0 tens + 7 ones.

307 = 300 + 7.

f) 540

540 = 5 hundreds + 4 tens + 0 ones.

540 = 500+ 40.

2. Write numerals for each number word.

a) forty-one 41

b) twenty-nine 29

c) sixty-five 65

d) one hundred and ninety 190

e) five hundred and two 502

f) two hundred and ninety-seven 297

g) three hundred and forty-six 346

h) one thousand, six hundred and twelve 1612

i) two thousand and sixty-three 263

3. On a separate piece of paper, write number words for each numeral (for example, the number word for 2137 is "two thousand, one hundred and thirty-seven").

a) 952  b) 3000  c) 4700  d) 6040  e) 2981  f) 5862

BONUS:

4. On a separate piece of paper, represent the number 275 in four different ways: by sketching a base-10 model, with number words, and in expanded form (two ways).

5. In the number 2735, what is the sum of the tens digit and the thousands digit?

# NS4-6: Comparing and Ordering Numbers

1. Write the number in each box. Write the name of each number on the line below. Then circle the larger number in each pair.

a) (i) 268

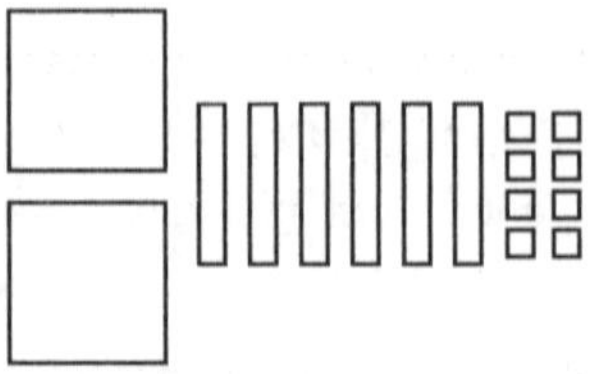

two hundred and sixty eight.

(ii) Greater 354

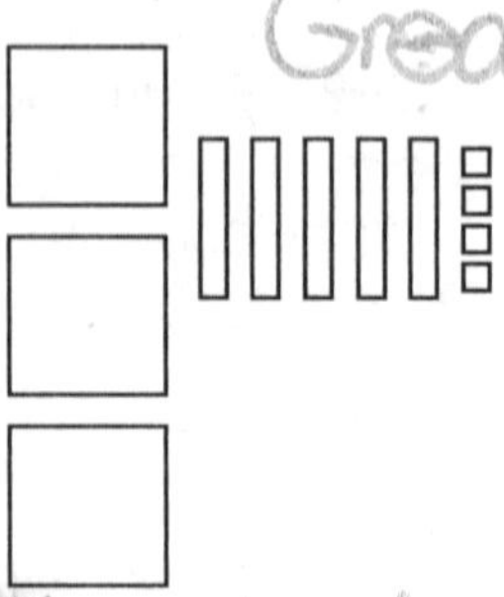

three hundred and fifty four

b) (i) Greater 2362

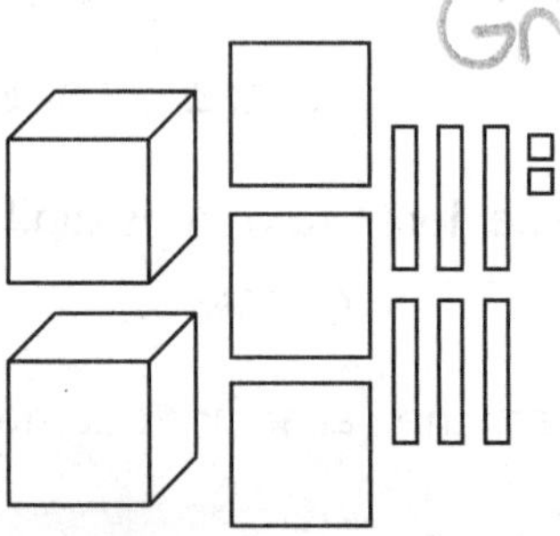

two thousand, three hundred, and sixty two.

(ii) 1350

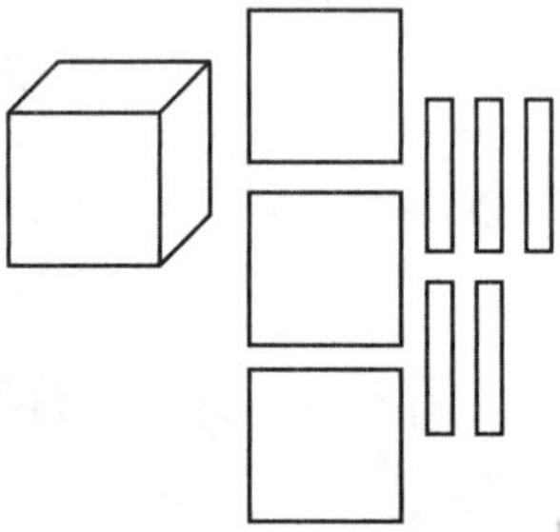

one thousand, three hundred and fifty.

2. Explain how you knew which numbers in question 1 were greater.

Because I looked in the thousands/hundreds place and I look at both of the numbers and saw which one was greater.

3. Write the number in each box. Then circle the larger number in each pair.
(HINT: If there is the same number of thousands, count the number of hundreds or tens.)

a) (i) 424

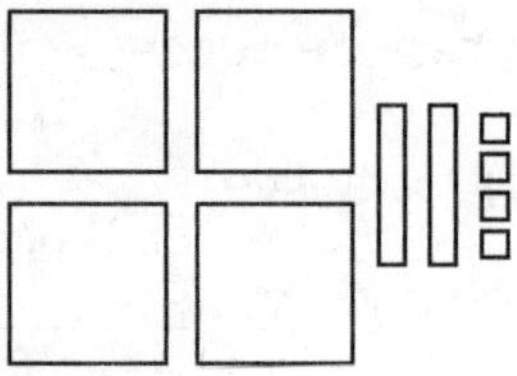

(ii) 224

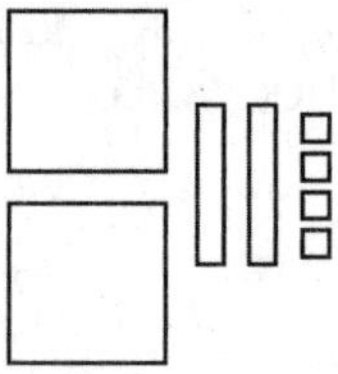

b) (i) 1232

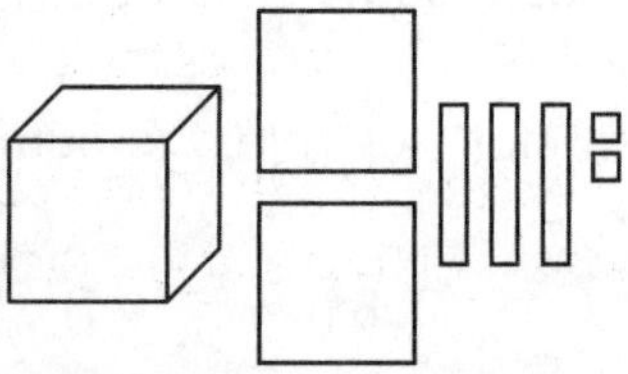

(ii) 123

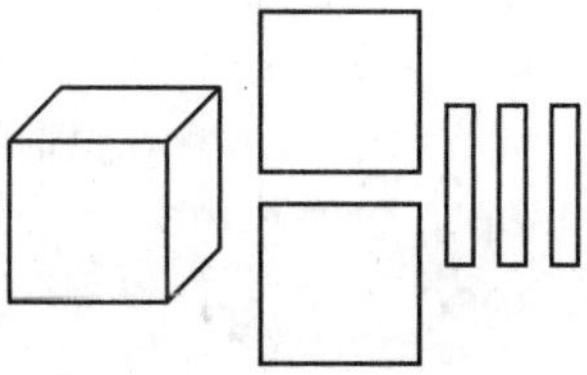

4. On a separate piece of paper, draw base-10 models for the following pairs of numbers. Circle the larger number.

a) four hundred and sixteen 460

b) one thousand three hundred 1007

5. Locate the numbers on the number line below. Cross out the smaller number.

a) 53 and 56

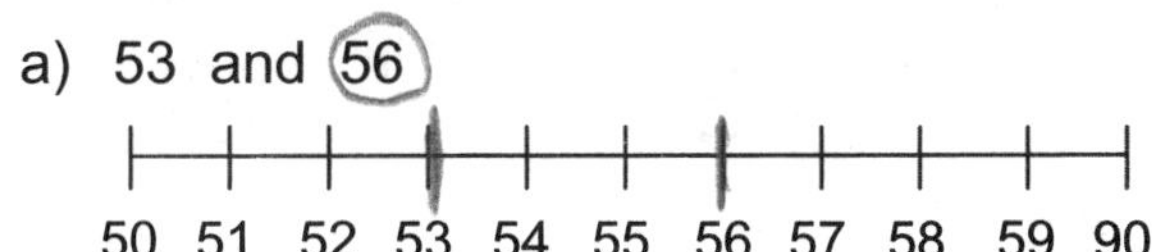


b) 91 and 97

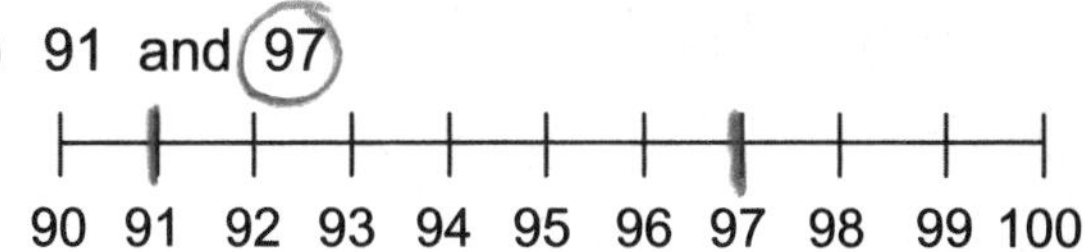


6. Which number is greater? Explain how you know on a separate piece of paper.

a) 47 or 74 b) 26 or 21

7. Circle the larger number in each pair.

a) 42 or forty five b) sixty four or 46 c) eleven or 17

8. Circle the greater number. (HINT: Look at the hundreds digit: <u>2</u>34.)

a) 614 or 714 b) 297 or 197 c) 364 or 864

9. Circle the greater number. (HINT: If the hundreds digits are the same, look at the tens digit: 2<u>3</u>4.)

a) 423 or 413 b) 770 or 769 c) 347 or 353

10. Circle the greater number. (HINT: If the hundreds and tens digits are the same, look at the ones digit: 23<u>4</u>.)

a) 237 or 233 b) 541 or 542 c) 900 or 909

11. Circle the greater number.

a) 342 432 243 b) 162 216 261 c) 745 547 754

12. Answer the following questions on a separate piece of paper. Explain your answers.

a) The school library has 762 books. The town library has 967 books. Which library has more books?

b) Montreal is 539 km away. Ottawa is 399 km away. Which city is further away?

13. Circle the greater number. (HINT: Compare the thousands digits first, then the hundreds, tens, and ones.)

a) 2175 or 3603 b) 4221 or 5012 c) 6726 or 6591 d) 3728 or 3729

e) 8175 or 8123 f) 5923 or 6000 g) 7327 or 7329 h) 4802 or 4952

14. On a separate piece of paper, say which number in each pair is greater. Explain how you know.

a) 7129 or 8235 b) 4212 or 4510 c) 9852 or 9851 d) 2423 or 294

15. List all the numbers you can make with the digits 9, 4, and 0. Then circle the greater number. How did you find your answer? (HINT: See how many numbers you can make that start with 9, then with 4, then with 0.) 940, 904, 409, 490, 094, 049.

BONUS:

16. Create the greatest possible number using these numbers. (Use each number only once!)

a) 4, 1, 6, 9 9641 b) 4, 0, 8, 1 8410 c) 7, 4, 8, 6 8764

17. What is the greatest number less than 1000 whose digits are all different?

# NS4-7: Mental Math

Add the numbers in questions 1 to 5 mentally by adding the ones digit first, and then the tens digit.

1. a) 10 + 3 = 13 b) 10 + 7 = 17 c) 5 + 10 = 15 d) 10 + 1 = 11
   e) 9 + 10 = 19 f) 10 + 4 = 14 g) 10 + 8 = 18 h) 10 + 2 = 12

2. a) 10 + 20 = 30 b) 40 + 10 = 50 c) 10 + 80 = 90 d) 10 + 50 = 60
   e) 30 + 10 = 40 f) 10 + 60 = 70 g) 10 + 10 = 20 h) 70 + 10 = 80

3. a) 10 + 25 = 35 b) 10 + 67 = 77 c) 10 + 31 = 41 d) 10 + 82 = 92
   e) 10 + 43 = 53 f) 10 + 51 = 61 g) 10 + 68 = 78 h) 10 + 21 = 31
   i) 10 + 11 = 21 j) 10 + 19 = 29 k) 10 + 44 = 54 l) 10 + 88 = 98

4. a) 20 + 30 = 50 b) 40 + 20 = 60 c) 30 + 30 = 60 d) 50 + 30 = 80
   e) 20 + 50 = 70 f) 40 + 40 = 80 g) 50 + 40 = 90 h) 40 + 30 = 70
   i) 60 + 30 = 90 j) 20 + 60 = 80 k) 20 + 70 = 90 l) 60 + 40 = 100

5. a) 20 + 23 = 43 b) 32 + 24 = 56 c) 51 + 12 = 63 d) 12 + 67 = 79
   e) 83 + 14 = 97 f) 65 + 24 = 89 g) 41 + 43 = 84 h) 70 + 27 = 97
   i) 31 + 61 = 92 j) 54 + 33 = 87 k) 28 + 31 = 59 l) 42 + 55 = 97

6. a) 9 + 3 = 12 b) 9 + 7 = 16 c) 6 + 9 = 15 d) 4 + 9 = 13
   e) 9 + 9 = 18 f) 5 + 9 = 14 g) 9 + 2 = 11 h) 9 + 8 = 17

7. a) 8 + 2 = 10 b) 8 + 6 = 14 c) 8 + 7 = 15 d) 4 + 8 = 12
   e) 5 + 8 = 13 f) 8 + 3 = 11 g) 9 + 8 = 17 h) 8 + 8 = 16

8. a) 40 − 10 = 30 b) 50 − 10 = 40 c) 70 − 10 = 60 d) 20 − 10 = 10
   e) 40 − 20 = 20 f) 60 − 30 = 30 g) 40 − 30 = 10 h) 60 − 50 = 10

9. a) 57 − 34 = 23 b) 43 − 12 = 31 c) 62 − 21 = 41 d) 59 − 36 = 23
   e) 87 − 63 = 24 f) 95 − 62 = 33 g) 35 − 10 = 25 h) 17 − 8 = 9

# NS4-7: Mental Math *(continued)*

**Multiples of Ten**

In the exercises below, you will learn several ways to use multiples of ten in mental addition or subtraction.

**I** You can write one number in expanded form and add on one multiple of 10 at a time:

425 + 312 = 425 + 300 + 10 + 2 = 725 + 10 + 2 = 735 + 2 = 737

927 – 216 = 927 – 200 – 10 – 6 = 727 – 10 – 6 = 717 – 6 = 711

Sometimes you will need to carry:
625 + 193 = 625 + 100 + 90 + 3 = 725 + 90 + 3 = 815 + 3 = 818

1. Warm up.

a) 427 + 100 = b) 325 + 10 = c) 932 + 5 = d) 632 + 200 =

e) 719 + 30 = f) 527 + 300 = g) 973 – 30 = h) 453 – 20 =

i) 688 – 70 = j) 712 – 400 = k) 372 + 90 = l) 589 + 60 =

2. Write the second number in expanded form and add or subtract one digit at a time. The first one is done for you.

a) 243 + 152 = 243 + 100 + 50 + 2 = 395

b) 342 + 226 = ______ = ______

c) 487 + 122 = ______ = ______

3. Add or subtract mentally (one digit at a time).

a) 372 + 214 = b) 578 + 221 = c) 586 – 423 =

**II** If one of the numbers you are adding or subtracting is close to a number with a multiple of 10, add or subtract the multiple of 10 and then add or subtract an adjustment factor:

425 + 198 = 425 + 200 – 2 = 625 – 2 = 623

723 + 23 = 723 + 20 + 3 = 743 + 3 = 746

**III** Sometimes in subtraction, it helps to think of a multiple of 10 as a sum of 1 and a number consisting entirely of 9s (for example, 100 = 1 + 99; 1000 = 1 + 999). You never have to borrow or exchange when you are subtracting from a number consisting entirely of 9s:

100 – 26 = 1 + 99 – 26 = 1 + 73 = 74 ← Do the subtraction, using 99 instead of 100, and then add 1 to your answer.

1000 – 724 = 1 + 999 – 724 = 1 + 275 = 276

4. Use the tricks you have just learned to solve these problems.

a) 735 + 99 = b) 421 + 304 = c) 100 – 67 = d) 1000 – 975 =

# NS4-8: Regrouping

Carl has 5 tens strips and 17 ones squares. He exchanges 10 ones squares for 1 tens strip:

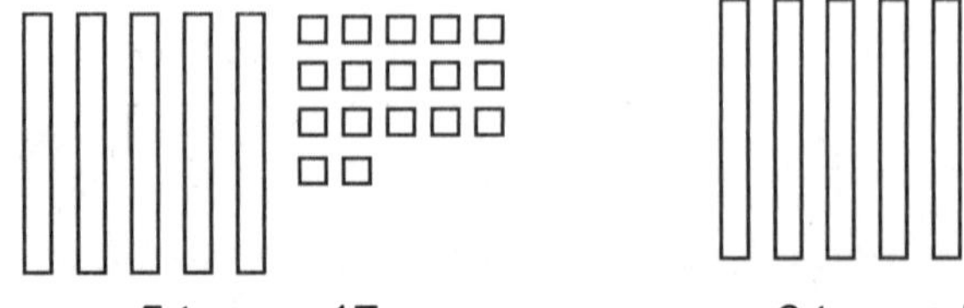

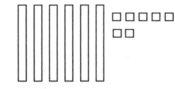

5 tens + 17 ones = 6 tens + 7 ones

---

1. Exchange 10 ones squares for 1 tens strip.

a) 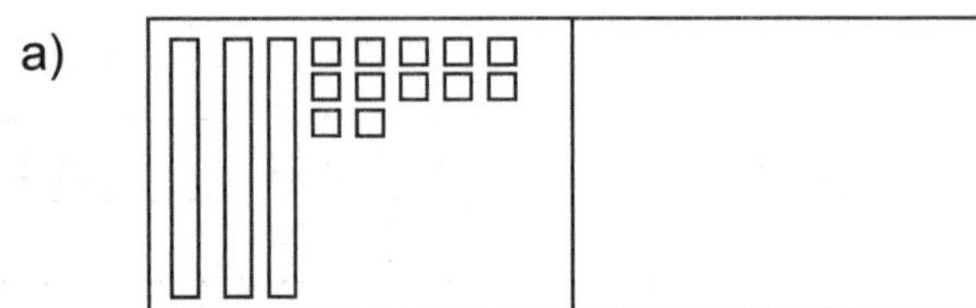

___ tens + ___ ones = ___ tens + ___ ones

b) 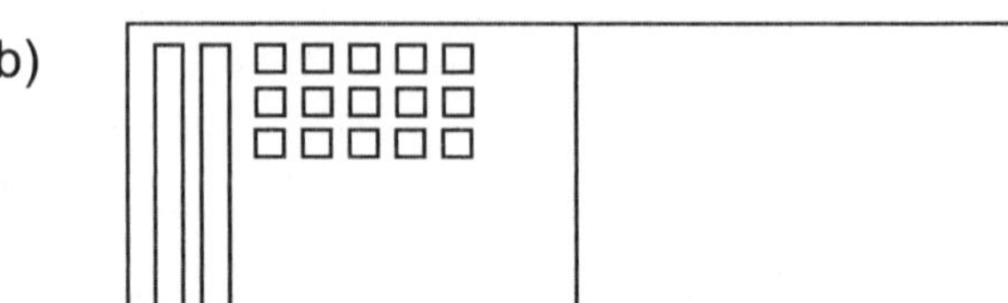

___ tens + ___ ones = ___ tens + ___ ones

c) 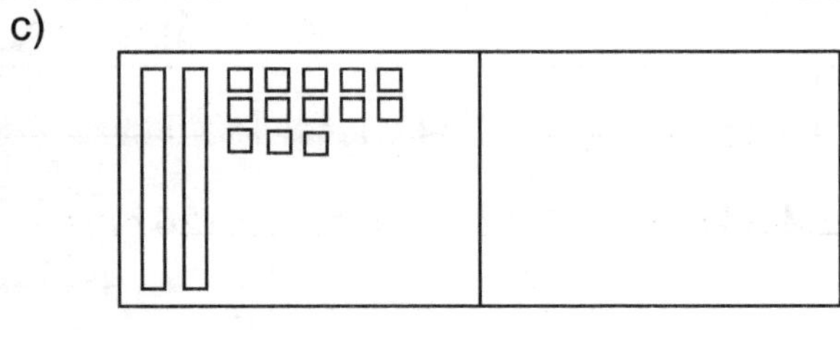

___ tens + ___ ones = ___ tens + ___ ones

d) 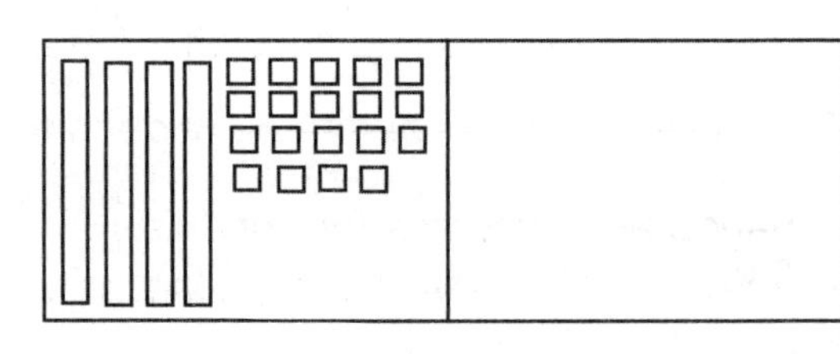

___ tens + ___ ones = ___ tens + ___ ones

2. Complete the charts by exchanging as many ones for tens as you can. REMEMBER: 10 ones = 1 ten, 20 ones = 2 tens, 30 ones = 3 tens, and so on. The first one is done for you.

a)

| Tens | Ones |
|---|---|
| 6 | (2)5 |
| 6 + (2) = 8 | 5 |

= 85

b)

| Tens | Ones |
|---|---|
| 8 | 12 |
| | |

=

c)

| Tens | Ones |
|---|---|
| 5 | 31 |
| | |

=

d)

| Tens | Ones |
|---|---|
| 7 | 17 |
| | |

=

e)

| Tens | Ones |
|---|---|
| 6 | 29 |
| | |

=

f)

| Tens | Ones |
|---|---|
| 1 | 52 |
| | |

=

3. Exchange ones for tens.

a) 23 ones = ___ tens + ___ ones
b) 56 ones = ___ tens + ___ ones
c) 86 ones = ___ tens + ___ ones
d) 58 ones = ___ tens + ___ ones
e) 18 ones = ___ tens + ___ ones
f) 72 ones = ___ tens + ___ ones
g) 80 ones = ___ tens + ___ ones
h) 7 ones = ___ tens + ___ ones
i) 98 ones = ___ tens + ___ ones

# NS4-8: Regrouping *(continued)*

Mehmet has 2 hundreds squares, 15 tens strips, and 6 ones squares. He exchanges 10 tens strips for 1 hundreds square:

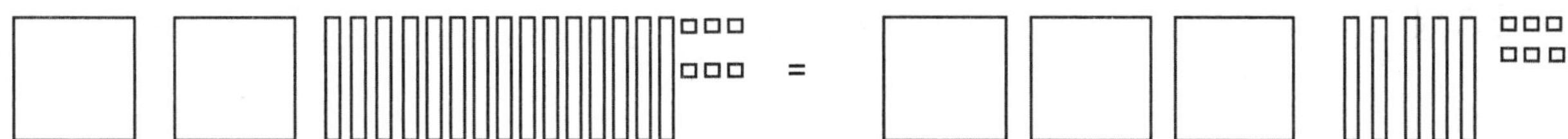

2 hundreds + 15 tens + 6 ones = 3 hundreds + 5 tens + 6 ones

---

4. Complete the charts by exchanging 10 tens for 1 hundred.

a)

| Hundreds | Tens |
|---|---|
| 5 | 11 |
| 5 + 1 = 6 | 1 |

b)

| Hundreds | Tens |
|---|---|
| 2 | 15 |
| | |

c)

| Hundreds | Tens |
|---|---|
| 6 | 17 |
| | |

d)

| Hundreds | Tens |
|---|---|
| 6 | 12 |
| | |

e)

| Hundreds | Tens |
|---|---|
| 2 | 17 |
| | |

f)

| Hundreds | Tens |
|---|---|
| 5 | 10 |
| | |

5. Exchange as many tens for hundreds as you can. REMEMBER: 10 tens = 1 hundreds, 20 tens = 2 hundreds, 30 tens = 3 hundreds, and so on.

a) 3 hundreds + 13 tens + 4 ones = ____ hundreds + ____ tens + ____ ones

b) 8 hundreds + 21 tens + 1 ones = ____ hundreds + ____ tens + ____ ones

c) 3 hundreds + 10 tens + 5 ones = ______________________________

d) 1 hundreds + 34 tens + 7 ones = ______________________________

e) 4 hundreds + 51 tens + 0 ones = ______________________________

6. Exchange tens for hundreds or ones for tens. The first one is done for you.

a) 4 hundreds + 2 tens + 19 ones = 4 hundreds + 3 tens + 9 ones

b) 7 hundreds + 25 tens + 2 ones = ______________________________

c) 2 hundreds + 43 tens + 6 ones = ______________________________

d) 7 hundreds + 1 tens + 28 ones = ______________________________

e) 7 hundreds + 0 tens + 61 ones = ______________________________

f) 0 hundreds + 26 tens + 3 ones = ______________________________

Maya has 1 thousands cube, 11 hundreds squares, 1 tens strip, and 2 ones squares.

She exchanges 10 hundreds squares for 1 thousand cube:

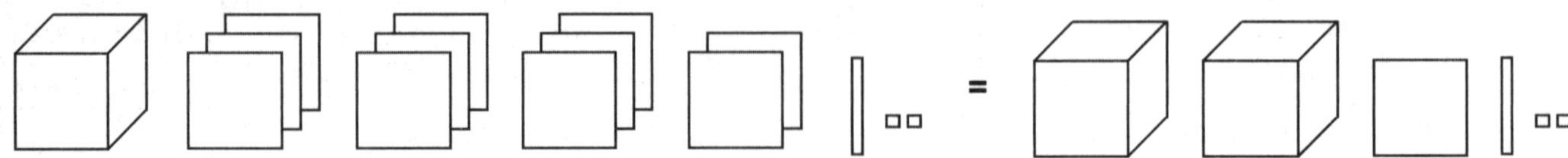

1 thousand + 11 hundreds + 1 ten + 2 ones = 2 thousands + 1 hundred + 1 ten + 2 ones

7. Complete the charts by exchanging 10 hundreds for 1 thousand.

a)

| Thousands | Hundreds |
|---|---|
| 3 | 12 |
| 3 + 1 = 4 | 2 |

b)

| Thousands | Hundreds |
|---|---|
| 4 | 13 |
| | |

c)

| Thousands | Hundreds |
|---|---|
| 7 | 14 |
| | |

8. Exchange 10 hundreds for 1 thousand. The first one is done for you.

a) 5 thousands + 12 hundreds + 3 tens + 1 one = 6 thousands + 2 hundreds + 3 tens + 1 one

b) 3 thousands + 15 hundreds + 1 ten + 6 ones = ____ thousands + ____ hundreds + ____ tens + ____ ones

c) 6 thousands + 14 hundreds + 6 tens + 5 ones = ____________________

d) 2 thousands + 18 hundreds + 0 tens + 7 ones = ____________________

e) 8 thousands + 10 hundreds + 1 ten + 0 ones = ____________________

9. Exchange hundreds for thousands, tens for hundreds, or ones for tens. The first one is done for you.

a) 3 thousands + 16 hundreds + 5 tens + 1 one = 4 thousands + 6 hundreds + 5 tens + 1 one

b) 6 thousands + 6 hundreds + 23 tens + 5 ones = ____________________

c) 4 thousands + 1 hundred + 3 tens + 19 ones = ____________________

Show your work for the remaining questions on a separate piece of paper.

d) 5 thousands + 21 hundreds + 1 ten + 9 ones

e) 7 thousands + 6 hundreds + 17 tens + 7 ones

10. Roger wants to build a model of three thousand, two hundred and thirty-five. He has 3 thousands cubes, 2 hundreds squares, and 24 ones squares. Can he build the model? Use diagrams and numbers to explain your answer.

# NS4-9: Adding Two-Digit Numbers

1. Find the **sum** of the numbers by drawing a picture and by adding the digits (use base-10 materials to help you). Do not worry about drawing the model in too much detail.

a) 15 + 43

| | With base-10 materials | | With numerals | |
|---|---|---|---|---|
| | Tens | Ones | Tens | Ones |
| 15 | | | 1 | 5 |
| 43 | | | 4 | 3 |
| sum | | | 5 | 8 |

b) 35 + 42

| | With base-10 materials | | With numerals | |
|---|---|---|---|---|
| | Tens | Ones | Tens | Ones |
| 35 | | | | |
| 42 | | | | |
| sum | | | | |

c) 31 + 27

| | With base-10 materials | | With numerals | |
|---|---|---|---|---|
| | Tens | Ones | Tens | Ones |
| ___ | | | | |
| ___ | | | | |
| sum | | | | |

d) 13 + 24

| | With base-10 materials | | With numerals | |
|---|---|---|---|---|
| | Tens | Ones | Tens | Ones |
| ___ | | | | |
| ___ | | | | |
| sum | | | | |

2. Add the numbers by adding the digits.

a) 3 4 + 4 3

b) 7 7 + 1 2

c) 5 4 + 3 5

d) 1 0 + 4 9

e) 1 6 + 2 3

3. On a separate piece of paper, add the numbers by drawing a picture (use base-10 materials to help you) **and** by lining up the digits.

a) 16 + 21 b) 52 + 24 c) 81 + 11 d) 43 + 31 e) 75+ 14 f) 61 + 16

# NS4-10: Adding with Regrouping (or Carrying)



1. Add the numbers below by drawing a picture and by adding the digits. Use base-10 materials to show how to combine the numbers and how to regroup. (The first one is done for you.)

a) 16 + 25

| | With base-10 materials | | With numerals | |
|---|---|---|---|---|
| | Tens | Ones | Tens | Ones |
| 25 | | | 1 | 6 |
| 17 | | | 2 | 5 |
| sum | | exchange 10 ones for 1 ten | 3 | 11 |
| | after regrouping | | 4 | 1 |

b) 25 + 37

| With base-10 materials | | With numerals | |
|---|---|---|---|
| Tens | Ones | Tens | Ones |
| | | | |
| | | | |
| | | | |
| | | | |

c) 29 + 36

| With base-10 materials | | With numerals | |
|---|---|---|---|
| Tens | Ones | Tens | Ones |
| | | | |
| | | | |
| | | | |
| | | | |

d) 17 + 35

| With base-10 materials | | With numerals | |
|---|---|---|---|
| Tens | Ones | Tens | Ones |
| | | | |
| | | | |
| | | | |
| | | | |

e) 27 + 26

| With base-10 materials | | With numerals | |
|---|---|---|---|
| Tens | Ones | Tens | Ones |
| | | | |
| | | | |
| | | | |
| | | | |

f) 19 + 8

| With base-10 materials | | With numerals | |
|---|---|---|---|
| Tens | Ones | Tens | Ones |
| | | | |
| | | | |
| | | | |
| | | | |

2. Add the ones digits. Show how you would exchange 10 ones for 1 ten. The first question is done for you.

a) [1] 15 + 18 = [3]

b) [ ] 64 + 16 = [ ]

c) [ ] 75 + 19 = [ ]

d) [ ] 66 + 17 = [ ]

e) [ ] 15 + 38 = [ ]

3. Add the numbers by regrouping (or carrying). The first one is done for you.

a) $\overset{1}{3}6 + 18 = 54$

b) 37 + 18

c) 59 + 18

d) 37 + 43

e) 57 + 26

f) 63 + 29

g) 58 + 47

h) 18 + 77

i) 59 + 13

j) 75 + 16

# NS4-11: Adding Three-Digit Numbers

Dalha adds 152 + 273 using base-10 materials:

| | | | | | | |
|---|---|---|---|---|---|---|
| **152** | = | 1 hundred | + | 5 tens | + | 2 ones |
| **+ 273** | = | 2 hundreds | + | 7 tens | + | 3 ones |
| | = | 3 hundreds | + | 12 tens | + | 7 ones |

Then, to get the final answer, Dalha exchanges 10 tens for 1 hundred:

= 4 hundreds + 2 tens + 7 ones

1. Add the numbers using base-10 materials or a picture (and record your work).

a)
353 = _____ hundreds + _____ tens + _____ ones
+ 164 = _____ hundred + _____ tens + _____ ones
= _____ hundreds + _____ tens + _____ ones
after regrouping = _____ hundreds + _____ ten + _____ ones

b)
462 = _____ hundreds + _____ tens + _____ ones
+ 375 = _____ hundreds + _____ tens + _____ ones
= _____ hundreds + _____ tens + _____ ones
after regrouping = _____ hundreds + _____ tens + _____ ones

2. Add. You will need to carry. The first one is started for you.

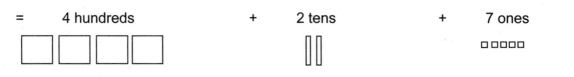

a)
```
  1
  5 2 6
+ 2 9 3
-------
    1 9
```

b) 645 + 183

c) 374 + 462

d) 482 + 477

e) 284 + 595

3. Add. You will need to carry into the tens.

a) 328 + 14

b) 247 + 516

c) 915 + 45

d) 346 + 205

e) 218 + 348

# NS4-11: Adding Three-Digit Numbers *(continued)*

4. Add, carrying where necessary.

   a) $\begin{array}{r} 564 \\ +\ 153 \\ \hline \end{array}$ b) $\begin{array}{r} 248 \\ +\ 424 \\ \hline \end{array}$ c) $\begin{array}{r} 526 \\ +\ 348 \\ \hline \end{array}$ d) $\begin{array}{r} 164 \\ +\ 672 \\ \hline \end{array}$ e) $\begin{array}{r} 444 \\ +\ 209 \\ \hline \end{array}$ f) $\begin{array}{r} 856 \\ +\ 134 \\ \hline \end{array}$

5. Add by lining the numbers up correctly in the grid. The first one is started for you.

   a) 288 + 265 b) 272 + 213 c) 643 + 718 d) 937 + 25

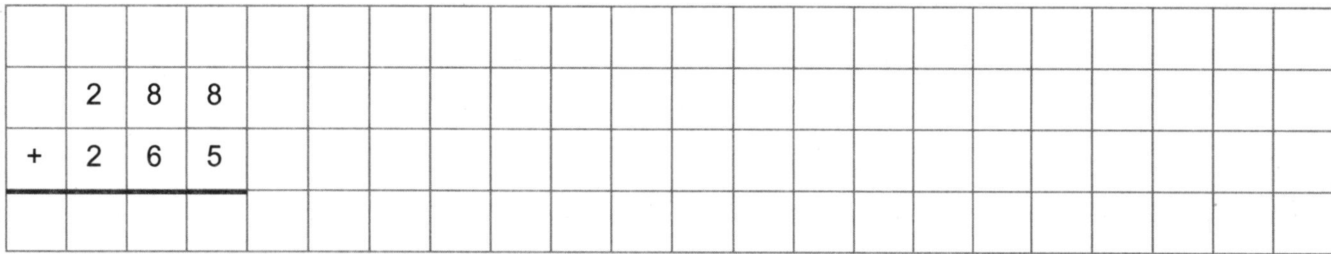


   e) 146 + 273 f) 816 + 925 g) 369 + 119 h) 847 + 910

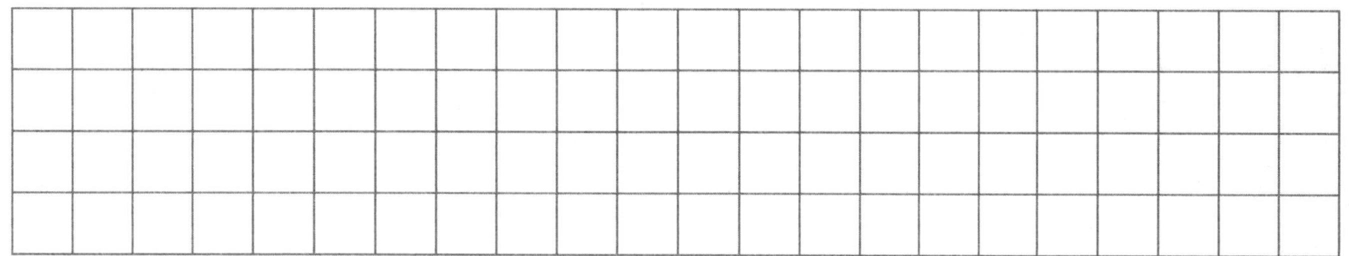

6. Use the pattern in your answers to parts a), b), and c) to find the sums in parts d) and e) without adding.

   a) $\begin{array}{r} 9 \\ +\ 9 \\ \hline \end{array}$ b) $\begin{array}{r} 99 \\ +\ 99 \\ \hline \end{array}$ c) $\begin{array}{r} 999 \\ +\ 999 \\ \hline \end{array}$ d) $\begin{array}{r} 9999 \\ +\ 9999 \\ \hline \end{array}$ e) $\begin{array}{r} 99999 \\ +\ 99999 \\ \hline \end{array}$

7. A glass can holds 255 mL of water. How much water can 2 glasses hold?

8. Alice's class raised $312 for charity. Sophie's class raised $287.

   a) Whose class raised more money? How do you know?

   b) How much money did the two classes raise altogether?

9. At a summer camp, 324 children are enrolled in baseball. There are 128 **more** children enrolled in swimming than in baseball.

   a) How many children are enrolled in swimming?

   b) How much children are enrolled in lessons altogether?

10. What is the greatest number you can add to 275 without having to regroup any place value?

# NS4-12: Adding Four-Digit Numbers

Amber adds 1852 + 2321 using base-10 materials:

| | | | | | | | | |
|---|---|---|---|---|---|---|---|---|
| **1852** | = | 1 thousand | + | 8 hundreds | + | 5 tens | + | 2 ones |
| **+ 2321** | = | 2 thousands | + | 3 hundreds | + | 2 tens | + | 1 ones |
| | = | 3 thousands | + | 11 hundreds | + | 7 tens | + | 3 ones |

Then, to get the final answer, Amber exchanges 10 hundreds for 1 thousand:

= 4 thousands + 1 hundred + 7 tens + 3 ones

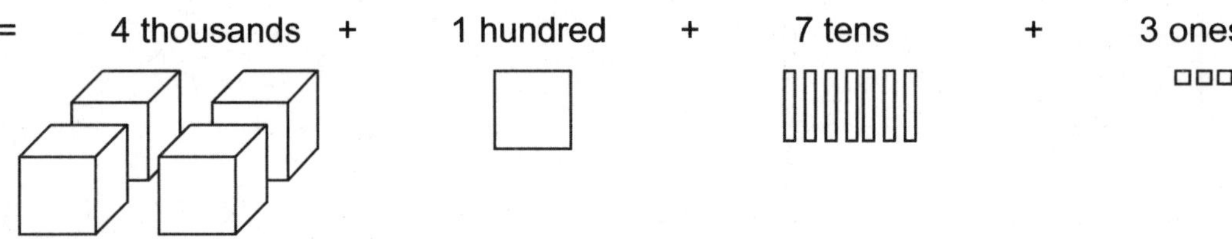

1. Add the numbers using base-10 materials or a picture. Record your work below.

a)

| | | | | | | | | | | | |
|---|---|---|---|---|---|---|---|---|---|---|---|
| 2543 | = | _____ | thousands + | _____ | hundreds + | _____ | tens + | _____ | ones |
| + 3621 | = | _____ | thousands + | _____ | hundreds + | _____ | tens + | _____ | ones |
| | = | _____ | thousands + | _____ | hundreds + | _____ | tens + | _____ | ones |
| after regrouping | = | _____ | thousands + | _____ | hundreds + | _____ | tens + | _____ | ones |

b)

| | | | | | | | | | |
|---|---|---|---|---|---|---|---|---|---|
| 3824 | = | _____ | thousands + | _____ | hundreds + | _____ | tens + | _____ | ones |
| + 1654 | = | _____ | thousands + | _____ | hundreds + | _____ | tens + | _____ | ones |
| | = | _____ | thousands + | _____ | hundreds + | _____ | tens + | _____ | ones |
| after regrouping | = | _____ | thousands + | _____ | hundreds + | _____ | tens + | _____ | ones |

2. Add. You will need to regroup or carry. The first one is started for you.

a)
```
   5 2 6 5
 + 2 9 1 2
 ---------
     1 7 7
```
b)
```
   6 4 5 4
 + 1 8 3 3
 ---------
```
c)
```
   3 7 4 7
 + 2 6 2 1
 ---------
```
d)
```
   1 8 2 1
 + 2 7 7 2
 ---------
```
e)
```
   1 8 2 4
 + 5 7 7 3
 ---------
```

## NS4-12: Adding Four-Digit Numbers *(continued)*

3. Add. You will need to carry into the hundreds.

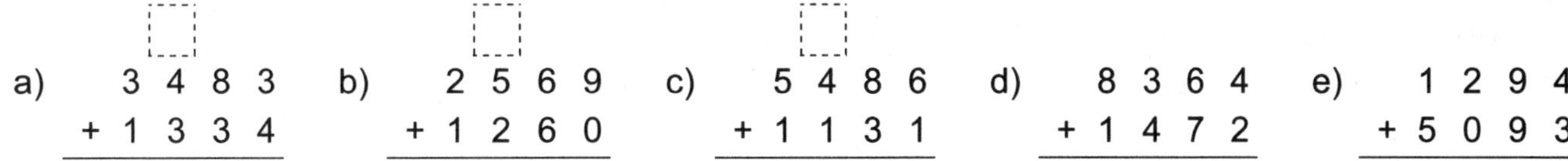

a) 3483 + 1334  b) 2569 + 1260  c) 5486 + 1131  d) 8364 + 1472  e) 1294 + 5093

4. Add. You will need to carry into the tens.

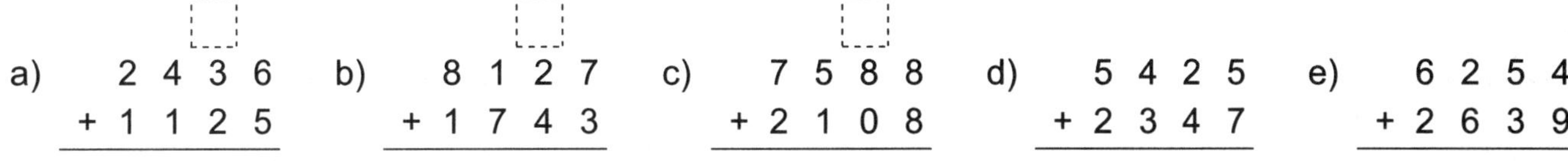

a) 2436 + 1125  b) 8127 + 1743  c) 7588 + 2108  d) 5425 + 2347  e) 6254 + 2639

5. Add (carrying where necessary).

a) 2354 + 2831  b) 4683 + 1742  c) 3831 + 4833  d) 6525 + 1533  e) 3844 + 2723

f) 3546 + 4822  g) 7624 + 1601  h) 5640 + 3712  i) 2925 + 1751  j) 3245 + 3431

6. Add by lining the numbers up correctly in the grid. In some questions you may have to carry twice.

a) 4534 + 2542  b) 6754 + 1360  c) 3214 + 4852  d) 2509 + 6621

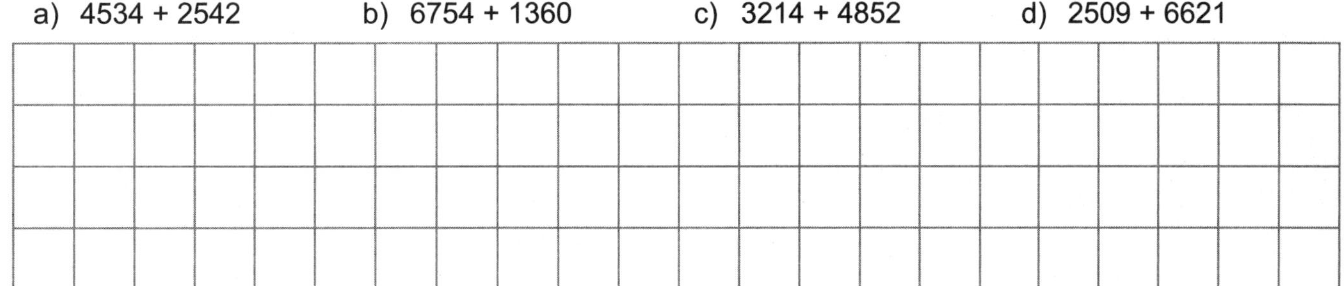

7. Emma flies 2457 km on one day and 1357 km the next day. How many kilometres did she fly in the two days?

8. 2375 people attended a science fair one day, and 3528 people attended the next day. How many people attended the fair on both days?

9. The human heart beats 4200 times in an hour. How many times does it beat in 3 hours?

# NS4-13: Subtraction

Bradley subtracts 48 – 32 using base-10 materials. He makes a model of 48. Then he takes away 3 tens and 2 ones (because 32 = 3 tens + 2 ones):

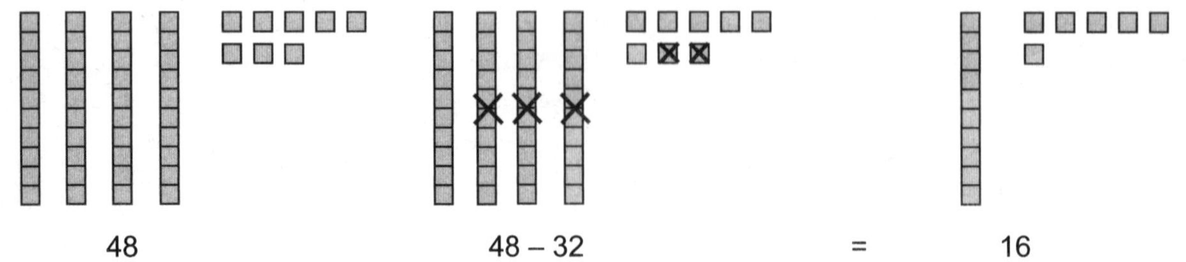


1. Perform the subtractions by crossing out tens strips and ones squares. Draw your final answer in the right-hand box. The first one is done for you.

a)

| 39 – 18 | = 21 |
|---|---|

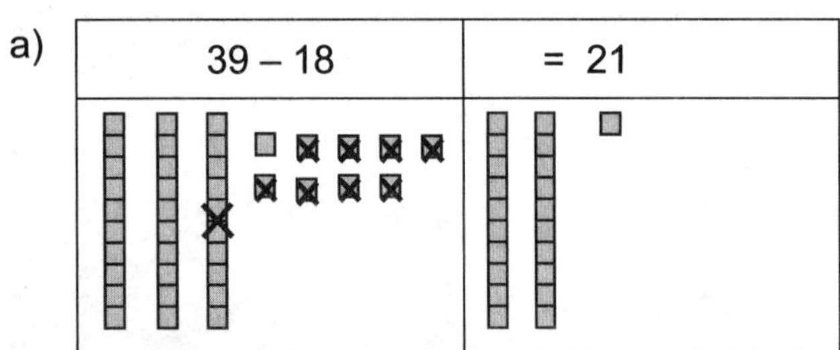

b)

| 25 – 11 | = |
|---|---|

c)

| 43 – 21 | = |
|---|---|

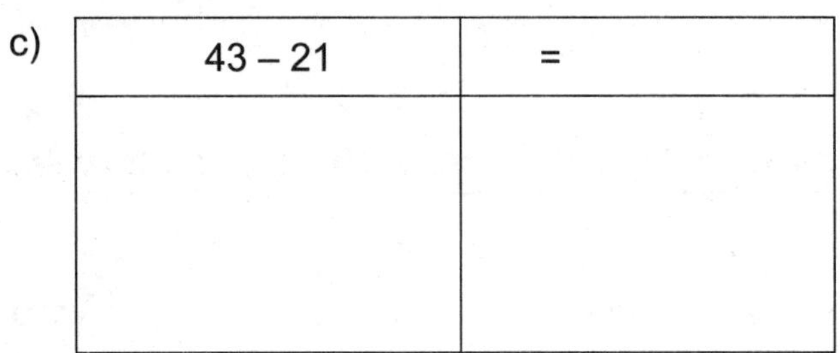

d)

| 45 – 32 | = |
|---|---|

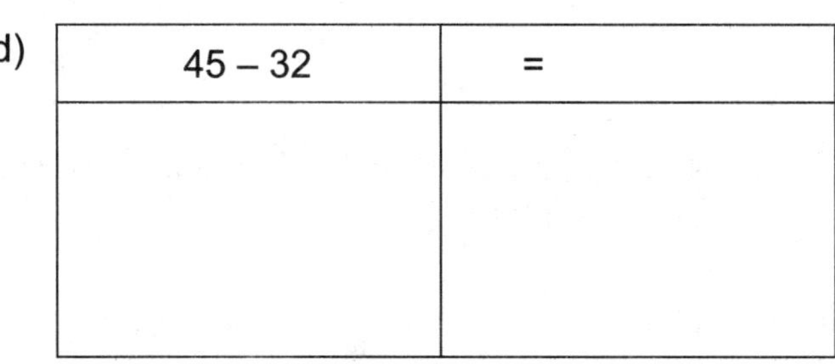

2. Write the number of tens and ones in each number. Then subtract each pair of numbers.

a) 45 = 4 tens + 5 ones
− 32 = 3 tens + 2 ones
= 1 tens + 3 ones
= 13

b) 57 = ___ tens + ___ ones
− 34 = ___ tens + ___ ones
= ___ tens + ___ ones
=

c) 84 = ___ tens + ___ ones
− 63 = ___ tens + ___ ones
= ___ tens + ___ ones
=

d) 89 = ___ tens + ___ ones
− 56 = ___ tens + ___ ones
=
=

e) 77 = ___ tens + ___ ones
− 44 = ___ tens + ___ ones
=
=

f) 67 = ___ tens + ___ ones
− 45 = ___ tens + ___ ones
=
=

3. Subtract by writing the number of tens and ones in each number.

a)
36 = 30 + 6
− 24 = 20 + 4
= 10 + 2
= 12

b)
84 =
− 52 =
=
=

c)
98 =
− 37 =
=
=

d)
73 =
− 12 =

e)
16 =
− 14 =

f)
88 =
− 33 =

4. Subtract the numbers by subtracting the digits.

a) 54 − 23 b) 86 − 73 c) 36 − 15 d) 64 − 32 e) 95 − 42 f) 89 − 40

5. a) Draw a picture of 543 using hundreds squares, tens strips, and ones squares. Show how you would subtract 543 – 421.

b) Now subtract the numbers by lining up the digits and subtracting. Do you get the same answer?

BONUS: Extend your knowledge of using patterns.

6. a) 274 − 132 b) 825 − 424 c) 936 − 423 d) 712 − 510 e) 980 − 120

7. How would you subtract the following numbers? Write what you think each answer might be.

a) 7532 − 4121 b) 65356 − 44245 c) 955763 − 523011

8. The world's tallest tree is 110 m. The Skylon Tower in Niagara Falls is 156 m. How much taller is the Skylon Tower than the tallest tree?

# NS4-14: Subtracting by Regrouping

Farkan subtracts 46 − 18 using base-10 materials.

Step 1:
Farkan represents 46 with base-10 materials.

| Tens | Ones |
|---|---|
| 4 | 6 |

Here is how Farkan uses numerals to show his work:

  46
− 18

Step 2:
8 (the ones digit of 18) is greater than 6 (the ones digit of 46) so Farkan regroups 1 tens strip as 10 ones squares.

| Tens | Ones |
|---|---|
| 3 | 16 |

Here is how Farkan shows the regrouping:

 3 16
 ~~4~~ ~~6~~
− 1 8

Step 3:
Farkan subtracts 18 (he takes away 1 tens strip and 8 ones squares).

| Tens | Ones |
|---|---|
| 2 | 8 |

And now Farkan can subtract 16 – 8 ones and 3 – 1 tens:

 3 16
 ~~4~~ ~~6~~
− 1 8
 2 8

---

1. Farkan does not have enough ones to subtract. Help him by exchanging 1 tens strip for 10 ones squares. Using Steps 1 and 2 above, show how he would rewrite his subtraction statement.

a) 63 − 26

| Tens | Ones |
|---|---|
| 6 | 3 |

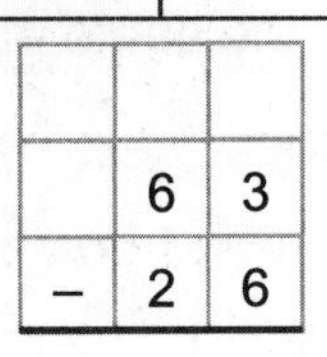

| | | |
|---|---|---|
| | | |
| | 6 | 3 |
| − | 2 | 6 |

| Tens | Ones |
|---|---|
| 5 | 13 |

| | | |
|---|---|---|
| | 5 | 13 |
| | ~~6~~ | ~~3~~ |
| − | 2 | 6 |

b) 74 − 39

| Tens | Ones |
|---|---|
| 7 | 4 |

| | | |
|---|---|---|
| | | |
| | 7 | 4 |
| − | 3 | 9 |

| Tens | Ones |
|---|---|
| | |

| | | |
|---|---|---|
| | | |
| | 7 | 4 |
| − | 3 | 9 |

c) 42 − 19

| Tens | Ones |
|---|---|
| 42 | 19 |

| | | |
|---|---|---|
| | | |
| | 4 | 2 |
| − | 1 | 9 |

| Tens | Ones |
|---|---|
| | |

| | | |
|---|---|---|
| | | |
| | 4 | 2 |
| − | 1 | 9 |

d) 65 − 27

| Tens | Ones |
|---|---|
| 6 | 5 |

| | | |
|---|---|---|
| | | |
| | 6 | 5 |
| − | 2 | 7 |

| Tens | Ones |
|---|---|
| | |

| | | |
|---|---|---|
| | | |
| | 6 | 5 |
| − | 2 | 7 |

2. Subtract by regrouping (or borrowing). The first one is done for you.

a)

| | 3 | 13 |
|---|---|---|
| | ~~4~~ | ~~3~~ |
| − | 2 | 7 |
| | 1 | 6 |

b)

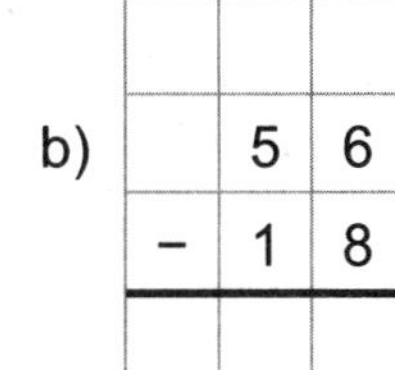

| | | |
|---|---|---|
| | 5 | 6 |
| − | 1 | 8 |
| | | |

c)

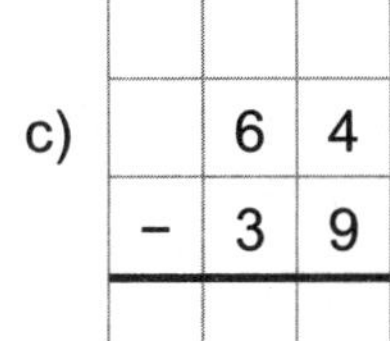

| | | |
|---|---|---|
| | 6 | 4 |
| − | 3 | 9 |
| | | |

d)

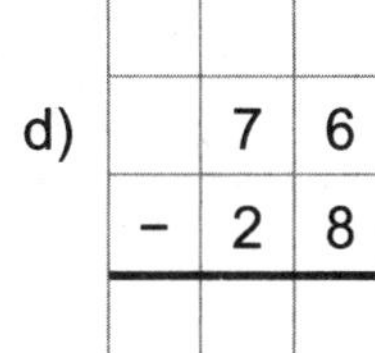

| | | |
|---|---|---|
| | 7 | 6 |
| − | 2 | 8 |
| | | |

e)

| | | |
|---|---|---|
| | 5 | 5 |
| − | 3 | 7 |
| | | |

3. For the questions where you need to regroup, write "Help!" in the space provided. How do you know you have to regroup?

a) 54 − 19 Help! 4 is less than 9

b) 77 − 56 OK

c) 85 − 53 ________

d) 95 − 18 ________

e) 66 − 54 ________

f) 84 − 17 ________

g) 24 − 12 ________

h) 47 − 19 ________

i) 54 − 16 ________

4. To subtract 348 −194, Sara exchanges 1 hundreds square for 10 tens strips:

| Hundreds | Tens | Ones |
|---|---|---|
| 3 | 4 | 8 |

| Hundreds | Tens | Ones |
|---|---|---|
| 2 | 14 | 8 |

| Hundreds | Tens | Ones |
|---|---|---|
| 1 | 5 | 4 |

On a separate piece of paper, draw a picture to show how you would exchange 1 hundreds square for 10 tens strips to subtract the following numbers:

a) 415 − 122 b) 546 − 162 c) 853 − 271 d) 532 − 241

5. Subtract by borrowing from the **hundreds**. The first one is started for you.

a)

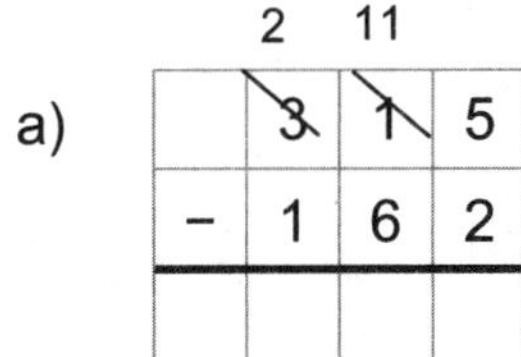

| | 2 | 11 | |
|---|---|---|---|
| | ~~3~~ | ~~1~~ | 5 |
| − | 1 | 6 | 2 |
| | | | |

b)

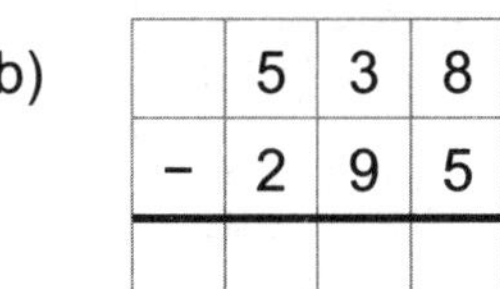

| | | | |
|---|---|---|---|
| | 5 | 3 | 8 |
| − | 2 | 9 | 5 |
| | | | |

c)

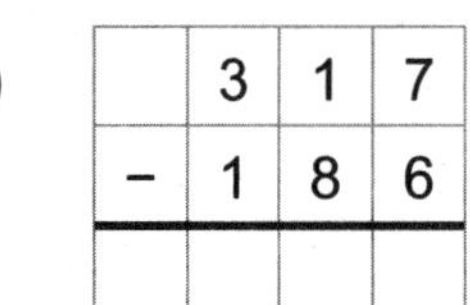

| | | | |
|---|---|---|---|
| | 3 | 1 | 7 |
| − | 1 | 8 | 6 |
| | | | |

d)

| | | | |
|---|---|---|---|
| | 9 | 4 | 2 |
| − | 5 | 7 | 0 |
| | | | |

6. The length of Whistling Cave on Vancouver Island is 782 m. The length of Grueling Cave is 697 m. How much longer is Whistling Cave than Grueling Cave?

7. Subtract by borrowing from the **tens**. The first one is started for you.

a) 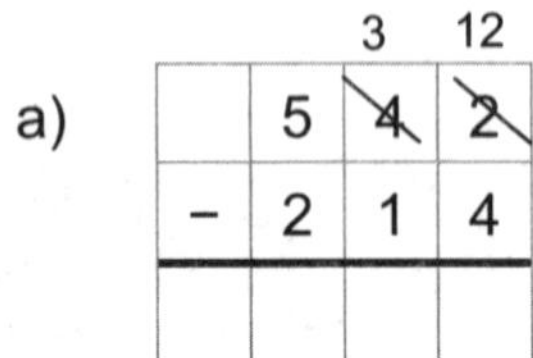

b)

| | 7 | 8 | 4 |
|---|---|---|---|
| − | 4 | 3 | 6 |
| | | | |

c)

| | 8 | 5 | 2 |
|---|---|---|---|
| − | 4 | 1 | 4 |
| | | | |

d)

| | 9 | 4 | 0 |
|---|---|---|---|
| − | 2 | 2 | 2 |
| | | | |

8. For the questions below, you will have to borrow **twice**—from the hundreds and from the tens (i.e., exchange 1 ten for 10 ones and 1 hundred for 10 tens).

Example:

| Step 1: | Step 2: | Step 3: | Step 4: | Step 5: |
|---|---|---|---|---|
| 4 14 | 4 14 | 14<br>7 ~~4~~ 14 | 14<br>7 ~~4~~ 14 | 14<br>7 ~~4~~ 14 |
| 8 ~~5~~ ~~4~~ | 8 ~~5~~ ~~4~~ | ~~8~~ ~~5~~ ~~4~~ | ~~8~~ ~~5~~ ~~4~~ | ~~8~~ ~~5~~ ~~4~~ |
| − 3 6 7 | − 3 6 7 | − 3 6 7 | − 3 6 7 | − 3 6 7 |
| | 7 | 7 | 8 7 | 4 8 7 |

a)

| | 6 | 3 | 4 |
|---|---|---|---|
| − | 1 | 5 | 6 |
| | | | |

b)

| | 5 | 8 | 5 |
|---|---|---|---|
| − | | 9 | 6 |
| | | | |

c)

| | 5 | 0 | 2 |
|---|---|---|---|
| − | 2 | 3 | 5 |
| | | | |

d)

| | 8 | 5 | 4 |
|---|---|---|---|
| − | 3 | 7 | 7 |
| | | | |

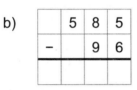

9. To subtract 3245 − 1923, Sara exchanges 1 thousands cube for 10 hundreds squares:

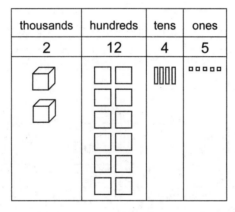

| thousands | hundreds | tens | ones |
|---|---|---|---|
| 3 | 2 | 4 | 5 |

| thousands | hundreds | tens | ones |
|---|---|---|---|
| 2 | 12 | 4 | 5 |

| thousands | hundreds | tens | ones |
|---|---|---|---|
| 2 | 3 | 2 | 2 |

On a separate piece of paper, draw a picture to show how you would exchange 1 thousands cube for 10 hundreds squares to subtract the following numbers:

a) 3652 − 1721 b) 5438 − 2716 c) 8652 − 4921 d) 7745 − 4832

10. Subtract by borrowing from the thousands. The first one is done for you:

a)

| | 7<br>~~8~~ | 13<br>~~3~~ | 6 | 4 |
|---|---|---|---|---|
| − | 4 | 8 | 3 | 1 |
| | 3 | 5 | 3 | 3 |

b)

| | 5 | 6 | 9 | 3 |
|---|---|---|---|---|
| − | 2 | 7 | 1 | 1 |
| | | | | |

c)

| | 5 | 7 | 5 | 8 |
|---|---|---|---|---|
| − | 2 | 9 | 4 | 2 |
| | | | | |

d)

| | 3 | 8 | 7 | 6 |
|---|---|---|---|---|
| − | 1 | 9 | 2 | 7 |
| | | | | |

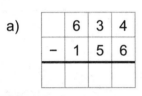

11. In some of the questions below, you will need to borrow from either the thousands, the hundreds, or the tens column. (How do you know when you need to borrow?) In others you will not need to borrow. Do parts e) through h) on a separate piece of paper.

a)

| | 3 | 3 | 1 | 7 |
|---|---|---|---|---|
| − | 1 | 4 | 0 | 5 |
| | | | | |

b)

| | 6 | 4 | 6 | 8 |
|---|---|---|---|---|
| − | 2 | 1 | 7 | 2 |
| | | | | |

c)

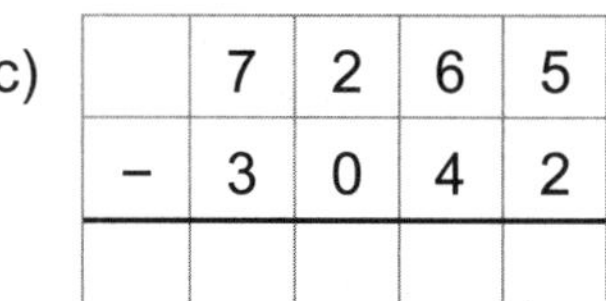

| | 7 | 2 | 6 | 5 |
|---|---|---|---|---|
| − | 3 | 0 | 4 | 2 |
| | | | | |

d)

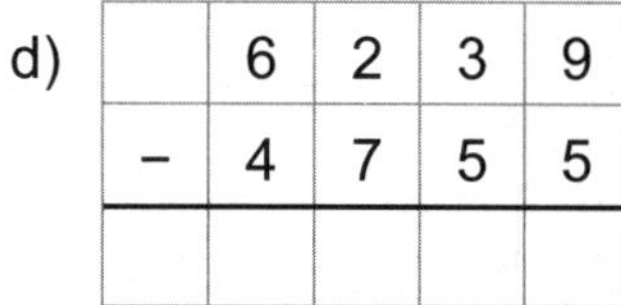

| | 6 | 2 | 3 | 9 |
|---|---|---|---|---|
| − | 4 | 7 | 5 | 5 |
| | | | | |

e) 8504 − 1230 f) 4484 − 2511 g) 5354 − 1061 h) 8946 − 3508

12. In the questions below, you will have to borrow three times (that is, exchange 1 ten for 10 ones, 1 hundred for 10 tens, and 1 thousand for 10 hundreds).

Step 1:

```
     4 12
 6 2 5̸ 2̸
-1 4 7 4
```

Step 2:

```
     4 12
 6 2 5̸ 2̸
-1 4 7 4
       8
```

Step 3:

```
    14
   1 4̸ 12
 6 2̸ 5̸ 2̸
-1 4 7 4
     7 8
```

Step 4:

```
 5 11 14
   1̸  4̸ 12
 6̸ 2̸ 5̸ 2̸
-1 4 7 4
   7 7 8
```

Step 5:

```
 5 11 14
   1̸  4̸ 12
 6̸ 2̸ 5̸ 2̸
-1 4 7 4
 4 7 7 8
```

a)

| | 8 | 5 | 3 | 2 |
|---|---|---|---|---|
| − | 2 | 7 | 5 | 4 |
| | | | | |

b)

| | 7 | 6 | 4 | 1 |
|---|---|---|---|---|
| − | 4 | 7 | 5 | 3 |
| | | | | |

c)

| | 6 | 1 | 3 | 0 |
|---|---|---|---|---|
| − | 2 | 2 | 8 | 3 |
| | | | | |

d)

| | 4 | 3 | 0 | 2 |
|---|---|---|---|---|
| − | 1 | 7 | 2 | 3 |
| | | | | |

13. In the questions below you will have to borrow two or three times (i.e., exchange 1 ten for 10 ones, 1 hundred for 10 tens. and 1 thousand for 10 hundreds).

Step 1:

```
 0 10
 1̸ 0̸ 0 0
-   3 4 1
```

Step 2:

```
     9
 0 1̸0 10
 1̸ 0̸ 0̸ 0
-   3 4 1
```

Step 3:

```
    9   9
 0 1̸0 1̸0 10
 1̸ 0̸  0̸  0̸
-   3  4  1
```

Step 4:

```
    9   9
 0 1̸0 1̸0 10
 1̸ 0̸  0̸  0̸
-   3  4  1
    6  5  9
```

a)

| | 1 | 0 | 0 | 0 |
|---|---|---|---|---|
| − | | 4 | 5 | 7 |
| | | | | |

b)

| | 1 | 0 | 0 |
|---|---|---|---|
| − | | 7 | 5 |
| | | | |

c)

| | 1 | 0 | 0 | 0 |
|---|---|---|---|---|
| − | | 6 | 3 | 3 |
| | | | | |

d)

| | 1 | 0 | 0 | 0 |
|---|---|---|---|---|
| − | | 8 | 8 | 9 |
| | | | | |

14. The border between the United States and Canada is 8963 km long. The total length of the Great Wall of China, including its branches, is 6324 km. How much longer than the Great Wall of China is the Canada–United States border?

15. Anna earned $2352 during her summer vacation. Janet earned $1780. How much more money did Anna earn?

# NS4-15: Concepts in Number Sense

Answer the following questions on a separate piece of paper:

1. In a class of 62 children, 17 are boys. How many girls are in the class? Show your work. How can you check your answer using addition?

2. Here are the heights of some of Canada's tallest buildings.
   a) Write the heights in order from least to greatest.
   b) How much higher than the Calgary Tower is the Scotia Plaza?
   c) How much higher than the shortest tower is the tallest tower?

| Heights of buildings | |
|---|---|
| First Canadian Place, Toronto | 298 m |
| Scotia Plaza, Toronto | 275 m |
| Calgary Tower, Calgary | 191 m |

3. The equation 5 + 7 = 12 is part of a fact family of equations. The other equations in the family are 7 + 5 = 12, 12 – 5 = 7, and 12 – 7 = 5. Write all the equations in the fact family for . . .
   a) 3 + 8 = 11 b) 7 – 3 = 4 c) 19 + 5 = 24

4. Use the numbers 1, 2, 3, 4, 5, 6 to make the greatest sum possible and the greatest difference.

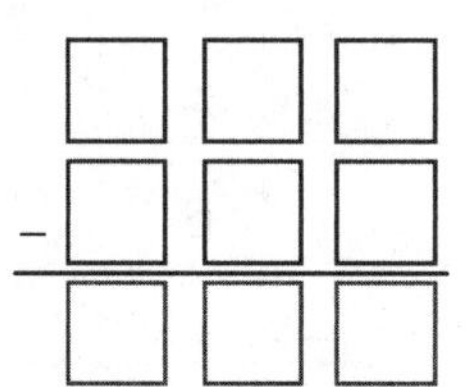

5. Find the error in Ezra's sum.

```
  2
  45
+ 27
  81
```

6. Leonardo da Vinci, the great Italian inventor and artist, lived from 1452 to 1519.
   a) How old was he when he died?
   b) Leonardo painted his masterpiece, the Mona Lisa, in 1503. How old was he then?

7. Write the number that is . . .
   a) 10 less than 1000 b) 10 more than 1000
   c) 100 less than 1000 d) 100 more than 1000

8. How do you think you would add or subtract the numbers? Write what you think the answer might be.

```
a)   2 3 1 7    b)   2 2    c)   3 2 4    d)   9 2 5 4    e)   5 2 3 1 8
   + 4 1 3 2         3 6         1 1 2       - 3 0 1 2       - 3 1 1 0 2
                   + 2 1       + 4 2 2
```

9. Pens cost 49¢. Erasers cost 45¢. Ben has 95¢. Does he have enough money to buy a pen and an eraser? (Explain your answer.)

10. Josh wants to add the numbers below. He starts by adding the ones digits.

```
  1
  35
+ 47
   2
```

Explain why Josh wrote the number 1 here.

# NS4-16: Arrays

When you multiply a pair of numbers, the result is called the product of the numbers. You can represent a product using an **array**.

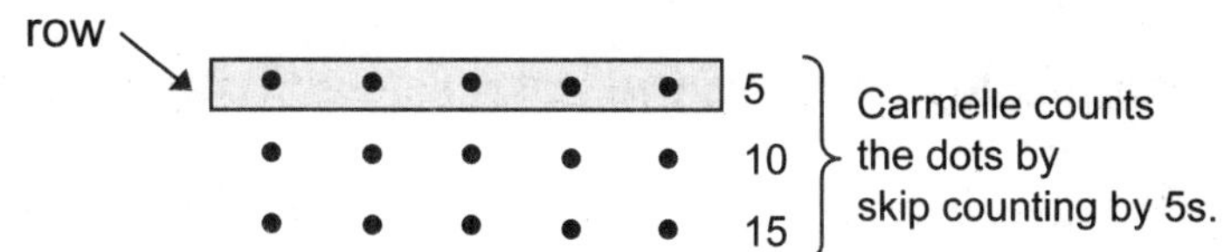


In the array shown above, there are 3 **rows** of dots and there are 5 dots **in each row**.

Carmelle writes a multiplication statement for the array: **3 × 5 = 15** (3 rows of 5 dots is 15 dots)

---

1. How many rows are there? How many dots are in each row? Write a multiplication statement and find the answer by skip counting (or by counting the dots individually).

a) 3 rows
4 dots in each row
3 × 4 = 12

b) ___ rows
___ dots in each row
___

c) ___
___
___

2. Write a product for each array.

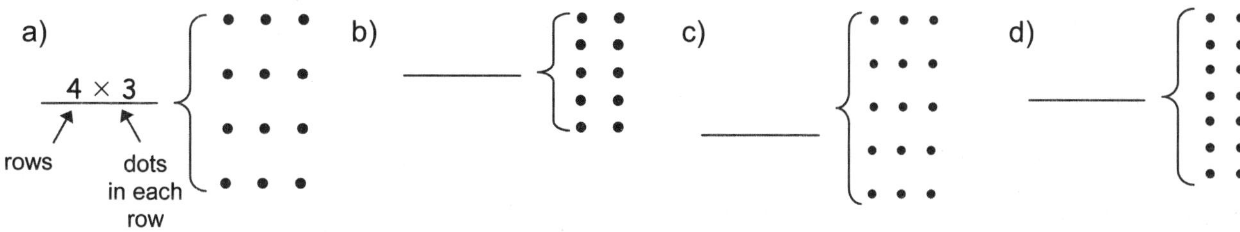


3. Draw an array and write a multiplication statement for each question.

a) 2 rows; 6 dots in each row b) 3 rows; 7 dots in each row c) 2 rows; 3 dots in each row

Answer the questions on a separate piece of paper.

4. Draw arrays for the following products:

a) 5 × 5 b) 3 × 5 c) 2 × 4 d) 4 × 3 e) 7 × 4 f) 8 × 3 g) 1 × 6 h) 0 × 5

5. Use counters or draw arrays (of dots or squares) to solve each question. Write a multiplication statement for each question.

a) In a garden, there are 6 rows of plants. There are 5 plants in each row. How many plants are there altogether?

b) Paul lines up 7 chairs in each row. There are 3 rows of chairs. How many chairs are there altogether?

c) Jenny planted 8 seeds in each row. There are 4 rows of seeds. How many seeds did Jenny plant?

6. Draw arrays for the products 4 × 3 (4 rows, 3 dots in each row) and 3 × 4 (3 rows, 4 dots in each row). Are the products 4 × 3 and 3 × 4 the same or different? How do you know? What about 5 × 6 and 6 × 5?

# NS4-17: Multiplication and Addition

Multiplication is a short way of writing addition: $4 \times 5 = \underbrace{5 + 5 + 5 + 5}_{\text{add 5 four times}}$

1. Write a sum for each product. The first one is done for you.

a) $3 \times 4 = 4 + 4 + 4$ b) $2 \times 8 =$ c) $5 \times 6 =$

d) $4 \times 2 =$ e) $3 \times 5 =$ f) $9 \times 3 =$

g) $5 \times 7 =$ h) $6 \times 1 =$ i) $1 \times 8 =$

2. Write a product for each sum. The first one is done for you.

a) $4 + 4 + 4 = 3 \times 4$ b) $5 + 5 + 5 =$ c) $4 + 4 =$

d) $7 + 7 + 7 + 7 =$ e) $9 + 9 =$ f) $8 + 8 + 8 =$

g) $2 + 2 + 2 =$ h) $9 + 9 + 9 + 9 =$ i) $1 + 1 + 1 =$

j) $6 + 6 + 6 + 6 + 6 =$ k) $8 + 8 + 8 + 8 + 8 + 8 =$ l) $3 + 3 + 3 =$

3. Write a sum and a product for each picture. The first one is done for you.

a) 2 boxes; 2 pencils in each box

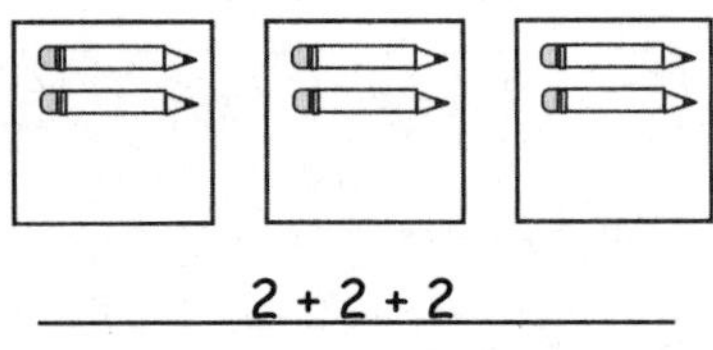

$2 + 2 + 2$

$3 \times 2$

b) 3 boxes; 4 pencils in each box

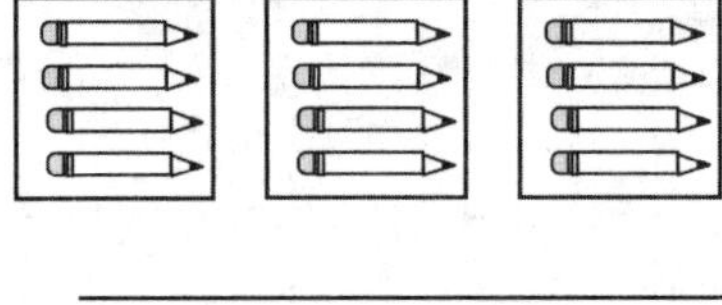

c) 4 boxes; 3 pencils in each box

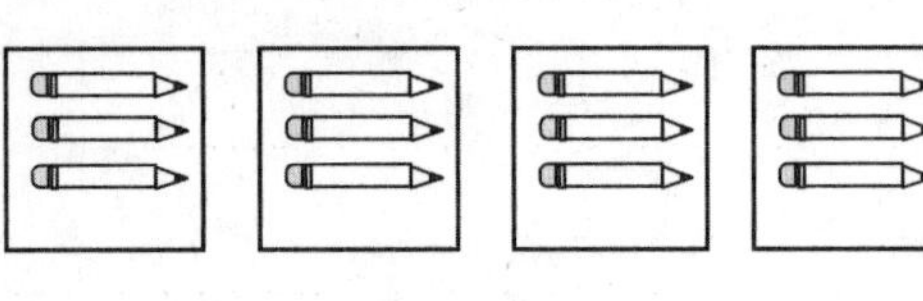

d) 2 boxes; 5 pencils in each box

4. Write a sum and a product for each phrase.

a) 6 cars
5 people in each car

b) 3 packets
7 erasers in each packet

c) 7 plates
4 cookies on each plate

5. Add the numbers.

NOTE:
Write your subtotals in the boxes provided. If necessary, add by counting on your fingers.

Example: 4 + 5 + 7 = ___ → add 4 + 5 (= 9) → 4 + 5 + 7 = ___ (9) → add 9 + 7 (= 16) → 4 + 5 + 7 = 16 (9)

a) 2 + 3 + 5 = ___ b) 3 + 3 + 7 = ___ c) 5 + 4 + 3 = ___

d) 6 + 4 + 2 = ___ e) 8 + 3 + 4 = ___ f) 9 + 1 + 6 = ___

g) 4 + 3 + 3 + 2 = ___ h) 4 + 5 + 5 + 3 = ___ i) 6 + 7 + 3 + 5 = ___

6. Write a sum for each picture. Then, add the numbers to find out how many apples there are altogether. Check that your answer is correct by counting the apples.

a) 3 boxes; 3 apples in each box

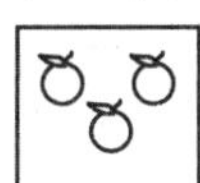 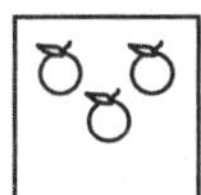 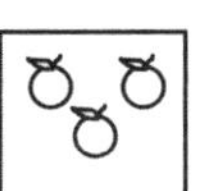

_______________

b) 4 boxes; 2 apples in each box

 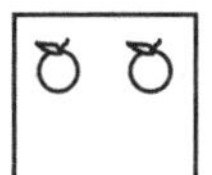 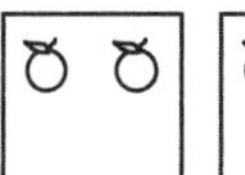 

_______________

c) 4 boxes; 4 apples in each box

 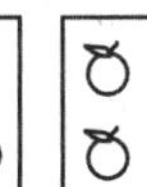 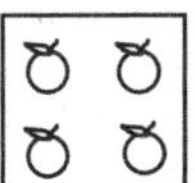 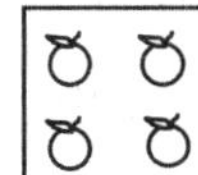 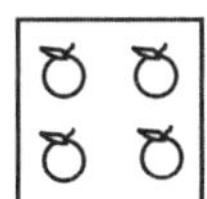

_______________

d) 3 boxes; 5 apples in each box

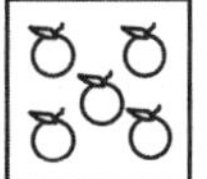 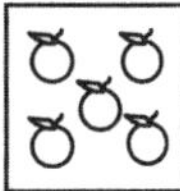 

_______________

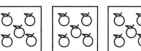

7. On a separate piece of paper, draw a picture and write an addition statement and a multiplication statement for your picture.

a) 6 vans
7 people in each van

b) 6 bags
5 books in each bag

c) 8 boxes
4 pens in each box

d) 5 boats
4 kids in each boat

8. On a separate piece of paper, write an addition statement and a multiplication statement for each question.

a) 6 plates
8 cookies on each plate

b) 7 packets
3 gifts in each packet

c) 4 baskets
7 bananas in each basket

# NS4-18: Multiplying by Skip Counting and Adding On

Amy finds the product of **3** and **5** by skip counting on a number line.

She counts off three 5s:  **3 × 5 = 5 + 5 + 5 = 15**

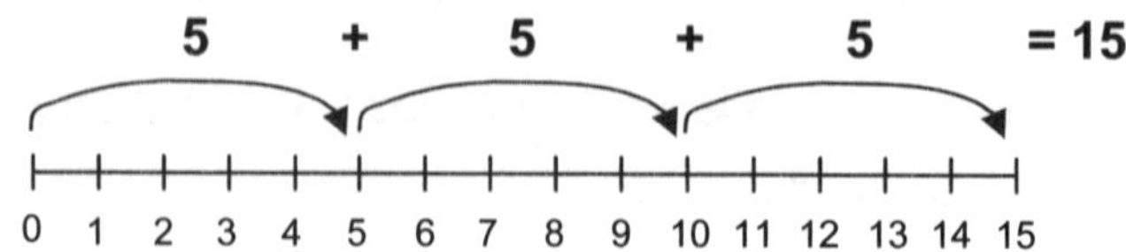


From the picture, Amy can see that the product of 3 and 5 is 15.

---

1. Show how to find the products by skip counting. Use arrows like the ones in Amy's picture.

   a) 4 × 3 = 

   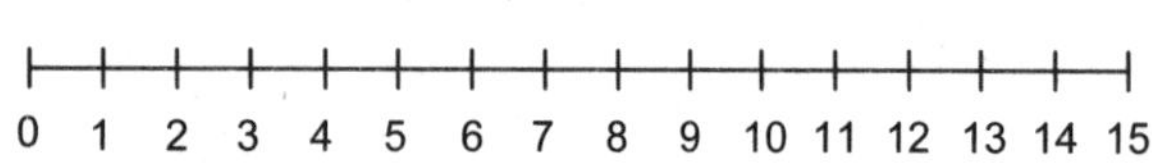
   

   b) 7 × 2 =

   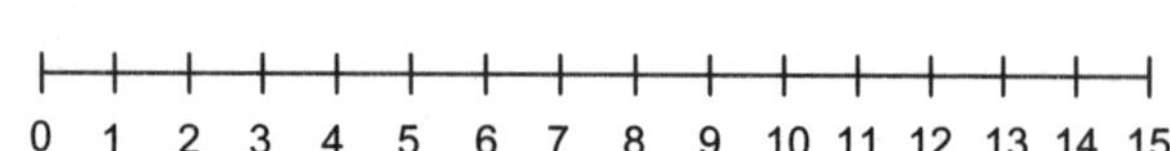
   

2. Use the number line to skip count by 4s, 6s, and 7s. Fill in the boxes as you count.

   **0** 1 2 3 4 5 6 7 8 9 **10** 11 12 13 14 15 16 17 18 19 **20** 21 22 23 24 25 26 27 28 29 **30** 31 32 33 34 35 36 37 38 39 **40** 41 42

   a) 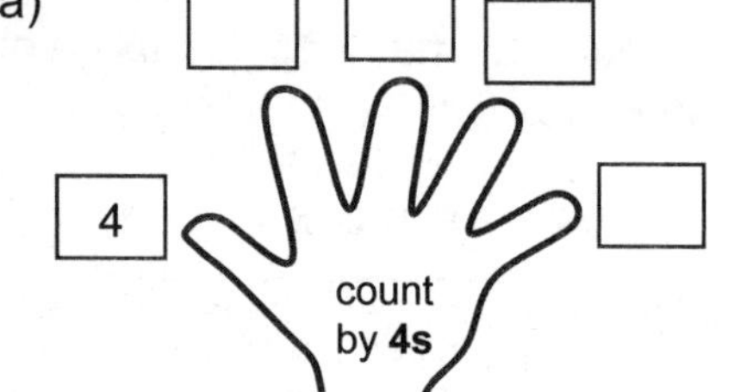
   

   b) 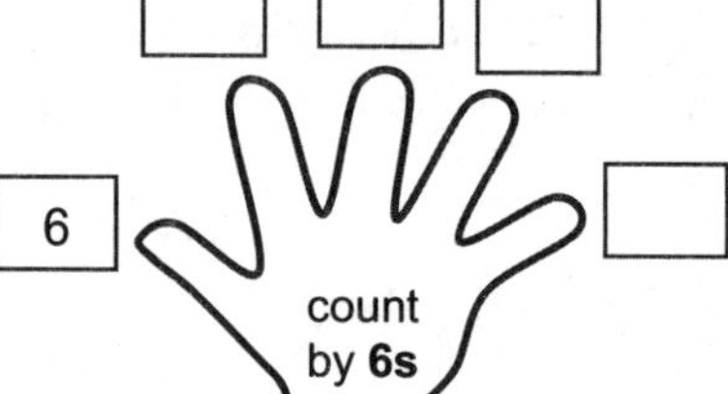
   

   c) 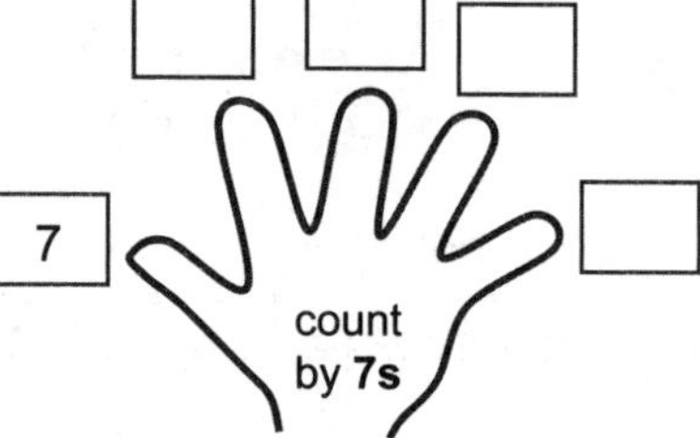
   

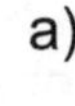

3. Find the products by skip counting on your fingers. Use the hands from question 2 to help.

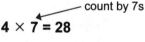

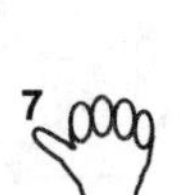

until you raise 4 fingers → **4 × 7 = 28** ← count by 7s

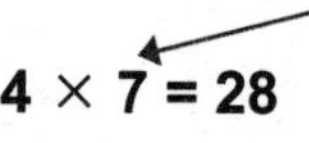

| | | | | |
|---|---|---|---|---|
| a) 4 × 5 = | b) 5 × 2 = | c) 4 × 4 = | d) 6 × 2 = | e) 7 × 1 = |
| f) 7 × 3 = | g) 3 × 3 = | h) 6 × 1 = | i) 2 × 7 = | j) 5 × 5 = |
| k) 2 × 2 = | l) 7 × 6 = | m) 2 × 1 = | n) 4 × 6 = | o) 3 × 6 = |

4. Find the number of items in each picture. (How can you use skip counting to help?) On a separate piece of paper, write a multiplication statement for each picture.

   a) 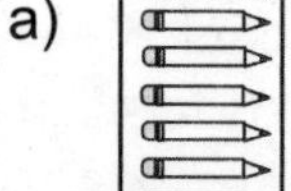 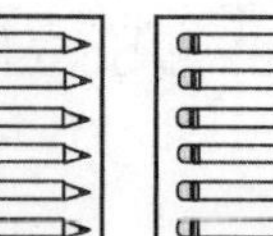 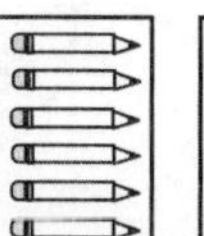 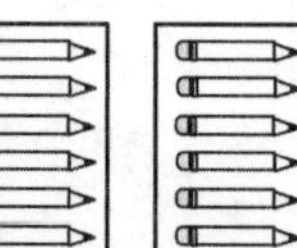 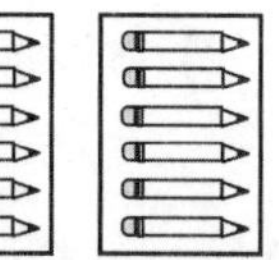

   b) 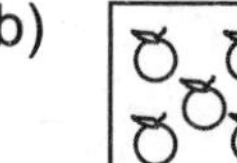 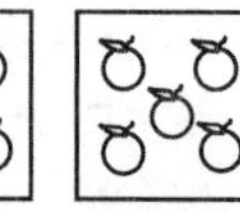 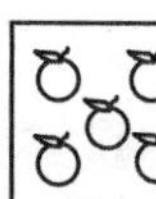  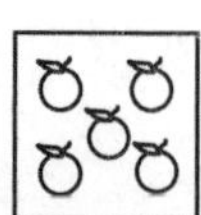

5. Find the total number of pie slices in each question. Write a multiplication statement as your answer (on a separate piece of paper).

   a) 4 pies; 5 slices in each pie.
   b) 6 pies; 6 slices in each pie
   c) 7 pies; 6 slices in each pie

# NS4-18: Multiplying by Skip Counting and Adding On *(cont'd)*

Stacy knows how to find $4 \times 5$ by adding four 5s ($5 + 5 + 5 + 5 = 20$). Her mother asks her how she can find $5 \times 5$ quickly (without adding five 5s).

Stacy knows that $5 \times 5$ is one more 5 than $4 \times 5$. She shows this in two ways.

**with a picture**

five 5s — four 5s — plus one more 5

**by adding**

$5 \times 5 = 5 + 5 + 5 + 5 + 5$

five 5s — four 5s — plus one more 5

Stacy knows that **$5 \times 5 = 4 \times 5 + 5$** (four 5s, plus one more 5)

So she finds $5 \times 5$ by adding 5 to 20 ($4 \times 5 = 20$): $5 \times 5 = \mathbf{20} + 5 = \mathbf{25}$

---

1. Use each array to write a multiplication statement. The first one is done for you.

a) $4 \times 4$ (rows, dots in each row) — $3 \times 4$ + 4

$4 \times 4 = 3 \times 4 + 4$

b) ______ ______ + ______

______

2. Draw an array (on a separate piece of paper) or use counters to show that . . .

a) $4 \times 6 = 3 \times 6 + 6$ b) $6 \times 7 = 5 \times 7 + 7$ c) $4 \times 7 = 3 \times 7 + 7$

3. Show how to turn each product into a smaller product and a sum. The first one is done for you.

a) $5 \times 6 = 6 + 6 + 6 + 6 + 6$
$= 4 \times 6 + 6$
$= 24 + 6 = 30$

b) $6 \times 6 =$
$=$
$=$

Show your work for the remaining questions on a separate piece of paper.

c) $6 \times 2 =$ d) $7 \times 2 =$ e) $6 \times 3 =$ f) $7 \times 3 =$ g) $8 \times 3 =$

4. In each question, you are given two products. Find the larger product by adding a number to the smaller one. Be sure to show your work. Use separate paper for parts d) to f).

a) If $8 \times 5 = 40$, what is $9 \times 5$?
$9 \times 5 = 8 \times 5 + 5$
$= 40 + 5 = 45$

b) If $6 \times 4 = 24$, what is $7 \times 4$?

c) If $6 \times 7 = 42$, what is $7 \times 7$?

d) If $8 \times 6 = 48$, what is $9 \times 6$? e) If $7 \times 8 = 56$, what is $7 \times 9$? f) If $9 \times 4 = 36$, what is $9 \times 5$?

PARENT: Please give your child a copy of the section "How to Learn Your Times Tables in 5 Days" (pp. xviii – xx of the Introduction). Review the material for 20 minutes a day for a week.

# NS4-19: Multiples of 10

To multiply 3 × 20, Christie makes 3 groups containing 2 **tens** strips (20 = 2 tens):

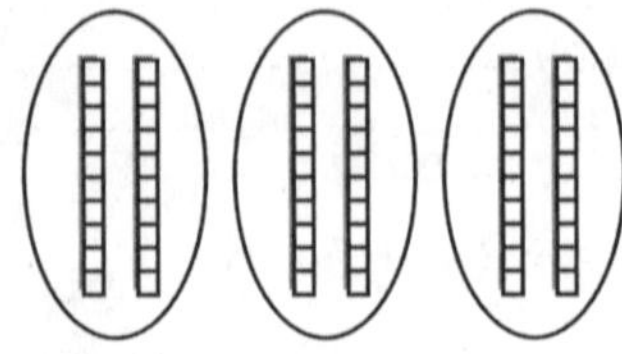

3 × 20 = 3 × 2 tens = 6 tens = 60

To multiply 3 × 200, Christie makes 3 groups containing 2 **hundreds** squares (200 = 2 hundreds):

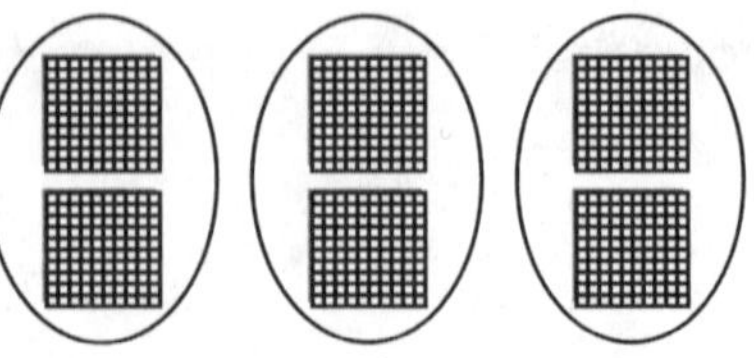

3 × 200 = 3 × 2 hundreds = 6 hundreds = 600

Christie notices a pattern: **3 × 2 = 6** **3 × 20 = 60** **3 × 200 = 600**

---

1. Draw a model for each multiplication statement, then calculate the answer. The first one is started for you.

   a) 4 × 20

   4 × 20 = 4 × ____ tens = ____ tens = ____

   b) 2 × 30

   2 × 30 = 2 × ____ tens = ____ tens = ____

2. On a separate piece of paper, draw a model for each statement and then calculate the answer.

   a) 4 × 200
   = 4 × ____ hundreds = ____ hundreds = ____

   b) 2 × 300
   = 2 × ____ hundreds = ____ hundreds = ____

3. Complete the pattern by multiplying.

   a) 2 × 2 = ______
   2 × 20 = ______
   2 × 200 = ______

   b) 5 × 1 = ______
   5 × 10 = ______
   5 × 100 = ______

   c) 2 × 4 = ______
   2 × 40 = ______
   2 × 400 = ______

   d) 3 × 3 = ______
   3 × 30 = ______
   3 × 300 = ______

4. Regroup to find the answer. The first one is done for you.

   a) 3 × 70 = 3 × 7 tens = 21 tens = 2 hundreds + 1 tens = 210
   b) 3 × 50 = 3 × ____ tens = ____ tens = ____ hundreds + ____ tens = ____
   c) 5 × 50 = 5 × ____ tens = ____ tens = ____ hundreds + ____ tens = ____
   d) 4 × 60 = 4 × ____ tens = ____ tens = ____ hundreds + ____ tens = ____

5. Multiply.

   a) 4 × 30 = ____ b) 5 × 30 = ____ c) 4 × 40 = ____ d) 2 × 50 = ____
   e) 3 × 500 = ____ f) 4 × 500 = ____ g) 3 × 60 = ____ h) 6 × 400 = ____
   i) 2 × 700 = ____ j) 6 × 70 = ____ k) 8 × 40 = ____ l) 2 × 900 = ____

6. Draw a base-10 model (using cubes to represent thousands) to show 4 × 1000 = 4000.

7. Knowing that 3 × 2 = 6, how can you use this fact to multiply 3 × 2000? Explain your answer on a separate piece of paper.

# NS4-20: Mental Math

To multiply 3 × 23, Rosa rewrites 23 as a sum:

23 = 20 + 3

She multiplies 20 by 3: 3 × 20 = 60

Then she multiplies 3 × 3: 3 × 3 = 9

Finally she adds the result: 60 + 9 = 69

The picture shows why Rosa's method works:

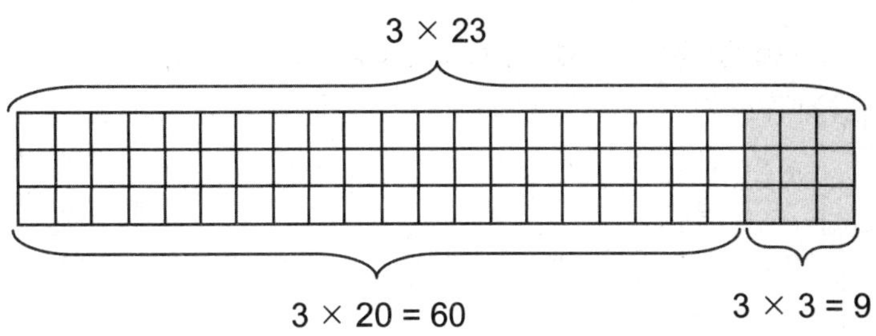


**3 × 23 = 3 × 20 + 3 × 3 = 60 + 9 = 69**

---

1. Use the picture to write the multiplication statement as a sum. The first one is started for you.

a)

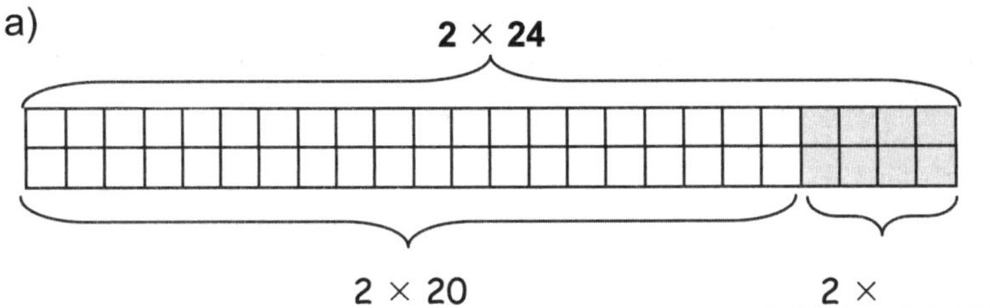


2 × 20 ______ 2 × ______

2 × 24 = 2 x ______ + 2 × ______

b)

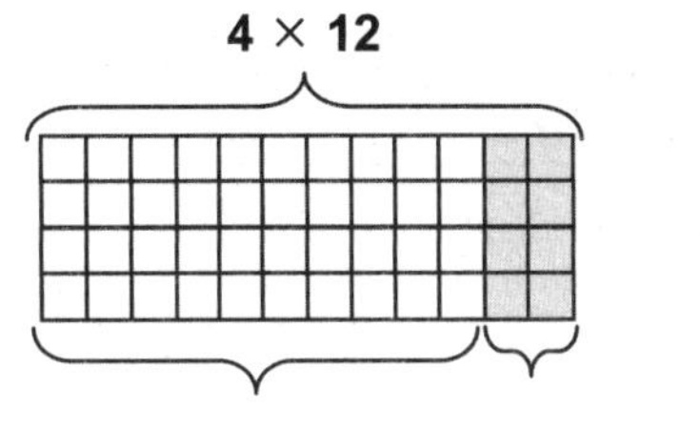


______ ______

4 × 12 = ______ + ______

2. Multiply using Rosa's method. The first one is done for you.

a) 3 × 13 = 3 × 10 + 3 × 3 = 30 + 9 = 39

b) 3 × 21 = ______

c) 2 × 14 = ______

d) 2 × 24 = ______

3. Multiply in your head.

a) 3 × 12 = ______ b) 2 × 31 = ______ c) 4 × 12 = ______ d) 5 × 11 = ______

e) 4 × 21 = ______ f) 2 × 43 = ______ g) 2 × 32 = ______ h) 3 × 33 = ______

4. Use Rosa's method to write each multiplication statement as a sum.

a) 3 × 213 = 3 × 200 + 3 × 10 + 3 × 3 = 600 + 30 + 9 = 639

b) 2 × 231 = ______

c) 2 × 342 = ______

d) 3 × 121 = ______

5. Multiply in your head.

a) 4 × 112 = ______ b) 2 × 234 = ______ c) 3 × 233 = ______ d) 5 × 111 = ______

e) 3 × 132 = ______ f) 2 × 422 = ______ g) 4 × 212 = ______ h) 3 × 333 = ______

6. Yen planted 223 pine seedlings in each of 3 rows. How many seedlings did she plant altogether?

# NS4-21: The Standard Method for Multiplication



To multiply 3 × 32, Ron uses a chart:

Step 1:
He multiplies the ones digit of 42 by 3.

| Hundreds | Tens | Ones |
|---|---|---|
| | 4 | 2 |
| | | 3 |
| | | 6 |

Step 2:
He multiplies the tens digit of 42 by 3.

| Hundreds | Tens | Ones |
|---|---|---|
| | 4 | 2 |
| | | 3 |
| | 12 | 6 |

Step 3:
He exchanges 10 tens for 1 hundred.

| Hundreds | Tens | Ones |
|---|---|---|
| | 4 | 2 |
| | | 3 |
| 1 | 2 | 6 |

1. Use Ron's method to complete the multiplications.

Step 1: Multiply the ones. Step 2: Multiply the tens. Step 3: Exchange.

a)

| Hundreds | Tens | Ones |
|---|---|---|
| | 3 | 2 |
| | | 4 |
| | | |

| Hundreds | Tens | Ones |
|---|---|---|
| | 3 | 2 |
| | | 4 |
| | | |

| Hundreds | Tens | Ones |
|---|---|---|
| | 3 | 2 |
| | | 4 |
| | | |

b)

| Hundreds | Tens | Ones |
|---|---|---|
| | 3 | 4 |
| | | 2 |
| | | |

| Hundreds | Tens | Ones |
|---|---|---|
| | | |
| | | |
| | | |

| Hundreds | Tens | Ones |
|---|---|---|
| | | |
| | | |
| | | |

Clara uses a faster method than Ron's method to multiply. She performs Step 2 and Step 3 of Ron's method as a single step:

Step 1:
She multiplies the ones digit of 42 by 3.

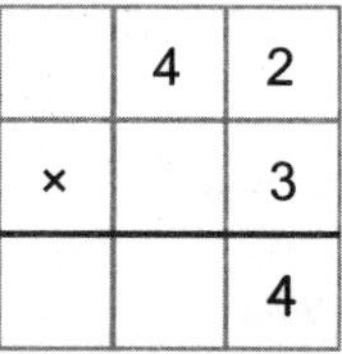


Step 2:
She multiplies the tens digit of 42 by 3 and exchanges 10 tens for 1 hundred.

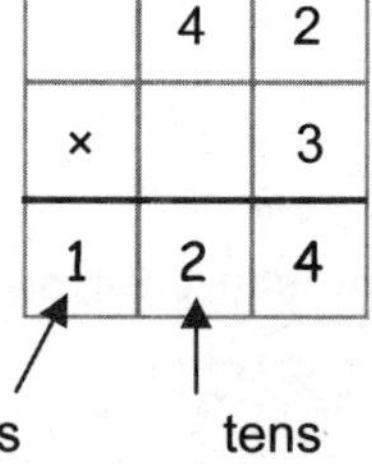


2. Use Clara's method to find the products.

a)

| | 3 | 1 |
|---|---|---|
| × | | 4 |
| | | |

b)

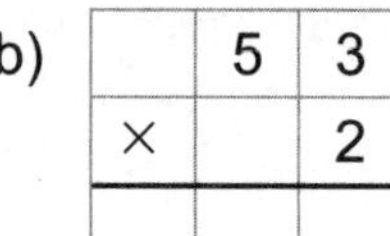


c)

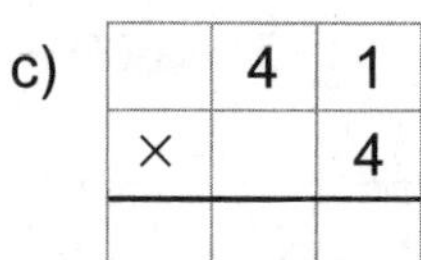


d)

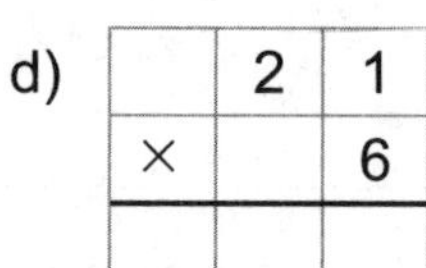


e)

| | 3 | 1 |
|---|---|---|
| × | | 3 |
| | | |

f)

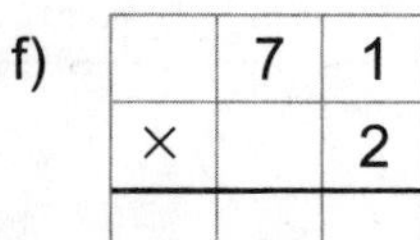


g)

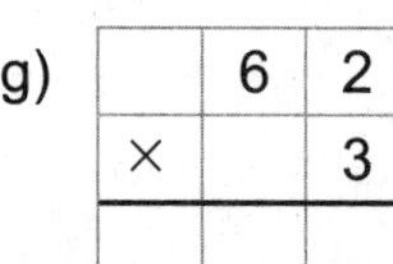


h)

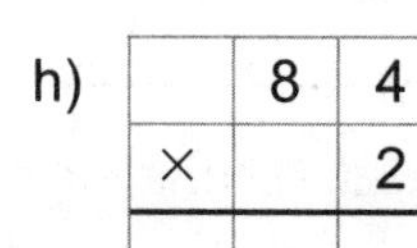


i)

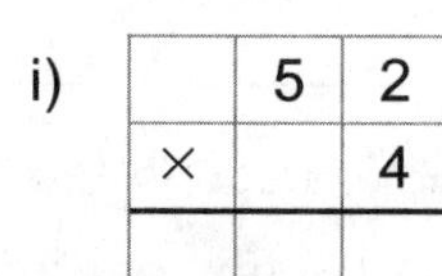


j)

| | 2 | 2 |
|---|---|---|
| × | | 2 |
| | | |

3. Find the following products. Show your work on a separate piece of paper.

a) 3 × 62  b) 2 × 74  c) 5 × 21  d) 4 × 62  e) 3 × 45

# NS4-22: Carrying

To multiply 3 × 24, Helen makes a chart:

**Step 1:**
She multiplies the ones digit of 24 by 3.

| | Tens | Ones |
|---|---|---|
| | 2 | 4 |
| × | | 3 |
| | | 12 |

**Step 2:**
She multiplies the tens digit of 24 by 3.

| | Tens | Ones |
|---|---|---|
| | 2 | 4 |
| × | | 3 |
| | 6 | 12 |

**Step 3:**
She exchanges 10 ones for 1 hundred.

| | Tens | Ones |
|---|---|---|
| | 2 | 4 |
| × | | 3 |
| | 6 + 1 = 7 | 2 |

1. Use Helen's method to complete the multiplications.

1: Multiply the ones.

| | Tens | Ones |
|---|---|---|
| | 1 | 5 |
| × | | 3 |
| | | |

2: Multiply the tens.

| | Tens | Ones |
|---|---|---|
| | 1 | 5 |
| × | | 3 |
| | | |

3: Exchange.

| | Tens | Ones |
|---|---|---|
| | 1 | 5 |
| × | | 3 |
| | | |

Jane uses a faster method than Helen's to multiply:

**Step 1:**
She multiples the ones digit of 24 by 3 (4 × 3 = 12). She exchanges 10 ones for 1 ten and writes the 1 at the top of the tens column.

| | | |
|---|---|---|
| | 1 | |
| | 2 | 4 |
| × | | 3 |
| | | 2 |

**Step 2:**
She multiples the tens digit of 24 by 3 (3 × 2 tens = 6 tens). She adds 1 ten to the result (6 + 1 = 7 tens).

| | | |
|---|---|---|
| | 1 | |
| | 2 | 4 |
| 1 | | 3 |
| | 7 | 2 |

2. Using Jane's method, complete the first step of the multiplications. The first one is done for you.

a)

| | | |
|---|---|---|
| | 2 | |
| | 1 | 4 |
| × | | 5 |
| | | 0 |

b) 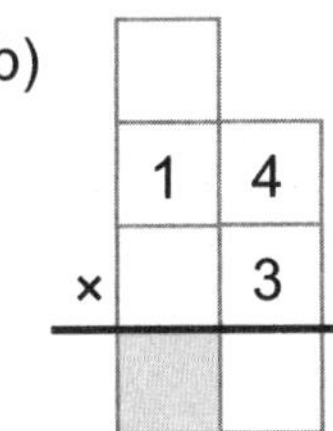

| | | |
|---|---|---|
| | | |
| | 1 | 4 |
| × | | 3 |
| | | |

c) 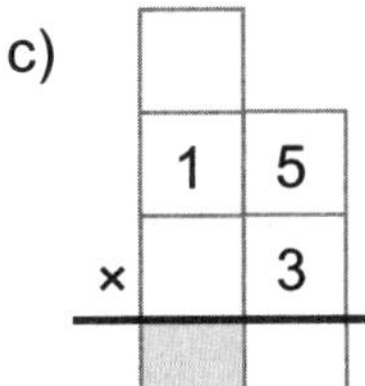

| | | |
|---|---|---|
| | | |
| | 1 | 5 |
| × | | 3 |
| | | |

d) 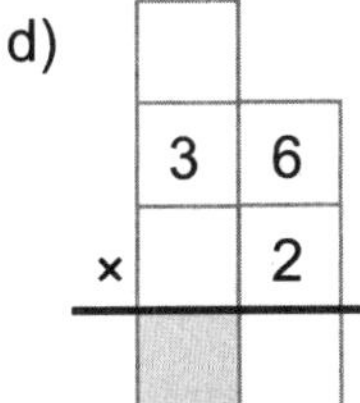

| | | |
|---|---|---|
| | | |
| | 3 | 6 |
| × | | 2 |
| | | |

e) 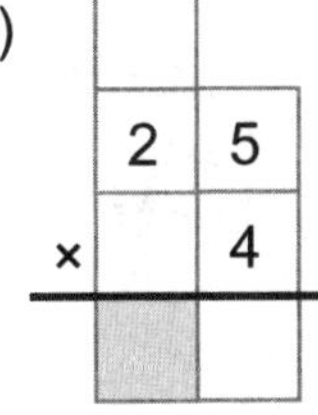

| | | |
|---|---|---|
| | | |
| | 2 | 5 |
| × | | 4 |
| | | |

3. Using Jane's method, complete the second step of the multiplications.

a)

| | | |
|---|---|---|
| | 1 | |
| | 2 | 4 |
| × | | 4 |
| | | 6 |

b) 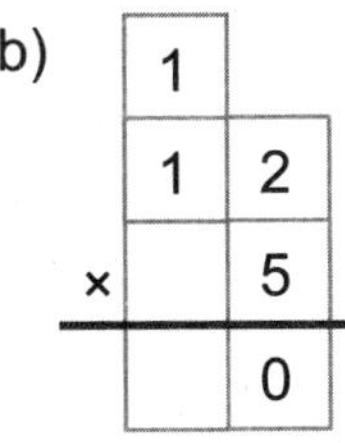

| | | |
|---|---|---|
| | 1 | |
| | 1 | 2 |
| × | | 5 |
| | | 0 |

c) 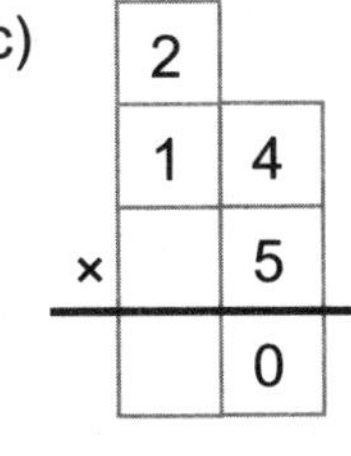

| | | |
|---|---|---|
| | 2 | |
| | 1 | 4 |
| × | | 5 |
| | | 0 |

d) 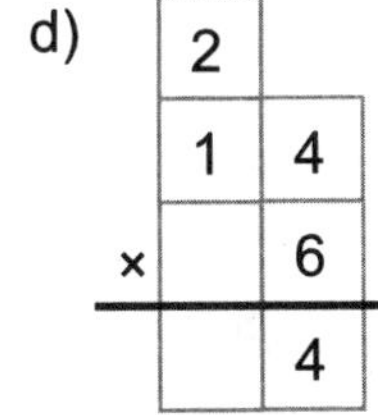

| | | |
|---|---|---|
| | 2 | |
| | 1 | 4 |
| × | | 6 |
| | | 4 |

e) 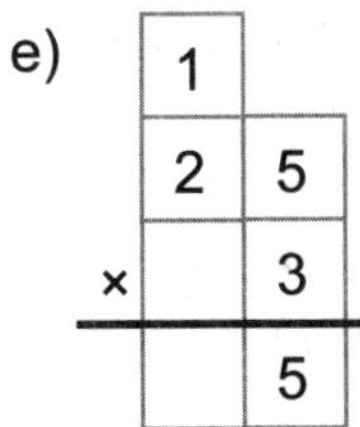

| | | |
|---|---|---|
| | 1 | |
| | 2 | 5 |
| × | | 3 |
| | | 5 |

4. Using Jane's method, complete the first and second step of the multiplications.

a)

| | | |
|---|---|---|
| | | |
| | 2 | 5 |
| × | | 2 |
| | | |

b) 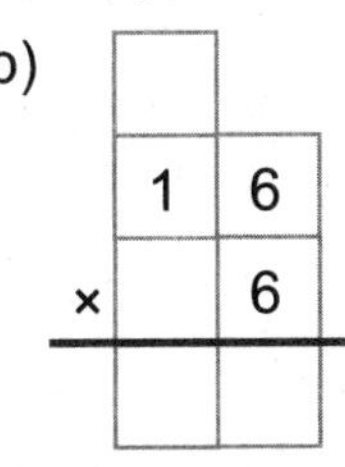

| | | |
|---|---|---|
| | | |
| | 1 | 6 |
| × | | 6 |
| | | |

c)

| | | |
|---|---|---|
| | | |
| | 3 | 5 |
| × | | 4 |
| | | |

d)

| | | |
|---|---|---|
| | | |
| | 3 | 5 |
| × | | 3 |
| | | |

# NS4-23: Multiplying a Three-Digit Number by a One-Digit Number

Kim multiplies 2 × 213 in 3 different ways:

**1. With a chart**

| | hundreds | tens | ones |
|---|---|---|---|
| | 2 | 1 | 3 |
| × | | | 2 |
| | 4 | 2 | 6 |

**2. In expanded form**

$$
\begin{array}{r}
200 + 10 + 3 \\
\times\ 2 \\
\hline
= 400 + 20 + 6 \\
= 426
\end{array}
$$

**3. With base-10 materials**

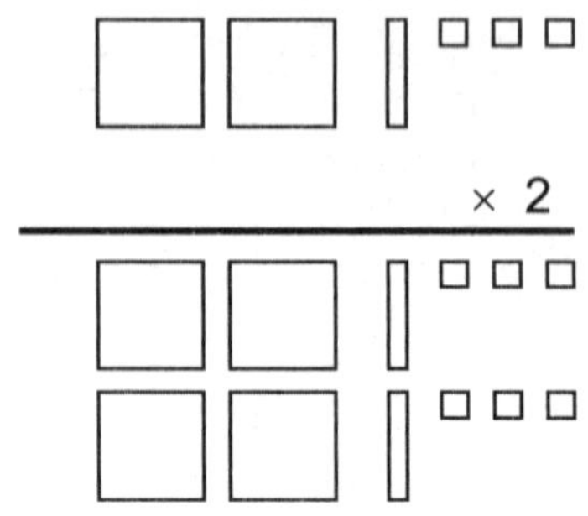

---

1. Rewrite the multiplication statement in expanded notation. Then perform the multiplication.

a) 321 × 3 ______ + ______ + ______ × 3 = ______ + ______ + ______ = ________

b) 432 × 2 ______ + ______ + ______ × 2 = ______ + ______ + ______ = ________

2. Draw a picture on a separate piece of paper to show the result of the multiplications.

a) 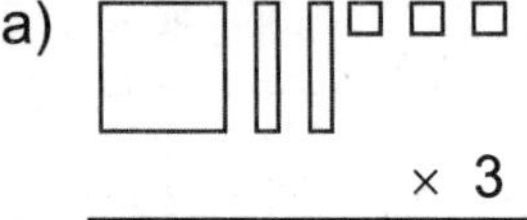 × 3

b) 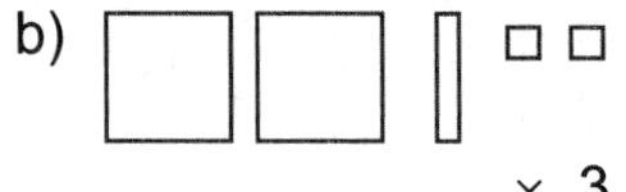 × 3

c) 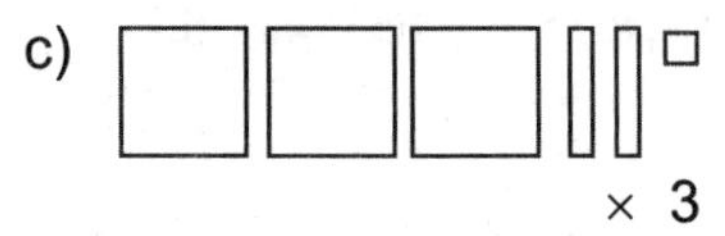 × 3

3. Multiply.

a) 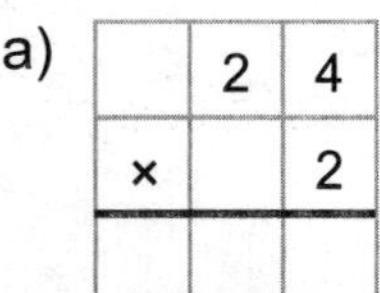

b)

| 2 | 1 | 3 |
|---|---|---|
| × | | 3 |
| | | |

c)

| 1 | 2 | 2 |
|---|---|---|
| × | | 4 |
| | | |

d)

| 3 | 2 | 3 |
|---|---|---|
| × | | 3 |
| | | |

e)

| 4 | 1 | 3 |
|---|---|---|
| × | | 2 |
| | | |

4. Multiply by exchanging ones for tens.

a) 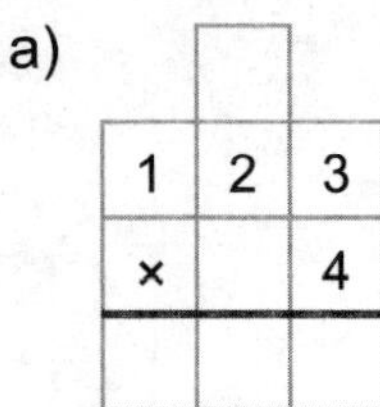

b)

| | | |
|---|---|---|
| 3 | 2 | 5 |
| × | | 3 |
| | | |

c) 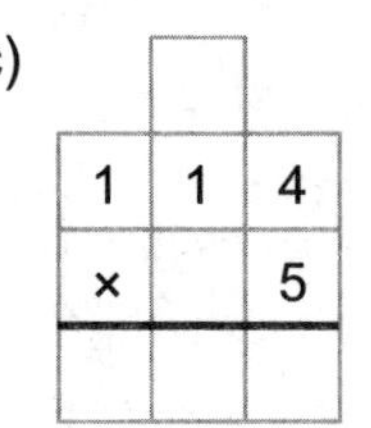

d) 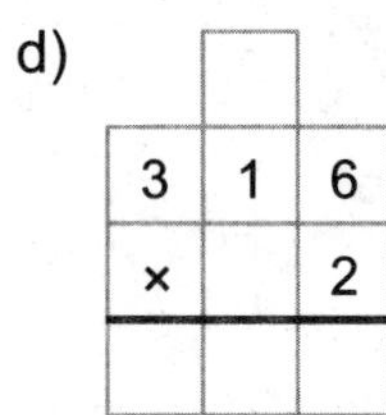

e) 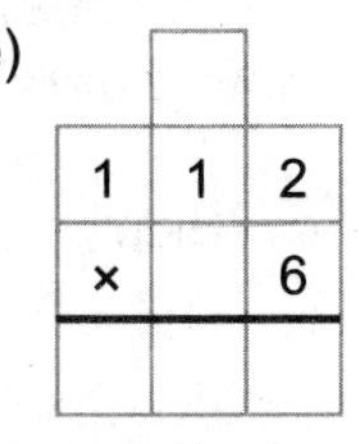

5. Multiply by exchanging tens for hundreds. In the last question, you will also exchange ones for tens.

a) 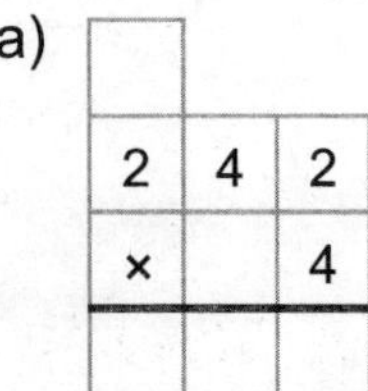

b) 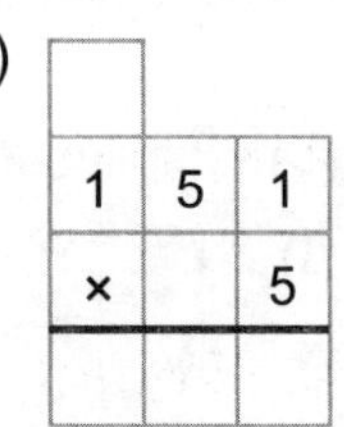

c) 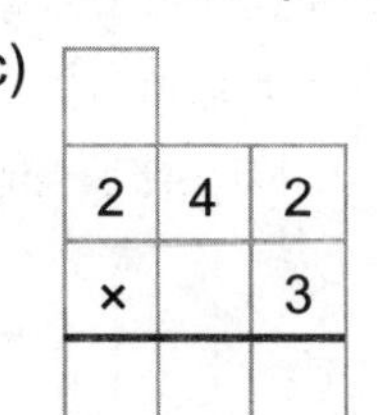

d) 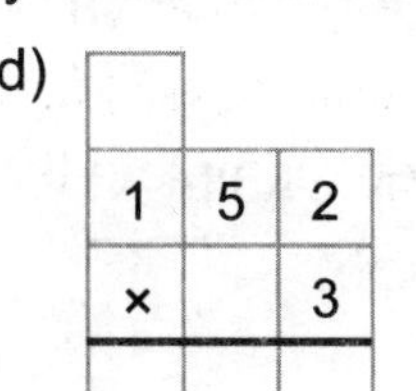

e) 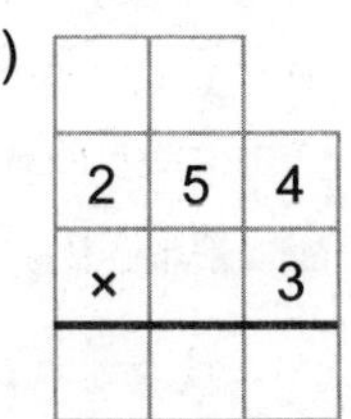

6. On a separate piece of paper, multiply . . .

a) 4 × 242 b) 5 × 312 c) 7 × 123 d) 8 × 314 e) 9 × 253 f) 6 × 241

# NS4-24: Concepts in Multiplication



Show your work for these questions on a separate piece of paper. Be sure to explain your answers.

1. A common octopus has 240 suckers on each arm. How many suckers does an octopus have in total?

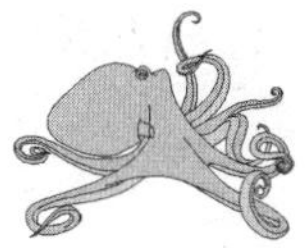

2. A glass holds 176 mL of water. How many millilitres are needed to fill 6 glasses?

3. On average, every North American uses 240 L of water each day.
   a) How much does each North American use in 1 week?
   b) How much water would a family of 4 use in 1 day?

4. The **product** of 3 and 2 is 6 (3 × 2 = 6). The **sum** of 3 and 2 is 5 (3 + 2 = 5). Which is greater, the **sum** or the **product**?

5. Try finding the **sum** and the **product** of different pairs of numbers (such as 3 and 4, 2 and 5, 5 and 6, 1 and 7). What do you notice? Is the product always greater than the sum?

6. Kyle multiplied two numbers. The product was one of the numbers. What was the other?

7. Write all the pairs of numbers you can think of that multiply to give 20. (For an extra challenge, find all the pairs of numbers that multiply to give 40.)

8. An insect called a cicada can burrow into the ground and stay there for 10 years.
   a) How many months can a cicada stay in the ground?
   b) Some cicadas have been known to stay in the ground for 20 years. How can you use your answer in part a) to find out how many months are in 20 years?

9. There are 3 ways to put 4 dots into rows so that each row contains the same number of dots. How many ways can you put the following number of dots into equal rows? Use counters or pictures to help you find all the possibilities.

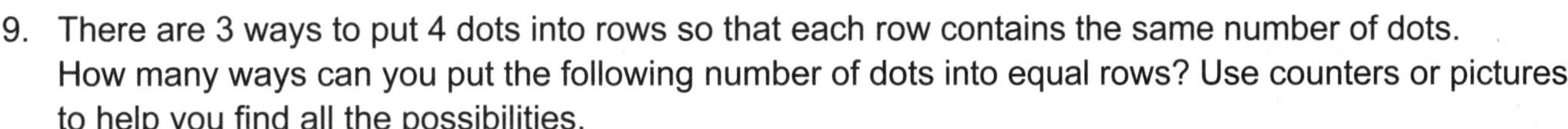

   a) 6 dots  b) 8 dots  c) 12 dots  d) 16 dots

10. Roger rides a horse around a hexagonal field with each side 325 m long. How far did he ride?

11. a) Skip count by 10 thirteen times. What number did you strop counting at?
    b) Use your answer in part a) to find the product of 10 × 13. ________
    c) When you multiply 13 by 10, how many zeroes do you add to 13? ___________
    d) Skip count by 100 thirteen times. What number did you stop counting at?_________
    e) Use your answer in part d) to find the product of 100 × 13. ___________
    f) When you multiply 13 by 100, how many zeroes do you add to 13? ____________
    g) Find the products.

| i) 17 × 10 = | ii) 10 × 14 = | iii) 22 × 10 = | iv) 10 × 57 = |
|---|---|---|---|
| v) 19 × 100 = | vi) 100 × 63 = | vii) 100 × 78 = | viii) 95 × 100 = |

# NS4-25: Rounding on a Number Line

1. Draw an arrow to the 0 or 10 to show whether the circled number is closer to **0** or **10**.

a) 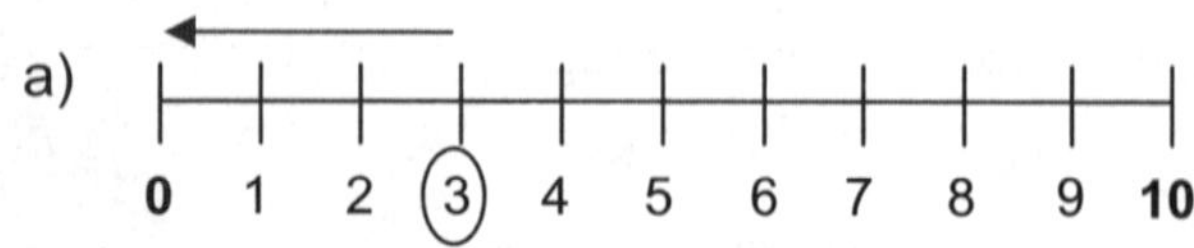


b) 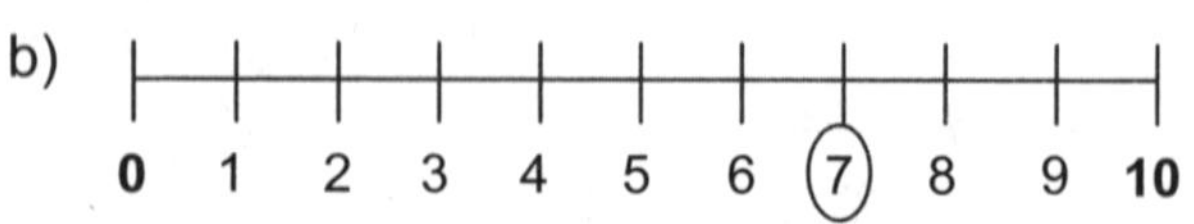


c) 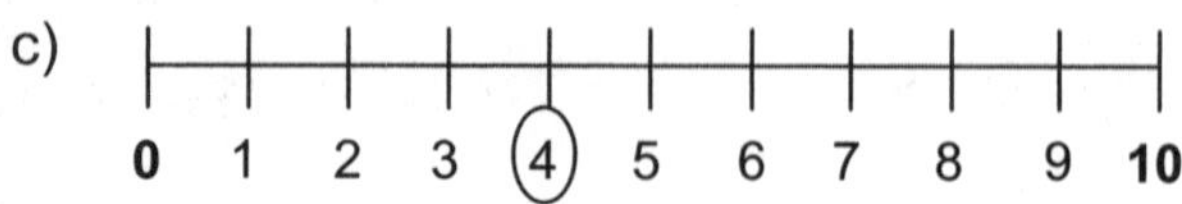


d) 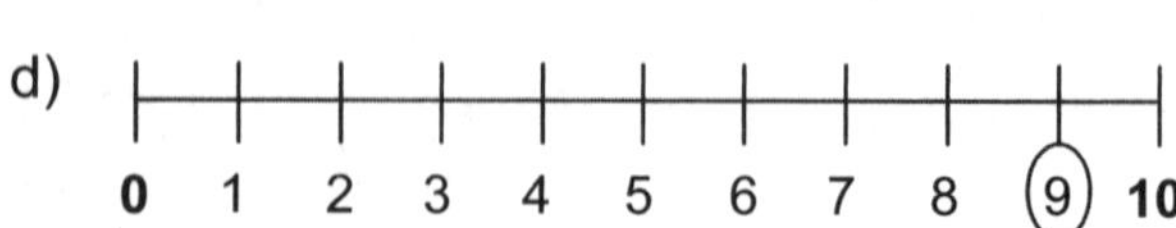


2. a) Which one-digit numbers are closer to 0? ______________

   b) Which are closer to 10? ______________

   c) Why is 5 a special case? ________________________________________

3. Draw an arrow to show if you would round to **10** or **20** or **30**.

a) 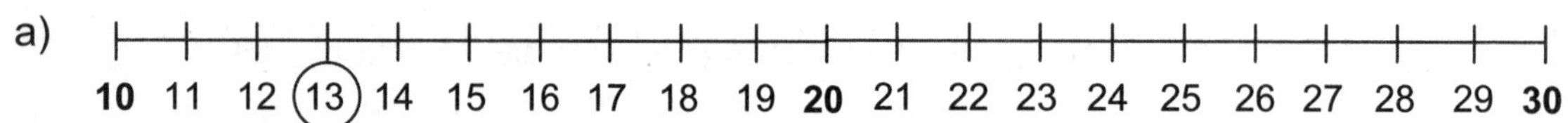


b) 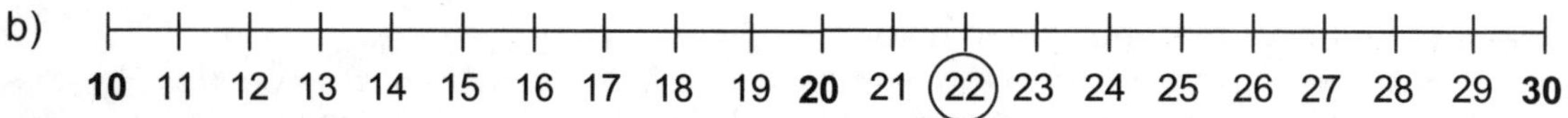


c) 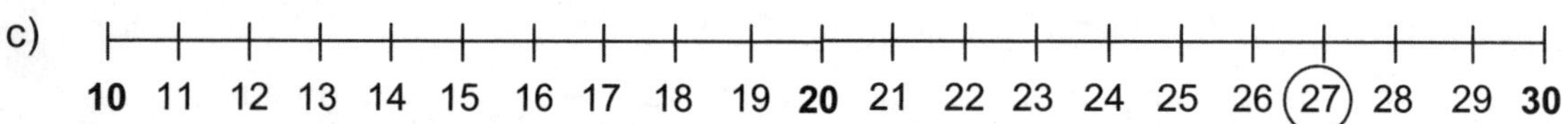


4. Circle the correct answer.

a) The number 28 is closer to 20 or 30

b) The number 34 is closer to 30 or 40

c) The number 56 is closer to 50 or 60

d) The number 79 is closer to 70 or 80

5. Draw an arrow to show which multiple of 10 the number in the circle is closest to.

a) 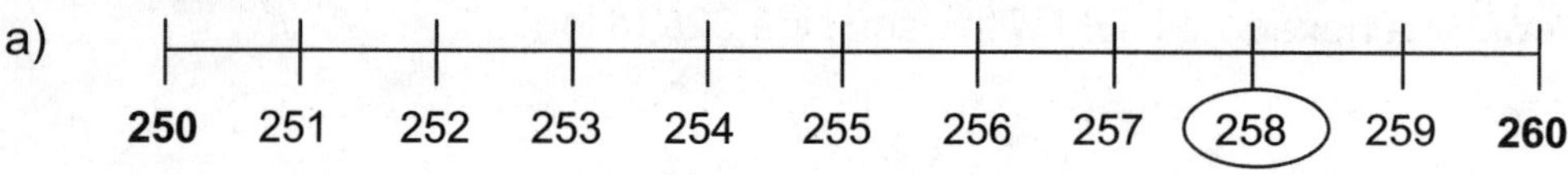


b) 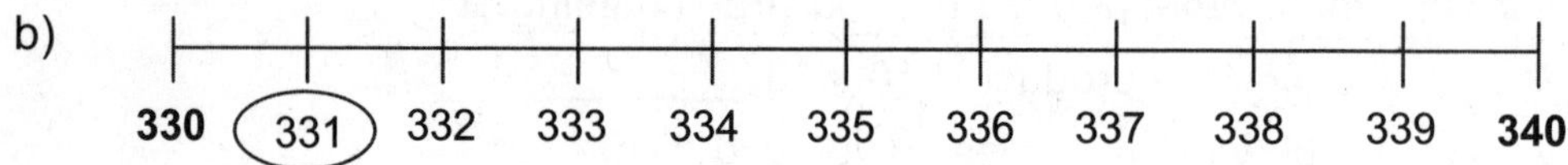


8. Circle the correct answer.

a) The number 168 is closer to 160 or 170

b) The number 385 is closer to 380 or 390

9. Round to the nearest tens place. Write the solution in the box.

a) 455 [ ]  b) 762 [ ]  c) 984 [ ]

10. Draw an arrow to show whether the circled number is closer to 0 or 100.

a) 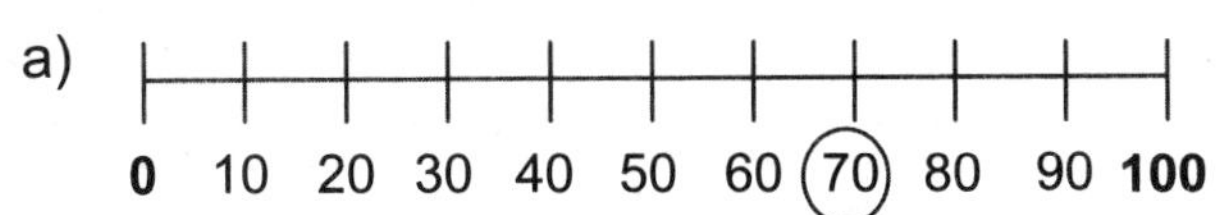


b) 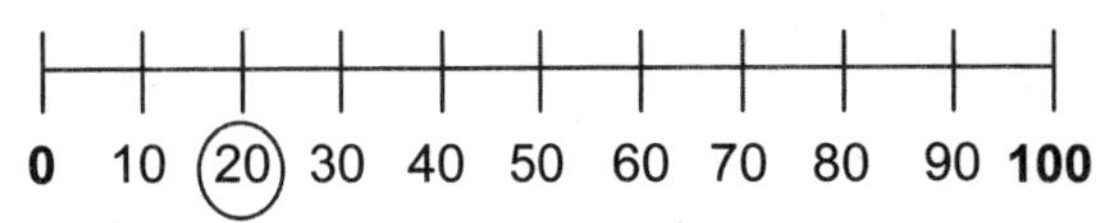


c) 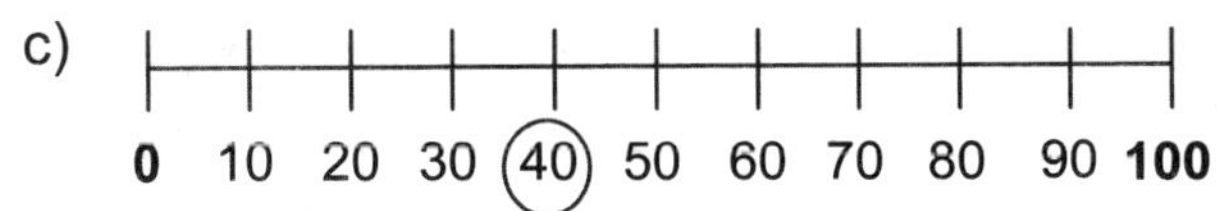


d) 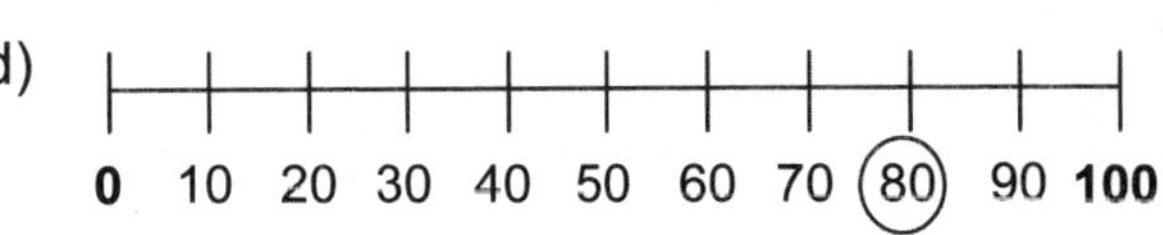


11. Is 50 closer to 0 or to 100? Why is 50 a special case? Explain on a separate piece of paper.

12. Circle the correct answer.

a) The number 80 is closer to 0 or 100

b) The number 20 is closer to 0 or 100

c) The number 40 is closer to 0 or 100

d) The number 10 is closer to 0 or 100

13. On the number line, draw an arrow to show if you would round the number up or down.

a) 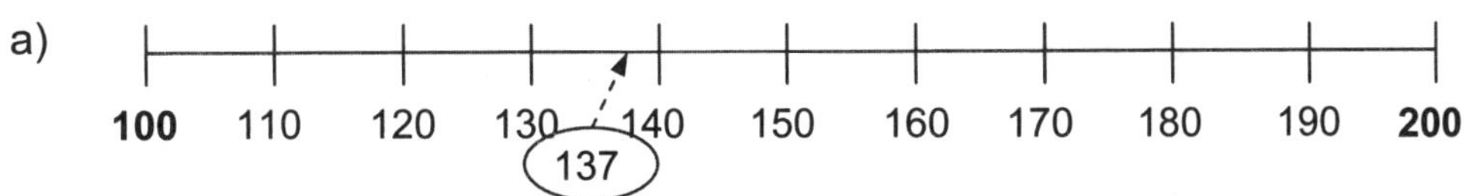


b) 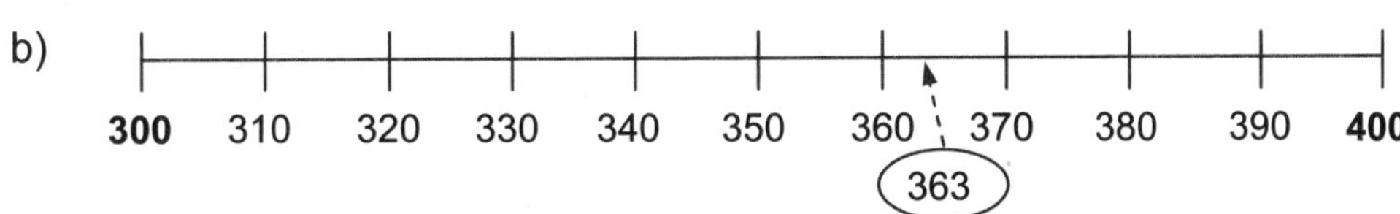


14. Circle the correct answer.

a) The number 153 is closer to 100 or 200

b) The number 729 is closer to 700 or 800

c) The number 319 is closer to 300 or 400

d) The number 586 is closer to 500 or 600

15. On separate paper, write a rule for rounding a three-digit number to the nearest hundreds.

16. Draw an arrow to show if you would round up or round down to the nearest thousands.

a) 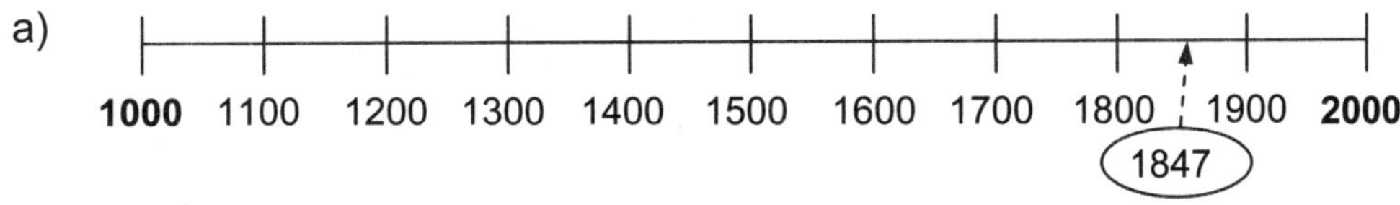


b) 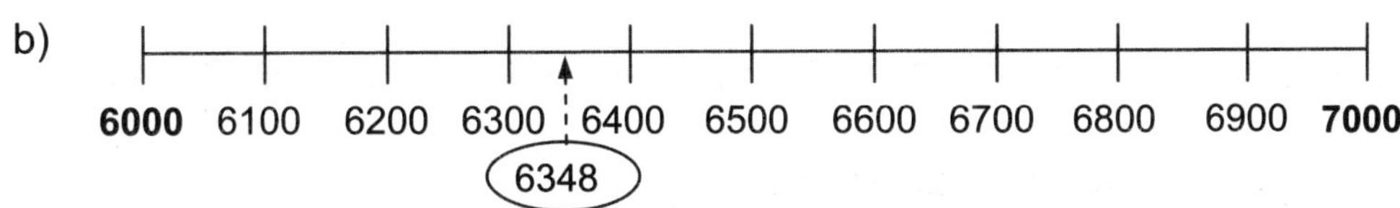


17. Circle the correct answer.

a) The number 2953 is closer to 2000 or 3000

b) The number 7293 is closer to 7000 or 8000

c) The number 5521 is closer to 5000 or 6000

d) The number 3190 is closer to 3000 or 4000

# NS4-26: Rounding

**REMEMBER:**
If the number in the ones digit is
0, 1, 2, 3, or 4, you round **down**
5, 6, 7, 8, or 9, you round **up**

1. Round to the nearest **tens** place.

a) 16 ☐ b) 23 ☐
c) 72 ☐ d) 66 ☐
e) 81 ☐ f) 93 ☐
g) 11 ☐ h) 52 ☐ i) 97 ☐
j) 68 ☐ k) 37 ☐ l) 43 ☐

2. Round to the nearest tens place (underline the ones digit first).

a) 14<u>5</u> 150 b) 172 ☐ c) 321 ☐
d) 255 ☐ e) 784 ☐ f) 667 ☐
g) 441 ☐ h) 939 ☐ i) 318 ☐
j) 527 ☐ k) 985 ☐ l) 534 ☐
m) 758 ☐ n) 845 ☐ o) 293 ☐

3. Round the following numbers to the nearest hundreds place (underline the tens digit first).

**REMEMBER:** 3<u>4</u>5
To round to the nearest hundreds, look at the tens digit.

a) 3<u>4</u>0 300 b) 870 ☐
c) 650 ☐ d) 170 ☐ e) 150 ☐
f) 240 ☐ g) 620 ☐ h) 710 ☐
i) 710 ☐ j) 580 ☐ k) 930 ☐

4. Round to the nearest hundreds place (underline the tens digit first).

a) 148 ☐ b) 218 ☐ c) 321 ☐
d) 668 ☐ e) 543 ☐ f) 282 ☐
g) 374 ☐ h) 857 ☐ i) 547 ☐

5. Round to the nearest thousands place (underline the hundreds digit first).

**REMEMBER:** 1<u>4</u>85
To round to the nearest thousands, look at the hundreds digit.

a) 2757 ☐ b) 9052 ☐
c) 6831 ☐ d) 3480 ☐ e) 5543 ☐
f) 4740 ☐ g) 8193 ☐ h) 2607 ☐

# NS4-27: Estimating Sums and Differences

1. To estimate sums and differences up to one hundred, we will follow these steps:
   - Round each number to the nearest tens.
   - Add or subtract the rounded number.

   Follow the first example.

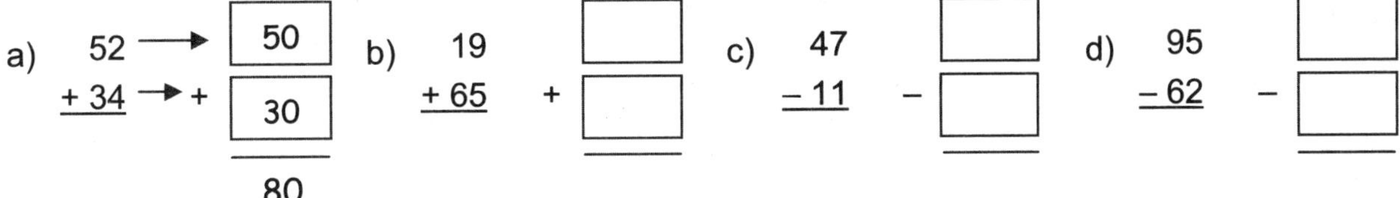

2. Try these questions on a separate piece of paper.

   a) 32 + 11 =   b) 74 – 32 =   c) 37 + 25 =   d) 84 + 28 =   e) 25 + 37 =

3. Round to the nearest hundreds then find the sum or difference. (HINT: Do not look at the ones digit—the tens digit will tell you to round up or down!)

   a) 281 – 123 =   b) 366 + 217 =   c) 855 + 132 =

4. To estimate sums and differences up to one thousand, we will follow these steps:
   - Round each number to the nearest hundreds.
   - Add the sum of the rounded numbers.

   Follow the first example.

   a) 170 → 170; + 340 → + 34; 500
   b) 190 + 650
   c) 470 – 110
   d) 950 – 620

5. Try these questions on a separate piece of paper.

   a) 540 + 210 =   b) 550 – 330 =   c) 210 + 770 =   d) 750 + 220 =   e) 380 + 420 =

6. Round to the nearest hundreds then find the sum or difference. (HINT: Look at the tens.)

   a) 871 – 543 =   b) 283 + 483 =   c) 689 + 214 =

7. To estimate sums and differences up to ten thousand, we will follow these steps:
   - Round each number to the nearest thousands.
   - Add the sum of the rounded numbers.

   Follow the first example.

   a) 1275 → 1000; + 3940 → + 4000; 5000
   b) 4729 – 3132
   c) 2570 + 6234
   d) 9172 – 4529

8. Round to the nearest hundreds then find the sum or difference.

   a) 3272 + 1976 =   b) 3581 – 1926 =   c) 4821 – 3670 =

# NS4-28: Estimating

Ms. Taylor's Grade 6 class was collecting used books for charity.

Anita collected 21 books and Mark collected 28 books. They estimated how many books they collected altogether.

First they rounded the numbers to the nearest tens:

2 1 → round to the nearest tens → 2 0

2 8 → round to the nearest tens → 3 0

Then they added the results:

$$\begin{array}{r} 20 \\ +\ 30 \\ \hline 50 \end{array}$$

---

Answer the following questions on a separate page (if necessary).

1. Round the number of books collected to the nearest **tens** then add to find the sum.
   a) Kishon collected 24 books and Jasjit collected 32 books. Estimate how many books they collected altogether.
   b) Mumtaz collected 75 books and Elizabeth collected 18 books.
   c) Annisha collected 31 books and Christina collected 56 books.

2. The Grade 8 classes at Carleton Village Public School collected books to raise money for charity. Round the number of books collected to the nearest **hundreds** then find the sum.
   a) Class 8A collected 243 books and class 8B collected 456 books. About how many books did 8A and 8B collect altogether?
   b) Class 8C collected 645 books and class 8D collected 129 books. About how many books did 8C and 8D collect altogether?
   c) About how many more books did 8C collect than 8D?
   d) About how many books did all the Grade 8s (8A, 8B, 8C, 8D) collect altogether?

3. A store has the following items for sale:

   **A.** sofa - \$472 **B.** arm chair - \$227 **C.** table - \$189 **D.** desk - \$382 **E.** lamp - \$112

   a) What could you buy if you had \$800 to spend? Estimate to find out. Then add the actual price to check.
   b) List a different set of items you could buy.

4. Estimate the following sums and differences. Then add or subtract to find the actual sum or difference. How far off was your estimate?

   a) 376 + 212 b) 875 – 341 c) 907 – 588

5. Explain why rounding to the nearest hundred is not helpful for the following question. What is a better method of estimation?

   Amy has \$318 and Claudia has \$279. How much more money does Amy have?

# ME4-1: Estimating Lengths in Centimetres

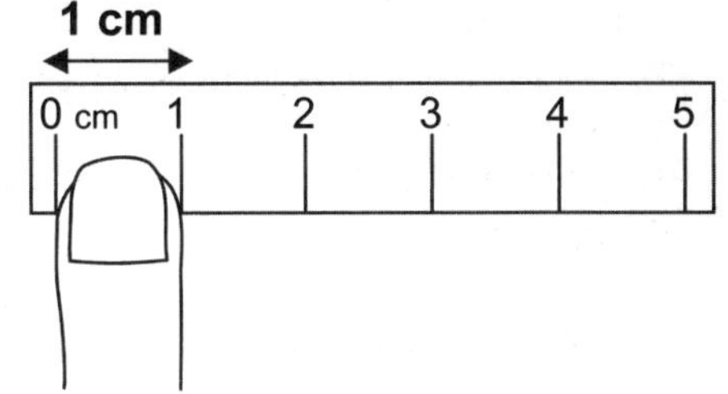


1. A centimetre (cm) is a unit of measurement for **length** (or **height** or **thickness**). Hold up your thumb to a ruler. Line up the edge of your thumb with the zero on the ruler:

   Your thumb is approximately the length of one centimetre.

   Now measure the following objects **using your thumb**:

   a) My pencil is approximately ______ cm long. b) My shoe is about ______ cm long.

2. Pick other objects to measure with your thumb.

   a) My ___________ is approximately _____cm. b) My ___________ is approximately _____cm.

3. 

   A toonie is about 3 cm wide.

   How many toonies would you need to line up to make . . .
   (HINT: Skip count by 3s.)

   a) 15 cm? _________ b) 30 cm? _________ c) 60 cm? _________

4. Hold up your right hand to a ruler. Line up your thumb at the zero (0) marker on the ruler:

   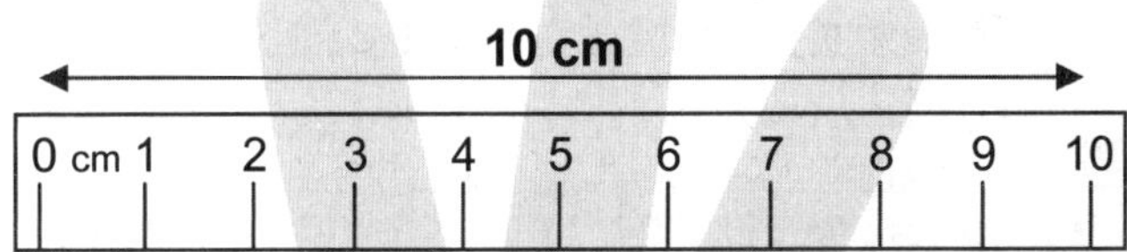


   Your hand should be approximately 10 cm long.

   Now measure the following objects using your right hand:

   a) My table is approximately ________ cm long. b) My arm is approximately ________ cm long.

5. Pick other objects to measure with your hand.

   a) ______________________________________________ is approximately _______cm long.

   b) ______________________________________________ is approximately _______cm long.

BONUS:
Estimate the height of a friend in centimetres without measuring. Then measure the height using your hand (to count by 10 cm). Finally, use a metre stick to check your result. How close were you?
(HINT: Measure your friend against a wall to get an accurate result.)

Estimate: __________ cm Hand measurement: _________cm Actual measurement: _______cm

# ME4-2: Measuring in Centimetres

Midori counts the number of centimetres between the arrows by counting the number of "hops" it takes to move between them:

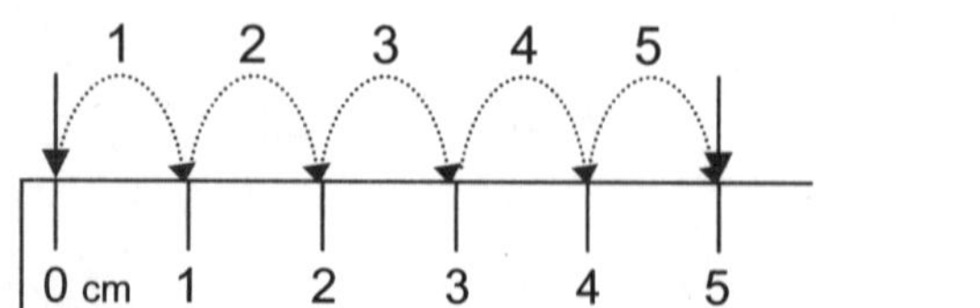


5 cm

1. Measure the distance between the two arrows on each ruler by counting the number of centimetres between them.

a) 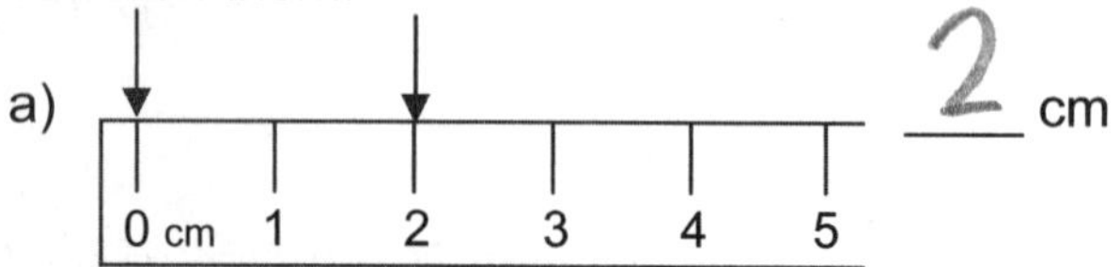

2 cm

b) 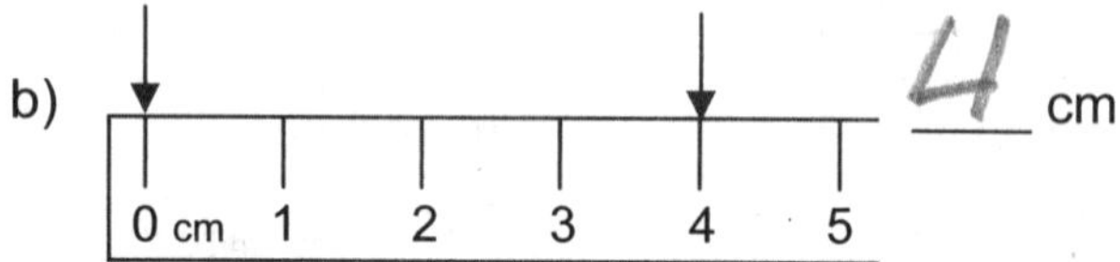

4 cm

2. Measure the distance between the arrows, but count carefully since the first arrow is not at the beginning of the ruler.

a) 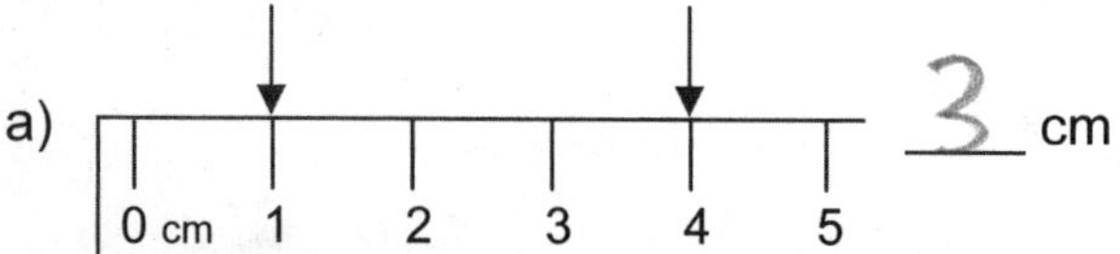

3 cm

b) 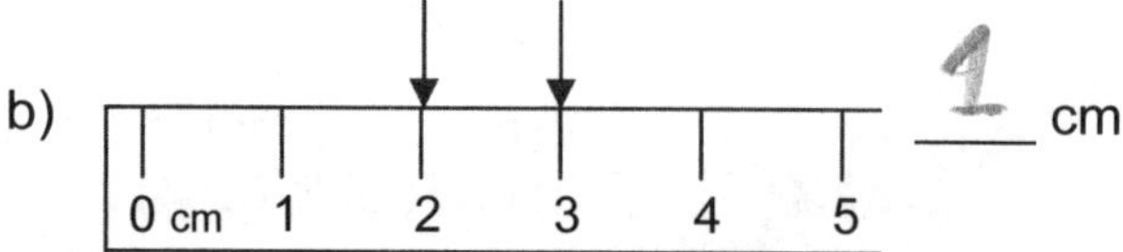

1 cm

3. Measure the distance between the arrows. The centimetre marks on the rulers are not numbered.

a) 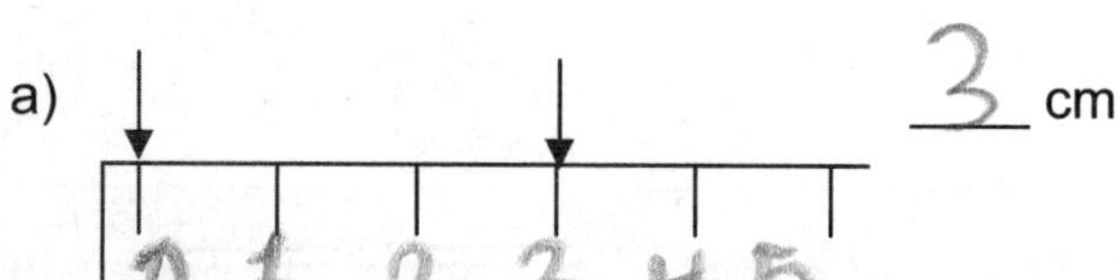
3 cm

b) 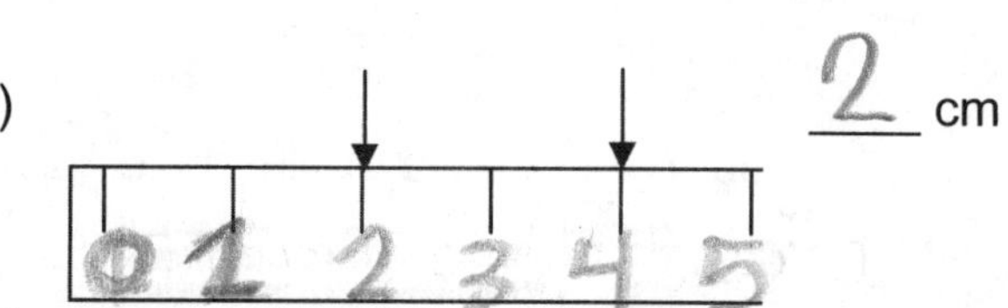
2 cm

4. Measure the length of each line or object by marking the beginning and the end of the line or object along the ruler and counting the number of centimetres between them.

a) 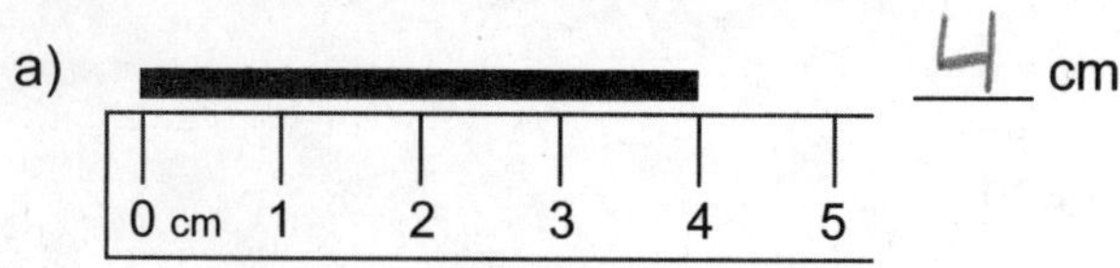

4 cm

b) 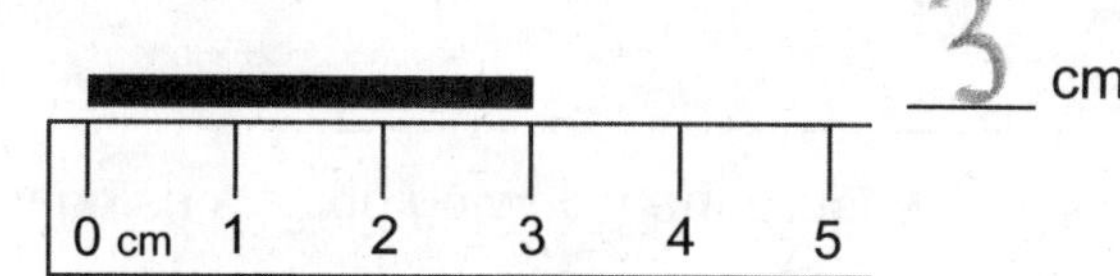

3 cm

c) 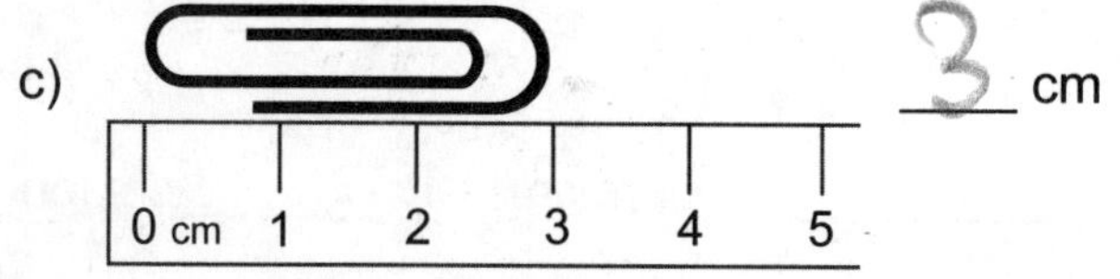

3 cm

d) 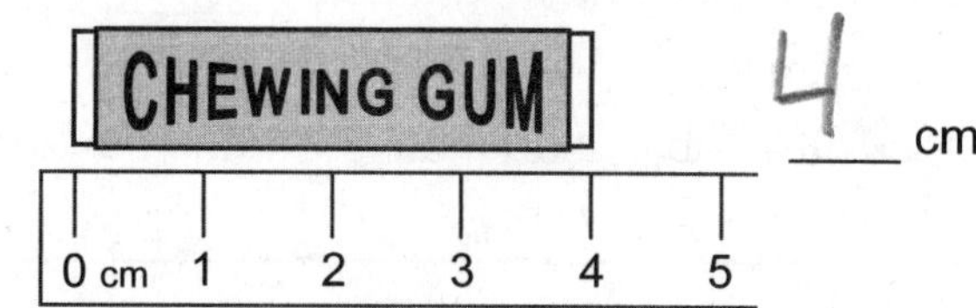

4 cm

5. Measure the length of the line and object below. Be careful! The centimetre marks on these rulers are not numbered.

a) 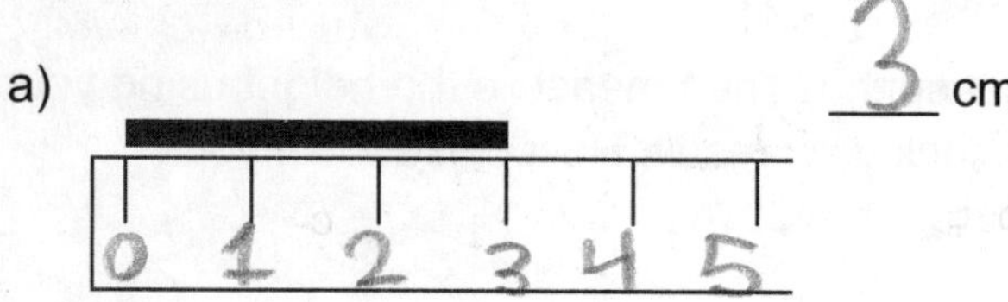
3 cm

b) 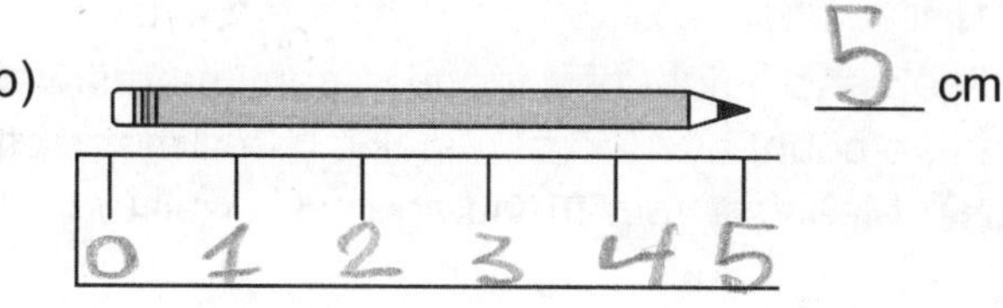
5 cm

# ME4-3: Drawing and Measuring in Centimetres

1. Measure the length of each line using your ruler.

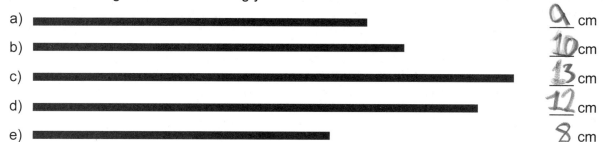

a) 9 cm
b) 10 cm
c) 13 cm
d) 12 cm
e) 8 cm

2. Measure the length of each object using your ruler. Be sure to set the beginning of the object along the "0" on your ruler.

a)  3 cm

b) 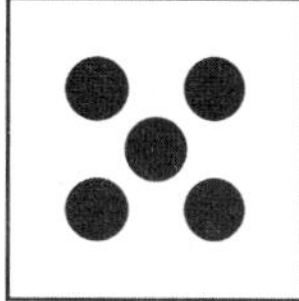 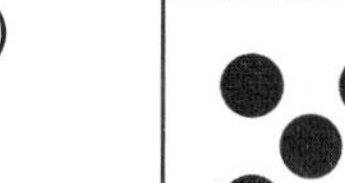 2 cm

3. Measure all the sides of each shape.

a) 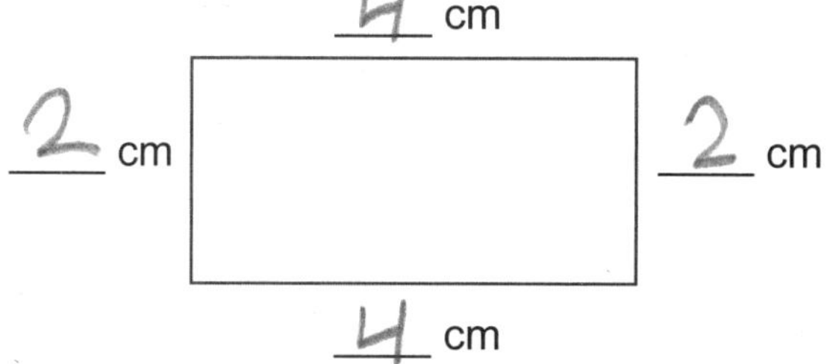

b) 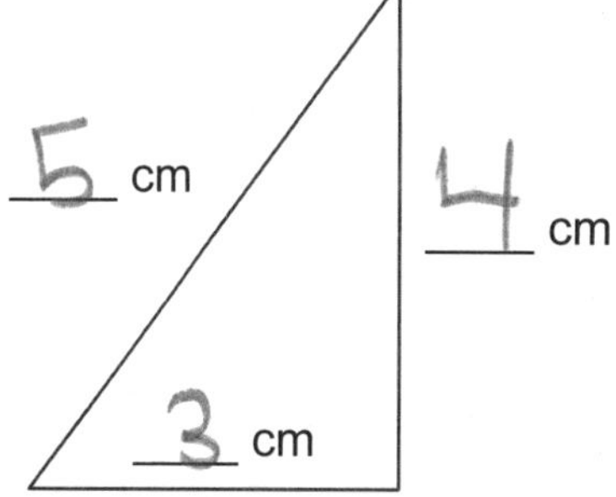

4. Draw two arrows on each ruler that are the given distance apart. The first question is done for you.
(HINT: You may find this easier if you place one of your arrows on the left edge.)

a) 4 cm apart

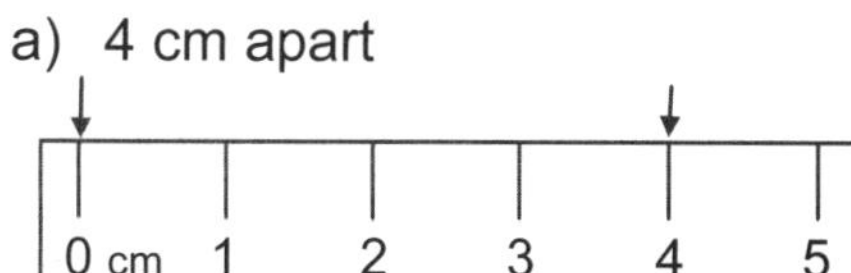

b) 3 cm apart

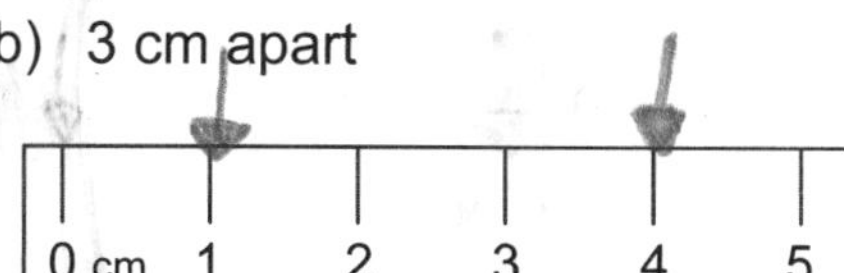

c) 5 cm apart

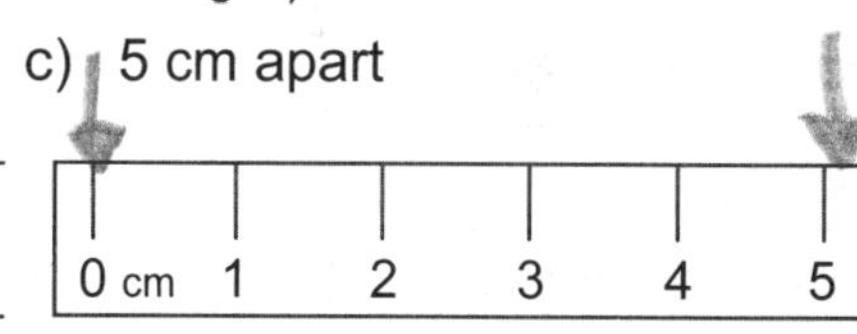

5. Using a ruler or straight edge, draw a line starting from the left edge of the ruler and ending at the given length.

a) 1 cm long

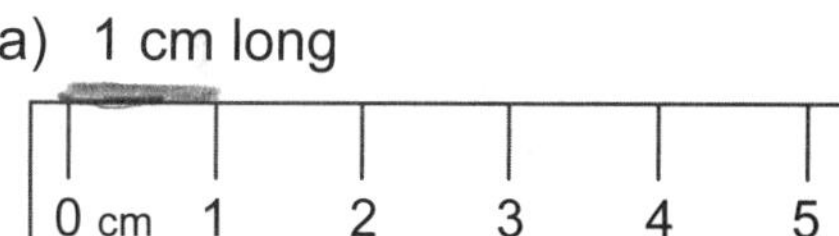

b) 4 cm long

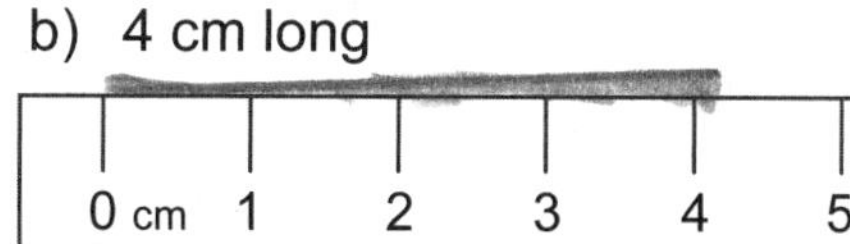

c) 2 cm long

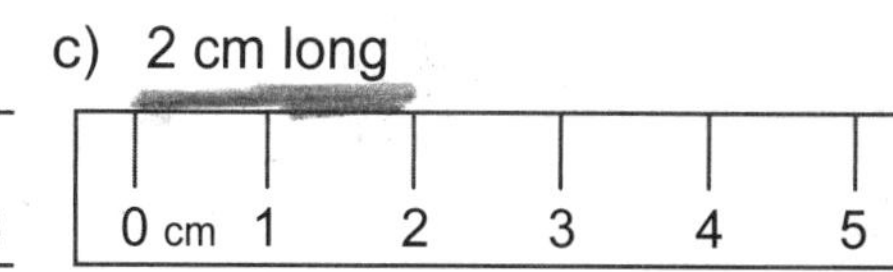

6. On a separate sheet of paper, draw a line starting from the "0" mark of the ruler and ending at the given length.

a) 3 cm long  b) 4 cm long  c) 5 cm long  d) 10 cm long

7. On a separate piece of paper, draw each object to the exact measurement given.

a) a caterpillar, 4 cm long  b) a leaf, 11 cm long  c) a feather, 8cm long

8. BONUS: On grid paper, draw a rectangle with a length of 5 cm and a width of 2 cm.

# ME4-4: Estimating in Millimetres

On many rulers, you can measure objects in both centimetres (cm) and millimetres (mm). If you look at a ruler with millimetre measurements, you can see that 1 cm is equal to 10 mm:

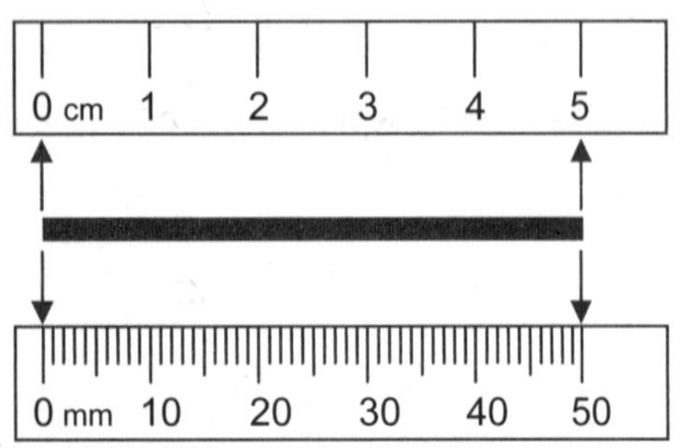


Here is a line that we can measure using both a millimetre ruler and a centimetre ruler. How long is it in millimetres? How long is it in centimetres?

The line is _____ cm long, or _____ mm long.

To convert a measurement from centimetres to millimetres, we have to multiply the measurement by ___.

---

1. Remember that your thumb is about 1 cm wide. This means that it is also about 10 mm wide. Using this fact, measure the following objects using your thumb. Then convert your measurement to millimetres. The first question is done for you.

a) CHEWING GUM

The gum measures about _5_ thumbs.

So, the gum is approximately _50_ mm long.

b)

The crayon measures about _2_ thumbs.

So, the crayon is approximately _20_ mm long.

c)

The pencil measures about _5_ thumbs.

So, the pencil is approximately _50_ mm long.

d)

The thumbtack measures about _1_ thumbs.

So, the thumbtack is approximately _10_ mm long.

2. If you lay a dime flat on your desk it is about 1 mm high. A stack of 10 dimes would be about 10 mm high. So, a stack of 10 dimes would also be 1 cm high.

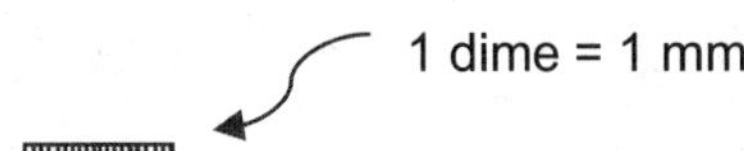

How many dimes would be in a stack that is . . .

a) 2 cm high? 20 dimes

b) 3 cm high? 30 dimes

c) 5 cm high? 50 dimes

d) 10 cm high? 100 dimes

3. Jamelia has 4 stacks of dimes, each about 1 cm high. About how much money does Jamelia have? Explain how you found your answer. 40 dimes. 40 ¢
10 dimes = 1 cm 40 dimes = 4 cm

4. A toonie is about 2 mm thick. Josie has a stack of toonies 10 mm high. How much money does Josie have? $5. 2 mm = 2$ 10 mm = $5
2 4 6 8 10
1 2 3 4 5 = $5

# ME4-5: Millimetres and Centimetres



Mei-Ling wants to measure a line that is 23 mm long. Rather than counting every millimetre, Mei-Ling counts by 10s until she reaches 20. Then she counts on by 1s:

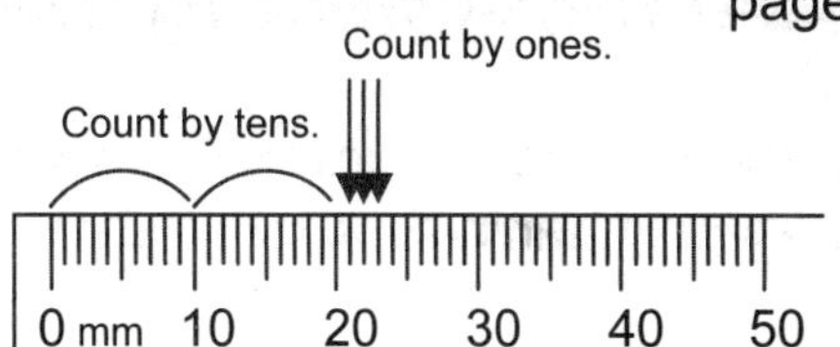


1. Measure the distance between the two arrows on each ruler by counting the number of millimetres between them.

a) 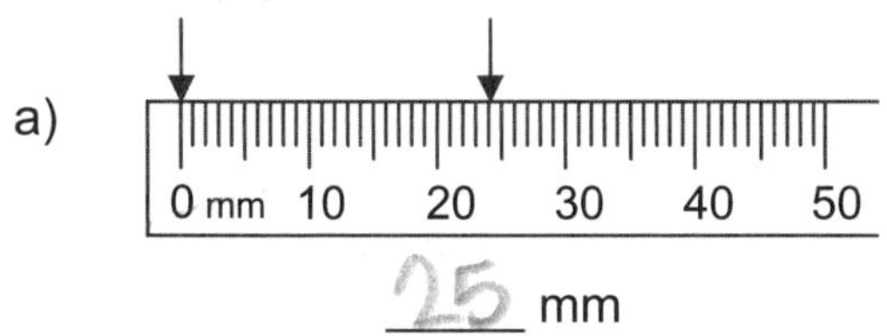

25 mm

b) 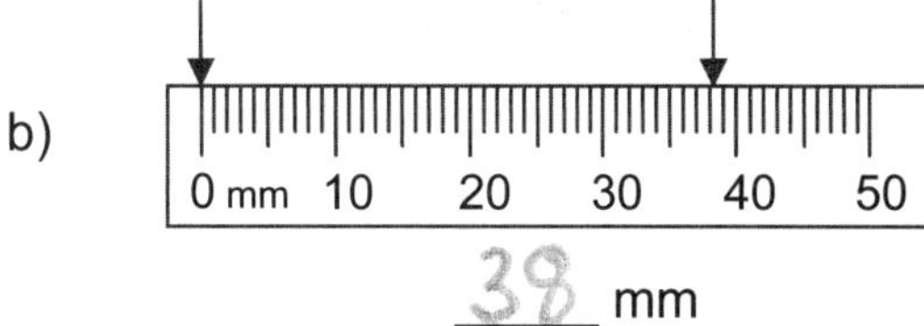

38 mm

2. Measure the length of each line by marking the beginning and the end of the line along the ruler and counting the number of millimetres between your marks.
(HINT: Rather than count every millimetre, you should find it quicker to count from the nearest "ten.")

a) 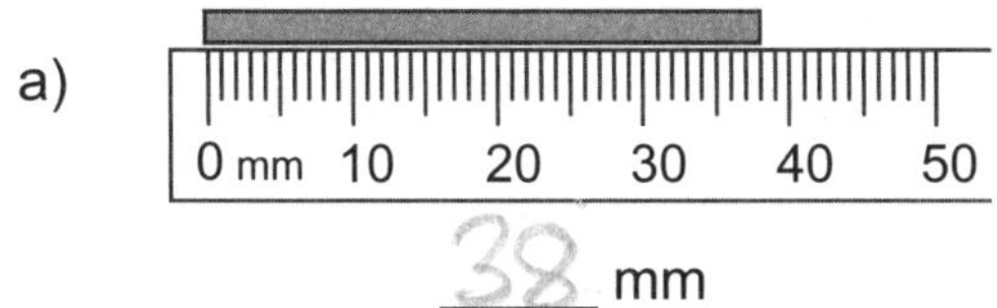

38 mm

b) 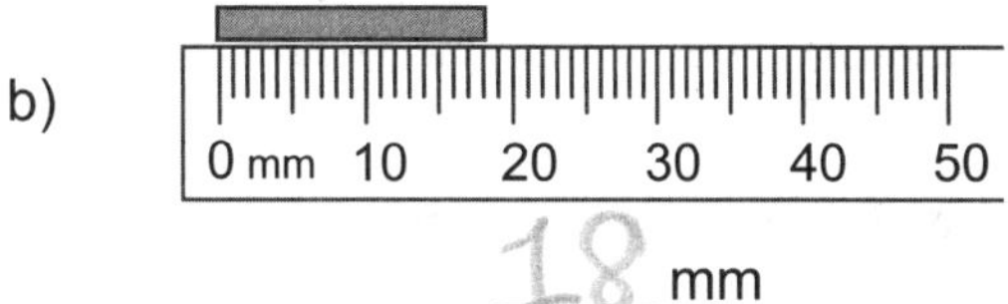

18 mm

3. Using a straight edge, draw a line starting from the zero mark of the ruler and ending at the given length.

a) 16 mm long

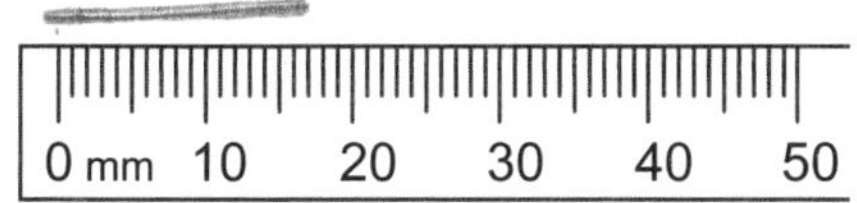


b) 41 mm long

4. On a separate piece of paper, use a ruler to draw the following objects to the exact millimetre:
   a) a line, 20 cm long
   b) a line, 27 mm long
   c) a line, 52 mm long
   d) a beetle, 30 mm long
   e) a pencil, 70 mm long
   f) a bicycle, 28 mm long

5. For each line below, estimate whether the length is **less than** 30 mm or **more than** 30 mm and place a check mark in the appropriate column.

| | **Less than 30 mm** | **More than 30 mm** |
|---|---|---|
| a) ✓ | | more |
| b) ✓ | less | |
| c) ✓ | | more |
| d) ✓ | less | |
| e) ✓ | less | |

6. How good were your estimates? For each estimate you made in question 5, measure the length of the line and record your measurement in millimetres.

   a) 50 mm  b) 20 mm  c) 45 mm  d) 25 mm  e) 10 mm

7. For each pair of lines estimate whether the distance between them is **less than** 20 mm or **more than** 20 mm and indicate your response by placing a check mark in the appropriate column.

| | Less than 20 mm | More than 20 mm |
|---|---|---|
| a) | | more |
| b) | less | |
| c) | | more |
| d) | less | |
| e) | | more |

8. How good were your estimates? For each estimate you made in question 7, measure the distance between the pair of lines and record your measurement in millimetres.

   a) 52 mm  b) 5 mm  c) 45 mm  d) 12 mm  e) 25 mm

9. Measure the following lines using both centimetres and millimetres:

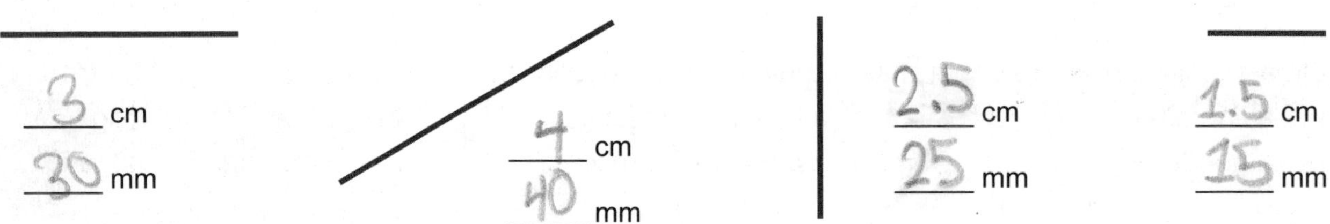

10. Measure the sides of the rectangles in centimetres. Then measure the distance between the two diagonal corners in centimetres and millimetres. (The dotted line is a guide for where you should place your ruler.)

a) 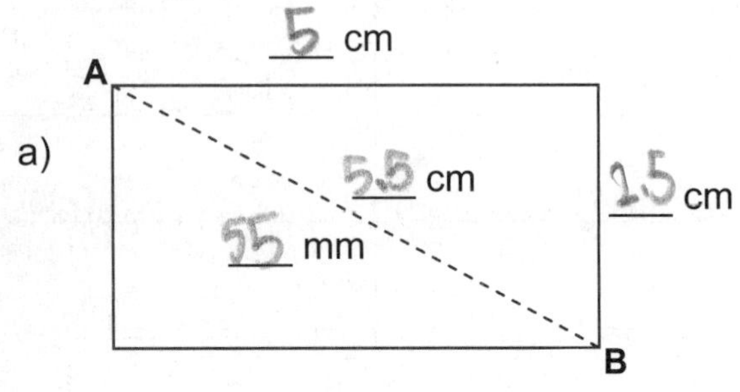

b) 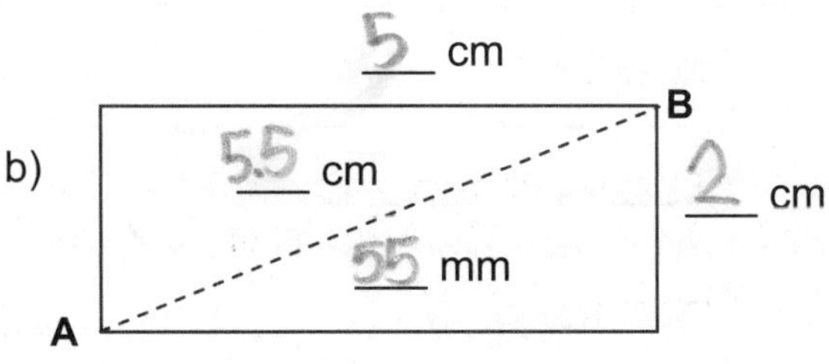

# ME4-6: Comparing Centimetres and Millimetres



1. How many millimetres (mm) are there in one centimetre (cm)? ________________

2. What fraction of a centimetre (cm) is a millimetre (mm)? ________________

3. To change a measurement from centimetres (cm) into millimetres (mm), what should you multiply the measurement by? ________________

4. Fill in the missing numbers for the following charts:

| mm | cm |
|---|---|
| | 11 |
| | 57 |
| | 5 |

| mm | cm |
|---|---|
| | 7 |
| | 12 |
| | 35 |

| mm | cm |
|---|---|
| | 112 |
| | 170 |
| | 293 |

| mm | cm |
|---|---|
| | 8 |
| | 257 |
| | 32 |

5. To change a measurement from millimetres to centimetre, what number do you have to divide by? ______

a) 40 ÷ 10 = ______ b) 60 ÷ 10 = ______ c) 2100 ÷ 10 = ______ d) 90 ÷ 10 = ______

e) 320 mm = ______ cm f) 30 mm = ______ cm g) 910 mm = ______ cm h) 650 mm = ______ cm

6. Fill in the following tables:

| cm | mm |
|---|---|
| 5 | |
| | 80 |
| 12 | |
| | 140 |

| cm | mm |
|---|---|
| 19 | |
| 1 | |
| | 180 |
| | 2700 |

| cm | mm |
|---|---|
| 7 | |
| | 10 |
| | 90 |
| | 11020 |

7. Circle the greater measurement in each pair by converting one of the measurements so that both units are the same.
(HINT: It is easy to convert centimetres to millimetres—just multiply the measurement by 10.)

a) 5 cm 70 mm b) 83 cm 910 mm c) 45 cm 53 mm

d) 2 cm 12 mm e) 60 cm 6200 mm f) 72 cm 420 mm

8. Estimate the width and length (in centimetres) of each rectangle. Then measure each quantity exactly in millimetres using a ruler.

a)

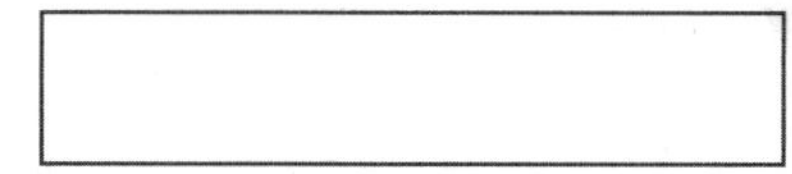

b)

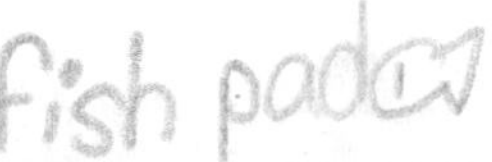

9. Complete the following table. Using your ruler, draw the second line so that the pair of lines are spaced apart according to the information provided in the table. The first question is done for you.

| | Distance apart | |
|---|---|---|
| | In cm | In mm |
| | 4 | 40 |
| | 3 | |
| | | 80 |
| | 7 | |
| | | 60 |

10. In the space provided, draw a line that is between 3 cm and 4 cm. How long is your line in millimetres?

11. In the space provided, draw a line that is between 6 cm and 7 cm. How long is your line in millimetres?

12. On a separate piece of paper, draw a line that is a whole number of centimetres long and is between . . .

a) 45 mm and 55 mm  b) 65 mm and 75 mm  c) 17 mm and 23 mm

13. Write a measurement in millimetres that is between . . .

a) 7 cm and 8 cm ________  b) 12 cm and 13 cm ________  c) 27 cm and 28 cm ________

14. Write a measurement in centimetres that is between . . .

a) 67 mm and 75 mm ________  b) 27 mm and 39 mm ________

c) 52 mm and 7 cm ________  d) 112 mm and 13 cm ________

15. On grid paper, draw a rectangle with a length of 60 mm and a width of 2 cm.

16. Peter says 5 mm is longer than 2 cm because 5 is greater than 2. Is he right?

# ME4-7: Decimetres



Remember that your hand is about 10 cm wide.
10 centimetres is equal to 1 decimetre (dm):

So there are 10 cm in 1 dm. (Similarly, 10 mm are equal to 1 cm.)

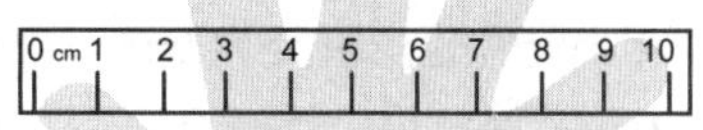

10 cm = 1 dm

1. Are the following objects more than 1 dm long, or less than 1 dm? Place a check mark in the appropriate column. You can use your hand to help you estimate. REMEMBER: 1 dm = 10 cm.

| | Less than 1 dm | More than 1 dm |
|---|---|---|
| my arm | | |
| a paperclip | | |
| my pencil | | |
| the height of my bedroom door | | |

2. How many centimetres are in 1 dm? ______________

3. What fraction of a decimetre (dm) is a centimetre? ______________

4. To change a measurement from decimetres (dm) to centimetres (cm), what should you multiply the measurement by? ______________

5. To change a measurement from centimetres to decimetres what should you divide by? ___________

6. Fill in the missing numbers for the following charts:

| cm | dm |
|---|---|
| 150 | 15 |
| | 23 |
| | 32 |

| cm | dm |
|---|---|
| 90 | |
| | 510 |
| 400 | |

| cm | dm |
|---|---|
| 610 | |
| | 1 |
| 780 | |

7. In the space provided, draw a line that is between 1 dm and 2 dm long.

a) How long is your line in centimetres?________ b) How long is your line in millimetres?______

8. Write a measurement in centimetres that is between . . .

a) 4 dm and 5 dm _________ b) 3 dm and 4 dm _________ c) 7 dm and 8 dm _________

Explain how you found your answer to part c) on a separate piece of paper.

9. Write a measurement in decimetres that is between . . .

a) 72 cm and 82 cm ________ b) 27 cm and 35 cm ________ c) 68 cm and 74 cm _________

10. If 1 dm is the same length as 10 cm, how many decimetres would there be in 100 cm? ___________

11. There are 10 mm in 1 cm. There are 10 cm in 1 dm. How many millimetres are in 1 dm?___________

How do you know? How could you check your answer?

# ME4-8: Metres



A **metre** is a unit of measurement for **length** (or **height** or **thickness**) that is equal to 100 cm.

A metre stick is 100 cm long:

1. When you spread your fingers, the distance between your little finger and your thumb is about 10 cm, or 1 dm. How many of your hands would fit into 100 cm? _______ How many decimetres is 100 cm?_______

2. Ten interlocking centimetre cubes are 10 cm long:

   How many groups of ten cubes would make 1 m? _______ How many decimetres is 1 m?______

**You can estimate metres using parts of your body.**

- A giant step is about one metre long.
- A 9-year-old child is about one metre tall.
- If you stretch your arms out, the distance between the tips of your fingers (your arm span) is about one metre.

3. Take a giant step and ask a friend to measure your step with a piece of string. Hold the string up to a metre stick. Is your step more or less than one metre? _____________

4. Ask a friend to measure your arm span using a piece of string. Is your arm span more or less than one metre? _____________

5. Stand against a wall and ask a friend to mark your height with chalk. Measure your height in centimetres using a metre stick. Your height is ___________ cm. Are you taller than 1 m? _______

6. Estimate the following distances to the nearest metre and then measure the actual distance with a metre stick or measuring tape:

   a) The length of your window. Estimate: ____ m Actual: ____ m _____ cm

   b) The length of your table. Estimate: ____ m Actual: ____ m _____ cm

   c) The distance from the floor to the door handle. Estimate: ____ m Actual: ____ m _____ cm

Answer the following questions on a separate piece of paper:

7. Khalid is a member of his high school track team. The track is 400 m long, so every time Khalid does a lap, he covers a distance of 400 m:

   a) Khalid runs 2 times around the track. How many metres has he travelled?

   b) Khalid finished practice after running 4 laps. How many metres did he run?

   c) Khalid is planning on competing for the 1500 m race at the Metro Finals. About how many times around the track is this?

8. A small city block is about 100 m long. Write the name of a place you can walk to from your home (a store, a park, your friend's home). Approximately how far away from your home is the place you named? How could you check your estimate?

Roger has a tree in his backyard. The tree is 3 m tall:
Another way to represent this height is by saying that the tree is 300 cm tall.
We could also say that the tree is 3000 mm tall.

Which do you think is the best measurement to use in describing the tree? ____________________

9. See if you can figure out the pattern in the following table. Then complete the table.

| m | 1 | 2 | 3 | 4 | 5 | 6 |
|---|---|---|---|---|---|---|
| dm | 10 | 20 | | | | |
| cm | 100 | 200 | | | | |
| mm | 1000 | 2000 | | | | |

10. To convert a measurement from metres to centimetres, what do you have to multiply your measurement by? ________________ Explain your answer on a separate piece of paper.

11. To convert a measurement from metres to millimetres, what do you have to multiply your measurement by? ________________ Explain your answer on a separate piece of paper.

12. Convert the following measurements:

| m | cm |
|---|---|
| 1 | |
| 14 | |
| 80 | |

| m | mm |
|---|---|
| 2 | |
| 19 | |
| 21 | |

| cm | mm |
|---|---|
| 3 | |
| 65 | |
| 106 | |

13. Sheena decided to measure her bedroom window with a metre stick and a measuring tape.
    - When she measured with the metre stick, the height of the window was 2 m with 15 cm extra.
    - When she measured with the measuring tape, she got a measurement of 215 cm.

    a) Was there a difference in the two measurements? Explain your answer on a separate piece of paper.

    b) What are the benefits of using multiple units of measurement?

14. Convert the measurement given in centimetres to a measurement using multiple units.

    a) 513 cm = __5__ m __13__ cm        b) 217 cm = _____ m ______ cm

    c) 367 cm = _____ m ______ cm        d) 481 cm = _____ m ______ cm

    e) 796 cm = _____ m ______ cm        f) 343 cm = _____ m ______ cm

15. Convert the following multiple units of measurements to a single unit.

    a) 3 m 71 cm = __371__ cm        b) 4 m 51 cm = _____ cm        e) 3 m 45 cm = _____ cm

    c) 8 m 91 cm = _____ cm        d) 9 m 27 cm = _____ cm        f) 7 m 50 cm = _____ cm

16. Linda says that to convert a measurement like 4 m 30 cm to a single unit of measurement, you take the metre measurement of 4 and multiply it by 100 and then add it to the remaining 30 cm. Is Linda correct? Why does Linda multiply by 100?

# ME4-9: Kilometres

A **kilometre** (km) is a unit of measurement for **length** that is equal to 1000 m.

1. a) Count by 100s to find out how many times you need to add 100 to make 1000.

   100 , ______ , ______ , ______ , ______ , ______ , ______ , ______ , ______ , ______

   b) A football field is about 100 m long.
   How many football fields long is one kilometre?

2. a) Skip count by 50s to find out how many times you need to add 50 to make 1000.

   b) An Olympic swimming pool is 50 m long.
   How many pools long is one kilometre?

3. Count by 10s to find the number of times you need to add 10 to make each number.

   a) 100 = ______ tens  b) 200 = ______ tens  c) 300 = ______ tens

   d) 400 = ______ tens  e) 500 = ______ tens  f) 600 = ______ tens

4. Using the pattern in question 3, how many times would you need to add 10 to make 1000?

5. A school bus is about 10 m long. How many school buses, lined up end to end, would be . . .

   a) close to one kilometre?  b) close to 2 km?

6. Continue the pattern to find out how many times you need to add 2 to make 1000.

   a) 100 = 50 twos  b) 200 = 100 twos  c) 300 = 150 twos  d) 400 = 200 twos

   e) 500 = ______ twos  f) 600 = ______ twos  g) 700 = ______ twos  h) 800 = ______ twos

   i) 900 = ______ twos  j) 1000 = ______ twos

7. A tall adult is about 2 m high. How many adults, lying head to foot, would make one kilometre?

8. You can travel 1 km if you walk for 15 minutes at a regular speed. Can you name a place (a store, a park, your friend's home) that is about 1 km from your home?

9. BONUS: If you lined up the following objects would they be (i) close to 1 km, (ii) less than 1 km, or (iii) more than 1 km? Explain your answer on a separate piece of paper.

   a) 1000 pencils  b) 1000 buses  c) 1000 JUMP books  d) 1000 baseball bats

   (HINT: First decide if the individual object is close to a metre, less than a metre or more than a metre.)

Hien plans to visit different relatives in Saskatchewan. He uses a map that shows how many kilometres are between each of the places he wants to visit.

The numbers beside each line mark the length of the road between those cities in kilometres.

One kilometre (km) is the same distance as 1000 m.

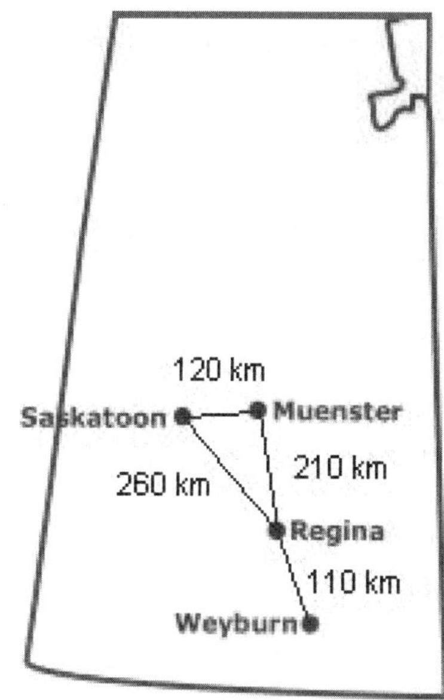


Use the map to answer the following questions:

10. Fill in the blanks to describe how far apart these different cities are in kilometres.

    a) Saskatoon and Muenster are _____________ km apart.

    b) Regina and Weyburn are _____________ km apart.

    c) Muenster and Regina are _____________ km apart.

    d) Sasktoon and Regina are _____________ km apart.

11. How far would Hien be travelling if he made the following trips? You will need to use addition to solve these problems.

    a) Start in Saskatoon and drive through Muenster to Regina. You would travel _____________ km.

    b) Start in Saskatoon and drive through Regina to Weyburn. You would travel _____________ km.

    c) Start in Weyburn and drive through Regina to Muenster. You would travel _____________ km.

    d) Start in Regina and drive through Muenster and Saskatoon back to Regina. You would travel _____________ km.

12. How many more kilometres is the distance between Regina and Saskatoon than the distance between Regina and Muenster?

BONUS:

13. Look at a map of Canada and use the scale on the map to estimate the distance between the city or town you live in and Regina. If you live in Regina, pick another city. Ask your parent to check the actual distance in kilometres.

    My estimate: _________ km Actual distance: _________ km

14. How far would you travel if you drove from your home town to Regina and then back home again?

    (Use the actual distance) _________ km

# ME4-10: Ordering and Assigning Appropriate Units

1. When you are choosing the best unit of measure, it is important to remember just how different each unit of measurement really is!

   For each of the following questions, you will need to pick an appropriate unit of measurement. Then you will need to explain why you chose the unit of measurement.
   REMEMBER: You can refer to the guidelines provided.

|  |  |  |  |  |
|---|---|---|---|---|
| the thickness of a dime is about 1 mm | the width of your thumb is about 1 cm | the width of your hand is about 1 dm | the height of the average 9-year-old child is about 1 m | the distance you can walk in 15 minutes is about 1 km |

   a) The length of an eraser. The best unit of measure would be ____________________ .

   b) The distance travelled on a plane flight from Halifax to Moncton. The best unit of measurement would be ____________________ .

   c) The length of a subway car. The best unit of measurement would be ____________________ . Explain why you chose this unit.

2. Match the word with the symbol. Then match the object with the most appropriate unit of measurement. The first one is done for you.

a)

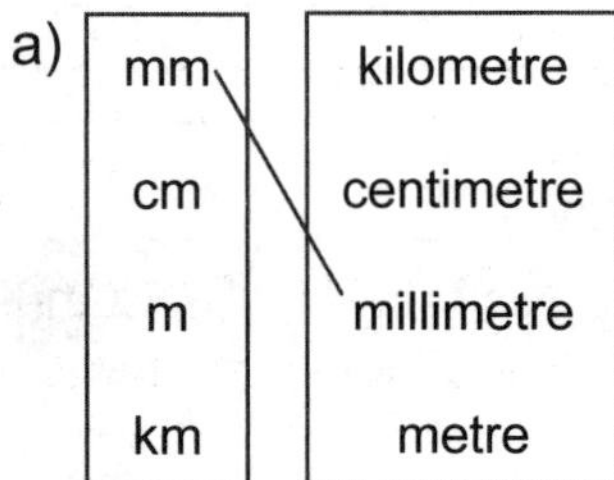

| Symbol | Word | Object |
|---|---|---|
| mm | kilometre | book |
| cm | centimetre | length of your street |
| m | millimetre | height of your room |
| km | metre | length of an ant |

b)

| Symbol | Word | Object |
|---|---|---|
| km | metre | door |
| cm | millimetre | distance to Montreal |
| m | kilometre | pencil |
| mm | centimetre | postage stamp |

3. Number the following items from smallest to largest (1 = smallest, 2 = middle, 3 = largest). What unit would you use to measure each item?

a)   

b)   

4. For the following questions, circle the unit of measurement that makes the statement correct:

   a) Your front door is about 2 **dm** / **m** high.

   b) The length of your shoe is close to 1 **dm** / **cm**.

   c) The thickness of your JUMP workbook is about 10 **mm** / **cm**.

   d) The height of the CN Tower is about 553 **dm** / **m**.

5. For each of the following questions, you need to decide which unit of measurement would make the statement correct. Remember to use the tools provided in question 1 to help you estimate.

   a) The thickness of a piece of construction paper is about 1 _____ .

   b) In the wintertime the schools might close if more than 50 _____ of snow has fallen overnight.

   c) An average adult bicycle is about 2 _____ long.

   d) It is more than 500 _____ from Toronto to Montreal.

   e) The length of your arm from your wrist to your shoulder is about 0.5 _____ .

6. This chart lists the lengths of some Canadian rivers and the provinces in which they are located. Order them from longest (1) to shortest (5).

| River | Length |
|---|---|
| Clearwater (Saskatoon | 187 km |
| Bloodvein (Manitoba) | 200 km |
| Kicking Horse (British Columbia) | 67 km |
| Jacques Cartier (Quebec) | 128 km |
| Athabasca (Alberta) | 168 km |

1. ______________________
2. ______________________
3. ______________________
4. ______________________
5. ______________________

7.

| Snake | Length |
|---|---|
| garter snake (G) | 150 cm |
| coral snake (C) | 25 cm |
| fox snake (F) | 100 cm |
| boa snake (B) | 2 m |

The chart shows the lengths of some snakes at the zoo.

Put the animals (G, C, F, B) on the number line in order from shortest to longest.

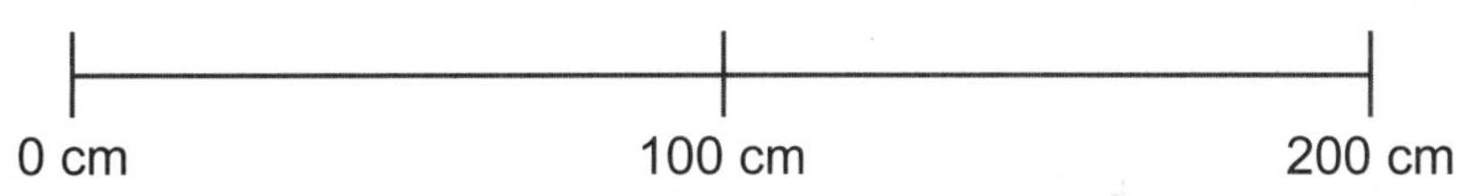


8. What would you use to measure the following distances—metres or kilometres? (HINT: If you think it will takes less than 1000 steps, you can measure in metres but if you think it will take more than 1000 steps you should use kilometres.)

   a) From your bedroom to the kitchen: _____

   b) From your home to the nearest school: _____

   c) Between Toronto and Ottawa: _____

   d) From your home to the CN Tower: _____

   e) From your home to the public library: _____

   f) From your home to your best friend's home: _____

   g) From your home to the grocery store: _____

   h) Around the local park: _____

9. Some BIG and SMALL facts about Canada! Choose which unit (kilometres, metres, or centimetres) belongs to complete each sentence. Read carefully!

   a) The Red Deer River flows from Alberta to Saskatchewan. It is 724 ______ long.

b) Hamilton, Ontario is 68 _____ away from Toronto, Ontario.

c) The sea otter can reach a length of 150 _____.

d) The city of Stewart, British Columbia gets a lot of snowfall. On average, it receives about 660 _____ of snowfall every year.

e) Toronto's Abby Hoffman won the gold medal in the 800 _____ race at the Pan-American Games in both 1963 and 1971.

f) The CN Tower, at 553 _____, is the world's tallest free-standing structure.

g) The Douglas Fir tree can grow to a height of 100 ______.

h) An Atlantic cod is about 1 ______ long and can swim in water that is 305 ______ deep.

i) The width of a maple leaf is approximately 16 ______.

10. Order the measurements from least to greatest.
(HINT: Change them all to the smallest unit.)

a) 3 dm    b) 25 cm    c) 327 mm    d) 235 mm

11. Draw a line to match up the most appropriate unit of measurement with the object.

| | |
|---|---|
| the length of your eyelashes | kilometres |
| the distance from Toronto to Vancouver | centimetres |
| your height | millimetres |

12. Which unit of measurement would you use for the following?

a) Length of a postage stamp: ______________________

b) Distance from your home to the park: ______________________

c) Length of a subway car: ______________________

d) Length of your hair: ______________________. Explain your thinking.

e) Distance travelled on a plane flight from Halifax to Moncton: ______________________
Explain your thinking.

BONUS:

13. Find any object in your home. Write down what unit of measure would be best for measuring it. Explain why it would be the best unit of measure.

# ME4-11: Perimeter

Maria makes a figure using toothpicks: 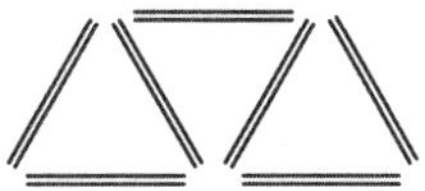

She counts the number of toothpicks around the outside of the figure:

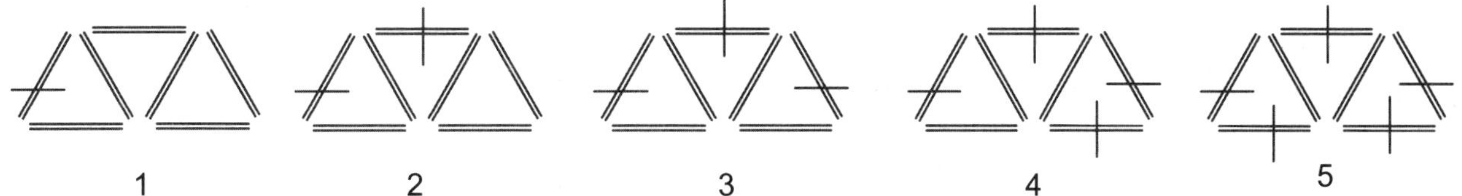


The distance around the outside of a shape is called the **perimeter** of the shape. The perimeter of Maria's figure, measured in toothpicks, is **5 toothpicks**.

---

1. Count the number of toothpicks around the outside of the figure. (Mark the toothpicks as you count, so you do not miss any!) Write your answer in the circle provided.

2. Count the number of edges around the **outside** of the figure, marking the edges as you count.

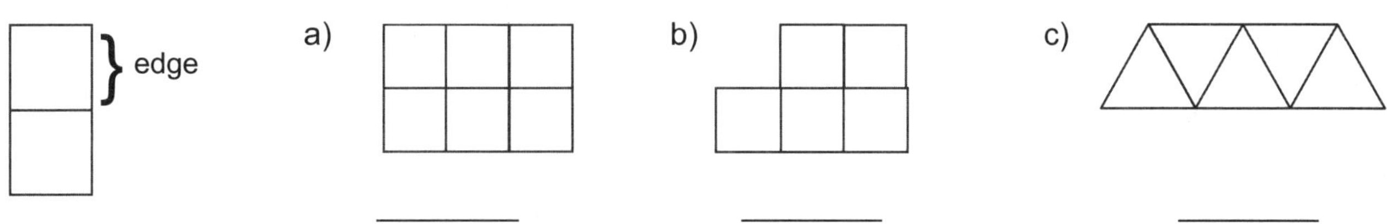


3. Each edge in the figure is 1 cm long. Find the perimeter in centimetres.

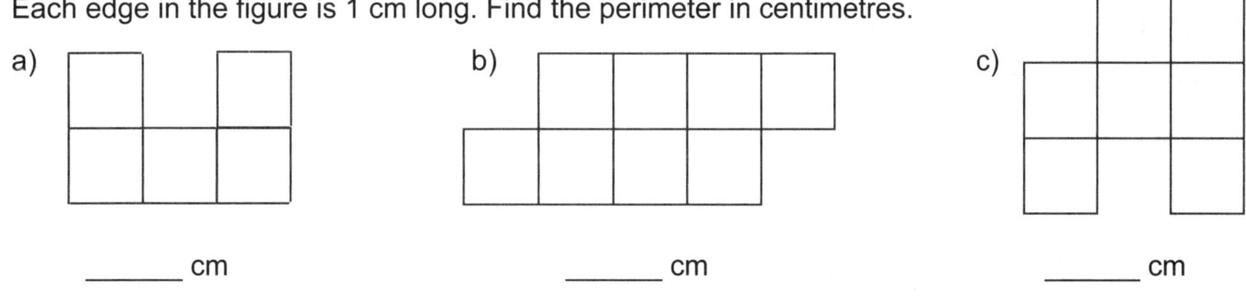


4. The picture shows the designs for 2 gardens. Find the perimeter of each garden by writing an addition statement.

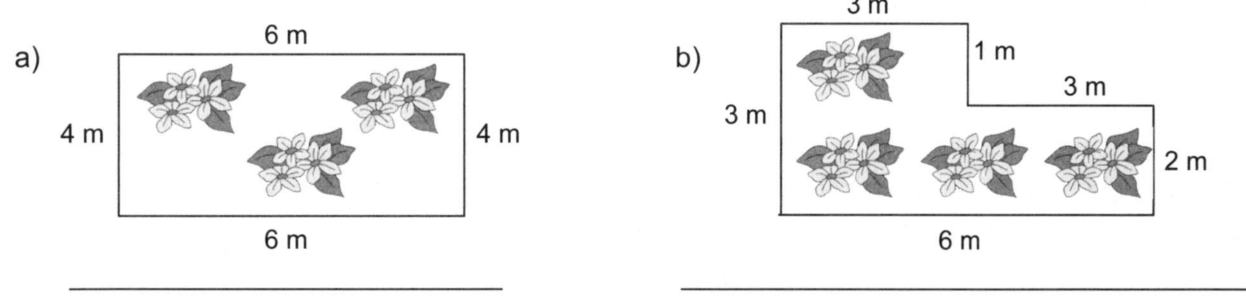

# ME4-11: Perimeter *(continued)*

5. Write the perimeter of each figure in the sequence (assume each edge is 1 unit).

   a) How does the perimeter change each time a square is added? ____________________

   b) If the sequence was continued, what would the perimeter of the 5th figure be? ____________

   c) If the sequence was continued, what would the perimeter of the 6th figure be? ____________

   d) If the sequence was continued, what would the perimeter of the 7th figure be? ____________

6. Write the perimeter of each figure in the sequence below.

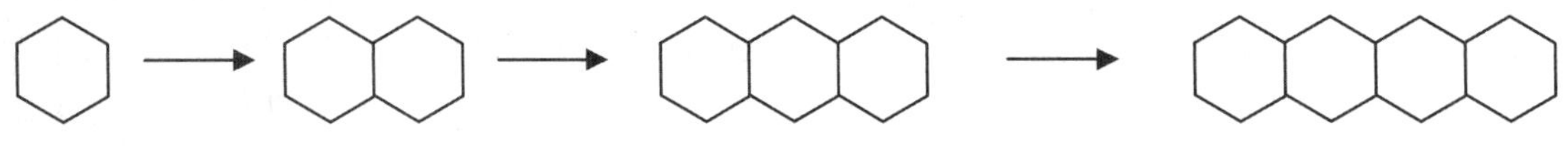

   a) How does the perimeter change each time a hexagon is added? ____________________

   b) If the sequence was continued, what would the perimeter of the 5th figure be? ____________

   c) If the sequence was continued, what would the perimeter of the 6th figure be? ____________

   d) If the sequence was continued, what would the perimeter of the 7th figure be? ____________

7. a) Add one square so that the perimeter of the shape increases by 2.

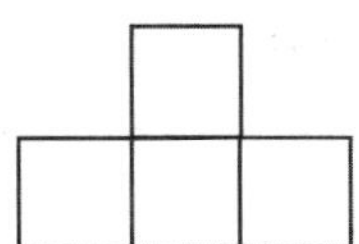

   Perimeter now: ________

   New perimeter: ________

   b) Add one square so that the perimeter of the shape stays the same.

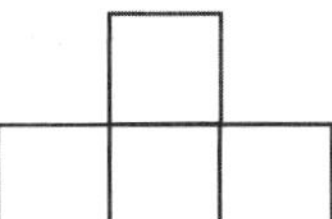

   Perimeter now: ________

   New perimeter: ________

8. Add squares to the following figure so the perimeter becomes 18 units:

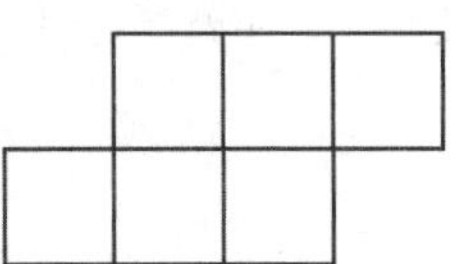

9. Add two squares to the following figure so that . . .

   a) its perimeter stays the same

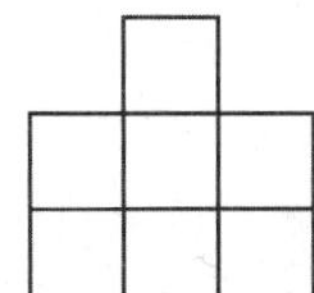

   b) its perimeter increases by 2 units

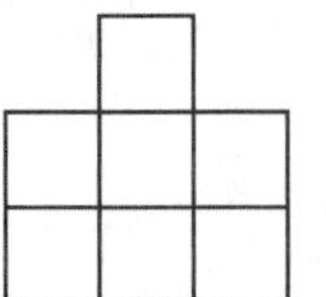

10. On a separate piece of paper, explain the meaning of perimeter.

11. Can two different shapes have the same perimeter? Explain your thinking on grid paper.

# ME4-12: Exploring Perimeter

1. Each edge is 1 cm long. Write the total length of each side beside the figure (one side is done for you). Then write an addition statement and find the perimeter.

2 cm

Perimeter: 

2. Each edge is 1 cm long. Write the total length of each side in centimetres as shown in the first figure. Then write an addition statement and find the perimeter. Do not miss any edges!
(HINT: Try grouping small numbers together so you can write a shorter addition statement.)

a)

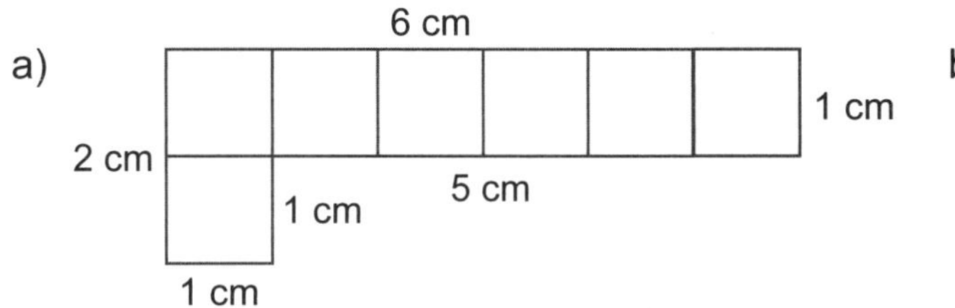


b)

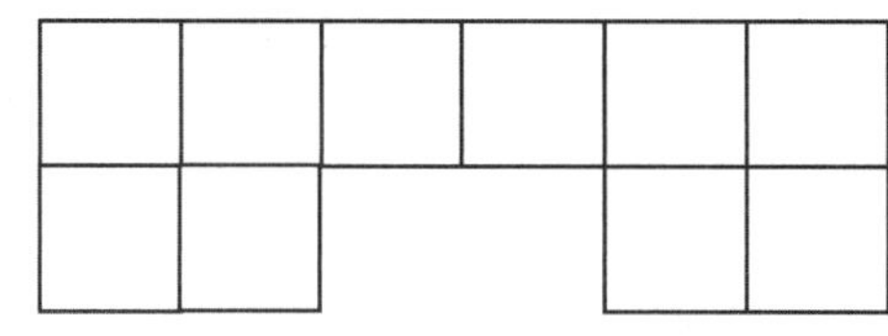

Perimeter: ____________________

Perimeter: ____________________

3. Each edge is 1 unit long. Write the length of each side beside the figure (do not miss any edges). Then use the side lengths to find the perimeter.

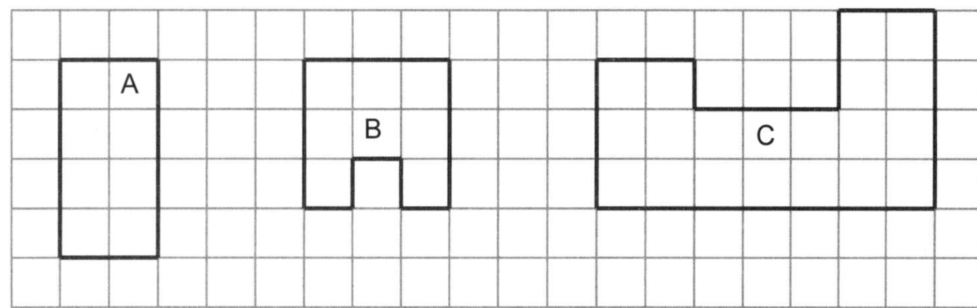


4. Draw your own figure and find the perimeter.

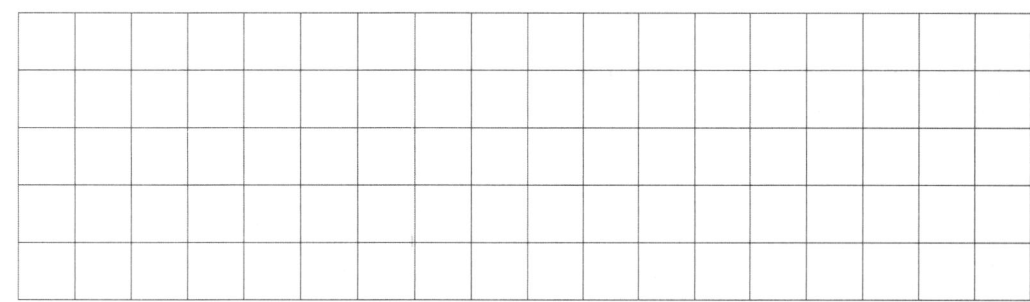

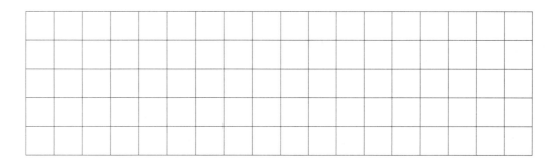

5. On grid paper, draw your own figures and find their perimeters. Try making letters or other shapes!

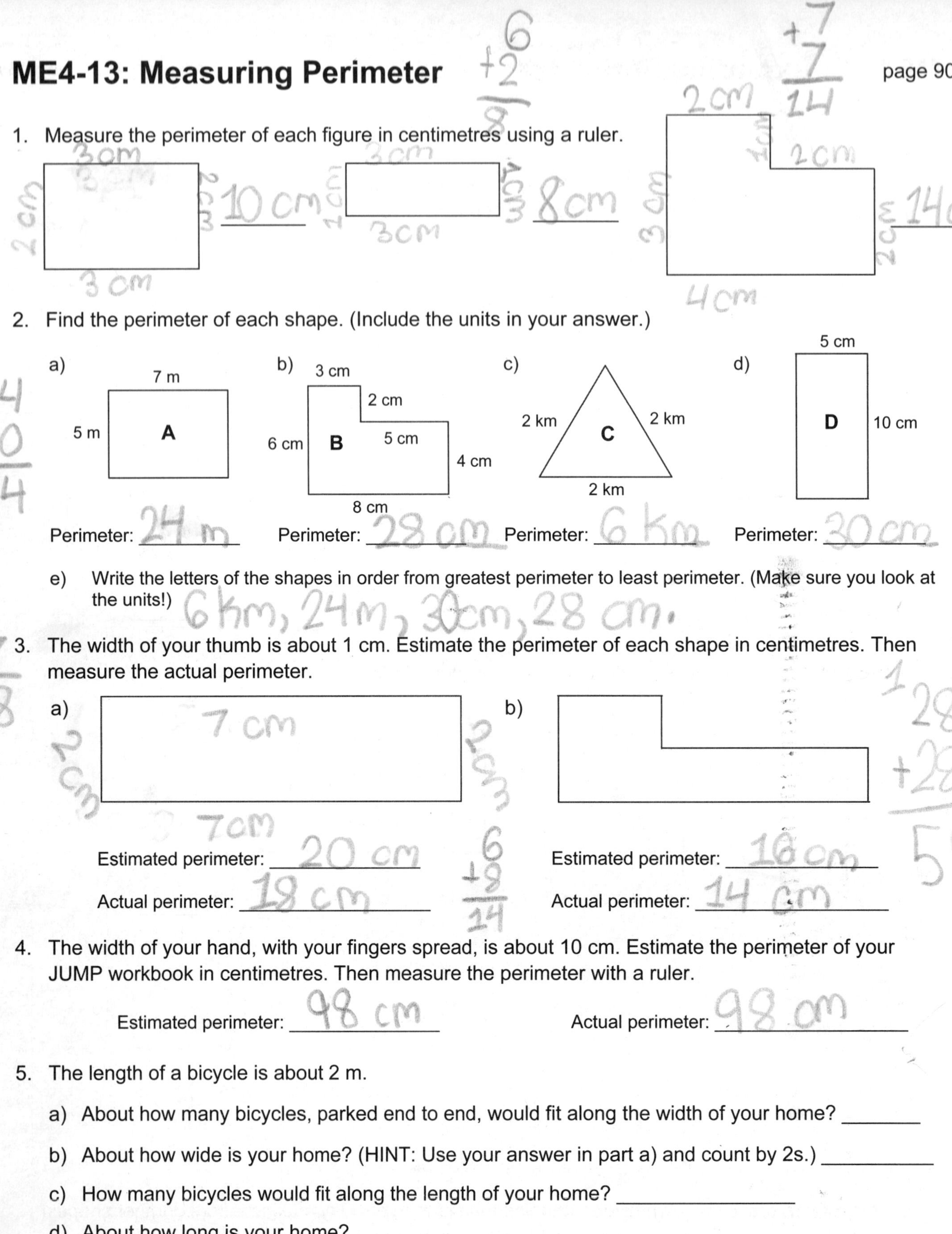

# ME4-13: Measuring Perimeter

1. Measure the perimeter of each figure in centimetres using a ruler.

______ ______ ______

2. Find the perimeter of each shape. (Include the units in your answer.)



Perimeter: ______ Perimeter: ______ Perimeter: ______ Perimeter: ______

e) Write the letters of the shapes in order from greatest perimeter to least perimeter. (Make sure you look at the units!)

3. The width of your thumb is about 1 cm. Estimate the perimeter of each shape in centimetres. Then measure the actual perimeter.

a)

Estimated perimeter: ______

Actual perimeter: ______

b)

Estimated perimeter: ______

Actual perimeter: ______

4. The width of your hand, with your fingers spread, is about 10 cm. Estimate the perimeter of your JUMP workbook in centimetres. Then measure the perimeter with a ruler.

Estimated perimeter: ______ Actual perimeter: ______

5. The length of a bicycle is about 2 m.

a) About how many bicycles, parked end to end, would fit along the width of your home? ______

b) About how wide is your home? (HINT: Use your answer in part a) and count by 2s.) ______

c) How many bicycles would fit along the length of your home? ______

d) About how long is your home? ______

e) What is the approximate perimeter of your home? ______

6. The length of a square room is about 3 ½ bicycles. REMEMBER: A bike is about 2 m long.
   a) About how many metres long is the room? ____________
   b) What is the approximate perimeter of the room? _____________

Answer the remaining questions on a separate piece of paper.

7. Estimate the perimeter of a room in your home. Explain how you estimated the perimeter.

8. The length of a school bus is about 10 m. Estimate the width and length of your block, then the perimeter. (Show your work.)

9. What units (centimetres, metres, or kilometres) would you use to measure the perimeter of . . .
   a) a house? b) a book? c) a school yard? d) a provincial park?
   e) a calculator? f) a city? g) a basketball court? h) a country?

10. How could you measure the perimeter of a round object (like a plate or a can) using a piece of string and a ruler?

11. A pentagon has sides that are 5 cm long. What is its perimeter?

12. How could you find the perimeter of a square with sides that are 5 cm long without drawing a picture?

13. The picture shows two ways (A and B) to make a rectangle using 4 squares:

    A B

    a) Which figure has the shorter perimeter? How do you know?
    b) Copy each figure onto grid paper (or make the figures using square tiles). Are there any other ways to make a rectangle using 4 squares? Explain your answer.

14. On grid paper, show all the ways you can make a rectangle using . . .
    a) 6 squares b) 10 squares c) Can you make a rectangle with 9 squares?
    d) Which of the rectangles in part b) has the greatest perimeter? What is it?

15. On grid paper, draw 3 different figures with a perimeter of 8. (The figures do not have to be rectangles.)

16. Sally arranges 4 square posters (each with sides that are 1 m) in a row: 1 m

    She wants to make borders for her posters out of ribbon.
    a) Ribbon costs 15¢ for each meter. How much will the border cost?
    b) Sally wants to arrange 8 square posters in a rectangular array. How many different rectangles can she make? For which arrangement would the border be the least expensive? Explain how you know.

# ME4-14: Investigations

Serge buys 12 m of fence to make a vegetable garden. Each section of fence is 1 m long. He wants to find the width and length of all rectangles with a perimeter of 12. Serge starts by assuming the width of the garden is 1 m, then 2 m, and then 3 m:

1 m ? 1 m

The widths add to 2 m.
The missing lengths are 12 – 2 = 10 m altogether.
Each length is 10 ÷ 2 = 5 m.

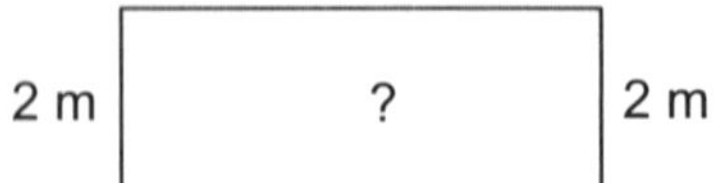


The widths add to 4 m.
The missing lengths are 12 – 4 = 8 m altogether.
Each length is 8 ÷ 2 = 4 m.

---

1. 3 m 3 m Perimeter = 12 m

Complete Serge's calculations.

a) The widths add to __________ m.

b) The missing lengths are ____________________ altogether.

c) Each length is ____________________________________ .

2. Using the information given, find the lengths of the missing sides in each figure (note that the pictures are not drawn to scale). Draw a picture and show your work for parts c) and d) on a separate piece of paper.

a) Perimeter = 10 m

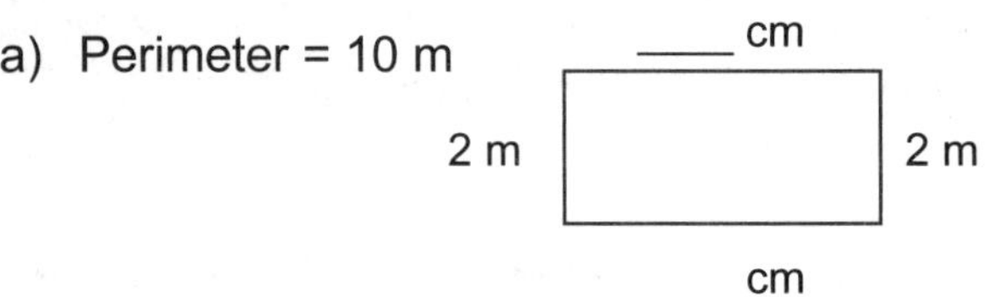


b) Perimeter = 12 m

4 m
____ cm ____ cm
4 m

c) Width = 1 m; Perimeter = 10 m

d) Width = 3 m; Perimeter = 14 m

3. Use Serge's method to find all rectangles with the given perimeter (with lengths and widths that are whole numbers). Show your work on a separate piece of paper.

| Width | Length |
|---|---|
| | |
| | |
| | |
| | |
| Perimeter = 10 units | |

| Width | Length |
|---|---|
| | |
| | |
| | |
| | |
| Perimeter = 12 units | |

| Width | Length |
|---|---|
| | |
| | |
| | |
| | |
| Perimeter = 16 units | |

| Width | Length |
|---|---|
| | |
| | |
| | |
| | |
| Perimeter = 18 units | |

4. On a geoboard or grid paper make rectangles with the following widths and lengths. Record the perimeter of . . .

a) width = 3; length = 3
Perimeter = ________

b) width = 3; length = 4
Perimeter = ________

c) width = 3; length = 5
Perimeter = ________

d) By what amount does the perimeter of the rectangle change when the length increases by 1 unit? ______________________________

e) Will the perimeter of the rectangle change by the same amount as you found in part d) if you start with a different width? Explain your thinking on a separate piece of paper.

# ME4-15: Counting Coins



1. Write the name and value of each coin.

Name: __________

Value: __________

Name: __________

Value: __________

Name: __________

Value: __________

Name: __________

Value: __________

2. Answer the following questions:

   a) How many pennies do you need to make 1 nickel? ____________________

   b) How many pennies do you need to make 1 dime? ____________________

   c) How many nickels do you need to make 1 dime? ____________________

   d) How many nickels do you need to make 1 quarter? ____________________

   e) How many pennies do you need to make 1 quarter? ____________________

   f) How many dimes do you need to make 1 quarter if you already have one nickel?

   ____________________

3. Count by 5s starting from the given numbers.

   a) 80, _____, _____, _____ b) 40, _____, _____, _____ c) 60, _____, _____, _____

   d) 70, _____, _____, _____ e) 105, _____, _____, _____ f) 120, _____, _____, _____

4. Count by 5s starting from the given numbers.

   a) 55, ____, ____, ____, ____ b) 75, ____, ____, ____, ____ c) 85, ____, ____, ____, ____

5. Count by 10s starting from the given numbers.

   a) 30, _____, _____, _____ b) 60, _____, _____, _____ c) 80, _____, _____, _____

   d) 70, _____, _____, _____ e) 100, _____, _____, _____ f) 120, _____, _____, _____

6. Count by 10s starting from the given numbers.

   a) 55, ____, ____, ____, ____ b) 70, ____, ____, ____, ____ b) 85, ____, ____, ____, ____

7. Count by the first number given, then by the second number after the vertical line.

a) 5, ___, ___, ___, ___ | ___, ___, ___
count by 5s | continue counting by 1s

b) 5, ___, ___, ___ | ___, ___, ___
count by 5s | continue counting by 1s

8. Count by the first number given, then by the second number after the vertical line. The first one is started for you.

a) (10¢) (10¢) (5¢) (5¢) (5¢) (5¢) (5¢)

5, ___, ___ | ___, ___, ___, ___, ___
count by 10s | continue counting by 5s

b) (10¢) (10¢) (10¢) (5¢) (5¢) (5¢) (5¢)

___, ___, ___ | ___, ___, ___, ___
count by 10s | continue counting by 5s

9. Complete each pattern by counting by 25s, then from the second number after the vertical line.

a) (25¢) (25¢) (25¢) (10¢) (10¢)

___, ___, ___ | ___, ___
count by 25s | count by 10s

b) (25¢) (25¢) (25¢) (5¢) (5¢)

___, ___, ___ | ___, ___
count by 25s | count by 5s

10. Complete each pattern by counting by the first number given, then by the following numbers given.

a) 25, 50, 75 | 80, 85 | 86
count by 25s | count by 5s | count by 1s

b) ___, ___ | ___, ___ | ___, ___, ___
count by 25s | count by 10s | count by 5s

c) ___, ___ | ___, ___ | ___, ___
count by 25s | count by 10s | count by 5s

d) ___, ___, ___ | ___, ___ | ___, ___
count by 25s | count by 10s | count by 1s

BONUS:

___, ___ | ___, ___, ___ | ___, ___ | ___, ___
count by 25s | count by 10s | count by 5s | count by 1s

11. Complete each pattern by counting by the first number given, then by the other number after the coin changes. The first one is done for you.

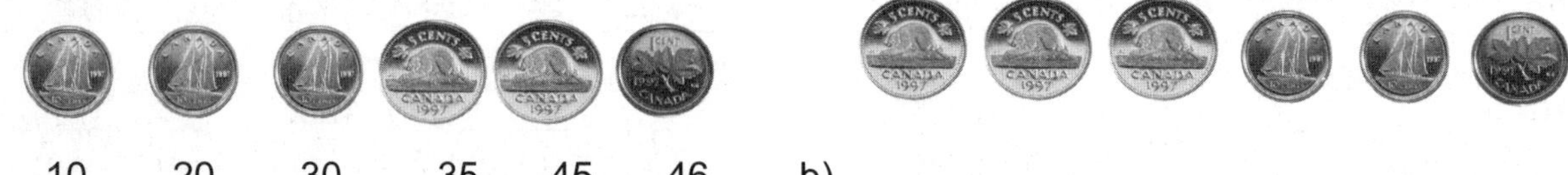

a) 10, 20, 30, 35, 45, 46

b) ___, ___, ___, ___, ___, ___

BONUS:

Complete the pattern by counting by the first coin, then by the second coin, and then by the third coin.

___, ___, ___, ___, ___, ___, ___, ___, ___, ___, ___, ___, ___

12. Complete each pattern by counting by the first number given, then by the following numbers given.

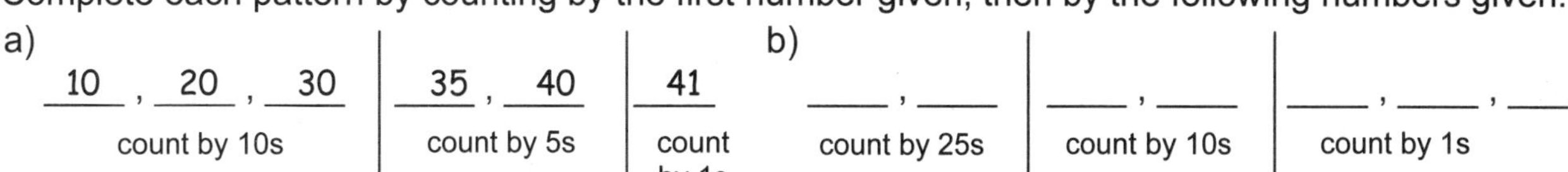


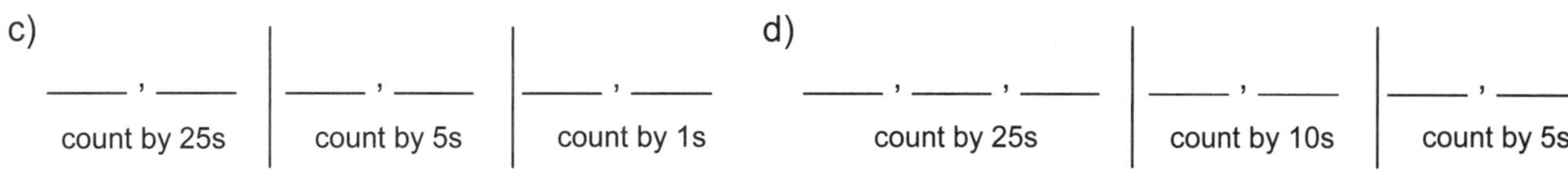


BONUS:

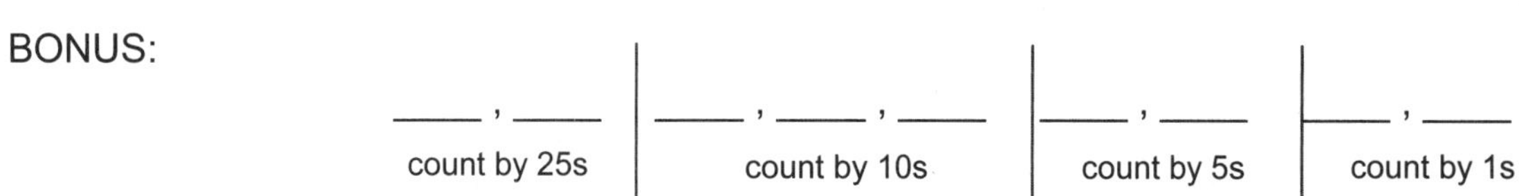


13. Write the total amount of money in cents for the number of coins given in the charts below. (HINT: Count by the greater amount first.)

a)

| Nickels | Pennies |
|---|---|
| 7 | 4 |

Total amount =

b)

| Quarters | Dimes |
|---|---|
| 4 | 2 |

Total amount =

c)

| Quarters | Nickels |
|---|---|
| 6 | 6 |

Total amount =

BONUS:

| Quarters | Nickels | Pennies |
|---|---|---|
| 3 | 1 | 2 |

Total amount =

| Quarters | Dimes | Nickels |
|---|---|---|
| 2 | 2 | 5 |

Total amount =

| Quarters | Dimes | Nickels | Pennies |
|---|---|---|---|
| 2 | 1 | 2 | 6 |

Total amount =

| Quarters | Dimes | Nickels | Pennies |
|---|---|---|---|
| 5 | 3 | 4 | 9 |

Total amount =

14. Count the given coins and write the total amount. (HINT: Count by the greater amount first.)

a) Total amount =

b) Total amount =

c) Total amount =

d) Total amount =

BONUS: Total amount =

# ME4-16: Counting by Different Denominations

1. Fill in the missing amounts, counting by 5s.

| | | |
|---|---|---|
| a) 14, ____ , 24 | b) 30, ____ , ____ , 45 | c) 67, ____ , ____ , 82 |
| d) 18, ____ , ____ , 33 | e) 71, ____ , ____ , 86 | f) 45, ____ , ____ , 60 |

2. Fill in the missing amounts, counting by 10s.

| | | |
|---|---|---|
| a) 63, ____ , 83 | b) 24, ____ , ____ , 54 | c) 39, ____ , ____ , 69 |

3. For each of the questions below, write in the missing coin to complete the addition statement. The possibilities for each question are listed.

| | | |
|---|---|---|
| a) 10¢ 5¢ ◯ = 16¢ <br> 10¢ or 1¢ | b) 10¢ 5¢ ◯ = 20¢ <br> 10¢ or 5¢ | c) 10¢ 10¢ ◯ = 21¢ <br> 10¢ or 1¢ |
| d) 25¢ 25¢ ◯ = 75¢ <br> 25¢ or 10¢ | e) 25¢ 10¢ ◯ = 40¢ <br> 10¢ or 5¢ | f) 10¢ 5¢ ◯ = 40¢ <br> 25¢ or 5¢ |

4. For each question, draw in the number of additional **nickels** needed to make the total.

| | | |
|---|---|---|
| a) 10¢ = 20¢ | b) 1¢ 1¢ = 12¢ | c) 10¢ 10¢ 1¢ = 31¢ |
| d) 10¢ 5¢ 1¢ = 26¢ | e) 25¢ 5¢ = 45¢ | f) 5¢ 5¢ = 40¢ |

5. For each question, draw in the number of additional **dimes** needed to make the total.

| | | |
|---|---|---|
| a) 25¢ 5¢ = 50¢ | b) 25¢ 1¢ 25¢ 1¢ = 62¢ | c) 10¢ 10¢ 5¢ = 35¢ |
| d) 10¢ 5¢ 1¢ = 46¢ | e) 25¢ 25¢ = 80¢ | f) 5¢ 5¢ = 50¢ |
| g) 25¢ 25¢ 5¢ 5¢ = 80¢ | h) 25¢ 25¢ 25¢ 5¢ = 90¢ | i) 25¢ 25¢ 25¢ 5¢ = 110¢ |

6. For each question, draw in the number of additional **coins** needed to make each total.

| | |
|---|---|
| a) How many dimes? (25¢) (25¢) + = 80¢ | b) How many nickels? (25¢) (5¢) + = 40¢ |
| c) How many dimes? (10¢) (10¢) + = 40¢ | d) How many quarters? (25¢) (25¢) + = 100¢ |

BONUS:

7. For each question, draw the number of **additional** coins needed to make each total. You can only use **two** coins for each question, either (i) a penny and a nickel, (ii) a penny and a dime, or (iii) a nickel and a dime.

| | |
|---|---|
| a) 21¢ (10¢) | b) 35¢ (10¢) (5¢) |
| c) 50¢ (25¢) (10¢) | d) 41¢ (25¢) (10¢) |
| e) 17¢ (10¢) (1¢) | f) 65¢ (25¢) (25¢) |

8. For each question, draw the number of additional coins needed to make each total. You can only use **two** coins for each question, either a loonie or a toonie.

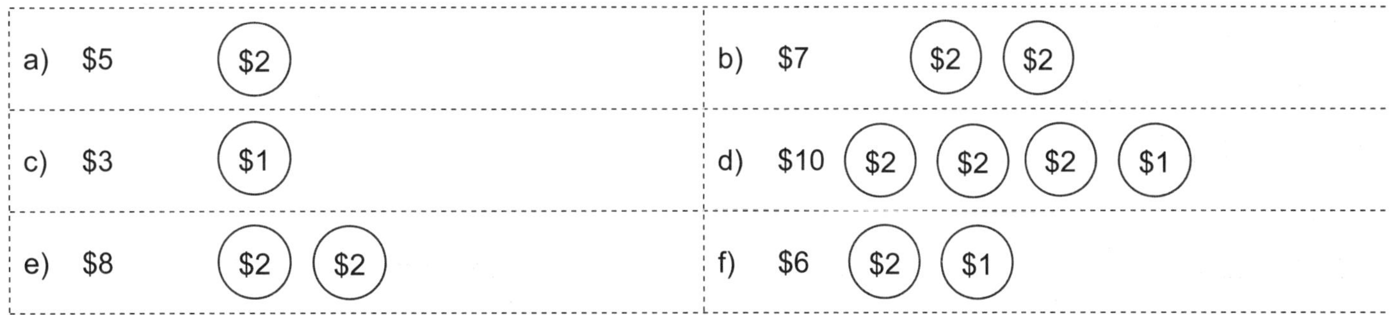

| | |
|---|---|
| a) $5 ($2) | b) $7 ($2) ($2) |
| c) $3 ($1) | d) $10 ($2) ($2) ($2) ($1) |
| e) $8 ($2) ($2) | f) $6 ($2) ($1) |

Answer the following questions on a separate piece of paper:

9. Draw a picture to show the extra coins each child will need to pay for the item they want. (Try to use the fewest coins.)
   a) Tashi has 25¢. He wants to buy a pencil for 45¢.
   b) Rosie has 19¢. She wants to buy a pen for 35¢.
   c) Zoltan has 3 quarters, 1 dime, and 1 nickel. He wants to buy a notebook for 98¢.
   d) Jane has 3 toonies. She wants to buy a plant for ten dollars.
   e) Marzuk has 2 toonies and 1 loonie. He wants to buy a book for seven dollars and twenty-five cents.

10. Can you make 80¢ using only . . . a) dimes and quarters? b) nickels and quarters?
    In each case, explain why or why not.

11. Make up a problem like one of the problems in question 9 and solve it.

# ME4-17: Least Number of Coins



1. Use the least number of coins to make the totals. (HINT: Start by seeing how many dimes you need.)

| | |
|---|---|
| a) 12¢ (10¢)(1¢)(1¢) *correct* (5¢)(5¢)(1¢)(1¢) *incorrect* | b) 16¢ |
| c) 22¢ | d) 37¢ |

2. Use the least number of coins to make the totals.

| | |
|---|---|
| a) 15¢ | b) 20¢ |

3. Use the least number of coins to make the totals.
(HINT: Start by seeing how many dimes you need (if any), then nickels, and then pennies.)

| | |
|---|---|
| a) 17¢ | b) 24¢ |
| c) 11¢ | d) 15¢ |
| e) 19¢ | f) 17¢ |

4. Fill in the amounts. 2 quarters = ____ ¢ 3 quarters = ____ ¢ 4 quarters = ___ ¢

5. For each amount, what is the greatest amount you could pay in quarters without exceeding the amount? (Draw the quarters to show your answer.)

| **Amount** | **Greatest amount you could pay in quarters** | **Amount** | **Greatest amount you could pay in quarters** |
|---|---|---|---|
| a) 35¢ | | b) 53¢ | |
| c) 78¢ | | d) 83¢ | |
| e) 59¢ | | f) 64¢ | |
| g) 49¢ | | h) 31¢ | |
| i) 82¢ | | j) 95¢ | |
| k) 29¢ | | l) 72¢ | |

# ME4-17: Least Number of Coins *(continued)*

6. For each amount, find the greatest amount you could pay in quarters. Represent the amount remaining using the least number of coins. The first one is done for you.

| Amount | Amount paid in quarters | Amount remaining | Amount remaining in coins |
|---|---|---|---|
| a) 83¢ | 75¢ | 83¢ - 75¢ = 8¢ | (5¢) (1¢) (1¢) (1¢) |
| b) 56¢ | | | |
| c) 33¢ | | | |
| d) 85¢ | | | |
| e) 97¢ | | | |

7. Use the **least** number of coins to make the totals. The first one is done for you. (HINT: Start by finding the greatest amount you can make in quarters, as in question 6.)

| | |
|---|---|
| a) 30¢ (10) (10) (10) *incorrect* (25) (5¢) *correct* | b) 76¢ |
| c) 40¢ | d) 55¢ |

BONUS:

8. On a separate piece of paper show how you could make 55¢ using the least number of coins. Use play money to help you.

9. Trade coins to make each amount with the least amount of coins. (For example, you can trade 2 nickels for 1 dime, 1 dime and 3 nickels for 1 quarter, 4 quarters for 1 loonie, or 1 toonie for 2 loonies.) Draw a picture to show your final answer on a separate piece of paper.

| | | |
|---|---|---|
| a) (5¢) (5¢) (5¢) (10¢) | b) (25¢) (25¢) (25¢) (25¢) | c) (5¢) (5¢) ($1) ($1) |
| d) (10¢) (10¢) (5¢) ($1) | e) (25¢) (10¢) (5¢) ($2) (25¢) (10¢) (25¢) (25¢) | |
| f) (10¢) (10¢) (5¢) ($1) ($1) ($1) ($1) (1¢) (1¢) (1¢) (1¢) (1¢) | | |

10. On a separate piece of paper, show how you could trade the amounts for the least number of coins.
    a) 5 quarters
    b) 4 dimes and 2 nickels
    c) 6 loonies
    d) 7 loonies and 5 dimes
    e) 9 loonies, 6 dimes, 2 nickels, and 5 pennies

 fish pad

# ME4-18: Dollar and Cent Notation

Shrey wants to buy stickers for his friends. The large stickers cost sixty-five cents and the small stickers cost thirty-five cents. Shrey can show the prices in two different ways:

| | Cents notation | Dollar (decimal) notation |
|---|---|---|
| sixty-five cents | 65¢ | $0.65 |
| thirty-five cents | 35¢ | $0.35 |

(In $0.65 and $0.35, arrows point from "dimes" to the tenths digit and from "pennies" to the hundredths digit.)

A dime is a **tenth** of a dollar.

A penny is a **hundredth** of a dollar.

1. For the given number of dimes and pennies in the T-tables, write the total amount of money in cents and in dollar (decimal) notation.

a)

| Dimes | Pennies |
|---|---|
| 3 | 4 |

= 34 ¢ = $ 0.34

b)

| Dimes | Pennies |
|---|---|
| 0 | 5 |

= ____ ¢ = $ ____

c)

| Dimes | Pennies |
|---|---|
| 4 | 3 |

= ____ ¢ = $ ____

d)

| Dimes | Pennies |
|---|---|
| 8 | 7 |

= ____ ¢ = $ ____

e)

| Dimes | Pennies |
|---|---|
| 5 | 4 |

= ____ ¢ = $ ____

f)

| Dimes | Pennies |
|---|---|
| 0 | 9 |

= ____ ¢ = $ ____

2. Count the given coins and write the total amount in cents and in dollar (decimal) notation.

a) 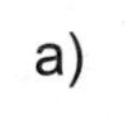     

Total amount = ____ ¢ = $ ____

b) 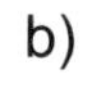   

Total amount = ____ ¢ = $ ____

c)      

Total amount = ____ ¢ = $ ____

d) 

Total amount = ____ ¢ = $ ____

e) 

Total amount = ____ ¢ = $ ____

f)

Total amount = ____ ¢ = $ ____

BONUS: 

Total amount = ____ ¢ = $ ____

# ME4-18: Dollar and Cent Notation *(continued)*

3. For the given amounts in cents, write the number of dollars, dimes, and pennies in the chart. Then write the amounts in dollars. The first one is done for you.

| Amount in ¢ | Dollars | Dimes | Pennies | Amount in $ |
|---|---|---|---|---|
| a) 143¢ | 1 | 4 | 3 | $ 1.43 |
| b) 47¢ | | | | |
| c) 325¢ | | | | |
| d) 3¢ | | | | |
| e) 816¢ | | | | |

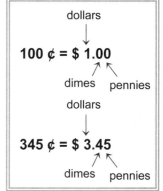

dollars ↓ **100 ¢ = $ 1.00** ↖ dimes ↖ pennies

dollars ↓ **345 ¢ = $ 3.45** ↖ dimes ↖ pennies

4. Complete each pattern by counting by the type of coin pictured. Write your answers in cent notation and in dollar notation.

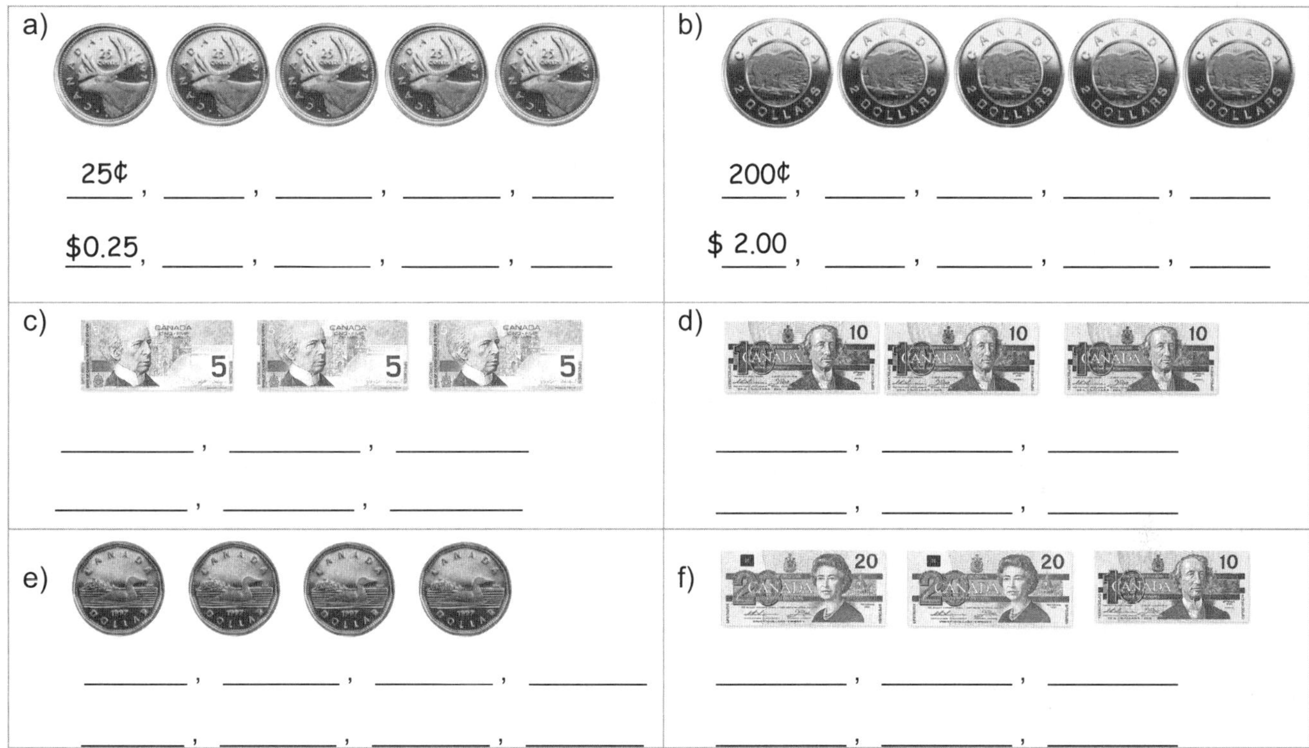


5. How much money would you have if you had the following coins? Write your answer in cent notation then in dollar notation. The first question is done for you.

a) 7 pennies = 7¢ = $0.07   b) 4 nickels = ____ = ____   c) 6 dimes = ____ = ____

d) 4 pennies = ____ = ____   e) 13 pennies = ____ = ____   f) 1 quarter = ____ = ____

g) 5 nickels = = ____ = ____   h) 3 quarters = ____ = ____   i) 8 dimes = ____ = ____

j) 6 toonies = ____ = ____   k) 4 loonies = ____ = ____   l) 7 loonies = ____ = ____

# ME4-19: Counting and Changing Units

1. In the given chart, first count the **dollar** amount and then count the **cent** amount. Write the total amount in dollar (decimal) notation. The first one is done for you.

| | Dollar amount | Cent amount | Total |
|---|---|---|---|
| a) | \$2 \$1 = \$3 | 25¢ 10¢ = 35¢ | \$3.35 |
| b) | \$2 \$2 \$2 = ____ | 5¢ 5¢ 1¢ = ____ | ____ |
| c) | \$2 \$2 = ____ | 10¢ 10¢ 5¢ = ____ | ____ |
| d) | \$2 \$2 \$2 = ____ | 25¢ 25¢ 5¢ = ____ | ____ |
| e) | CANADA 5 CANADA 5 = ____ | 5¢ 1¢ 1¢ = ____ | ____ |
| f) | CANADA 10 CANADA 10 = ____ | 5¢ 5¢ 1¢ = ____ | ____ |

2. Count the given coins. Write the total amount in cents and in dollars (decimals).

| | Coins | Cent notation | Dollar notation |
|---|---|---|---|
| a) | 25¢ 25¢ 25¢ 25¢ 5¢ | 105¢ | \$1.05 |
| b) | 25¢ 25¢ 25¢ 10¢ 10¢ 1¢ | ____ | ____ |
| c) | 25¢ 25¢ 25¢ 25¢ 25¢ 25¢ | ____ | ____ |
| d) | 25¢ 25¢ 25¢ 10¢ 10¢ 10¢ 5¢ | ____ | ____ |

3. Alicia paid for a pencil with 3 coins. The pencil cost \$0.75. Which coins did she use?

4. Alan bought a pack of markers for \$3.50. He paid for it with 4 coins. Which coins did he use?

5. Tanya's daily allowance is \$5.25. Her mom gave her 4 coins. Which coins did she use?

# ME4-20: Converting Between Dollar and Cent Notation

**Dollar notation** and **cent notation** are related in the following ways:

$1.00 = 100¢ $0.50 = 50¢ $0.05 = 5¢ $3.82 = 382¢

1. Write each number of cents in dollar notation.

a) 64¢ = ______ b) 99¢ = ______ c) 3¢ = ______ d) 56¢ = ______

2. Write each amount of money in cents notation.

a) $0.98 = ______ b) $0.55 = ______ c) $0.03 = ______ d) $0.75 = ______

3. Write each number of cents in dollar notation. The first one is done for you.

a) 300¢ = $3.00 b) 4¢ = ______ c) 7¢ = ______ d) 90¢ = ______

e) 600¢ = ______ f) 1000¢ = ______ g) 1200¢ = ______ h) 1600¢ = ______

4. Write each amount of money in cents notation. The first one is done for you.

a) $3.00 = 300¢ b) $0.60 = ______ c) $0.08 = ______ d) $1.00 = ______

e) $7.00 = ______ f) $12.00 = ______ g) $15.00 = ______ h) $14.00 = ______

5. Write each number of cents in dollar notation.

a) 254¢ = ______ b) 103¢ = ______ c) 216¢ = ______ d) 375¢ = ______

e) 144¢ = ______ f) 205¢ = ______ g) 218¢ = ______ h) 465¢ = ______

6. Write each amount of money in cents notation.

a) $1.99 = ______ b) $1.11 = ______ c) $1.51 = ______ d) $1.37 = ______

e) $2.34 = ______ f) $2.70 = ______ g) $6.55 = ______ h) $8.08 = ______

BONUS:

7. Circle the greater amount of money in each pair.

a) 175¢ or $1.73 b) $1.00 or 101¢ c) 6¢ or $0.04

d) $5.98 or 597¢ e) 650¢ or $6.05 f) $0.87 or 187¢

8. Circle the larger amount of money in each pair.

a) three dollars and eighty-five cents or three dollars and twenty-eight cents

b) nine dollars and seventy cents or nine dollars and eighty-two cents

c) eight dollars and seventy-five cents or 863¢

d) twelve dollars and sixty cents or $12.06

9. Which is a greater amount of money: 168¢ or $1.65? Explain how you know.

fish pad

# ME4-21: Canadian Bills and Coins

Jenny is looking over some coins and bills and figures out how much each one is worth by reading the number of cents or dollars printed on each one:

She then makes up a chart with the **names** of the different coins and how much each is **worth**:

| Penny | Nickel | Dime | Quarter | Loonie | Toonie |
|---|---|---|---|---|---|
| 1 cent | 5 cents | 10 cents | 25 cents | 100 cents | 200 cents |
| $0.01 | $0.05 | $0.10 | $0.25 | $1.00 | $2.00 |
| 1¢ | 5¢ | 10¢ | 25¢ | 100¢ | 200¢ |

1. Circle all the **correct** forms of writing amounts of money. Cross out the **incorrect** forms.

   Example: $1.00 ~~$4.56832~~

| | | | | | |
|---|---|---|---|---|---|
| 0.45¢ | 2.34$ | $15.958 | $10.05 | &18.66 | &56¢ |
| ¢23 | ¢676 | $85.32 | $0.95 | ¢36 | $0.17 |
| ¢15.18 | $25.30 | 36¢ | $18.50 | $95.99 | $12.3560 |

2. Match the picture of each coin to its correct value. Be careful! There are more answers than coins.

$3.00 $2.00 $1.00 25¢ 1¢ 10¢ $0.05 13¢ $0.75 15¢

3. Match the picture of each bill to its correct value. Be careful! There are more answers than bills.

$5.00 $20.00 $100.00 $10.00 $50.00 $1000.00 $500.00

# ME4-22: Making Change Using Mental Math



1. Calculate the change owing for each purchase. Subtract the amounts by counting up on your fingers if necessary.

a) Price of a pencil = 42¢
Amount paid = 50¢
Change = ________

b) Price of an eraser = 34¢
Amount paid = 50¢
Change = ________

c) Price of a sharpener = 81¢
Amount paid = 90¢
Change = ________

d) Price of a ruler = 56¢
Amount paid = 60¢
Change = ________

e) Price of a marker = 78¢
Amount paid = 80¢
Change = ________

f) Price of a notebook = 63¢
Amount paid = 70¢
Change = ________

g) Price of a folder = 67¢
Amount paid = 70¢
Change = ________

h) Price of a juice box = 49¢
Amount paid = 50¢
Change = ________

i) Price of a freezie = 26¢
Amount paid = 30¢
Change = ________

2. Count up by 10s to find the change owing from a dollar (100¢).

| Price paid | Change | Price paid | Change | Price paid | Change |
|---|---|---|---|---|---|
| a) 90¢ | | d) 40¢ | | h) 20¢ | |
| b) 70¢ | | e) 10¢ | | i) 60¢ | |
| c) 50¢ | | f) 30¢ | | j) 80¢ | |

3. Find the change owing for each purchase.
(HINT: Count up by 10s.)

a) Price of a lollipop = 50¢
Amount paid = $1.00
Change = ________

b) Price of an eraser = 60¢
Amount paid = $1.00
Change = ________

c) Price of an apple = 30¢
Amount paid = $1.00
Change = ________

d) Price of a banana = 60¢
Amount paid = $1.00
Change = ________

e) Price of a patty = 80¢
Amount paid = $1.00
Change = ________

f) Price of a pencil = 20¢
Amount paid = $1.00
Change = ________

g) Price of a gumball = 10¢
Amount paid = $1.00
Change = ________

h) Price of a juice box = 40¢
Amount paid = $1.00
Change = ________

i) Price of a popsicle = 70¢
Amount paid = $1.00
Change = ________

4. Find the smallest two-digit number ending in zero (for example, 10, 20, 30, 40) that is **greater** than the number given. Write your answer in the box provided. The first one is done for you.

a) 72 [80] b) 54 [ ] c) 47 [ ] d) 26 [ ] e) 58 [ ] f) 7 [ ]

5. Make change for the number written below. Follow the steps shown for 17¢.

Step 1: Find the smallest multiple of 10 greater than 17¢:

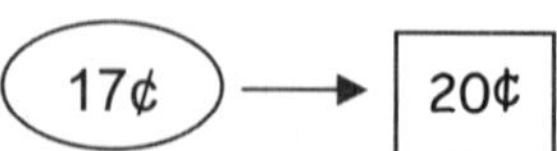


Step 2: Find the differences: 20 – 17 **and** 100 – 20

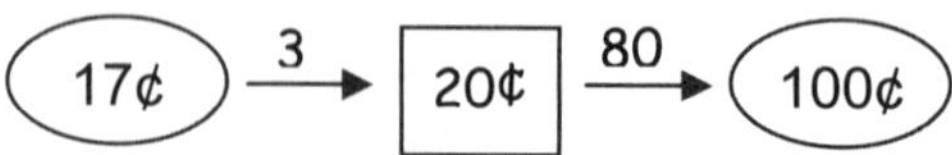


Step 3: Add the differences: 3¢ + 80¢ **Change = 83¢**

a) b)

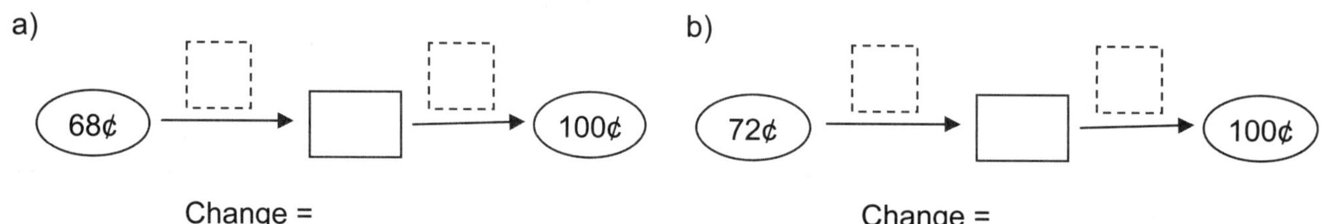


Change = ________ Change = ________

c)

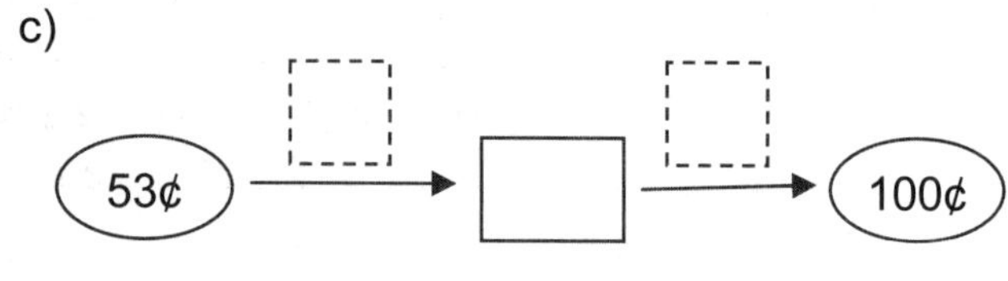


d)

Change = ________

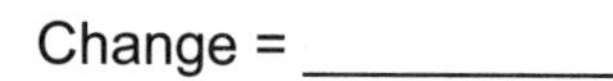

Change = ________

e)

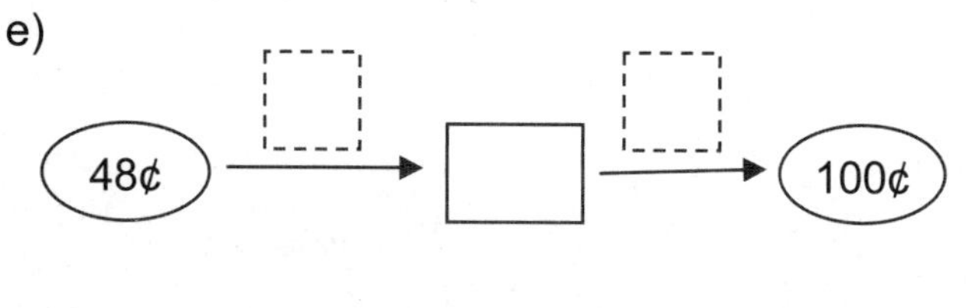


f)

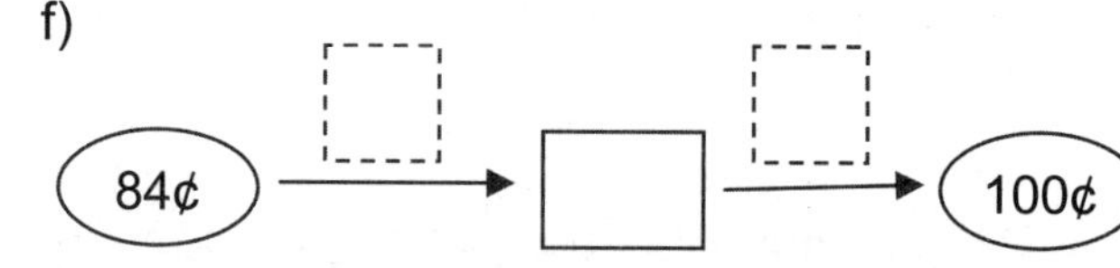


Change = ________ Change = ________

6. Find change from 100¢ for the following numbers. Try to do the work in your head.

a) 86¢ ______ b) 64¢ ______ c) 27¢ ______ d) 46¢ ______ e) 52¢ ______

f) 39¢ ______ g) 97¢ ______ h) 56¢ ______ i) 89¢ ______ j) 91¢ ______

BONUS:

7. Find the change for the following amounts. Do the work in your head.

a) Price: 37¢ Amount paid: 50¢
Change required: ________

b) Price: 58¢ Amount paid: 75¢
Change required: ________

# ME4-23: Adding Money

1. Add.

a)

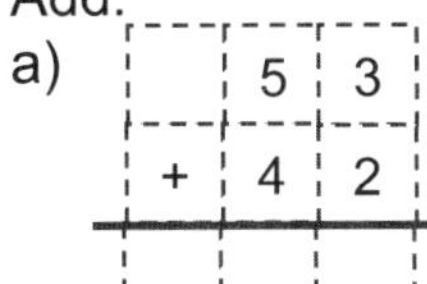

| | 5 | 3 |
|---|---|---|
| + | 4 | 2 |
| | | |

b)

| | 7 | 5 |
|---|---|---|
| + | | 2 |
| | | |

c)

| | 2 | 4 |
|---|---|---|
| + | 3 | 0 |
| | | |

d)

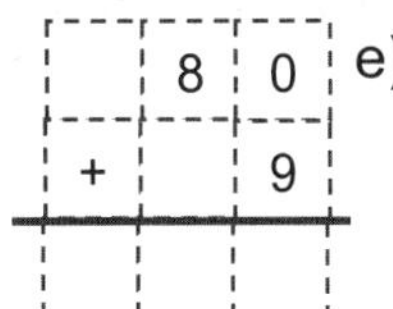

| | 8 | 0 |
|---|---|---|
| + | | 9 |
| | | |

e)

| | 6 | 3 |
|---|---|---|
| + | 1 | 6 |
| | | |

2. Answer the following word problems. Be sure to show your work.

a) Ari paid 23¢ for a doughnut and 35¢ for an apple. How much money did he spend in total?

| | 2 | 3 ¢ |
|---|---|---|
| + | 3 | 5 ¢ |
| | | |

b) Kunga paid 39¢ for a pencil and 50¢ for a colouring book. How much did he pay altogether?

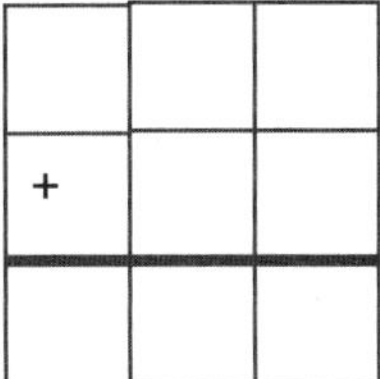

| | | |
|---|---|---|
| + | | |
| | | |

c) Minh bought a candy for 23¢ and a stick of gum for 26¢. How much money did he spend in total?

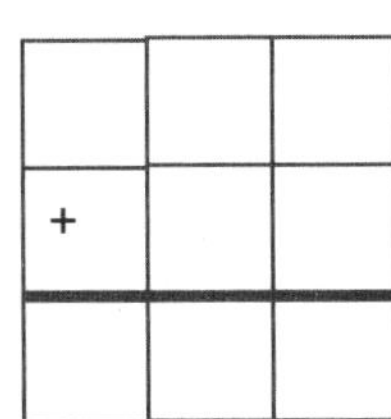

| | | |
|---|---|---|
| + | | |
| | | |

d) Atul paid 82¢ for a binder and 7¢ for a sticker. How much money did he spend in total?

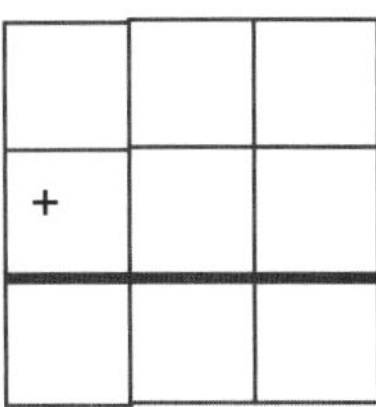

| | | |
|---|---|---|
| + | | |
| | | |

3. Shelly spent $12.50 on a blouse and $4.35 on a pair of socks. To find out how much she spent, she added the amounts using the following steps:

| $ | 1 | 2. | 5 | 0 |
|---|---|---|---|---|
| + $ | | 4. | 3 | 5 |
| | | . | | |

Step 1:
She lined up the numerals: she put dollars above dollars, dimes above dimes, and pennies above pennies.

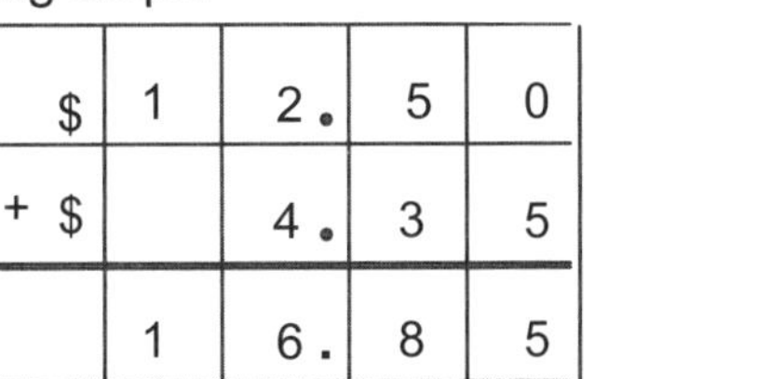

| $ | 1 | 2. | 5 | 0 |
|---|---|---|---|---|
| + $ | | 4. | 3 | 5 |
| | 1 | 6. | 8 | 5 |

Step 2:
She added the numerals, starting with the ones digits (the pennies).

| $ | 1 | 2. | 5 | 0 |
|---|---|---|---|---|
| + $ | | 4. | 3 | 5 |
| | 1 | 6. | 8 | 5 |

Step 3:
She added a decimal to show the amount in dollars.

4. Find the total by adding the dollar amounts.

a) $5.45 + $3.23

| $ | 5. | 4 | 5 |
|---|---|---|---|
| + $ | 3. | 2 | 3 |
| | . | | |

b) $22.26 + $15.23

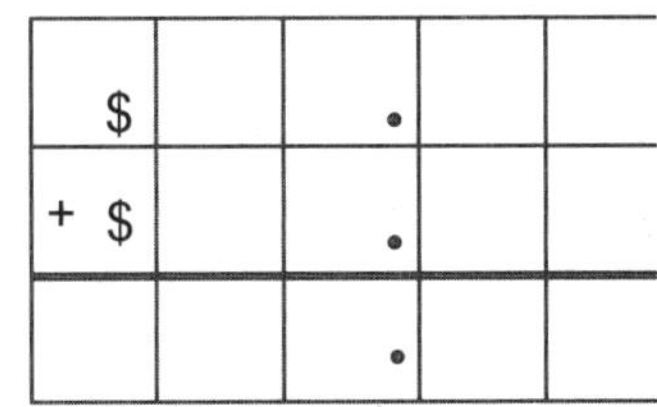

| $ | | . | |
|---|---|---|---|
| + $ | | . | |
| | | . | |

c) $18.16 + $20.32

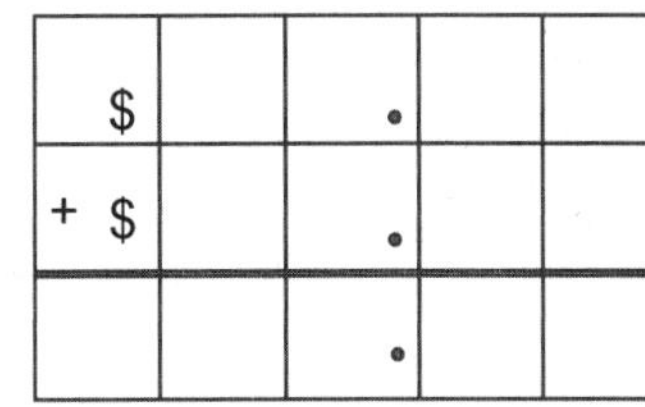

| $ | | . | |
|---|---|---|---|
| + $ | | . | |
| | | . | |

5. Solve the following word problems. Show your work on a separate piece of paper.

a) Abi wants to buy a pair of shoes that cost $24.24 and a pair of jeans that cost $20.34. How much money does she need to buy both items?

b) Alan bought a book for $14.25 and a box of candles for $10.14. How much did he spend in total?

6. In order to add the amounts, you will have to carry.

a)

| | | | | |
|---|---|---|---|---|
| $ | 1 | 3. | 6 | 0 |
| + $ | 2 | 5. | 5 | 5 |
| | | | | |

b)

| | | | | |
|---|---|---|---|---|
| $ | 1 | 8. | 2 | 5 |
| + $ | 5 | 3. | 1 | 2 |
| | | | | |

c)

| | | | | |
|---|---|---|---|---|
| $ | 4 | 5. | 2 | 0 |
| + $ | | 6. | 5 | 5 |
| | | | | |

d)

| | | | | |
|---|---|---|---|---|
| $ | 3 | 2. | 6 | 0 |
| + $ | 2 | 8. | 0 | 0 |
| | | | | |

e)

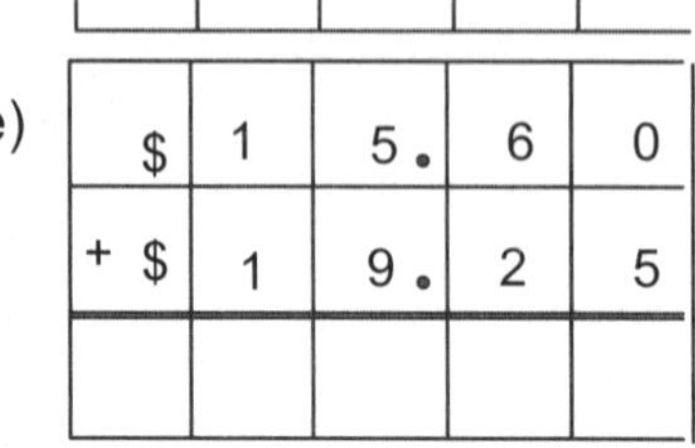

| | | | | |
|---|---|---|---|---|
| $ | 1 | 5. | 6 | 0 |
| + $ | 1 | 9. | 2 | 5 |
| | | | | |

f)

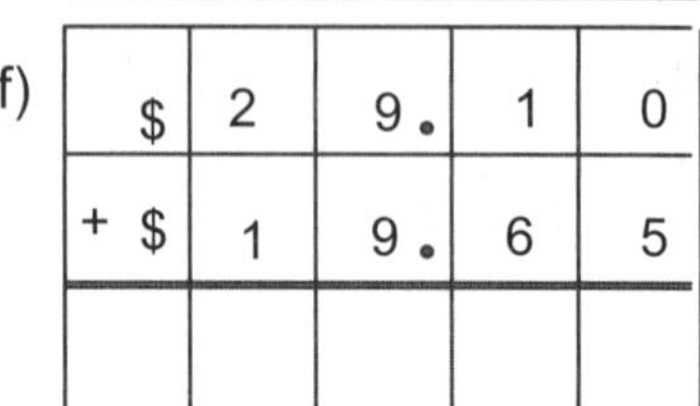

| | | | | |
|---|---|---|---|---|
| $ | 2 | 9. | 1 | 0 |
| + $ | 1 | 9. | 6 | 5 |
| | | | | |

Answer the following questions on a separate piece of paper:

7. Add. a) $14.72 + $15.29 b) $23.75 + $32.18

8. From her babysitting job on Sunday, Meera saved 6 toonies, 5 dimes, and 3 pennies. Kyle saved 1 five-dollar bill, 3 toonies, 2 dimes, and 4 pennies from his babysitting job. Who saved more money?

9. Anthony, Mike, Sandor, and Tory went to an animal shelter. They each bought a dog. The chart shows the price of each dog.
   - ✓ Anthony paid for his dog with 2 twenty-dollar bills, 1 toonie, 1 loonie, 2 quarters, and 1 nickel.
   - ✓ Mike paid with 2 ten-dollar bills, 8 toonies, and 1 quarter.
   - ✓ Sandor paid with 1 twenty-dollar bill, 1 ten-dollar bill, 1 loonie, and 3 quarters.
   - ✓ Tory paid with 2 twenty-dollar bills, 4 toonies, 1 loonie, and 3 dimes.

   Find the amount each child paid. Then match their names with the dog they bought.

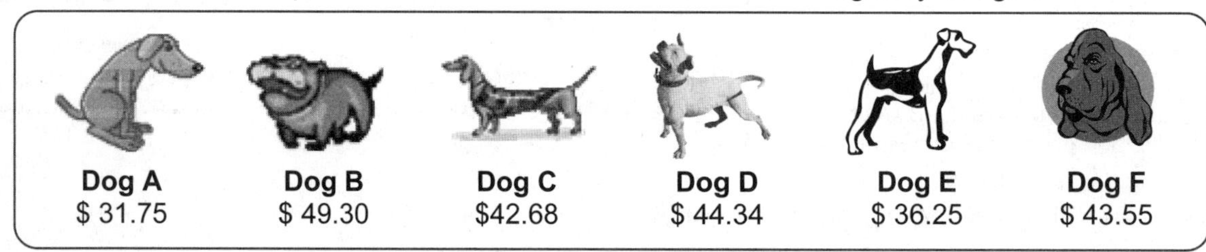


10. Keylan sold cookies for his class field trip. On the first day, he collected 5 toonies, 4 loonies, 6 quarters, 5 dimes, 3 nickels, and 5 pennies. How much money did he collect in total?

11. Mansa goes out with her friends on Sunday. Her allowance is $18.
    a) If she spends $12.00 watching a movie in a movie theatre, will she have enough money left to buy a magazine, which costs $3.29?
    b) If she buys a book for $7.50 and a cap for $ 9.00, will she have enough money left to buy a subway ticket, which costs $ 2.25?

12. Try to find the answers mentally.
    a) How much do 3 roses cost at $1.25 each?
    b) How many lemons, each costing 30¢, could you buy with $1.00?
    c) Sketch pads cost $5.25. How many could you buy if you had $26.00?

# ME4-24: Subtracting Money

1. Find the remaining amounts by subtracting.

a) 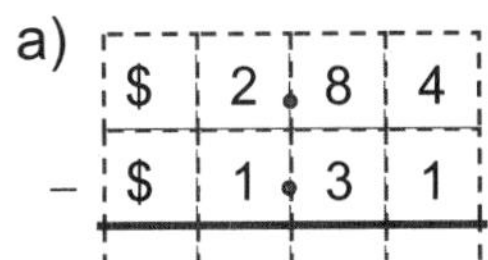

| | $ | 2. | 8 | 4 |
|---|---|---|---|---|
| − | $ | 1. | 3 | 1 |
| | | . | | |

b) 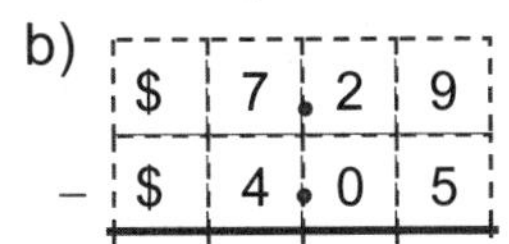

| | $ | 7. | 2 | 9 |
|---|---|---|---|---|
| − | $ | 4. | 0 | 5 |
| | | . | | |

c) 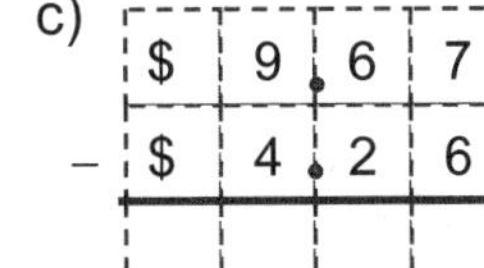

| | $ | 9. | 6 | 7 |
|---|---|---|---|---|
| − | $ | 4. | 2 | 6 |
| | | . | | |

d) 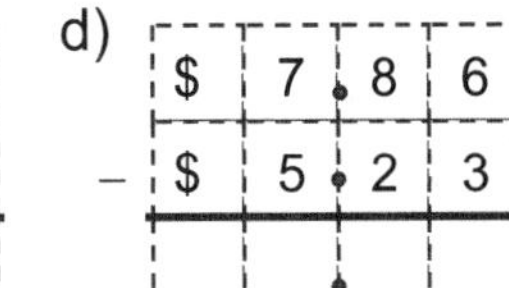

| | $ | 7. | 8 | 6 |
|---|---|---|---|---|
| − | $ | 5. | 2 | 3 |
| | | . | | |

e) 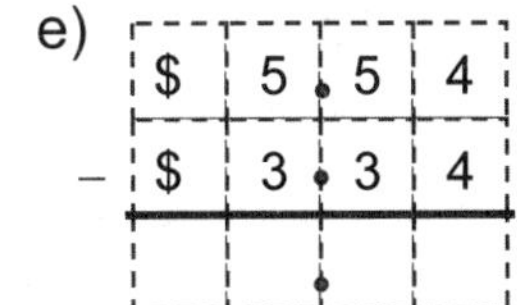

| | $ | 5. | 5 | 4 |
|---|---|---|---|---|
| − | $ | 3. | 3 | 4 |
| | | . | | |

2. Answer the following word problems. Show your work.

a) Val has $1.85. He lends $1.45 to his friend. How much money does he have left?

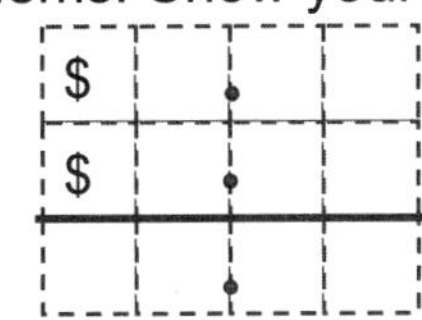

| $ | . | | |
|---|---|---|---|
| $ | . | | |
| | . | | |

______________________

b) Anu lost 56¢ from her pocket. She had $1.98 before she lost her money. How much money does she have left?

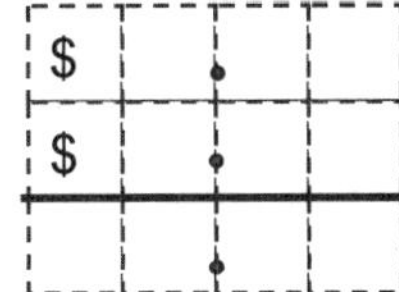

| $ | . | | |
|---|---|---|---|
| $ | . | | |
| | . | | |

______________________

3. Subtract the given money amounts by borrowing once or twice.

An example is done for you:

Step 1:

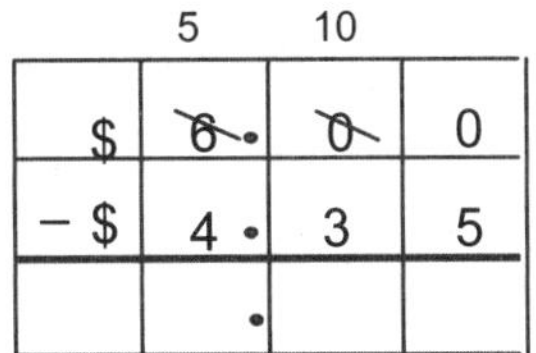

| | 5 | 10 | |
|---|---|---|---|
| $ | ~~6~~. | ~~0~~ | 0 |
| − $ | 4. | 3 | 5 |
| | . | | |

Step 2:

| | 5 | 9 ~~10~~ | 10 |
|---|---|---|---|
| $ | ~~6~~. | ~~0~~ | ~~0~~ |
| − $ | 4. | 3 | 5 |
| $ | 1. | 6 | 5 |

a)

| $ | 7. | 0 | 0 |
|---|---|---|---|
| − $ | 4. | 4 | 5 |
| | | | |

b) 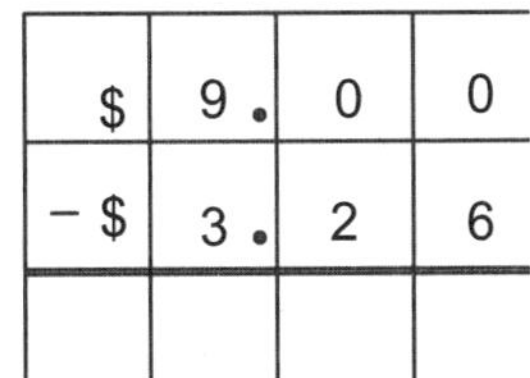

| $ | 9. | 0 | 0 |
|---|---|---|---|
| − $ | 3. | 2 | 6 |
| | | | |

c)

| $ | 9. | 0 | 4 |
|---|---|---|---|
| − $ | 8. | 9 | 5 |
| | | | |

d)

| $ | 5 | 3. | 0 | 0 |
|---|---|---|---|---|
| − $ | 2 | 2. | 3 | 1 |
| | | | | |

e) 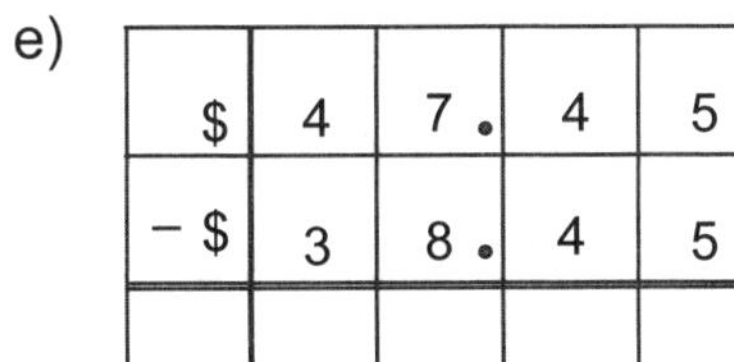

| $ | 4 | 7. | 4 | 5 |
|---|---|---|---|---|
| − $ | 3 | 8. | 4 | 5 |
| | | | | |

f)

| $ | 2 | 7. | 4 | 8 |
|---|---|---|---|---|
| − $ | 1 | 3. | 6 | 6 |
| | | | | |

Answer the following questions in a separate piece of paper:

4. Chris spent $4.23 on his lunch. He paid for it with a five-dollar bill. Calculate his change.

5. Betty has $6.75 and Karen has $4.23. How much more money does Betty have than Karen?

6. Anya goes to a grocery store with $10.00. She wants to buy vegetables for $3.50, juice for $4.00, and cereal for $4.50. Does she have enough money to buy all these items? If not, by how much is she short?

7. Mark has $25.00. He wants to buy a shirt that costs $14.95 and a pair of pants that cost $16.80. How much more money does he need to buy the pants and shirt?

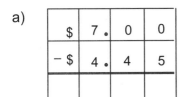

# ME4-25: Estimating

1. For each collection of coins and bills estimate the amount to the nearest dollar and then count the precise amount.

| | Estimate total (to the nearest dollar) | Actual total |
|---|---|---|
| a) | | |
| b) | | |
| c) | | |
| d) | | |

2. Round the given cent amounts to the nearest tens place. The first one is done for you.

**REMEMBER:**

If the number in the **ones** digit is

**0, 1, 2, 3, or 4**, you round **down**

**5, 6, 7, 8, or 9**, you round **up**

a) 54¢ 50¢ b) 35¢

c) 82¢ d) 66¢

e) 45¢ f) 71¢

g) 19¢ h) 18¢ i) 89¢

j) 14¢ k) 38¢ l) 56¢

3. Circle the amount where the **cent** amount is less than 50¢. The first one is done for you.

a) $8.45 (45 is less than 50) b) $6.80 c) $2.24 d) $8.74 e) $9.29 f) $5.55

g) $4.45 h) $3.50 i) $5.40 j) $9.29 k) $5.49 l) $7.51

4. Round the given amounts to the nearest dollar amount.

**REMEMBER:**

If the cent amount is **less than** 50¢, you round **down**.

If the cent amount is **equal to or greater than** 50¢, you round **up**.

a) $5.65 $6.00 b) $13.32

c) $22.75 d) $6.55

e) $37.35 f) $12.22

g) $48.15 h) $411.50 i) $4.24

j) $35.42 k) $29.75 l) $45.89

5. Estimate the following sums and differences by rounding each amount to the nearest dollar amount before performing the operation. The first one is done for you.

a) $5.49 + $3.20

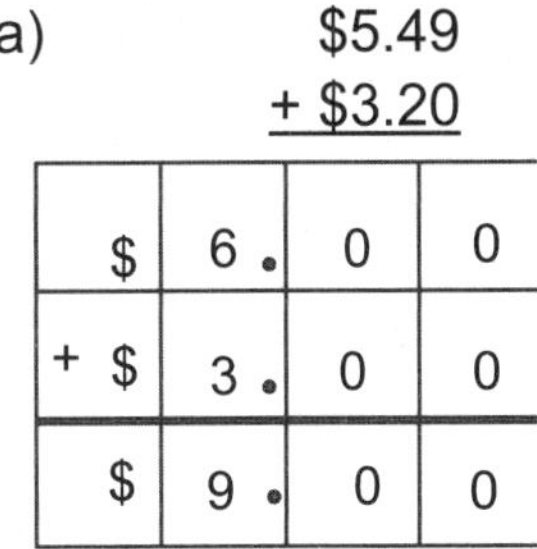


b) $9.53 − $2.14

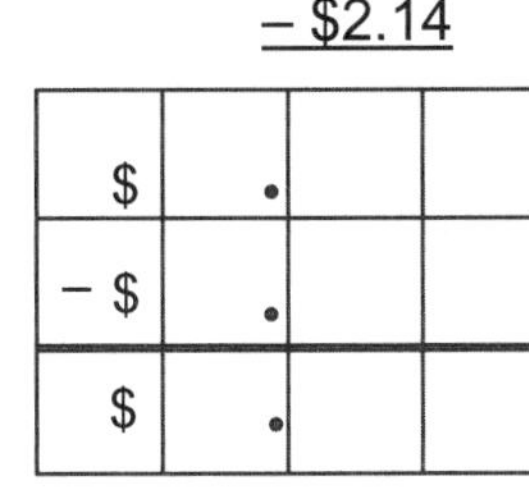

c) $2.75 + $5.64

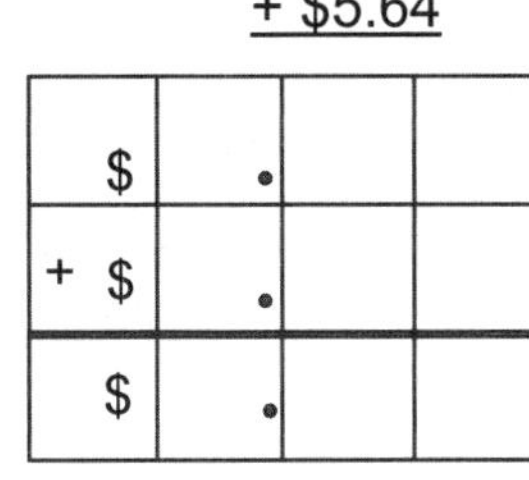

d) $7.78 − $2.85

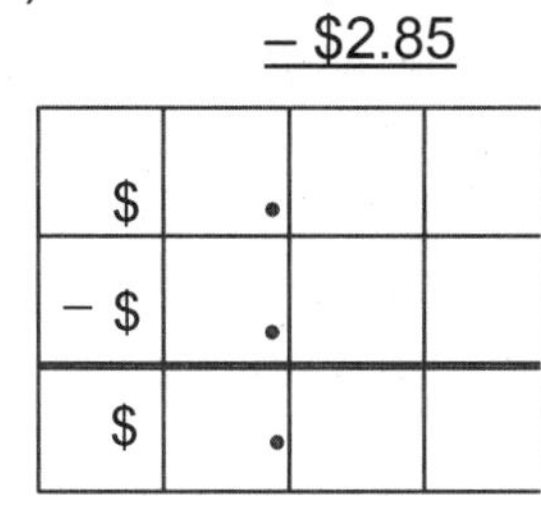

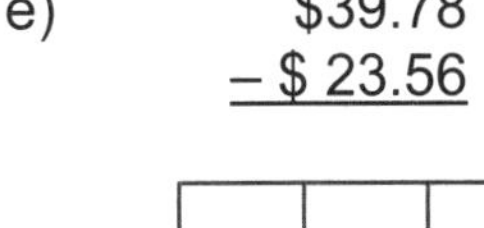

e) $39.78 − $ 23.56

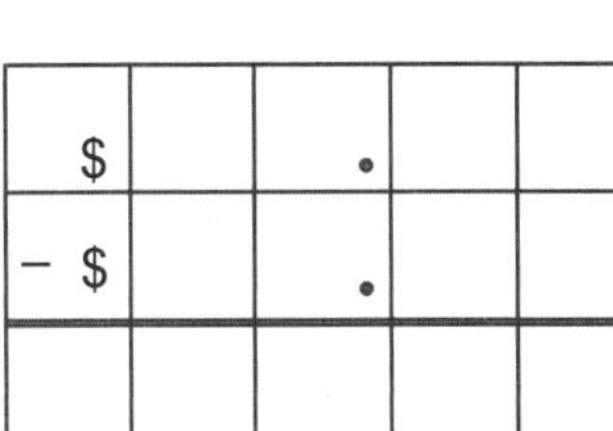

f) $26.78 + $13.45

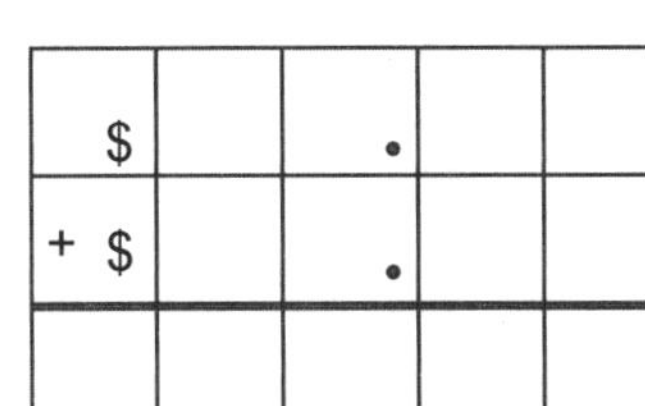

g) $26.65 + $15.33

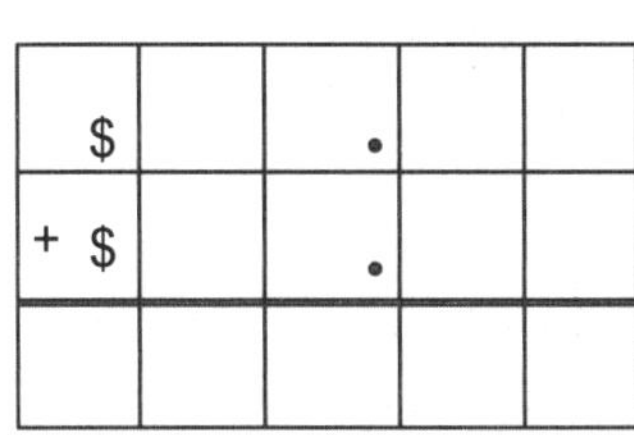

Solve the following word problems by rounding and estimating. Show all your work on a separate piece of paper.

6. Jasmine has $10.00. She buys a paintbrush for $2.27. Estimate her change.

7. Tony spends $12.35 and Sayaka spends $26.91 at the grocery store. About how much more did Sayaka spend than Tony?

8. Todd invited some friends over to his house for a Halloween party. He spent $8.64 on pop, $6.95 on vegetables and dip, $12.64 on chips, and $14.36 on ice cream. About how much did he spend altogether?

9. Donna bought school supplies for her three children. Each child's supplies cost $13.78. About how much money did Donna spend?

10. For each problem below, make an estimate and then find the **exact** amount.

    a) Dianna has $4.26. Erick has $2.34. How much more money does Dianna have?

    b) Maribel has $19.64. Sharon has $7.42. How much money do they have altogether?

11. Jason saved $16.95 this week. He wants to buy a present for his mom and a book for himself. The present for his mom costs $8.77 and the book costs $6.93. Does he have enough money to buy the book and the gift?

12. Explain why rounding to the nearest dollar isn't helpful for the following question: "Patrick has $7.23. Jill has $6.95. About how much more money does Patrick have than Jill."

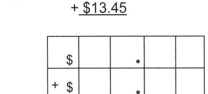

# PDM4-1: Introduction to Classifying Data



**Data** is facts or information.

For example, your eye colour is a **piece** of data, and so is your height. The different heights of you and your friends are a **group** of data.

A group of data can be organized into **categories**. We organize data into categories using **attributes**. For example, here are some attributes (and categories) you could use to organize information about you and your friends.

- Eye colour ("brown" or "green")
- Grade ("grade 4" or "grade 5")
- Height ("120 cm" or "130 cm")

---

1. Animals: dog, horse, giraffe, goldfish, pig, tiger, cow, cat

   Categories: House pets ____ Farm animals ____ Zoo animals ____

   a) Underline the animals that are zoo animals.

   b) Circle the animals that are house pets.

   c) Count and record how many are in each category.

2. Count how many are in each category. Read all the categories first.

   a) Objects: coin, tree, window, telephone pole, popsicle stick, staple, newspaper, gold necklace

      Categories: Wood ____ Glass ____ Metal ____

   b) Objects: strawberry, ocean, sky, grass, poppy, apple, leaf, heart, pickle, stop sign

      Categories: Green ____ Blue ____ Red ____

3. Match the data with the correct category.

   **A.** carrot, lettuce, cucumber
   **B.** rainy, snowy, foggy
   **C.** morning, evening, noon
   **D.** hammer, wrench, saw

   ____ Weather forecasts
   ____ Tools
   ____ Vegetables
   ____ Times of day

4. Can you think of another piece of data for each category in question 3?

   a) Weather forecasts: ______________________

   b) Tools: ______________________

   c) Vegetables: ______________________

   d) Times of day: ______________________

5. Can you add an appropriate piece of data to each group? Which category name best describes the group of data? The first one is done for you.

   a) blue, yellow, green, purple, ___red___

      Category name: ___colours___

   b) grape, apple, plum, mango, ____________

      Category name: ____________

   c) math, gym, music, spelling, ____________

      Category name: ____________

   d) verb, object, noun, adverb, ____________

      Category name: ____________

6. Heather wants to sort her T-shirts into 2 different categories: those **with** patterns and those **without** patterns.

   Here are her T-shirts. Notice that each one has been given a letter:

   a) Use the following table to help Heather sort her T-shirts. The first two are sorted for you.

| Category | T-shirt (by letter) |
|---|---|
| T-shirts **with** pattern | A, |
| T-shirts **without** pattern | B, |

   b) Use your table to answer the following questions:

   How many patterned T-shirts does Heather have? ________

   How many T-shirts without patterns does Heather have? ________

   c) Use the following table to sort Jessica's T-shirts. Notice that some of Jessica's T-shirts are in more than one category. The first two T-shirts are sorted for you.

| T-shirt | A | B | C | D | E | F | G | H | I | J |
|---|---|---|---|---|---|---|---|---|---|---|
| dark colour | | ✓ | | | | | | | | |
| light colour | ✓ | | | | | | | | | |
| with pattern | ✓ | | | | | | | | | |

   How many T-shirts does Jessica have that are a dark colour AND have a pattern? ________

   d) Think of the T-shirts that you own. What is a different way you could sort them?

   Name the **categories** you would use to sort them.________________________________

   Would you need a table like Heather's or like Jessica's? ________________________________

# PDM4-2: Using Venn Diagrams to Classify Data

A piece of data can have more than one attribute. A Venn diagram is a good way to see which objects share an attribute.

Jessica used a Venn diagram to sort her T-shirts in another way:

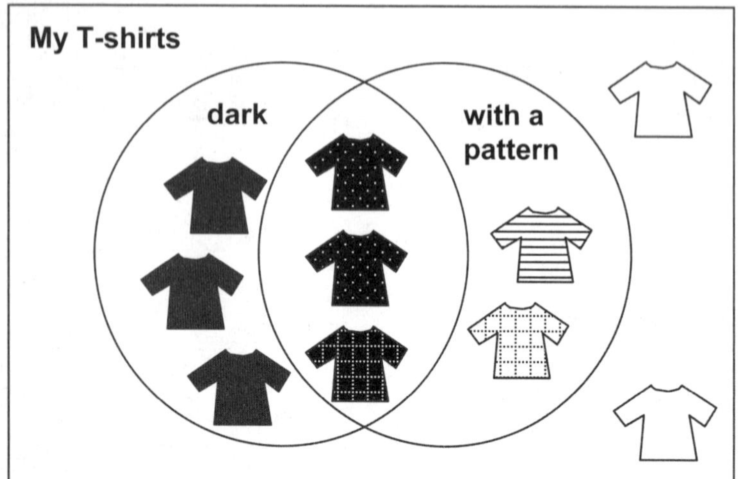


She labelled the data "My T-shirts."

She labelled one circle "dark."

She labelled the other circle "with a pattern."

The T-shirts in the overlap are dark AND patterned. They are **in both** categories.

The T-shirts outside the circles are NOT dark and NOT patterned. They are **not in either** of the categories.

1. Look at the following shapes:

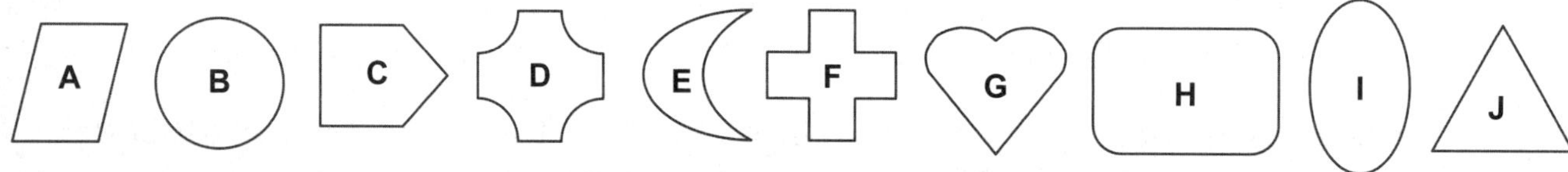


Complete the following table, then use the information to complete the Venn diagram:

| Shape | Straight sides only | Curved sides only | Both straight and curved sides |
|---|---|---|---|
| A | ✓ | | |
| B | | | |
| C | | | |
| D | | | |
| E | | | |
| F | | | |
| G | | | |
| H | | | |
| I | | | |
| J | | | |

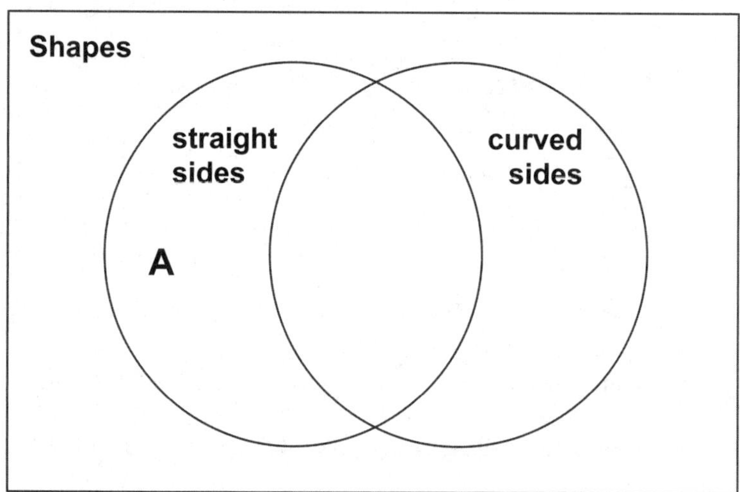

2. 

Bradley loves to learn about space. Using the Internet with help from his father, he collects the following information about the planets in our solar system:

| Planet | Number of moons | Days needed to orbit the Sun |
|---|---|---|
| Mercury (A) | 0 | 88 |
| Venus (B) | 0 | 225 |
| Earth (C) | 1 | 365 |
| Mars (D) | 2 | 687 |
| Jupiter (E) | 16 | 4 344 |
| Saturn (F) | 20 | 10 768 |
| Uranus (G) | 15 | 30 660 |
| Neptune (H) | 8 | 60 152 |
| Pluto (I) | 1 | 91 579 |

a) Look at the number of moons each planet has. Which planets have more than 10 moons?

List their letters. ______________________________

b) Look at the orbit time for each planet. Which planets orbit the Sun in fewer than 10 000 days?

List their letters. ______________________________

c) Do any planets fall into **both** categories? That is, they have more than 10 moons and take fewer than 10 000 days to orbit the Sun?

If so, circle this planet's letter in both the lists above.

d) Now place **all** the planets—by letter—into the following Venn diagram.

Pay particular attention to the planet you have circled. Where will it go? 

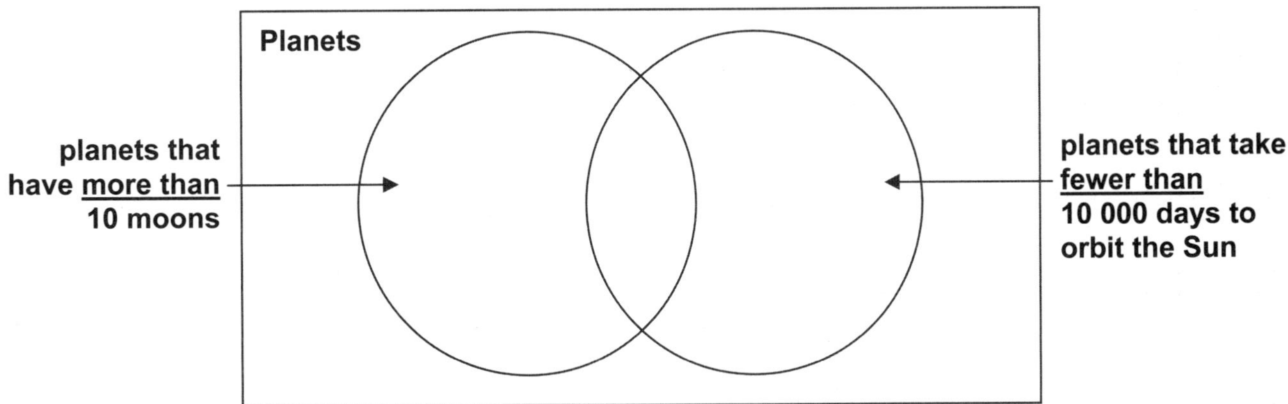

3. Iain has a part-time job at a pet store. As a school project, he decides to organize the animals in the store into the following Venn diagram:

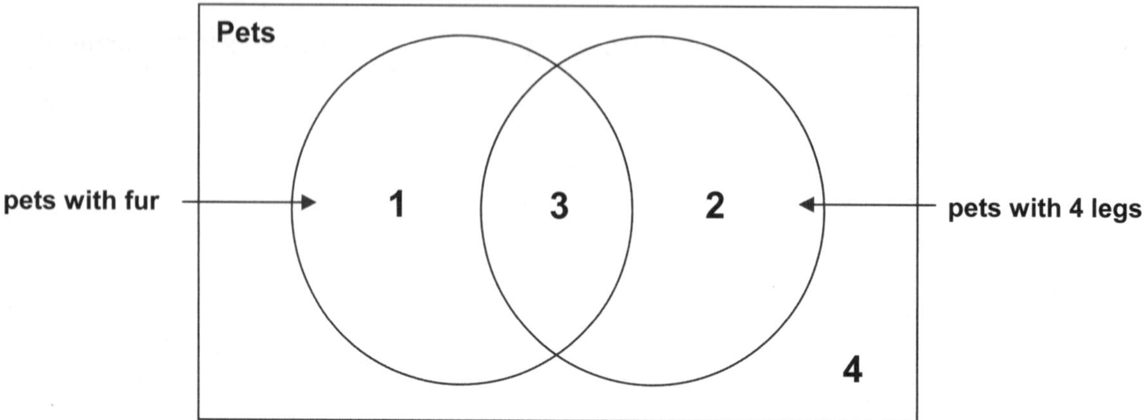


Can you help him classify these animals by giving the section where they belong?

cat – ☐ gerbil – ☐ fish – ☐

dog – ☐ lizard – ☐ turtle – ☐

4. Survey 10 friends to see where they would fit into the following Venn diagram. Then, on a separate piece of paper, redraw the Venn diagram and include your friends' names in the appropriate spot.

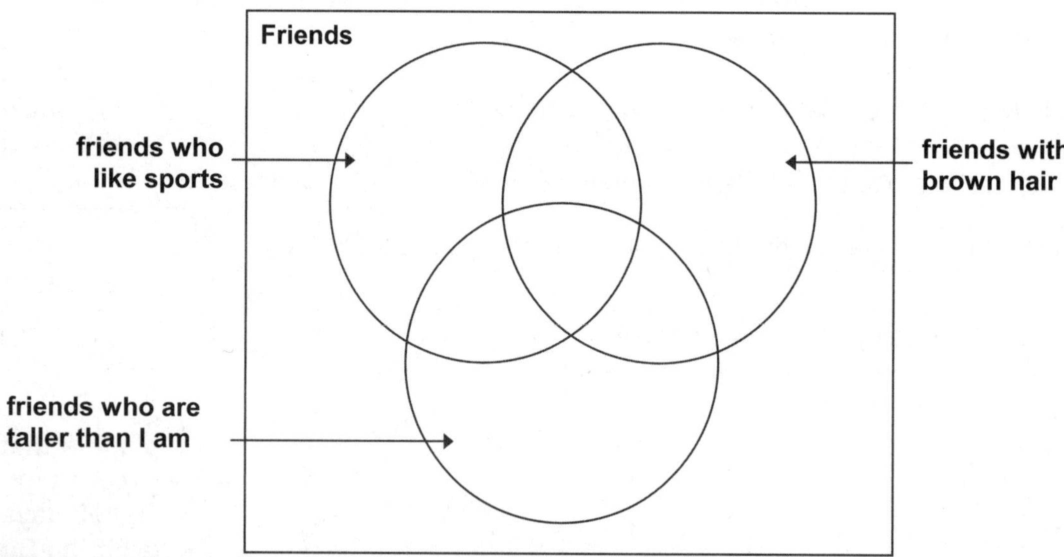


BONUS:
What is true about the friends in the middle section of the diagram?

# PDM4-3: Revisiting Tallies

A **tally** is a useful way to record and count data. In a tally, each stroke represents 1:

/ = 1    // = 2    /// = 3    //// = 4    𝍸 = 5

𝍸 / = 6    𝍸 // = 7    𝍸 /// = 8    𝍸 //// = 9    𝍸 𝍸 = 10

Every fifth stroke is made sideways. This makes it easy to use skip counting by 5s to count a tally:

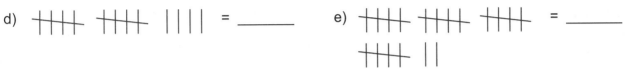

𝍸 𝍸 𝍸 𝍸 𝍸 𝍸 //
5, 10, 15, 20, 25, 30, 32

---

1. Provide the number that matches the given tally.

a) 𝍸 = ____    b) ||| = ____    c) 𝍸 | = ____

d) 𝍸 𝍸 |||| = ____

e) 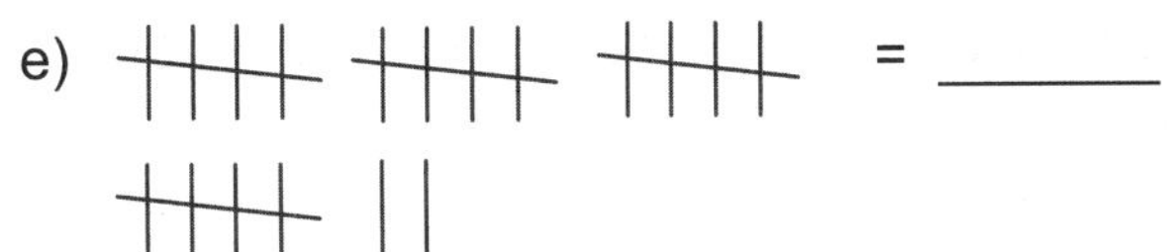 = ____

f) 𝍸 𝍸 𝍸 𝍸 𝍸 | = ____

g) 𝍸 𝍸 𝍸 | = ____

2. Provide the tally that matches the given number.

a) 4 =    b) 7 =    c) 9 =

d) 21 =    e) 13 =

3. Using your knowledge of tallies, complete the following data chart:

| | Roses | Petunias | Lilies | Tulips | Carnations |
|---|---|---|---|---|---|
| **Tally** | 𝍸 𝍸 ||| | | 𝍸 𝍸 | ||| | |
| **Count** | ____ | 7 | ____ | ____ | 9 |

# PDM4-4: Revisiting Pictographs

A **pictograph** uses a **symbol** to represent data.

This pictograph shows that Josef read 5 books and Alexander read 3 books in December.

**Number of Books Read in December**
Josef 📖📖📖📖📖
Alexander 📖📖📖

Josef read 50 books in a year and Alexander read 30—but 50 and 30 are too many symbols to draw!

A **scale** can be used to show greater numbers in a pictograph. When you use a scale, the value of each symbol is a number greater than 1. The scale is usually a skip counting number, like 2, 5, or 10.

A **key** tells what the scale is:

**Number of Books Read in 1 Year**
Josef 📖📖📖📖📖
Alexander 📖📖📖
1 📖 means 10 books

OR

**Number of Books Read in 1 Year**
Josef 📖📖📖📖📖📖📖📖📖📖
Alexander 📖📖📖📖📖📖
1 📖 means 5 books

1. Using the pictograph given below, answer the following questions:

SCALE: 1☼ = 2 days of sun

| Month | Number of sunny days | Count<br>number of suns x 2 = number of sunny days |
|---|---|---|
| April | ☼ ☼ ☼ ☼ ☼ | 5 x 2 = 10 sunny days in April |
| May | ☼ ☼ ☼ ☼ | |
| June | ☼ ☼ ☼ ☼ ☼ ☼ ☼ ☼ | |
| July | ☼ ☼ ☼ ☼ ☼ ☼ ☼ ☼ ☼ ☼ ☼ ☼ | |
| August | ☼ ☼ ☼ ☼ ☼ ☼ ☼ ☼ ☼ | |

a) Complete the last column of the chart above.

b) How many sunny days were there in July? _____ in May? _____

c) Which month had 18 sunny days? __________ d) Which month was the sunniest? ________

e) June has 30 days. How many days in June **were not** sunny? _____

How do you know? ____________________________________________

____________________________________________________________

Complete the following questions on a separate piece of paper:

f) Describe 2 other things you can tell from reading this pictograph.

g) Explain why a book and a sun are good choices to use for the symbols in the pictographs on this page.

# PDM4-4: Revisiting Pictographs *(continued)*

2. You have counted and tallied the seeds of three plants. Count your tally and then create a pictograph to show the number of seeds on each plant.

**Your tally**

| **Plant** | **Number of seeds** | |
|---|---|---|
| rose | 卌 卌 卌 卌 卌 卌 卌 卌 卌 卌 | = ______ seeds |
| dandelion | 卌 卌 卌 卌 | = ______ seeds |
| pansy | 卌 卌 | = ______ seeds |

**Your pictograph**

**KEY:** (seed) = 10 seeds

| **Plant** | **Number of seeds** |
|---|---|
| rose | |
| dandelion | |
| pansy | |

3. In a box of candies, there are three different colours: blue (B), green (G), and yellow (Y).

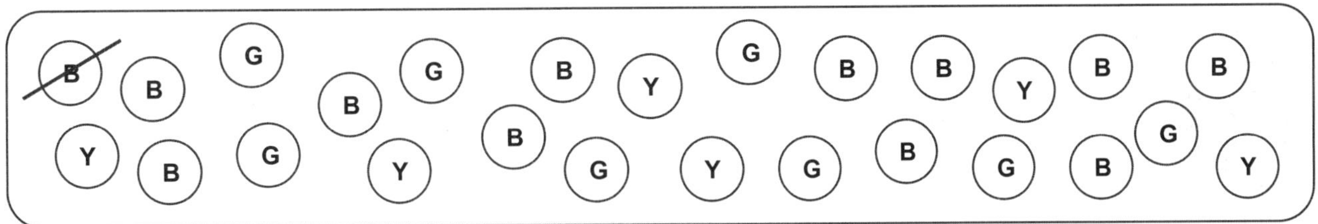

Use the chart to tally the candies (the first one is done for you) and then create a pictograph using the following key:

**KEY:** ⊙ = 2 candies

| **Colour** | **Tally** | **Pictograph** |
|---|---|---|
| blue | \| | |
| green | | |
| yellow | | |

# PDM4-5: Choosing a Pictograph Scale and Symbol

Manuel has counted the flowers in his garden:

| Flower | dandelion | buttercup | daisy |
|---|---|---|---|
| Height | 15 | 25 | 40 |

He wants to display his data in a pictograph. The numbers are large, though, so he needs a scale.

He looks for a skip counting number that will work well with these numbers.

- A scale of 2 means 20 symbols are needed for the daisy. That is too many symbols.
- He can count to all three numbers by 5s. A scale of 5 will work.
- If he uses half symbols, a scale of 10 will work too.

Manuel thinks about what symbol he could use.

- For a scale of **5**, all the symbols will be whole symbols, so he chooses a flower for the symbol.
- For a scale of **10**, he needs half symbols. It is hard to draw half a flower. He chooses a circle.

**Number of Flowers**
dandelion ❀❀❀
buttercup ❀❀❀❀❀
daisy ❀❀❀❀❀❀❀❀
1 ❀ means 5 flowers

**Number of Flowers**
dandelion ●◖
buttercup ●●◖
daisy ●●●●
1 ● means 10 flowers

---

1. Which scale and which symbol is best for the data?

a) 12, 6, 8 ☐ scale of 2 ☐ scale of 5 ☐ scale of 10

b) 30, 90, 60 ☐ scale of 2 ☐ scale of 5 ☐ scale of 10

c) 9, 12, 6 ☐ scale of 2 ☐ scale of 3 ☐ scale of 5

d) 25, 10, 35 ☐ scale of 2 ☐ scale of 3 ☐ scale of 5

2. Why symbol is best for the data?

a) number of nights ☐ ● ☐ 🚹 ☐ ☾

b) number of valentines ☐ ✦ ☐ ♡ ☐ ■

c) number of friends ☐ ☺ ☐ ☆ ☐ ●

3. Which symbol will work best?

a) You need whole symbols and half symbols. ☐ 👂 ☐ ▲

b) You need whole symbols and quarter symbols. ☐ ⊞ ☐ ☺

# PDM4-6: Pictographs (Advanced)

1. Theresa surveyed 20 of her friends to find out about their favourite reading material. She gave the results to her sister in the form of a pictograph but forgot to include the key. Can you help her sister understand Theresa's data?

**My Friends' Reading Preferences**

| Favourite reading material | Number of friends |
|---|---|
| mysteries | 📖 📖 |
| adventure | 📖 📖 📖 |
| science fiction | 📖 |
| comic books | 📖 📖 📖 |
| magazines | 📖 |

a) Count the number of books in Theresa's pictograph. How many books are there altogether? _____

b) Does each book represent one friend? _____ Explain how you know on a separate piece of paper.

c) Knowing there are 20 friends in Theresa's survey, how many friends do you think each book represents?

📖 = ______ friends

d) Using the **scale** you found, count the number of friends in each category and write your counts in the chart. The total should be 20 friends. If not, try a different scale.

e) What strategies did you use to find Theresa's key? Outline them on a separate piece of paper.

ACTIVITIES:

2. If there were 40 friends in Theresa's survey, how many friends would each book represent? Explain your reasoning on a separate piece of paper.

3. Choose something you can **count** and group it in categories. (For example, the number of students in your swimming class whose first names begin with a letter from A to H, from I to P, and Q to Z; or how many of 50 pennies have a date like this: "before 1980," "198__," "199__," or "200__"?)

   Collect and record your data. Display your data in a pictograph. What new information can you find using your pictograph?

4. Choose some things that you can **measure** and group them in categories. (For example, how many of the books on a shelf are about 2 cm thick, about 3 cm thick, and about 4 cm thick?)

   Collect your data and display it in a pictograph. What new information can you find?

5. Conduct an experiment to collect data. (For example, roll a die 50 times. How many times did it land on 1 or 2? on 3 or 4? on 5 or 6?)

   Display your data in a pictograph. Think of a way to change the experiment. (For example, use the categories "rolls 1," "rolls 2," and "rolls 3, 4, 5, or 6.") Predict how your data will change, then do the new experiment and display the data.

# PDM4-7: Revisiting Bar Graphs

A **bar graph** has 4 parts: a vertical and horizontal **axis,** a **scale**, **labels** (including a title) and **data** (shown by the bars). Bar graphs tend to be drawn on square **grids**.

The bars in a bar graph can be either vertical or horizontal. The scale tells how much each square on the axis represents. The labels indicate what the data in the bars is. You can then use the scale to measure the value of the data represented by particular bars.

---

1. This bar graph gives the average temperature for Vancouver (in °C) at different times of the year:

   Use the graph to answer the questions.

   a) In Vancouver, the coldest months are

   ____________ – ____________.

   b) In Vancouver, the warmest months are

   ____________ – ____________.

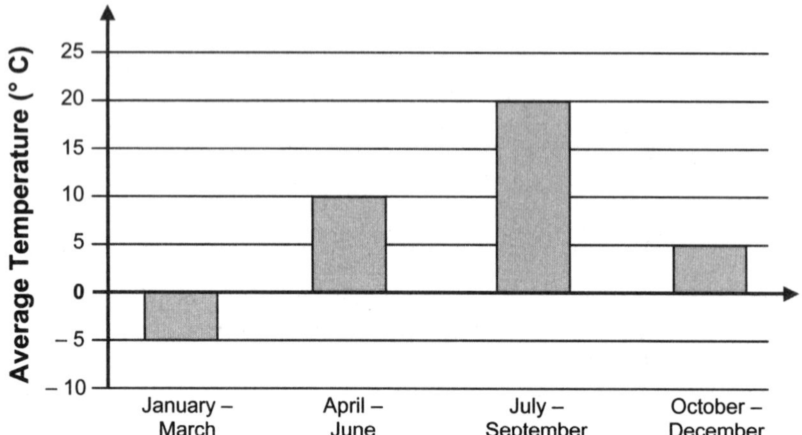


2. This bar graph gives the average total snowfall for Guelph (in centimetres) at different times of the year:

   Use the graph to answer the questions.

   a) The average total snowfall from January – March is _____ cm.

   b) The average total snowfall is 200 cm for the months of

   ____________ – ____________.

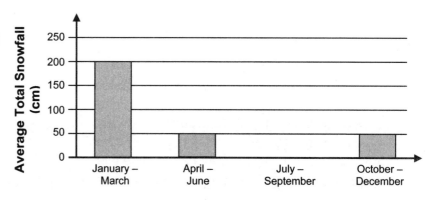

   c) The average total snowfall **over the whole year** is ______ cm.

Average Total Snowfall (cm)
250
200
150
100
50
0
January – March
April – June
July – September
October – December
Time of Year

3. Determine the values of the other bars on the graphs.

a)

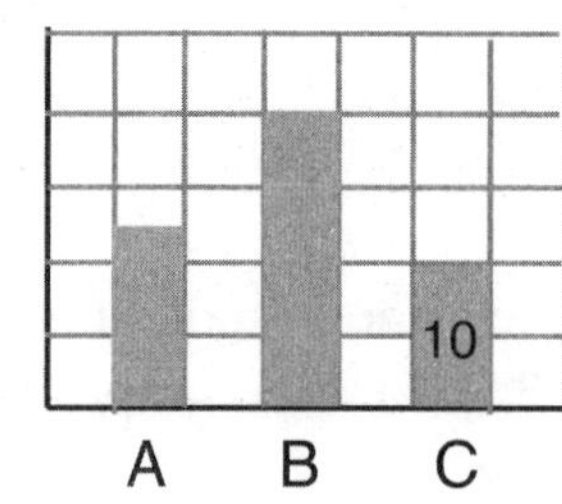


b)

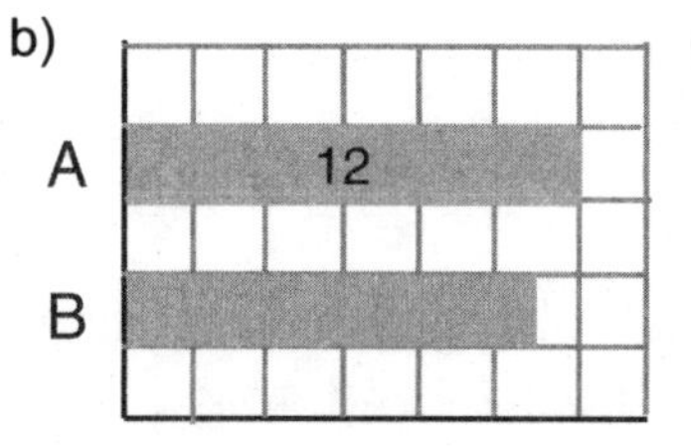


c)

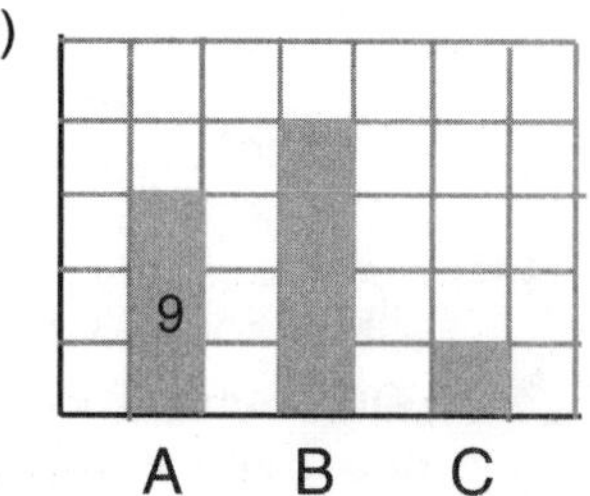


4. Toss a coin ten times.

   a) Make a bar graph to show the number of heads and tails you tossed.

   b) Did you flip as many tails as you expected? Explain.

5. The following students wrote a spelling test. Their marks (out of 20) were as follows:

| | | | | | | | |
|---|---|---|---|---|---|---|---|
| Adam | 10 | Akeila | 15 | Joanne | 20 | Shey | 20 |
| Ben | 10 | Fabiola | 15 | Beth | 20 | Sally | 5 |
| Kim | 20 | Rosa | 10 | Sahar | 20 | Imran | 20 |
| Jenny | 5 | Abdul | 20 | Ken | 5 | Noomph | 20 |
| Shawn | 15 | Cesar | 10 | Sharla | 15 | Aidan | 10 |

Organize the above results into a bar graph, keeping in mind that the bars in this graph run **horizontally**.

The first one is done for you.

NOTE: If you want to create a tally of the data, use a separate piece of paper or the space below.

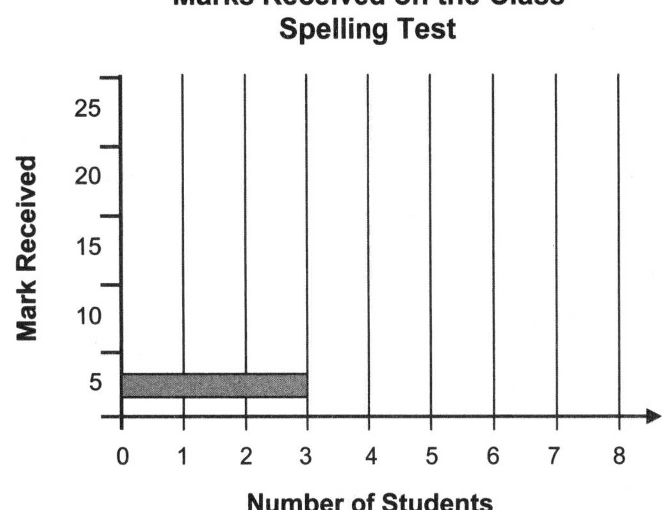


6. Complete the following chart. Then, on a separate piece of paper, create a bar graph to display the data. Be sure to include a title and label your axes. Do you want to make a horizontal or a vertical bar graph? What scale works best?

**Survey Question**: How many brothers and sisters do you have?

| Number of brothers and sisters | Tally | Count |
|---|---|---|
| 0 | 𝍷𝍷𝍷𝍷 | ____ |
| 1 | 𝍸 𝍸 | ____ |
| 2 | 𝍸 𝍸 𝍸 𝍷 | ____ |
| 3 | 𝍸 𝍷𝍷𝍷 | ____ |
| 4 | 𝍷𝍷𝍷 | ____ |
| more than 4 | 𝍸 | ____ |

# PDM4-8: Introduction to Pie Charts

NOTE: Review naming fractions before you complete this worksheet.

1. Janice likes reading and has collected many of her favourite books. As a pie graph, her collection looks like this:

**Janice's Book Collection**

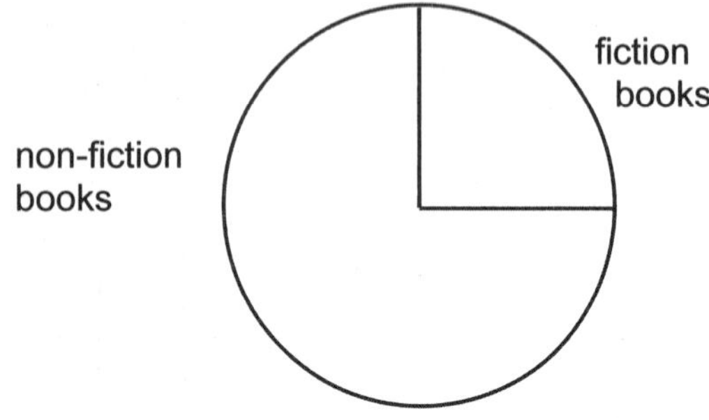


a) Which does Janice prefer: fiction or non-fiction?

b) What fraction of her collection is fiction?

c) What fraction is non-fiction?

d) If Janice had 20 books altogether, how many would be fiction? (HINT: How can you divide 20 into 4 equal parts?)

2. Can you help Ming read the following pie graph?

**My Friends' Favourite Juices**

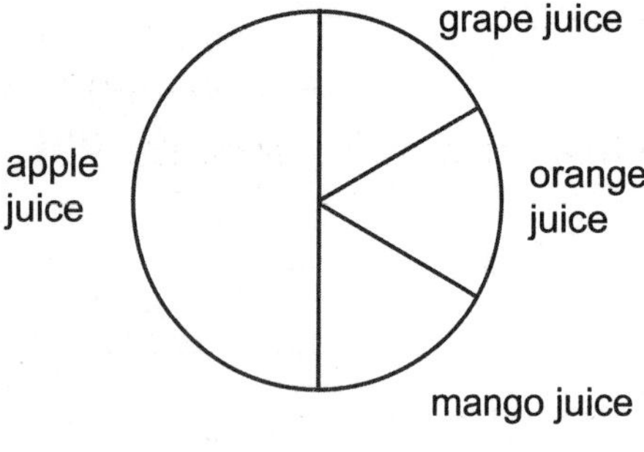


a) What juice is the most popular?

b) What fraction of Ming's friends prefer orange juice? Be careful!

c) What fraction prefer grape juice?

d) If Ming surveyed 12 friends, how many liked apple juice the best?

# PDM4-9: Revisiting Surveys



1. George did a survey of his friends' favourite sports. Once he had collected and organized his data, he created a bar graph to display it. Here is his graph:

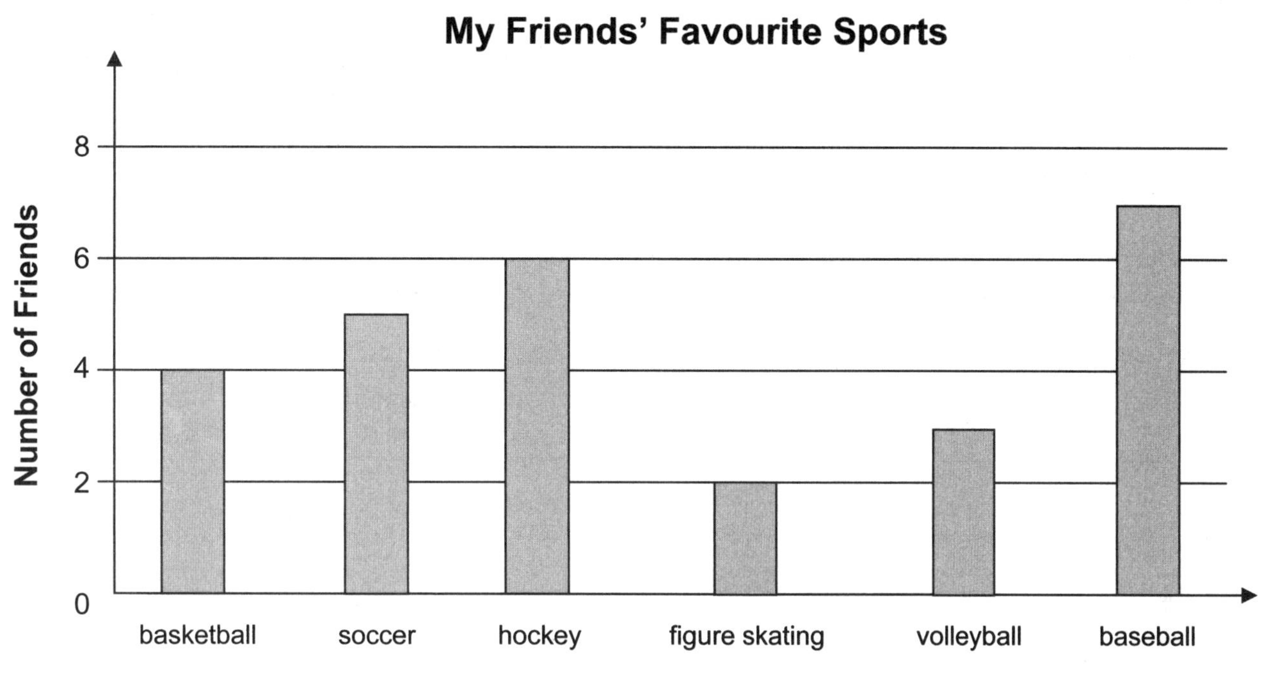


Answer the following questions on a separate piece of paper:

a) Can you guess what George's original tally sheet might have looked like? Try to recreate it.

b) Instead of using a bar graph or tally sheet, how could George have displayed his data? Explain your ideas in detail.

2. In each case, which method would you use to find the type of data?

- **a survey?**
- **measuring?**
- **counting?**
- **an experiment?**
- **researching in books or on the Internet?**

a) How far people can jump. ____________________

b) How fast different animals can run. ____________________

c) How many students in a class have each colour of hair. ____________________

d) The favourite sports of your friends. ____________________

e) How many people can count to 100 in 1 minute or less. ____________________

- ✓ Data you collect yourself is called **first-hand data**. Some ways you can collect first-hand data are by measuring items, by conducting an experiment, and by conducting a survey.
- ✓ Data collected by someone else is called **second-hand data**. You can find second-hand data in books and magazines, and on the Internet.

**Writing a Survey Question**

1. Decide what you want to know. (For example, "I would like to know the favourite flavour of ice cream of my friends.")
2. The question should have no more than 3 to 5 possible responses. If appropriate, one of the responses could be "other."

Example:

| | |
|---|---|
| What is your favourite flavour of ice cream? | ✗ This **is not** a good survey question. You could get a different answer from each person. |
| What flavours of ice cream do you like?<br>☐ vanilla ☐ chocolate ☐ strawberry ☐ other | ✗ This **is not** a good survey question. The person could say more than one flavour. |
| Which is your favourite flavour of ice cream:<br>☐ vanilla ☐ chocolate ☐ strawberry ☐ other | ✓ This **is** a good survey question. Each person will only give one answer. |

---

1. Write a survey question to find out what pizza toppings people like best.

   ______________________________________________?

   ☐ ____________ ☐ ____________ ☐ ____________ ☐ other

2. Write a survey question to find out what activity people like the best: skateboarding, rollerblading, bicycling, walking, or scootering.

   ______________________________________________?

3. Write a different survey question that you could ask your friends.

   ______________________________________________?

4. Conduct a survey of your friends to answer one of questions 1, 2, or 3. Record your data using a tally chart. Display your data in a bar graph with a scale of 2, 3, or 5.

REMEMBER: Here are the steps for planning a survey:

Decide: i) **What** you want to know. ii) **Who** you will survey and **how many** people you will survey.

iii) **When** and **where** you will conduct your survey. iv) **How** you will record your data.

Then **write** your survey question, **predict** what the response to your survey will be, and **conduct** your survey. Were the results of your survey what you expected?

# PDM4-11: Designing Your Own Survey

Now it is your turn to do a survey. Record all of your ideas, data, observations, and conclusions on a separate piece of paper.

Here are some suggestions to help you get started. NOTE: Be sure to keep in mind all that you have learned about writing survey questions (see PDM4-10 for details).

1. A survey usually asks a particular question. For example: How do you get to school? What is your favourite colour? How big is your family?

   **Ask yourself:** What question will my survey ask?

2. It is sometimes a good idea to offer people a sample of possible answers. For example: Do you walk to school or do you take the bus?

   **Ask yourself:** What are some of the responses I expect?

3. Before doing a survey, it can be interesting to try to predict the result. What answer do you think will be the most common? the least common? For example, do you think most of your friends walk to school or do they take the bus?

   **Ask yourself:** What are my predicted results?

4. Next, you will need to create a tally sheet to keep track of the responses you get. For example:

| How do you get to school? | Tally |
|---|---|
| walk | |
| take the bus | |
| ride my bike | |

5. Now that you have collected your survey data, you display it.

   **Ask yourself:** Would I prefer to use a bar graph or a pictograph? If I use a bar graph, will it be horizontal or vertical? What scale should I use? If I use a pictograph, what symbol might work best? What will my key be?
   NOTE: Do not forget to label everything clearly and include a descriptive title.

6. Finally, you should use your results to draw some conclusions about your original survey question.

   **Ask yourself:** Did people respond as I expected? Were the results a surprise? Did I learn anything interesting from my survey?

# PDM4-12: Reading and Manipulating Found Data

1. During the Olympic Games, Geoff kept track of the gold medals won by the following countries:

| Korea | Italy | Greece | Brazil | Canada |
|---|---|---|---|---|
| 𝍸 \|\|\|\| | 𝍸 𝍸 | 𝍸 \| | \|\|\|\| | \|\|\| |
| 9 | ____ | ____ | ____ | ____ |

a) Before answering the questions, count the tally results and add the numbers to the chart above. The first one is done for you.

b) How many gold medals did Brazil win? _____ c) How many gold medals did Greece win? _____

You can **compare** and **order** the data for each country to find new information.

d) Which country listed above won the **most** gold medals? __________ e) the least? __________

f) List the countries in order of gold medals won (greatest to least).

________________________________________________

You can **add**, **subtract**, or **multiply** data from the chart to find new information.

g) How many gold medals did Geoff's countries win altogether? ____________________

h) How many more medals did Italy win than Brazil? ____________________

h) Which country won three times as many gold medals as Canada? ____________________

2. Three students collected data and made graphs of their data:

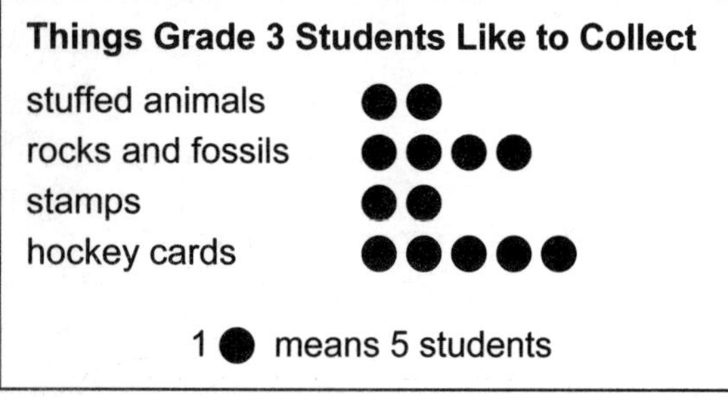


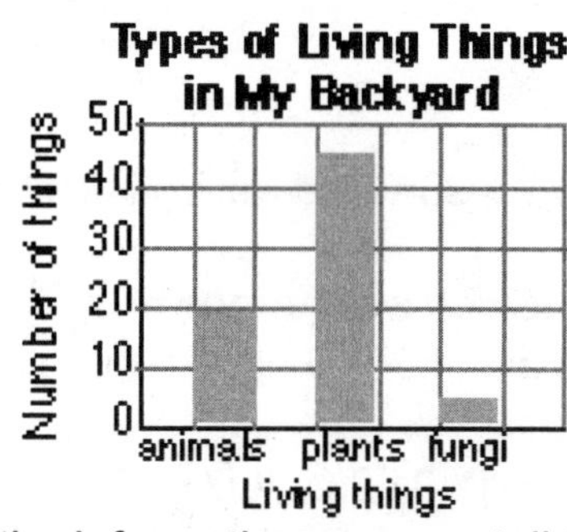


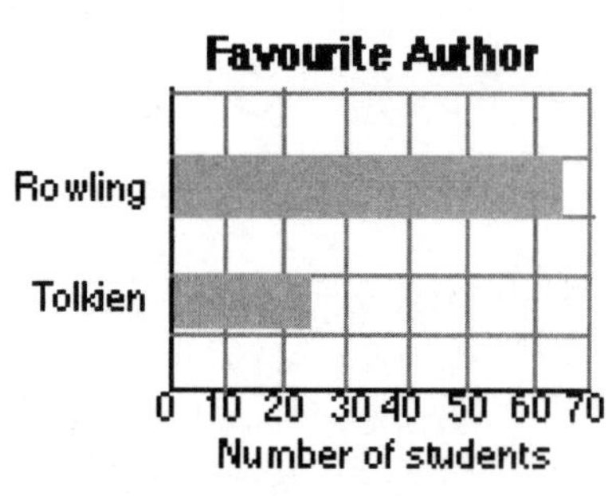


a) On a separate piece of paper, list all the information you can tell from each graph, including new information you can find by comparing, ordering, adding, subtracting, multiplying, or dividing data amounts.

b) On grid paper, make a new graph of one of these graphs **using a different scale**.

# G4-1: Sides and Vertices of 2-D Figures

All polygons have sides (or "edges") and vertices (the "corners" where the sides meet).

NOTE: A polygon is a 2-D (flat) shape with sides made of straight lines.

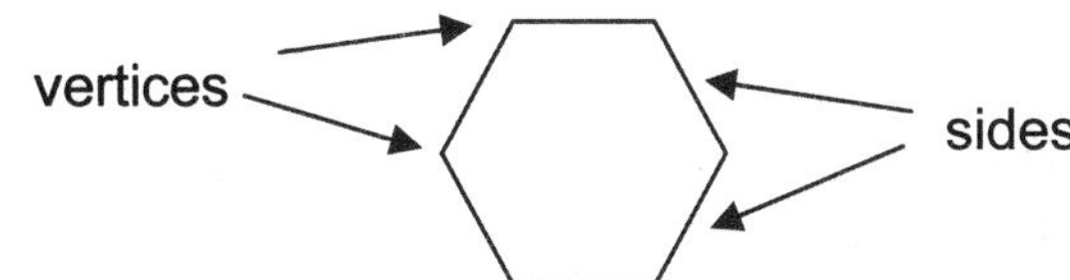


To find the number of:

a) **SIDES**
Move clockwise around the polygon, and put a tick mark on each side as you count it. This ensures that you (1) count all the sides and (2) count each side only once.

Example: 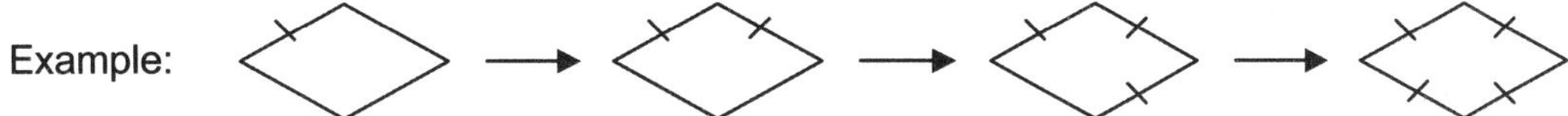

This shape has **4** sides.

b) **VERTICES**
Move clockwise around the polygon, and circle each vertex as you count it. This ensures that you count all the vertices only once.

Example: 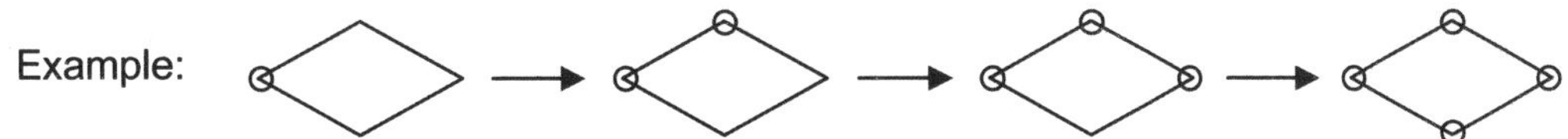

This shape has **4** vertices.

---

1. Using the method above, find the number of sides and vertices in each of the following figures:

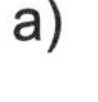

a)  ____ sides ____ vertices

b) 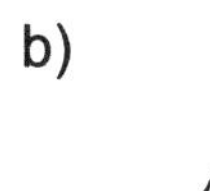 ____ sides ____ vertices

c)  ____ sides ____ vertices

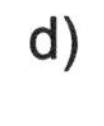

d) 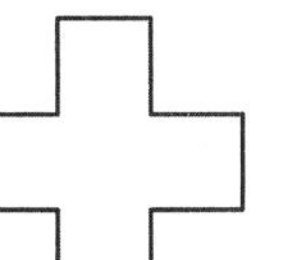 ____ sides ____ vertices

e) 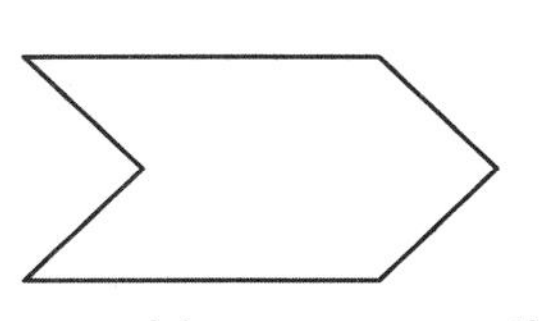 ____ sides ____ vertices

f) 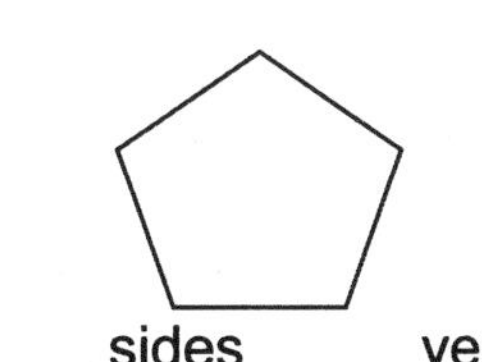 ____ sides ____ vertices

g) 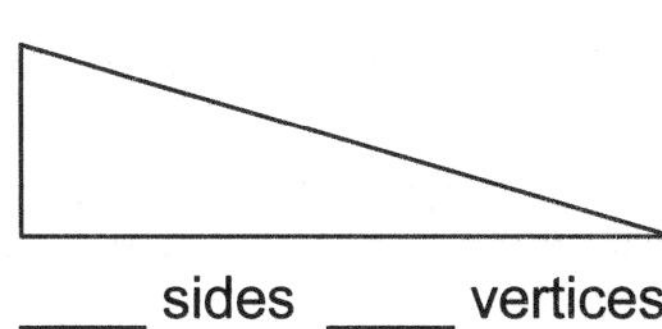 ____ sides ____ vertices

h) 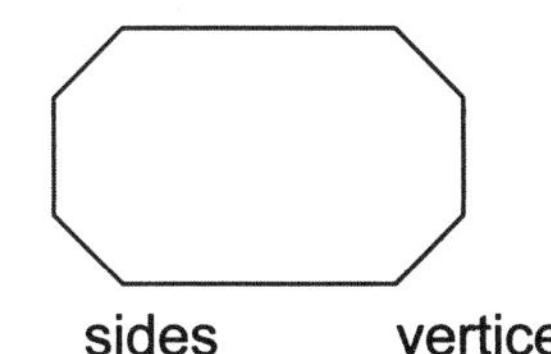 ____ sides ____ vertices

i) 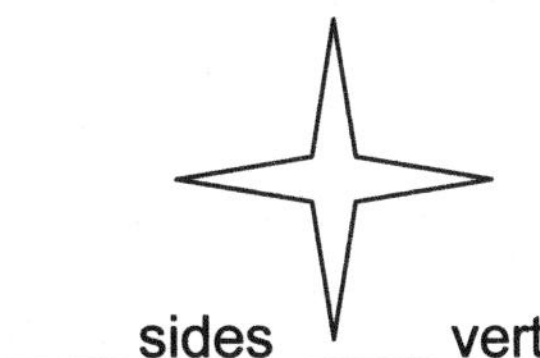 ____ sides ____ vertices

j) 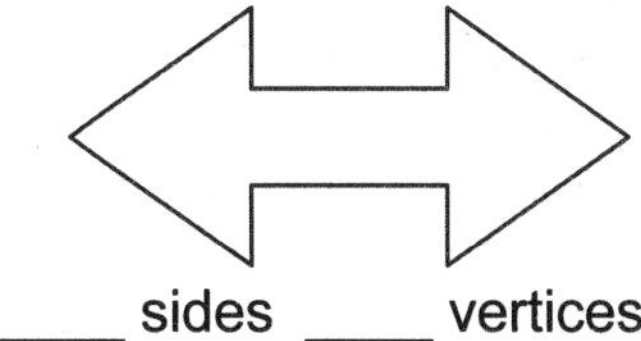 ____ sides ____ vertices

2. Helen names the shapes according to how many sides they have. Write the number of sides for each shape.

a) ___ sides **triangle**

b) ___ sides **quadrilateral**

c) ___ sides **pentagon**

d) ___ sides **hexagon**

3. Complete the chart. Find as many shapes as you can for each shape name.

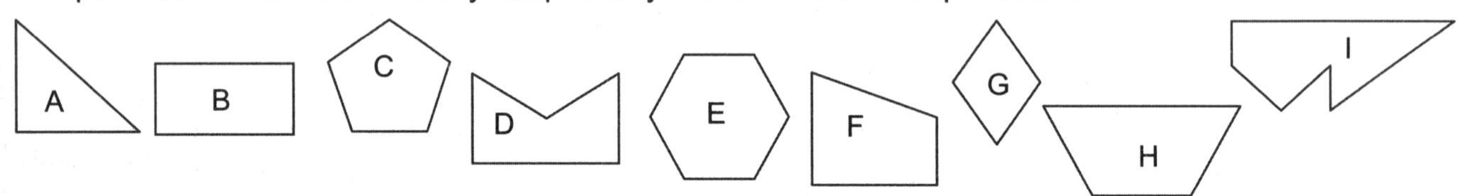


| Shapes | Letters |
|---|---|
| triangles | |
| quadrilaterals | |

| Shapes | Letters |
|---|---|
| pentagons | |
| hexagons | |

4. Using a ruler, draw a polygon with . . .
   a) 3 sides
   b) 4 sides

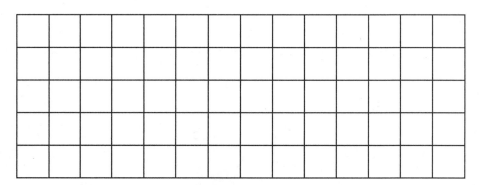

5. The following figures have both straight and curved sides. Fill in the missing numbers.

a) _____ vertices
_____ curved sides
_____ straight sides

b) _____ vertices
_____ curved sides
_____ straight sides

BONUS:

6. On grid paper, draw a polygon with . . . a) 5 sides b) 6 sides
   Can you draw a polygon in which the number of sides does not equal the number of vertices?

7. How many sides do 2 quadrilaterals and 3 pentagons have altogether? How did you find your answer? (Did you use a calculation? a picture? a model?)

# G4-2: Introduction to Angles

An **angle** is formed when two lines cross:

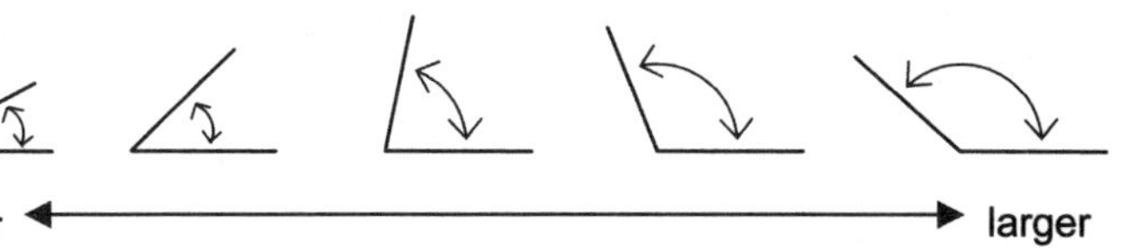


The lines that form an angle are called "arms" and the point where the two lines cross (that is, the point where the angle is formed) is called the "vertex."

When you talk about the **size** of an angle, you are actually talking about the space between the lines.

smaller ← → larger

**RIGHT ANGLES**

Right angles are a special type of angle—they are found in many important places, including the corners of squares, rectangles, and some triangles:

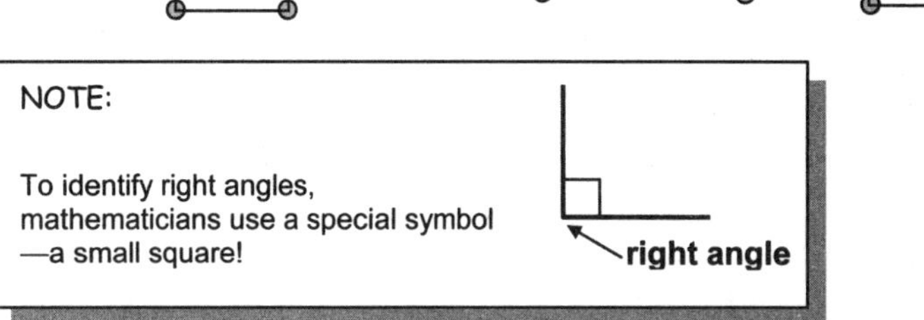


You can always check for right angles using the corner of a piece of paper:

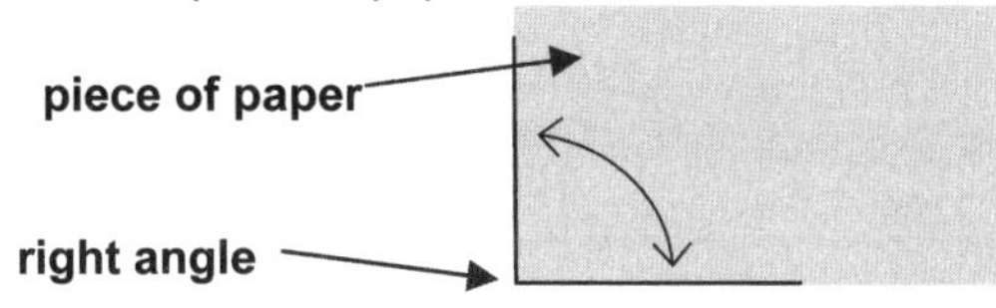


NOTE:

To identify right angles, mathematicians use a special symbol —a small square!

right angle

---

1. Mark each angle as (i) a **right angle**; (ii) **less than** a right angle; OR (iii) **greater than** a right angle. Check your answers with the corner of a piece of paper.

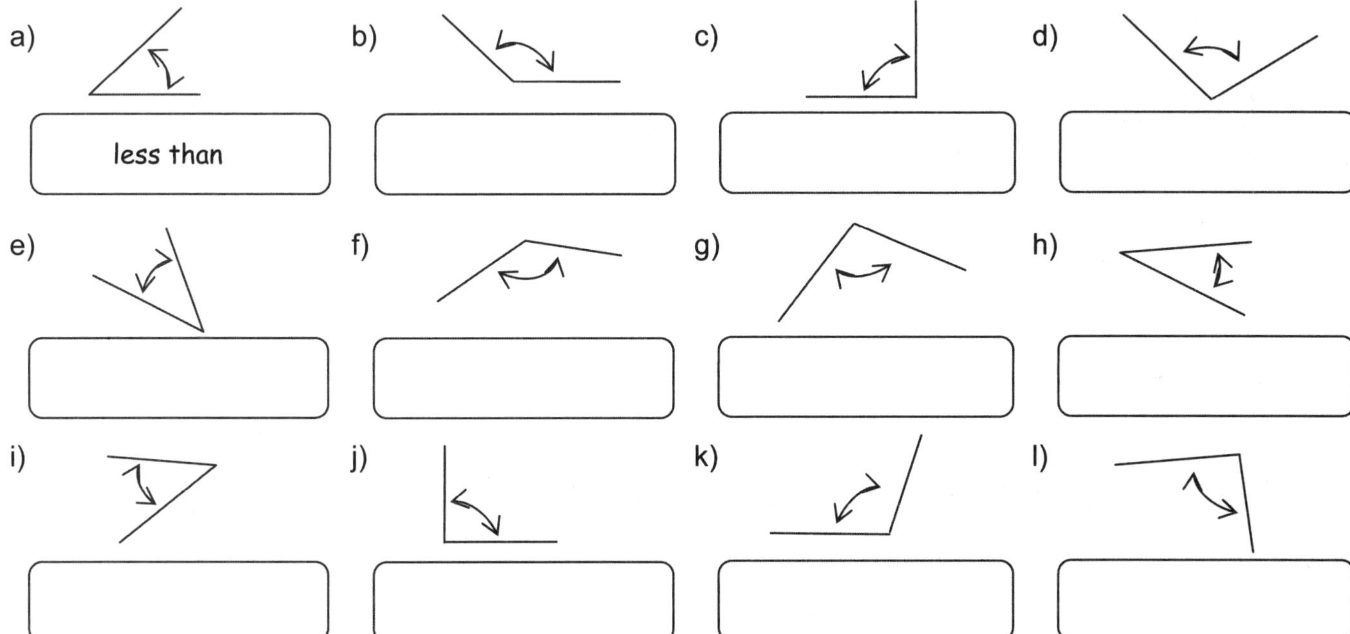


2. Using a pair of pencils, make an angle that is a) a little less than a right angle, and b) a little more than a right angle. Sketch your angles on a separate piece of paper.

3. Mark the angles that are **right angles** with a small square. (You can check with the corner of a piece of paper.) Cross out the angles that are not right angles.

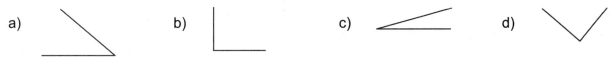

 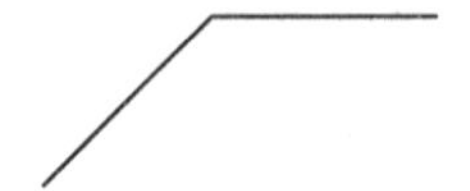 f)  g) 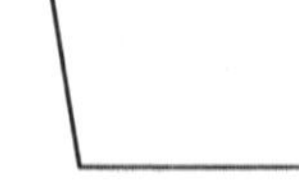 h) 

4. Draw two **different** right angles, marking them properly with a small square (see the NOTE on the previous page for details).

**Right angle #1** **Right angle #2**

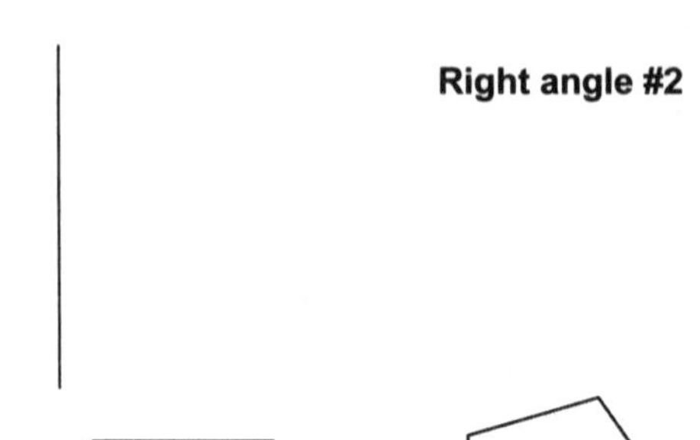

5. Circle the figure that has no right angles. 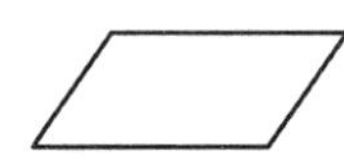 

6. Mark (with a small square) the right angle in each figure.

a) 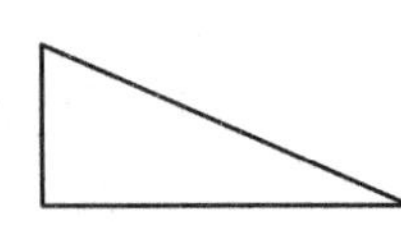 b) 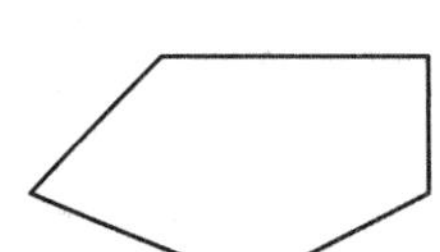 c)  d) 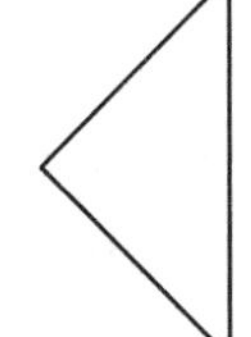

7. Mark (with a small square) all the right angles in the following figures. Then circle the figures that have **two** right angles.

 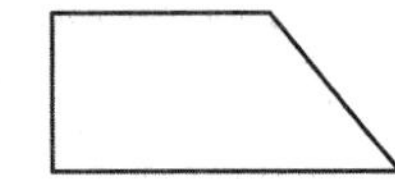 b) 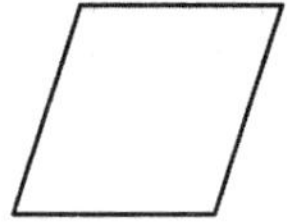 c) 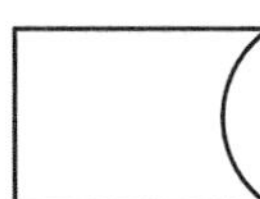

d)  e) 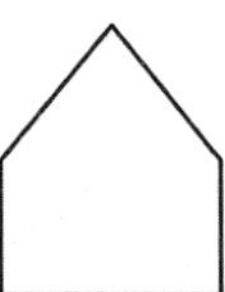 f) 

Show your work for the following questions on a separate piece of paper:

8. Many letters of the alphabet have **right** angles: The letter “T” has 2 right angles.
   a) Draw at least 5 letters with right angles. Mark all the right angles.
   b) Which letter of the alphabet do you think has the most right angles?

9. Angles that are less than a right angle are called **acute** angles. Many letters of the alphabet have **acute** angles: The letter “N” has 2 acute angles.
   a) Draw at least 5 letters with acute angles. Mark all the acute angles with dots.
   b) Can you find a letter that has both a right angle and an acute angle?

10. Angles that are greater than a right angle are called **obtuse** angles: The letter “A” has 2 obtuse angles. Draw an “A” and mark the obtuse angles.

# G4-3: Measuring Angles



To measure an angle, you use a **protractor**. A protractor has 180 subdivisions around its circumference. The subdivisions are called degrees. 45° is short form for "forty-five degrees."

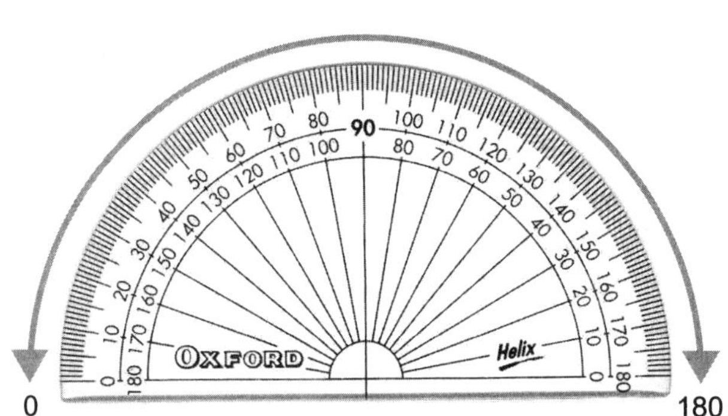


There are 180 subdivisions (180°) around the outside of a protractor.

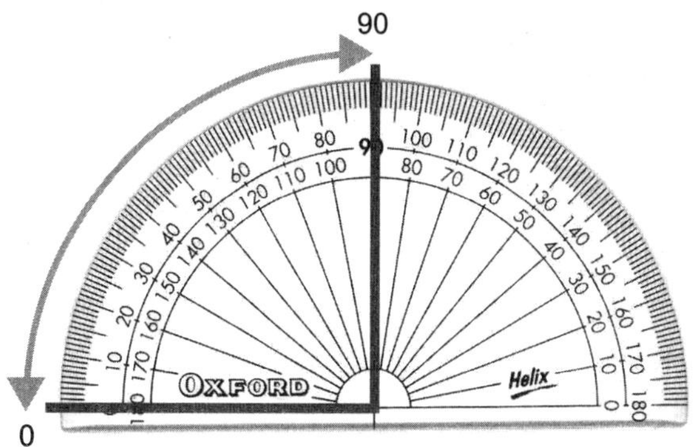


There are 90° in a right angle (or a square corner).

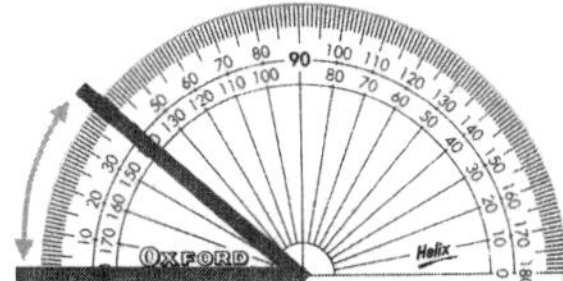
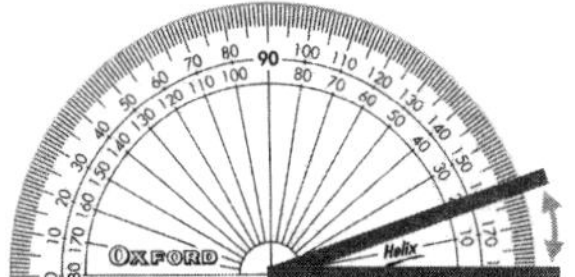

An angle can be less than 90° . . .

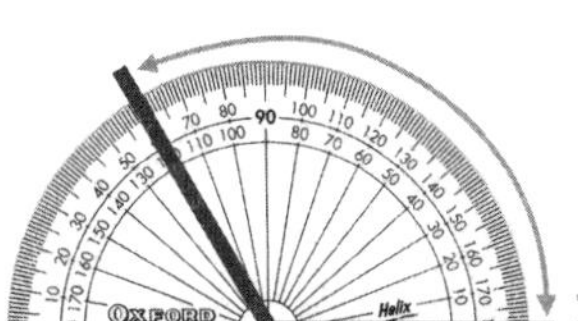
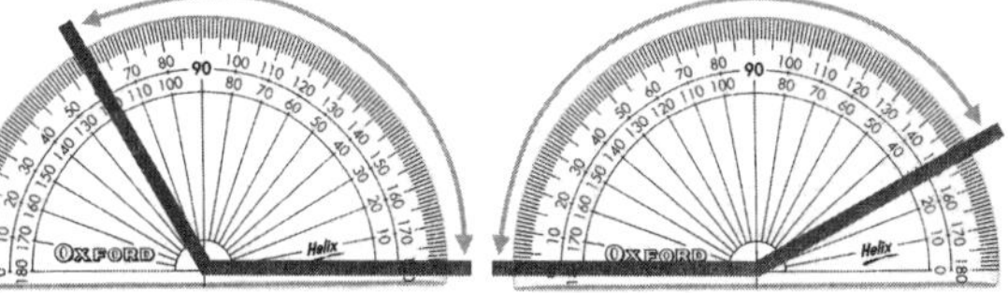

. . . or more than 90°.

---

1. Without using a protractor, identify each angle as "less than 90°" or "more than 90°."

m) 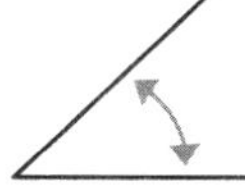

_______________

n) 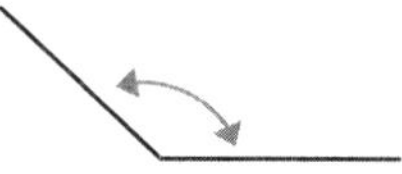

_______________

o) 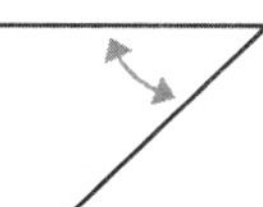

_______________

p) 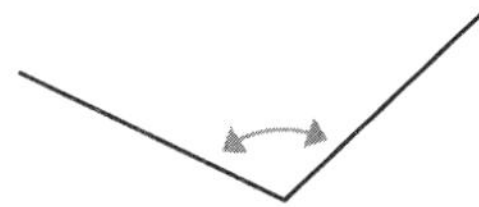

_______________

q) 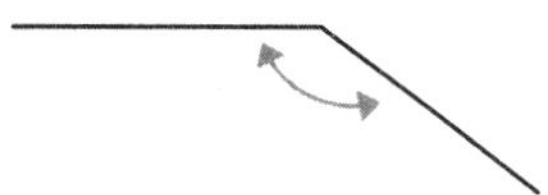

_______________

r) 

_______________

s) 

_______________

t) 

_______________

u) 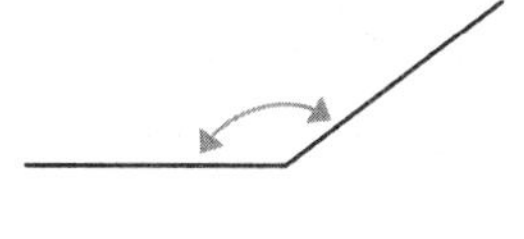

_______________

**A protractor has two scales.** These exercises will help you decide which scale to use.

2. Identify the angle as "less than 90°" or "more than 90°." Circle the **two** numbers that the arm of the angle passes through. Pick the correct measure of the angle (that is, if you said the angle is "less than 90°," pick the number that is less than 90). The first one is done for you.

a)

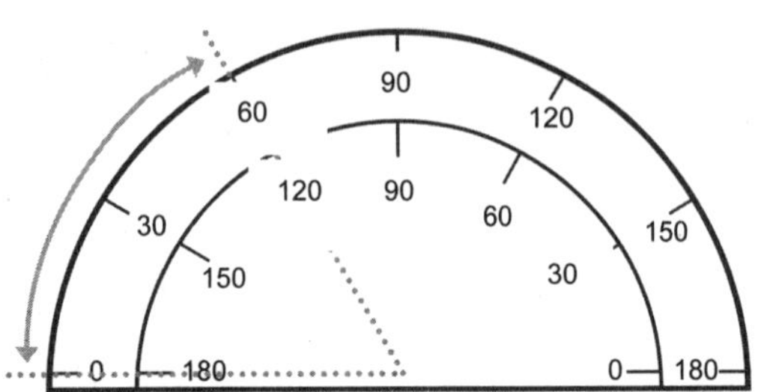


The angle is: less than 90°

The angle is: 60°

b)

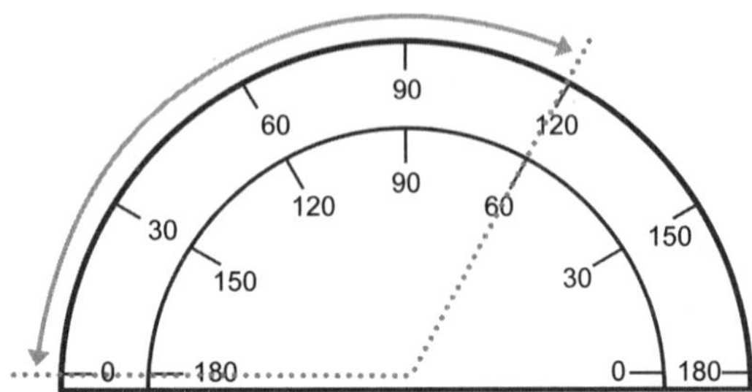


The angle is: ____________________

The angle is: __________

c)

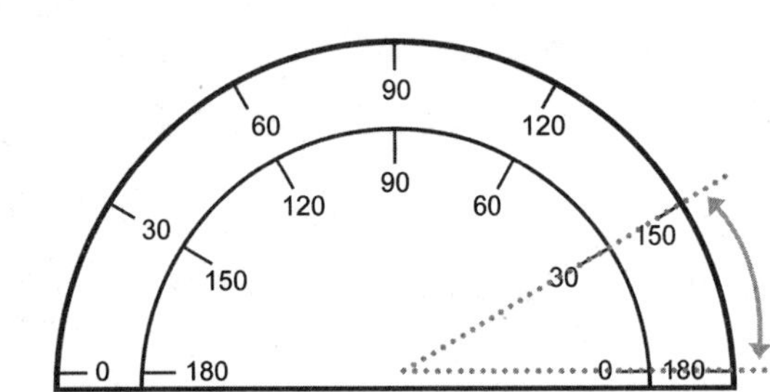


The angle is: ____________________

The angle is: __________

d)

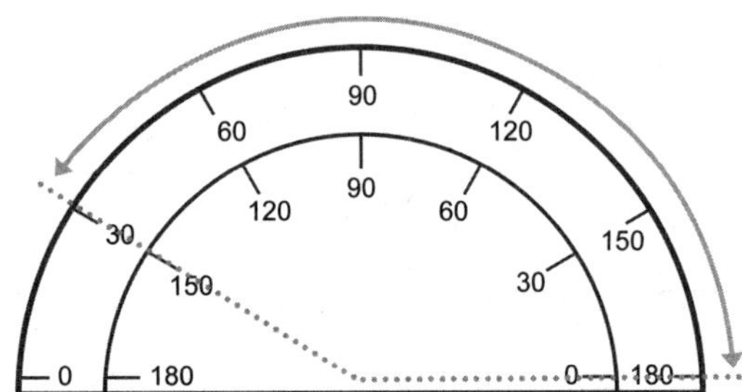


The angle is: ____________________

The angle is: __________

3. Identify the angle as "less than 90°" or "more than 90°." Circle the **two** numbers that the arm of the angle passes through. Pick the correct measure of the angle (that is, if you said the angle is "less than 90°," pick the number that is less than 90).

a)

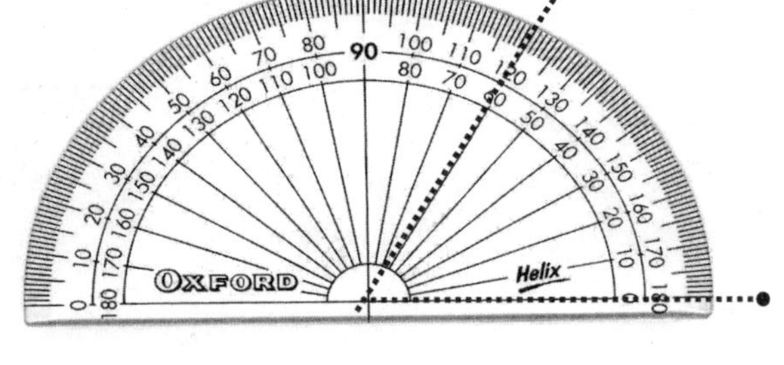


____________________

b)

____________________

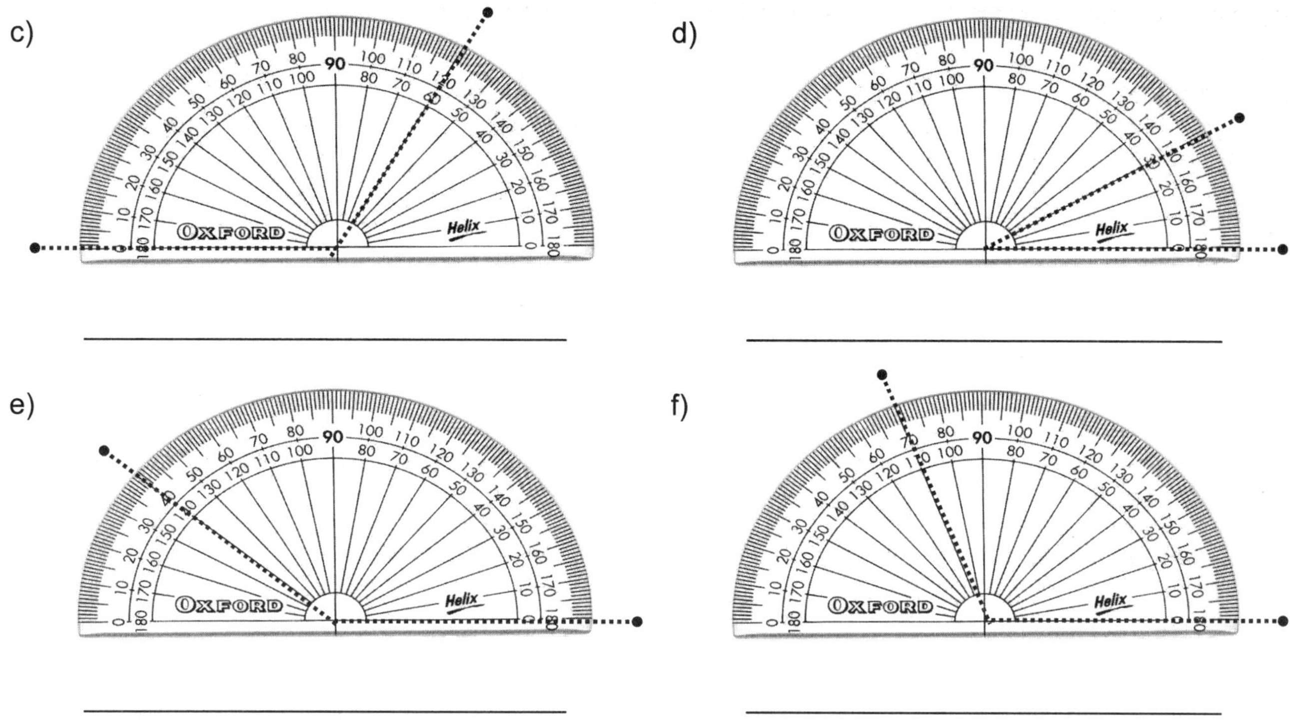

c) d) e) f)

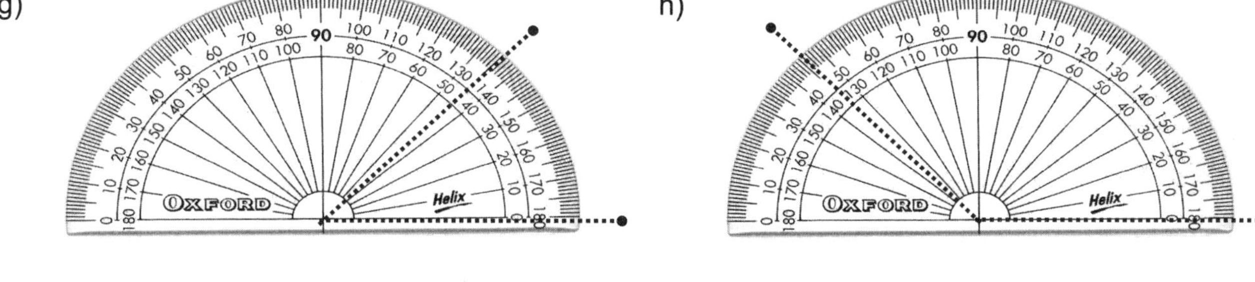

g) h)

4. Measure the angles using a protractor, and write your answers in the boxes.

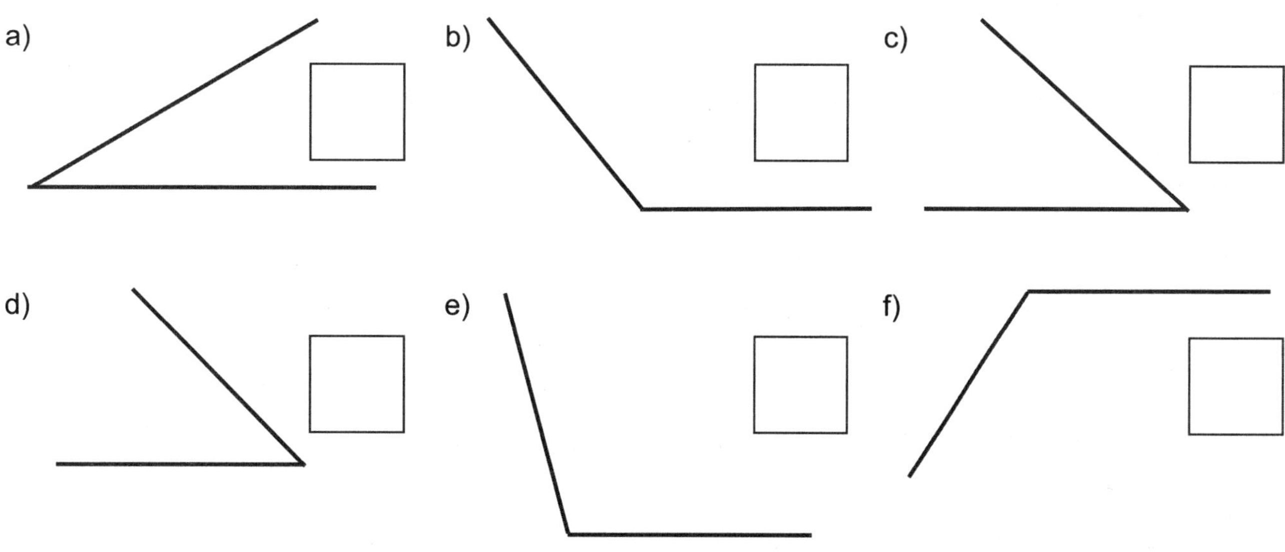

a) b) c) d) e) f)

# G4-3: Measuring Angles *(continued)*

5. Draw 5 angles on grid paper and use a protractor to measure the angles.

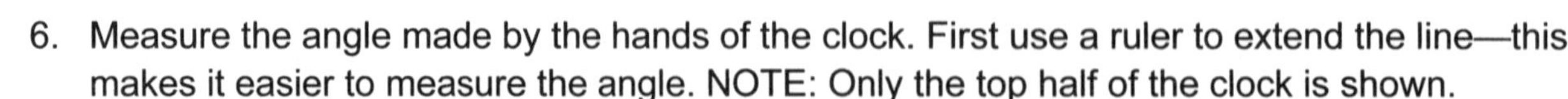

6. Measure the angle made by the hands of the clock. First use a ruler to extend the line—this makes it easier to measure the angle. NOTE: Only the top half of the clock is shown.

a)

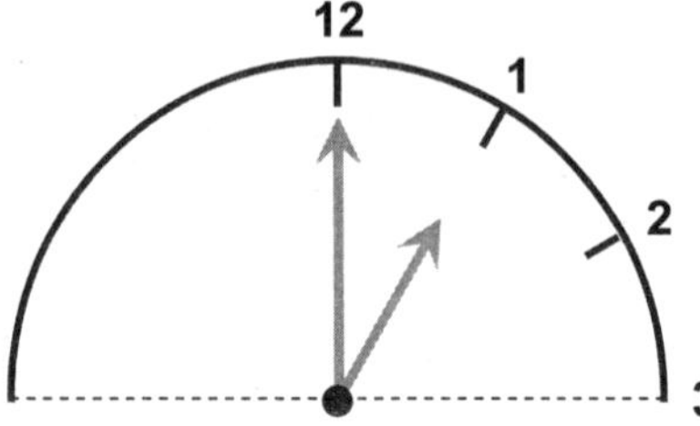


b)

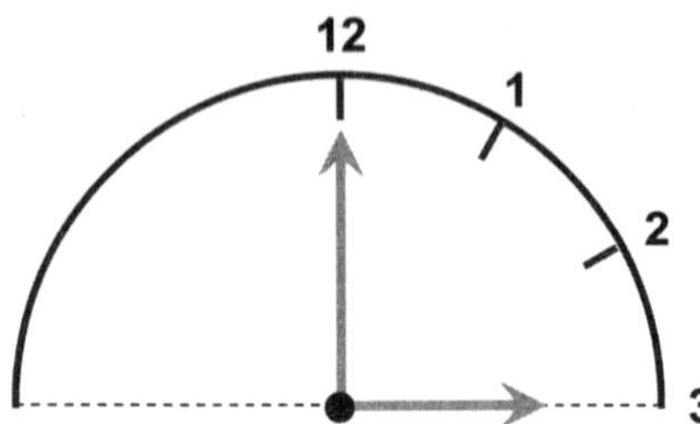


7. In question 6, you found the angle between the hands of the clock at 1 o'clock. How can you use this information to find the angle between the hands of the clock at 2 o'clock? Explain on a separate piece of paper.

8. Find the angles made by the hands of the clock at the following times . . . without measuring! Explain your answers on a separate piece of paper.

a) b)

c)

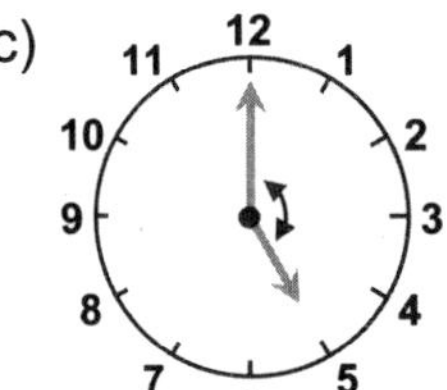

d) e)

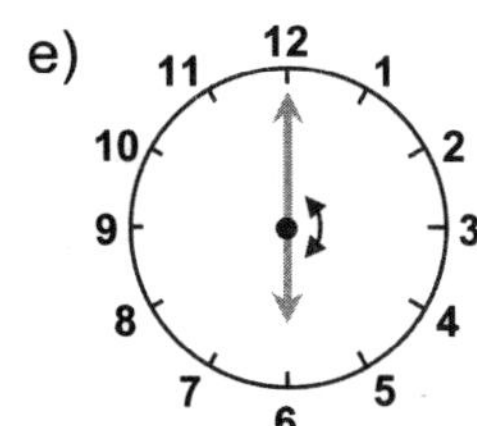

Clare makes a 60° angle as follows:

Step 1:
She draws a base line and places the protractor on the base line as shown.

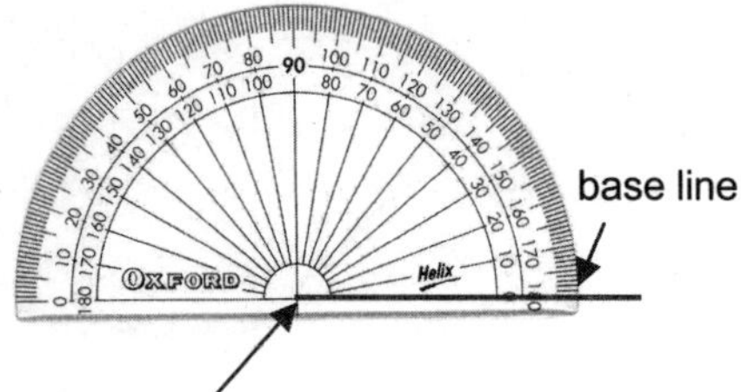


She lines up the centre cross on the protractor with the end of the base line.

Step 2:
She makes a mark at 60°.

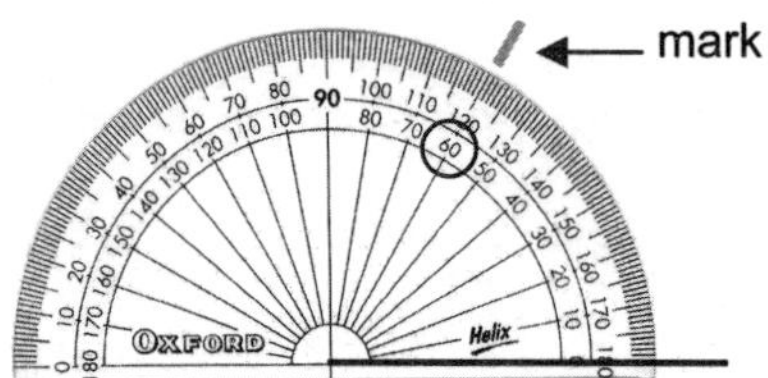


Step 3:
Using a ruler, she joins the end point of the base line to her mark.

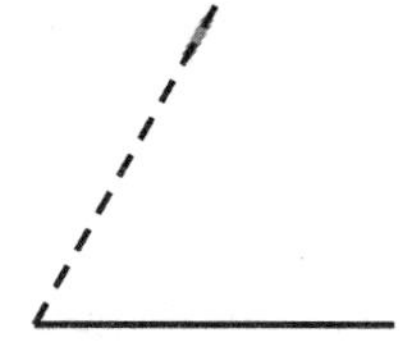

9. On a separate piece of paper, use a protractor to construct the following angles:

a) 60° b) 40° c) 50° d) 20° e) 45°

f) 90° g) 120° h) 75° i) 115° j) 150°

# G4-4: Parallel Lines

**Parallel lines** are like railway tracks (on a straight section of track); that is, they are . . .

- ✓ straight
- ✓ always the same distance apart

No matter how long they are, parallel lines will **never** meet.

NOTE: Lines of different lengths can still be parallel (as long as they are both straight and are always the same distance apart).

NOTE:

Mathematicians use arrows to indicate that certain lines are parallel:

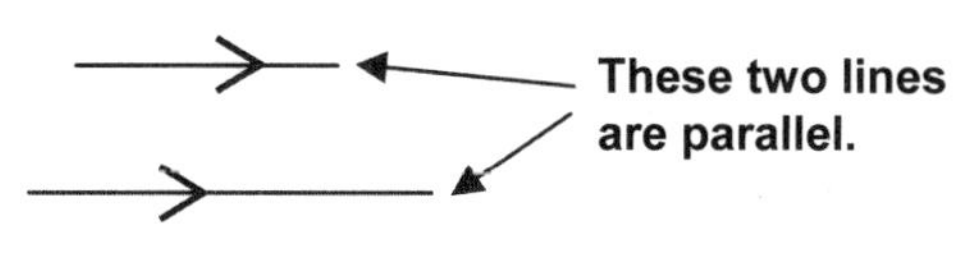
These two lines
are parallel.

1. Mark any pairs of lines that are parallel with arrows.

a) 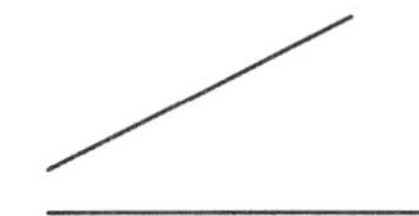

b) 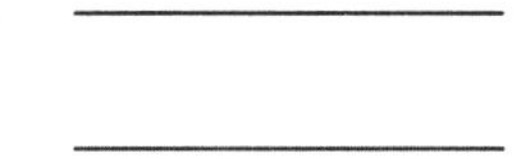

c) 

d) 

e) 

f) 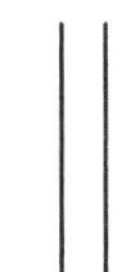

g) 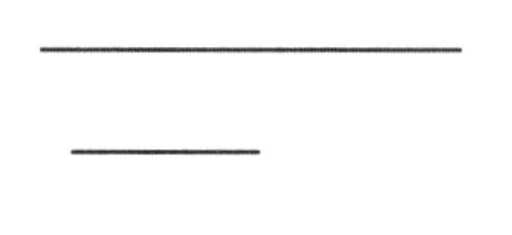

h)

BONUS:
Select one of the pairs of lines that **are not** parallel. Write the corresponding letter. 

How do you know these lines are not parallel? Give as many reasons as you can.

2. Draw a second line—parallel to the first—beside each of the lines below. Be sure to use a ruler!

a) 

b) 

BONUS:
Use a ruler to draw a second line. This time, however, make the second line parallel to the first line **and** the same length.

3. The following pairs of lines are parallel. In each case, join the dots to make a quadrilateral. The first one is done for you.

a) 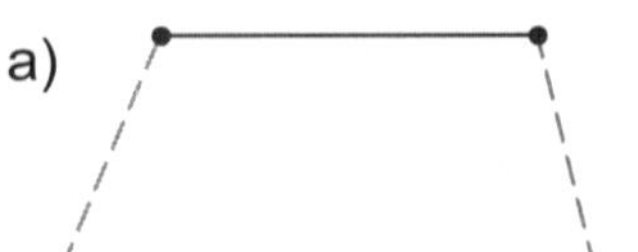 b) c) d)

In each case, are the original two lines still parallel? ________

4. Each of the shapes below has **one pair** of parallel sides. Put an "X" through the sides that are **NOT parallel**. The first one is done for you.

a) 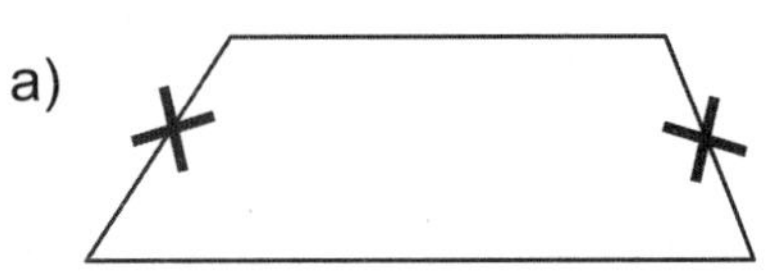

b) 

c) 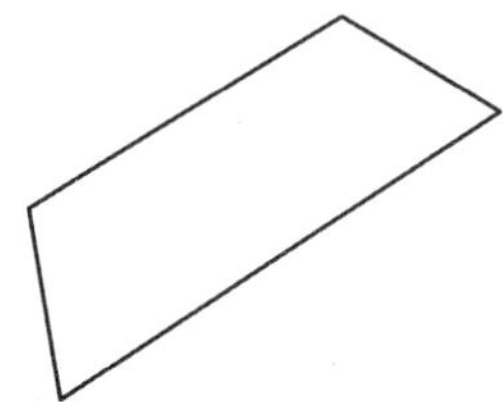

d) 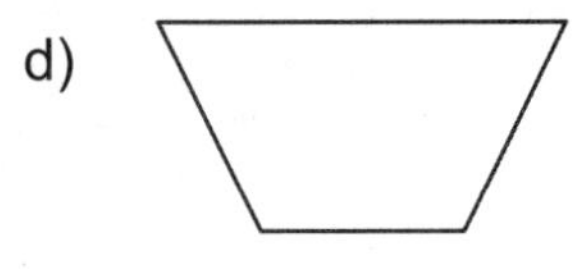

e) 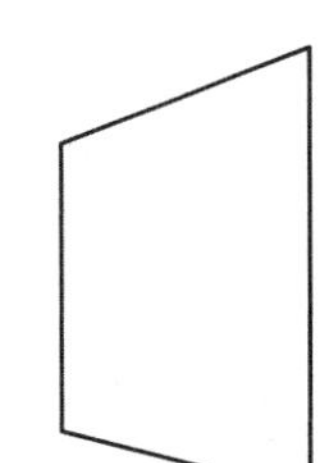

f) 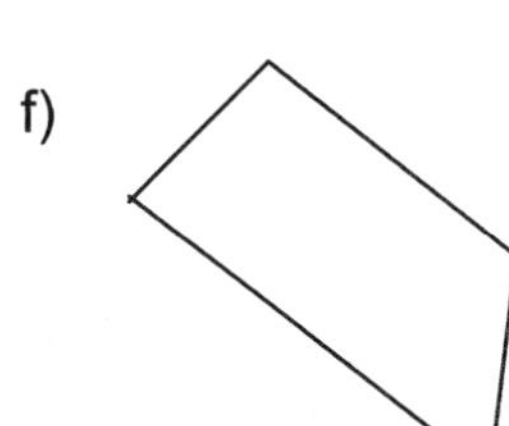

g) 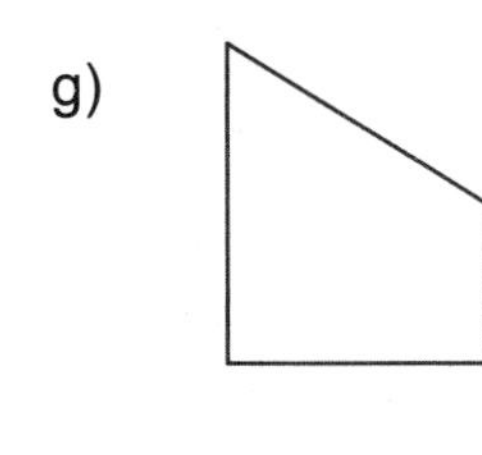

NOTE:

If a figure contains **more than a single pair** of parallel lines, you can avoid confusion by using a different number of arrows on each pair.

Example: 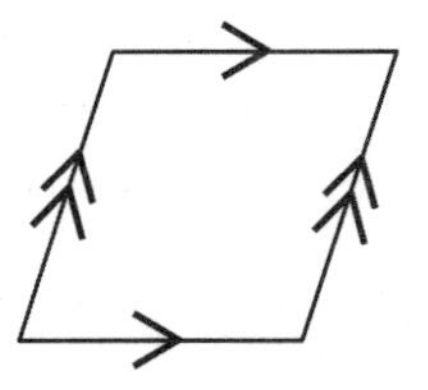

5. Using arrows, mark all the pairs of parallel lines in the figures.

a) 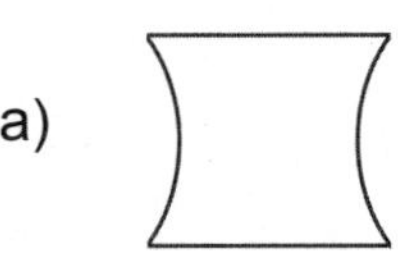

____ pairs

b) 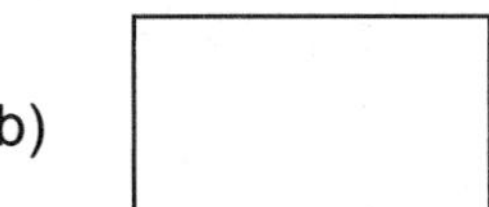

____ pairs

c) 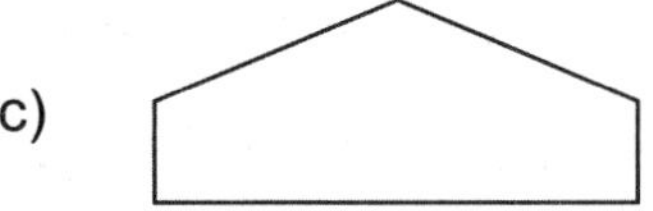

____ pairs

d) 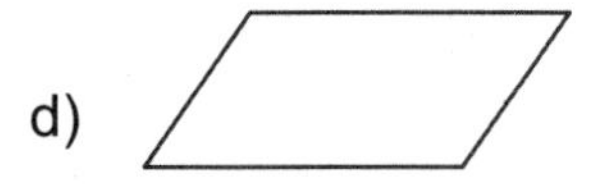

____ pairs

6. Find a picture in a magazine or newspaper that has a pair of parallel lines. Mark the lines with a coloured pencil.

# G4-5: Quadrilaterals

A polygon with four sides is called a **quadrilateral**.

Example:

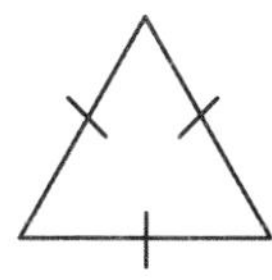

3 sides
NOT a quadrilateral

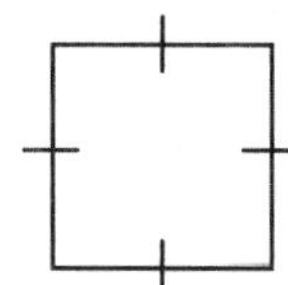

4 sides
**quadrilateral**

4 sides
**quadrilateral**

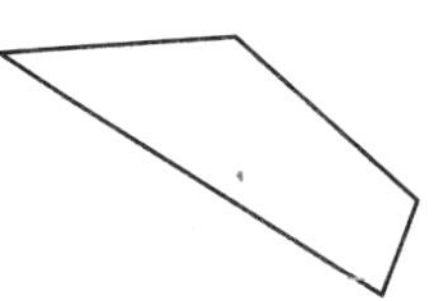

4 sides
**quadrilateral**

---

1. Based on the properties of the following figures, fill in the chart.

A

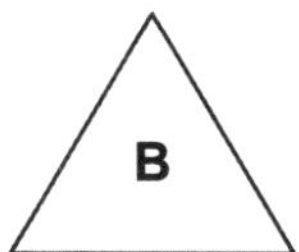


C

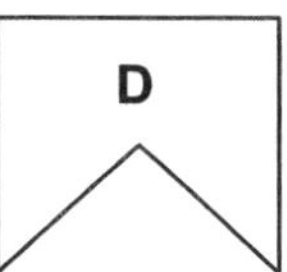

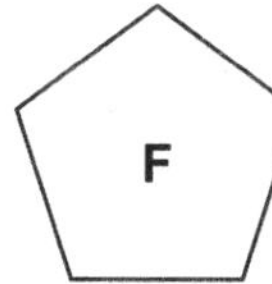


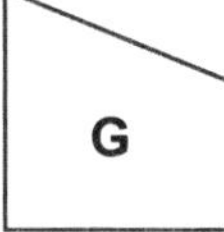


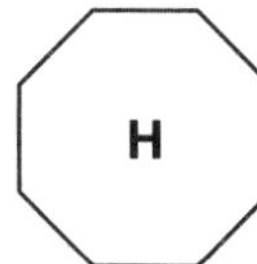


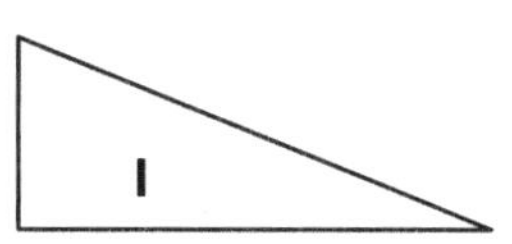


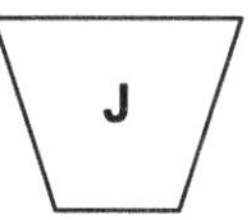


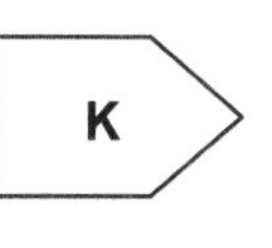

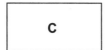

| Property | Shape with property |
|---|---|
| quadrilateral | |
| non-quadrilateral | |

2.

B

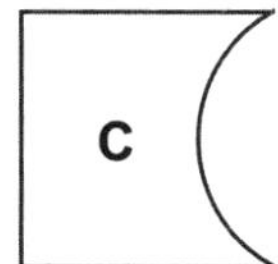


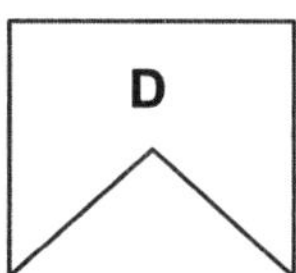


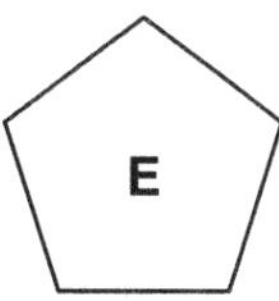


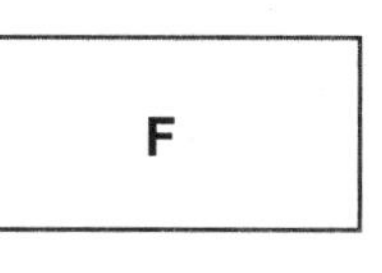


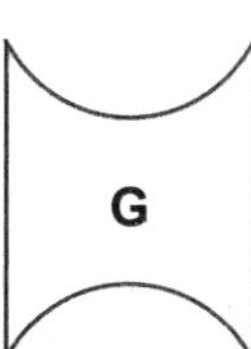


a) Which shapes are polygons? REMEMBER: A polygon has straight sides.

b) Which shapes have sides that are all the same length? (Check with a ruler.)

c) Which shapes have at least one curved side?

d) What do shapes D and E have in common?

e) What do shapes B, C, F, and G have in common?

f) Which shape does not belong in this group: A, B, C, and G?

g) Pick your own group of shapes and say what they have in common.

# G4-6: Properties of Shapes

Some quadrilaterals have no pairs of parallel lines. Some have one pair of parallel lines. Parallelograms have TWO pairs of parallel lines:

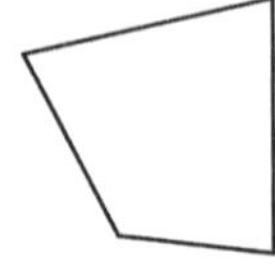

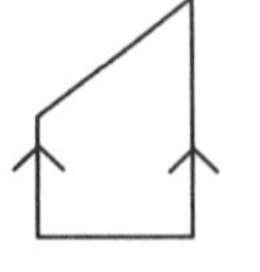

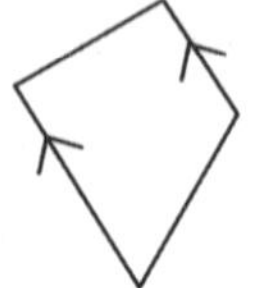

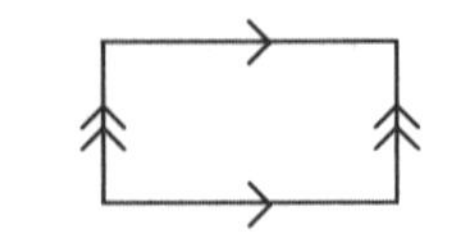

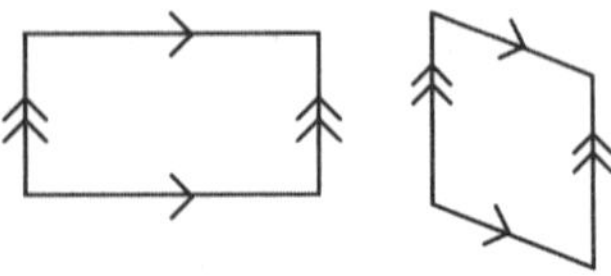

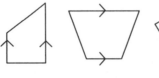

**NO** pairs of parallel lines | **ONE** pair of parallel lines | **TWO** pairs of parallel lines

---

1. For each of the shapes, mark the parallel lines with arrows. Mark any pairs of sides that are not parallel with "X"s. Under each quadrilateral, write how many **pairs** of edges are parallel.

A ________

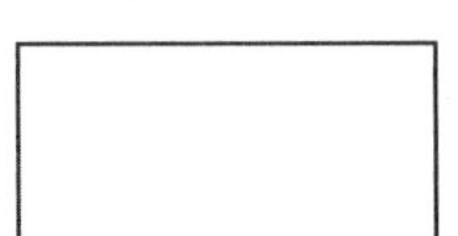

B

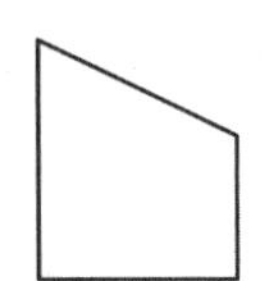

C ________

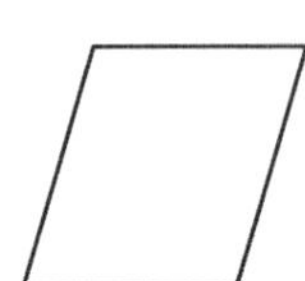

D ________

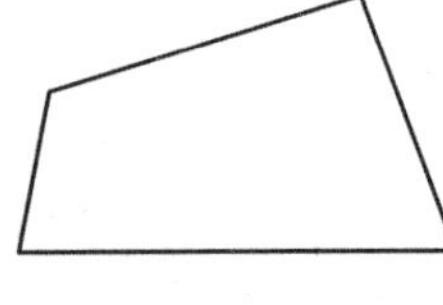

E ________

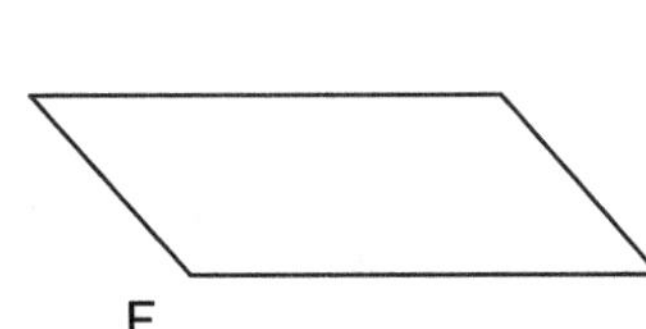

F

G ________

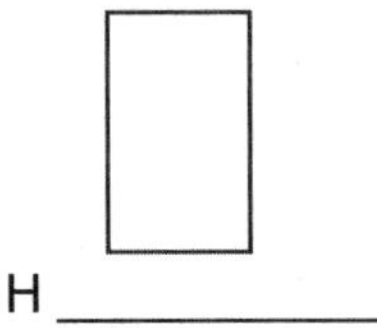

H ________

2. Sort the shapes A through H into the chart by writing the letter in the correct column.

| No pairs of parallel sides | One pair of parallel sides | Two pairs of parallel sides |
|---|---|---|
| | | |

3. Using the figures below, complete the two charts. Start by marking the right angles and parallel lines in each figure.

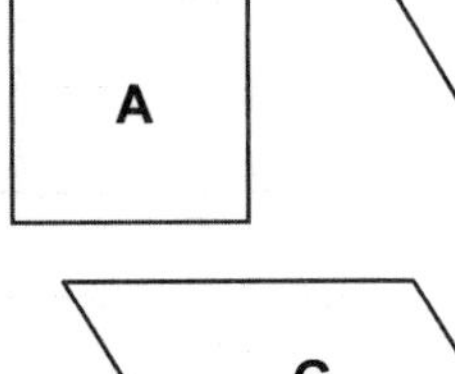


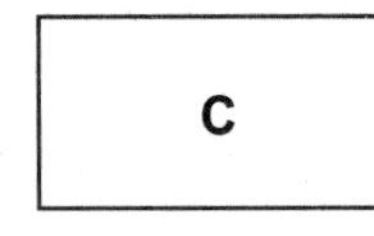


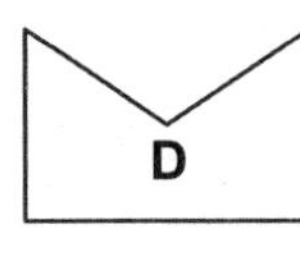


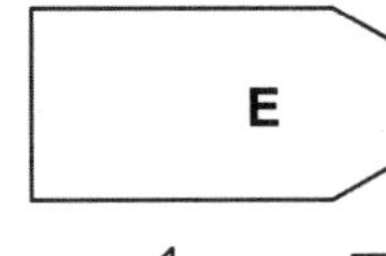

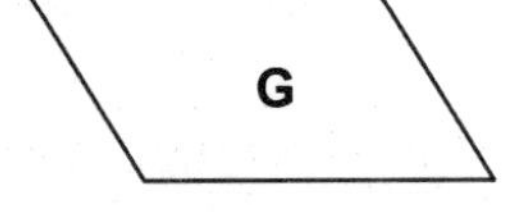


H

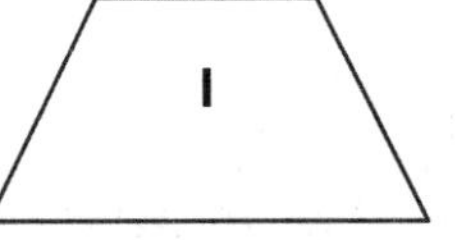


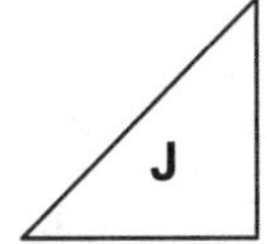


K

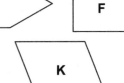

a)

| Property | Shapes with property |
|---|---|
| no right angles | |
| 1 right angle | |
| 2 right angles | |
| 4 right angles | |

b)

| Property | Shapes with property |
|---|---|
| no parallel lines | |
| 1 pair | |
| 2 pairs | |

NOTE: A shape with all sides the same length is called **equilateral**. ("Equi" comes from a Latin word meaning "equal" and "lateral" means "sides.")

4. Using your ruler, measure the sides of the shapes. Circle those that are equilateral.

a)

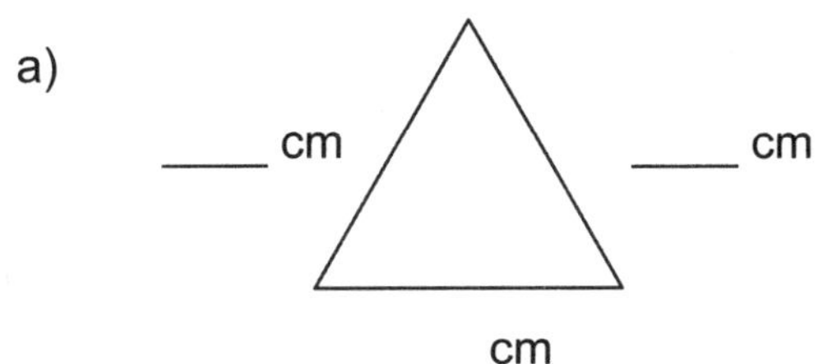


b)

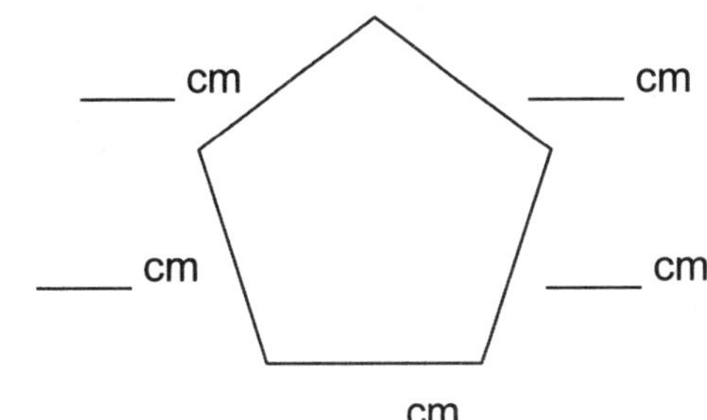


c)

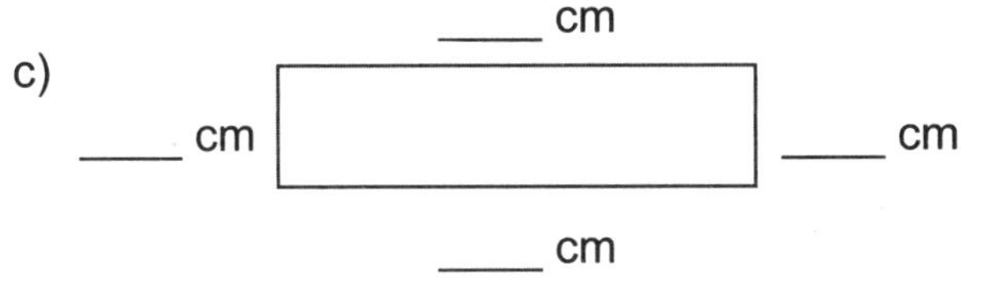


d)

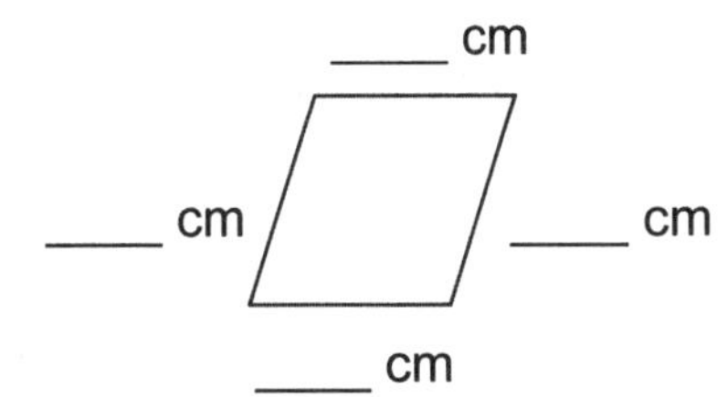


5. Complete the charts. Use shapes A to J for each chart. Start by marking the right angles and parallel lines in each figure. If you are not sure if a figure is equilateral, measure its sides with a ruler.

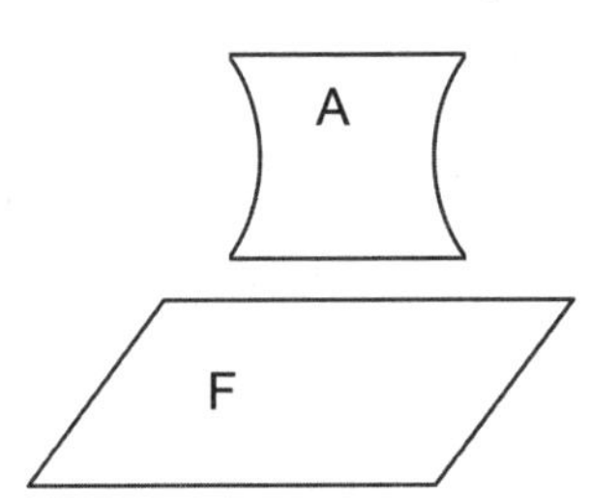


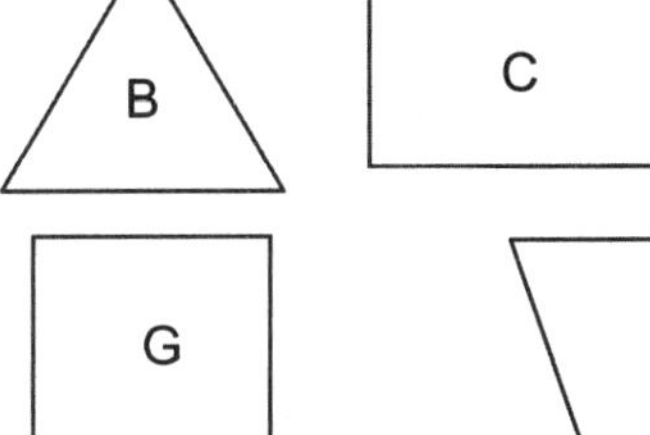


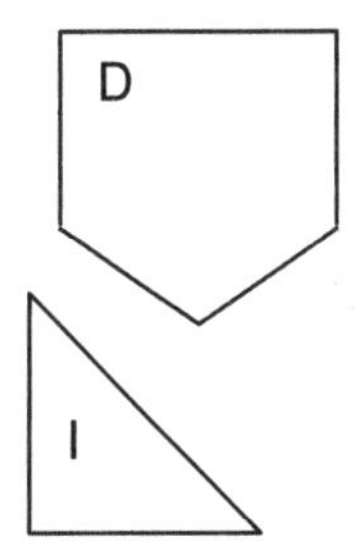


E

H

J

a)

| Property | Shapes with property |
|---|---|
| equilateral | |
| not equilateral | |

b)

| Property | Shapes with property |
|---|---|
| no right angle | |
| 1 right angle | |
| 2 right angles | |
| 4 right angles | |

c)

| Property | Shapes with property |
|---|---|
| no parallel sides | |
| 1 pair of parallel sides | |
| 2 pairs of parallel sides | |
| 3 pairs of parallel sides | |

d)

| Shape name | Shapes with property |
|---|---|
| triangle | |
| quadrilateral | |
| pentagon | |
| hexagon | |

# G4-7: Special Quadrilaterals

A **quadrilateral** (shape with 4 sides) with two pairs of parallel sides is called a **parallelogram**.

**Parallelogram**:
A quadrilateral with two pairs of parallel sides.

Some quadrilaterals have special names:

**rhombus**
a parallelogram with 4 equal sides

**rectangle**
a parallelogram with 4 right-angles

**square**
a parallelogram with 4 right-angles and 4 equal sides

**trapezoid**
a quadrilateral with only one pair of parallel sides

1. a) Mark the angles that are right angles in the quadrilaterals.
   b) Measure the length of each side with a ruler and write it onto the pictures. Use this to help you decide on the best (or most specific) name for each quadrilateral.

____ cm

____ cm ____ cm

____ cm

____ cm

____ cm ____ cm

____ cm

Name: ______________________ Name: ______________________

2. Match the name of the quadrilateral to the best description.

| | |
|---|---|
| square | a parallelogram with 4 right angles |
| rectangle | a parallelogram with 4 equal sides |
| rhombus | a parallelogram with 4 right angles and 4 equal sides |

3. Name the shapes. (HINT: Use the words "rhombus," "square," "parallelogram," and "rectangle.")

______________ ______________ ______________ ______________

Answer the following questions on a separate piece of paper.

4. Describe any similarities or differences between a . . .
   a) rhombus and a parallelogram b) rhombus and a square c) trapezoid and a parallelogram

5. a) Why is a square a rectangle? b) Why is a rectangle not a square?
   c) Why is a trapezoid not a parallelogram?

# G4-7: Special Quadrilaterals *(continued)*

6. Mark all the right angles in each quadrilateral. Then identify each quadrilateral as a square, a rectangle, a parallelogram, or a rhombus.

 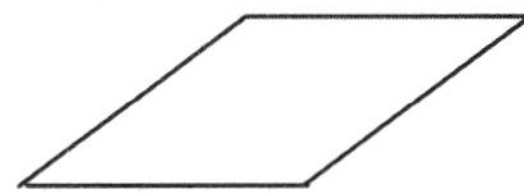  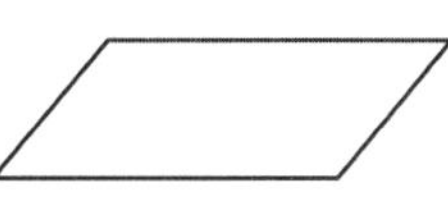

______________ ______________ ______________ ______________

7. For each quadrilateral, say how many **pairs** of sides are parallel. Then identify each quadrilateral as a square, a rectangle, a parallelogram, or a trapezoid.

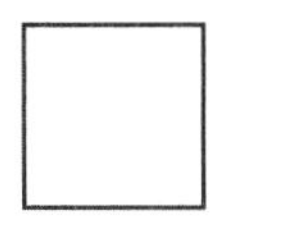  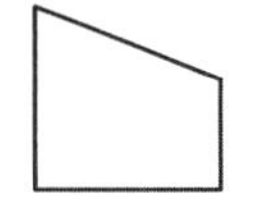 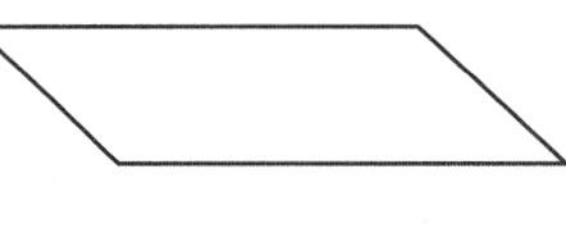

__________ __________ __________ __________

__________ __________ __________ __________

8. 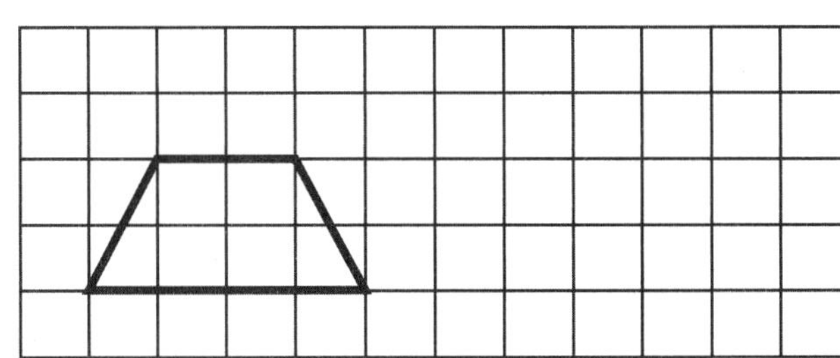

The shape on the grid is a trapezoid.

a) On the grid, draw a second trapezoid that has 2 right angles. Mark the right angles.

b) On a separate piece of paper, say how you know both shapes are trapezoids.

9. Use the words "all," "some," or "no" for each statement.

a) __________ squares are rectangles

b) __________ trapezoids are parallelograms

c) __________ parallelograms are trapezoids

d) __________ parallelograms are rectangles

Answer the remaining questions on a separate piece of paper:

10. If a shape has 4 right angles, which two special quadrilaterals might it be?

11. If a quadrilateral has all equal sides, which two special quadrilaterals might it be?

12. Write 3 different names for a square.

13. On grid paper draw a quadrilateral with . . .
    a) no right angles
    b) one right angle
    c) two right angles

14. On grid paper draw a quadrilateral with . . .
    a) no parallel sides
    b) one pair of parallel sides
    c) two pairs of parallel sides and no right angles
    d) 4 right angles and 2 pairs of equal sides

15. a) I have 4 equal sides, but no right angles. What am I?
    b) I have 4 right angles, but my sides are not all equal. What am I?
    BONUS: c) I have exactly 2 right angles. Which special quadrilateral **must** I be?

# G4-8: Tangrams

PARENT:
Your child will need a copy of page xxi: Tangram from the Introduction. Your child may need your help cutting out the shapes. (It is important that the shapes be cut out accurately.)

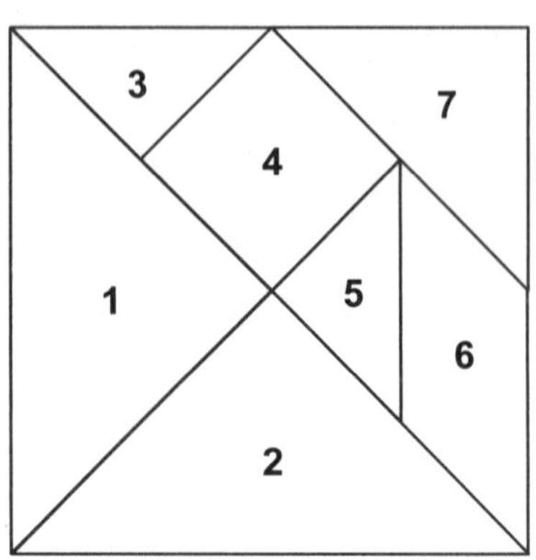


A **tangram** is an ancient Chinese puzzle. The tangram is a square cut into seven pieces called tans.

1. Which tans are quadrilaterals? ______________

2. Which tans are triangles? ______________

   Which are the same size and shape? ______________ ______________

3. Which tans are parallelograms? ______________ Explain how you know on a separate piece of paper.

4. 3 5 The figure shows how to make a square using tans 3 and 5. On a separate piece of paper, show how to make a square using . . .

   a) tans 1 and 2 b) tans 3, 5, and 7

   NOTE: Trace around your tans to show how you made each figure.

5. 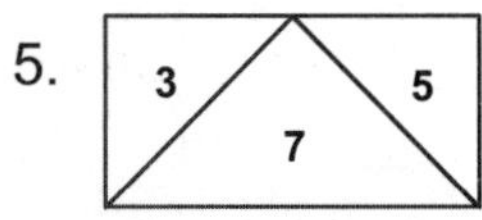


   The figure shows how to make a rectangle using tans 3, 5, and 7. On a separate piece of paper, show how to make rectangles using . . .

   a) tans 3, 4, and 5 b) tans 1, 2, 3, 5, and 7 c) tans 1, 3, 5, 6, and 7

6. Show how to make a parallelogram that is not a square using . . .

   a) tans 3 and 5 b) tans 1 and 2 c) tans 3, 5, and 6

7. Show different ways to make a trapezoid. How many ways can you find? Pick one of your shapes and explain how you knew it was a trapezoid.

8. Make a pentagon from tans 3, 4, 5, and 7.

9. Predict the shapes you can make using the tans listed in the chart (look for triangles, quadrilaterals, pentagons, hexagons, trapezoids, and parallelograms).

| Tan pieces | Predicted shapes possible | Shapes made |
|---|---|---|
| 5, 6 | | |
| 3, 5, 6 | | |
| 3, 5, 6, 7 | | |

# G4-9: Congruency



Shapes are **congruent** if they are **the same size and shape**. Congruent shapes can be different colours and shades. These pairs of shapes are congruent:

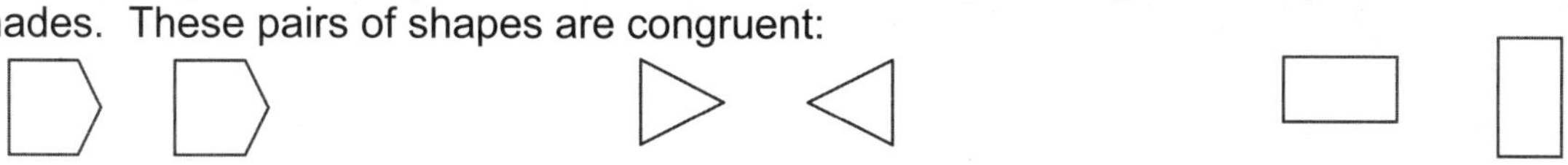

1. Write **congruent** or **not congruent** under each pair of shapes.

a) 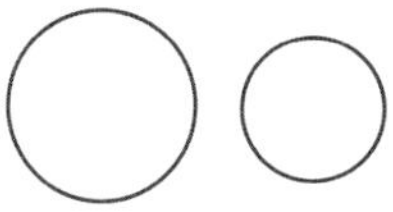 not congruent

b) ______________

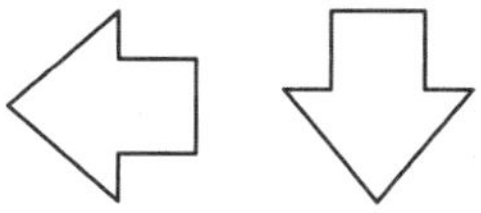

c) ______________

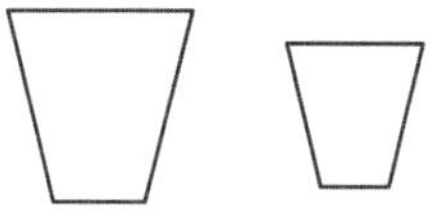

2. Circle the pairs of shapes that are congruent.

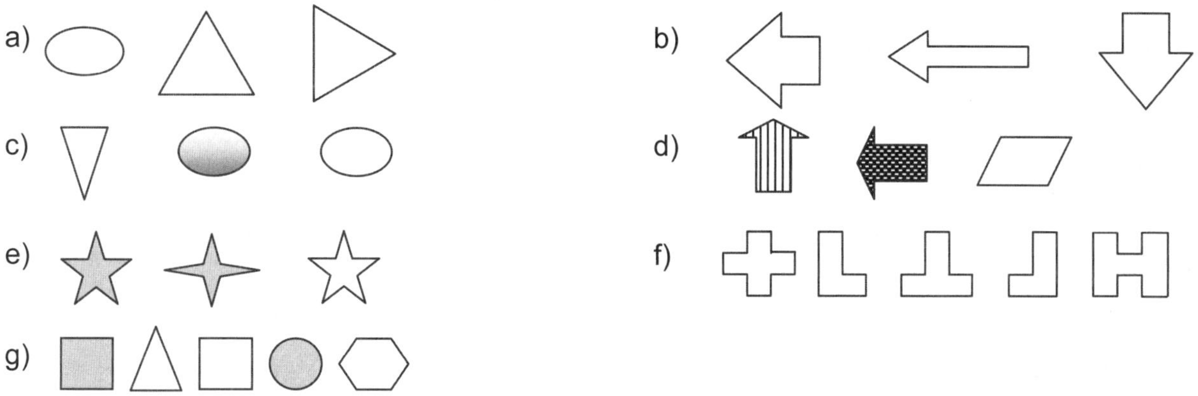

a)

b)

c)

d)

e)

f)

g)

3. Two pairs of shapes are congruent. Show which pairs of shapes are congruent by writing the same letters in each pair. (HINT: You will need the letters A and B.)

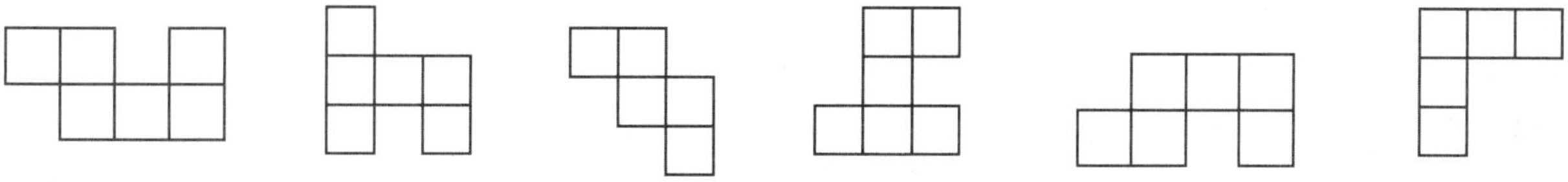

4. Shade regions in the right-hand grid to make the two figures congruent.

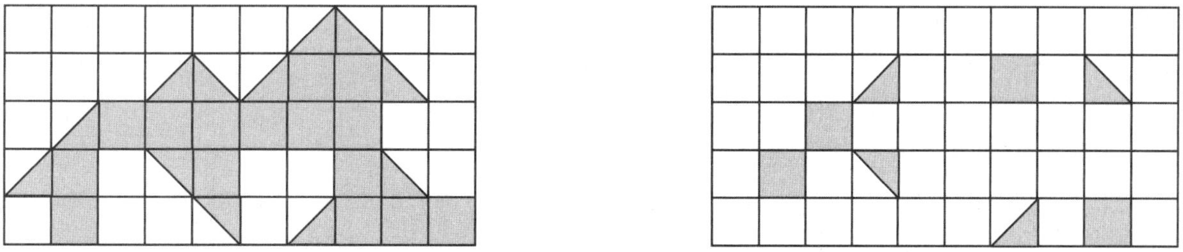

5. Are these pairs of shapes congruent?

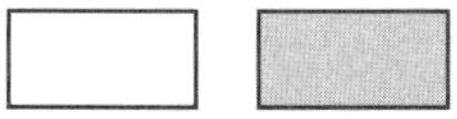

__________ because ______________________________

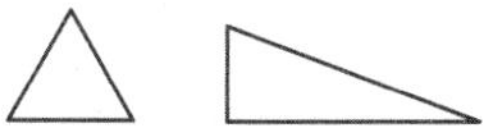

__________ because ______________________________

6. Find two congruent shapes in your home. How can you check that they are congruent?

# G4-9: Congruency *(continued)*

3. Draw rectangles that are **congruent** to the ones shown.

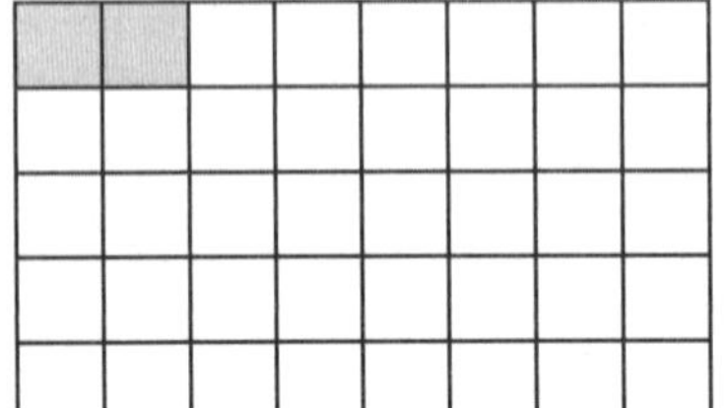

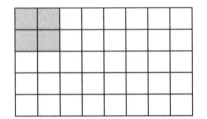

4. Draw a second shape that has the same area as the one given but is NOT congruent.

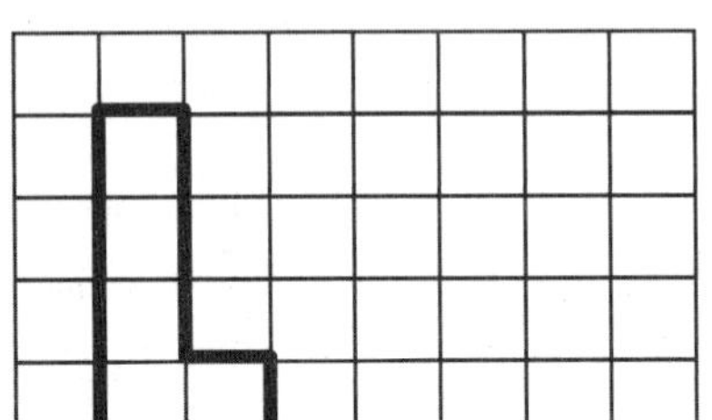

Draw a second figure that is the same shape as the one below but is NOT congruent.

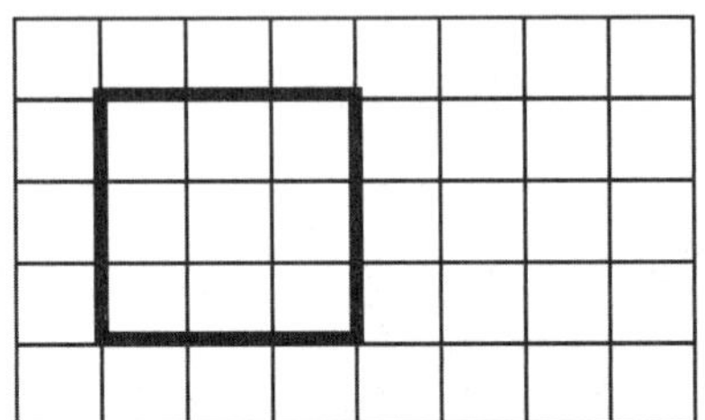

5. Add the following:

a) 2 lines to make 3 congruent squares

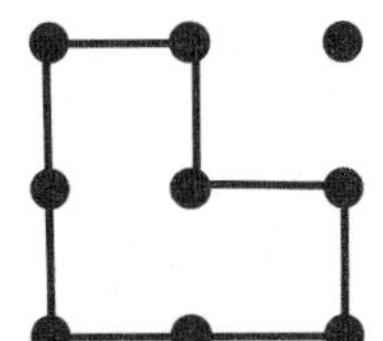

b) 3 lines to make 4 congruent triangles

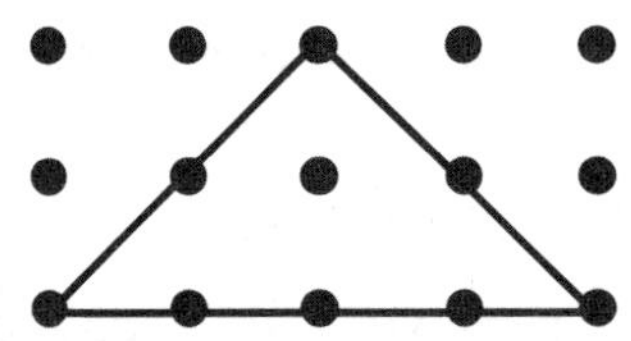

c) 2 lines to make 3 congruent rectangles

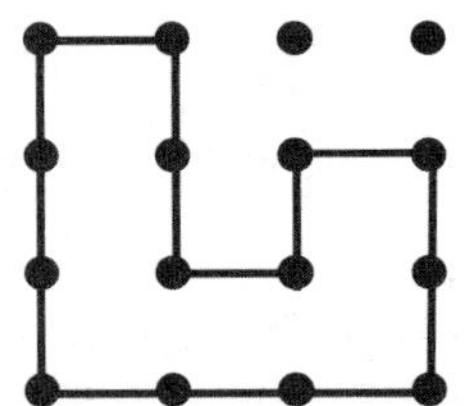

6. Some of the shapes below are congruent. Find any shapes that are congruent to Shape A and label them with the letter "A." If you can find any other shapes that are congruent to each other, label them all with the same letter. (HINT: You will need to use the letters B, C, and D.)

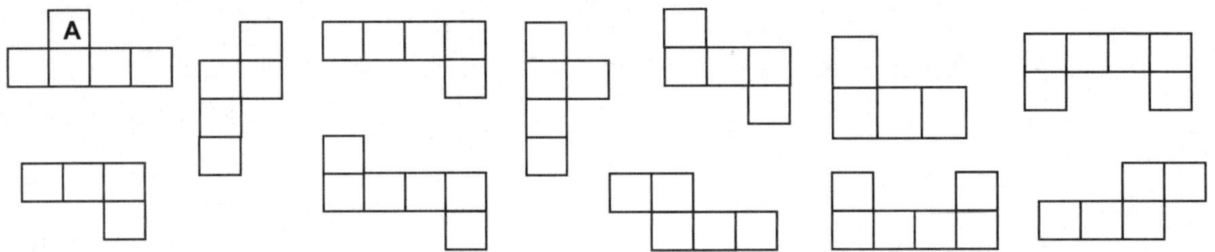


7. Cross out all the shapes that are congruent to the shape on the left. Then count the shapes that you **did not** cross out (including the shape on the left).

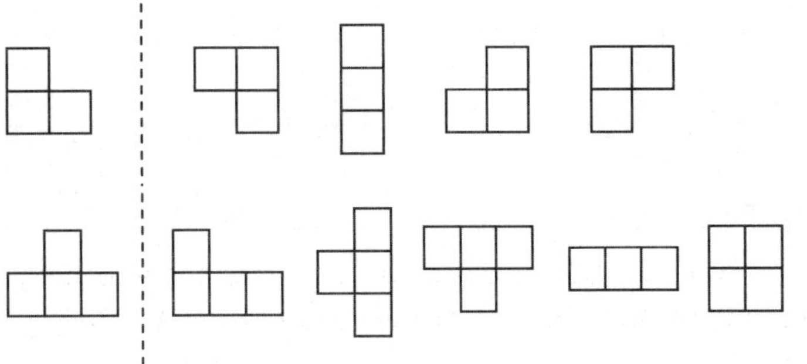

non-congruent shapes

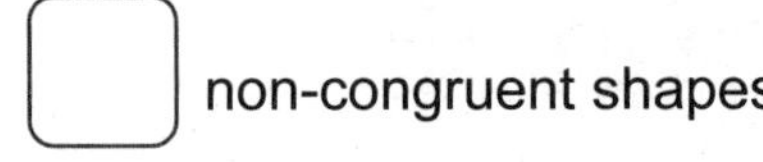

non-congruent shapes

# G4-9: Congruency *(continued)*

8. Look at the shapes from left to right. If you find a shape that is congruent to a shape you have already looked at, cross it out. How many non-congruent shapes are left? The first one is done for you.

a) 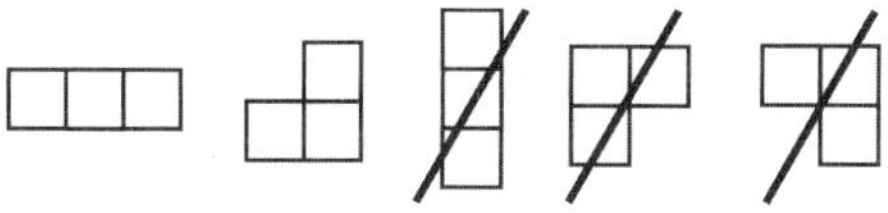 2 non-congruent shapes

b) 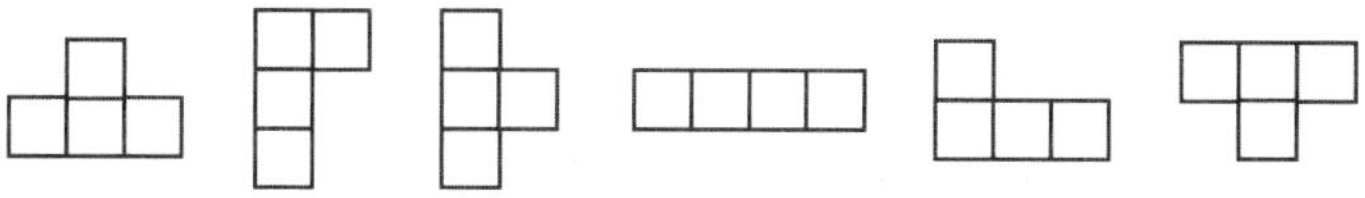 non-congruent shapes

c) 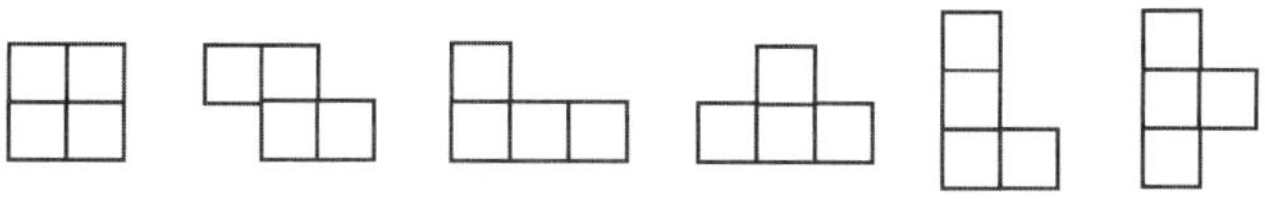 non-congruent shapes

9. Starting with the shape on the left, add a square to each shape in the position shown by the arrow. If you create a shape that is congruent to a shape you have already made, cross it out. How many non-congruent shapes did you make?

Example: 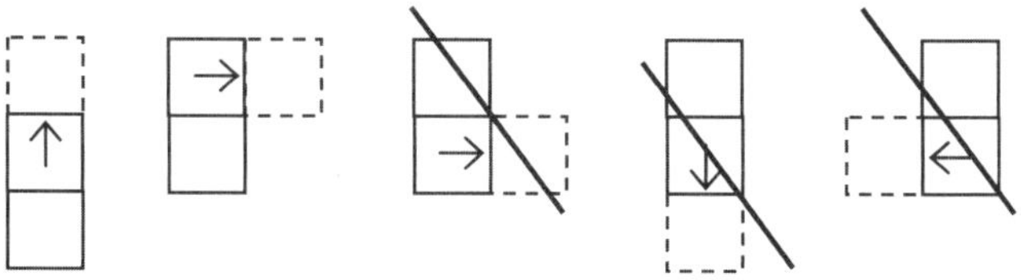 2 non-congruent shapes

a) 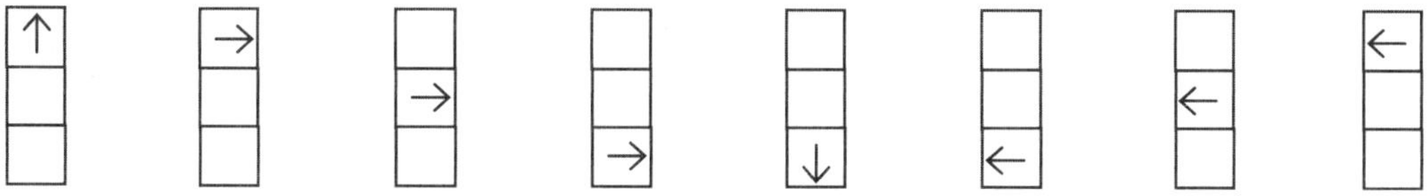 non-congruent shapes

b) 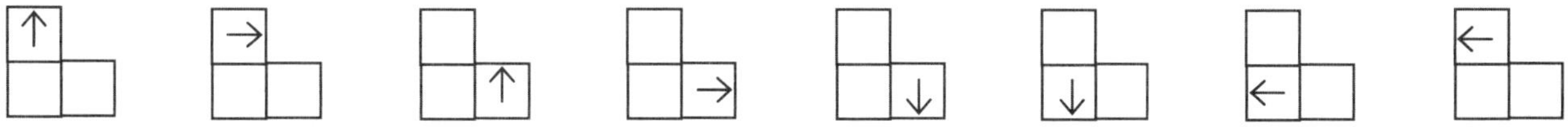 non-congruent shapes

BONUS:

10. On grid paper, show how many different (non-congruent) shapes you can make by adding one square to the original figure.
(HINT: Make copies of the shape, and add one square to each copy as in question 2.)

a)

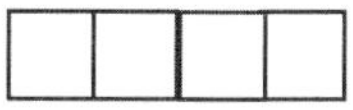

b)

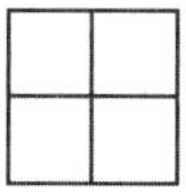

c)

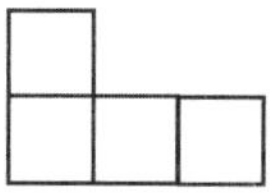

11. 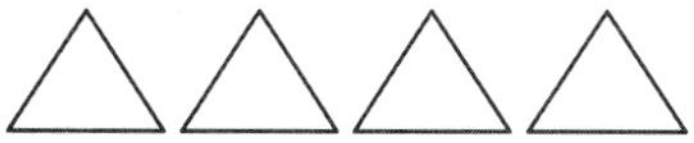 Show how many non-congruent shapes you can make by placing 4 equilateral triangles edge to edge. (Use pattern blocks to help you find the answer.)

# G4-10: Similarity

Example:
How many times greater is number A than number B?

A = 5, B = 20, B is 4 times greater than A.

Two shapes are similar if they are the same **shape**. (They do not need to be the same size.)

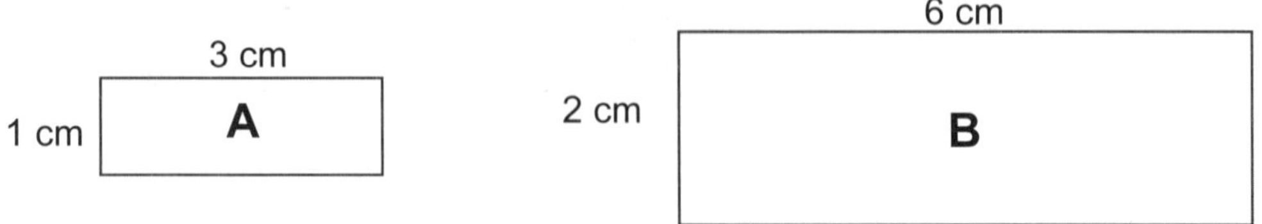


Example:
Rectangles A and B are similar. The width of B (2 cm) is 2 times the width of A (1 cm). Since A and B are the same shape; the length of B must **also** be 2 times the length of A.

---

1. Rectangles A and B are similar. How can you find the length of B without using a ruler?

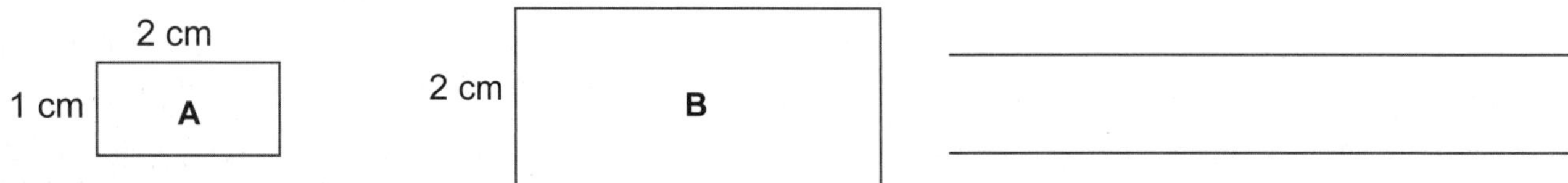


2. Rectangles A and B are similar. How many times the width of A is the width of B? (Do not forget to include the units!)

   a) Width of A: 1 cm  Width of B: 3 cm
   The width of B is ______ times the width of A.

   b) Width of A: 2 cm  Width of B: 6 cm
   The width of B is ______ times the width of A.

   c) Width of A: 2 cm  Width of B: 10 cm
   The width of B is ______ times the width of A.

   d) Width of A: 3 cm  Width of B: 12 cm
   The width of B is ______ times the width of A.

3. Rectangles A and B are similar. Find the length of B.

   a) Width of A: 1 cm  Width of B: 2 cm
   Length of A: 3 cm  Length of B: ________

   b) Width of A: 1 cm  Width of B: 3 cm
   Length of A: 5 cm  Length of B: ________

   c) Width of A: 2 cm  Width of B: 6 cm
   Length of A: 4 cm  Length of B: ________

   d) Width of A: 5 cm  Width of B: 10 cm
   Length of A: 10 cm  Length of B: ________

4. Rectangles A and B are similar. Draw rectangle A on grid paper. Then draw rectangle B.

   a) Width of A: 1 unit
   Length of A: 2 units
   Width of B: 2 units

   b) Width of A: 1 unit
   Length of A: 2 units
   Width of B: 3 units

   c) Width of A: 2 units
   Length of A: 3 units
   Width of B: 4 units

5. Draw a trapezoid similar to A with a base that is 2 times as long as the base of A. (A is 1 unit high. How high should the new figure be?)

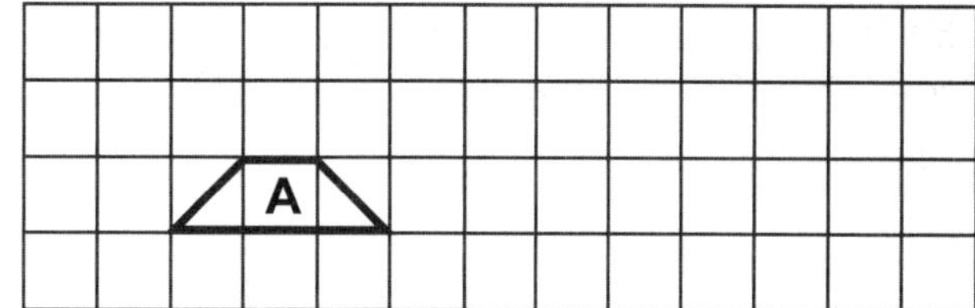


6.

a) Draw a shape that is **similar** to the original. Make the base 2 times as long. How high should you make the new shape?

b) Find the area (in square units) of each original shape, then the area of each new shape.

Area of A: ________ Area of B: ________ Area of C: ________ Area of D: ________

Area of the new shape: ________ Area of the new shape: ________ Area of the new shape: ________ Area of the new shape: ________

c) When the base and the height of a shape are doubled, what happens to the area of the shape?

7. Are shapes A and B similar? Explain how you know.
(HINT: Are all the sides in B twice as long as the sides in A?)

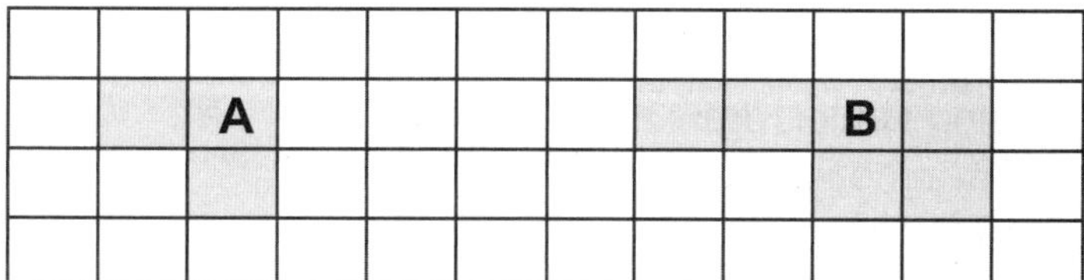


8. Which of these shapes are similar? How do you know?

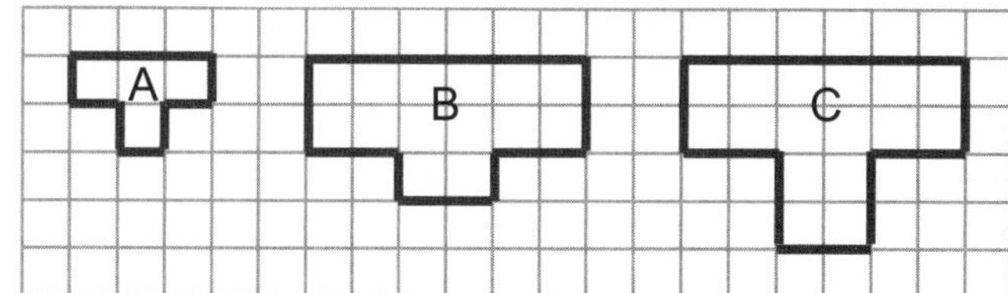


9. Draw a parallelogram on grid paper. Then, draw a similar parallelogram that is exactly twice as high as the first.

10. Draw a right angle triangle on grid paper. Then, draw a similar triangle that is exactly three times as high as the first.

11. Two polygons are similar if they have the **same** angles. Use a protractor and a ruler to construct two triangles that are similar but not congruent.

12. Can a trapezoid and a square ever be similar? Explain.

# G4-11: Symmetry

Some shapes have lines of **symmetry**. Tina uses a mirror to check for symmetry in shapes. She places the mirror across half the shape and checks to see if the half reflected in the mirror makes her picture "whole" again:

Tina also checks if a shape has a line of symmetry by cutting the shape out and then folding it. If the halves of the shapes on either side of the fold match exactly, Tina knows that the fold shows a line of symmetry:

1. Complete the picture so it has a **horizontal** line of symmetry.

   Then draw the line of symmetry.

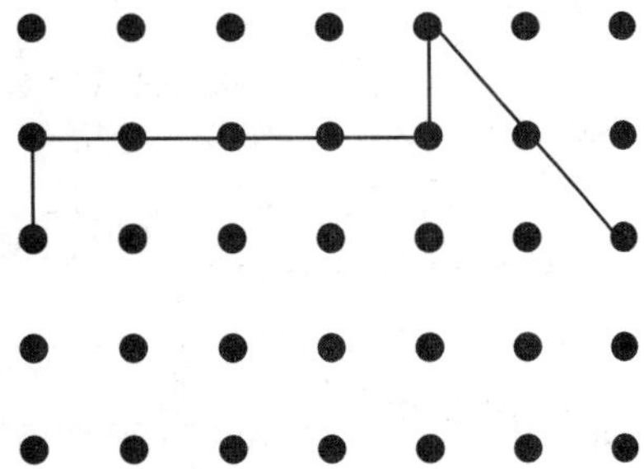

2. Complete the picture so it has a **vertical** line of symmetry.

   Then draw the line of symmetry.

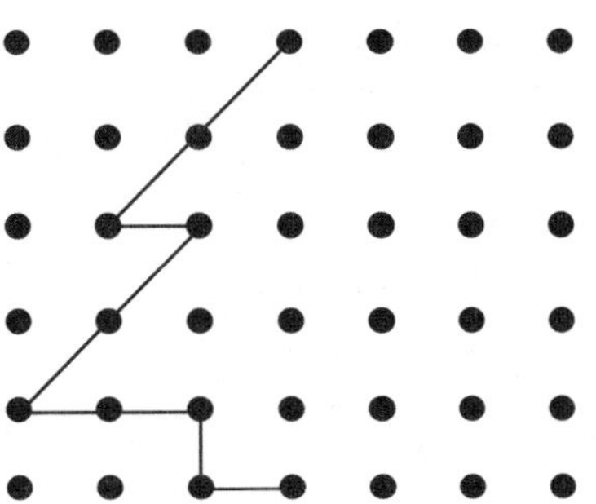

3. Using a ruler, draw a **horizontal** line of symmetry through each of the following figures.

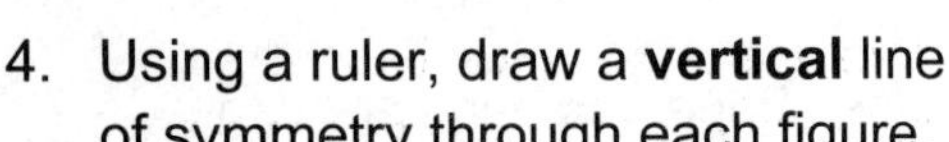

a) 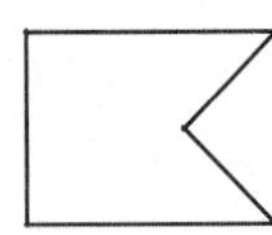

b) 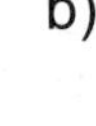 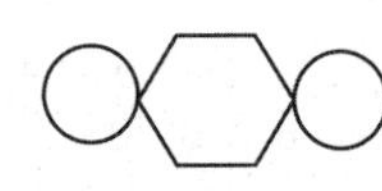

4. Using a ruler, draw a **vertical** line of symmetry through each figure.

a) 

b)  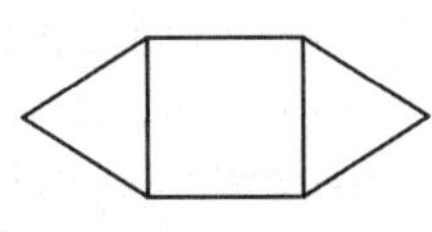

5. Using a ruler, draw dotted lines to show any horizontal **and/or** vertical lines of symmetry in the following figures.

   NOTE: Some figures may have both kinds of symmetry, while some may have neither.

a) 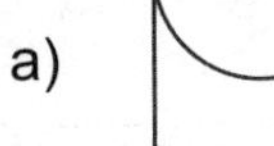 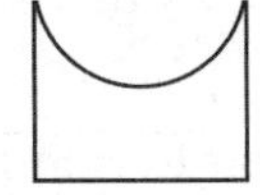

b) 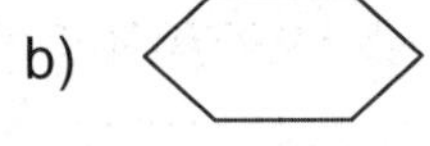 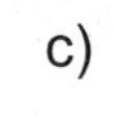

c) 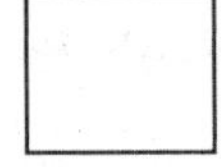 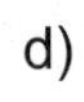

d) 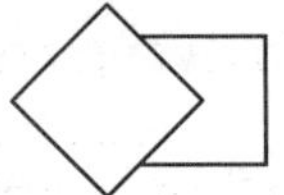 

e) 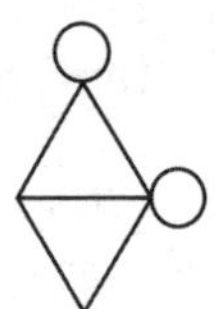

# G4-11: Symmetry *(continued)*

6. Many letters of the alphabet have lines of symmetry:  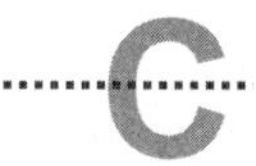

   a) Draw at least 5 letters of the alphabet and show their lines of symmetry.

   b) Can you find a letter with 2 or more lines of symmetry?

7. a) **First predict** how many lines of symmetry each shape will have and write it into the chart. Write your best guess.

| Shape | Predicted number of lines of symmetry | Actual number of lines of symmetry |
|---|---|---|
| square | | |
| rectangle | | |
| rhombus | | |
| parallelogram | | |

   b) How will you check how many lines of symmetry each shape has?

   c) Either fold a photocopy of the shapes or use a mirror to check how many lines of symmetry they have. Draw the lines of symmetry onto the shapes on the page and fill in the chart.

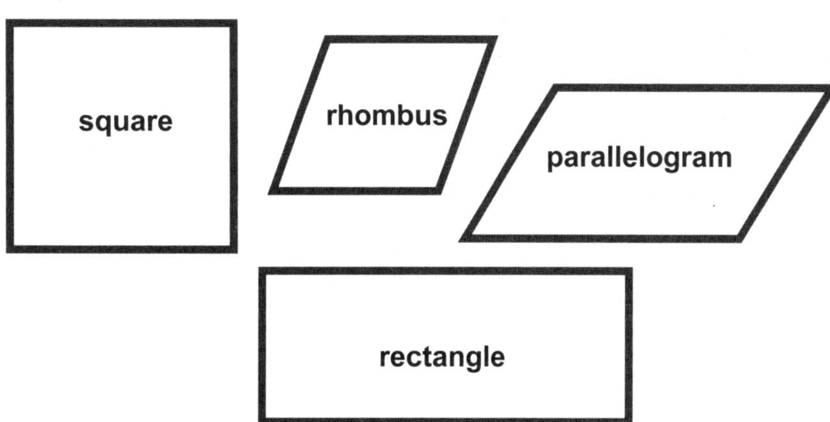


8. A square can be divided by a diagonal line and half shaded in **four** different ways:

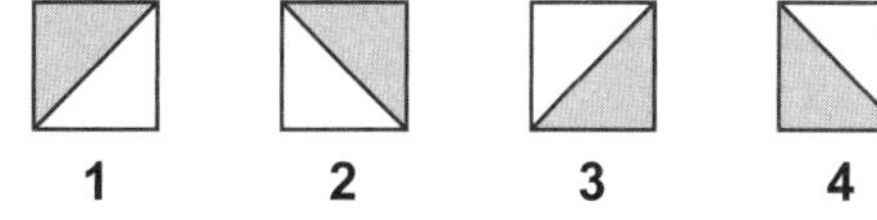


   a) For each of the 4-square grids below, choose a mixture of half-shaded squares. Then draw in any lines of symmetry you see—do not forget to check in all directions: vertically, horizontally, **and** diagonally! The first three are done for you.

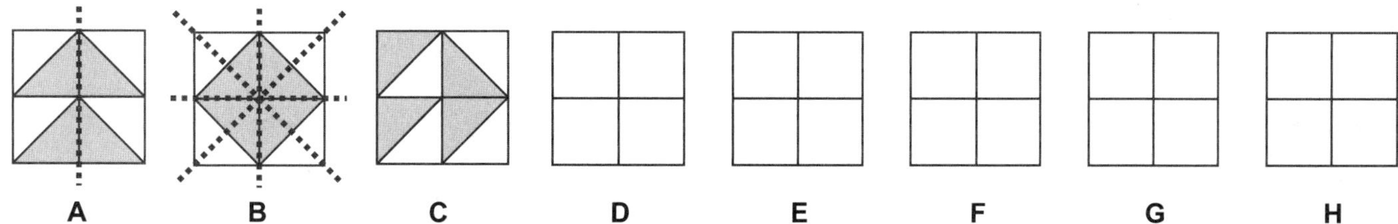


   b) Complete the following chart based on the number of lines of symmetry you found:

| **Number of lines of symmetry** | 0 | 1 | 2 | 4 |
|---|---|---|---|---|
| **Letter beneath grid** | C, | A, | | B, |

# G4-11: Symmetry *(continued)*

9. a) Draw a line of symmetry through the triangle **parallel to line** A.

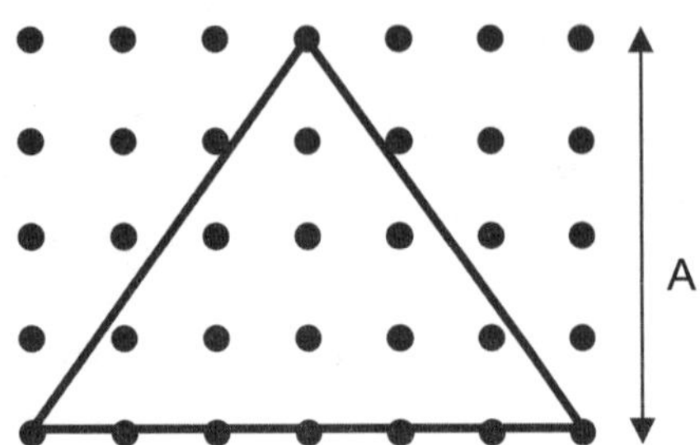


b) Draw a line through the rectangle that is parallel to B, but is **not** a line of symmetry.

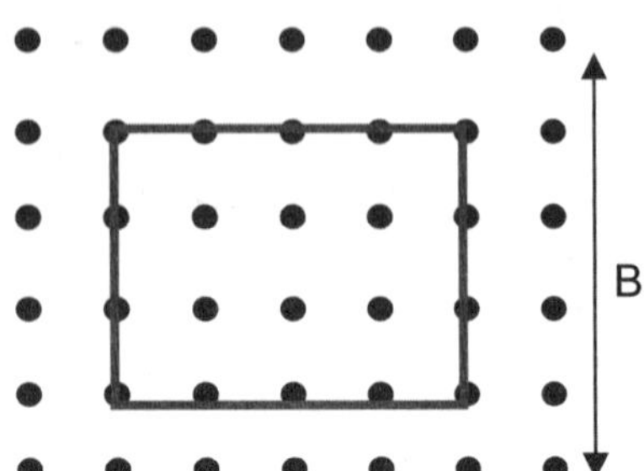


10. Decode the words written in "mirror code" by filling in the missing half of each letter.

a) b) c)

11. On a separate piece of paper, write a word in mirror code and ask a friend to decode it. REMEMBER: Check that all the letters you use have either horizontal or vertical lines of symmetry.

12. Draw all the lines of symmetry for each shape. Then complete the chart. NOTE: "Regular" means "having equal sides and equal angles."

equilateral triangle

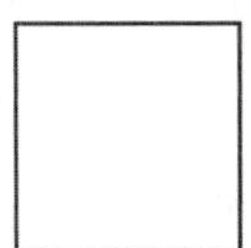
square

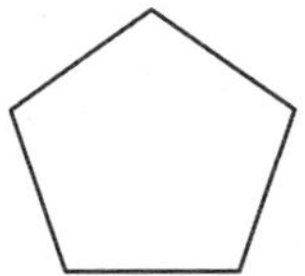
regular pentagon

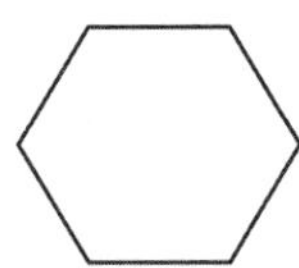
regular hexagon

| a) **Figure** | **Triangle** | **Square** | **Pentagon** | **Hexagon** |
|---|---|---|---|---|
| number of edges | | | | |
| number of lines of symmetry | | | | |

b) On a separate piece of paper, describe any relation you see between lines of symmetry and the number of edges.

13. Find a picture in a magazine that has at least one line of symmetry. Mark the line with a pencil.

BONUS:

14. Sudha drew a mirror line on a square. Then she drew and shaded a reflection of the corner of the square in the mirror line:

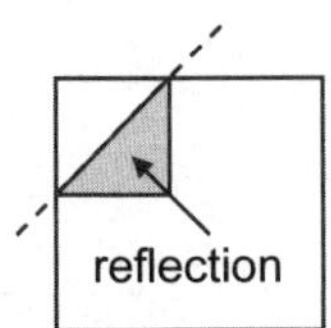


a) Draw a large square on grid paper. Draw a mirror line on the square and reflect part of the square in the line.

b) Can you place the mirror line so that the two parts of the square on either side of the mirror line make . . .

i) a rectangle ii) a hexagon (a shape with 6 sides) iii) an octagon (a shape with 8 sides)

# G4-12: Comparing Shapes

1. Complete the chart by commenting on the properties of the following figures, how they are the **same**, and how they are **different**.

**Figure 1** 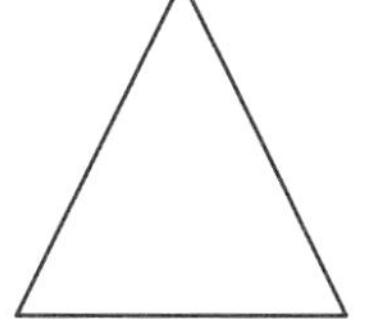 **Figure 2** 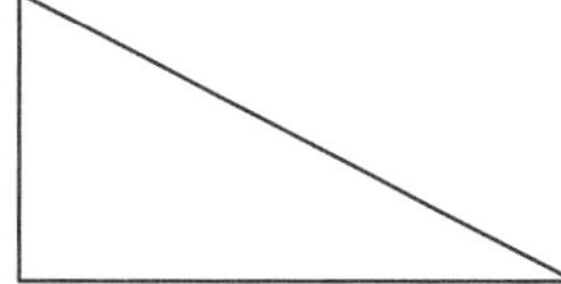

a) Compare the two shapes above by filling out the following chart:

| Property | Figure 1 | Figure 2 | Same? | Different? |
|---|---|---|---|---|
| number of **vertices** | | | | |
| number of **edges** | | | | |
| number of **pairs of parallel sides** | | | | |
| number of **right angles** | | | | |
| any lines of **symmetry**? | | | | |
| number of lines of **symmetry**? | | | | |
| Is the figure **equilateral**? | | | | |

b) By simply looking at the following figures, can you say how they are the same and different?

**Figure 1**

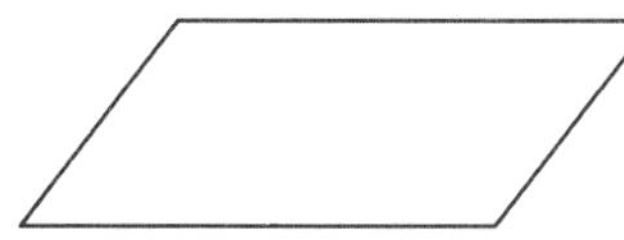

**Figure 2**

| Property | Same? | Different? |
|---|---|---|
| number of **vertices** | | |
| number of **edges** | | |
| number of **pairs of parallel sides** | | |
| number of **right angles** | | |
| any lines of **symmetry**? | | |
| number of lines of **symmetry**? | | |
| Is the figure **equilateral**? | | |

2. On a separate piece of paper, draw two figures and compare them using a chart (as in question 1).

3. Looking at the figures, can you comment on their **similarities** and **differences**?
Show your work on a separate piece of paper. Be sure to mention the following properties:

✓ the number of **vertices**
✓ the number of **edges**
✓ the number of **pairs of parallel sides**
✓ the number of **right angles**
✓ number of **symmetries**
✓ whether the figure is **equilateral**

**Figure 1** 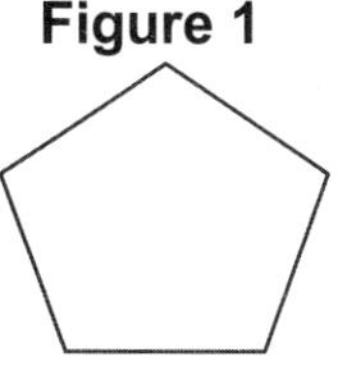 **Figure 2**

# G4-13: Sorting and Classifying Shapes



1. Using pairs of properties that a figure might have (for instance, "I have 4 vertices" and "I have a vertical line of symmetry"), we are going to sort the following figures using a Venn diagram:

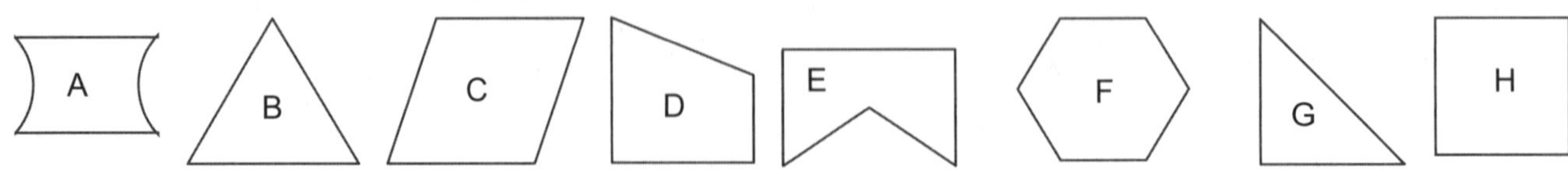


a)

| Property | Figures with this property |
|---|---|
| 1. I am a quadrilateral | C, D, H |
| 2. I have at least 2 right angles | D, E, H |

Which figures share both properties? __________

Using the information in the chart above, complete the following Venn diagram:

property 1

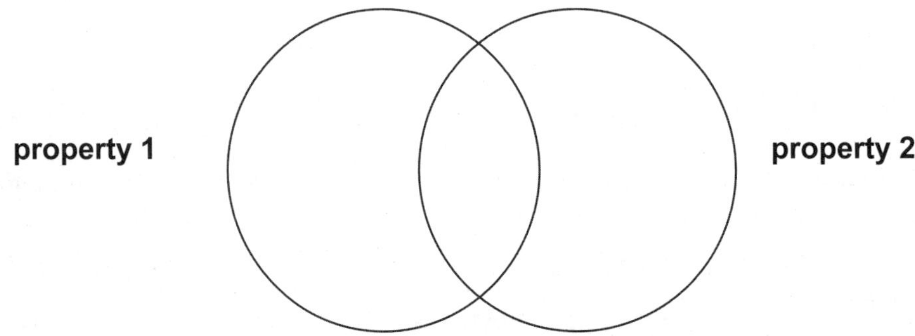

property 2

b) Complete the chart.

| Property | Figures with this property |
|---|---|
| 1. I am a quadrilateral. | |
| 2. All of my sides are the same length. | |

Which figures share both properties? __________

Using the information in the chart above, complete the following Venn diagram:

property 1

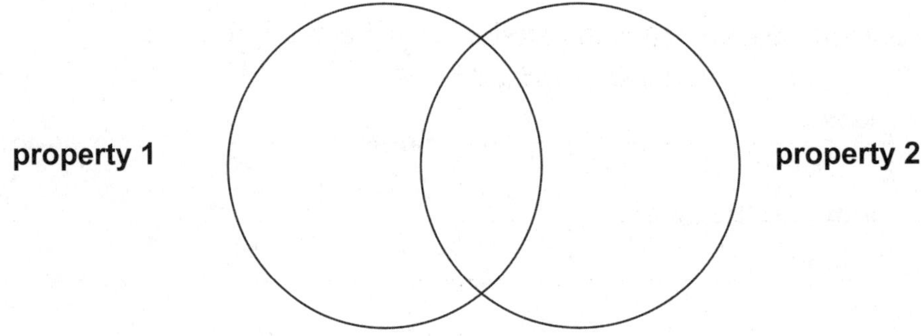

property 2

c) Complete the chart.

| Property | Figures with this property |
|---|---|
| 1. I have 4 or 5 vertices. | |
| 2. I have at least 1 right angle. | |

Which figures share both properties? __________

Using the information in the chart above, complete the following Venn diagram:

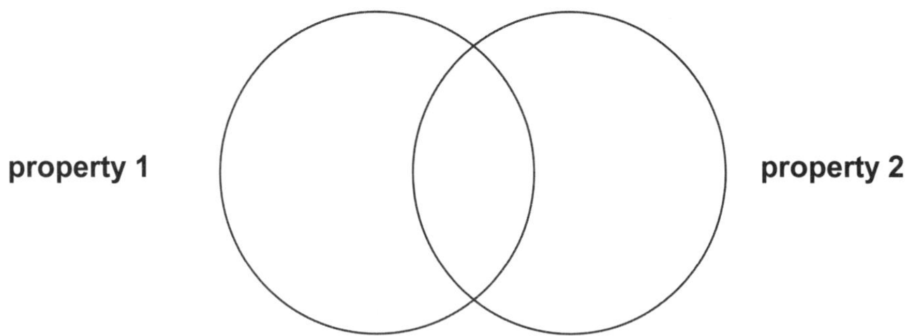


2. Using two properties of your own, make a chart and a Venn diagram as in question 1. Show your work on a separate piece of paper. You might want to choose from the following properties:
    - ✓ number of vertices
    - ✓ number of pairs of parallel sides
    - ✓ number of edges
    - ✓ number of right angles
    - ✓ lines of symmetry
    - ✓ equilateral

3. Record the properties of each shape. Write "yes" in the column if the shape has the given property. Write "no" otherwise.

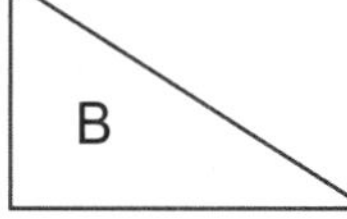

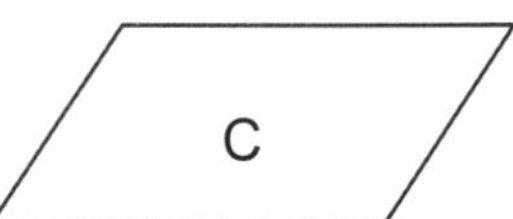

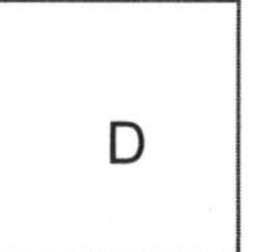

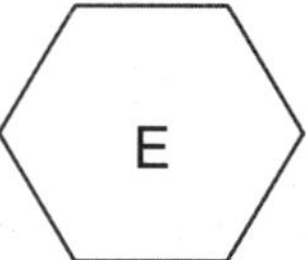


| Shape | Quadrilateral | Equilateral | Two pairs of parallel sides | At least one right angle |
|---|---|---|---|---|
| A | | | | |
| B | | | | |
| C | | | | |
| D | | | | |
| E | | | | |

# G4-13: Sorting and Classifying Shapes *(continued)*

4. On a separate piece of paper, describe each figure completely. In your description you should mention the following properties:

   ✓ number of sides
   ✓ number of vertices
   ✓ number of pairs of parallel sides
   ✓ number of right angles
   ✓ number of lines of symmetry
   ✓ Is the figure equilateral?

   a) b)

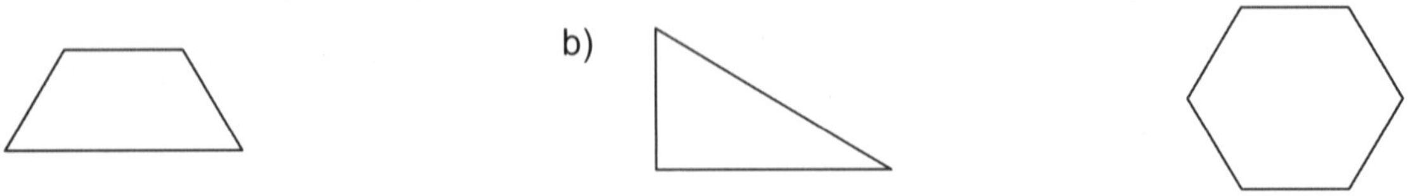

5. On a separate piece of paper, name all the properties the figures have in common. Then describe any differences.

   a) b) c)

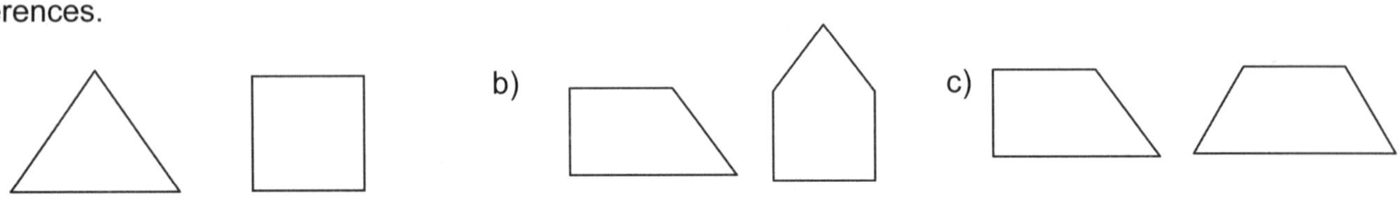

6. Count the vertices and edges in the figures. Mark any right angles with a square. Mark any pairs of parallel sides with arrows. Write "T" (for true) if **both** figures have the property in common. Otherwise, write "F" (for false).

   a) b)

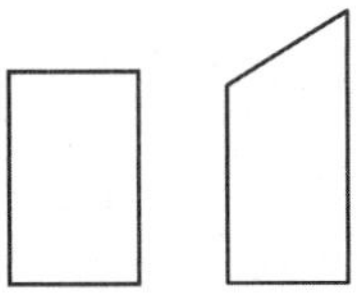

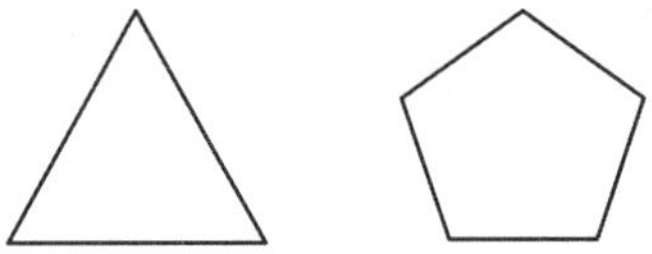

   Both figures have . . .

   a)
   ____ 4 vertices
   ____ 2 pairs of parallel sides
   ____ 4 sides
   ____ 2 right angles

   b)
   ____ 3 vertices
   ____ 5 sides
   ____ no right angles
   ____ equilateral

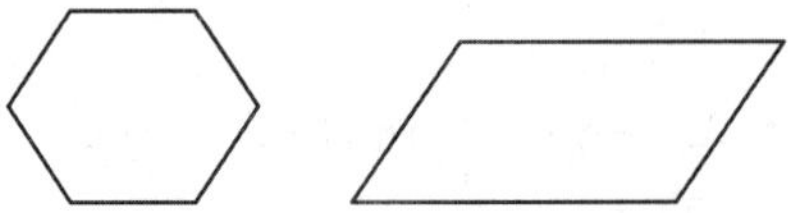

   c)
   ____ quadrilateral
   ____ at least one right angle
   ____ at least one pair of parallel sides
   ____ 2 pairs of parallel sides

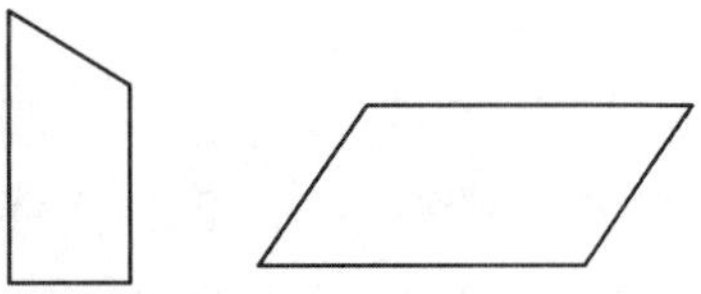

   d)
   ____ 6 vertices
   ____ at least 2 pairs of parallel sides
   ____ no right angles
   ____ equilateral

7. Name the shapes based on the descriptions.

   a) I have three sides. All of my sides are the same length. I am an ______________________.
   b) I have four equal sides. None of my angles are right angles. I am a ______________________.
   c) I am a quadrilateral with two pairs of parallel sides. I am a ______________________.
   d) I am a quadrilateral with exactly one pair of parallel sides. I am a ______________________.

# G4-14: Puzzles and Problems

Write your answers for the problems on a separate piece of paper.

1. How many right angles are there in this figure?

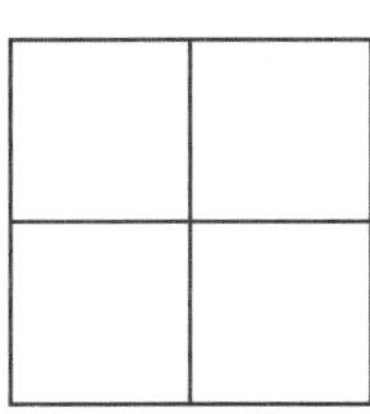

2. On a separate piece of paper, name all the quadrilaterals in this shape:

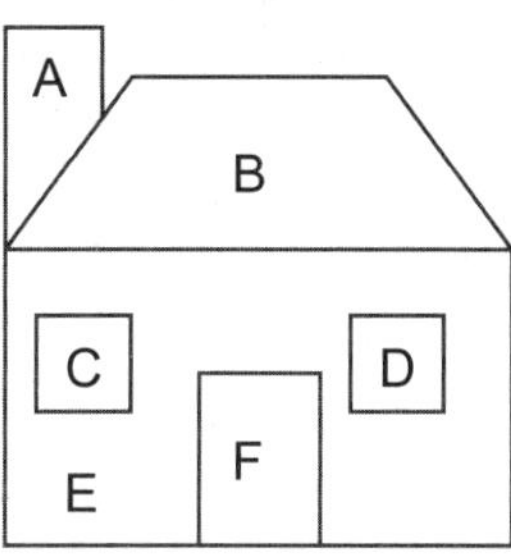


3. Which of the quadrilaterals have only 1 name? Which have 2? Which have 3? Write as many names as you can for each figure.

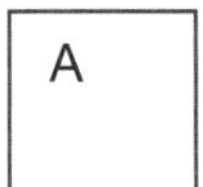

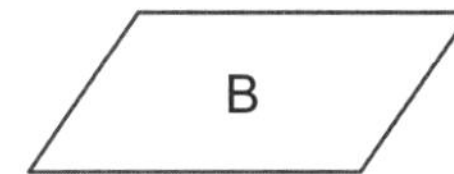

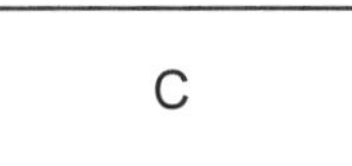

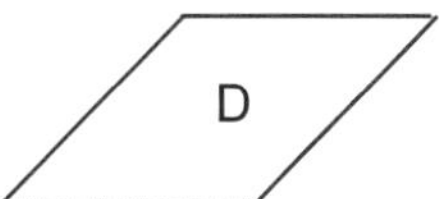

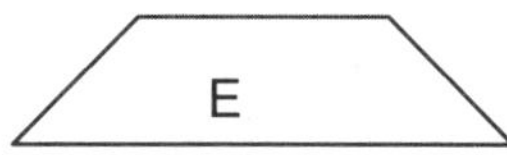


4. Nick and Jessica's gardens are similar shapes. How long is the base of Jessica's garden?

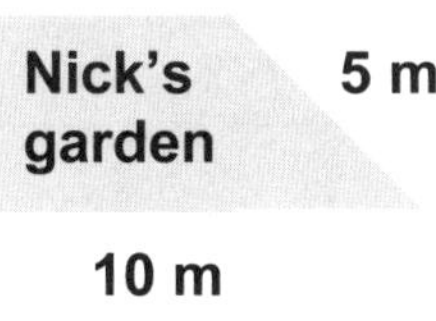

5. Triangle A and Triangle B are the same height. Which triangle is similar to A? How do you know?

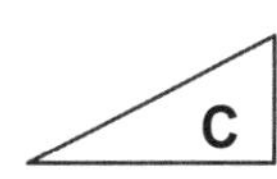


6. Which shapes are congruent? Which are similar? Explain how you know.

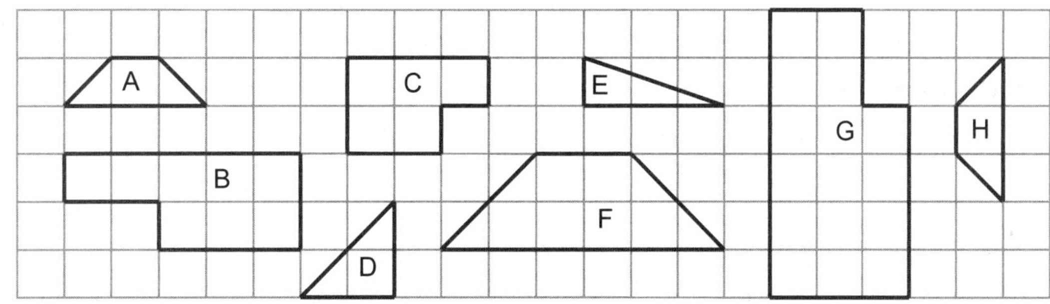


7. Draw a trapezoid on grid paper and find any lines of symmetry.

8. Use a ruler and compass to construct a triangle with two 60° angles.
   a) Measure the third angle of the triangle. What do you notice?
   b) Measure all 3 sides of the triangle. What do you notice?

# LSS4-1: Lists

NOTE:
Review the meaning of the terms "less than," "greater than," "odd," "even," "multiples of 2," and "multiples of 3" before completing this worksheet. REMEMBER: Zero is an even number and is also a multiple of any number.

---

1. Write the numbers from 0 to 9 in order.

2. Write all the numbers from 0 to 9 that are . . .

a) greater than 5
b) greater than 4
c) less than 5
d) greater than 9
e) less than 3
f) greater than 1
g) less than 7
h) greater than 7
i) less than 9
j) even numbers
k) odd numbers
l) multiples of 4
m) multiples of 2
n) multiples of 3
o) multiples of 7

3. Make two lists: one for condition (i) and one for condition (ii). Part a) is done for you. Circle the numbers that appear on both lists to find the numbers from 0 to 9 that are . . .

a) even numbers smaller than 7

(i) even numbers: (0), (2), (4), (6), 8

(ii) numbers less than 7: (0), 1, (2), 3, (4), 5, (6)

answer: 0, 2, 4, 6

b) odd numbers greater than 2

(i) odd numbers:

(ii) numbers greater than 2:

answer:

Show your work for the remaining questions on a separate piece of paper.

c) odd numbers less than 8
d) even numbers less than 9
e) odd numbers greater than 4 and less than 8
f) numbers greater than 3
g) even numbers less than 9 that are multiples of 2
h) multiples of 4
i) numbers between 0 and 9 that are multiples of both 2 and 3
j) odd numbers less than 9 that are multiples of 5
k) odd numbers that are multiples of 3

# LSS4-2: Organized Lists

Many problems in mathematics and science have more than one solution. If a problem involves two quantities, you can be sure you have not missed any possible solutions if you list the values of one of the quantities in increasing order.

For instance, to find all the ways you can make 35¢ with dimes and nickels, start by assuming you have no dimes, then 1 dime, and so on up to 3 dimes (4 would be too many).

In each case, count by 5s to 35 to find out how many nickels you need to make 35¢.

Step 1:

| Dimes | Nickels |
|---|---|
| 0 | |
| 1 | |
| 2 | |
| 3 | |

Step 2:

| Dimes | Nickels |
|---|---|
| 0 | 7 |
| 1 | 5 |
| 2 | 3 |
| 3 | 1 |

1. Fill in the amount of pennies, nickels, or dimes you need to made the following amounts:

a) 19¢

| Nickels | Pennies |
|---|---|
| 0 | |
| 1 | |
| 2 | |
| 3 | |

b) 45¢

| Dimes | Nickels |
|---|---|
| 0 | |
| 1 | |
| 2 | |
| 3 | |
| 4 | |

c) 24¢

| Nickels | Pennies |
|---|---|
| 0 | |
| 1 | |
| 2 | |
| 3 | |
| 4 | |

d) 35¢

| Dimes | Nickels |
|---|---|
| 0 | |
| 1 | |
| 2 | |
| 3 | |

e) 80¢

| Quarters | Nickels |
|---|---|
| 0 | |
| 1 | |
| 2 | |
| 3 | |

f) 95¢

| Quarters | Nickels |
|---|---|
| 0 | |
| 1 | |
| 2 | |
| 3 | |

2.

| Quarters | Nickels |
|---|---|
| 0 | |
| 1 | |
| 2 | |

Kyle wants to find all the ways he can make 55¢ using quarters and nickels. He lists the number of quarters in increasing order. Why did he stop at 2 quarters?

________________________________________

________________________________________

3. On a separate piece of paper, make a chart to show all the ways you can make the given amount. (HINT: List values of the largest money denomination in increasing order, starting at 0.)

a) make 26¢ using nickels and pennies

b) make 70¢ using quarters and dimes

c) make 55¢ using dimes and nickels

d) make $11 using loonies and toonies

# LSS4-2: Organized Lists *(continued)*

4. On a separate piece of paper, make a chart to find all the pairs of numbers that add up to 9. (Do not forget to include 0: 0 + 9 = 9.)

5. If you add the number of marbles that Aidan and his friend Ben have, the total is 11. Neither of them has 0 marbles.
   a) What are the possible number of marbles that each of them can have?
   b) If Ben has more marbles than Aidan, what is the possible number of marbles that each boy can have?

6. Birds have 2 legs, cats have 4 legs, and bees have 6 legs. Complete the charts to find out how many legs each combination of 2 animals has.

a)

| Birds | Cats | Total number of legs |
|---|---|---|
| 0 | 3 | |
| 2 | 2 | |
| 2 | 0 | |

b)

| Birds | Bees | Total number of legs |
|---|---|---|
| 0 | 3 | |
| 2 | 1 | |
| 4 | 0 | |

7. On a separate piece of paper, make a chart like the ones in question 6 to solve each puzzle.
   a) 3 pets have 8 legs.
   Each pet is either a bird or a dog.
   How many birds and dogs are there?
   b) 4 pets have 10 legs.
   Each pet is either a bird or cat.
   How many birds and cats are there?
   c) 4 things you can ride have 9 wheels.
   Each is either a tricycle or a bicycle.
   How many bicycles and tricycles are there?
   d) 5 things you can ride have 13 wheels.
   Each is either a tricycle or a bicycle.
   How many bicycles and tricycles are there?

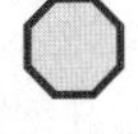

8. The chart shows all two-digit numbers whose digits add to 4. On a separate piece of paper, make a chart like the one shown to find all two-digit numbers whose digits . . .

   a) add to 3    b) add to 6    c) are the same

| Tens digit | Ones digit | Number |
|---|---|---|
| 1 | 3 | 13 |
| 2 | 2 | 22 |
| 3 | 1 | 31 |
| 4 | 0 | 40 |

BONUS:

9.

| Quarters | Dimes |
|---|---|
| 0 | |
| 1 | |
| 2 | |

Alicia wants to find all the ways she can make 70¢ using quarters and dimes. One of the entries on her chart will not work.

Which one is it?

EXTRA CHALLENGE:

10. Make a chart to show all the ways you can make 155¢ using nickels, dimes, and loonies.
Your chart will have to have 3 columns.
(HINT: Start with 0 loonies and 0 dimes, 0 loonies and 1 dime, etc.)

1. a) What number is 3 more than 4? ______ b) What number is 2 more than 7? ______

   c) What number is 3 less than 8? ______ d) What number is 2 less than 5? ______

   e) The sum of two numbers is 5. One number is 2. What is the other number? ________

   f) The sum of two numbers is 7. One number is 3. What is the other number? ________

   g) The sum of two numbers is 6. One number is 4. What is the other number? ________

2. Use the clues to find the answers: "I am a **two-digit** number . . . "

   a) my tens digit is 9 and my ones digit is 1

   _____ _____

   b) my ones digit is 5 and my tens digit is 7

   _____ _____

   c) my ones digit is 0 and my tens digit is 4

   _____ _____

   d) my ones digit is 5 and both of my digits are the same

   _____ _____

   e) my tens digit is 7 and my ones digit is 2 less than my tens digit

   _____ _____

   f) my ones digit is 2 and my tens digit is 3 more than my ones digit

   _____ _____

3. On a separate piece of paper make an organized list to find all solutions to the problem: "I am a **two-digit** number and . . . "

   a) the sum of my digits is 3 b) the sum of my digits is 5 c) both of my digits are the same

4. Read the statement and make an organized list to find all the possible solutions. Then read the second statement and circle the correct answer. The first one is done for you.

   "I am a **two-digit** number and . . . "

a)
- **The sum of my digits is 3.**
- My tens digit is 1 more than my ones digit.

| Tens | Ones |
|---|---|
| 3 | 0 |
| 2 | 1 |
| 1 | 2 |

The answer is 21.

b)
- **The sum of my digits is 2.**
- Both of my digits are the same.

| c) • **The sum of my digits is 3.**<br>• My ones digit is 1 more than my tens digit. | d) • **The sum of my digits is 4.**<br>• Both of my digits are the same. |
|---|---|

Answer the following questions on a separate piece of paper:

5. On a separate piece of paper, make a chart to solve the following problems: "I am a two-digit number and . . . "

   a) the sum of my digits is 5; my tens digit is one more than my ones digit

   b) the sum of my digits is 5; my tens digit is 3 less than my ones digit

   c) both of my digits are the same; I am greater than 50 and less than 60

   d) both of my digits are the same; I am greater than 90

   e) both of my digits are the same; if you multiply my digits you get 9

   f) both of my digits are the same; the sum of my digits is 12

6. What is the **hundreds** digit of a **three-digit** number . . .

   a) between 400 and 500?

   b) between 300 and 400?

   c) between 600 and 700?

   d) between 700 and 800?

   e) greater than 900?

   f) less than 200?

7. On a separate piece of paper, make a chart to solve the following problems: "I am a three-digit number and . . . "

   a) I am between 500 and 600; all of my digits are the same

   b) I am between 200 and 300; my ones digit is 3 times my hundreds digit; the sum of my digits is 10

   c) my hundreds digit, 9, is 3 times my ones digit; the sum of my digits is 14

   d) my ones digit, 8, is 2 times my tens digit and 4 times my hundreds digit

   e) I am between 800 and 900; my hundreds digit is 2 times my ones digit; the sum of my digits is 15

   f) I am between 800 and 900; my hundreds digit is 4 times my ones digit; the sum of my digits is 19

   g) I am between 300 and 400; my tens digit and my ones digit are the same; the sum of my digits is 9

   h) all of my digits are the same; the sum of my digits is 15

# LSS4-4: Arrangements, Combinations, and Puzzles

Show your work for the questions on this page on a separate piece of paper.

1. Show all the ways you can colour the flag with red (R), green (G), and blue (B), using one block of each colour.

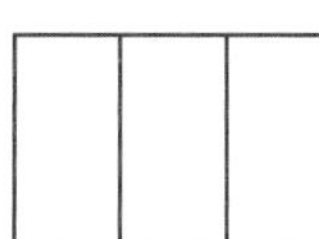

2. 

Using the numbered boxes above, show all the ways you can make a stack of **two** boxes so that a box with a lower number never sits on top of a box with a higher number.

3. A frog takes two long jumps (of equal length) and two shorter jumps (of equal length).

What lengths could the first and last jumps be if the frog jumps a total distance of

a) 10 m?

b) 16 m?

4. Using the digits from 0 to 9 (you can only use each digit once in each question), make . . .

a) the greatest number ____ ____ ____ ____

b) the lowest odd number ____ ____ ____ ____

c) the greatest number with 9 in the tens place ____ ____ ____ ____

d) the greatest even number with 4 in the thousands place ____ ____ ____ ____

5. Crayons come in boxes of 4 or 5. For each of the following numbers, can you buy a combination of boxes that will give you the number exactly? If you can buy the right combination of boxes, say how many of each type of box you must buy.
NOTE: For some of these questions, you need not buy boxes of both types.

a) 8 crayons
b) 10 crayons
c) 11 crayons
d) 14 crayons
e) 17 crayons
f) 18 crayons
g) 19 crayons
h) 21 crayons

6. The numbers 2 and 5 have a **product** of 10 (they **multiply** to give 10) and a **sum** of 7 (they **add** to give 7). Can you find two numbers that have . . .

a) a **product** of 8, and a **sum** of 6?
b) a **product** of 9, and a **sum** of 6?
c) a **product** of 12, and a **sum** of 7?
d) a **product** of 12, and a **sum** of 8?

7. Pick two numbers, one from each of the boxes to the right, so that . . .

a) the product of the two numbers is smallest
b) the product is the greatest
c) the product is closest to 20
d) the difference between the two numbers is smallest

| Box 1 | Box 2 |
|---|---|
| 7, 5, 1 | 3, 2, 9 |

Example: Gloria places 3 pennies in the following figure so that there is . . .

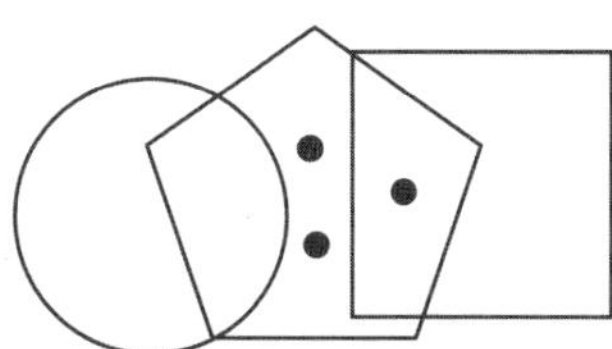

- an even number in the circle (REMEMBER: Zero is an even number.)
- an odd number in the square
- an odd number in the pentagon

8. Solve each puzzle by placing 3 pennies in the following shapes. Draw each solution (using dots to represent the pennies) in the shapes provided beside each question.

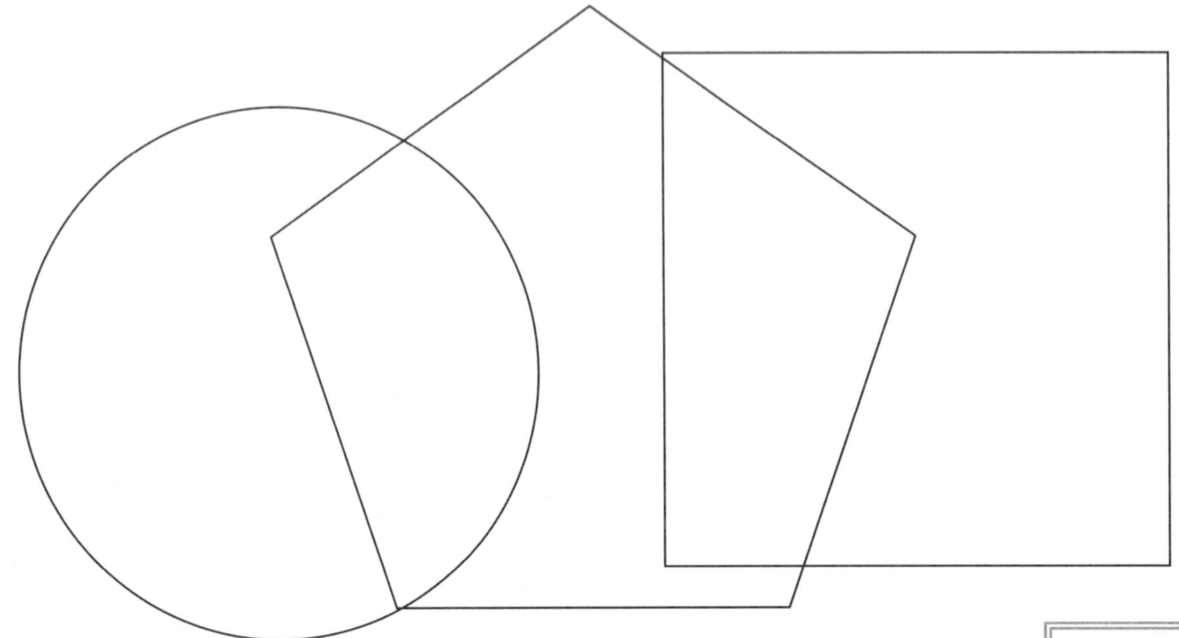

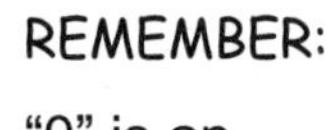

REMEMBER:
"0" is an **even number**.

Can you place 3 pennies so you have . . .

a) an **even** number in the circle,
an **even** number in the pentagon, and
an **even** number in the square?

b) an **odd** number in the circle,
an **even** number in the pentagon, and
an **even** number in the square?

c) an **even** number in the circle,
an **odd** number in the pentagon, and
an **even** number in the square?

d) an **even** number in the circle,
an **even** number in the pentagon, and
an **odd** number in the square?

e) an **odd** number in the circle,
an **even** number in the pentagon, and
an **odd** number in the square?

f) an **odd** number in the circle,
an **odd** number in the pentagon, and
an **odd** number in the square?

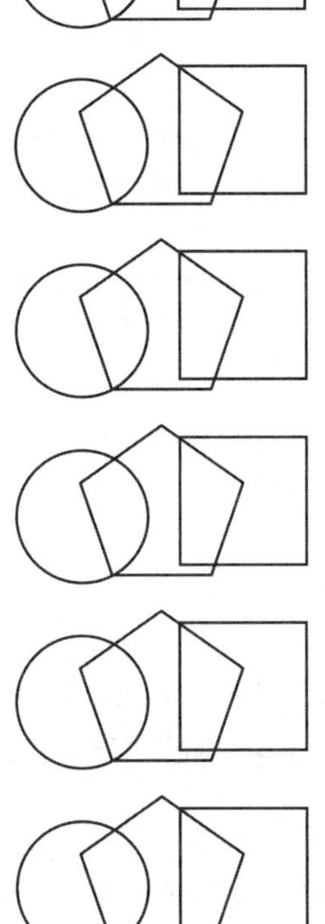

# PA4-18: Number Lines

Marie is on a bicycle tour 300 km from home. She can cycle 75 km each day. If she starts riding toward home on Tuesday morning, how far away from home will she be by Thursday evening?

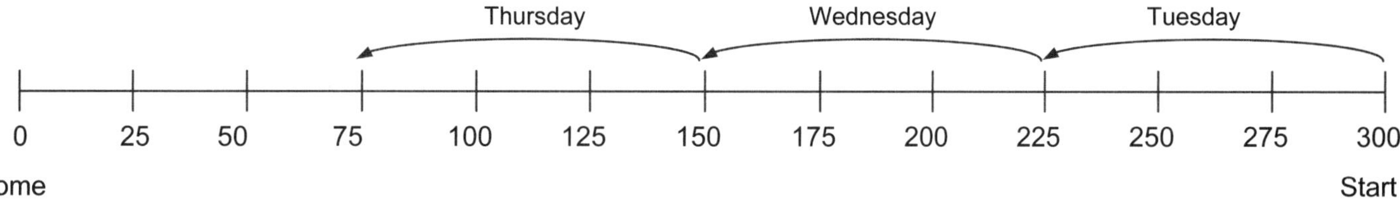


On Thursday evening, she will be 75 km from home.

---

1. On Wednesday morning, Ryan's campsite is 20 km from Mount Currie in British Columbia. He plans to walk 6 km toward the mountain each day. How far from the mountain will he be on Thursday evening?

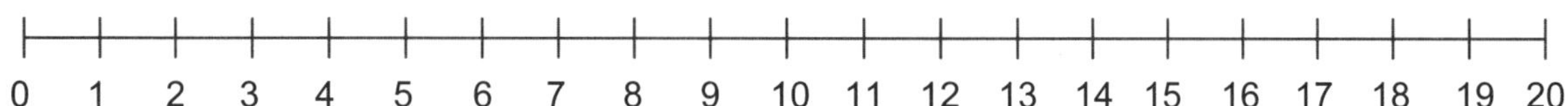


2. Jane is camping 50 km from her home. She can cycle 15 km every hour. How far from home will she be after 3 hours?

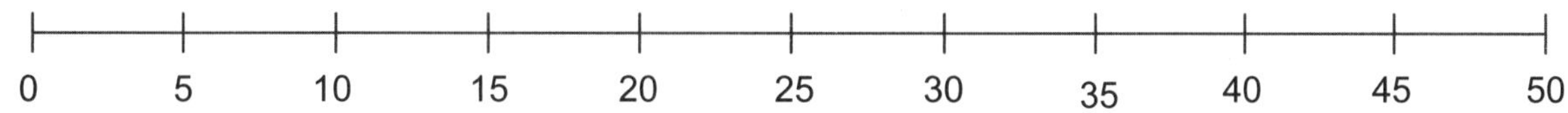


Draw number lines on grid paper to answer the following questions:

3. Midori is 16 blocks from home. She can walk 4 blocks in 1 minute. How many minutes will it take her to walk home?

4. James has entered a 250 km bicycle race. He can cycle 75 km each day. How far from the finish will he be after 3 days?

5. Wendy has to climb 5 walls in an obstacle course. The 1st wall is 100 m from the start. After that, each wall is 50 m further than the last. How far from the start is the 3rd wall?

6. Daniel plants 5 apple trees in a row. The nearest tree is 5 m from his house. The trees are 2 m apart. How far away from Daniel's house is the last tree?
(HINT: Put Daniel's house at "zero" on the number line.)

7. To build a fence, Ravi uses one post for every 3 m of fence. If he uses 6 posts altogether, how long is his fence? (Do not forget that there must be a post at each end of the fence.)

8. A painter's ladder has 12 steps. The painter spills red paint on every second step and blue paint on every third step. Which steps have red and blue paint on them?

# PA4-19: Describing and Creating Patterns

In the first sequence, each number is greater than the one before it. The sequence is always **increasing**: 7 8 10 15 21

In the second sequence, each number is less than the one before it. The sequence is always **decreasing**: 25 23 18 11 8

In the third sequence, the numbers **increase** and **decrease**. The **+** signs show where the sequence increases and the – signs show where it decreases:

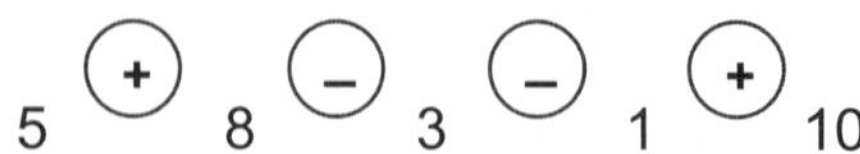


1. Write a **+** sign in the circle to show where the sequence **increases**. Write a – sign to show where it **decreases**. The first question is done for you.

a) 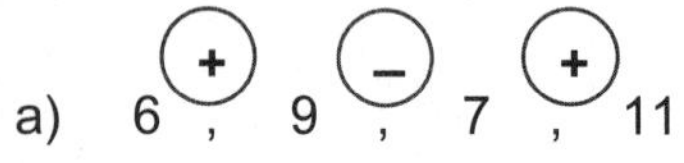


b) 1 , 5 , 7 , 2

c) 10 , 7 , 6 , 8

d) 2 , 5 , 1 , 7

e) 5 , 3 , 9 , 8

f) 2 , 5 , 9 , 12

g) 2 , 7 , 4 , 9

h) 11 , 15 , 18 , 13

i) 18 , 13 , 11 , 23

j) 28 , 36 , 49 , 52

k) 17 , 38 , 29 , 85

l) 53 , 64 , 96 , 98

2. Write a **+** sign in the circle to show where the sequence **increases**. Write a – sign to show where it **decreases**. Then write . . .

   an A beside the sequence if it **increases**

   a B beside the sequence if it **decreases**

   a C beside the sequence if it **increases** and **decreases**

a) 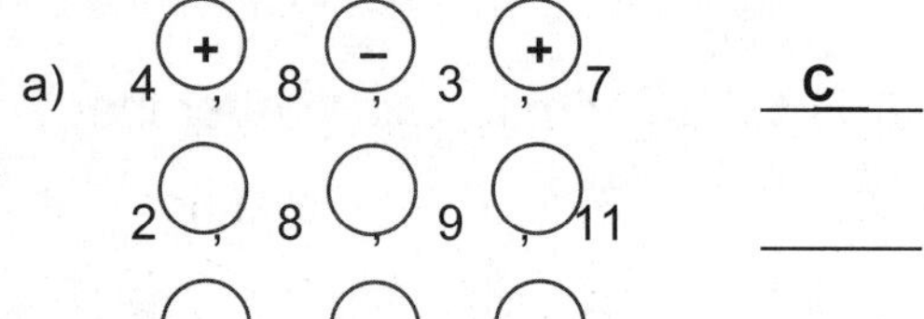


b) 7 , 5 , 3 , 2 ______

8 , 6 , 3 , 9 ______

1 , 4 , 7 , 11 ______

c) 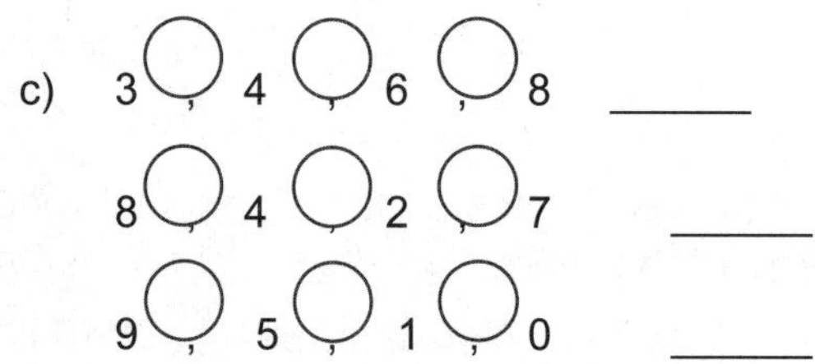


d) 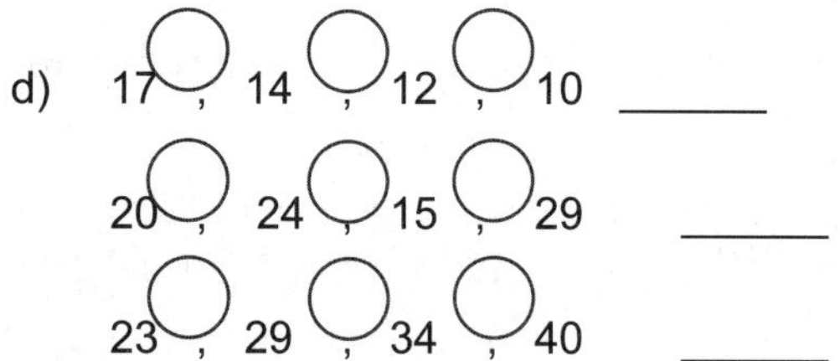

# PA4-19: Describing and Creating Patterns *(continued)*

3. Find the **amount** by which the sequence **increases** or **decreases**. (Write a number with a **+** sign if the sequence increases, and a – sign if it decreases.) The first one is done for you.

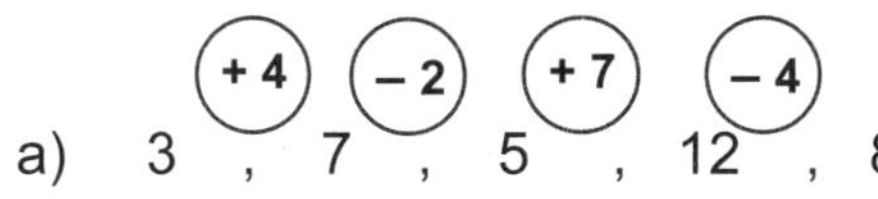


a) 3 , 7 , 5 , 12 , 8

b) 2 , 5 , 4 , 8 , 5

c) 3 , 6 , 7 , 11 , 13

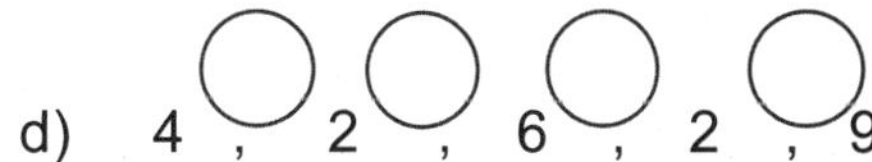

d) 4 , 2 , 6 , 2 , 9

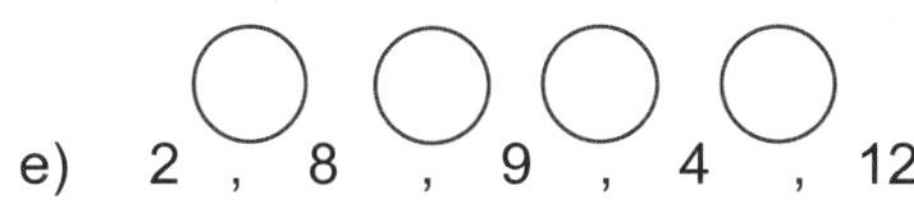

e) 2 , 8 , 9 , 4 , 12

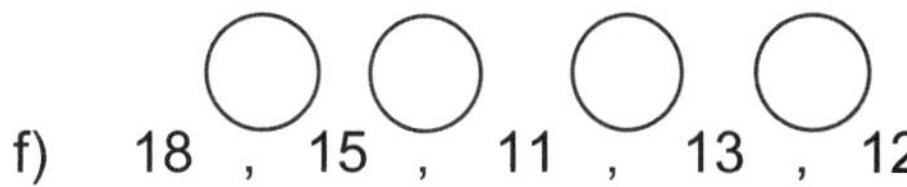

f) 18 , 15 , 11 , 13 , 12

g) 16 , 11 , 13 , 18 , 15

h) 28 , 31 , 24 , 31 , 38

4. Match each sequence with the sentence that describes it. This sequence . . .

a) A increases by 3 each time
B increases by different amounts

____ 9 , 12 , 15 , 18 , 21

____ 7 , 10 , 13 , 14 , 19

b) A increases by 4 each time
B increases by different amounts

____ 6 , 10 , 14 , 17 , 21

____ 5 , 9 , 13 , 17 , 21

c) A decreases by different amounts
B decreases by the same amount

____ 10 , 9 , 8 , 6 , 5

____ 11 , 10 , 9 , 8 , 7

d) A decreases by 5 each time
B decreases by different amounts

____ 35 , 30 , 25 , 20 , 15

____ 30 , 25 , 20 , 15 , 5

BONUS:

e) A increases by 5 each time
B decreases by different amounts
C increases by different amounts

____ 17 , 22 , 28 , 32 , 34

____ 17 , 14 , 10 , 9 , 6

____ 14 , 19 , 24 , 29 , 34

f) A increases and decreases
B increases by the same amount
C decreases by different amounts
D decreases by the same amount

____ 21 , 19 , 15 , 13 , 9

____ 10 , 13 , 9 , 7 , 5

____ 19 , 17 , 15 , 13 , 11

____ 9 , 12 , 15 , 18 , 21

5. Write a rule for each pattern (use the words **add** or **subtract**, and say what number the pattern starts with). Then choose one of the patterns and, on a separate piece of paper, explain how you found the rule.

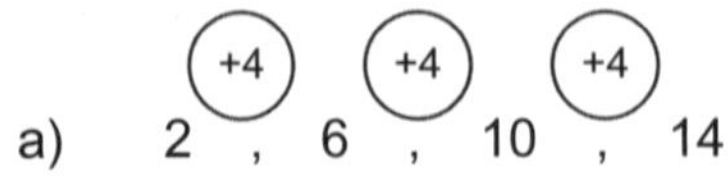


a) 2 , 6 , 10 , 14 start at 2, add 4

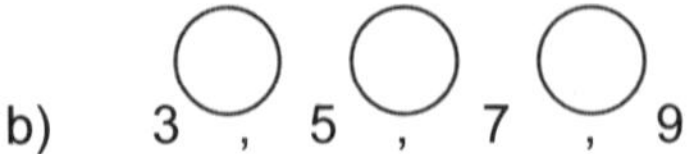

b) 3 , 5 , 7 , 9 __________

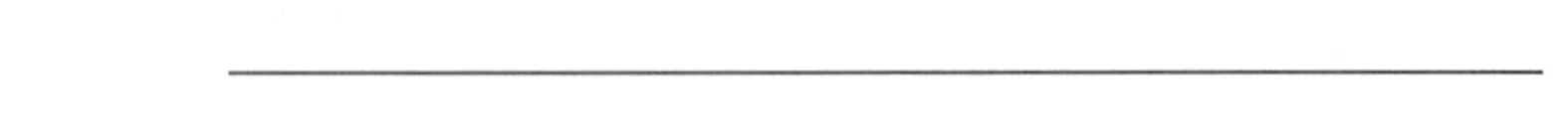

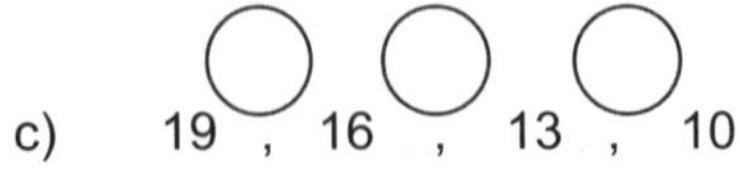

c) 19 , 16 , 13 , 10 __________

d) 33 , 28 , 23 , 18 __________

6. Write a rule for each pattern. Then choose one of the patterns and, on a separate piece of paper, explain how you know your rule is correct.
NOTE: One sequence does not have a rule—see if you can find it.

a) 8 , 11 , 14 , 17 __________

b) 14 , 10 , 6 , 2 __________

c) 25 , 21 , 18 , 17 , 11 __________

d) 61 , 65 , 69 , 73 __________

7. Describe each pattern as “increasing,” “decreasing,” or “repeating.”

a) 1 , 4 , 7 , 10 , 13 , 16 __________ b) 1 , 5 , 8 , 1 , 5 , 8 __________

c) 9 , 8 , 7 , 6 , 5 , 4 __________ d) 2 , 4 , 6 , 8 , 10 , 12 __________

e) 3 , 8 , 3 , 8 , 3 , 8 __________ f) 21 , 16 , 10 , 7 , 5 , 1 __________

Answer the following questions on a separate piece of paper:

8. Write the first 5 numbers in each pattern.
a) start at 6, add 3 b) start at 26, subtract 4 c) start at 39, add 5

9. Create an increasing number pattern. Give the rule for your pattern.

10. Create a decreasing number pattern. Give the rule for your pattern.

11. Create a repeating pattern using . . . a) letters b) shapes c) numbers

12. Create a pattern and ask a friend to find the rule for your pattern.

# PA4-20: Two-Dimensional Patterns

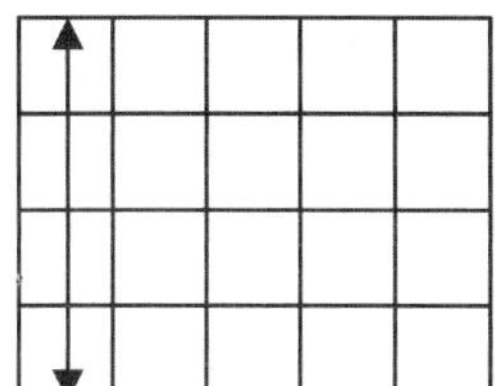

Columns run up and down.

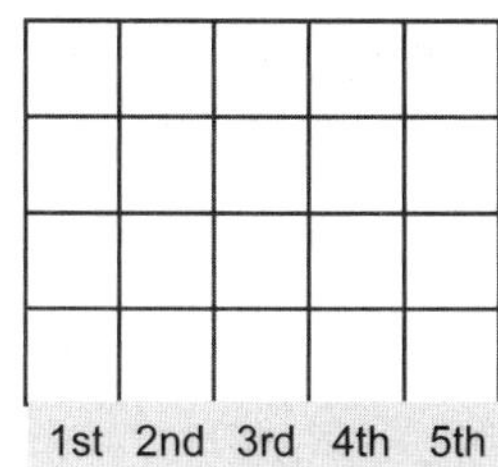


Columns are numbered left to right.

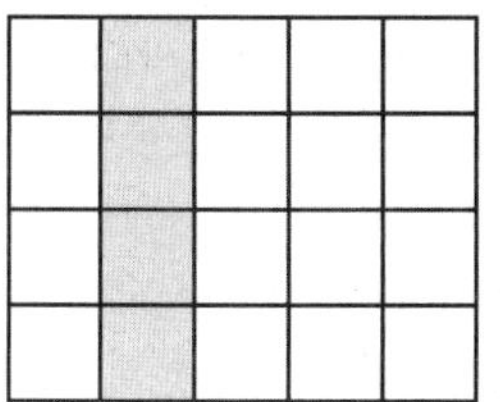

The 2nd column is shaded.

1. Shade . . .

a) 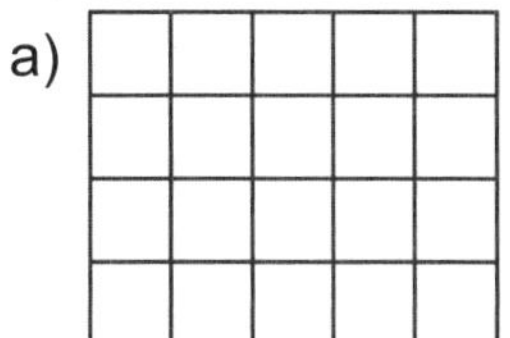

the 1st column

b) 

the 5th column

c) 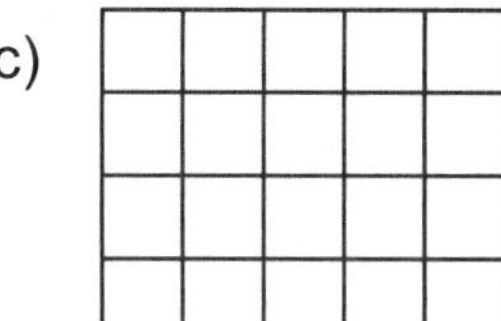

the 3rd column

d) 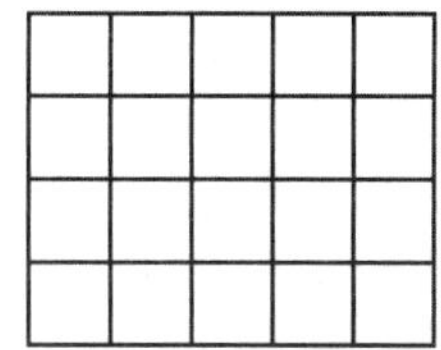

the 4th column

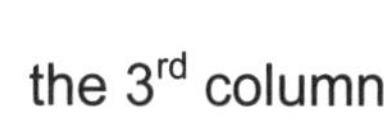

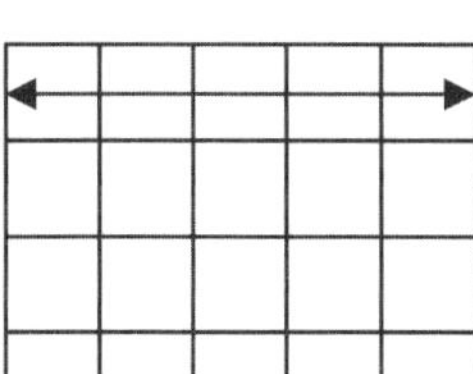

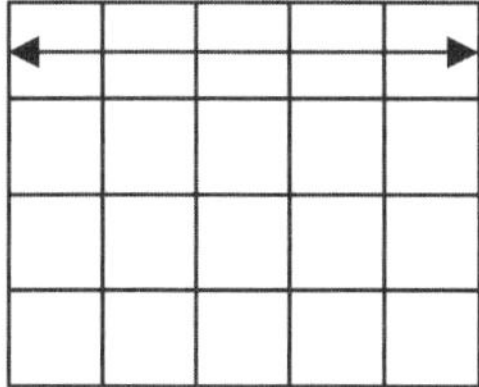

Rows run sideways.

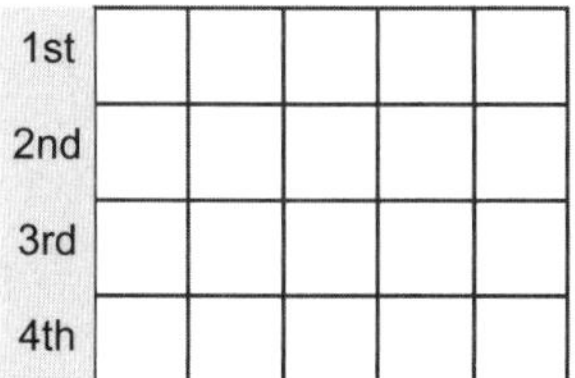


Rows are numbered from top to bottom (in this exercise).

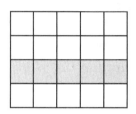

The 3rd row is shaded.

2. Shade . . .

a) 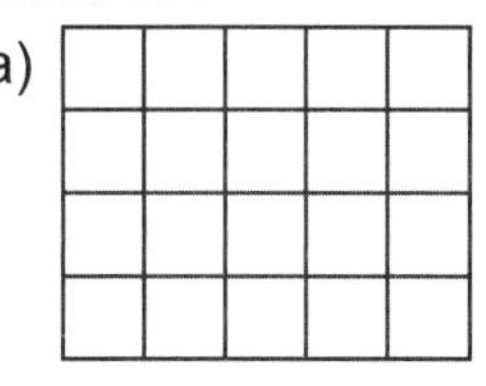

the 2nd row

b) 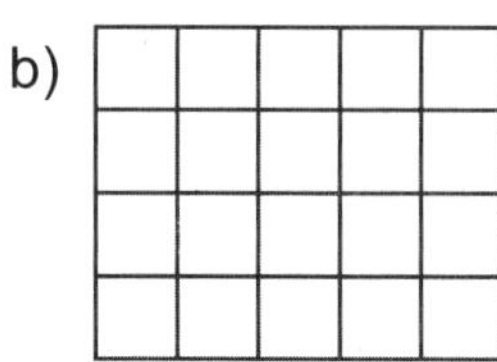

the 4th row

c) 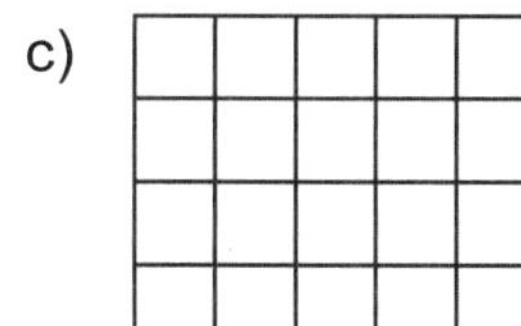

the 1st row

d) 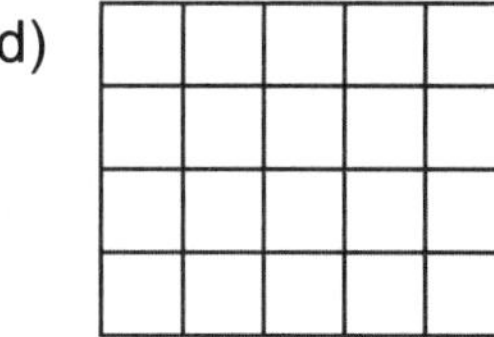

the 3rd row

3. Shade . . .

a) 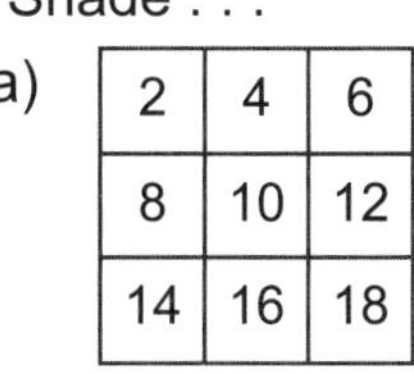

| 2 | 4 | 6 |
|---|---|---|
| 8 | 10 | 12 |
| 14 | 16 | 18 |

the 2nd row

b)

| 2 | 4 | 6 |
|---|---|---|
| 8 | 10 | 12 |
| 14 | 16 | 18 |

the 1st column

c)

| 2 | 4 | 6 |
|---|---|---|
| 8 | 10 | 12 |
| 14 | 16 | 18 |

the 3rd column

d)

| 2 | 4 | 6 |
|---|---|---|
| 8 | 10 | 12 |
| 14 | 16 | 18 |

the diagonals
(one is shaded)

4. On a separate piece of paper, describe the pattern in the numbers you shaded for each part of question 3.

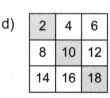

Describe the patterns you see in each chart below (remember to look horizontally, vertically, and diagonally).

You should use the words "rows," "columns," and "diagonals" in your answers.

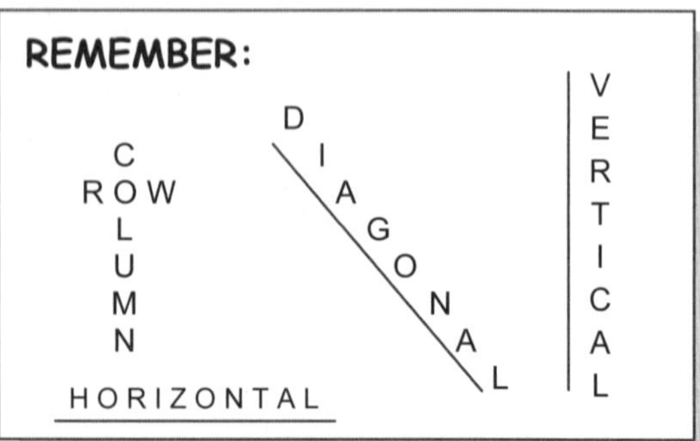


5.

| 2 | 4 | 6 |
|---|---|---|
| 4 | 6 | 8 |
| 6 | 8 | 10 |

6.

| 12 | 15 | 18 | 21 |
|---|---|---|---|
| 9 | 12 | 15 | 18 |
| 6 | 9 | 12 | 15 |
| 3 | 6 | 9 | 12 |

7. The patterns in the sequences can only be seen by reading down the first column, up the second column, down the third column, and so on. Fill in the missing shape or letter.

| X | Y | Y | X |
|---|---|---|---|
| Y | X | X | Y |
| Y | Y |  | Y |
| X | Y | Y | X |

| ○ | □ | □ | ○ |
|---|---|---|---|
| ○ | ○ | □ | □ |
| □ | ○ | ○ | □ |
| □ | □ |  | □ |

| A | C | C | A | B |
|---|---|---|---|---|
| A | B | C | A | C |
| B | A | A | C | C |
| C | A | A | C | C |
| C | C | B | C |  |

8.

| **+** | **1** | **2** | **3** | **4** | **5** | **6** |
|---|---|---|---|---|---|---|
| **1** | 2 | 3 |  |  |  |  |
| **2** |  | 4 |  |  |  |  |
| **3** |  | 5 |  |  |  |  |
| **4** |  |  |  |  |  |  |
| **5** |  |  |  |  |  |  |
| **6** |  |  |  |  |  |  |

Complete the addition chart. Describe the patterns you see in the rows, columns, and diagonals of the chart.

9. Place the letters A, B, and C so that each row and column has exactly one A, one B, and one C in it (in any order).

| A | B | C |
|---|---|---|
|   |   |   |
|   |   |   |

10. Place the letters A and B so that each row and each column has two As and two Bs in it.

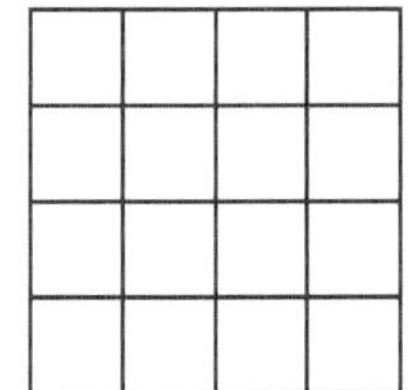

11. A gardener plants roses (R), lilies (L) and tulips (T) in rows in the pattern shown to the right:

    a) Complete the chart.

    b) In which row will the pattern in the second row be repeated? _______

| | | | | | |
|---|---|---|---|---|---|
| **Row 1** | L | R | T | T | L |
| **Row 2** | R | T | T | | |
| **Row 3** | | | | | |
| **Row 4** | | | | | |
| **Row 5** | | | | | |
| **Row 6** | | | | | |
| **Row 7** | | | | | |

PARENT: For the following exercises, your child will need a copy of page xvii: Hundreds Charts from the Introduction.

12. Shade any diagonal in a hundreds chart. Add the ones digit and the tens digit of each number you shaded. What do you notice? Does this work for every diagonal?

13. a) How many numbers from 1 to 20 are divisible by 4?

    b) How many numbers from 1 to 40 are divisible by 4?

    c) What do you notice about your answers in parts a) and b)? How can you use this information to find out how many numbers between 1 and 100 are divisible by 4?

14. a) Shade every third square on a hundreds chart. How can you describe the position of the squares you shaded?

    b) Mark every fifth square on the same chart with an "X."

    c) Write out the numbers between 1 and 100 that are multiples of 3 and 5. (These are the numbers shaded and marked with an "X.") Describe the pattern in the tens digit of the numbers and in the ones digits.

15. a) Shade the multiples of 9 on the hundreds chart. Describe the position of these numbers.

    b) Add the ones digit and the tens digit of each multiple of 9. What do you notice?

    c) What pattern do you see in the ones digits of the multiples of 9?

    d) What pattern do you see in the tens digits of the multiples of 9?

16. Complete the chart by inserting the whole numbers from 1 to 20 into the correct boxes.

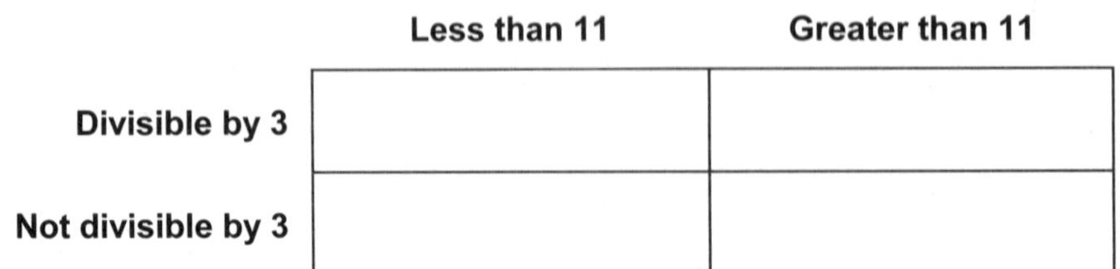

| | Less than 11 | Greater than 11 |
|---|---|---|
| **Divisible by 3** | | |
| **Not divisible by 3** | | |

17. Here are some number pyramids:

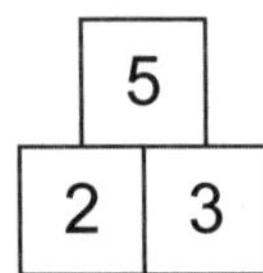

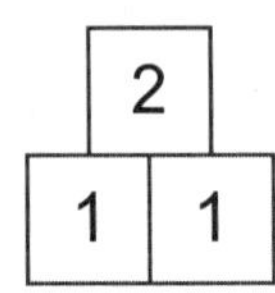

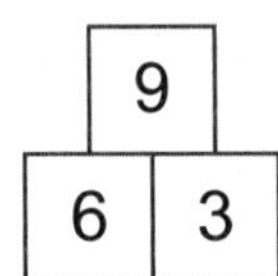

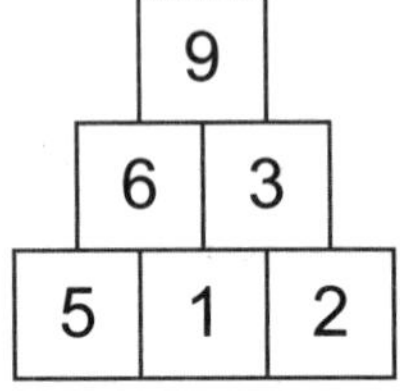


Can you find the rule by which the patterns in the pyramids were made? Describe it here.

18. Using the rule you described in question 17, find the missing numbers.

a) 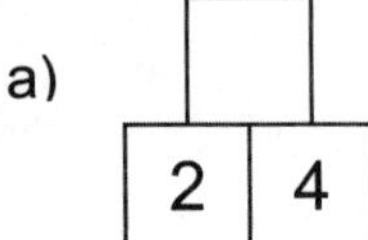


b) 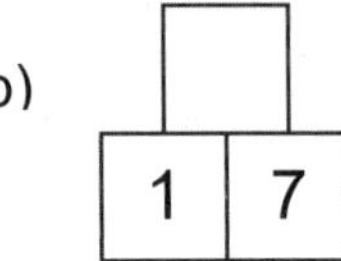


c) 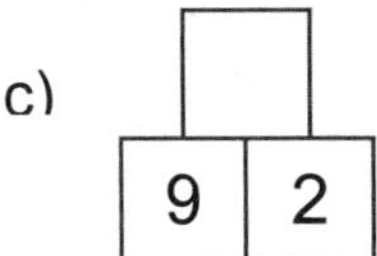


d) 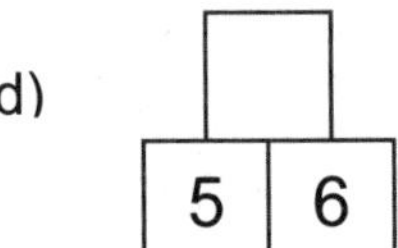


e) 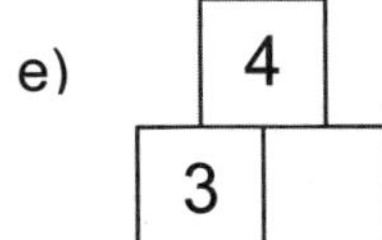


f) 7 / 4

g) 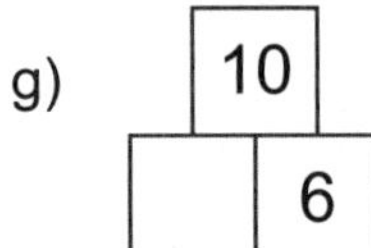


h) 12 / 7

i) 10 5

j) 16 / 11

BONUS:

k) 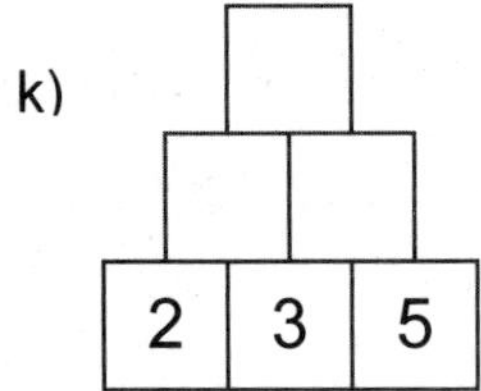


l) 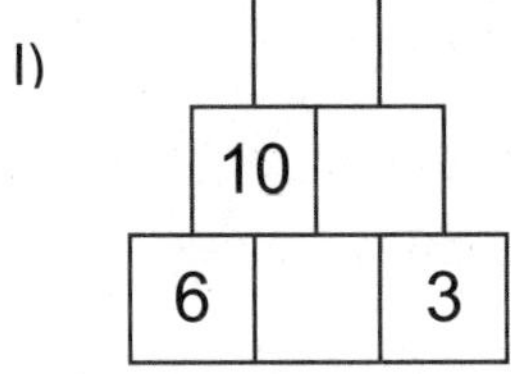


m) 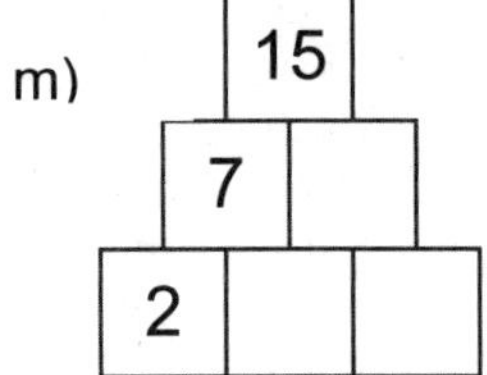


n) 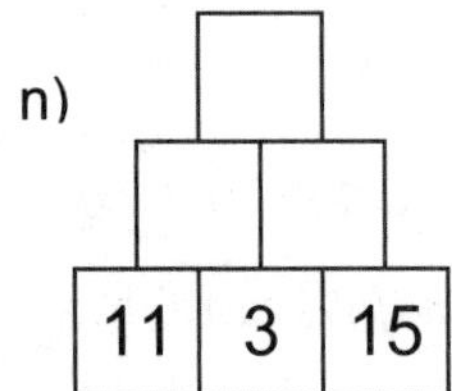


o) 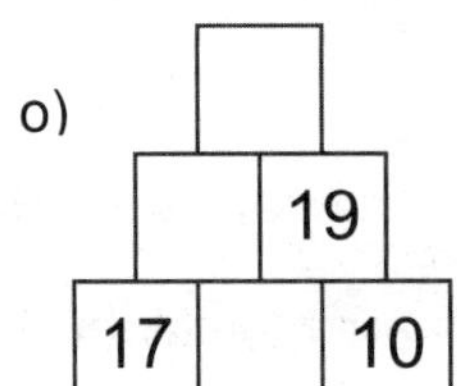


p) 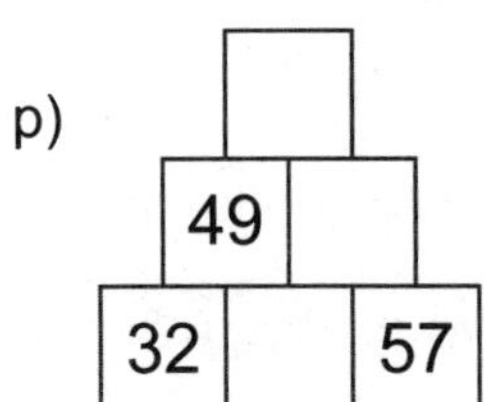

# PA4-21: Patterns in Times Tables

PARENT:
For this lesson your child will need a copy of page xvii: Hundreds Charts from the Introduction. Also, remind your child about the digits of a number:

tens digit ⟶ 7 3 ⟵ ones digit

---

**Patterns in the 2 Times Table**

1. a) On a hundreds chart, shade every second number (that is, shade the numbers you would say when counting by 2s: 2, 4, 6, and so on).
   The numbers you shaded are the **multiples** of 2 (up to 100).

   b) What patterns can you see in the **positions** of the multiples of 2? Use the words "rows," "columns," or "diagonals" in your answer.

   c) Look at the **ones digits** of the multiples of 2 in the third row of the hundreds chart:

| 21 | 2<u>2</u> | 23 | 2<u>4</u> | 25 | 2<u>6</u> | 27 | 2<u>8</u> | 29 | 3<u>0</u> |
|---|---|---|---|---|---|---|---|---|---|

   Underline the ones digits of the multiples of 2 in any other row. What do you notice?

   d) How can you tell whether a number between 1 and 100 is a multiple of 2 without counting?

   e) Without counting (or looking at the hundreds chart) circle the numbers that are multiples of 2.

   15 27 82 63 45 93 36 78 38 59

   f) The multiples of 2 (including zero) are called **even** numbers. Circle the even numbers.

   7 3 18 32 21 76 34 89 94 67

   g) Now look at the numbers you **did not** shade on the hundreds chart. What do you notice about these numbers?

   h) The numbers that are **not** multiples of 2 are called **odd** numbers. Circle the odd numbers.

   5 75 60 37 44 68 83 92 100

i) Pick an **even** number. Add two to your number. What kind of number do you get—even or odd? Will this always happen?

j) Pick an **odd** number. Add two to your number. What kind of number do you get—even or odd? Will this always happen?

k) Write out the first ten numbers for the following rule: "Start at 1 and add 2." What do you notice about the numbers in the sequence?

**Patterns in the 5 Times Table**

2. a) On a hundreds chart, shade every fifth number (that is, shade the numbers you would say when counting by 5s: 5, 10, 15, and so on).

   The numbers you shaded are the **multiples** of 5 (up to 100).

   b) What patterns can you see in the **positions** of the multiples of 5? Use the words "rows," "columns," or "diagonals" in your answer.

   c) Look at the **ones digits** of the multiples of 5 in the fourth row of the hundreds chart:

| 31 | 32 | 33 | 34 | 35 | 36 | 37 | 38 | 39 | 40 |
|---|---|---|---|---|---|---|---|---|---|

   Now look at the ones digits of the multiples of 5 in any other row. What do you notice?

   d) How can you tell whether a number between 1 and 100 is a multiple of 5 without counting up?

   e) Without counting up (or looking at the hundreds chart) circle the numbers that are multiples of 5.

   8 16 45 27 60 62 90 85 11 25

NOTE: Review Venn diagrams before completing this worksheet.

3 a)

| 10 | 25 | 15 | 37 | 86 | 49 | 5 | 79 | 24 |
|---|---|---|---|---|---|---|---|---|
| 50 | 6 | 17 | 61 | 40 | 36 | 65 | 8 | 96 |

Sort these numbers into the Venn diagram. The first number is done for you.

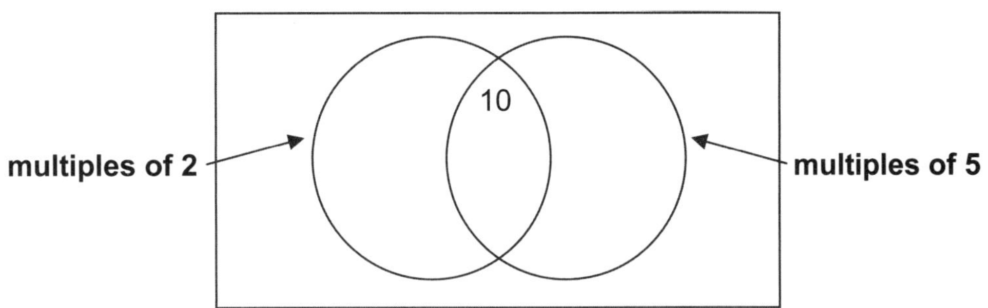


b) Think of two numbers from 50 to 100 that would go in the middle of the diagram. _____, _____

c) Think of two numbers from 50 to 100 that could not be placed in either circle. _____, _____

**Patterns in the 8 Times Table**

4. a) On a hundreds chart, shade every eighth number (that is, shade the numbers you would say when counting by 8s: 8, 16, 24, and so on).

The numbers you shaded are the **multiples** of 8 (up to 100).

b) Complete the following:

Write the first five multiples of 8 here (in increasing order).

0 8
1 6
___ ___
___ ___
___ ___
↑

Write the next five multiples of 8 here.

___ ___
___ ___
___ ___
___ ___
___ ___
↑

Look down the columns marked by the arrows. Can you see a pattern in the **ones** digits of the multiples of 8?

c) Can you see a pattern in the **tens** digits of the multiples of 8?

d) Use the pattern you found in parts b) and c) to write out the multiples of 8 from 88 to 160.

| | |
|---|---|
| 8 8 | ____ |
| 9 6 | ____ |
| 10 4 | ____ |
| ____ | ____ |
| ____ | ____ |

**Circle Charts**

Show your written work for the remaining questions on a separate piece of paper.

5. a) Underline the ones digits of the multiples of 4.

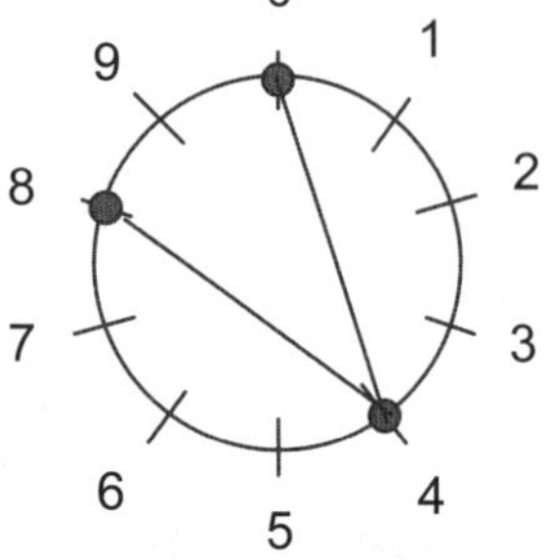


0   4   8   12   16   20   24

28   32   36   40   44   48

Mark the digits that you underlined with a dot on the circle chart. (The first three are marked for you.) Join the dots. What pattern do you see?

b) On a hundreds chart, circle the first 10 multiples of 6. Underline the ones digits of the numbers you underlined. Plot the ones digits on the circle chart and join the dots. What do you notice?

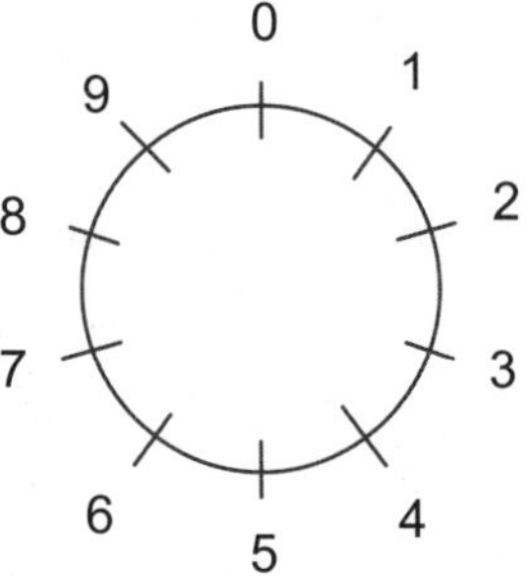


c) Repeat the exercise in part b) for the multiples of

d) Repeat the exercise in part b) for the multiples of 3.

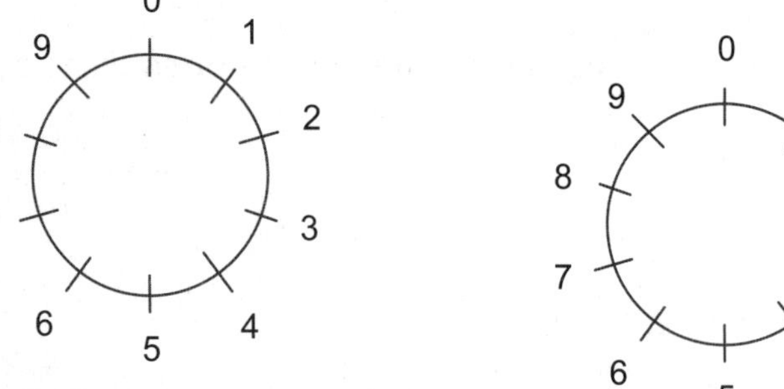

e) Which one-digit number (2, 5, 7, or 9) do you think will give the same pattern as the circle pattern for the number 3? Test your prediction on the circle.

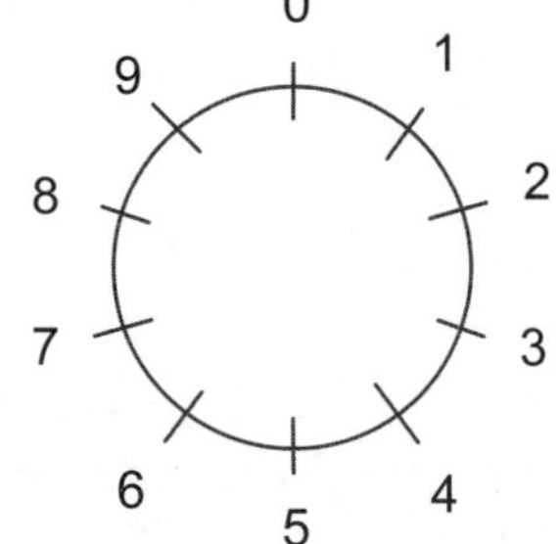


f) What one-digit number (2, 5, 7, or 9) do you think will give the same circle pattern as the numbers 4, 6, and 8? Draw a circle and test your prediction.

# PA4-22: Patterns with Increasing and Decreasing Steps

1. In the sequences, the step or gap between the numbers increases. Can you see a pattern in the way the gap increases? Use the pattern to extend the sequence.

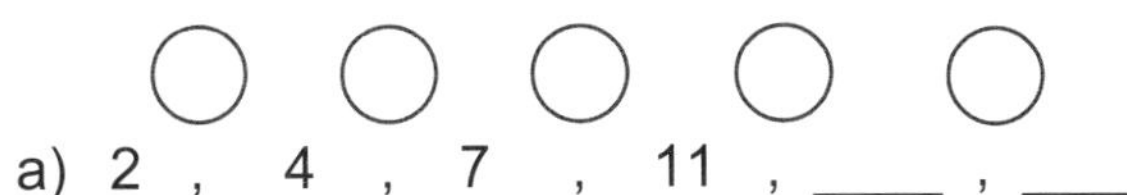

a) 2 , 4 , 7 , 11 , ____ , ____

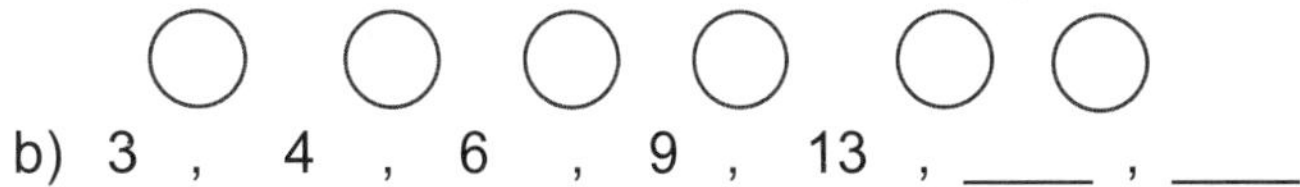

b) 3 , 4 , 6 , 9 , 13 , ____ , ____

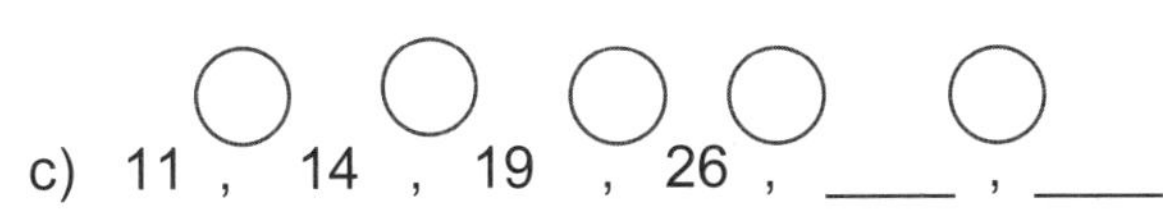

c) 11 , 14 , 19 , 26 , ____ , ____

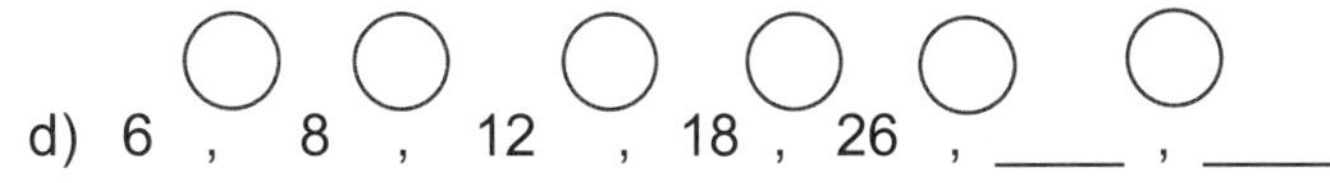

d) 6 , 8 , 12 , 18 , 26 , ____ , ____

2. In the sequences, the gap between the numbers decreases. Can you see a pattern in the way the gap decreases? Use the pattern to extend the sequence.

a) 17 , 16 , 14 , 11 , ____ , ____

b) 32 , 30 , 26 , 20 , ____ , ____

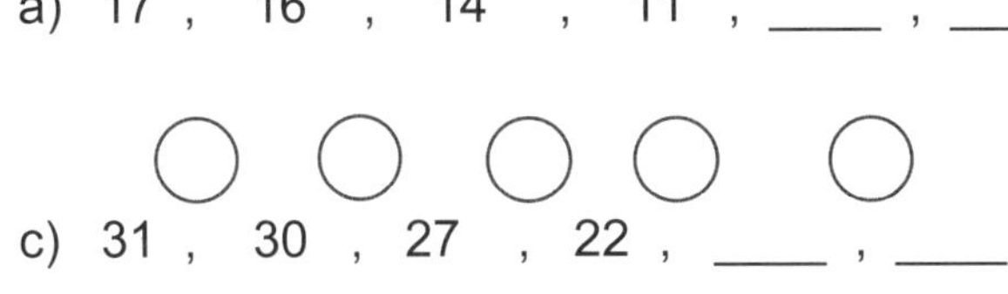

c) 31 , 30 , 27 , 22 , ____ , ____

d) 110 , 105 , 95 , 80 , 60 , ____ , ____

3. Complete the T-table for Figure 3 and Figure 4. Then use the pattern in the gap to predict the number of squares needed for Figure 5 and Figure 6.

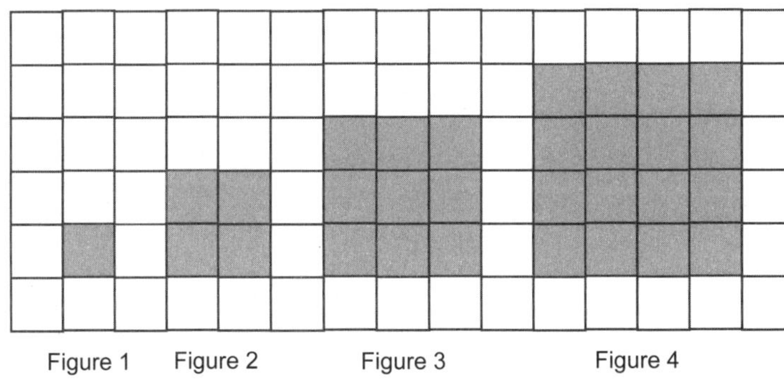


| Figure | Number of squares |
|---|---|
| 1 | 1 |
| 2 | 4 |
| 3 | |
| 4 | |
| 5 | |
| 6 | |

Write the number of squares added each time here.

4. On a separate piece of paper, make a T- table to predict how many squares will be needed for Figure 5.

Figure 1 Figure 2 Figure 3

# PA4-22: Patterns with Increasing and Decreasing Steps *(continued)*

5. On a separate piece of paper make a T-table to predict how many dots will be needed for Figure 6.

Figure 1

Figure 2

Figure 3

6. Jane is training for the cross-country run. She begins by training for 10 minutes on Monday, and each day she trains for 2 minutes longer. How many minutes in all did she train in the first four days?

NOTE: Review multiplication and dividing by 2 before answering the questions.

7. Ahmed made a pattern starting at 2, and multiplied each term by a fixed number.

   2, 4, 8, 16, ___, ___, ___, ___

   a) **What** number did Ahmed multiply each term by?

   b) Continue Ahmed's pattern.

   c) Find the gap between the numbers. What do you notice?

8. Joe had $400. He spent half of his money each week, so after 1 week, he had $200 and after 2 weeks he had $100. How much money did he have after 4 weeks?

BONUS:

9. Olivia and Krishna save the amounts shown.

   a) What is the pattern rule for the amount Krishna saves?

   b) What is the pattern rule for the amount Olivia saves?

   c) Who do you think will save more by the end of the seven weeks?

   d) Continue the pattern to see if you are right.

| Week | Olivia | Krishna |
|---|---|---|
| 1 | $1 | $15 |
| 2 | $2 | $20 |
| 3 | $4 | $25 |
| 4 | $8 | $30 |
| 5 | | |
| 6 | | |
| 7 | | |

10. a) Describe how the gap changes in the pattern below.

    b) Continue the pattern. 3 , 6 , 4 , 7 , 5 , 8 , ___ , ___ , ___

# PA4-23: Patterns with Larger Numbers



1. Use addition or multiplication to complete the following charts. (There are 60 seconds in a minute, 52 weeks in a year, and 365 days in a year.)

a)

| Minutes | Seconds |
|---|---|
| 1 | 60 |
| 2 | |
| 3 | |
| 4 | |
| 5 | |

b)

| Years | Weeks |
|---|---|
| 1 | 52 |
| 2 | |
| 3 | |
| 4 | |

c)

| Years | Days |
|---|---|
| 1 | 365 |
| 2 | |
| 3 | |
| 4 | |

Use T-tables to solve the following problems on a separate piece of paper:

2. There are 12 months in a year. How many months are there in 4 years?

3. A rabbit's heart beats 200 times a minute. How many times does it beat in 4 minutes?

4. A blue goose can fly 1500 km in 2 days. How far can it fly in 3 days? Explain how you found your answer.

5. Miguel earns $18 for the first hour he works. He earns $16 for each hour after that. How much does he earn for 5 hours of work?

6. Lisa earns $14 on Monday. She earns $25 each day after that. How much does she earn by Friday evening?

7. Halley's comet returns to Earth every 76 years. It was last seen in 1986. List the next three dates it will return to Earth.

8. Use multiplication or a calculator to find the first few products. Look for a pattern. Use the pattern to fill in the rest of the numbers.

a) 999 x 2 = ________

999 x 3 = ________

999 x 4 = ________

________ = ________

________ = ________

b) 6 x 9 = ________

6 x 99 = ________

6 x 999 = ________

________ = ________

________ = ________

c) 9 x 1 + 2 = ________

9 x 12 + 3 = ________

9 x 123 + 4 = ________

________ = ________

BONUS:

9. Using a calculator, can you discover any patterns like the ones in question 8?

# PA4-24: Equations

1. Find the number that makes the equation true (by guessing and checking) and write it in the box.

a) □ + 2 = 7 b) □ + 3 = 6 c) □ + 2 = 10

d) 9 – □ = 6 e) 17 – □ = 15 f) 8 – □ = 2

g) 2 × □ = 10 h) 5 × □ = 15 i) 3 × □ = 12

j) □ ÷ 3 = 2 k) □ ÷ 5 = 2 l) □ ÷ 2 = 4

m) 7 + 3 = 6 + □ = n) 10 – 3 = □ + 2

o) □ + □ = 8 p) □ + □ + 3 = 13

2. Find a set of numbers that make the equation true. (Some questions have more than one answer.)
NOTE: In a given question, congruent shapes represent the same number.

a) □ + □ + ○ = 5 b) □ + □ + ○ = 8

c) ◇ + ◇ + ○ + ○ = 8 d) □ + △ + ○ = 7

3. Find two answers for the equation.

□ + □ + ○ = 5 □ + □ + ○ = 5

Show your work for the remaining questions on a separate piece of paper.

4. How many answers can you find for the equation □ + □ + ○ = 7 ?

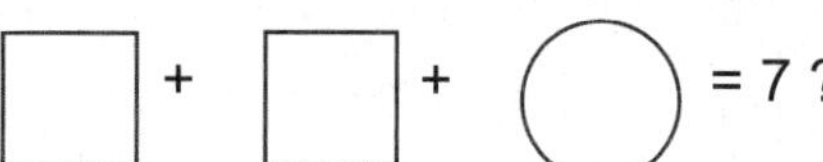

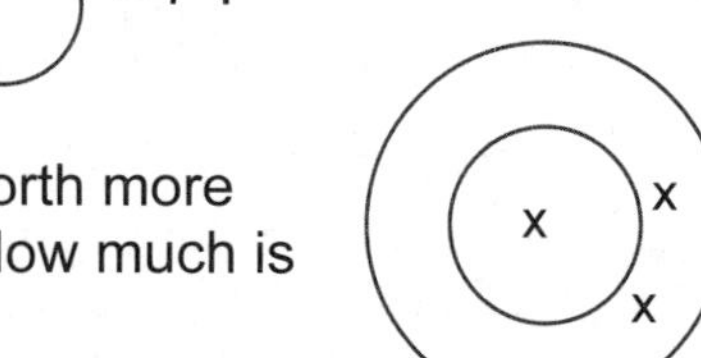

5. Raegan threw 3 darts and scored 8 points. The dart in the centre ring is worth more than the others. Each dart in the outer ring is worth more than one point. How much is each dart worth?
(HINT: How can an equation like the one in question 2. b) help you solve the problem?)

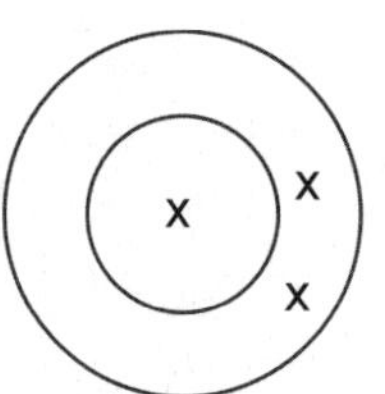

6. Paul threw 3 darts and scored 9 points. The dart in the centre ring is worth more than the others. Each dart in the outer ring is worth more than one point. How much is each dart worth?

7. If A + A = 6, what number does A represent?

8. Write an equation that tells you the relationship between the numbers in column A and column B. (The first two are done for you.)

a)

| A | B |
|---|---|
| 1 | 4 |
| 2 | 5 |
| 3 | 6 |

A + 3 = B

b)

| A | B |
|---|---|
| 1 | 2 |
| 2 | 4 |
| 3 | 6 |

A × 2 = B

c)

| A | B |
|---|---|
| 1 | 3 |
| 2 | 4 |
| 3 | 5 |

__________

d)

| A | B |
|---|---|
| 1 | 3 |
| 2 | 6 |
| 3 | 9 |

__________

e)

| A | B |
|---|---|
| 1 | 5 |
| 2 | 10 |
| 3 | 15 |

__________

9. 3 × [1] = 3; 3 × [2] = 6; 3 × [3] = 9; 3 × [4] = 12; 3 × [5] = 15;

When [ ] increases by 1, by how much does the **product** increase?

Answer the following questions on a separate piece of paper:

10. The fact family for the addition statement 2 + 4 = 6 is: 4 + 2 = 6; 6 – 4 = 2; and 6 – 2 = 4. Write the fact family of equations for the following statements:

a) 3 + 4 = 7 b) 5 + 4 = 9 c) 11 + 2 = 13 d) 23 + 5 = 28

11. The fact family for the multiplication statement 3 × 5 = 15 is: 5 × 3 = 15; 15 ÷ 3 = 5; and 15 ÷ 5 = 3. Write the fact family of equations for the following statements:

a) 5 × 2 = 10 b) 4 × 3 = 12 c) 8 × 4 = 32 d) 9 × 3 = 27

12. a) You can count the dots in an array by grouping them in "L"s as shown below. Write an addition statement and a multiplication statement for the arrays.

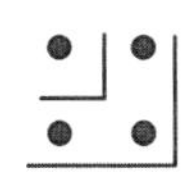

1 + 3 = 4

2 × 2 = 4

1 + 3 + 5= 9

3 × 3 = 9

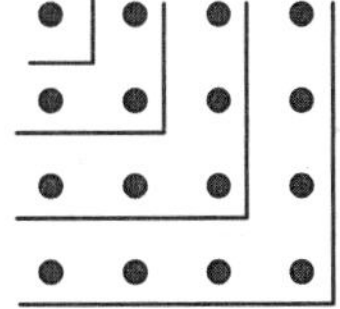

Addition statement: _______________

Multiplication statement: _______________

b) On grid paper draw a 5 × 5 array and draw "L"s to group the dots. Write an addition statement and a multiplication statement. Are the numbers in your statement all odd or all even?

c) How can you find 1 + 3 + 5 + 7 + 9 + 11 without adding? (HINT: Can you write an equivalent multiplication statement?)

# PA4-25: Puzzles and Problems

PARENT:
Give your child a copy of page xvii: Hundreds Charts, page xvi: Calendars from the Introduction, and some grid paper for drawing number lines and T-tables. Let your child decide which tool should be used for each question. (Note that some questions will not require any materials besides pencil and paper.)

Show your work for the following questions on a separate piece of paper:

1. 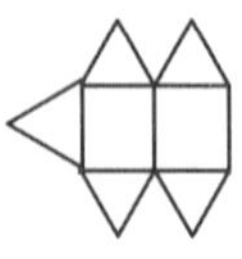 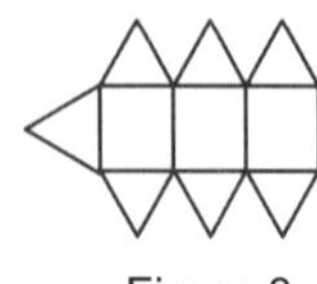

Figure 1 Figure 2 Figure 3

How many triangles will be needed for Figure 6?

2. Marie saves \$17 in October. She saves \$3 every month after that. How much does she save by the end of January?

3. April $1^{st}$ is a Monday. Andrea has a piano lesson every $5^{th}$ day of the month. Peter has a lesson every Friday. On what days of the month do they both have lessons?

4. Sue makes ornaments using squares and triangles. She has 12 squares. How many triangles will she need to use to make ornaments with all 12 squares?

   How did you solve the problem?
   Did you use a T-table? a picture? a model?

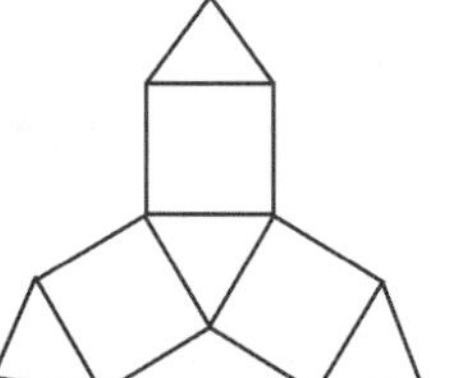

5. Hank has to climb 7 walls in an obstacle course. The $1^{st}$ wall is 200 m from the start. After that, each wall is 50 m further than the last. How far from the start is the $5^{th}$ wall?

6. Continue the patterns.

   a) 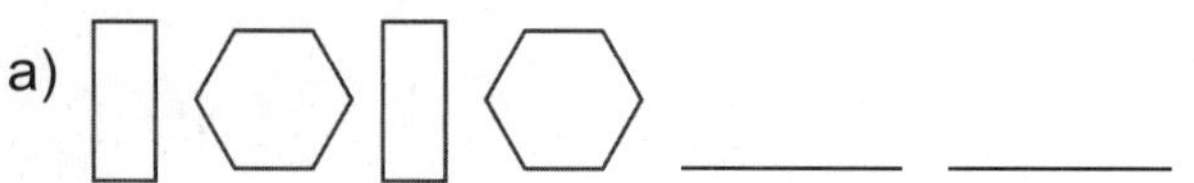 ______ ______

   b) K Q A 10 K Q A ____ ____ ____

   c) 001, 010, 100, 001, ____, ____, ____

   d) 000, 001, 011, 111, 000, ____, ____, ____

   e) 010, 020, 030, 010, ____, ____, ____

   f) 030, 060, 090, 030, ____, ____, ____

   g) M N M M N N M M M ____ ____ ____

   h) 2 T 22 T 222 ____ ____ ____ ____ ____

   i) AA, AB, AC, AD, ____, ____

   j) ________ ________ ________

7. What strategy would you use to find the 23rd shape in this pattern? What is the shape?

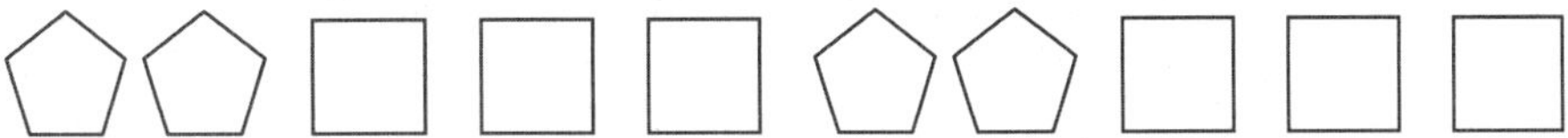

8. Find the mystery number.
   a) I am greater than 21 and less than 26. I am a multiple of 3. What am I?
   b) I am greater than 29 and less than 33. I am a multiple of 4. What am I?
   c) I am less than 15. I am a multiple of 3 **and** a multiple of 4. What am I?

9. Extend each pattern.
   a) 3427 3527 3627 ________ ________ ________
   b) 4234 5235 6236 ________ ________ ________
   c) 1234 2345 3456 ________ ________ ________

10. Sam and Kiana run up 12 steps with muddy shoes.
    a) Sam steps on every 3rd step and Kiana steps on every 4th step. Which steps have both of their footprints on them?
    b) If Sam's right foot lands on the 3rd step, on which steps does his left foot land?

11. Make a pattern by shading squares in a hundreds chart. Describe any patterns you see in the numbers you have shaded.

12.

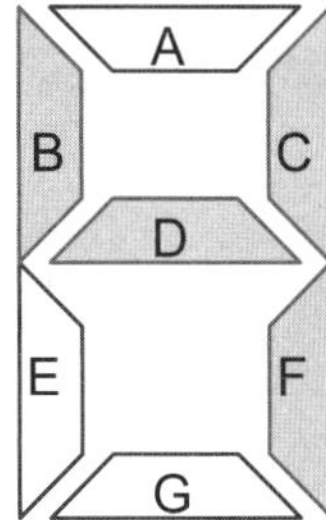


On a digital watch or calculator, numbers are made from bars in the shape of trapezoids. The number 4, shown in the picture, is made from the trapezoids B, D, C, and F.

a) On a separate piece of paper, list the trapezoids that are needed to make each of the numbers from 0 to 9.

b) Which trapezoid is used most often? (Do not forget to count the trapezoids in the list for the number 4.)

13. Every 2nd person who arrives at a book sale receives a free pen and every 3rd person receives a free book. Which of the first 15 people will receive a free pen and a book?

14. Emma makes a staircase using stone blocks. How many blocks will she need to build a stairway that is 6 steps high?

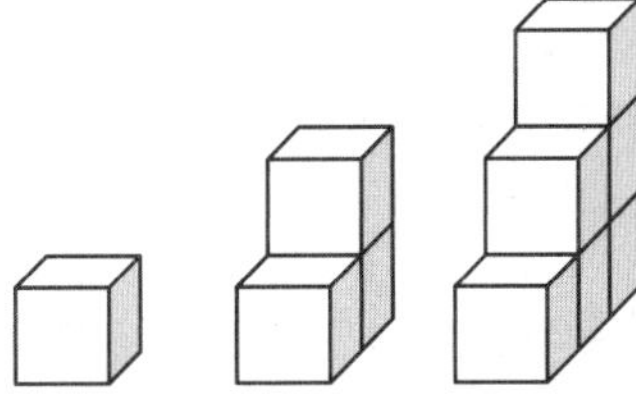

# NS4-29: Sharing—Knowing the Number of Sets

Kyla wants to share 16 cookies with three friends. She sets out four plates (one for herself and one for each of her friends). She puts one cookie at a time on the plates:

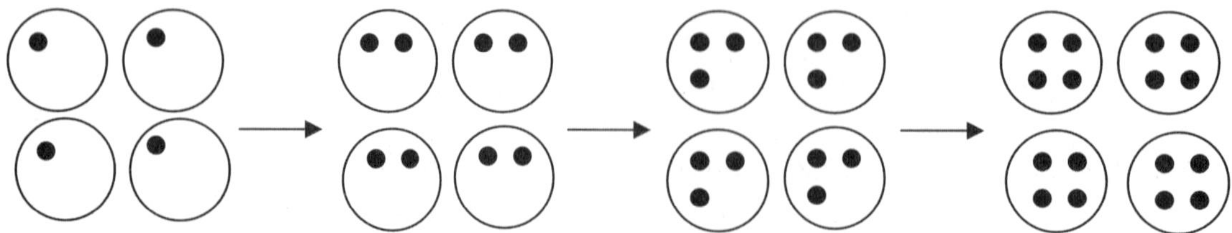

Each plate holds a **set** (or group) of 4 cookies. When 16 cookies are **divided** (or shared equally) into 4 sets, there are 4 cookies **in each set**.

---

1. Put an equal number of cookies on each plate. Draw circles for the plates and dots for the cookies. (HINT: Draw the plates, then place one cookie at a time.)

   a) 12 cookies; 3 plates

   b) 15 cookies; 5 plates

   c) 10 cookies; 2 plates

2. Draw dots (or lines) for the things being shared or divided equally. Draw circles (or rectangles) for the sets.

   a) 4 vans; 8 people
   How many people are in each van?

   b) 18 stickers; 6 kids
   How many stickers are there for each kid?

   c) 20 flowers; 5 plants
   How many flowers are on each plant?

   d) 6 boxes; 24 grapefruits
   How many grapefruits are in each box?

Solve the problems on a separate piece of paper. Use counters or draw pictures to model the problems.

3. 5 friends pick 20 cherries. How many cherries does each friend get?

4. Lauren's weekly allowance is $21. What is his daily allowance? (HINT: There are 7 days in a week.)

5. Eileen shared 12 stickers among her 4 friends and herself. How many stickers does each one of them get?

6. There are 16 apples in 8 trees. How many apples are in each tree?

# NS4-30: Sharing – Knowing the Number in Each Set

Saud has 30 apples.

He wants to give 5 apples to each of his friends: 

To find out how many friends he can give apples to, he starts by counting out 5 apples.

He then keeps counting out **sets** or **groups** of 5 apples until he has used all 30 apples: 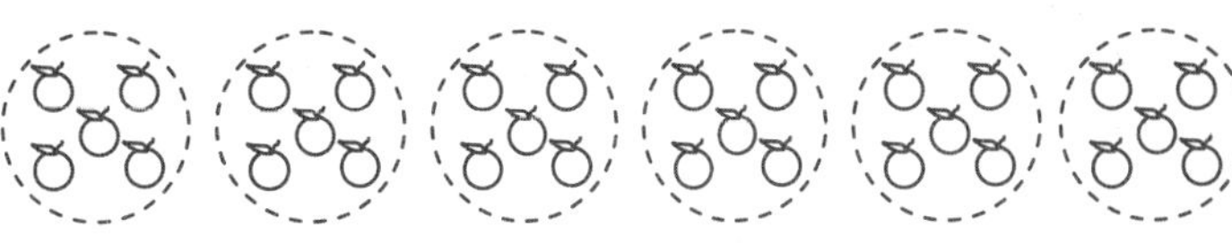

He can give apples to 6 friends. When 30 apples are divided into sets of 5 apples, there are 6 sets.

---

7. Divide the dots into equal sets by putting the correct number of dots in each set. The first one is done for you.

a)  4 dots in each set

b) ● ● ● ● ● ● ● ● ● ● 5 dots in each set

c)  3 dots in each set

8. Draw circles to divide these arrays into . . .

a) groups of 3

b) groups of 4

c) groups of 3

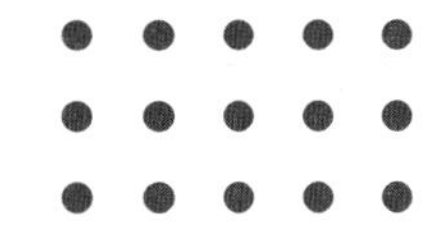

d) groups of 4

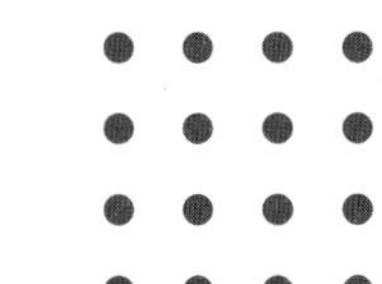

9. Draw dots (or lines) for the things being shared or divided equally. Draw circles (or rectangles) for the sets.

a) 15 apples; 5 apples in each box
How many boxes are there?

______ boxes

b) 25 stickers; 5 stickers for each kid
How many kids are there?

______ kids

Solve the problems on a separate piece of paper. Use counters or pictures to model the problem.

10. Shelly has 18 cookies. She wants to give 3 cookies to each of her siblings. How many siblings does she have?

11. Vinaya has 14 stamps. He puts 2 stamps on each envelope. How many envelopes does he have?

12. Ali earned 7 loonies for each hour of work. He earned 21 loonies in total. How many hours did he work? (HINT: Use circles for hours and dots for loonies.)

# NS4-31: Sets

Elisa has 12 glasses of water. A tray holds 3 glasses.

There are 4 trays: 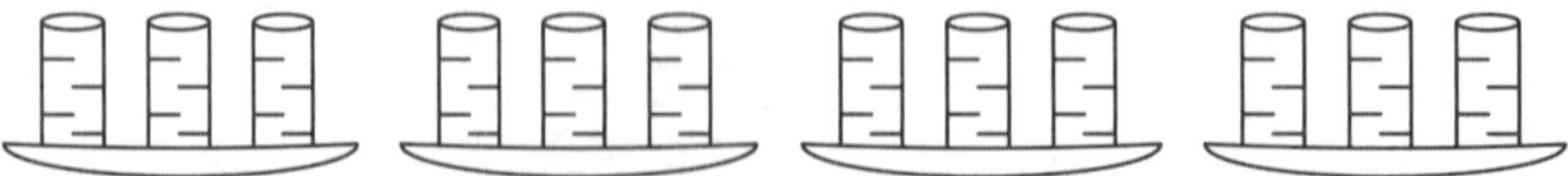

What has been shared or divided into **sets** or **groups**? (glasses)

How many sets are there? (There are 4 sets of glasses.)

How many of the things being divided are in each set? (There are 3 glasses in each set.)

---

1. a) 

What has been shared or divided into sets? ____________________

How many sets are there? _______

How many are in each set? _______

b) 

What has been shared or divided into sets? ____________________

How many sets are there? _______

How many are in each set? _______

2. Using circles for **sets** and dots for **things**, draw a picture to show . . .

a) 4 sets
6 things in each set

b) 6 groups
3 things in each group

c) 6 sets
2 things in each set

3. a) 20 toys; 4 toys for each kid; 5 kids

What has been shared or divided into sets? ________________

How many sets are there? _______ How many are in each set? _______

b) 7 friends; 21 pencils; 3 pencils for each friend.

What has been shared or divided into sets? ________________

How many sets are there? _______ How many are in each set? _______

c) 16 students; 4 desks; 4 students at each desk

What has been shared or divided into sets? _______________

How many sets are there? _______ How many are in each set? _______

d) 8 plants; 24 flowers; 3 flowers on each plant

What has been shared or divided into sets? _______________

How many sets are there? _______ How many are in each set? _______

e) 6 grapefruits in each box; 42 grapefruits; 7 boxes

What has been shared or divided into sets? _______________

How many sets are there? _______ How many are in each set? _______

f) 3 school buses; 30 kids; 10 kids in each school bus

What has been shared or divided into sets? _______________

How many sets are there? _______ How many are in each set? _______

g) 15 cows; 5 cows in each herd; 3 herds

What has been shared or divided into sets? _______________

How many sets are there? _______ How many are in each set? _______

h) 6 litters; 36 puppies; 6 puppies in each litter

What has been shared or divided into sets? _______________

How many sets are there? _______ How many are in each set? _______

BONUS:

4. Draw pictures for questions 3. a), b), and c) using **circles** for sets and **dots** for the things being divided.

REMEMBER:

In division problems, the word that tells you **what is being divided or shared** will almost always come right before the word "each" ("in each," "on each," "to each," "for each," or "at each").

For example, in the sentence "There are 4 kids in each boat," the word "kids" comes right before the phrase "in each boat."

# NS4-32: Two Ways of Sharing

Samuel has 15 cookies. There are two ways that he can share or **divide** his cookies equally:

I • He can decide how many **sets** (or **groups**) of cookies he wants to make.

Example:
Samuel wants to make 3 sets of cookies. He draws 3 circles:

He then puts one cookie at a time into the circles until he has placed all 15 cookies.

II • He can decide how many cookies he wants to put **in each set**.

Example:
Samuel wants to put 5 cookies in each set. He counts out 5 cookies:

He keeps counting out sets of 5 cookies until he has placed all 15 cookies in sets.

---

1. Share **20** dots equally. How many dots are in each set? (HINT: Place one dot at a time.)

   a) 4 sets

   There are _____ dots in each set.

   b) 5 sets

   There are _____ dots in each set.

2. Share the triangles equally among the sets. (HINT: Count the triangles first.)

   △△△
   △△△
   △△△
   △△△

   a)

   b)

3. Share the squares equally among the sets.

   □□□□□□□
   □□□□□□□

4. Group the lines so that there are 3 lines in each set. Write how many sets there are.

   a) | | | | | | | | |

   There are _____ sets.

   b) | | | | | | | | | | | |

   There are _____ sets

   c) | | | | | |

   There are _____ sets.

5. Group **18** dots so that . . .

   a) there are 6 dots in each set

   b) there are 9 dots in each set

6. In each question, groups of things or people are divided equally into sets.
   i) Write a word that tells you what has been divided into sets.
   ii) From the information given, state the number of sets or the number of people or things in each set.

   The first two questions are done for you.

   a) Vanessa has 25 pencils. She puts 5 pencils in each box.
      i) ______pencils______ ii) ______There are 5 pencils in each set.______
   b) There are 30 kids in 10 boats.
      i) ______kids______ ii) ______There are 10 sets of kids.______
   c) Ben has 36 stickers. He gives them to 6 friends.
      i) ____________ ii) ____________
   d) Donald has 12 books. He puts 3 on each shelf.
      i) ____________ ii) ____________
   e) There are 15 kids sitting at 3 tables.
      i) ____________ ii) ____________

   Answer the following questions on a separate piece of paper:

   f) 30 kids are in 2 school buses
   g) 9 fruit bars are shared among 3 kids
   h) 15 chairs are in 3 rows
   i) 20 kids are sitting at 5 tables

7. Divide the dots into sets.
   REMEMBER: If you know the number of sets, start by drawing circles for the sets. If you know the number of things in each set, fill one circle at a time with the correct number of dots.

   a) 15 dots; 5 sets
      ______ dots in each set
   b) 24 dots; 8 dots in each set
      ______ sets

   Answer the following questions on a separate piece of paper:

   c) 15 dots; 5 dots in each set
      ______ sets
   d) 8 dots; 4 sets
      ______ dots in each set
   e) 12 dots; 6 sets
      ______ dots in each set

8. 4 friends share 12 tickets. How many tickets does each friend get?

9. Pamela has 10 apples. She wants to give 2 apples to each of her friends. How many apples does each friend get?

# NS4-33: Division

When 15 things are divided into 5 sets, there are 3 things in each set.

We write: **15 ÷ 5 = 3**

We could also describe the picture as follows: 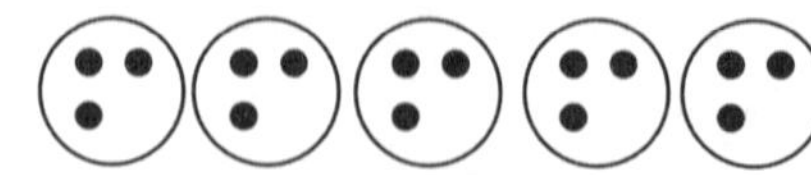

When 15 things are divided into sets of size 3, there are 5 sets (**15 ÷ 3 = 5**).

---

1. Fill in the blanks. Then write two division statements.

a)  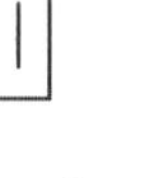

_____ lines _____ sets

_____ lines in each set

____________________

____________________

b) 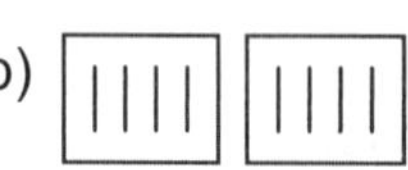 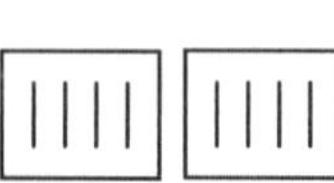

_____ lines _____ sets

_____ lines in each set

____________________

____________________

c) 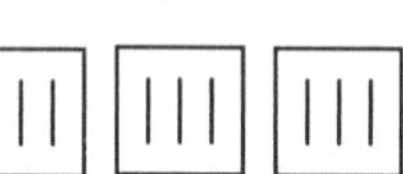 

_____ lines _____ sets

_____ lines in each set

____________________

____________________

2. Fill in the blanks. Then write two division statements. (HINT: Count the figures first.)

a) 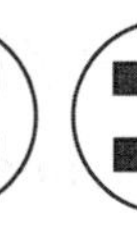 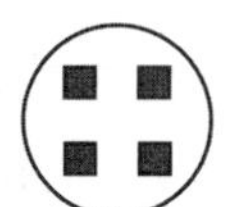 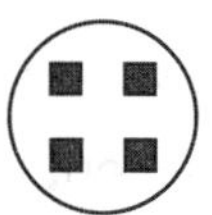

_____ sets

_____ dots in each set

____________________

____________________

b) 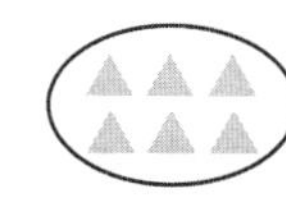 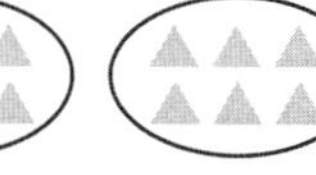

_____ sets

_____ triangles in each set

____________________

____________________

c)     

_____ sets

_____ stars in each set

____________________

____________________

3. Solve the problem by drawing a picture. Then write a division statement for your answer.

a) 6 circles; 3 dots in each set

____________________

How many sets are there? _____

b) 20 triangles; 4 sets

____________________

How many triangles are in each set? _____

4. Solve each problem on a separate piece of paper by drawing a picture. Then write a division statement for your answer. (HINT: Use dots or lines for things and circles or boxes for sets.)

a) 20 people; 5 cars—How many people are in each car?

b) 12 kids; 3 boats—How many kids are in each boat?

# NS4-34: Dividing by Skip Counting

Every **division** statement implies an **addition** statement.

For example, "15 divided into sets of size 3 gives 5 sets."

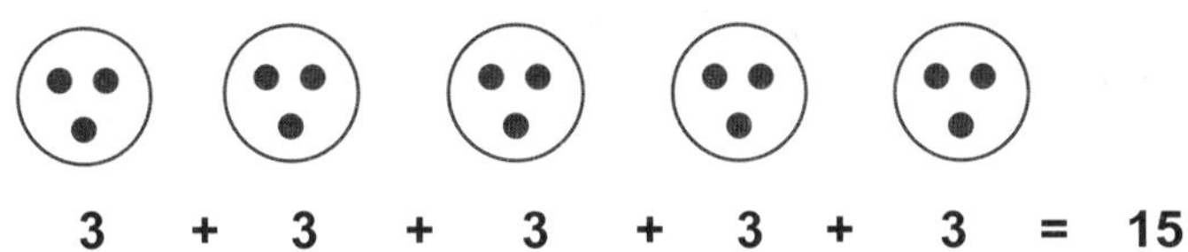


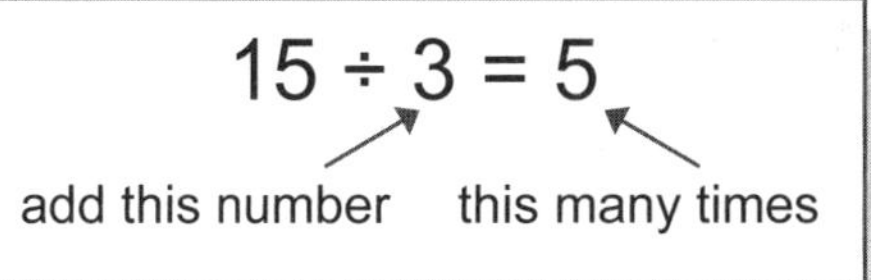


Hence, the division statement 15 ÷ 3 = 5 can be read as "add three five times."

---

1. Draw a picture and write an **addition** statement for each **division** statement. The first one is done for you. Solve parts d), e), and f) on a separate piece of paper.

a) 8 ÷ 2 = 4

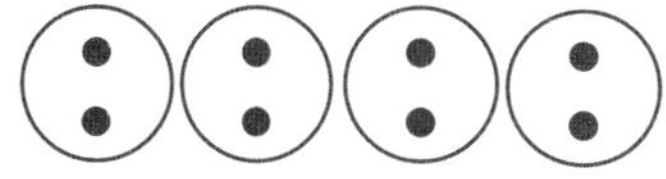

2 + 2 + 2 + 2 = 8

b) 9 ÷ 3 = 3

______________

c) 16 ÷ 4 = 4

______________

d) 35 ÷ 5 = 7 e) 10 ÷ 5 = 2 f) 36 ÷ 6 = 6

2. Draw a picture and write a **division** statement for each **addition** statement. The first one is done for you.

a) 4 + 4 + 4 + 4 = 16

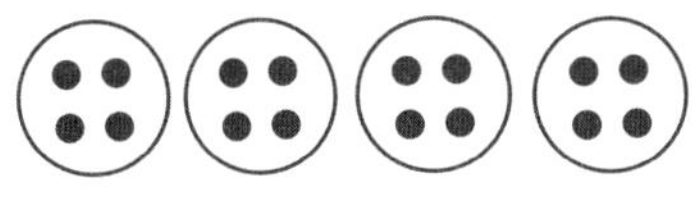

16 ÷ 4 = 4

b) 7 + 7 + 7 + 7 + 7 = 35

______________

Copy the remaining questions onto a separate piece of paper. Draw a picture and write a division statement for each one.

c) 6 + 6 + 6 = 18 d) 8 + 8 = 16 e) 9 + 9 + 9 = 27

3. You can solve the division problem **15 ÷ 3 = ?** by skip counting on the number line:

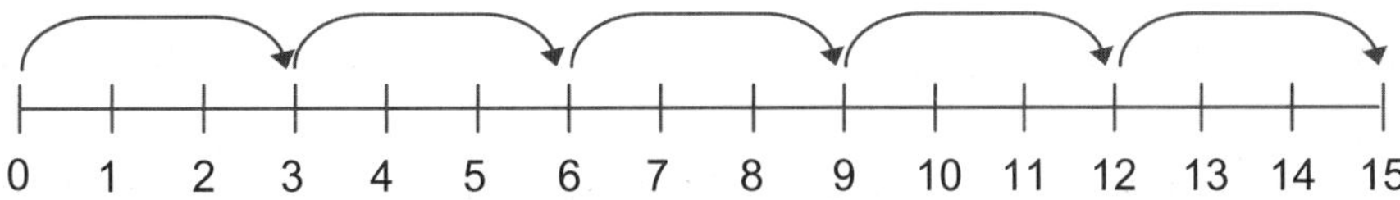


If you divide 15 into sets of size 3, how many sets do you get? The number line shows that it takes 5 skips of size 3 to get 15.

**3 + 3 + 3 + 3 + 3 = 15** so . . . **15 ÷ 3 = 5**

4. Use the number line to find the answer to the division statement. Be sure to draw arrows to show your skip counting.

a)

0 1 2 3 4 5 6 7 8

8 ÷ 2 = ____

b)

0 1 2 3 4 5 6 7 8 9 10 11 12 13 14 15 16

16 ÷ 8 = ____

5. What division statement does the picture represent?

a)

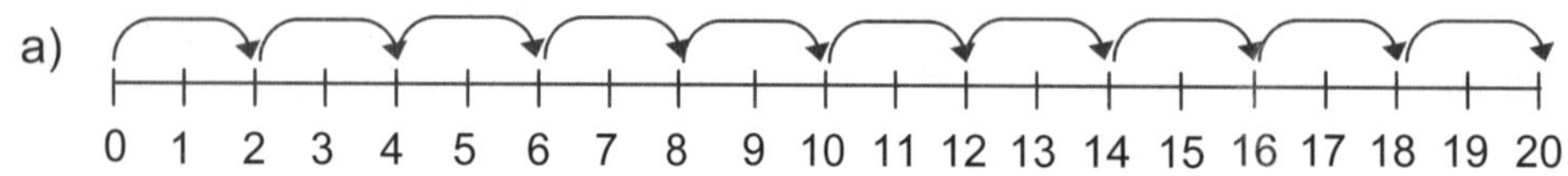


____________

b)

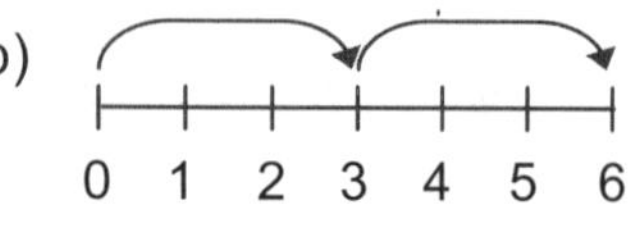


____________

NOTE:
Review skip counting on one hand by 6s, 7s, 8s, and 9s.

6. You can also find the answer to a division question by skip counting on your fingers.

For example, to find **45 ÷ 9**, count by 9s until you reach 45. The number of fingers you have up when you say "45" is the answer:

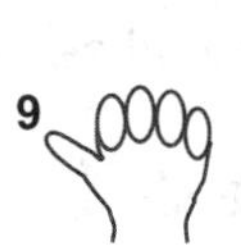

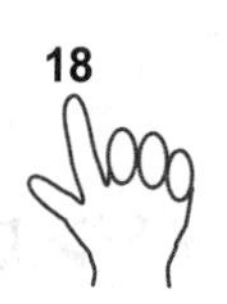

**So 45 ÷ 9 = 5**

Find the answers by skip counting on your fingers.

a) 14 ÷ 2 = ____ b) 18 ÷ 6 = ____ c) 24 ÷ 8 = ____ d) 21 ÷ 7 = ____ e) 35 ÷ 5 = ____

f) 45 ÷ 5 = ____ g) 32 ÷ 4 = ____ h) 40 ÷ 5 = ____ i) 24 ÷ 3 = ____ j) 16 ÷ 4 = ____

k) 36 ÷ 9 = ____ l) 28 ÷ 7 = ____ m) 12 ÷ 3 = ____ n) 18 ÷ 3 = ____ o) 35 ÷ 7 = ____

p) 18 ÷ 2 = ____ q) 24 ÷ 6 = ____ r) 12 ÷ 6 = ____ s) 18 ÷ 9 = ____ t) 32 ÷ 4 = ____

u) 14 ÷ 2 = ____ v) 18 ÷ 6 = ____ w) 24 ÷ 8 = ____ x) 21 ÷ 7 = ____ y) 35 ÷ 5 = ____

7. Seven friends share 28 tickets to a fair. How many tickets does each friend get?

8. 30 students sit in 6 rows. How many students are in each row?

9. Karen rides 9 km every hour. How long does it take her to ride 36 km?

# NS4-34: Dividing by Skip Counting *(continued)*

Daniel bought 12 fish from a pet store:

Daniel has 4 fishbowls. How many fish can he put in each fishbowl? Daniel counts by 4s on his fingers to find out:

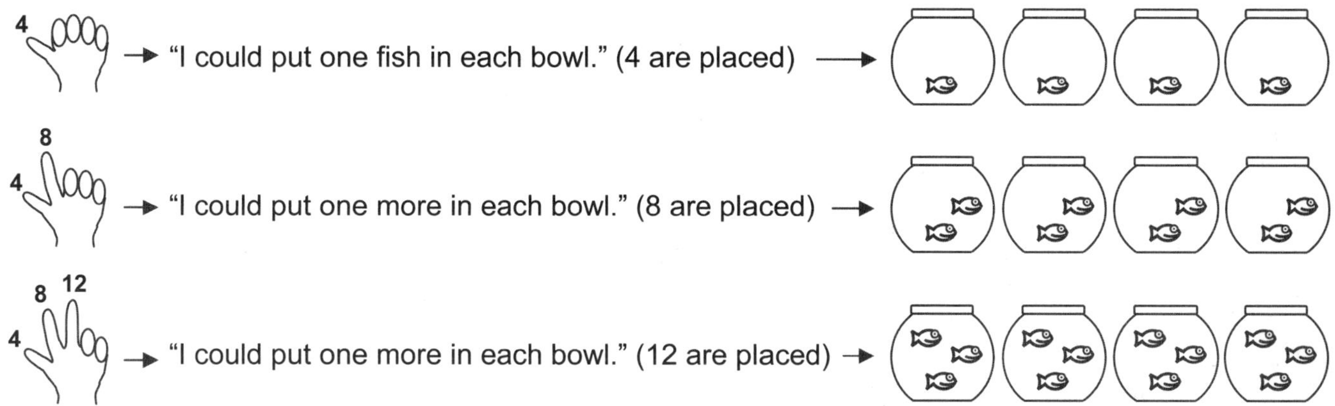


He has raised 3 fingers, so he knows that **12 ÷ 4 = 3**. He puts 3 fish in each fishbowl.

---

10. Draw circles to divide the objects in the number of equal sets given. (HINT: Count the objects. Then divide the number of objects by the number of sets to find the number of objects in each set.)

a) 

3 equal sets

b) ♡ ♡ ♡ ♡ ♡ ♡ ♡ ♡ ♡ ♡

5 equal sets

c) 

2 equal sets

d)

4 equal sets

e) ● ● ● ● ● ● ● ● ● ● ● ● ● ●

7 equal sets

f)

2 equal sets

g) 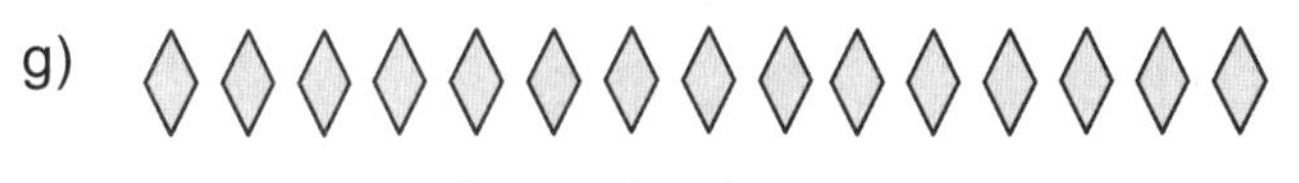

3 equal sets

h) O O O O O O O O O O O O

6 equal sets

BONUS:

i)

3 equal sets

j)

5 equal sets

k)

4 equal sets

11. Azul has 16 fish and 4 fish bowls. How many fish can he put in each bowl? Write a division question and find the answer by skip counting. Show your work on a separate piece of paper.

# NS4-35: Division, Multiplication, and Addition



Every division statement implies a multiplication statement. The statement

"10 divided into sets of size 2 gives 5 sets" (or **10 ÷ 2 = 5**)

can be rewritten as: "5 sets of size 2 equals 10" (**5 × 2 = 10** or **2 × 5 = 10**)

1. Write two multiplication statements and one division statement for each picture.

a)   

b)      

______________________ ______________________

2. Write two multiplication statements, two division statements, and one addition statement for each picture. Then answer the questions.

a)  

b) 

______________________ ______________________

______________________ ______________________

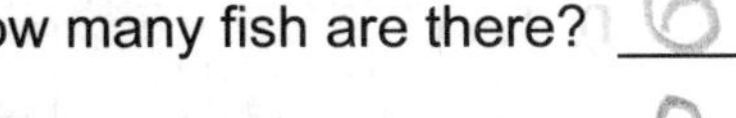

How many fish are there? 6

How many sets are there? 2

How many fish are in each set? 3

How many snails are there? 12

How many sets are there? 6

How many snails are in each set? 2

3. Find the answer to the division problem by first finding the answer to the multiplication statement. The first one is done for you.

a) 4 × [5] = 20  20 ÷ 4 = [5]

b) 6 × [2] = 12  12 ÷ 6 = [2]

c) 5 × [4] = 20  20 ÷ 5 = [4]

d) 6 × [5] = 30  30 ÷ 6 = [5]

e) 9 × [5] = 45  45 ÷ 9 = [5]

4. The picture shows that 2 sets of size 4 contain the same number of dots as 4 sets of size 2 (that is, 2 × 4 = 4 × 2).

a) On a separate piece of paper, draw a picture and explain how your picture shows that . . .

i) 6 × 3 = 3 × 6  ii) 8 × 2 = 2 × 8

b) Draw an array and explain how your picture shows that 5 + 5 + 5 + 5 = 4 + 4 + 4 + 4 + 4.

# NS4-36: Knowing When to Multiply or Divide



NOTE:
To solve word problems involving multiplication or division, you should ask . . .

- How many things are there altogether?
- How many sets are there?
- How many things are in each set?

You should also know (and be able to explain using pictures or concrete materials) that . . .

- when you know the number of sets and the number of things in each set, you multiply to find the total number of things
- when you know the total number of things and the number of sets, you divide to find the number of things in each set
- when you know the total number of things and the number of things in each set, you divide to find the number of sets

---

1. For each picture, fill in the blanks.

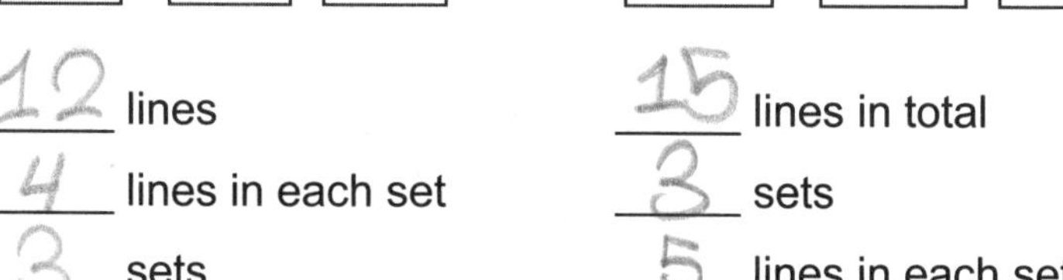

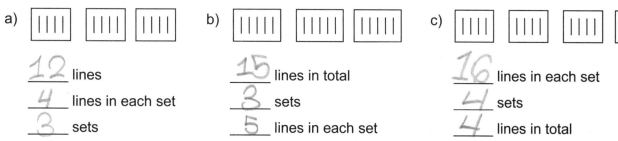

a) 12 lines
4 lines in each set
3 sets

b) 15 lines in total
3 sets
5 lines in each set

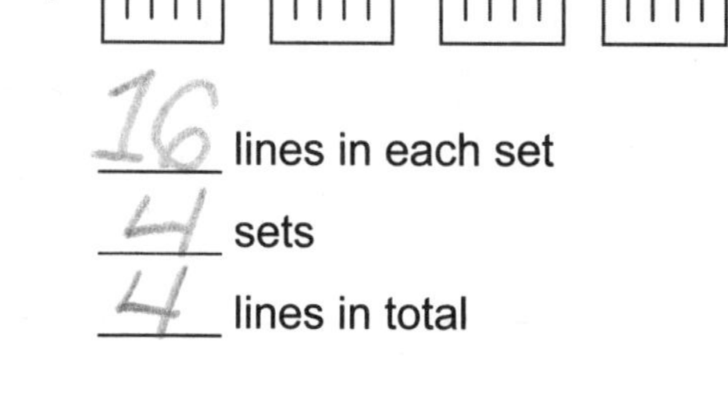

c) 16 lines in each set
4 sets
4 lines in total

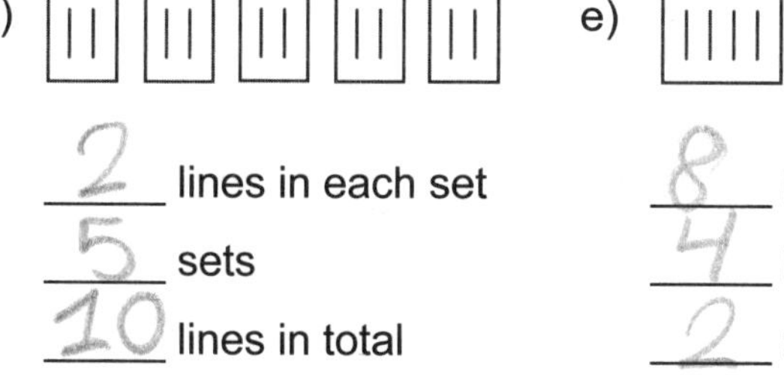

d) 2 lines in each set
5 sets
10 lines in total

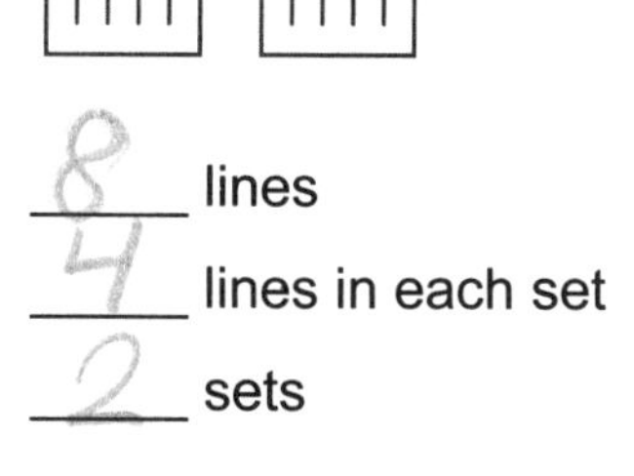

e) 8 lines
4 lines in each set
2 sets

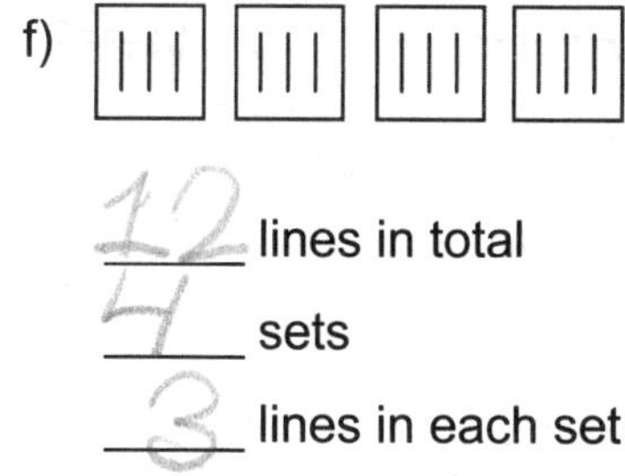

f) 12 lines in total
4 sets
3 lines in each set

2. On a separate piece of paper, draw a picture of the following sets:

a) 16 lines altogether; 4 lines in each set; 4 sets
b) 8 lines; 4 lines in each set; 2 sets
c) 6 sets; 3 lines in each set; 18 lines in total
d) 12 lines; 2 sets; 6 lines in each set

3. On a separate piece of paper, draw a picture of **and** write a division statement for the following sets:

a) 15 lines altogether; 3 lines in each set; 5 sets
b) 15 lines; 5 lines in each set; 3 sets
c) 9 sets; 3 lines in each set; 9 lines in total
d) 20 lines; 5 sets; 4 lines in each set

4. For each question, write a multiplication or a division statement to solve the problem.

a) 18 things in total
3 things in each set

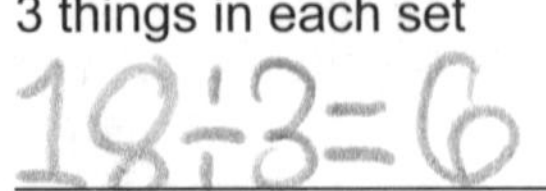

How many sets are there? 6

b) 5 sets
4 things in each set

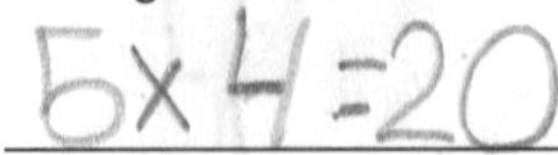

How many things are there in total? 20

c) 15 things in total
5 sets

How many things are in each set? 3

d) 8 sets
3 things in each set

How many things are there in total? 24

e) 6 things in each set
12 things in total

12÷6=2

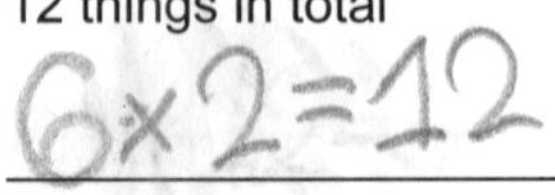

How many sets are there? 2

6x2=12

f) 5 sets
10 things in total

How many things are in each set? 2

5. Show your work for these problems in the space provided.

a) 20 people; 4 vans
How many people are in each van?

20÷4=5

b) 3 marbles in each jar; 6 jars
How many marbles are there in total?

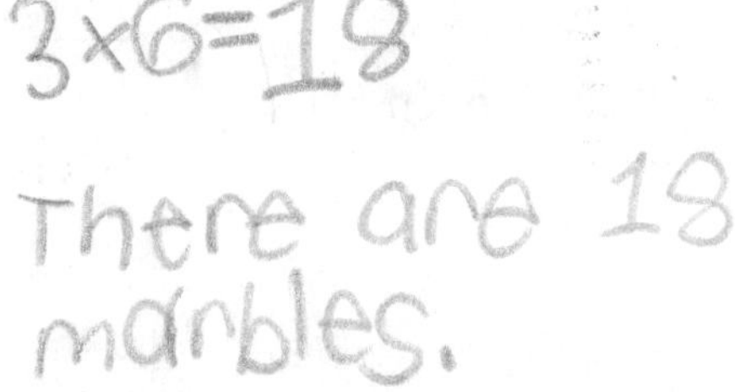


c) 15 flowers; 5 pots
How many flowers are in each pot?

15÷5=3

There are 3 flowers in each pot.

d) 4 chairs at each table; 2 tables
How many chairs are there in total?

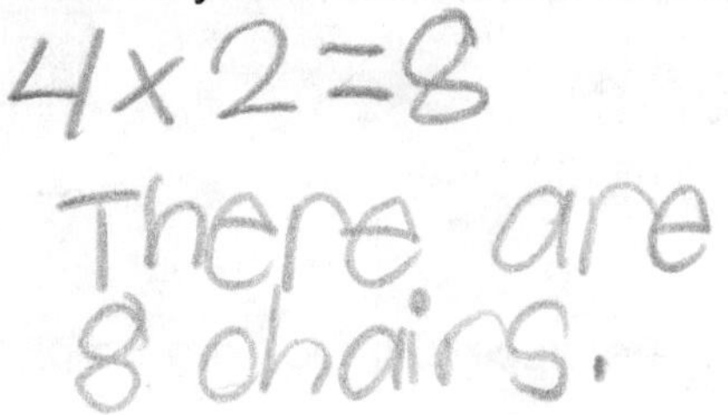


e) 18 pillows; 6 beds
How many pillows are on each bed?

18÷6=2

There are 2 pillows on each bed

f) 27 houses; 9 houses on each block
How many blocks are there in total?

27÷9=3

There are 3 blocks.

# NS4-37: Remainders

Ori wants to share 7 cookies with 2 friends. He sets out 3 plates: 1 for himself and 1 for each of his friends. He puts one cookie at a time on a plate:

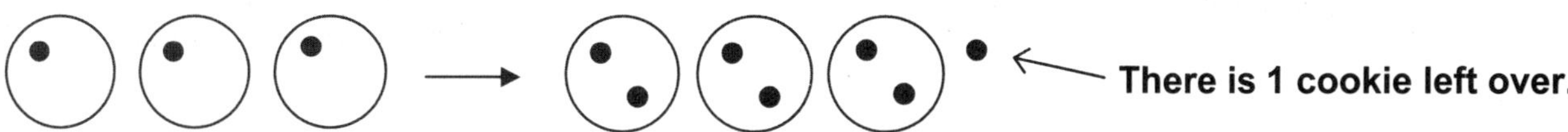
There is 1 cookie left over.

7 cookies can not be shared equally into 3 sets. Each friend gets 2 cookies, but 1 cookie is left over. This is the remainder:

**7 ÷ 2 = 3 Remainder 1 OR 7 ÷ 2 = 3 R 1**

---

1. Can you share 5 cookies equally on 2 plates? Show your work using dots for cookies and circles for plates.

2. For each question, share the dots as equally as possible among the circles. (HINT: In one question, the dots **can** be shared equally; there will be **no** remainder.)

   a) 7 dots in 2 circles

   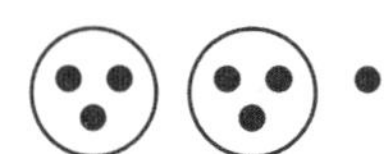

   3 dots in each circle; 1 dots remaining

   b) 10 dots in 4 circles

   2 dots in each circle; 2 dots remaining

   c) 12 dots in 6 circles

   2 dots in each circle; 0 dots remaining

   d) 15 dots in 4 circles

   3 dots in each circle; 3 dots remaining

Show your work for the remaining questions on a separate piece of paper.

3. Share the dots as equally as possible among the circles. Draw a picture and write a division statement for your picture. The first one is done for you.

   a) 7 dots in 2 circles  b) 11 dots in 4 circles  c) 15 dots in 3 circles

   d) 10 dots in 6 circles  e) 9 dots in 4 circles  f) 14 dots in 3 circles

4. Three friends want to share 10 apples. How many apples will each friend receive? How many apples will be left over?

5. Find two different ways to share 7 cookies into equal groups so that one is left over.

6. Fred, George, and Paul have less than 10 oranges and more than 3 oranges. They share the oranges evenly. How many oranges do they have? (Is there more than one answer?)

fish pad

# NS4-38: Finding Remainders on Number Lines

Paul has 14 oranges. He wants to give a bag of 4 oranges to each of his friends. He skip counts to find out how many friends he can share with:

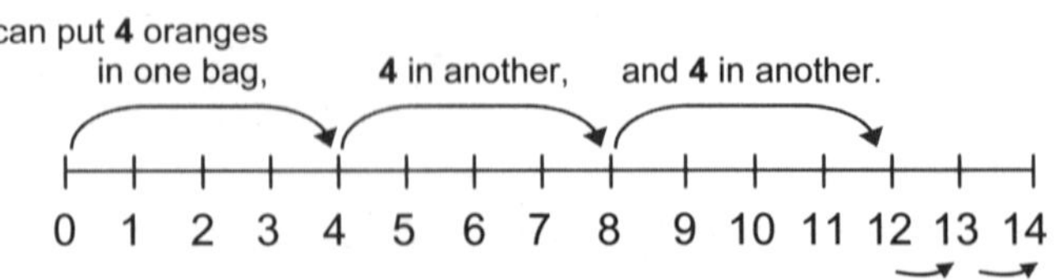


14 oranges divide into sets of size 4 gives 3 sets (with 2 oranges **remaining**):

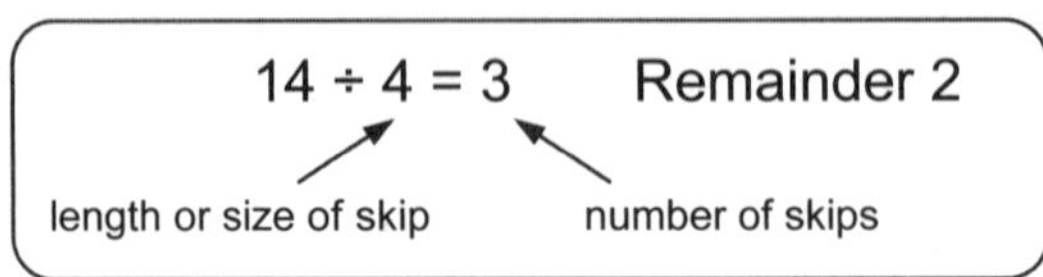


or 14 ÷ 4 = 3 R2

1. Paul drew each of the pictures below to solve a division problem. Fill in the missing numbers.

a) 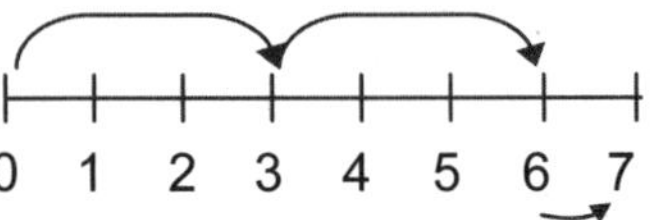


Size of skip = _____ Number of skips = ____

Remainder = _____

b) 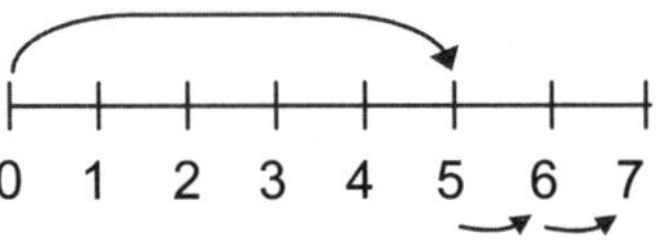


Size of skip = _____ Number of skips = _____

Remainder = _____

c) Size of skip = _______

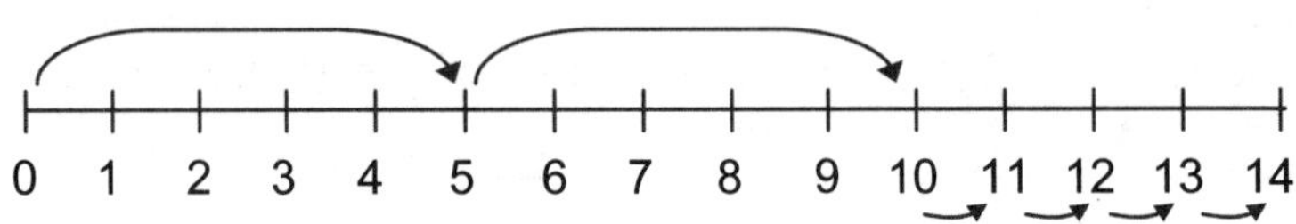


Number of skips = _______

Remainder = _______

2. Each of the pictures below shows a solution to a division problem. Fill in the number, then write a division statement for the picture.

a) 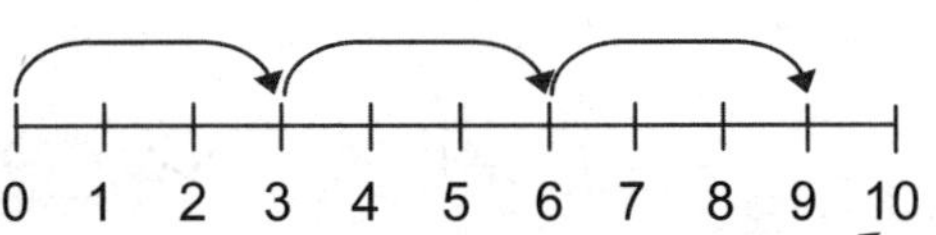


Size of skip = _____ Number of skips = _____

Remainder = ______

_______________________________

b) 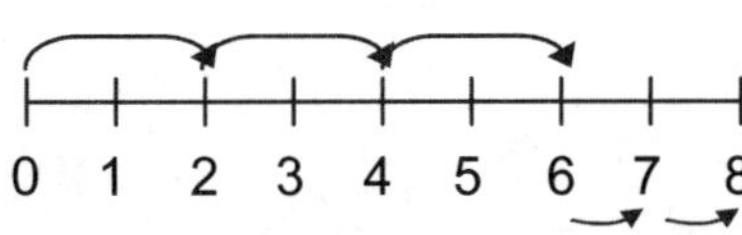


Size of skip = _____ Number of skips = _____

Remainder = ______

_______________________________

3. 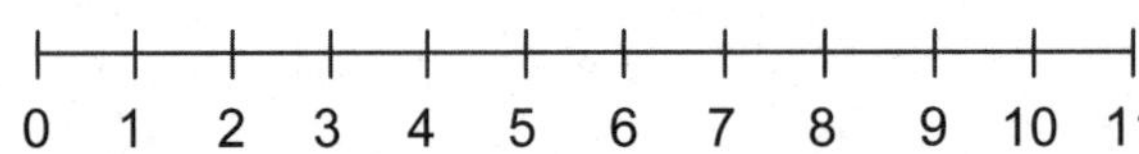


Jane has 11 oranges. She wants to give a bag of 4 oranges to each friend. How many bags can she make? How many oranges will be left over? Use the number line to solve the problem.

4. Draw a number line on grid paper to solve each problem.

   a) A ride at the fair costs 4 tickets. Liz has 13 tickets. How many rides can she take?

   b) Eli has 12 tickets for the fair. He wants to give 5 tickets to each friend. How many friends can he share with?

5. On grid paper, draw a number line picture to model the division.

   a) 5 ÷ 2 = 2 R1
   b) 9 ÷ 4 = 2 R1
   c) 11 ÷ 3 = 3 R2

# NS4-39: Finding Quotients and Remainders

Nina finds 13 ÷ 5 by skip counting on her fingers:

Step 1:
She counts by 5s to see how many times 5 will divide into 13.

She stops counting at 10 because she does not want to count past 13.

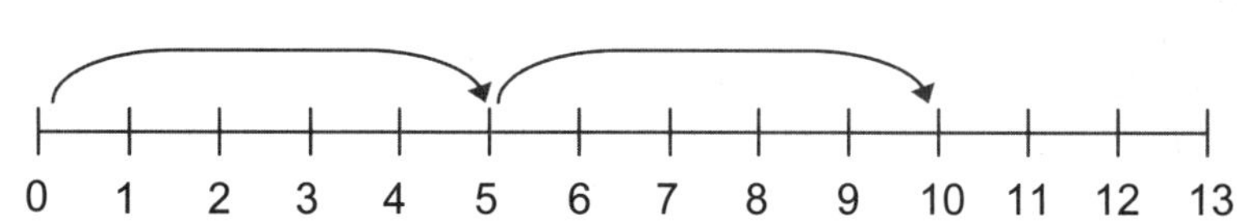


This is what her calculation would look like on a number line.

NOTE: We will return to Nina's calculation after you have practised the first step.

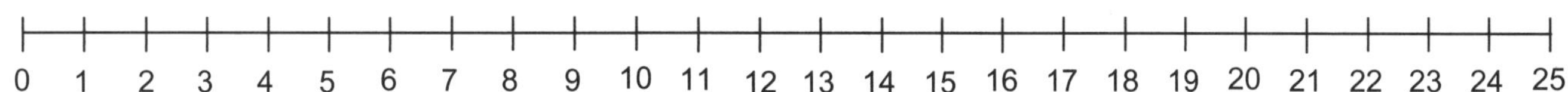


1. Count by 5s. Stop before you go past the number in bold.
   (HINT: Use the number line to help you see where to stop.)

   a) **17**: You stop at ______ b) **21**: You stop at ______ c) **12**: You stop at ______

   d) **9**: You stop at ______ e) **14**: You stop at ______ f) **24**: You stop at ______

   g) **16**: You stop at ______ h) **6**: You stop at ______ i) **21**: You stop at ______

2. Count by 2s. Stop before you go past the number in bold.

   a) **9**: You stop at ______ b) **5**: You stop at ______ c) **7**: You stop at ______

   d) **3**: You stop at ______ e) **11**: You stop at ______ f) **15**: You stop at ______

3. Count by 3s. Stop before you go past the number in bold.

   a) **11**: You stop at ______ b) **7**: You stop at ______ c) **8**: You stop at ______

   d) **13**: You stop at ______ e) **4**: You stop at ______ f) **10**: You stop at ______

4. Count by 4s. Stop before you go past the number in bold.

   a) **13**: You stop at ______ b) **21**: You stop at ______ c) **10**: You stop at ______

   d) **26**: You stop at ______ e) **6**: You stop at ______ f) **15**: You stop at ______

   g) **11**: You stop at ______ h) **17**: You stop at ______ i) **23**: You stop at ______

Step 2:
Nina raised 2 fingers when she was counting, so she knows 5 will divide into thirteen 2 times.

Two (the number of skips) is called the **quotient** of 13 ÷ 5.

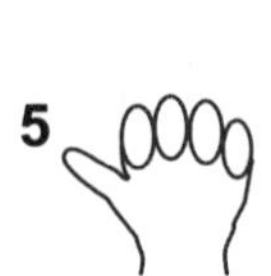

There are 2 skips = the quotient.

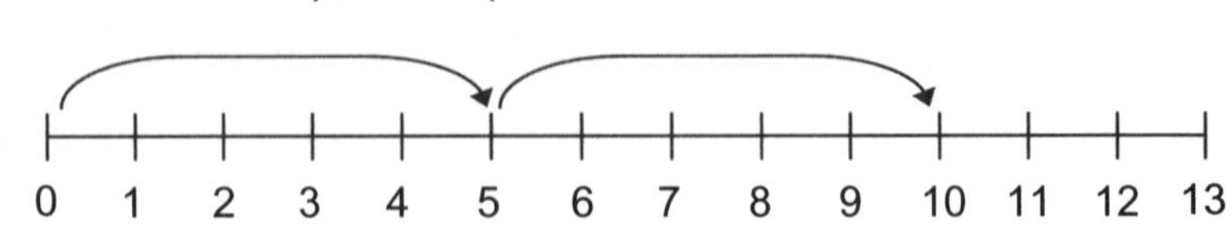


5. Find the quotient for each division problem.
(HINT: How many figures did you raise when you stopped counting?)

a) 16 ÷ 5 Quotient: ______
b) 22 ÷ 5 Quotient: ______
c) 10 ÷ 5 Quotient: ______
d) 7 ÷ 3 Quotient: ______
e) 11 ÷ 3 Quotient: ______
f) 9 ÷ 2 Quotient: ______
g) 5 ÷ 2 Quotient: ______
h) 17 ÷ 4 Quotient: ______

Step 3:
In a division problem, the number that is being divided or shared is called the **dividend**.

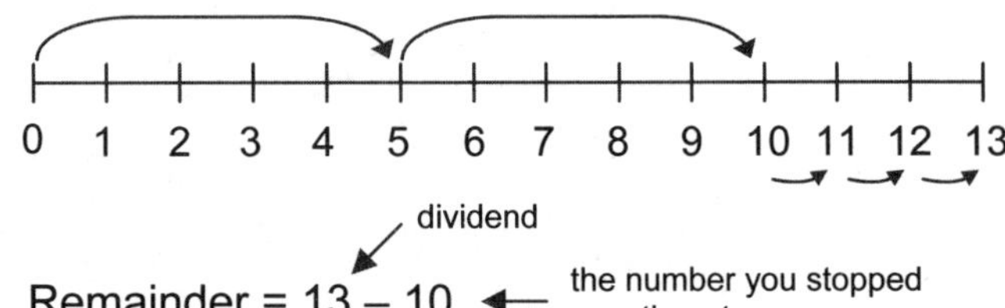


Nina notices that the remainder is just the dividend minus the number she stopped counting at (10).

Remainder = 13 – 10 (13: dividend; 10: the number you stopped counting at)

6. Count by 5s. Stop before you go past the dividend. Find the remainder by subtracting the number you stop at from the dividend.

a) 16 ÷ 5: You stop at ____ Remainder: ______
b) 22 ÷ 5: You stop at ____ Remainder: ______
c) 11 ÷ 5: You stop at ____ Remainder: ______
d) 7 ÷ 5: You stop at ____ Remainder: ______
e) 28 ÷ 5: You stop at ____ Remainder: ______
f) 33 ÷ 5: You stop at ____ Remainder: ______

7. Write the quotient in the first blank and the remainder in the second.
REMEMBER: The quotient is the number of fingers you raise.

a) 18 ÷ 5 = _____ R _____
b) 23 ÷ 5 = _____ R _____
c) 26 ÷ 5 = _____ R _____
d) 28 ÷ 5 = _____ R _____
e) 16 ÷ 5 = _____ R _____
f) 6 ÷ 5 = _____ R _____
g) 10 ÷ 3 = _____ R _____
h) 7 ÷ 3 = _____ R _____
i) 16 ÷ 3 = _____ R _____
j) 8 ÷ 2 = _____ R _____
k) 5 ÷ 2 = _____ R _____
l) 17 ÷ 4 = _____ R _____

8. You have 17 tickets to a school play-day. You want to give 5 tickets to each friend. How many friends can you share with? How many tickets will be left over?

# NS4-40: Long Division

Long division is a way of organizing the steps you follow when you divide by skip counting.

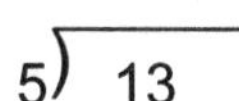 means 13 ÷ 5 divisor → 5) 13 ← dividend

---

1. The first step in long division is to find the quotient. To do this, skip count by the divisor. Stop counting before you reach the dividend. Write the number of skips (the quotient) in the box provided.

a) 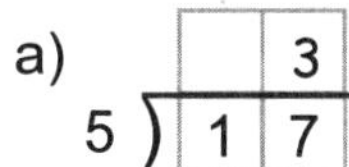
b) 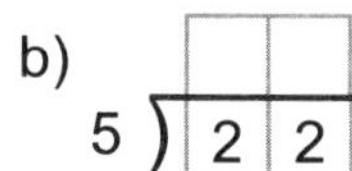
c) 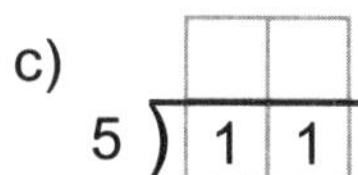
d) 5) 1 8

e) 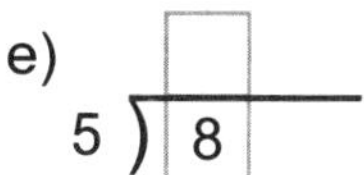
f) 3) 1 3
g) 3) 7
h) 2) 9

2. Repeat the step you learned in question 1. What number did you say when you stopped skip counting? Write your answer below the dividend.

a) 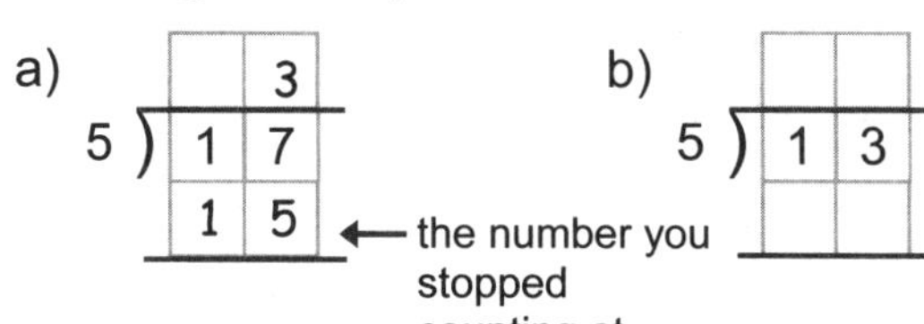

b) 5) 1 3
c) 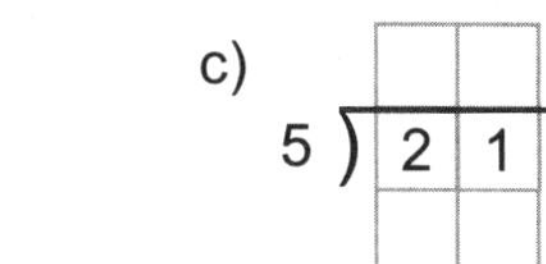
d) 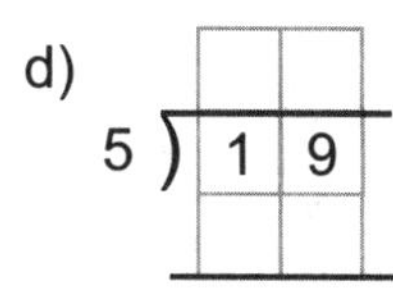

e) 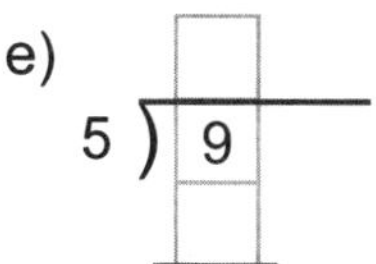
f) 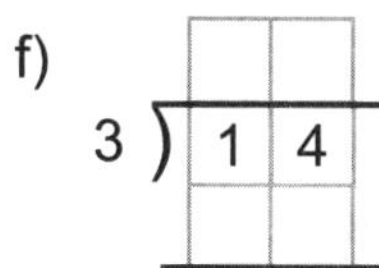
g) 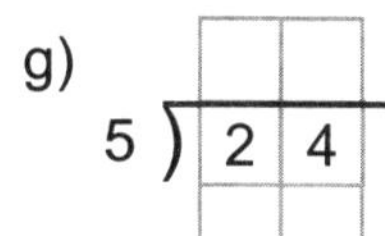
h) 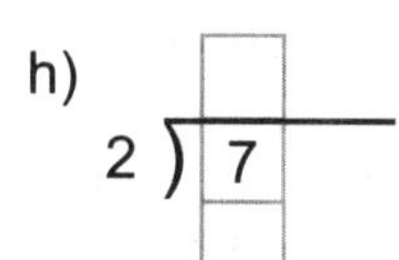

3. Repeat the steps you learned in questions 1 and 2, then subtract the number written below the dividend. Your answer is the remainder.

a) 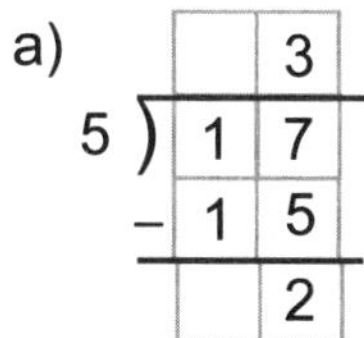
b) 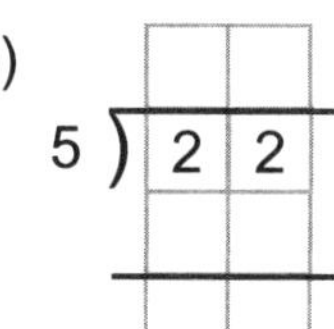
c) 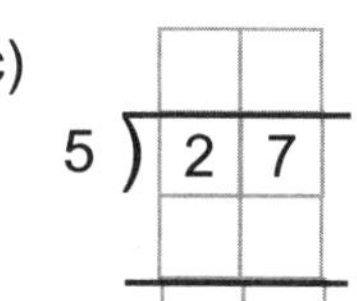
d) 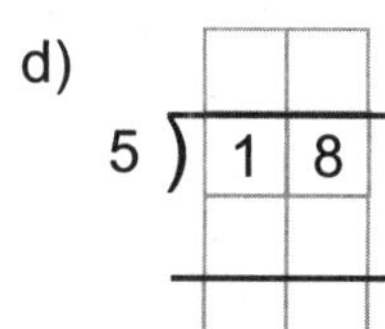

e) 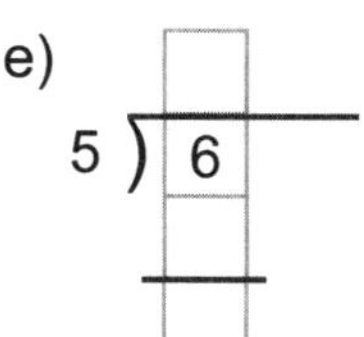
f) 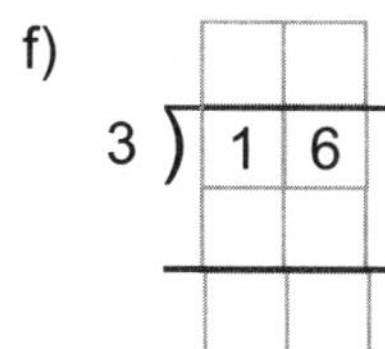
g) 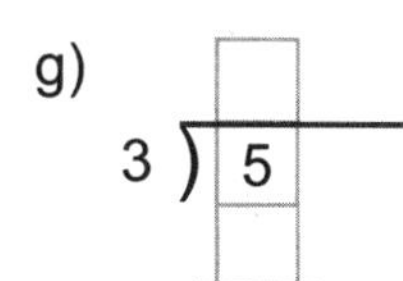
h) 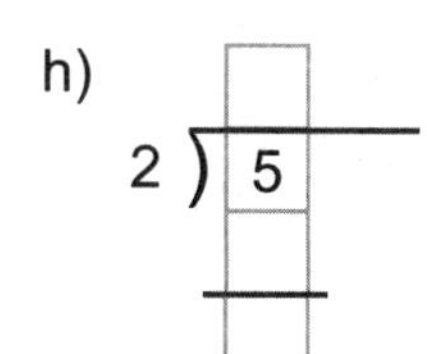

4. Copy the division questions onto grid paper and carry out the long division.

a) 5) 23 b) 5) 26 c) 3) 14 d) 3) 16 e) 2) 17 f) 4) 13

5. Richard wants to give 16 oranges to 5 friends. How many oranges will each friend get? How many will be left over?

# NS4-41: Dividing with Base-10 Materials *(continued)*

Alex wants to divide 74 animal stickers into 3 equal groups. He makes a model of 74 using base-10 materials:

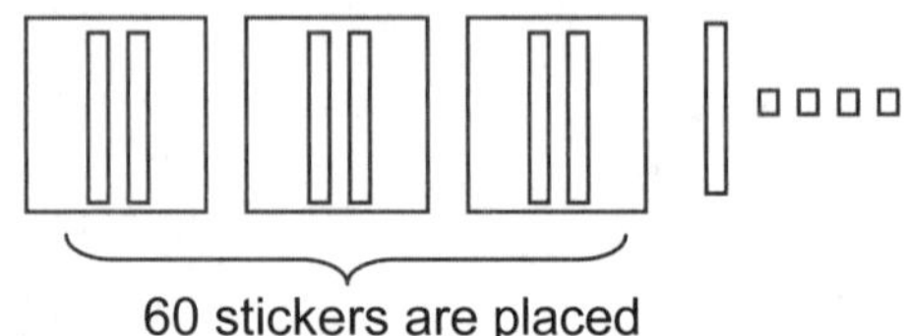

Step 1: He divides the tens strips into 3 equal groups.

60 stickers are placed

NOTE: We will look at Alex's next step after you have practised the first step.

1. Show the tens strips as equally as possible among the groups. Place the strips one at a time. Cross out the strips as you place then to show how many remain. (In one question, there is no remainder.)

a)

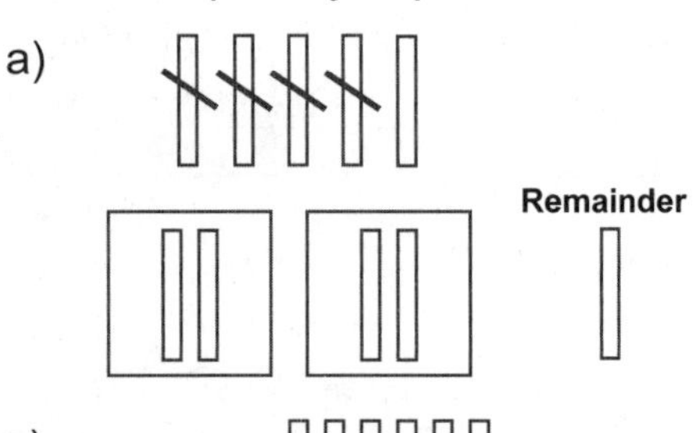

Remainder

b)

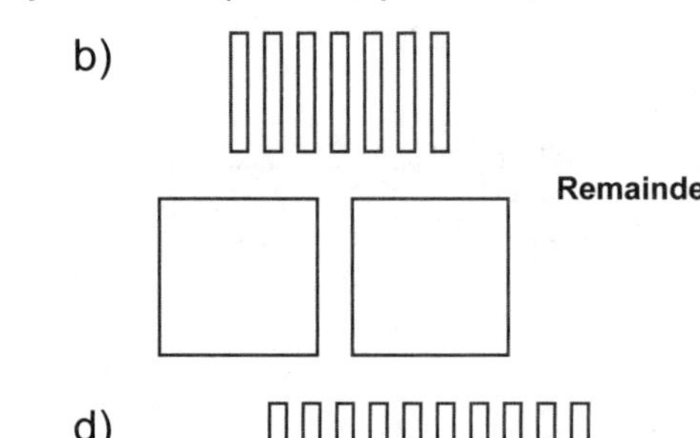

Remainder

c)

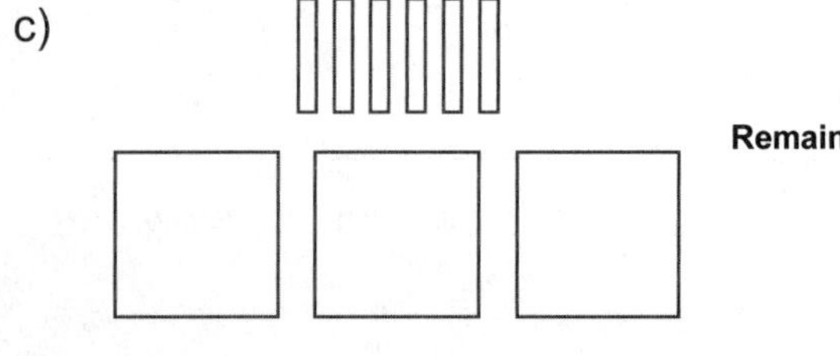

Remainder

d)

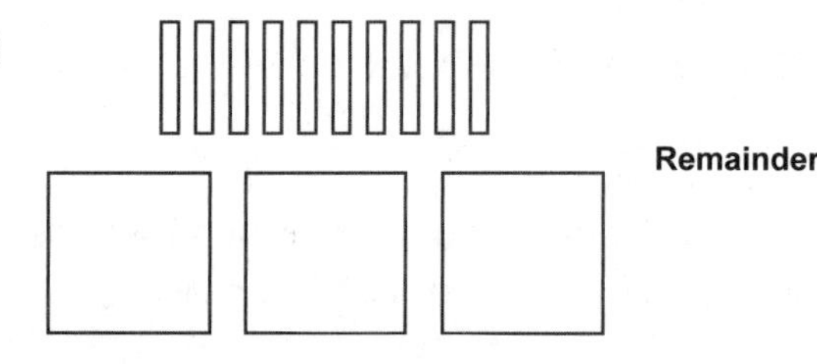

Remainder

2. Divide.

a) 8 tens strips into 3 groups

How many tens are in each group? ______

How many are left over? ______

b) 7 ten strips into 2 groups

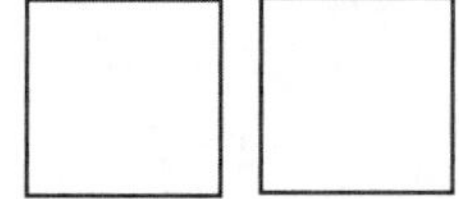

How many tens are in each group? ______

How many are left over? ______

3. Divide the tens strips equally among the groups. Cross out the tens strips as you place them to show how many tens and ones would be left over.

a)

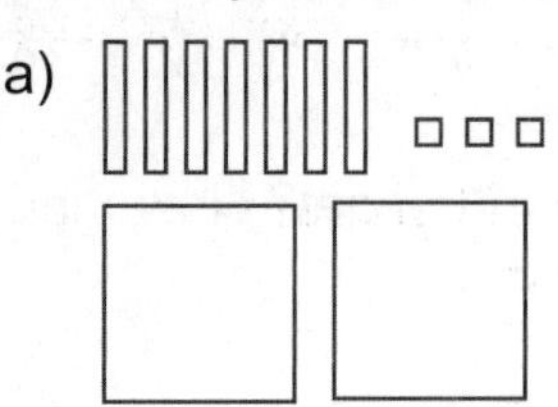

b)

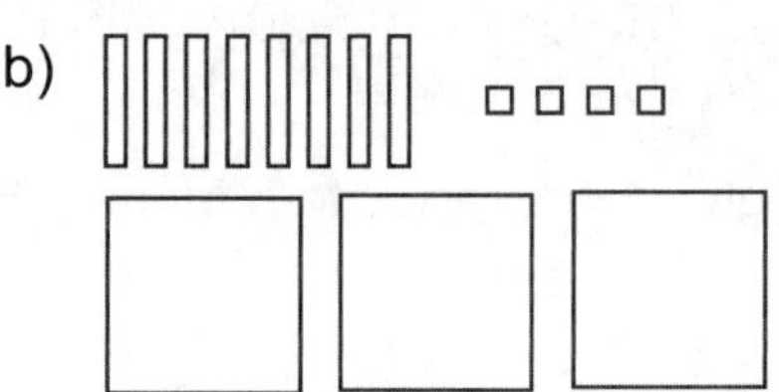

# NS4-41: Dividing with Base-10 Materials *(continued)*

Alex has divided his tens strips into 3 groups. 14 stickers are left over:

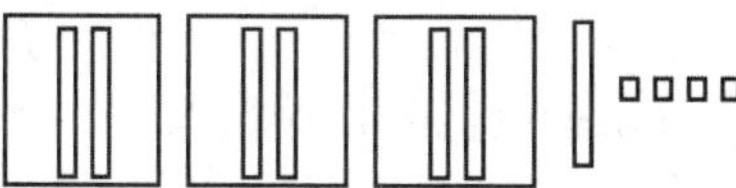

Step 2: He skip counts to find out how many of the 14 stickers he can put in each group.

**14 ÷ 3 = 4 R2**

He can put 4 stickers in each group with 2 left over.

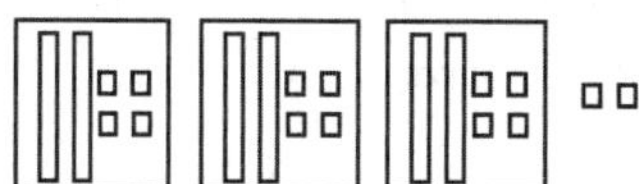

---

4. How many stickers does each picture represent?

a) 

b) 

c) 

d)

5. Each tens strip represents 10 stickers. Write a division statement to show how to divide the stickers into equal groups.

a)

How many stickers are there altogether? ___

Division statement: _______________

How many are in each group? ______

How many are left over? ______

b)

How many stickers are there altogether? ___

Division statement: _______________

How many are in each group? ______

How many are left over? ______

6. Draw a base-10 model to solve the problem.

Divide 54 stickers into 4 equal groups.

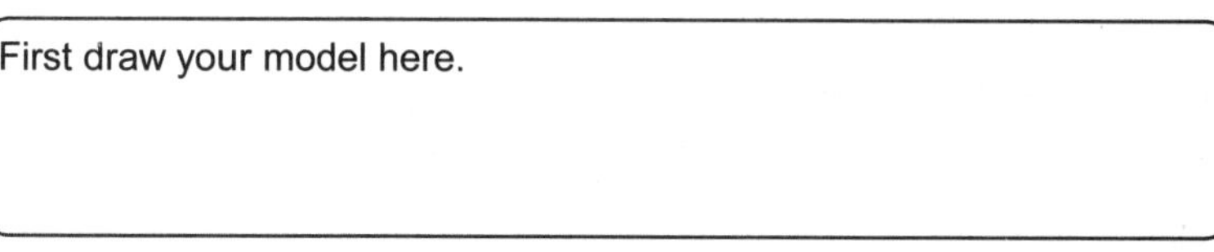


Step 1: Place the tens.

Step 2: Place the remainder.

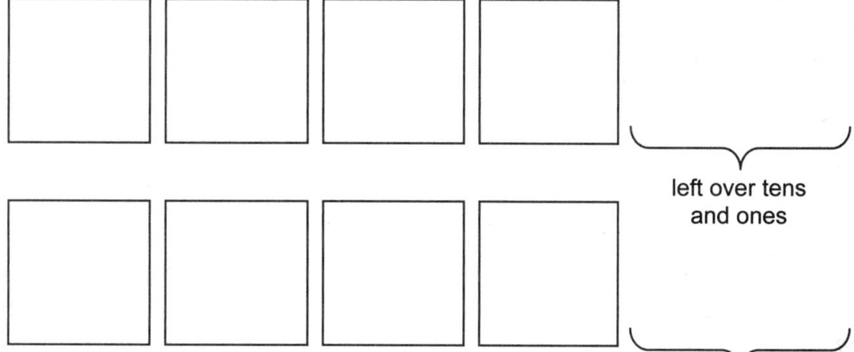


7. Use base-10 materials or draw a picture to solve the following problems. Write a division statement for each answer.

a) Divide 42 into 3 equal groups.

b) Divide 65 into 5 equal groups.

# NS4-41: Dividing with Base-10 Materials *(continued)*

8. Use skip counting to answer the questions.

   a) Divide 11 tens strips into 5 groups.
   How many are in each group? ______
   How many are left over? ______

   b) Divide 21 tens strips into 5 groups.
   How many are in each group? ______
   How many are left over? ______

   c) Divide 16 tens strips into 3 groups.
   How many are in each group? ______
   How many are left over? ______

   d) Divide 21 tens strips into 4 groups.
   How many are in each group? ______
   How many are left over? ______

   e) Divide 17 tens strips into 5 groups.
   How many are in each group? ______
   How many are left over? ______

   f) Divide 11 tens strips into 3 groups.
   How many are in each group? ______
   How many are left over? ______

9. Describe what each model represents. Assume each tens strip represents 10 stickers.

   a) 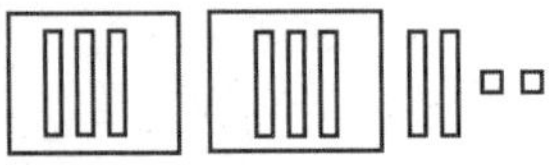
   How many stickers have been placed in each group? ______
   How many stickers have been placed altogether? ______
   How many stickers are left? ______

   b) 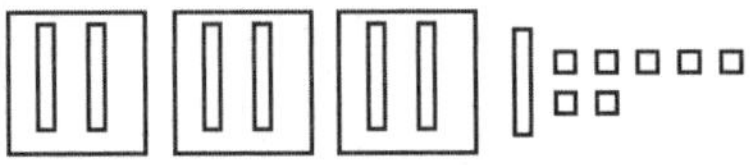
   How many stickers have been placed in each group? ______
   How many stickers have been placed altogether? ______
   How many stickers are left? ______

   c) 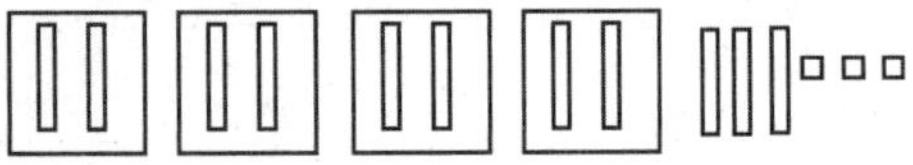
   How many stickers have been placed in each group? ______
   How many stickers have been placed altogether? ______
   How many stickers are left? ______

10. Divide the tens strips equally among the groups. (Use skip counting to help you decide how many to put in each group.) Cross out the tens strips as you place them to show how many tens and ones would be left over.

   a)

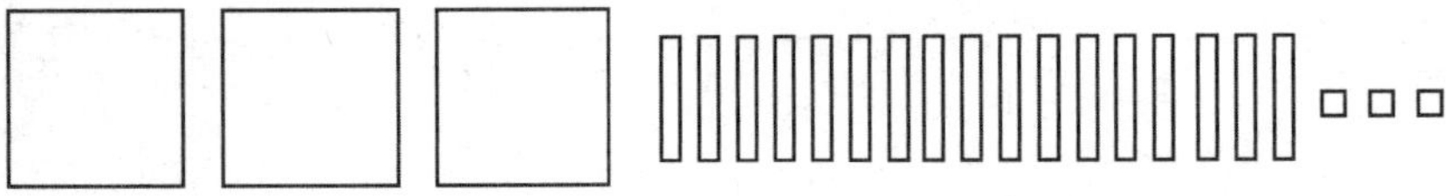

   b)

11. Use base-10 materials or a drawing to show how you would divide the base-10 materials into 4 groups if you had the following amounts. Make sure you show how many tens and ones would be left over. Write a division statement for your answer.

   a) 9 tens strips and 5 ones b) 10 tens strips and 0 ones c) 13 tens strips and 3 ones

12. Aron wants to divide 65 animal stickers into 3 equal groups. How many can he put in each group and how many will be left over? Solve the problem on a separate piece of paper using base-10 materials or a picture.

# NS4-42: Long Division—Two-Digits by One-Digit

Inez is preparing snacks for 4 classes. She needs to divide 93 apples into 4 equal groups. She will use long division and a model to solve the problem:

$4\overline{)93}$

She writes the number of groups she needs to make here. (→ 4)

She writes the number of apples here. (→ 93)

Step 1: Inez finds the number of tens strips she can put in each group by dividing 9 by 4 (9 ÷ 4 = 2).

$$\begin{array}{r}2\phantom{3}\\4\overline{)93}\end{array}$$

She needs 4 equal groups.

There are 3 ones.

There are 9 tens strips in the model.

Inez makes a base-10 model of the problem:

**93 = 9 tens + 3 ones**

Inez can divide 8 of the 9 tens strips into 4 equal groups of size 2.

1. Inez has written a division statement to solve a problem. How many groups does she want to make? How many tens strips and how many ones would she need to model the problem?

a) $3\overline{)85}$ Groups: 3 Tens strips: 8 Ones: 5

b) $4\overline{)92}$ Groups: ______ Tens strips: ______ Ones: ______

c) $5\overline{)86}$ Groups: ______ Tens strips: ______ Ones: ______

d) $2\overline{)87}$ Groups: ______ Tens strips: ______ Ones: ______

2. How many tens strips can be put in each group? (Use skip counting to find the answers.) Write your answer in the box above the tens digit of the dividend.

a) $3\overline{)75}$ (2)

b) $4\overline{)93}$

c) $5\overline{)62}$

d) $3\overline{)98}$

e) $4\overline{)82}$

f) $2\overline{)58}$

g) $3\overline{)87}$

h) $4\overline{)81}$

i) $6\overline{)83}$

j) $7\overline{)92}$

3. For each division statement, how many groups have been made and how many tens strips are in each group?

a) $3\overline{)75}$ (2) Groups: 3 Number of tens in each group: 2

b) $2\overline{)91}$ Groups: ______ Number of tens in each group: ______

c) $4\overline{)95}$ Groups: ______ Number of tens in each group: ______

d) $2\overline{)73}$ Groups: ______ Number of tens in each group: ______

4. Inez makes 3 groups with 5 tens strips in each group. How many tens strips are there altogether? Explain how you found your answer.

Step 2: Inez calculates the total number of tens strips that have been placed by multiplying the number of strips in each group (2) by the number of groups (4).

4 ) 9 3 (quotient 2) → 4 ) 9 3 (quotient 2, × ) with 8 below: 2 × 4 = 8 tens strips have been placed

In the model:

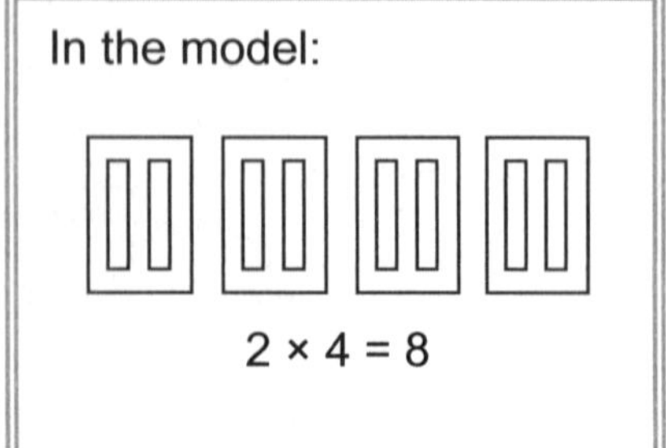


5. For each question, find how many tens have been placed by multiplying.

a) 3 ) 8 7 (quotient 2)

How many tens are in each group? ______

How many groups are there? ______

How many tens are placed altogether? ____

b) 4 ) 9 6 (quotient 2)

How many tens are in each group? ______

How many groups are there? ______

How many tens are placed altogether? ____

6. Use skip counting to find out how many tens can be placed in each group. Then use multiplication to find out how many tens have been placed.

a) 2 ) 7 3
b) 3 ) 8 2
c) 2 ) 9 5
d) 5 ) 9 8
e) 7 ) 8 1
f) 6 ) 6 3
g) 2 ) 7 1
h) 3 ) 7 5
i) 4 ) 9 3
j) 8 ) 8 5

Step 3: There are 9 tens strips. Inez has placed 8. She subtracts to find out how many are left over (9 – 8 = 1).

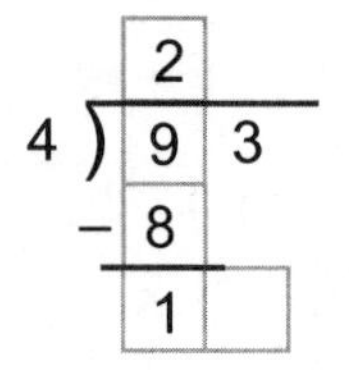


In the model:

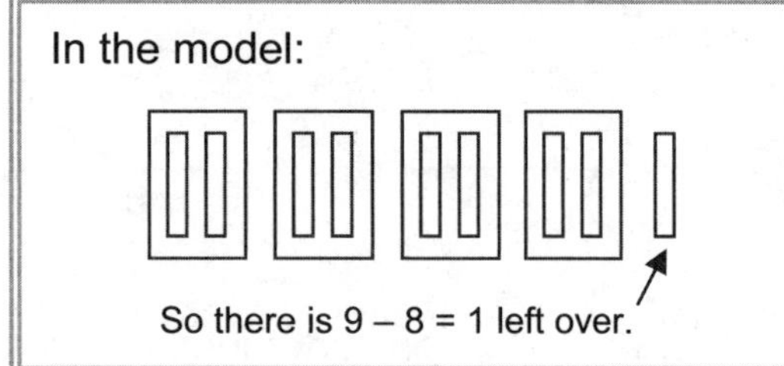


7. For each question, carry out all 3 steps of long division.

a) 6 ) 9 1
b) 3 ) 7 6
c) 2 ) 4 1
d) 4 ) 8 3
e) 3 ) 8 5
f) 4 ) 5 7
g) 8 ) 9 3
h) 2 ) 9 9
i) 3 ) 7 1
j) 4 ) 8 2

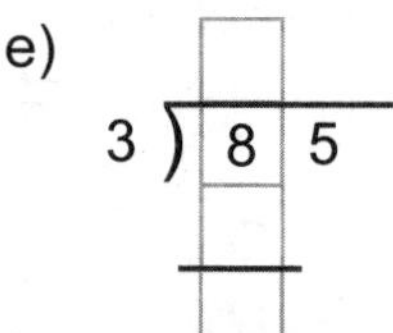

Step 4: There is one tens strip left over and 3 ones. So there are 13 ones left over. Inez writes the 3 beside the 1 to show this.

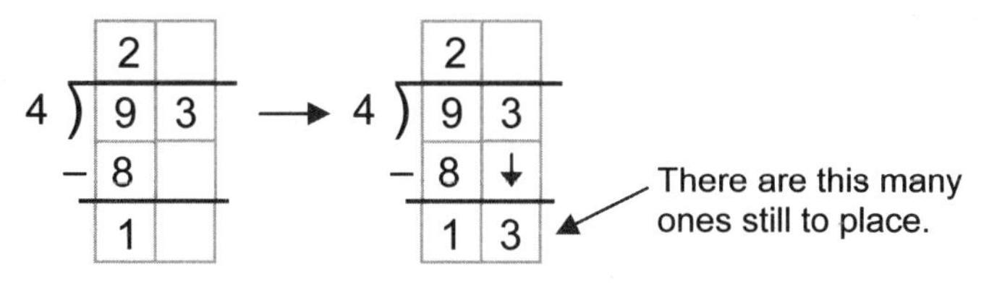
There are this many ones still to place.

In the model:

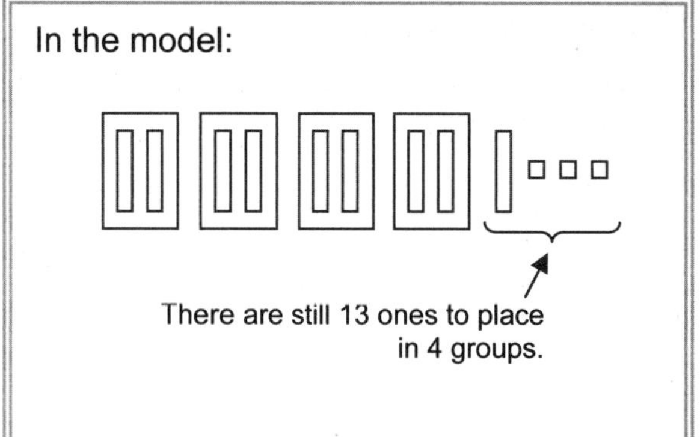
There are still 13 ones to place in 4 groups.

8. Carry out the first four steps of long division.

a) 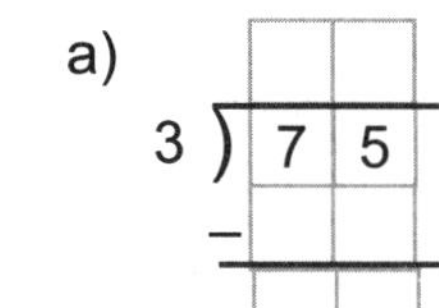
b) 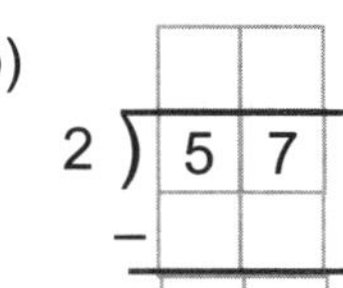
c) 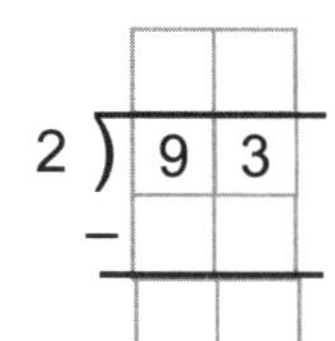
d) 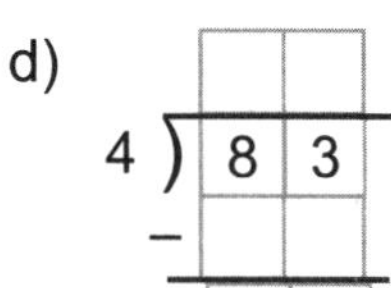
e) 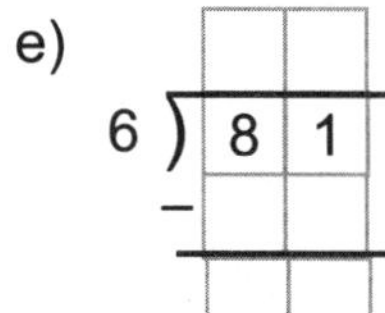

f) 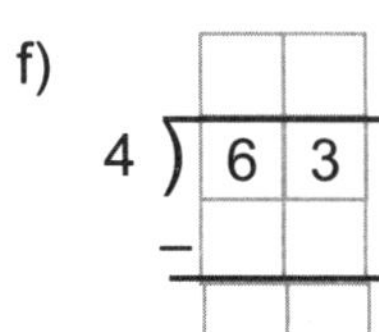
g) 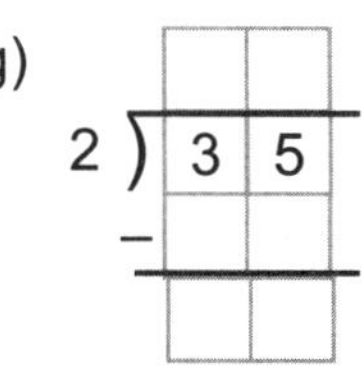
h) 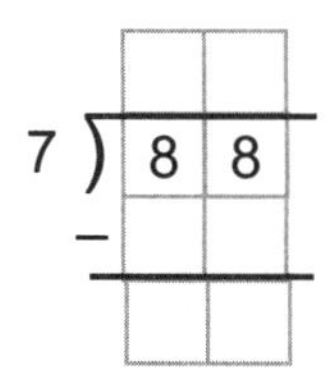
i) 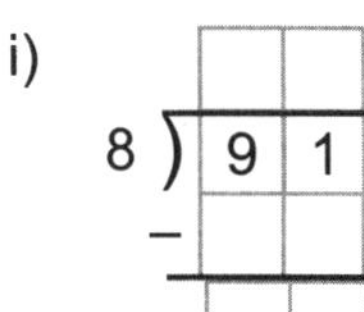
j) 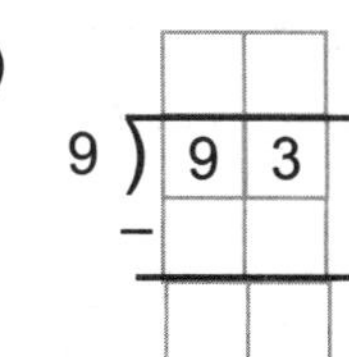

Step 5: Inez finds the number of ones she can put in each group by dividing 13 by 4.

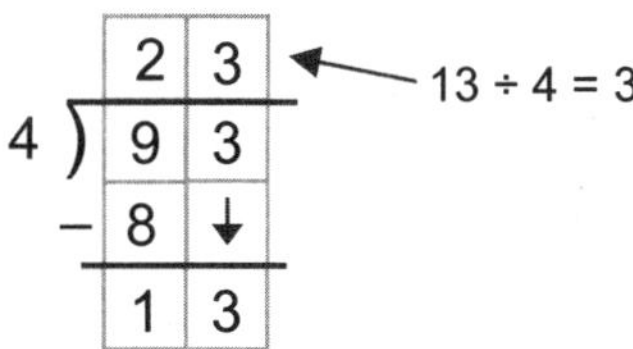
13 ÷ 4 = 3

In the model:

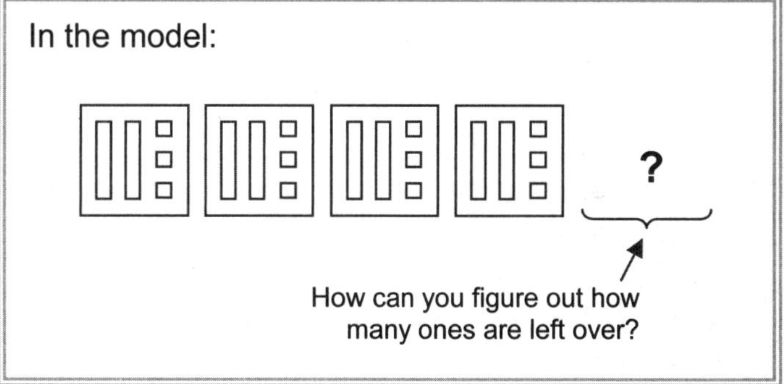
?
How can you figure out how many ones are left over?

9. Carry out the first five steps of long division.

a) 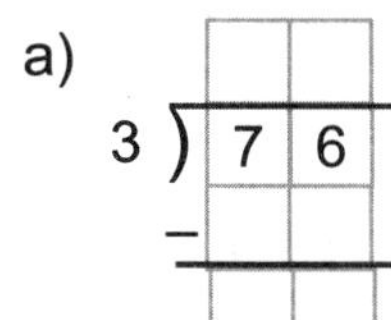
b) 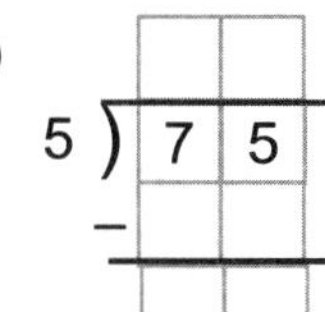
c) 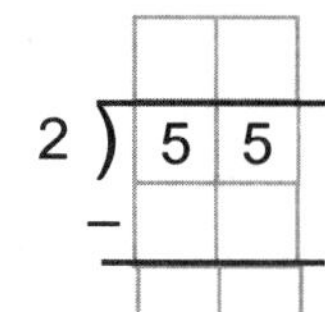
d) 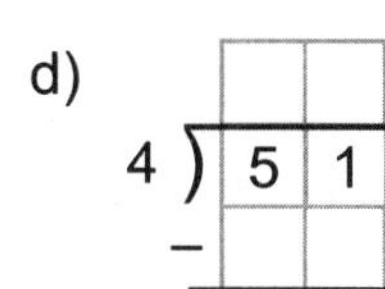
e) 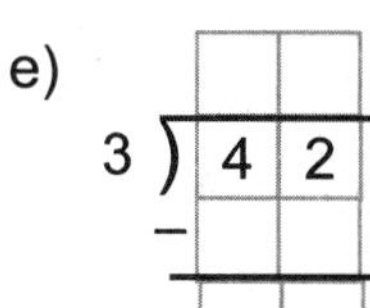

f) 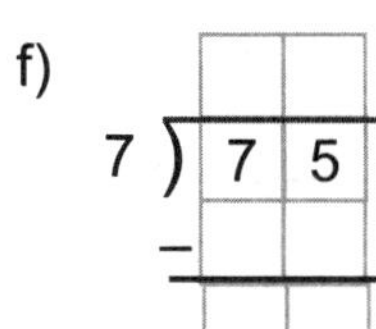
g) 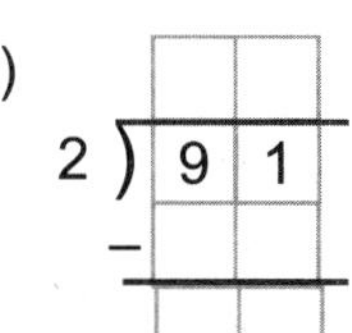
h) 3 ) 9 6
i) 9 ) 9 2
j) 2 ) 7 3

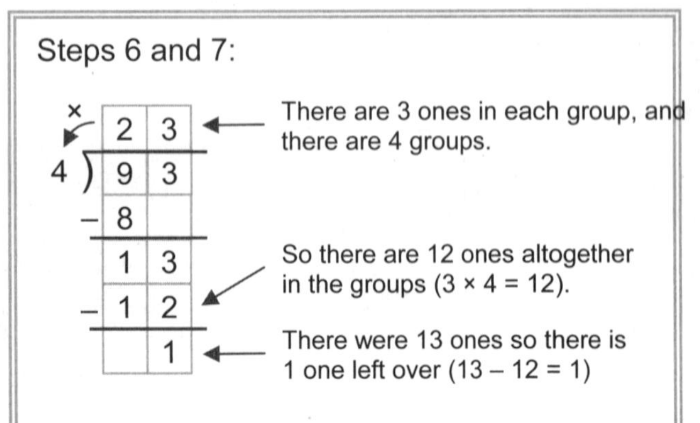

Steps 6 and 7:
There are 3 ones in each group, and there are 4 groups.
So there are 12 ones altogether in the groups (3 × 4 = 12).
There were 13 ones so there is 1 one left over (13 – 12 = 1)


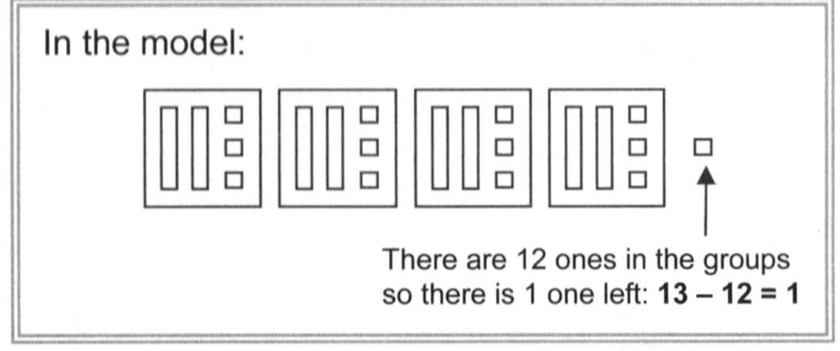

In the model:
There are 12 ones in the groups so there is 1 one left: 13 – 12 = 1


**The division statement and the model both show that Inez can give each class 23 apples with one left over.**

10. Carry out all 7 steps of long division.

a) 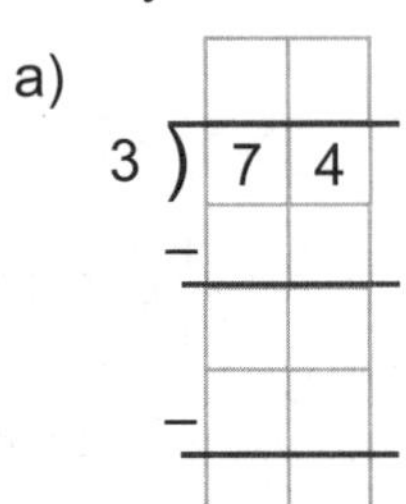
b) 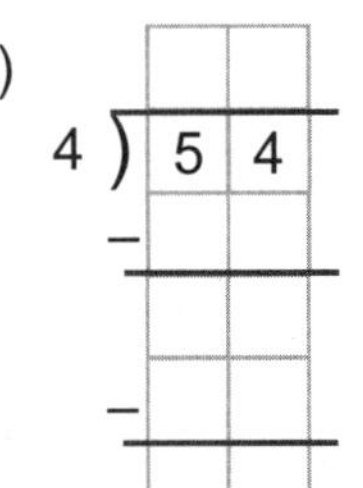
c) 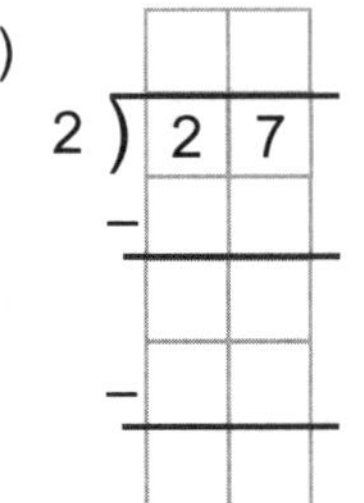
d) 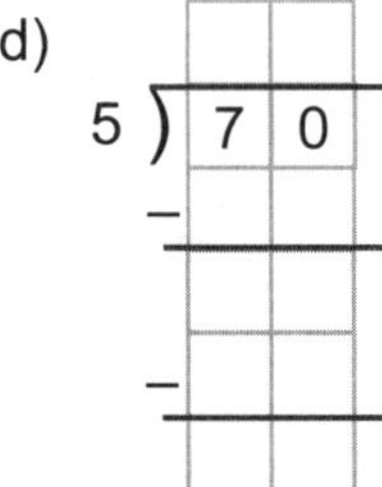
e) 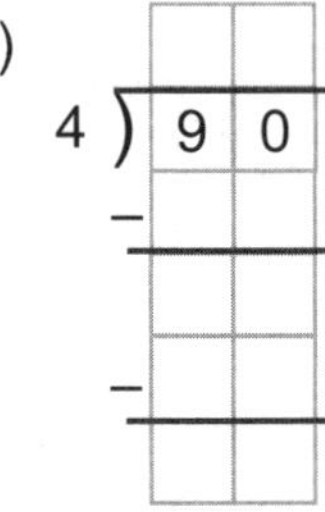

f) 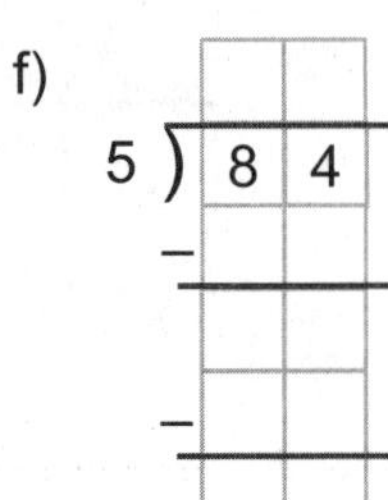
g) 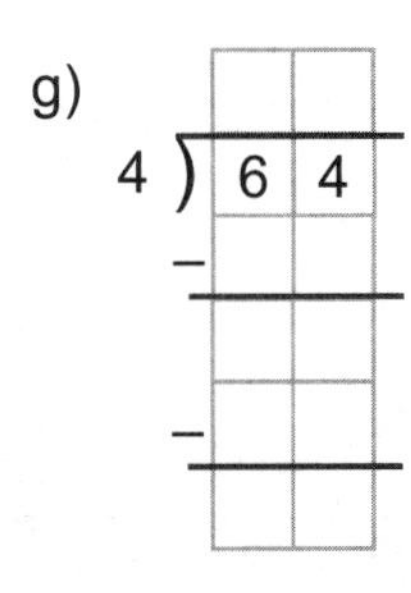
h) 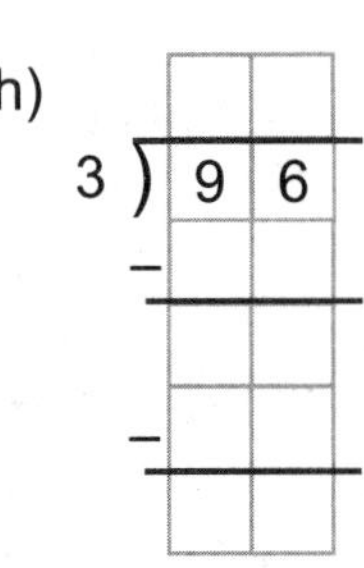
i) 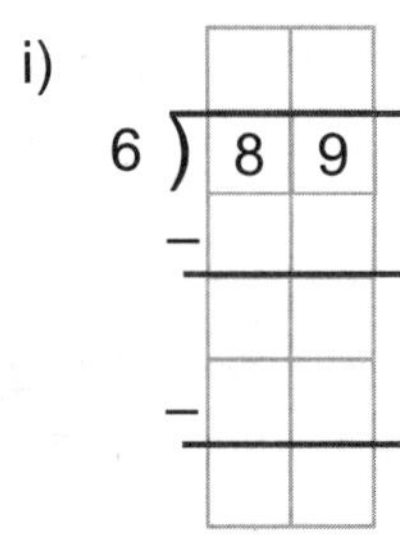
j) 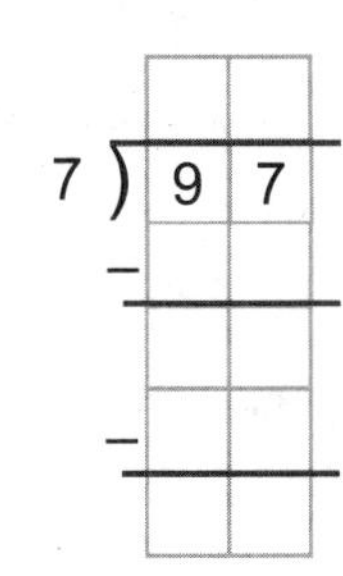

Show your work for the remaining questions on a separate piece of paper.

11. Sandra put 62 tomatoes into cartons of 5. How many tomatoes did she have left over?
12. How many weeks are there in 84 days?
13. Shawn can hike 8 km in a day. How many days will it take him to hike 96 km?
14. Alexa put 73 apples in bags of 6. Mike put 46 apples in bags of 4. Who had more apples left over?

For the questions, you will have to decide what to do with the remainder.

Example: Sally wants to put her collection of 53 shells into glass-covered trays. Each tray holds 4 shells. How many trays will she need? **53 ÷ 4 = 13 Remainder 1** She will need 14 trays (because she needs a tray to hold the one shell left over).

15. A canoe can hold 3 kids. How many canoes will 44 kids need?
16. Anne reads 5 pages before bed every night. She has 63 pages left to read in her book. How many nights will it take her to finish her book?
17. Ed wants to give 65 hockey cards to 4 friends. How many cards will each friend get?
18. Daniel wants to put 97 hockey cards into a scrap book. A page can hold 9 cards. How many pages will he need?

1. Find 512 ÷ 2 by drawing a base-10 model and by long division.

Step 1: Draw a base-10 model of 512.

Step 2: Divide the hundreds squares into 2 equal groups.

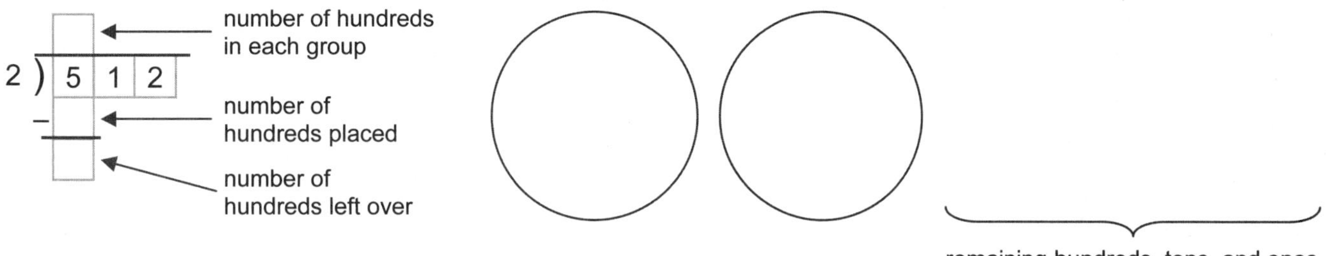


Step 3: Exchange the leftover hundreds square for 10 tens strips.

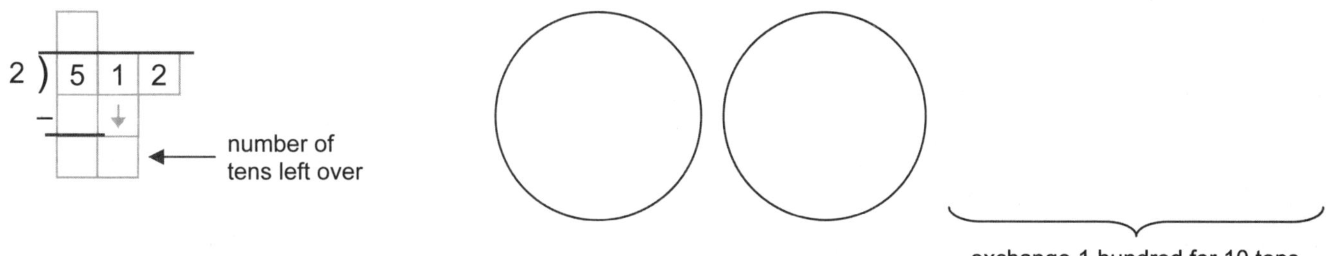


. Divide the tens strips into 2 equal groups.

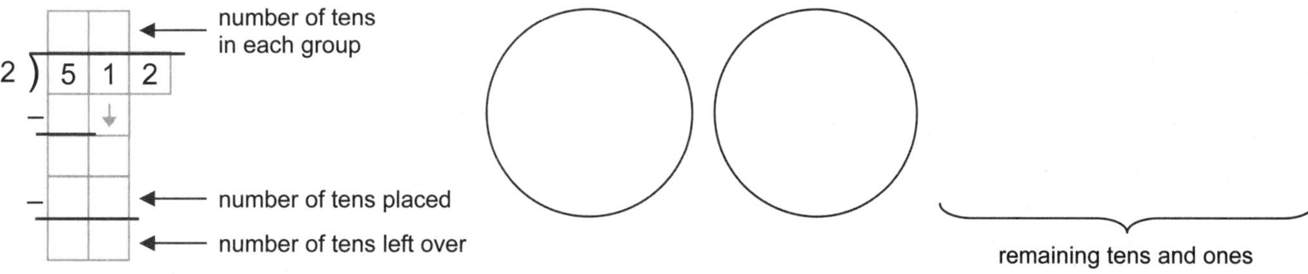


Step 5: Exchange the leftover tens strips for 10 ones squares.

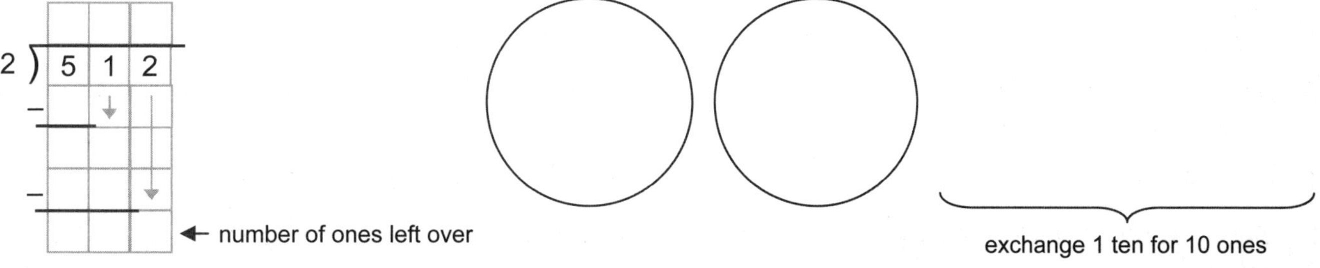

Steps 6 and 7: Divide the ones into 2 equal groups.

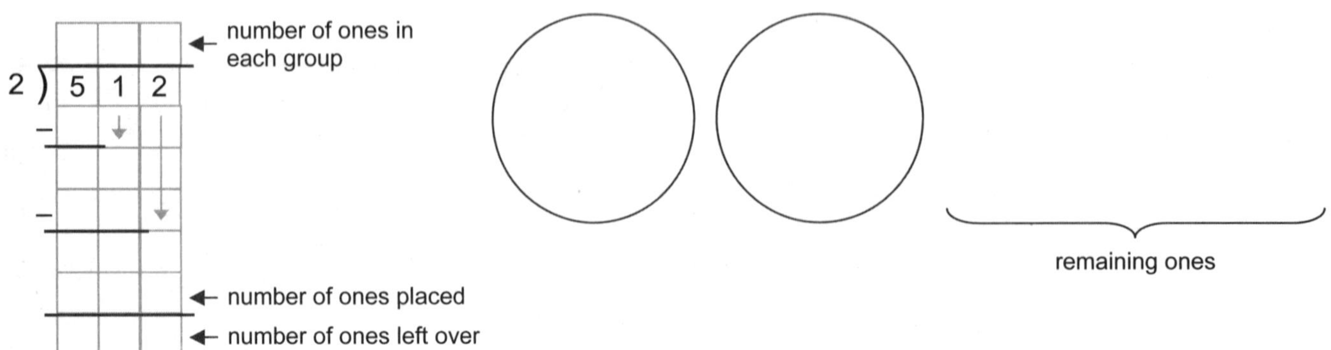


2. Divide.

a) 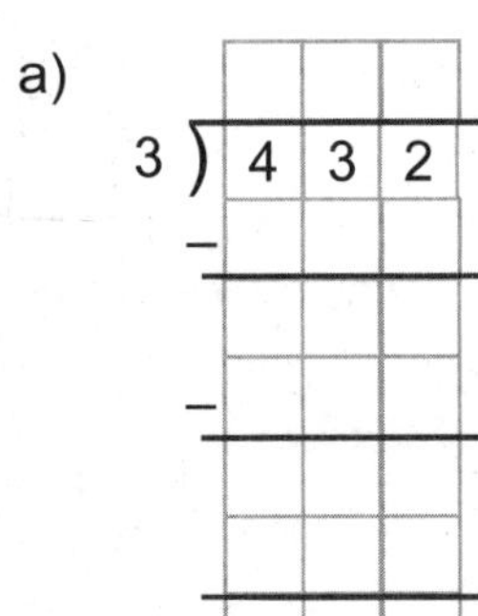


b) 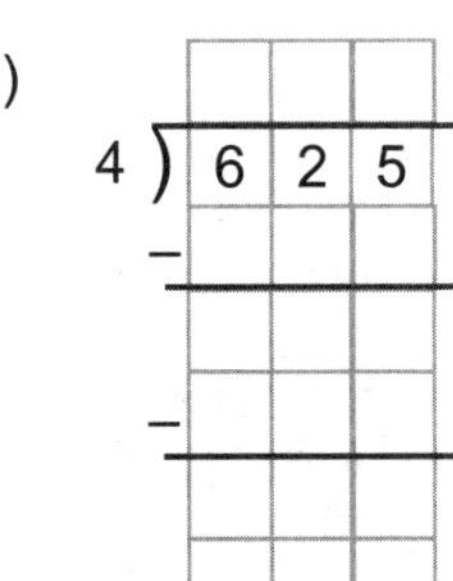


c) 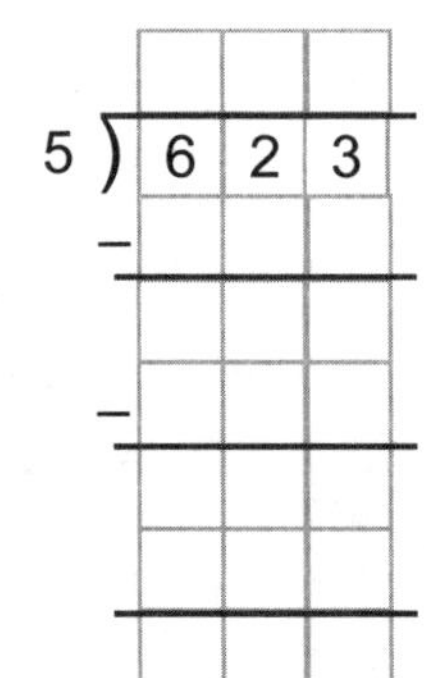


d) 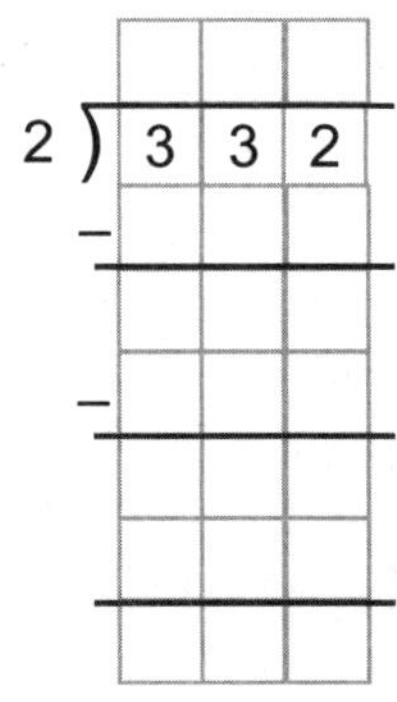


NOTE:
For each question below, there are fewer hundreds than the number of groups. Write a "0" in the hundreds position to show that no hundreds can be placed in equal groups. You should then perform the division as if the hundreds had automatically been exchanged for tens.

3. Divide. The first one is done for you.

a)

|   | 0 | 2 | 4 |
|---|---|---|---|
| 5 ) | 1 | 2 | 4 |
| − | 1 | 0 |   |
|   |   | 2 | 4 |
| − |   | 2 | 0 |
|   |   |   | 4 |

2 tens can be placed in each group
10 tens have been placed
2 tens are left over

b) 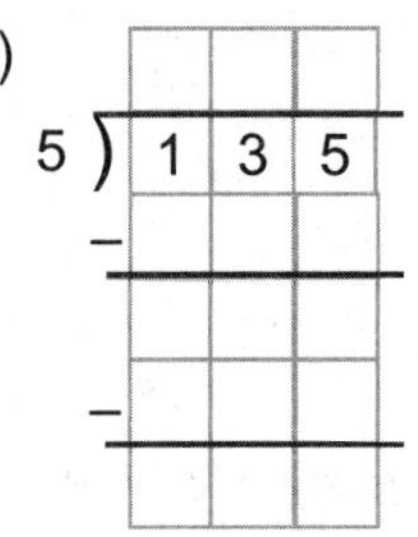


c) 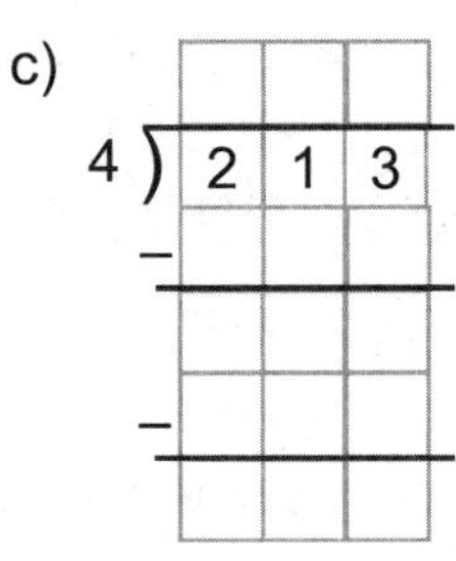


d) 3 ) 1 1 2

4. Divide. Show your work on a separate piece of paper.

a) 3 ) 217 b) 5 ) 678 c) 6 ) 724 d) 8 ) 172 e) 7 ) 225

5. An equilateral triangle has a perimeter of 465 cm. How long is each side?

6. Four friends earn a total of $612 shovelling snow. How much does each friend earn?

# NS4-44: Concepts in Multiplication and Division

NOTE:
Review the terms "multiples of" and "divisible by."

Example: The numbers (greater than 0) that are "multiples of" or "divisible by" 4 are the numbers you say when counting by 4: 4, 8, 12, 16, and so on.

---

Answer the following questions on a separate piece of paper:

1. Write one multiplication statement and two division statements in the same fact family as 6 x 8 = 48.

2. Find the mystery numbers.
   a) I am a multiple of 4. I am greater than 25 and less than 31.
   b) I am divisible by 3. I am between 20 and 26. I am an even number.

3. 140 kids attend a play on 4 buses. There are an equal number of kids on each bus.
   a) How many kids are on each bus?
   b) A ticket for the play costs $6. How much will it cost for one busload of kids to attend the play?

4. Find two different ways to share 14 apples in equal groups so there are 2 apples left over.

5. Find three numbers that give the same remainder when divided by 3.

6. A queen ant can lay one egg every ten seconds. How many eggs can she lay in . . .

   a) 1 minute? b) 2 minutes? c) 1 hour?

   How did you find your answers?

7. Six friends read 150 books for a read-a-thon. Each friend reads the same number of books. How many books did each friend read?

8. A 212-mL container of water is used to fill 4 glasses. How many millilitres are in each glass?

9. A square park has a perimeter of 680 m. How long is each side of the park?

10. A square park has sides of length 237 m. What is the perimeter of the park?

11. A pentagon with equal sides has a perimeter of 225 cm. How long is each side?

12. A robin lays **at least** 3 eggs and **no more than** 6 eggs.

   a) What is the least number of eggs 3 robin's nests would hold (if there were eggs laid in each nest)?
   b) What is the greatest number of eggs 3 robin's nests would hold?
   c) Three robin's nests contain 13 eggs. Draw a picture to show 2 ways the eggs could be shared among the nests.

# NS4-45: Equal Parts and Models of Fractions

Fractions name equal parts of a whole. The pie is cut into 4 equal parts. 3 parts out of 4 are shaded. $\frac{3}{4}$ of a pie is shaded.

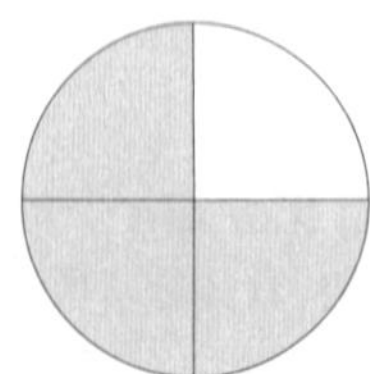

$\frac{3}{4}$

The **numerator** (3) tells you how many parts are counted.

The **denominator** (4) tells you how many parts are in a whole.

1. Name the fraction shown by the shaded part of each shape.

a) 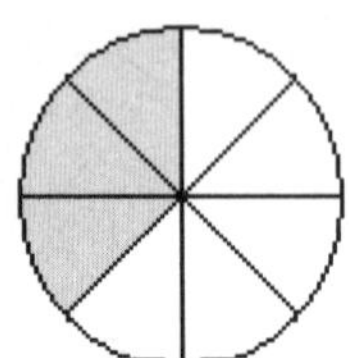

b) 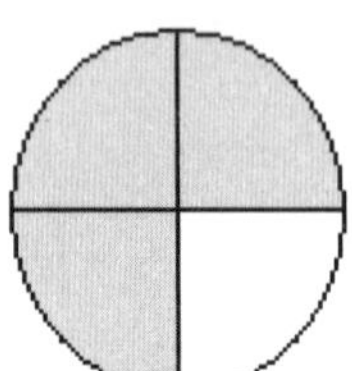

c) 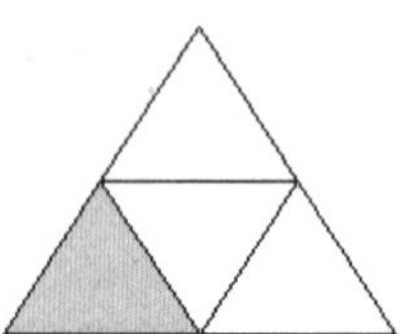

d) 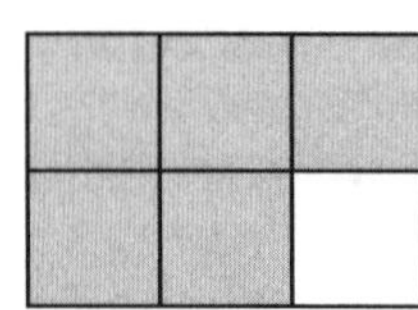

e) 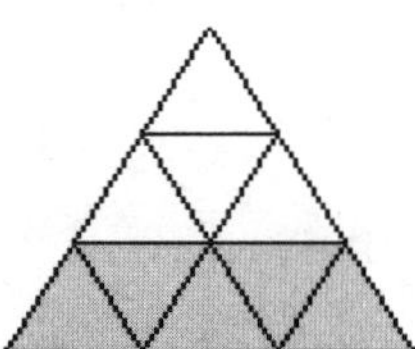

f) 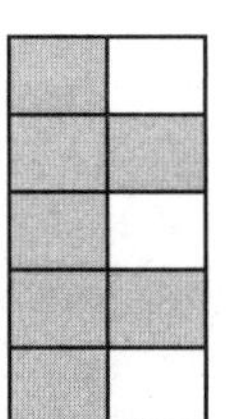

g) 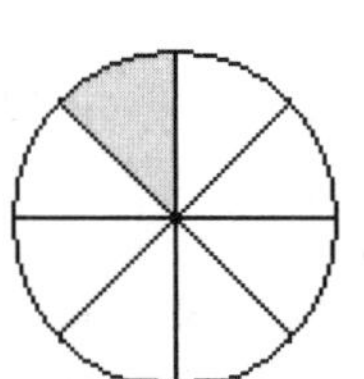

h) 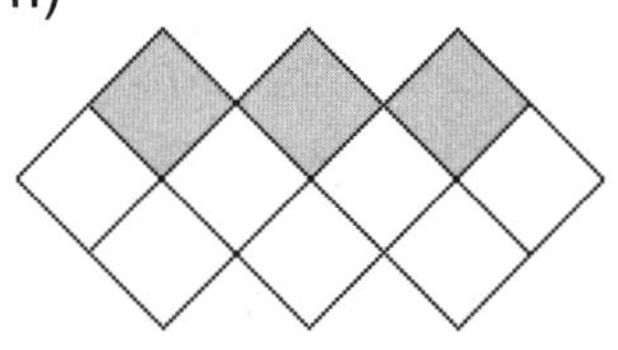

2. Shade the fractions that are named.

a) $\frac{3}{6}$ 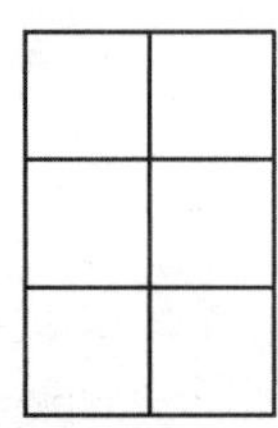

b) $\frac{2}{5}$ 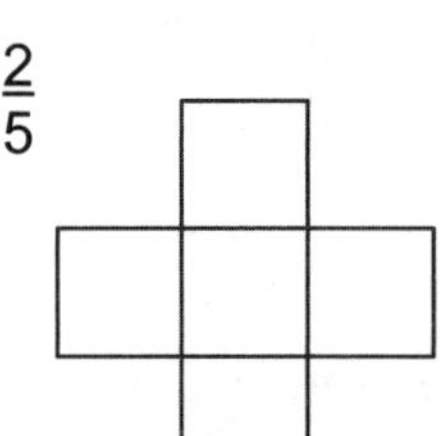

c) $\frac{5}{9}$ 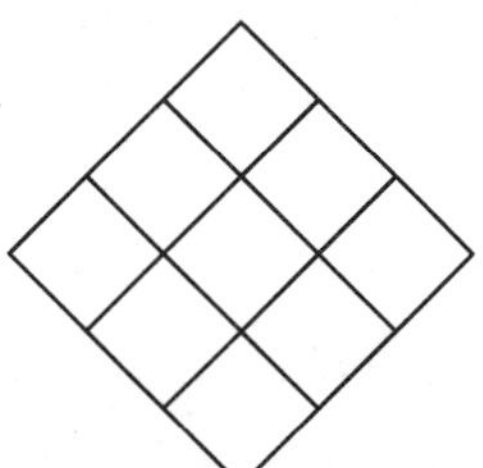

3. You have $\frac{3}{5}$ of a pie.

   a) What does the bottom (denominator) of the fraction tell you? ______________________

   ________________________________________________

   b) What does the top (numerator) of the fraction tell you? ______________________

   ________________________________________________

BONUS:

4. On a separate piece of paper, explain why each picture does or does not show $\frac{1}{4}$.

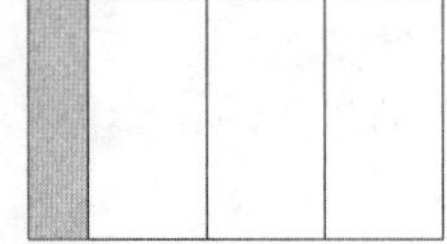

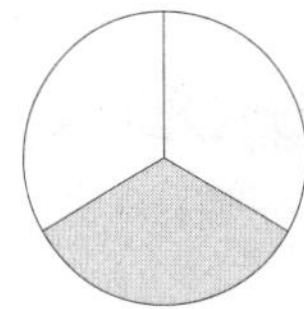

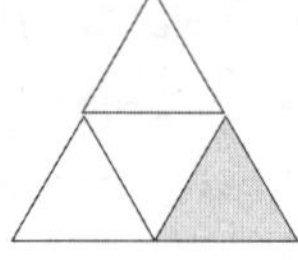

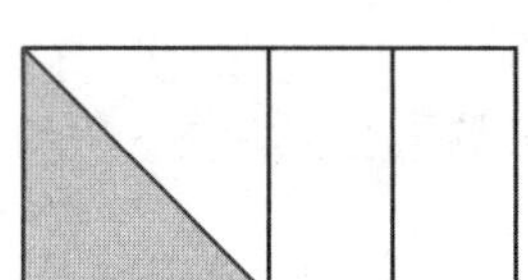

5. Use one of the following words to describe the parts in the figures below—"halves," "thirds," "fourths," "fifths," "sixths," "sevenths," "eighths," or "ninths."

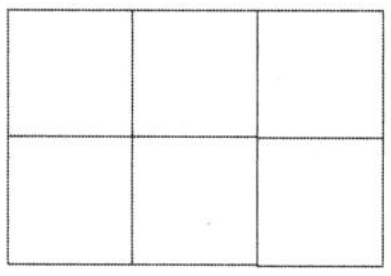

______ ______ ______

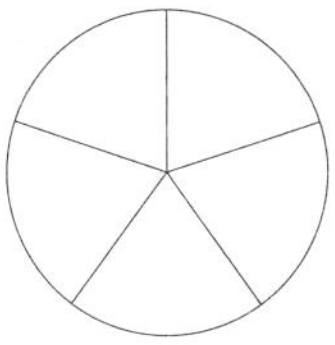

______ ______ ______

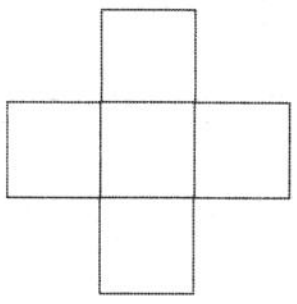

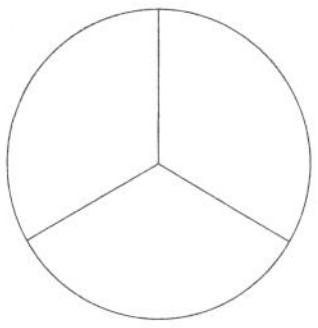

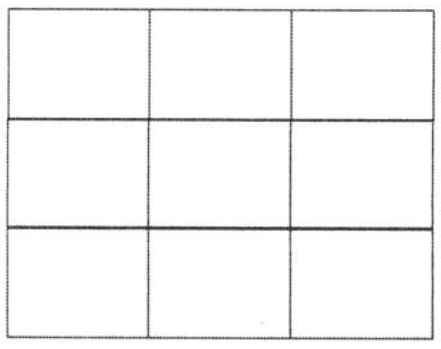

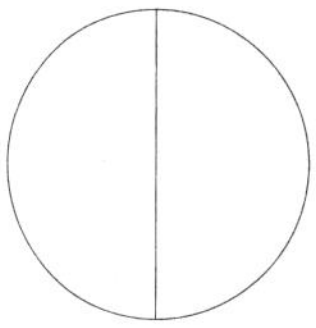

6. BONUS: On a separate piece of paper, sketch a pie cut in . . .

a) fifths b) thirds c) quarters (or fourths) d) tenths

7. Sketch a pie and cut it into fourths. How can you cut the pie into eighths?

NOTE: You will need a ruler for the exercises below.

8. Use a ruler to divide each line into equal parts.

a) 5 equal parts b) 3 equal parts c) 2 equal parts

9. Use a ruler to divide each box into equal parts.

a) 4 equal parts b) 5 equal parts

10. Using a ruler, find what fraction of each of the following boxes is shaded:

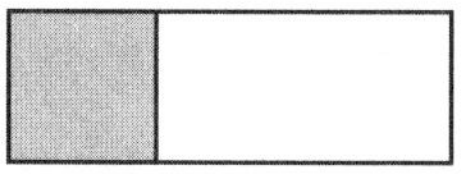

______ is shaded. ______ is shaded.

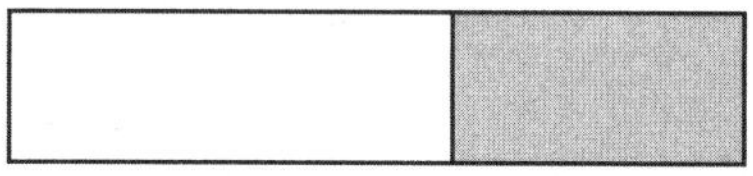

11. Using a ruler, complete the following figures to make a whole:

$\frac{1}{4}$ $\frac{1}{3}$ $\frac{1}{2}$

12. Each of the lines below is $\frac{1}{4}$ of a line. Using a ruler, fill in the rest to make a whole line.

a) ______ b) ______

# NS4-46: Equal Parts of a Set

Fractions can name parts of a set: $\frac{3}{5}$ of the figures are triangles, $\frac{1}{5}$ are squares, and $\frac{1}{5}$ are circles:

---

Answer questions 1, 2, and 3 on a separate piece of paper.

1. Using the words "figures," "shaded," "unshaded," "circles," "squares," and "triangles," write at least 3 fractions statements for each picture.

   a)

   b)

2. Can you describe the pictures in two different ways using the fraction $\frac{2}{7}$ ?

3. Draw a picture to solve each puzzle.

   a) There are 5 circles and squares. $\frac{3}{5}$ of the figures are squares. $\frac{2}{5}$ of the figures are shaded. Two circles are shaded.

   b) There are 5 triangles and squares. $\frac{3}{5}$ of the figures are shaded. $\frac{2}{5}$ of the figures are triangles. One square is shaded.

4. A soccer team wins 5 games and loses 3 games.

   a) How many games did the team play? _______________

   b) What **fraction** of the games did the team win? _______________

   c) Did the team win more than half its games? _______________

5. A basketball team wins 7 games, loses 2 games, and ties 3 games. What fractions of the games did the team . . .

   a) win? __________ b) lose? __________ c) tie? __________

6. A box contains 4 blue markers, 3 black markers, and 3 red markers. What fraction of the markers are **not** blue? ____________

BONUS:

7. Julie lives 3 km from her school. She has biked 1 km towards her school. What fraction of the distance to her school does she still have to bike?

8. Pia is 9 years old. She was born in Calgary, but she moved to Regina when she was 5. What fraction of her life did she live in Calgary?

# NS4-47: Parts and Wholes

1. What fraction is shaded? How do you know?

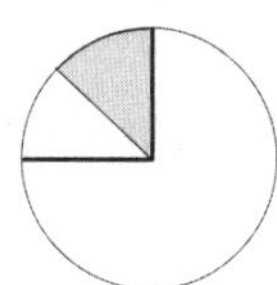

2. Draw lines from the point in the centre of the hexagon to the vertices of the hexagon. How many triangles cover the hexagon?

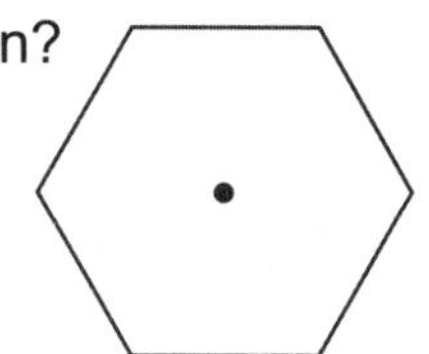

3. What fraction of each figure is the shaded part?

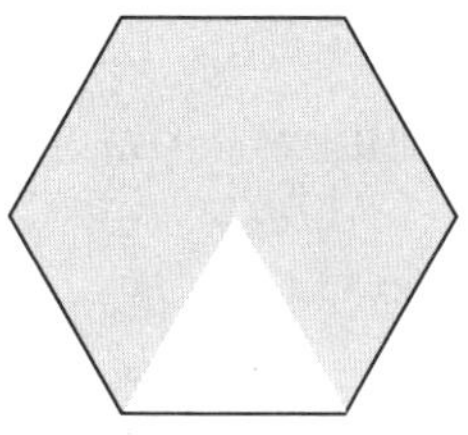 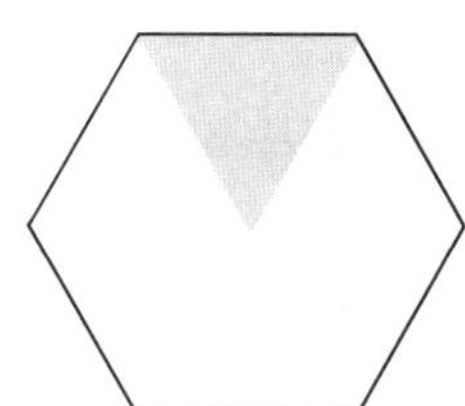 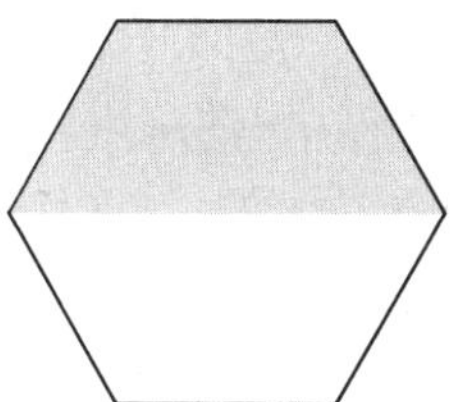 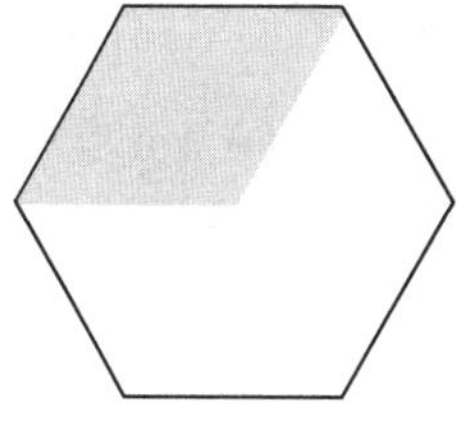

_______ _______ _______ _______

4. What fraction of each figure is the shaded piece?

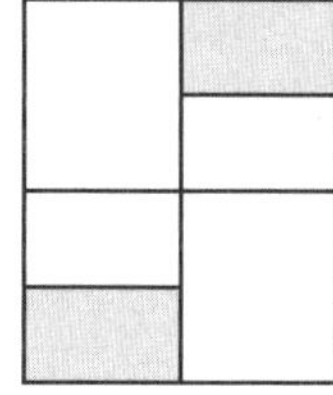 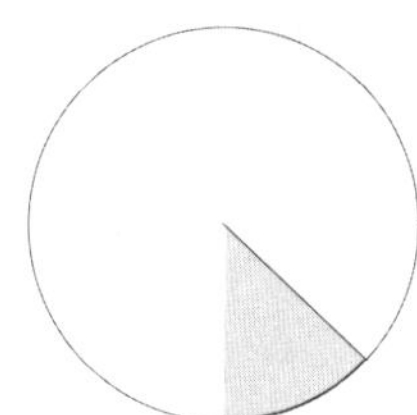 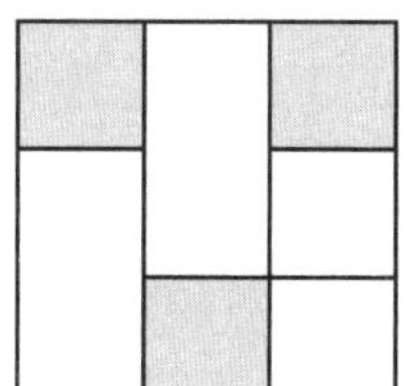 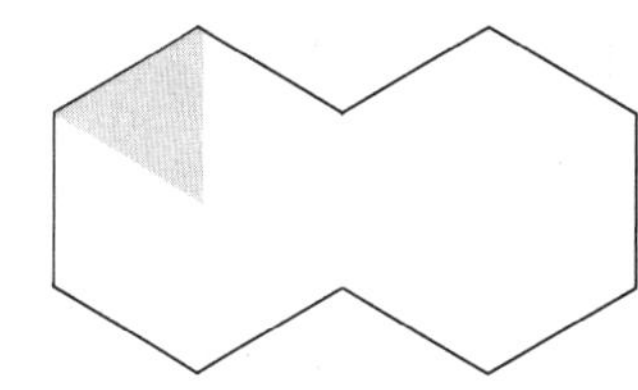

_______ _______ _______ _______

PARENT: For the remaining questions your child will need page xxii: Pattern Blocks from the Introduction.

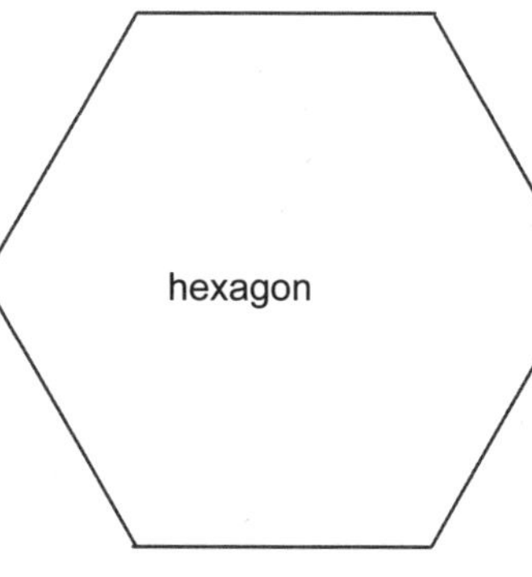


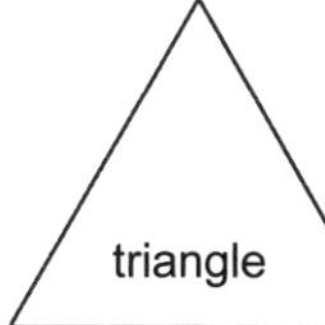

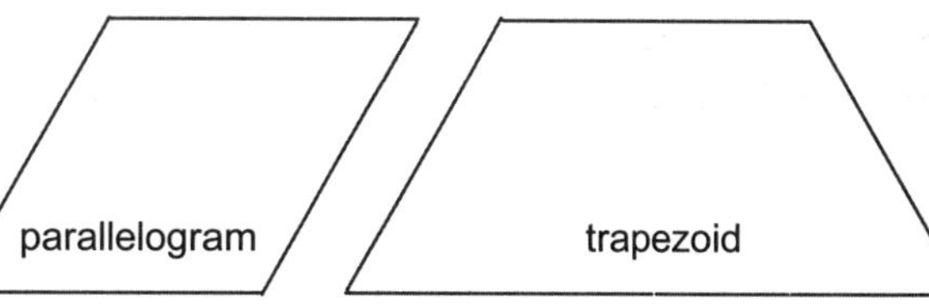


5. What fraction of the trapezoid is the triangle? (How many triangles will fit in the trapezoid?)

6. What fraction of the hexagon is the trapezoid?

7. What fraction of the hexagon is the parallelogram?

8. What fraction of two hexagons is the triangle?

9. What fraction of the hexagon is the triangle?

# NS4-48: Ordering and Comparing Fractions

1. What fraction has a larger numerator, $\frac{1}{4}$ or $\frac{3}{4}$? ________

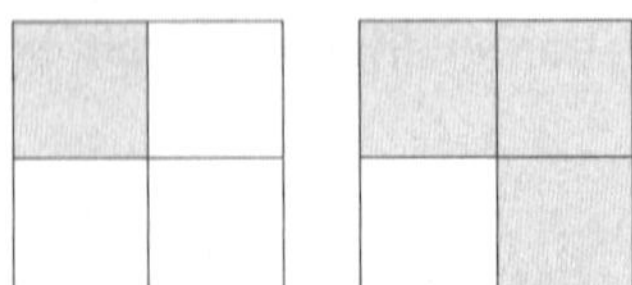

   Which fraction is larger? ________

   Explain your thinking. ________________________________________

   ________________________________________

2. Circle the larger fraction in each pair.

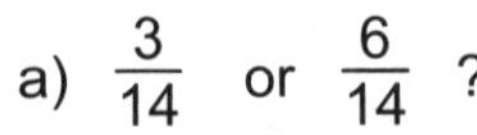

   a) $\frac{3}{14}$ or $\frac{6}{14}$ ?    b) $\frac{4}{12}$ or $\frac{7}{12}$ ?    c) $\frac{2}{9}$ or $\frac{5}{9}$ ?

3. Two fractions have the same **denominators** (bottoms) but different **numerators** (tops). How can you tell which fraction is larger?

   ________________________________________

   ________________________________________

   ________________________________________

4. Write the fractions in order from least to greatest on a separate piece of paper.

   a) $\frac{2}{3}, \frac{1}{3}, \frac{3}{3}$    b) $\frac{2}{10}, \frac{1}{10}, \frac{7}{10}, \frac{9}{10}, \frac{5}{10}$    c) $\frac{5}{17}, \frac{2}{17}, \frac{9}{17}, \frac{8}{17}, \frac{16}{17}$

5. a) Cut the square in half.

   What fraction of the square is each part? ________

   b) Next, cut each of these parts in half.

   What fraction of the square is each new part? ________

   c) As the denominator of the fraction **increases**, what happens to the size of each piece?

   ________________________________________

6. Which fraction is larger, $\frac{1}{2}$ or $\frac{1}{100}$? ________ Explain your thinking.

   ________________________________________

   ________________________________________

7. Circle the **biggest** fraction in each pair.

a) $\frac{1}{5}$ or $\frac{1}{7}$? b) $\frac{3}{15}$ or $\frac{3}{7}$? c) $\frac{2}{197}$ or $\frac{2}{297}$?

8. Fraction A and fraction B have the same **numerators** (tops) but different **denominators** (bottoms). How can you tell which fraction is larger?

______________________________________________

______________________________________________

9. Write the fractions in order from least to greatest.

a) $\frac{1}{5}$, $\frac{1}{2}$, $\frac{1}{4}$ b) $\frac{1}{5}$, $\frac{1}{8}$, $\frac{1}{7}$, $\frac{1}{2}$, $\frac{1}{3}$ c) $\frac{2}{3}$, $\frac{2}{5}$, $\frac{2}{7}$

10. Circle the **biggest** fraction in each pair.

a) $\frac{1}{3}$ or $\frac{1}{9}$? b) $\frac{7}{13}$ or $\frac{9}{13}$? c) $\frac{6}{15}$ or $\frac{6}{18}$?

11.

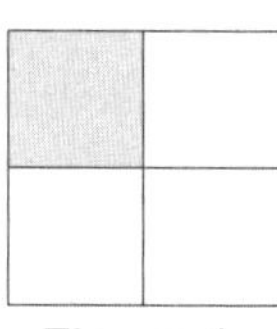

Figure 1

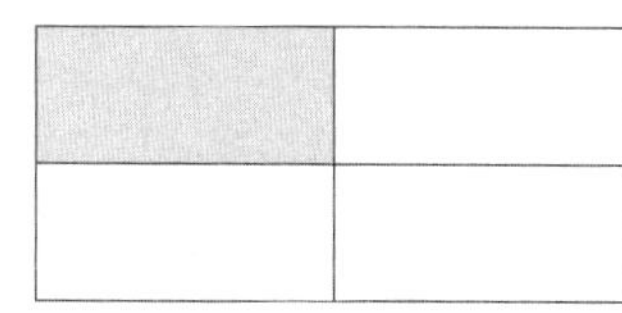

Figure 2

Is $\frac{1}{4}$ of Figure 1 the same as $\frac{1}{4}$ of Figure 2? Explain why or why not on a separate piece of paper.

12. Is it possible for $\frac{1}{4}$ of a pie to be bigger than $\frac{1}{3}$ of another pie? Show your thinking with a picture on a separate piece of paper.

13. ACTIVITY:

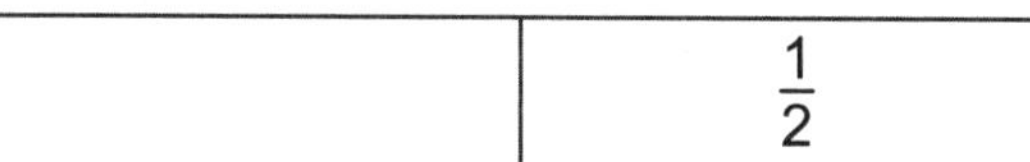


Cut 3 strips of paper of equal length. Fold one strip to make 2 equal parts. Mark the creases with a line and write $\frac{1}{2}$ as shown. Fold the second strip to make equal 3 parts. Mark the creases $\frac{1}{3}$ and $\frac{2}{3}$. Fold the third strip to make 4 equal parts. Mark the strips $\frac{1}{4}$, $\frac{2}{4}$, $\frac{3}{4}$. Line up the strips to answer the questions.

a) Which is greater, $\frac{2}{3}$ of a strip or $\frac{1}{2}$ of a strip?

b) Which is greater, $\frac{2}{3}$ or $\frac{3}{4}$?

c) Is $\frac{2}{3}$ closer to $\frac{1}{2}$ or to 1?

d) Which is greater, $\frac{1}{4}$ or $\frac{1}{3}$?

# NS4-49: Mixed Fractions



Alan and his friends ate the amount of pizza shown:

They ate two and one quarter pies altogether ($2\frac{1}{4}$ pies).

$2\frac{1}{4}$ is called a **mixed** fraction because it is a mixture of a whole number and a fraction.

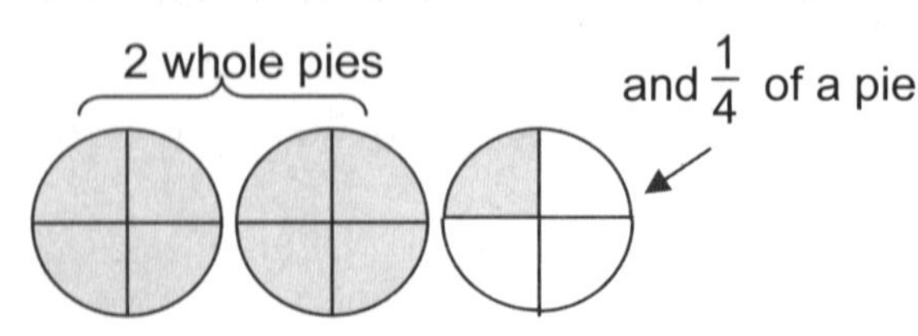


NOTE: Review naming fractions before completing the questions.

---

1. Write how many **whole** pies are shaded. The first one is done for you.

a) 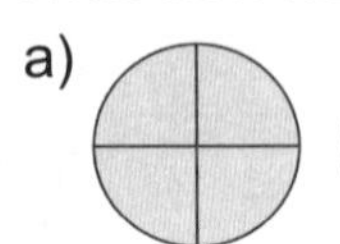 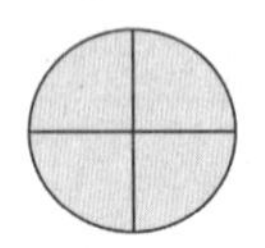 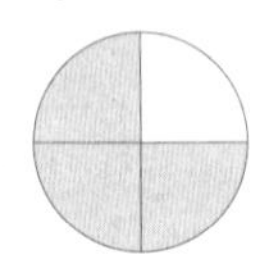

2 whole pies

b) 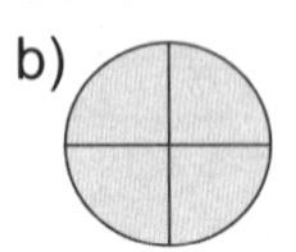 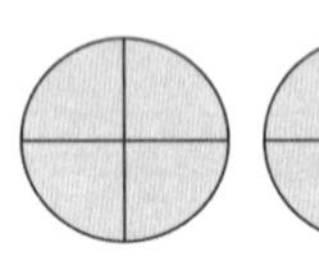 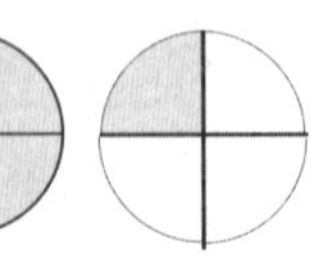 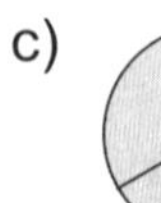

______ whole pies

c) 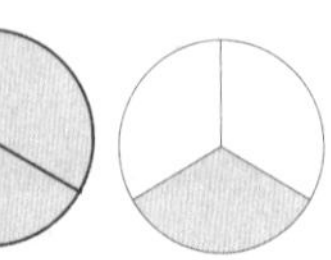

______ whole pie

2. Write the fractions as mixed fractions.

a)  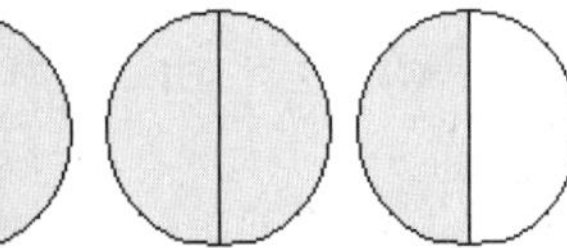

b) 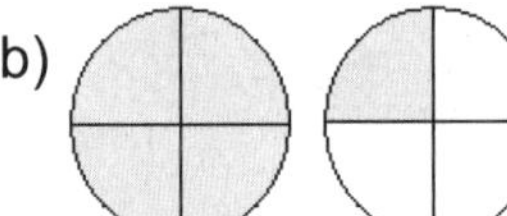

c) 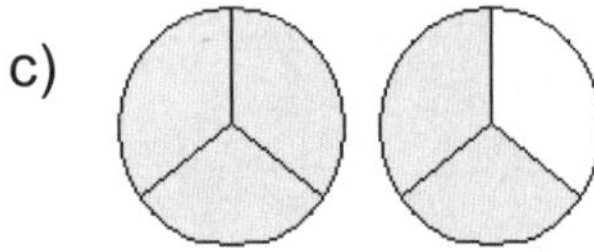

d) 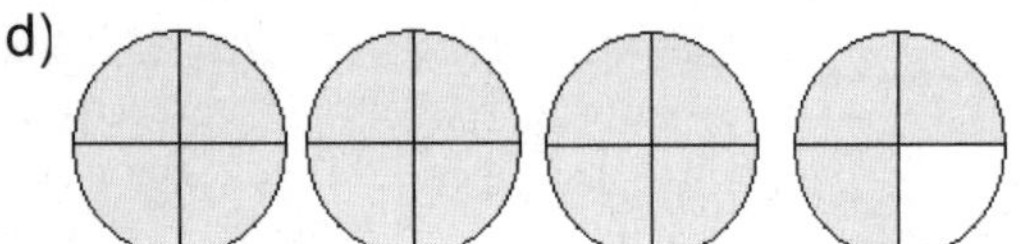

e) 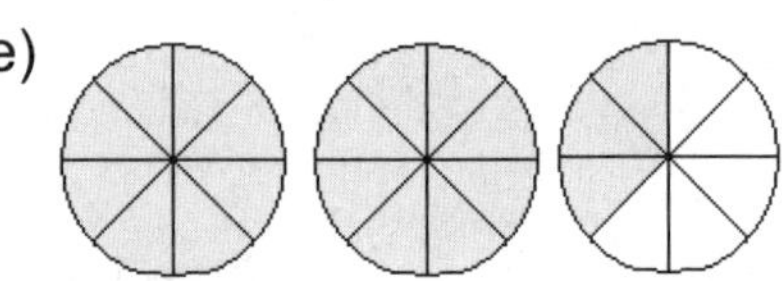

f) 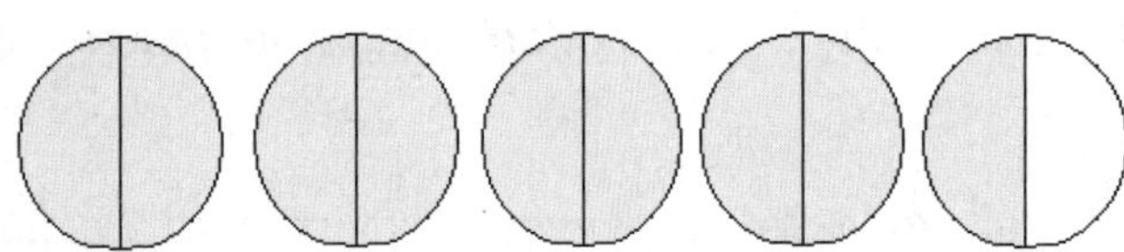

g) 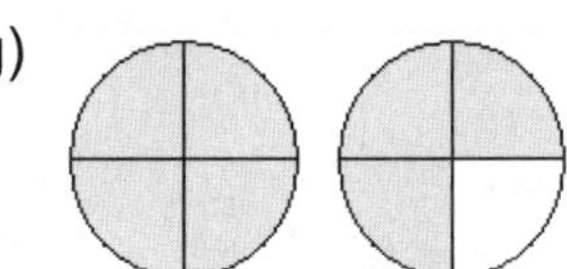

3. Shade one piece at a time until you have shaded the amount of pie given in bold. There may be more pies than you need.

a) $\mathbf{2\frac{1}{2}}$ 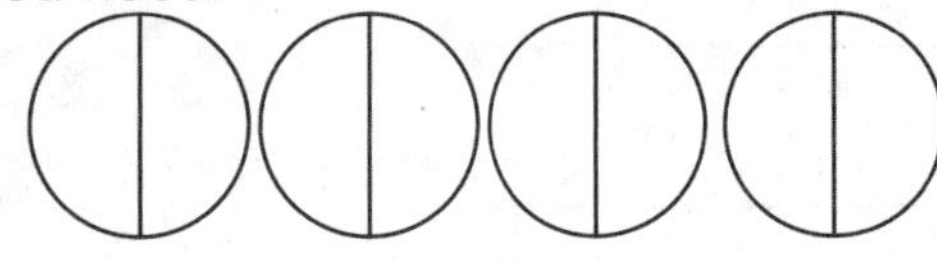

b) $\mathbf{3\frac{1}{2}}$ 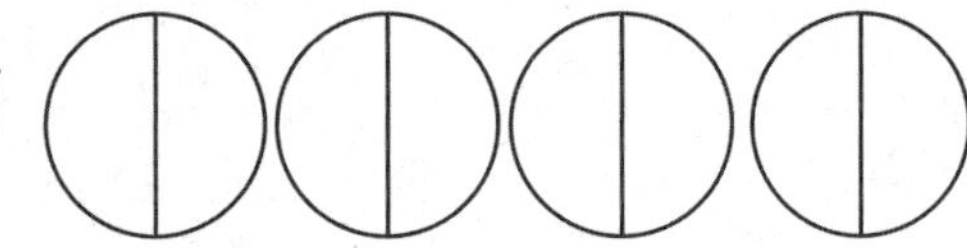

c) $\mathbf{1\frac{1}{2}}$ 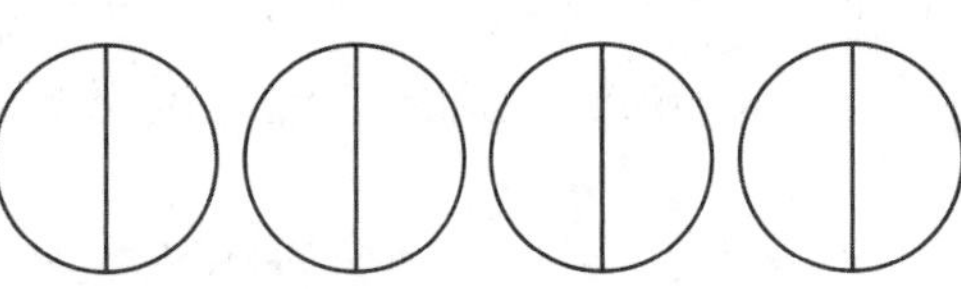

d) $\mathbf{2\frac{2}{3}}$ 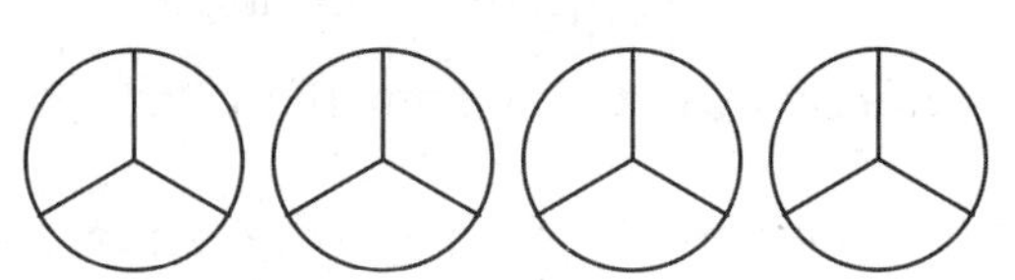

4. On a separate piece of paper, sketch . . . a) $2\frac{1}{2}$ pies b) $3\frac{1}{2}$ pies c) $2\frac{1}{4}$ pies

5. Which fraction represents more pie, $2\frac{1}{4}$ or $3\frac{1}{2}$? How do you know?

6. Is $2\frac{3}{4}$ closer to 2 or 3?

# NS4-50: Improper Fractions

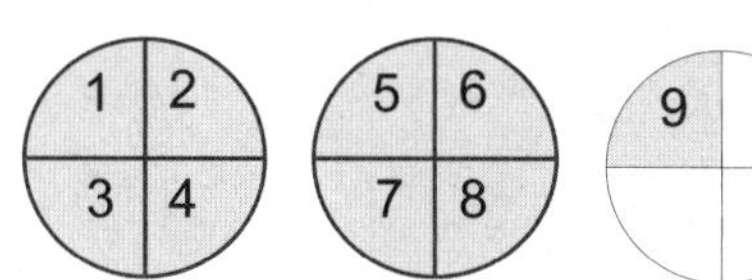


| **Improper fraction** | | **Mixed fraction** |
|---|---|---|
| $\mathbf{\frac{9}{4}}$ | = | $\mathbf{2\frac{1}{4}}$ |

Alan and his friends ate **9** quarter-sized pieces of pizza. Altogether they ate $\mathbf{\frac{9}{4}}$ pizzas.

When the numerator of a fraction is larger than the denominator, the fraction represents **more than** a whole. Such fractions are called **improper fractions**.

---

1. Write these fractions as **improper** fractions.

a)

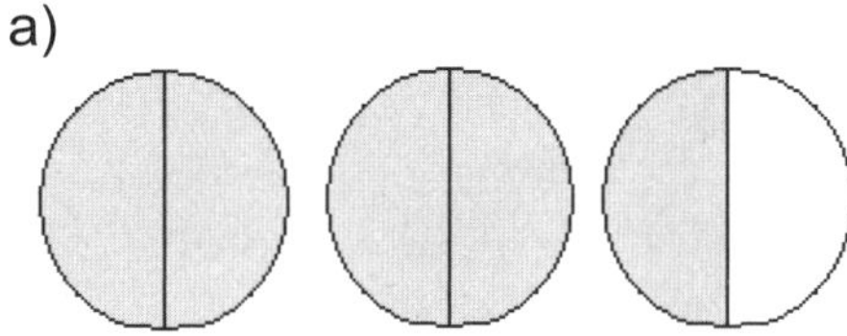

b)

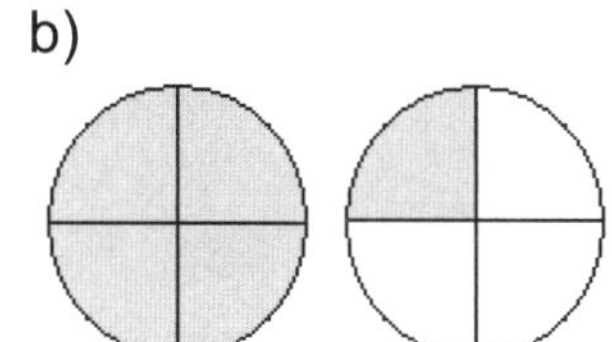

c)

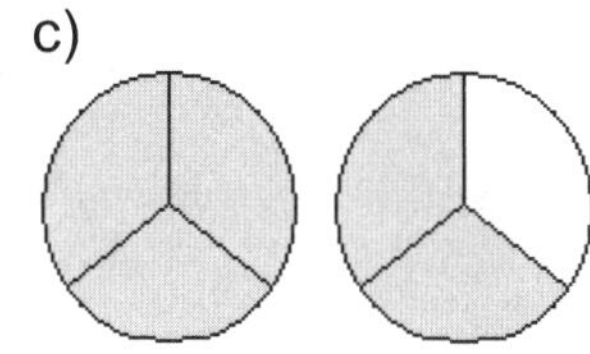

d)

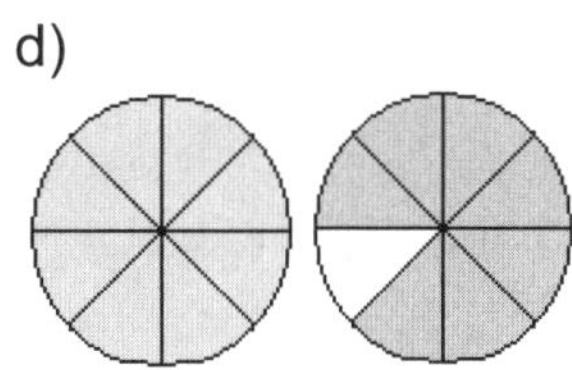

e)

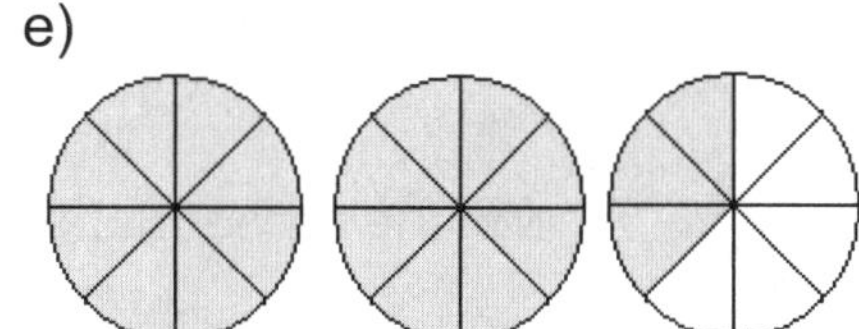

f)

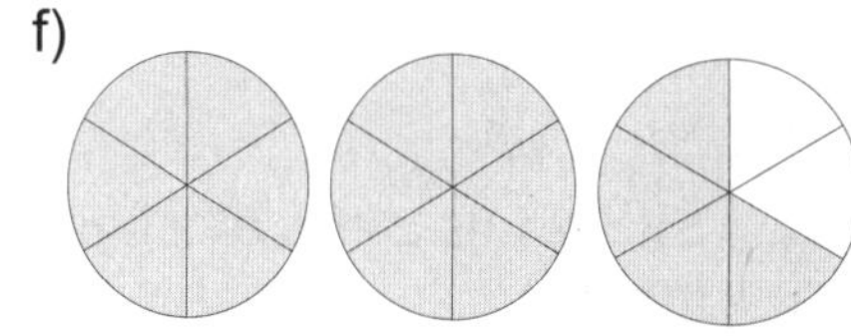

g) h)

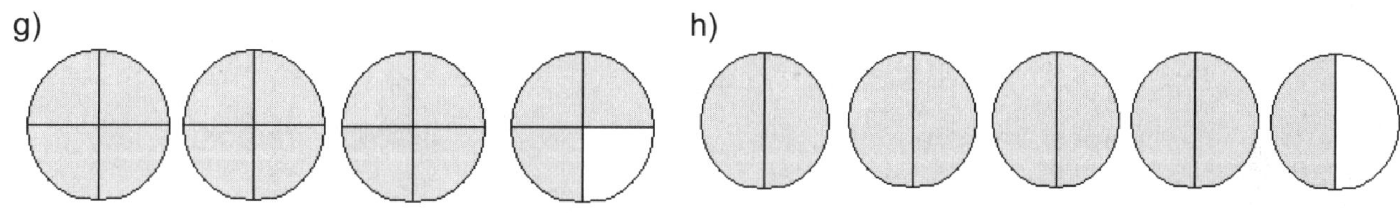

2. Shade one piece at a time until you have shaded the amount of pie given in bold.

a) $\mathbf{\frac{5}{2}}$

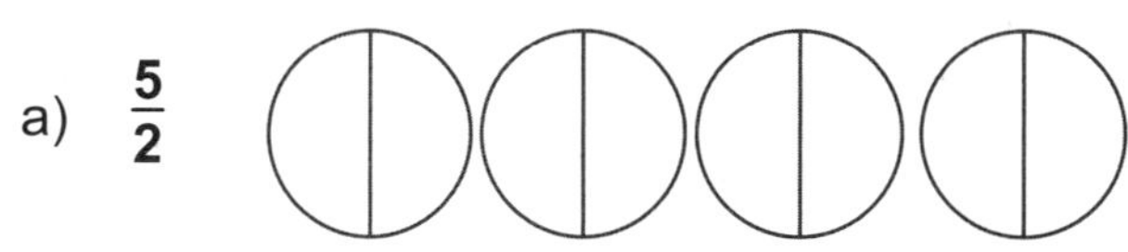

b) $\mathbf{\frac{7}{2}}$

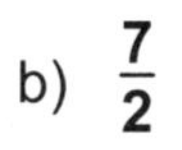

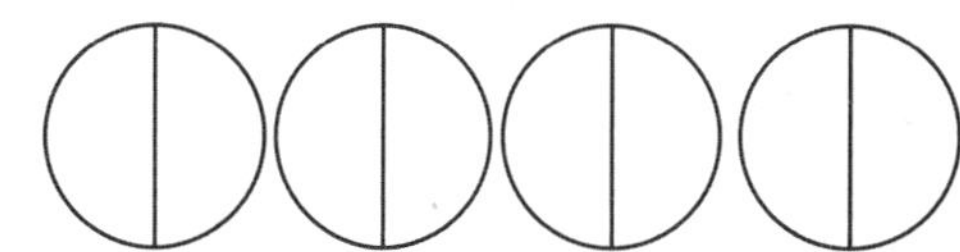

c) $\mathbf{\frac{8}{3}}$

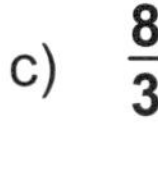

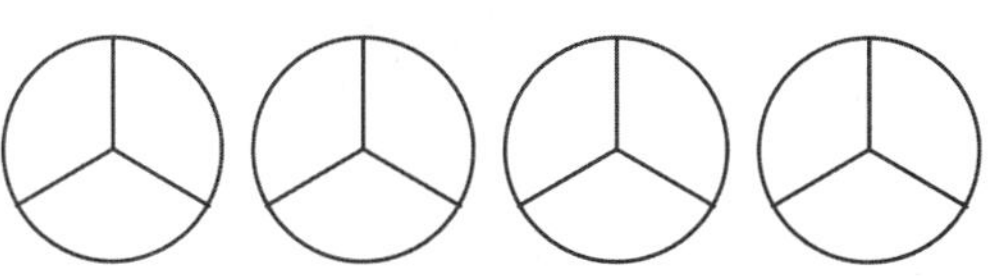

d) $\mathbf{\frac{13}{4}}$

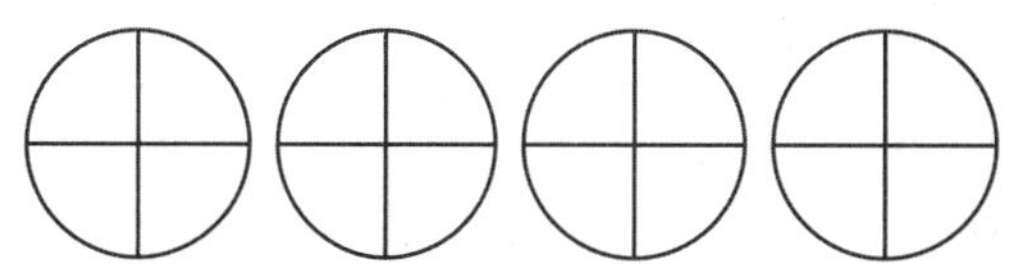

3. On a separate piece of paper, sketch . . . a) $\frac{3}{2}$ pies b) $\frac{9}{2}$ pies c) $\frac{10}{4}$ pies

4. Which fraction represents more pie, $\frac{5}{2}$ or $\frac{7}{2}$? How do you know?

5. Which fractions are more than a whole? How do you know? a) $\frac{3}{4}$ b) $\frac{9}{4}$ c) $\frac{7}{5}$

# NS4-51: Mixed and Improper Fractions



1. Write these fractions as **mixed** fractions and as **improper** fractions.

a) 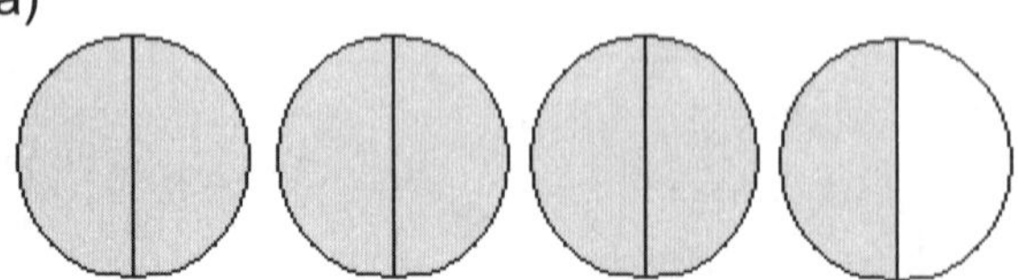

b) 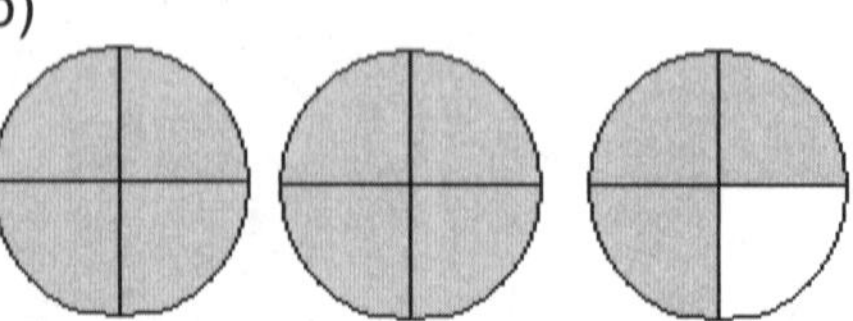

c) 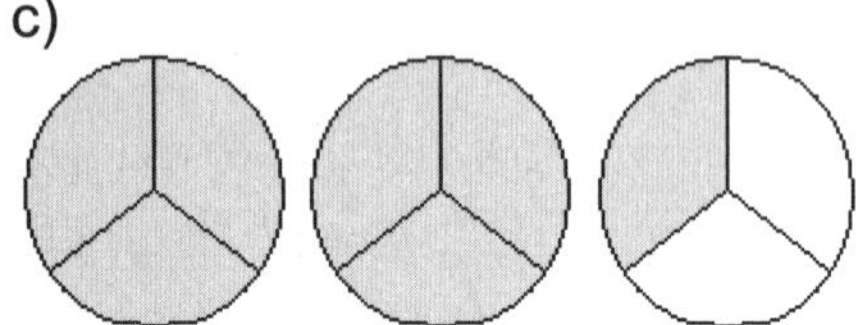

d) 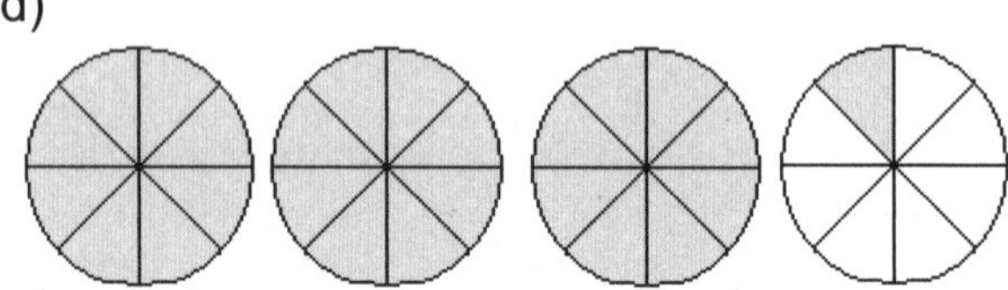

e) 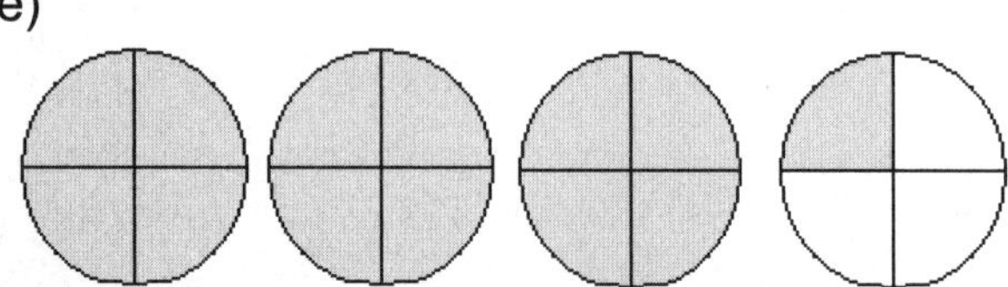

f) 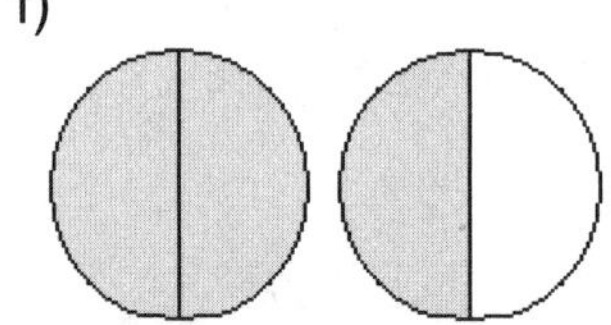

2. Shade one piece at a time until you have shaded the amount of pie given in bold. Then write an **improper** fraction for the amount of pie.

a) $\mathbf{2\frac{1}{2}}$ 

Improper fraction:

b) $\mathbf{3\frac{1}{4}}$ 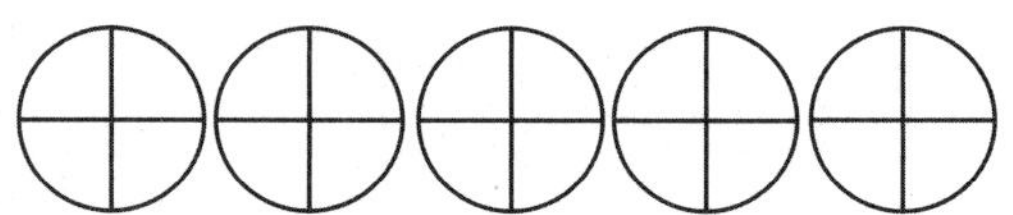

Improper fraction:

3. Shade one piece at a time until you have shaded the amount of pie given in bold. Then write a **mixed** fraction for the amount of pie.

a) $\mathbf{\frac{7}{3}}$ 

Mixed fraction:

b) $\mathbf{\frac{13}{6}}$ 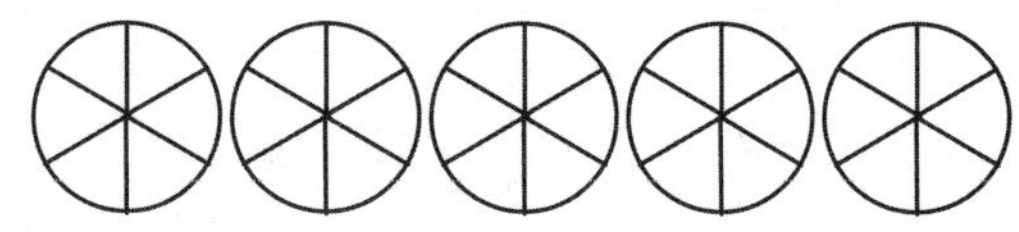

Mixed fraction:

4. Draw a picture to find out which fraction is greater.

a) $3\frac{1}{2}$ or $2\frac{1}{2}$ b) $\frac{7}{4}$ or $\frac{5}{4}$ c) $3\frac{1}{2}$ or $\frac{5}{2}$ d) $2\frac{1}{3}$ or $\frac{8}{3}$

5. How could you use division to find out how many **whole** pies are in $\frac{13}{4}$ of a pie? Explain your answer on a separate piece of paper.

# NS4-52: Investigating Proper and Improper Fractions

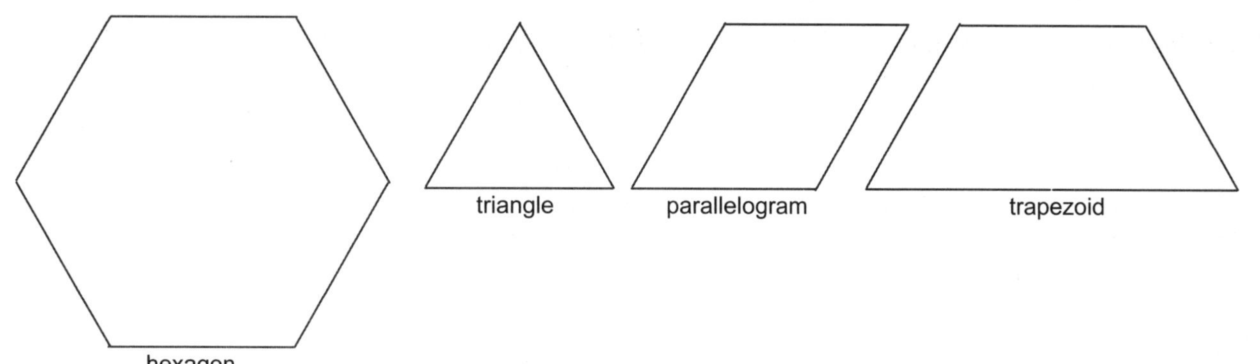


PARENT: Your child will need a copy of page xxii: Pattern Blocks from the Introduction for this exercise.

---

Euclid's bakery sells hexagonal pies. They sell pieces shaped like triangles, rhombuses, and trapezoids.

1. Make a model of the pies below with pattern blocks (place the smaller shapes on top of the hexagons) and write a mixed and improper fraction for each pie.

a) 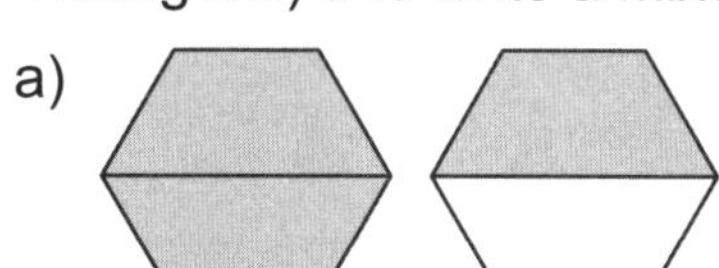

b) 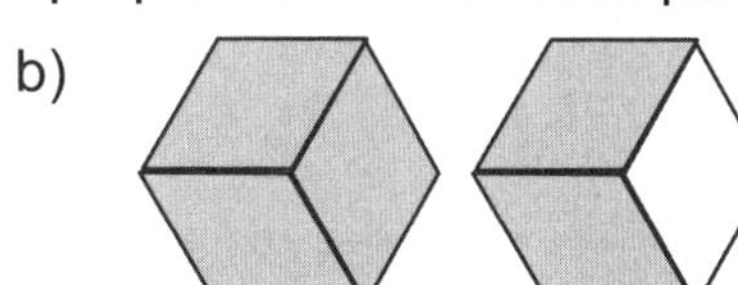

c) 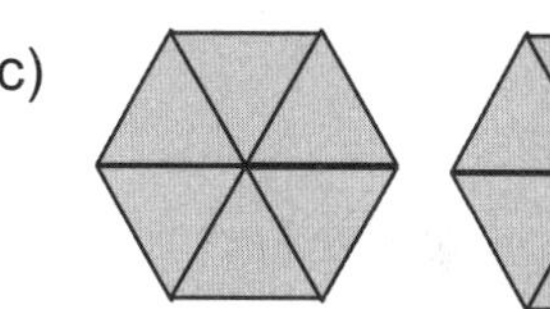 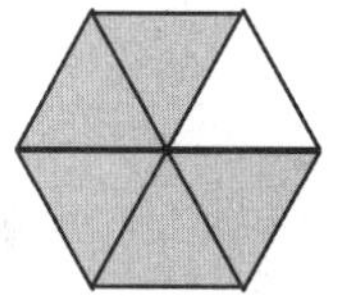

2. Using the hexagon as the whole pie and the triangles, rhombuses, and trapezoids as the pieces, make a pattern block model of the fractions below. Sketch you models on the grid. The first one is done for you.

a) $2\frac{1}{2}$ b) $1\frac{1}{2}$ c) $2\frac{1}{6}$ d) $1\frac{5}{6}$ e) $1\frac{2}{3}$ e) $3\frac{1}{3}$

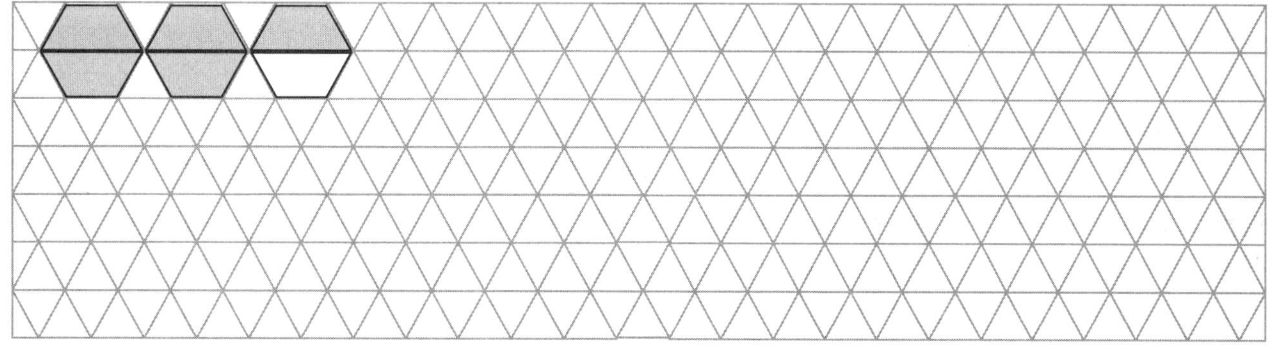

3. Make a pattern block model of the fractions. Sketch your model below.

a) $\frac{5}{2}$ b) $\frac{7}{6}$ c) $\frac{7}{3}$ d) $\frac{10}{3}$ e) $\frac{11}{6}$

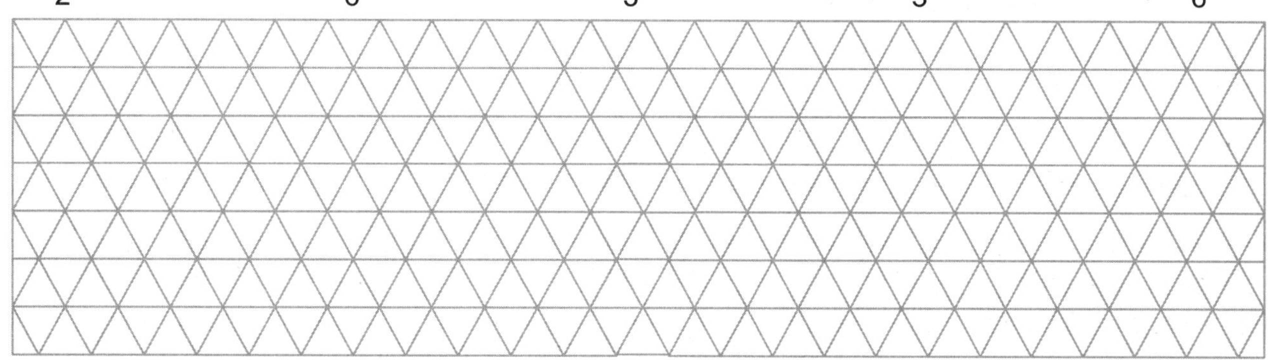

# NS4-52: Investigating Proper and Improper Fractions *(cont'd)*

4. Using the trapezoid as the whole pie, and triangles as the pieces, make a pattern block model of the fractions. Sketch your models on the grid. The first one is done for you.

a) $\frac{5}{3}$ b) $\frac{7}{3}$ c) $1\frac{2}{3}$ d) $2\frac{1}{3}$

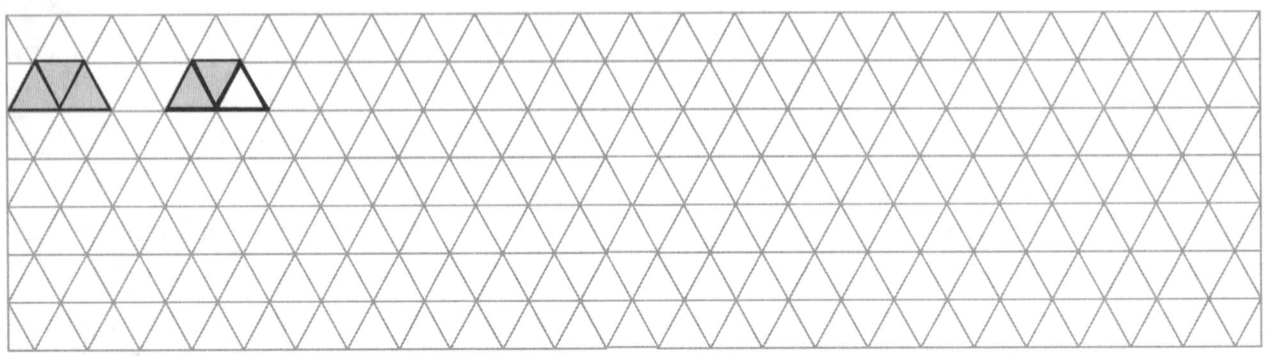

5. Which is a greater $\frac{3}{2}$ or $\frac{5}{2}$? How do you know?

6. Is $\frac{5}{2}$ greater than 1 whole pie or less than 1 whole pie? How do you know?

Use pattern blocks or a pie diagram to answer questions 7 and 8.

7. Which is greater? a) $\frac{5}{3}$ or $\frac{7}{3}$ ? b) $\frac{7}{3}$ or $\frac{5}{2}$ ? c) $2\frac{2}{3}$ or 3 ?

8. Which whole numbers is $\frac{7}{4}$ between?

9. Bottles come in packs of 6. How many bottles are in $2\frac{1}{2}$ packs?

10. Figure A is a model of 1 whole and Figure B is a model of $\frac{5}{2}$.

a) Ben says that Figure A represents more pie than Figure B. Is he correct? How do you know?

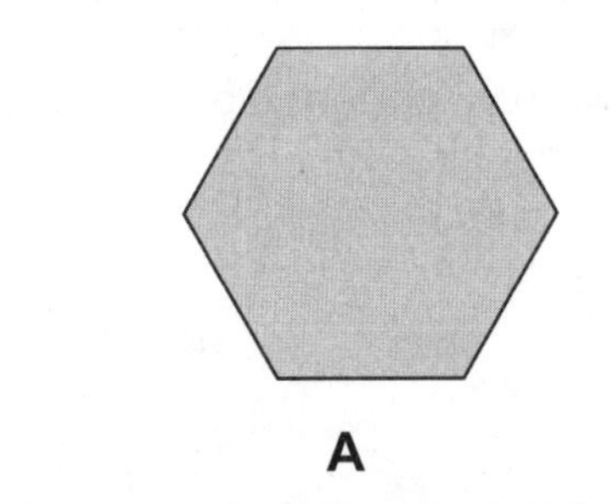

A

b) Ben says that because Figure A represents more pie than Figure B, 1 whole must be more than $\frac{5}{2}$. What is wrong with his reasoning?

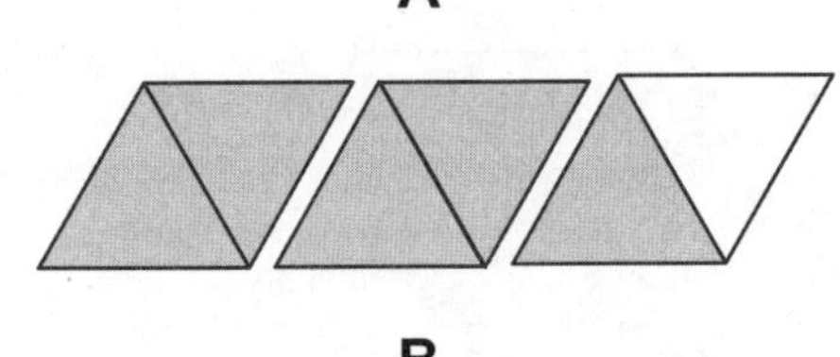

B

# NS4-53: Equivalent Fractions



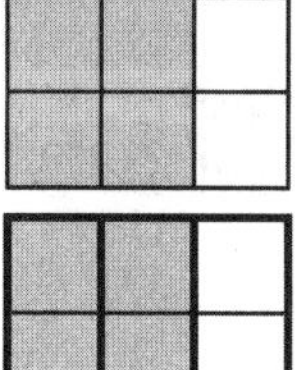

George shades $\frac{4}{6}$ of the squares in an array:

He draws heavy lines around the squares to group them into 3 equal groups: $\frac{2}{3}$ of the squares are shaded.

The pictures show that four sixths are equal to two thirds: $\frac{4}{6} = \frac{2}{3}$. Four sixths and two thirds are **equivalent fractions**.

---

1. Write an equivalent fraction.

a) 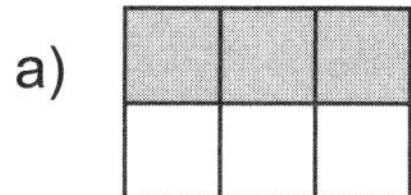

$\frac{3}{6} = \frac{\ }{2}$

b) 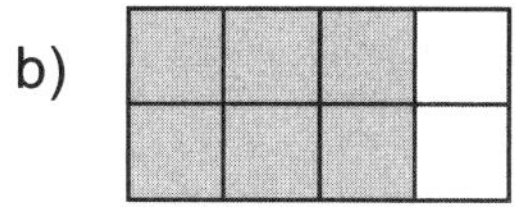

$\frac{6}{8} = \frac{\ }{4}$

c) 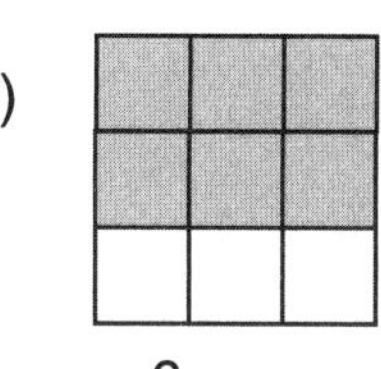

$\frac{6}{9} = \frac{\ }{3}$

2. Group the squares to show that . . .

a) 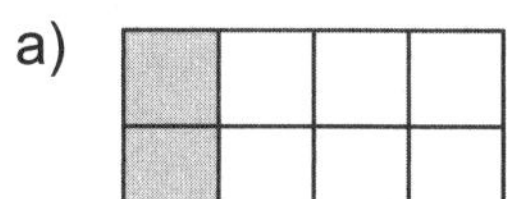

two eighths equal one fourth ( $\frac{2}{8} = \frac{1}{4}$ )

b) 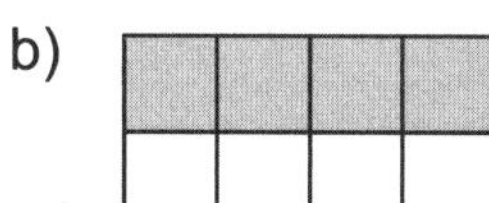

four eighths equal one half ( $\frac{4}{8} = \frac{1}{2}$ )

3. Group the squares to make an equivalent fraction.

a) 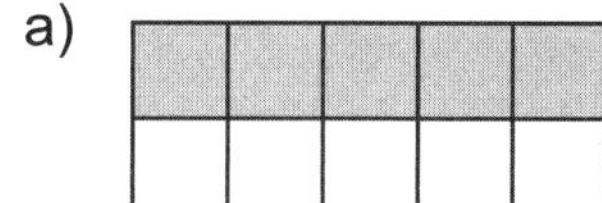

$\frac{5}{10} = \frac{\ }{2}$

b) 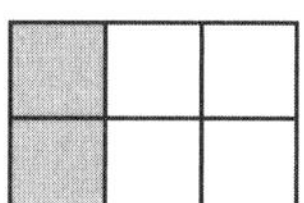

$\frac{2}{6} = \frac{\ }{3}$

c) 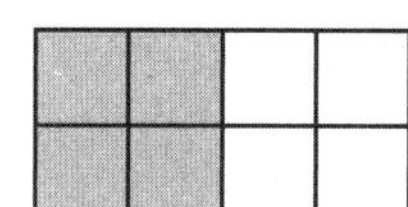

$\frac{4}{8} = \frac{\ }{2}$

4. Group the squares into sets of the same size and write an equivalent fraction.

a) 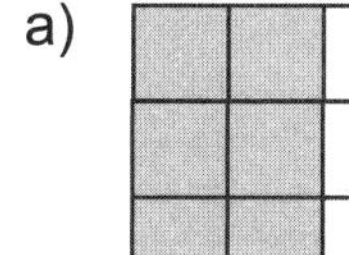

$\frac{6}{9} = \frac{\ }{\ }$

b) 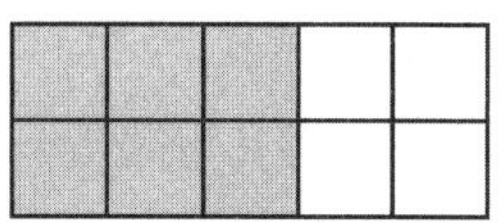

$\frac{6}{10} = \frac{\ }{\ }$

c) 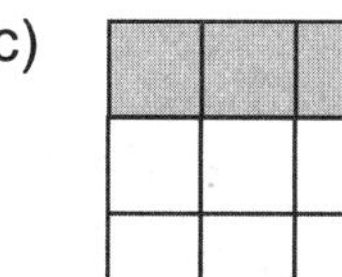

$\frac{3}{9} = \frac{\ }{\ }$

5. Make 2 copies of the array on grid paper. Show 2 different ways to group the squares into equal amounts. Are the fractions four eighths ( $\frac{4}{8}$ ), two fourths ( $\frac{2}{4}$ ), and one half ( $\frac{1}{2}$ ) the same or different?

# NS4-53: Equivalent Fractions *(continued)*

Candice has a set of grey and white buttons. Four of the six buttons are grey. Candice groups buttons to show that two thirds of the buttons are grey:

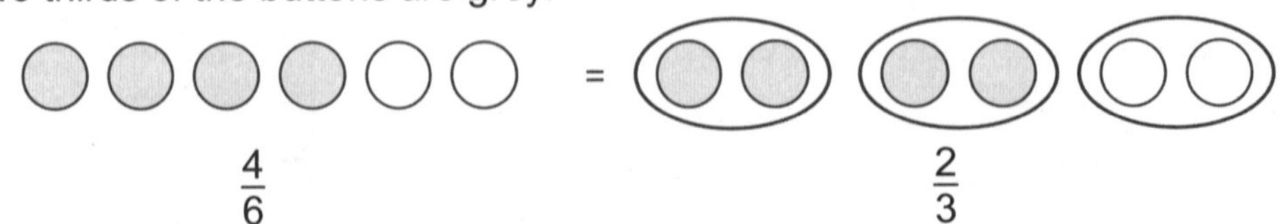

$\frac{4}{6}$ $\frac{2}{3}$

6. Group the buttons to make an equivalent fraction.

a) 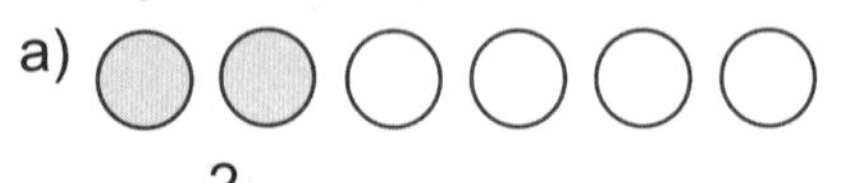

$\frac{2}{6} = \frac{}{}$

b) 

$\frac{2}{4} = \frac{}{}$

c) $\frac{3}{6} = \frac{}{}$

d) 

$\frac{3}{9} = \frac{}{}$

e) 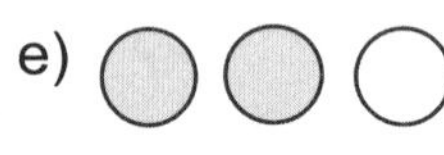 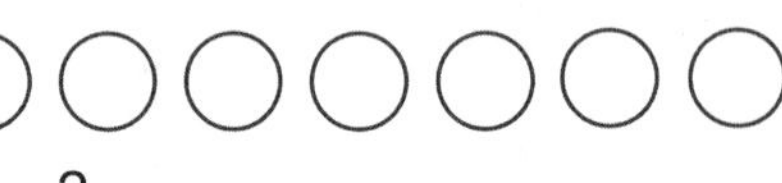

$\frac{2}{10} = \frac{}{}$

7. Group the circles to make an equivalent fraction. The grouping in the first question is done for you.

a) 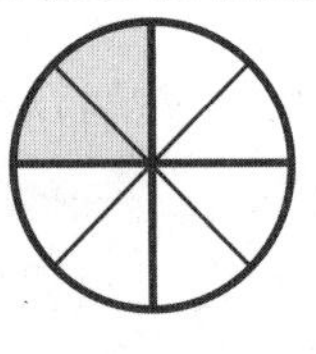

$\frac{2}{8} = \frac{}{4}$

b) 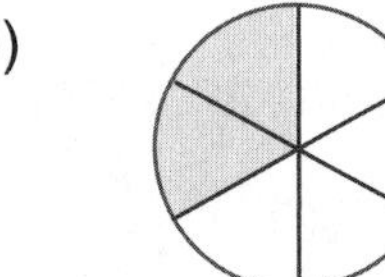

$\frac{2}{6} = \frac{}{3}$

c) 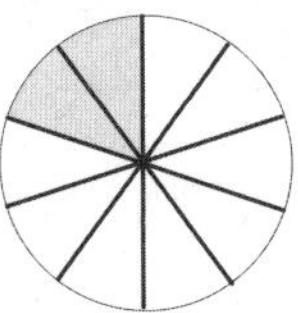

$\frac{2}{10} = \frac{}{5}$

8. Cut each pie into smaller pieces to make an equivalent fraction.

a) 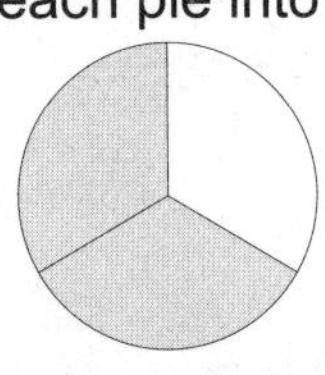

$\frac{2}{3} = \frac{}{6}$

b) 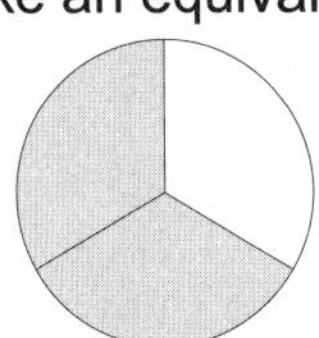

$\frac{2}{3} = \frac{}{9}$

c) 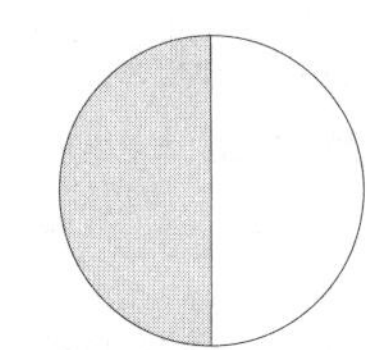

$\frac{1}{2} = \frac{}{4}$

9. Shade squares to make an equivalent fraction.

a) 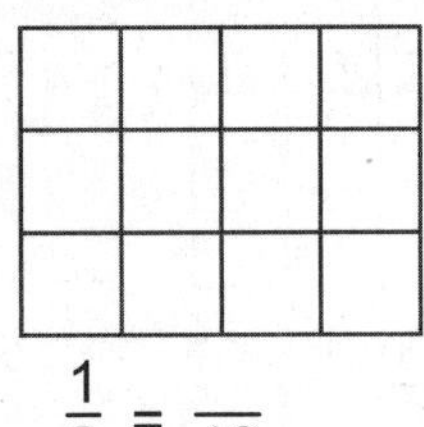

$\frac{1}{2} = \frac{}{12}$

b) 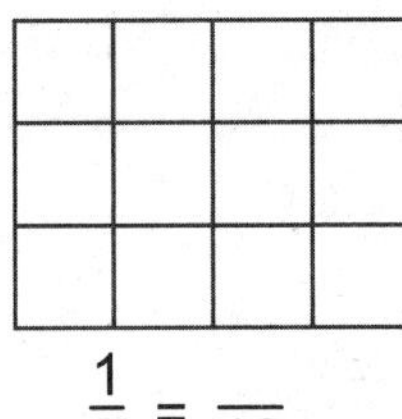

$\frac{1}{3} = \frac{}{12}$

c) 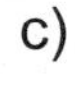 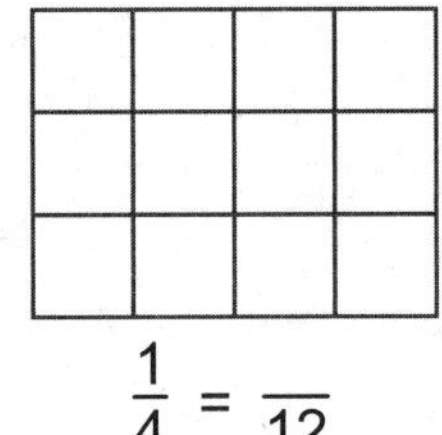

$\frac{1}{4} = \frac{}{12}$

10. On grid paper, draw shaded and unshaded circles (like the ones in question 6) and group the circles to show that . . .

a) six eighths is equivalent to three quarters

b) four fifths is equivalent to eight tenths

11. Dan says that $\frac{1}{2}$ is equivalent to $\frac{2}{4}$. Is he right? How do you know?

# NS4-54: Sharing and Fractions

Dan has 6 cookies. He wants to give $\frac{2}{3}$ of his cookies to his friends.
To do so, he shares the cookies equally on 3 plates:

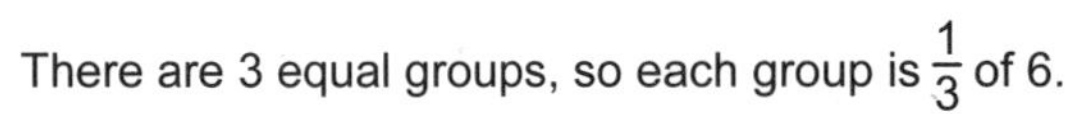

There are 3 equal groups, so each group is $\frac{1}{3}$ of 6.

There are 2 cookies in each group, so $\frac{1}{3}$ of 6 is 2.

There are 4 cookies in two groups, so $\frac{2}{3}$ of 6 is 4.

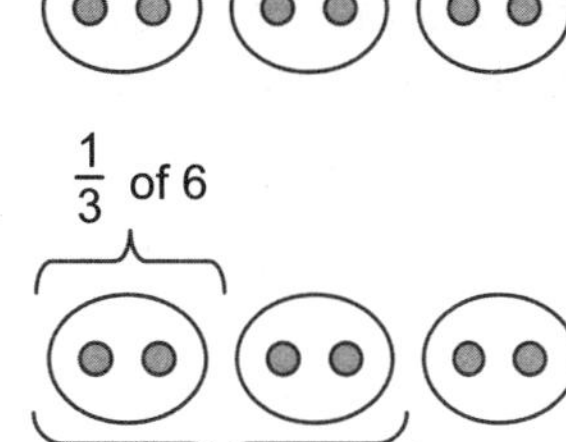


1. Write a fraction for the amount of dots shown. The first one is done for you.

a) 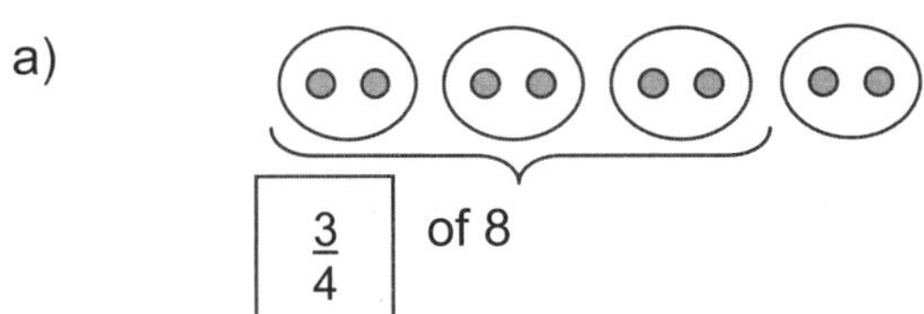
$\frac{3}{4}$ of 8

b) 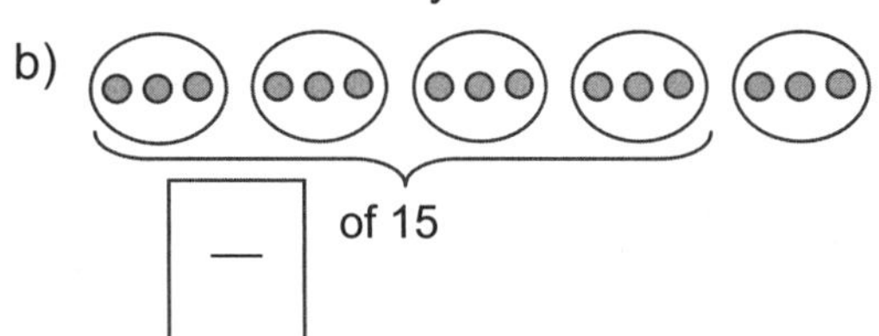
— of 15

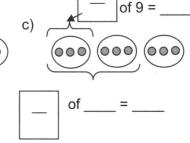

2. Fill in the missing numbers.

a) $\frac{1}{3}$ of 6= _____
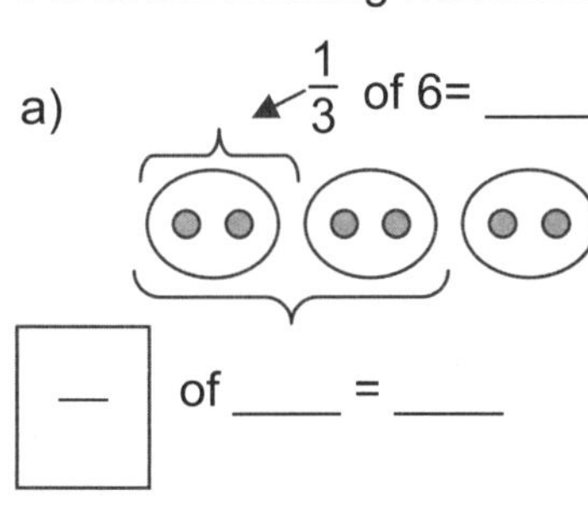
— of _____ = _____

b) — of 8 = _____
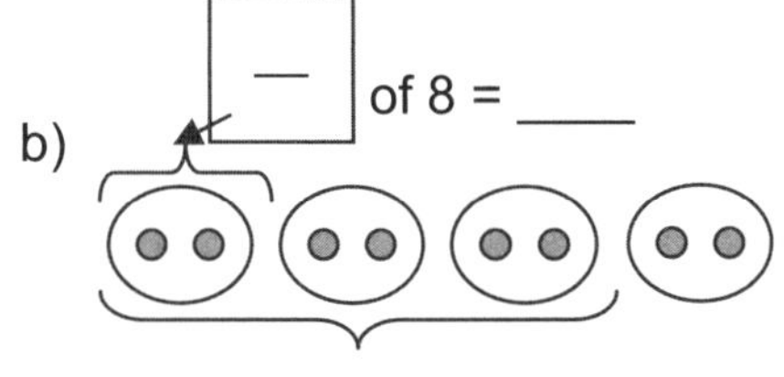
— of _____ = _____

c) — of 9 = _____

— of _____ = _____

d) 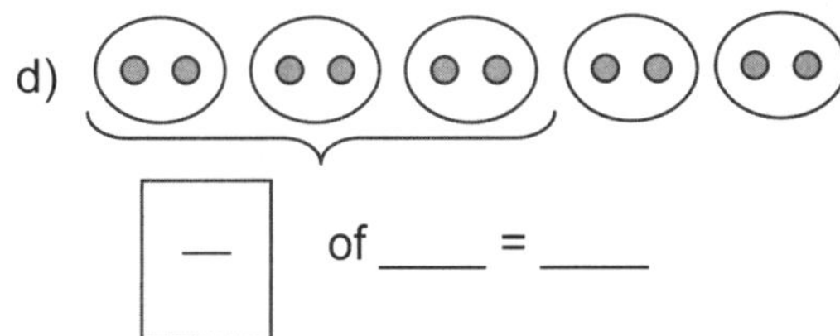
— of _____ = _____

e) 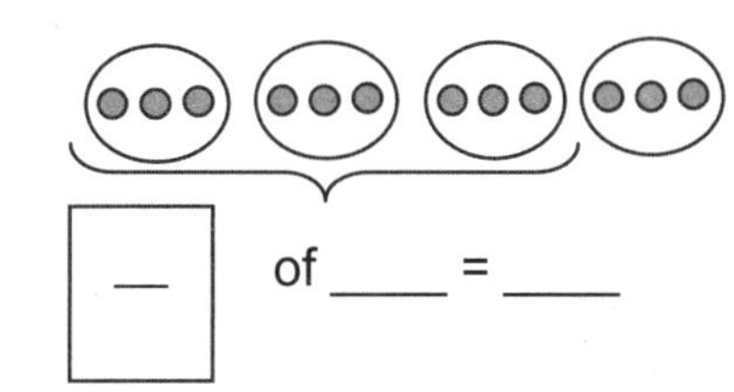
— of _____ = _____

3. Draw a circle to show the given amount.

a) $\frac{2}{3}$ of 6

b) $\frac{3}{4}$ of 8

c) $\frac{3}{5}$ of 10

d) $\frac{3}{4}$ of 12

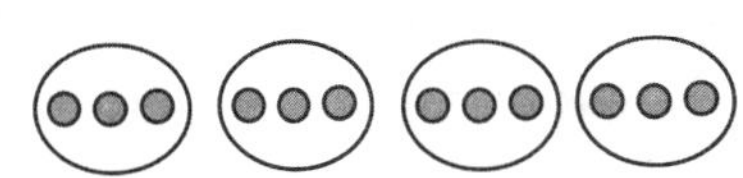

4. Fill in the correct number of dots in each circle, then draw a circle to show the given amount.

a) $\frac{2}{3}$ of 12

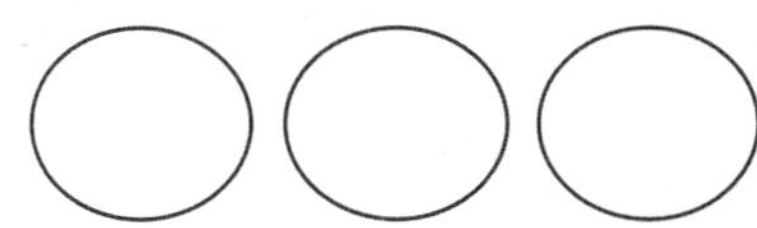

b) $\frac{2}{3}$ of 9

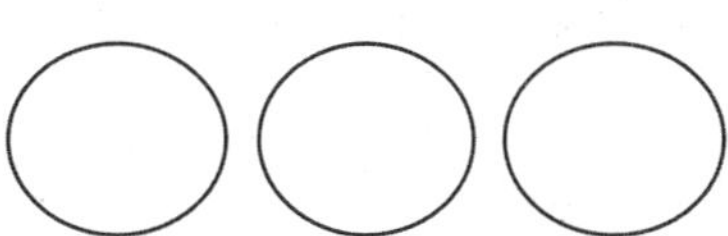

5. Dan wants to share some cookies with his friends. He uses plates to divide the cookies into equal groups. How many plates should Dan use to divide his cookies if he wants to give away . . .

a) $\frac{1}{2}$ of his cookies

_______ plates

b) $\frac{1}{3}$ of his cookies

_______ plates

c) $\frac{2}{3}$ of his cookies

_______ plates

d) $\frac{3}{5}$ of his cookies

_______ plates

e) $\frac{5}{6}$ of his cookies

_______ plates

f) $\frac{3}{4}$ of his cookies

_______ plates

6. Find the fraction of the whole amount by sharing the cookies equally. (HINT: Draw the correct number of plates and place the cookies one at a time. Then circle the correct amount.)

a) Find $\frac{1}{4}$ of 8 cookies.

$\frac{1}{4}$ of 8 is ________

b) Find $\frac{1}{2}$ of 10 cookies.

$\frac{1}{2}$ of 10 is ________

c) Find $\frac{2}{3}$ of 6 cookies.

$\frac{2}{3}$ of 6 is ________

d) Find $\frac{3}{4}$ of 12 cookies.

$\frac{3}{4}$ of 12 is ________

7. On a separate piece of paper, draw a picture to find . . .

a) $\frac{1}{3}$ of 12 b) $\frac{1}{2}$ of 10 c) $\frac{2}{3}$ of 9 d) $\frac{3}{4}$ of 12 e) $\frac{2}{3}$ of 12

8. Gerome finds 1/3 of 6 by dividing: 6 divided into 3 groups gives 2 in each group (6 ÷ 3 = 2). Find the fraction of each of the following numbers by writing an equivalent division statement. Then skip count to find the answer.

a) $\frac{1}{2}$ of 8

$8 \div 2 = 4$

b) $\frac{1}{2}$ of 10

_______________

c) $\frac{1}{2}$ of 16

_______________

d) $\frac{1}{2}$ of 20

_______________

e) $\frac{1}{3}$ of 9

_______________

f) $\frac{1}{3}$ of 15

_______________

g) $\frac{1}{4}$ of 12

_______________

h) $\frac{1}{6}$ of 18

_______________

# NS4-54: Sharing and Fractions *(continued)*

9. Complete the number statement using the words "twos," "threes," "fours," or "fives." Then draw a picture and complete the fraction statements. The first one is done for you.

| Number statement | Picture | Fraction statements |
|---|---|---|
| a) 6 = 3 twos | \|\| \|\| \|\| | $\frac{1}{3}$ of 6 = ____<br>$\frac{2}{3}$ of 6 = ____ |
| b) 12 = 4 ______ | | $\frac{1}{4}$ of 12 = ____<br>$\frac{2}{4}$ of 12 = ____<br>$\frac{3}{4}$ of 12 = ____ |
| c) 15 = 3 ______ | | $\frac{1}{3}$ of 15 = ____<br>$\frac{2}{3}$ of 15 = ____ |

10. Circle $\frac{1}{2}$ of each set of lines. (HINT: Count the lines and divide by 2.)

a) | | | | | |    b) | | | | | | | | | |    c) | | | |

11. Circle $\frac{1}{3}$ of each set of circles. Then circle $\frac{2}{3}$.

a) ○ ○ ○ ○ ○ ○    b) ○ ○ ○ ○ ○ ○ ○ ○ ○ ○ ○ ○

12. Circle $\frac{1}{4}$ of each set of triangles. Then circle $\frac{3}{4}$.

a) △ △ △ △    b) △ △ △ △ △ △ △ △ △ △ △ △

13. Shade $\frac{3}{5}$ of the boxes. (HINT: Shade $\frac{1}{5}$ of the boxes at a time.)

a)

| | | | | |
|---|---|---|---|---|
| | | | | |

b)

| | | | | | | | | | |
|---|---|---|---|---|---|---|---|---|---|
| | | | | | | | | | |

14. Andy finds $\frac{2}{3}$ of 12 as follows: First he divides 12 by 3. Then he multiplies the result by 2. Draw a picture using dots and circles to show why this would work. Then find $\frac{2}{3}$ of 15 using Andy's method.

15. Complete each statement by writing "more than half," "half," or "less than half."
(HINT: Start by finding half of the number by skip counting by 2s.)

a) 2 is ______________________ of 6    b) 3 is ______________________ of 8

c) 6 is ______________________ of 12    d) 7 is ______________________ of 10

16. A soccer team plays 12 games. They win 5 games. Did they win more than half their games? Explain your answer on a separate piece of paper.

17. Fill in the missing number to make a fraction that is **equal to** $\frac{1}{2}$:

a) $\frac{\square}{10}$ b) $\frac{\square}{6}$ c) $\frac{\square}{4}$ d) $\frac{\square}{8}$ e) $\frac{\square}{20}$

18. Complete each statement by writing "more than one third," "one third," or "less that one third." (HINT: Start by finding one third of the number by skip counting by 3s.)

a) 2 is ______________________ of 9 b) 4 is ______________________ of 9

c) 5 is ______________________ of 15 d) 6 is ______________________ of 12

19. Sarah has 8 pennies. She loses 2. To find out what fraction of her pennies she lost, she draws 8 dots (in groups of 2).

(••)(••)(••)(••) ⟵ It takes 4 groups of 2 to make 8. **So 2 is $\frac{1}{4}$ of 8.**

Complete each statement by first drawing a picture. The first one is done for you.

a) 2 is $\boxed{\frac{1}{3}}$ of 6 b) 2 is $\square$ of 4 c) 3 is $\square$ of 12

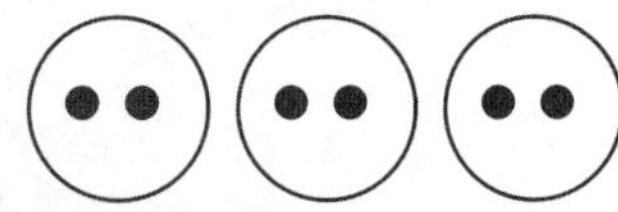

20. Gerald has 10 oranges. He gives away $\frac{3}{5}$ of the oranges.

a) How many did he give away?
b) How many did he keep?
c) How did you find your answer to part b)? (Did you use a calculation, a picture, a model, or a list?)

21. A kilogram of nuts cost $8.

How much would $\frac{3}{4}$ of a kilogram of nuts cost?

22. Beth is making a black and white patchwork. Two thirds of the quilt are completed.

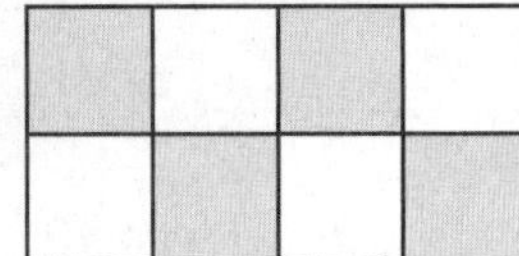

a) How many black squares will be in the finished quilt?
b) Is your answer reasonable? How could you check?

# NS4-55: Decimal Tenths

A tenth (or $\frac{1}{10}$) can be represented in different ways:

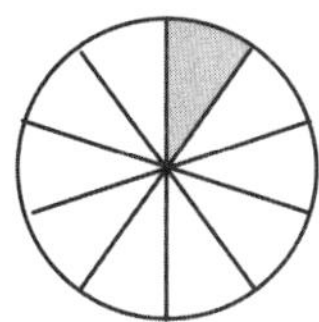
a tenth of a pie

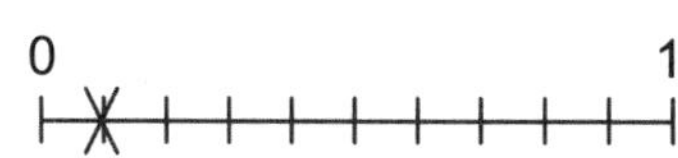

a tenth of the distance between 0 and 1

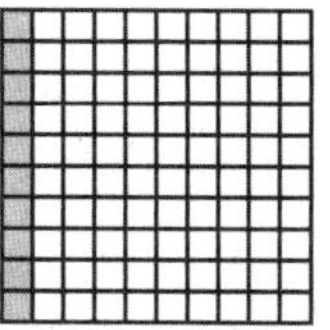
a tenth of a hundreds flat

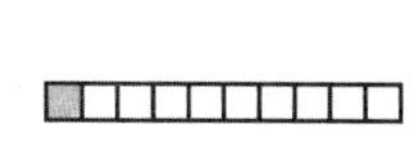
a tenth of a tens strip

Tenths commonly appears in units of measurement (a millimetre is a tenth of a centimetre).

Mathematicians invented the decimal as a short form for tenths: $\frac{1}{10}$ = 0.1, $\frac{2}{10}$ = 0.2 and so on.

---

1. Write a fraction in each box for the shaded part.

a) 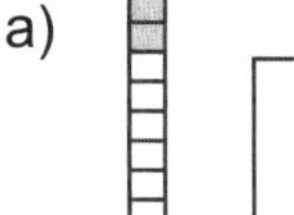 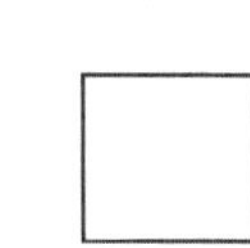 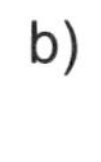
b) 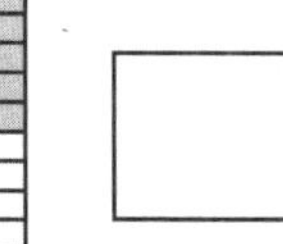
c) 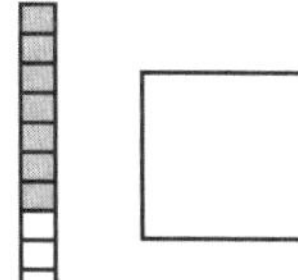
d) 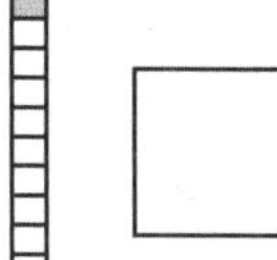

2. Write a fraction AND a decimal in the boxes for each shaded part.

a) 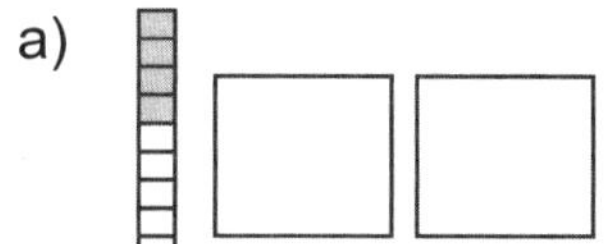 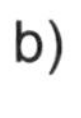
b) 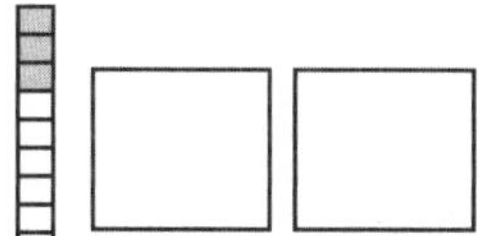
c) 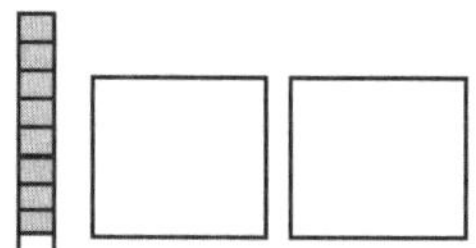
d) 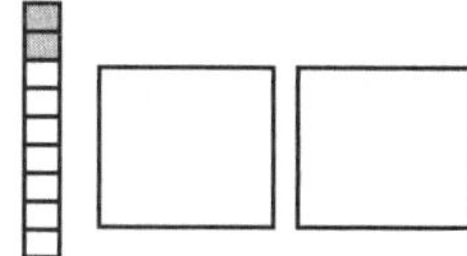

3. Write a fraction for each shaded part. Then add them together, and shade your answer. The first one is done for you.

a) 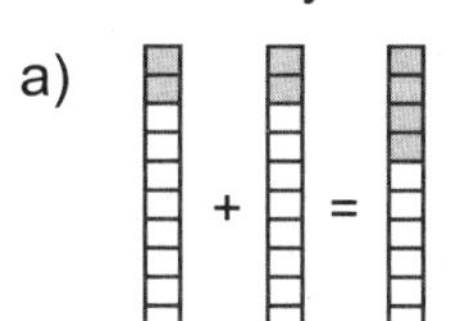 $\frac{2}{10} + \frac{2}{10} = \frac{4}{10}$
b) 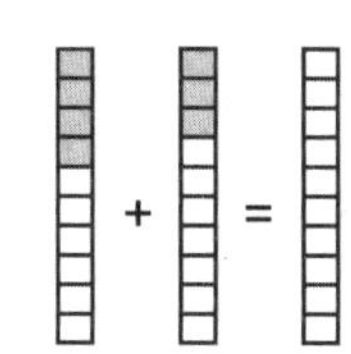
c) 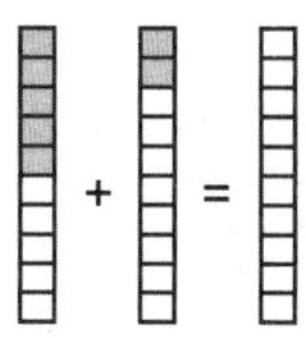
d)
e) 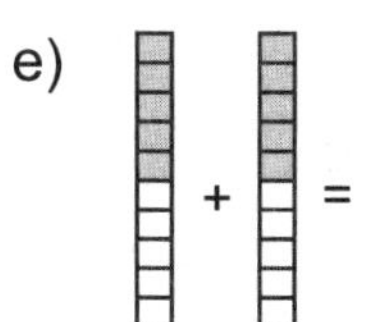
f)

4. In the chart, write the decimals that correspond to the fractions in question 3 above. Then solve.

| a) 0.2 + 0.2 = 0.4 | b) | c) |
|---|---|---|
| d) | e) | f) |

5. Continue the pattern: 0.2 , 0.4 , 0.6 , _______ , _______

# NS4-56: Decimal Tenths and Hundredths



Fractions with denominators that are multiples of ten (tenths, hundredths) commonly appear in units of measurement.

- A millimetre is a tenth of a centimetre (10 mm = 1 cm).
- A centimetre is a tenth of a decimetre (10 cm = 1 dm).
- A decimeter is a tenth of a metre (10 dm = 1 m).
- A centimetre is a hundredths of a metre (100 cm = 1 m).

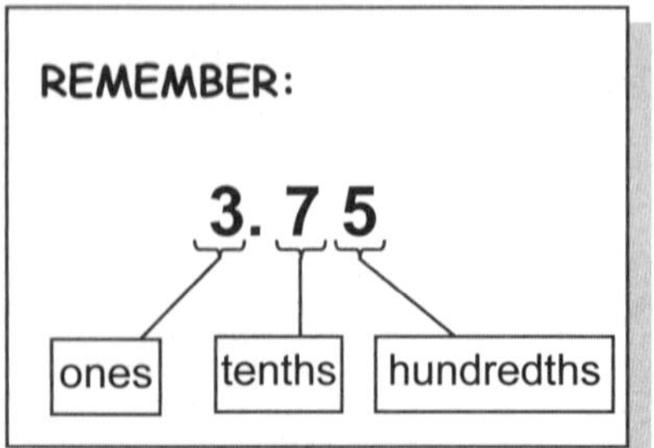


Decimals are short forms for fractions: the first digit to the right of a decimal tells you the number of tenths: 0.<u>7</u>3 (7 tenths). The second digit tells you the number of hundredths: 0.7<u>3</u> (3 hundredths).

---

1. Write the decimal that is given in words in decimal notation.

   a) 27 hundredths = 0.27 b) 32 hundredths = ________ c) 50 hundredths = ________

   d) 49 hundredths = ________ e) 87 hundredths = ________ f) 6 hundredths = ________

2. Say the name of the fraction to yourself (for example, the first fraction is "thirty-five hundredths"). Then write a decimal for the fraction.

   a) $\frac{35}{100}$ = 0.35 b) $\frac{17}{100}$ = c) $\frac{40}{100}$ = d) $\frac{5}{100}$ =

   d) $\frac{22}{100}$ = e) $\frac{89}{100}$ = f) $\frac{67}{100}$ = g) $\frac{1}{100}$ =

3. Count the number of shaded squares. (HINT: Count by 10s for each column or row that is shaded.) Write a fraction for the shaded part of the hundred square. Then write the fraction as a decimal.

a) 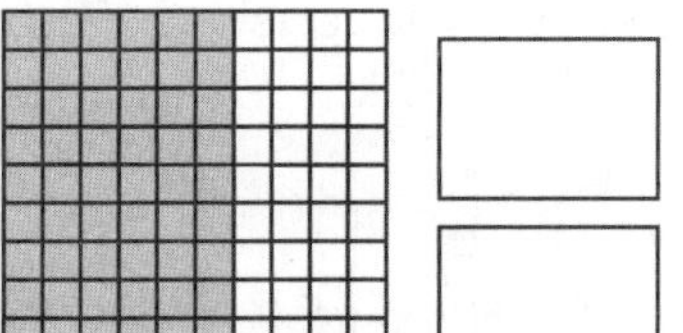

b) 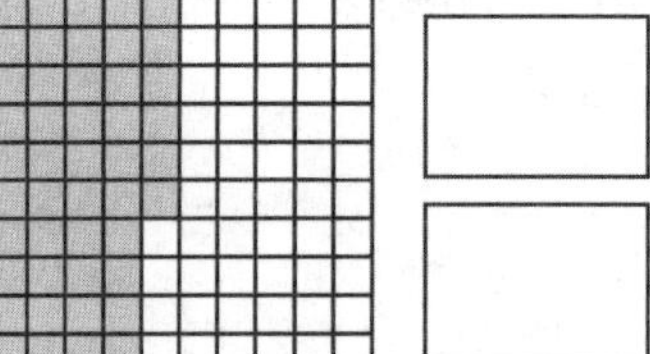

c) 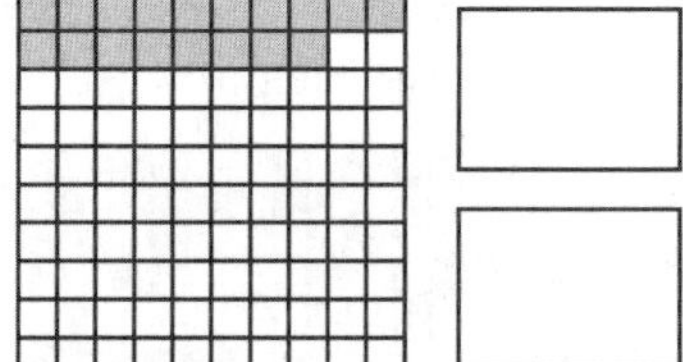

d) 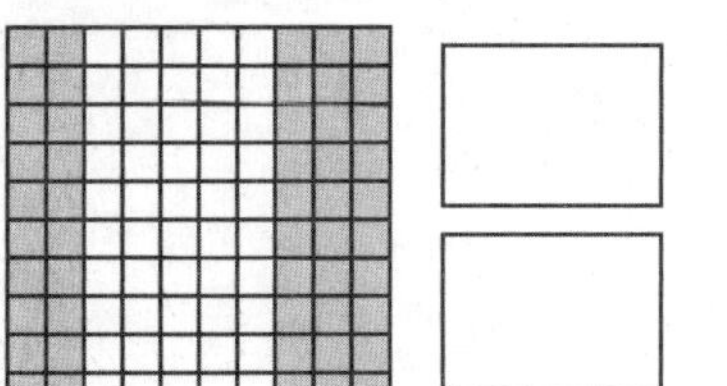

e) 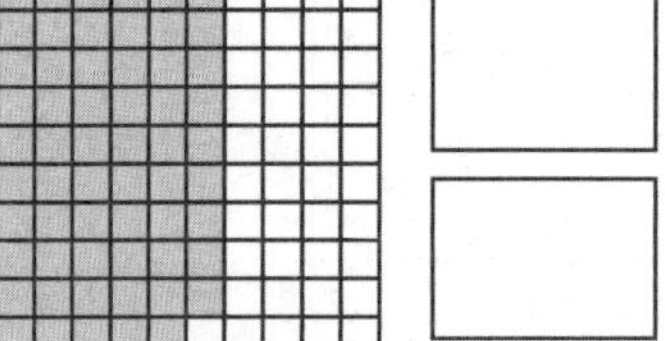

f) 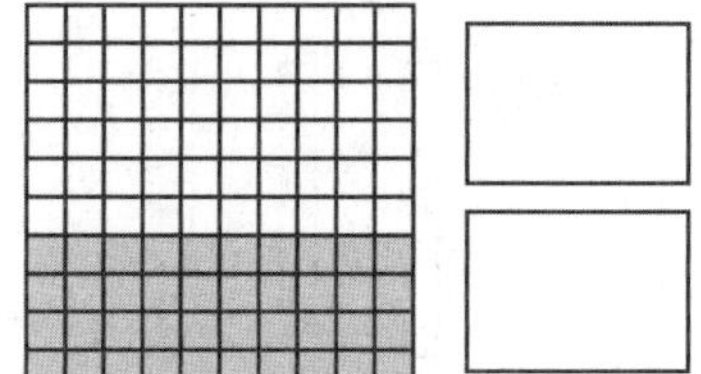

g) 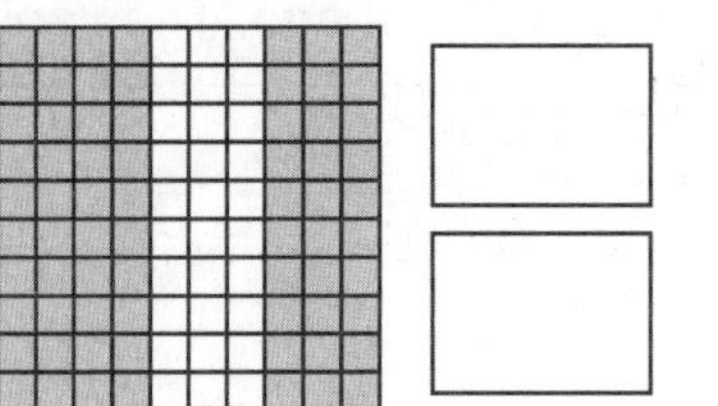

h) 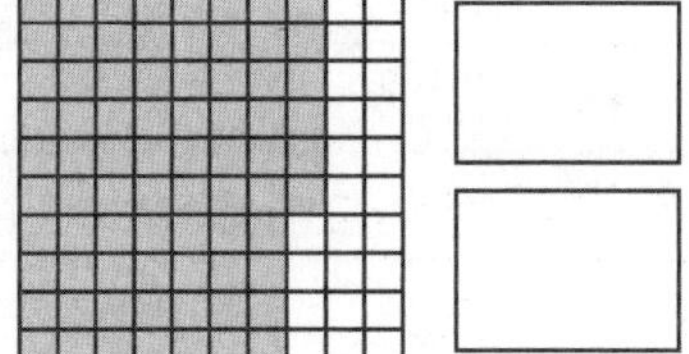

i) 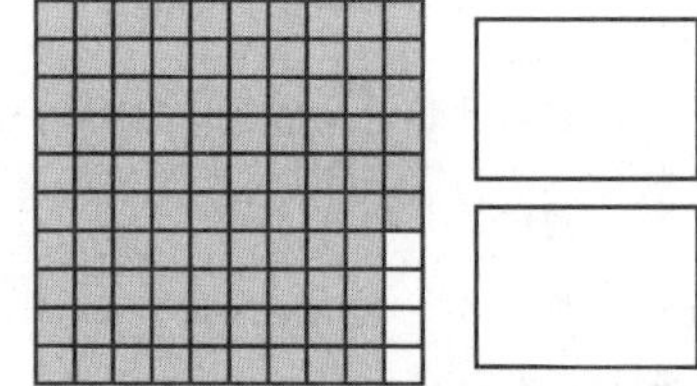

4. Convert the fraction to a decimal. Then shade that amount in the hundreds square.

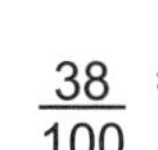

a) $\frac{38}{100}$ =

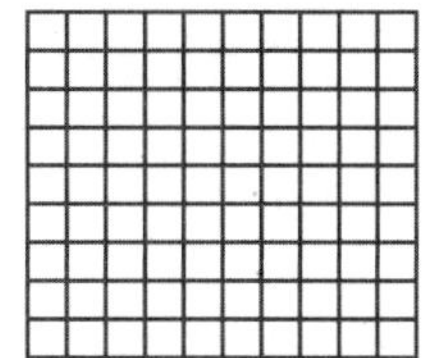

b) $\frac{45}{100}$ =

c) $\frac{70}{100}$ =

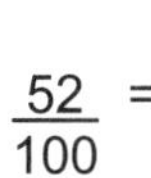

d) $\frac{52}{100}$ =

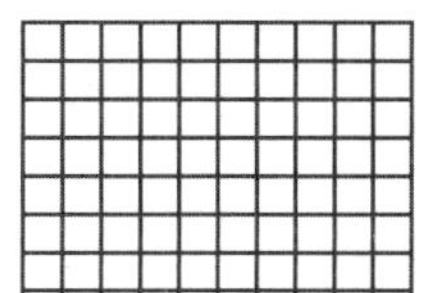

e) $\frac{13}{100}$ =

f) $\frac{5}{100}$ =

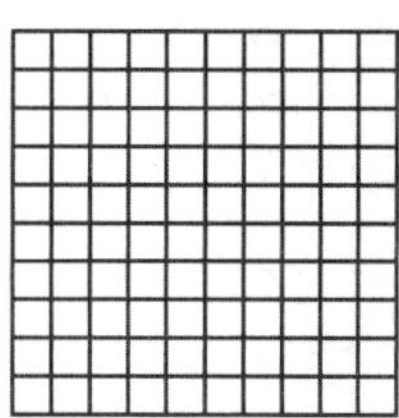

5. Write a fraction and a decimal for each shaded part.

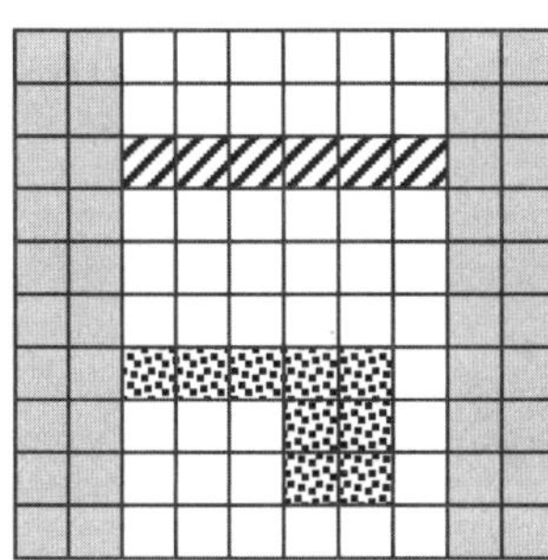

6. Create 3 designs of your own. Write a fraction and a decimal for each shaded part.

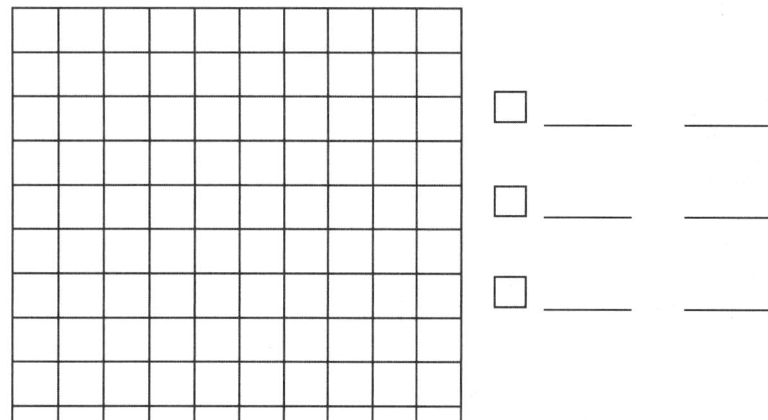

7. Write a fraction for the number of **hundredths**. Then draw a heavy line around each column and write a fraction for the number of **tenths**.

a)

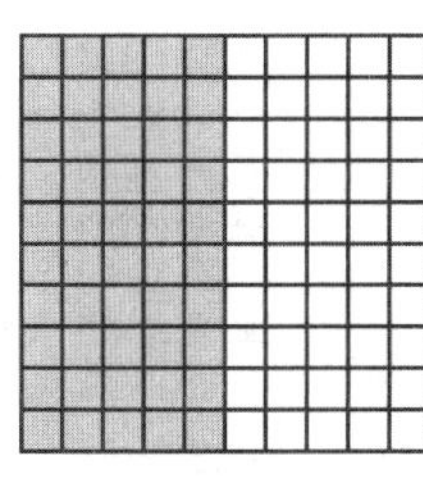

$\frac{\_\_\_}{100} = \frac{\_\_\_}{10}$

b)

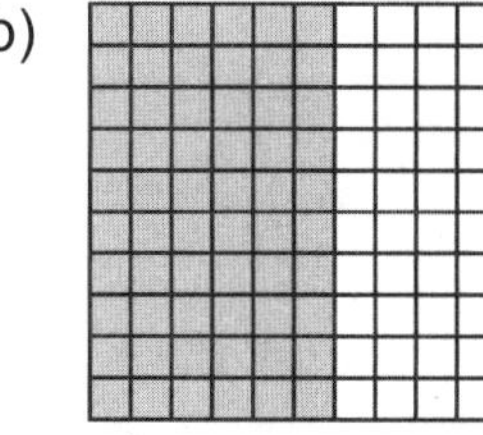

$\frac{\_\_\_}{100} = \frac{\_\_\_}{10}$

c)

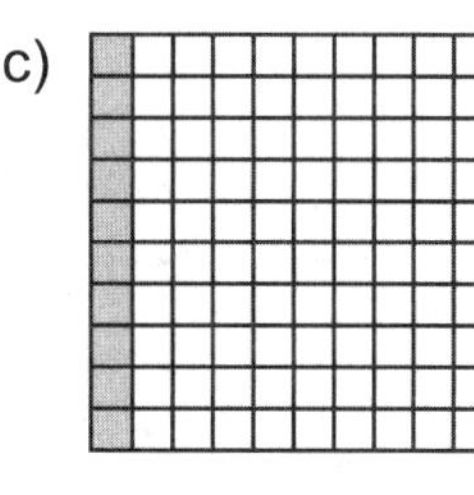

$\frac{\_\_\_}{100} = \frac{\_\_\_}{10}$

d)

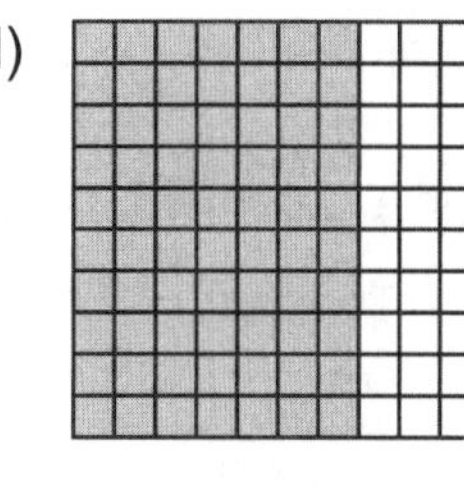

$\frac{\_\_\_}{100} = \frac{\_\_\_}{10}$

8. Brad says 0.20 is greater than 0.4 because 20 is greater than 4. Is he right? Explain your answer on a separate piece of paper.

9. Fill in the chart. The first one is done for you.

| Drawing | Fraction | Decimal | Equivalent decimal | Equivalent fraction | Drawing |
|---|---|---|---|---|---|
| | $\frac{5}{10}$ | 0.5 | 0.50 | $\frac{50}{100}$ | |
| | | | | | |
| | | | | | |
| | | | | | |

10. Use base-10 materials or a picture to answer the following questions. REMEMBER: $\frac{10}{100} = \frac{1}{10}$.

a) $\frac{2}{10} = \frac{\_\_\_}{100}$ b) $\frac{3}{10} = \frac{\_\_\_}{100}$ c) $\frac{7}{10} = \frac{\_\_\_}{100}$ d) $\frac{40}{100} = \frac{\_\_\_}{10}$ e) $\frac{\_\_\_}{10} = \frac{80}{100}$

f) $\frac{5}{10} = \frac{\_\_\_}{100}$ g) $\frac{60}{100} = \frac{\_\_\_}{10}$ h) $\frac{\_\_\_}{10} = \frac{70}{100}$ i) $\frac{30}{100} = \frac{\_\_\_}{10}$ j) $\frac{\_\_\_}{10} = \frac{50}{100}$

k) $\frac{1}{10} = \frac{\_\_\_}{100}$ l) $\frac{8}{10} = \frac{\_\_\_}{100}$ m) $\frac{4}{10} = \frac{\_\_\_}{100}$ n) $\frac{70}{100} = \frac{\_\_\_}{10}$ o) $\frac{\_\_\_}{10} = \frac{90}{100}$

11. Fill in the missing numbers.

a) 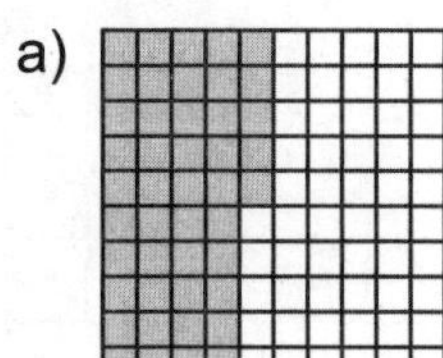

| Tenths | Hundredths |
|---|---|
| | |

$\frac{\_\_\_}{100}$ = 0 . ___ ___

b) 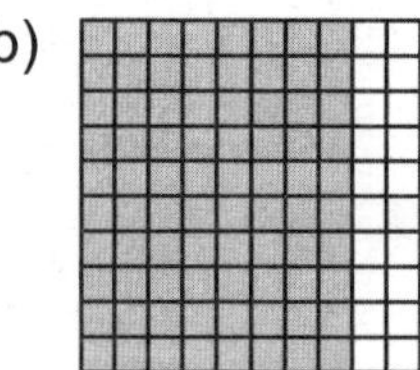

| Tenths | Hundredths |
|---|---|
| | |

$\frac{\_\_\_}{100}$ = 0 . ___ ___

c) 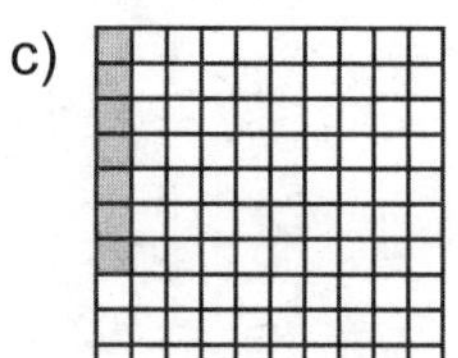

| Tenths | Hundredths |
|---|---|
| | |

$\frac{\_\_\_}{100}$ = 0 . ___ ___

d) 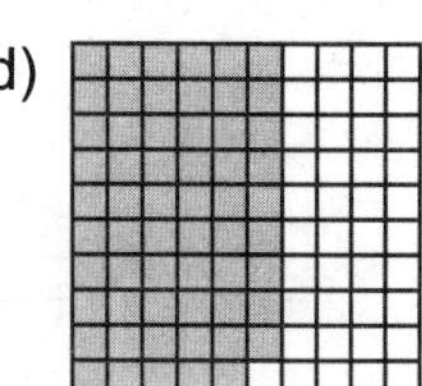

| Tenths | Hundredths |
|---|---|
| | |

$\frac{\_\_\_}{100}$ = 0 . ___ ___

12. Fill in the missing numbers.

a) 0.23 = ____tenths ______hundredths

b) 0.52 = ____tenths ______hundredths

c) 0.87 = ____tenths ______hundredths

d) 0.66 = ____tenths ______hundredths

e) 0.60 = ____tenths ______hundredths

f) 0.03 = ____tenths ______hundredths

13. Write the following numbers as a decimal:

a) 2 tenths 0 hundredths =

b) 0 tenths 5 hundredths =

c) 5 tenths 7 hundredths =

d) 6 tenths 4 hundredths =

e) 3 tenths 9 hundredths =

f) 0 tenths 1 hundredth =

14. Write the following decimals as fractions:

a) 0.7 = $\frac{\_\_}{10}$ b) 0.3 = $\frac{\_\_}{10}$ c) 0.5 = $\frac{\_\_}{10}$ d) 0.1 = $\frac{\_\_}{10}$ e) 0.9 = $\frac{\_\_}{10}$

15. Write the following decimals as fractions:

a) 0.23 = $\frac{\_\_\_}{100}$ b) 0.48 = $\frac{\_\_\_}{100}$ c) 0.66 = $\frac{\_\_\_}{100}$ d) 0.07 = $\frac{\_\_\_}{100}$ e) 0.01 = $\frac{\_\_\_}{100}$

16. Write the following decimals as fractions:

a) 0.2 = b) 0.35 = c) 0.04 = d) 0.8 = e) 0.6 =

f) 0.02 = g) 0.72 = h) 0.4 = i) 0.23 = j) 0.25 =

17. Change the following fractions to decimals by filling in the blanks:

a) $\frac{6}{10}$ = 0. ___ b) $\frac{3}{10}$ = 0. ___ c) $\frac{4}{10}$ = 0. ___ d) $\frac{8}{10}$ = 0. ___

18. Change the following fractions to decimals by filling in the blanks:

a) $\frac{82}{100}$ = 0. __ __ b) $\frac{7}{100}$ = 0. __ __ c) $\frac{77}{100}$ = 0. __ __ d) $\frac{9}{100}$ = 0. __ __

19. Circle the equalities that are incorrect. REMEMBER: The number of digits in the decimal must equal the number of zeroes in the denominator of the fraction.

$0.52 = \frac{52}{100}$ $0.8 = \frac{8}{10}$ $0.5 = \frac{5}{100}$ $\frac{17}{100} = 0.17$ $\frac{3}{100} = 0.03$

$0.7 = \frac{7}{100}$ $0.53 = \frac{53}{10}$ $0.64 = \frac{64}{100}$ $0.05 = \frac{5}{100}$ $0.02 = \frac{2}{10}$

# NS4-57: Decimals and Fractions Greater Than One

A hundreds square may be used to represent a whole. 10 is a tenth of 100, so a tens strip represents a tenth of the whole. 1 is a hundredth of 100, so a ones square represents a hundredth of the whole:

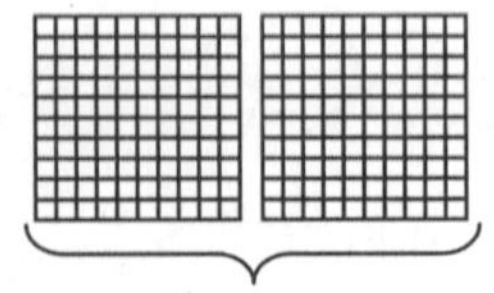
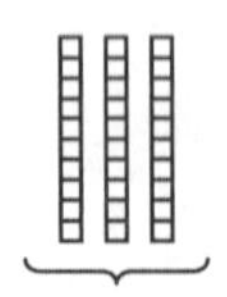
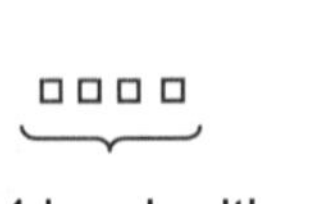

2 wholes   3 tenths   4 hundredths

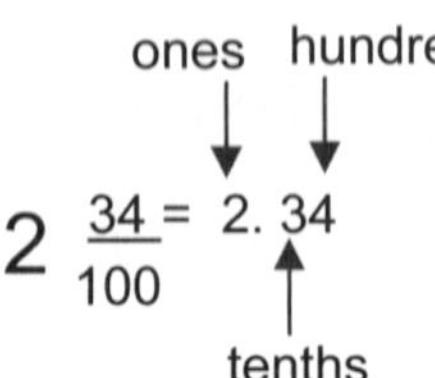


A mixed fraction can be written as a decimal.

---

1. Write a mixed fraction and a decimal for the base-10 models.

a) 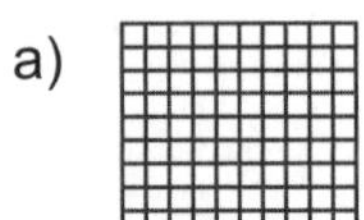 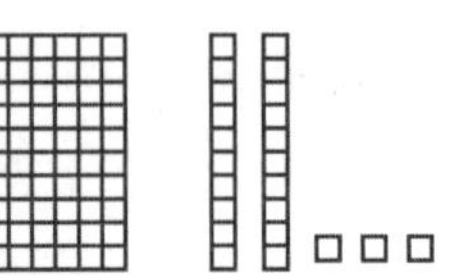 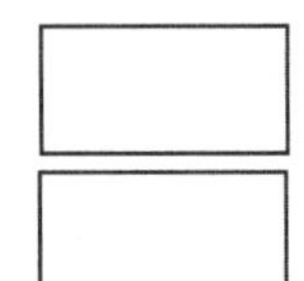

b) 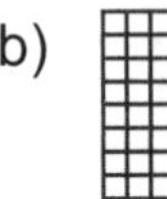 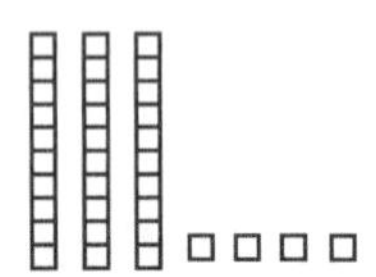 

c) 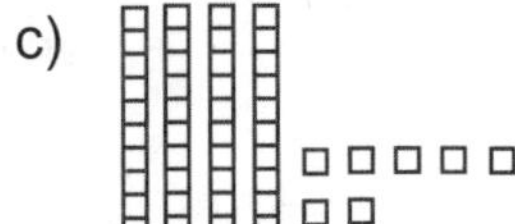 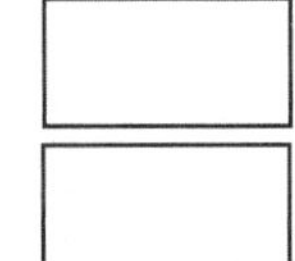

d) 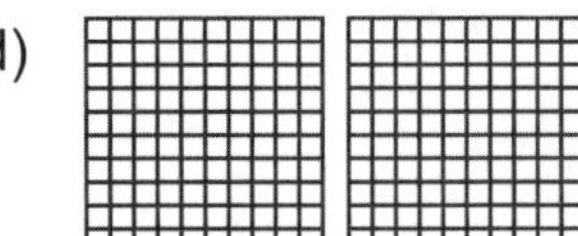 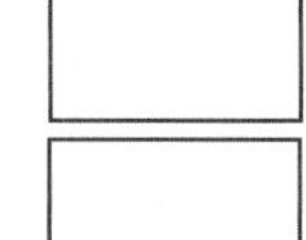

e) 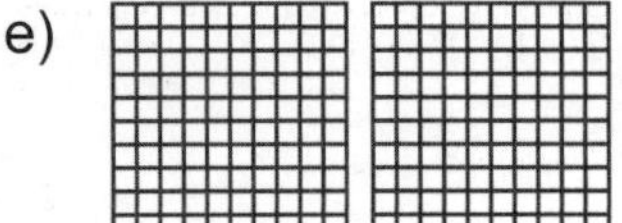 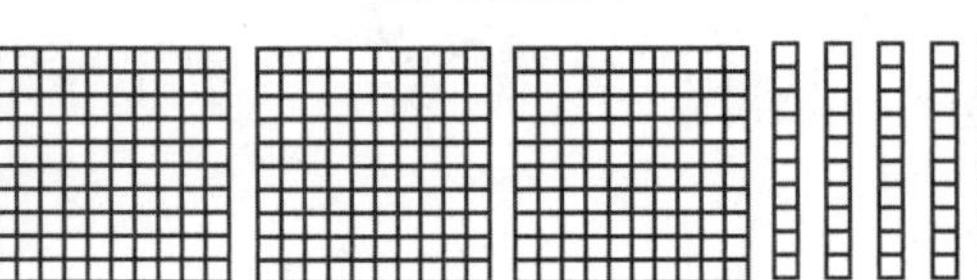 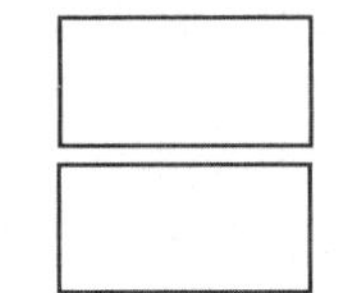

2. Draw a base-10 model (simplified versions of the ones in question 1) for the following decimals:

a) 3.21   b) 1.62

3. On a separate piece of paper, draw base-10 models for . . .

a) 2.35   b) 1.84   c) 3.02

4. Write a decimal and a mixed fraction for each of the pictures.

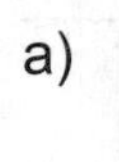

a) 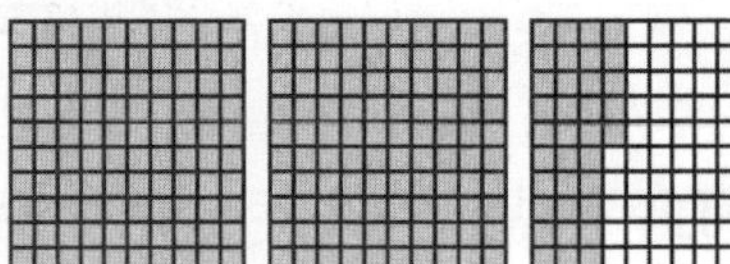 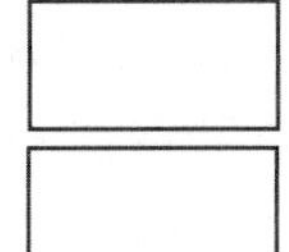

b) 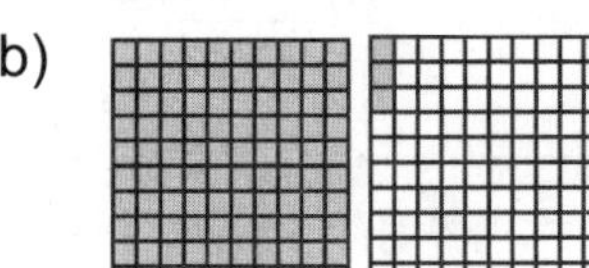 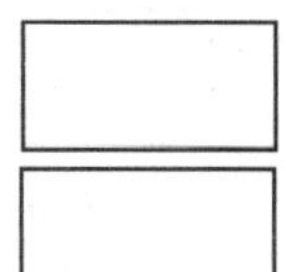

5. Write a decimal for each of the mixed fractions.

a) $1\frac{1}{2} =$   b) $2\frac{71}{100} =$   c) $8\frac{7}{10} =$   d) $4\frac{27}{100} =$

e) $3\frac{7}{100} =$   f) $17\frac{8}{10} =$   g) $27\frac{1}{10} =$   h) $38\frac{5}{100} =$

6. Which decimal represents a greater number? Explain your answer with a picture.

a) 6 tenths or 6 hundredths?   b) 0. 8 or 0. 08?   c) 1.02 or 1.20?

This number line is divided into tenths. The number represented by point A is $2\frac{3}{10}$ or 2.3.

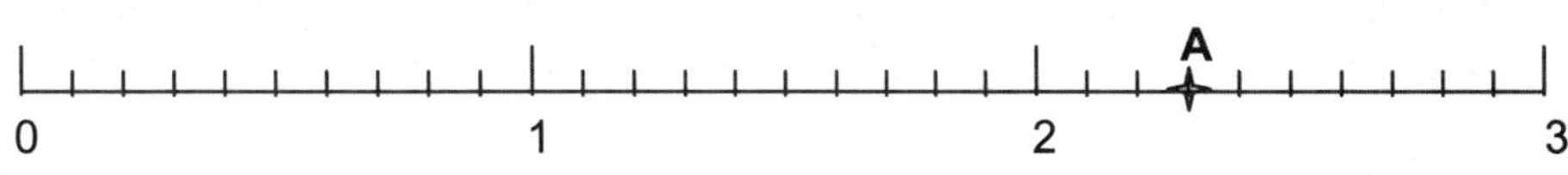


7. Write a fraction or mixed fraction for each point.

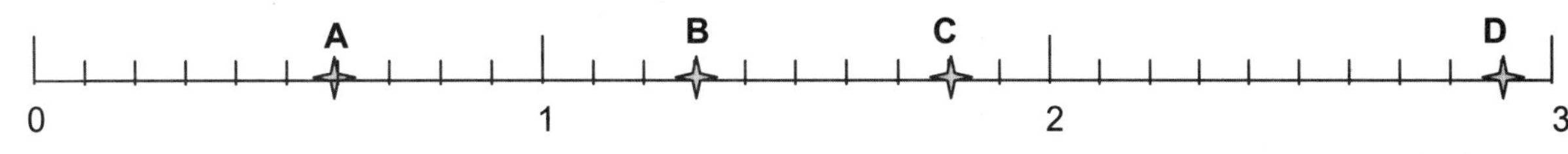


**A:** **B:** **C:** **D:**

8. Write a decimal and a fraction or mixed fraction for each point.

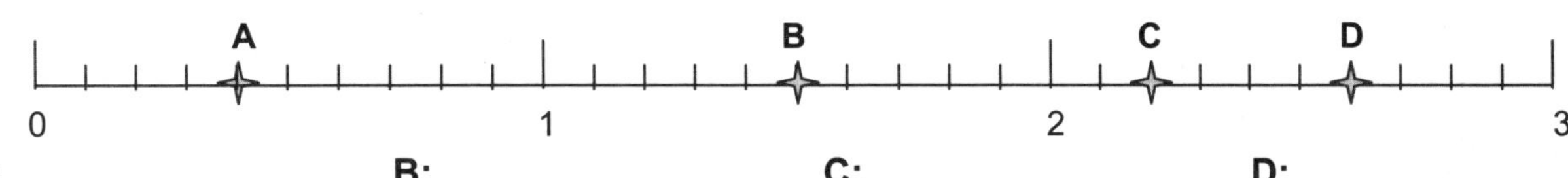


**A:** **B:** **C:** **D:**

9. Mark each point with an "X" and label the point with the correct letter.

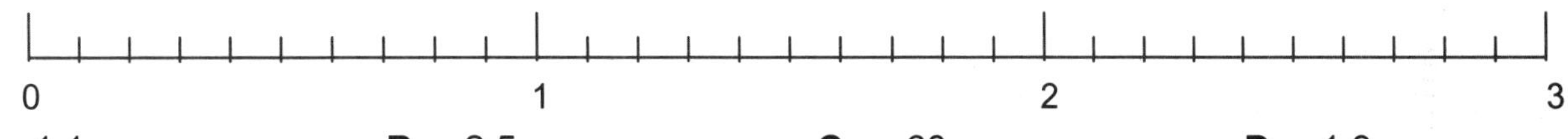


**A.** 1.1 **B.** 2.5 **C.** .60 **D.** 1.9

10. Mark each point with an "X" and label the point with the correct letter.

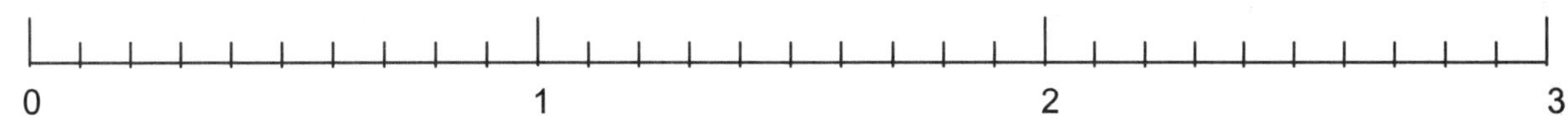


**A.** $1\frac{3}{10}$ **B.** $2\frac{1}{10}$ **C.** $1\frac{7}{10}$ **D.** $\frac{27}{10}$

11. Mark each point with an "X" and label the point with the correct letter.

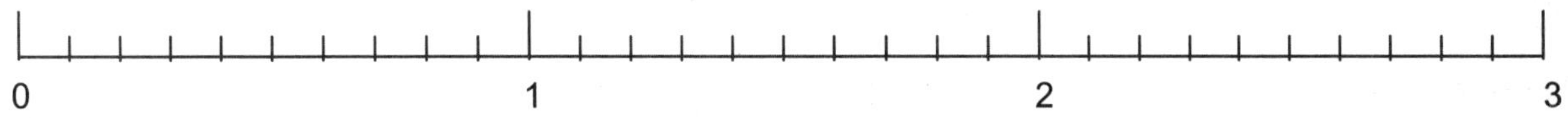


**A.** two and three tenths **B.** one and six tenths **C.** five tenths **D.** two decimal nine

12. Write the name of each point as a fraction in words.

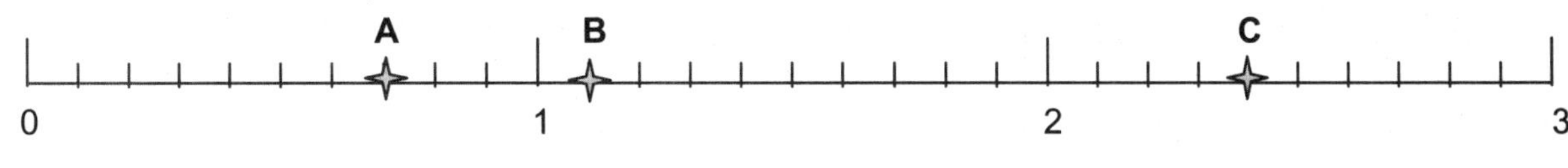


**A.** __________ **B.** __________ **C.** __________

BONUS:

13. Mark the following fractions and decimals on the number line:

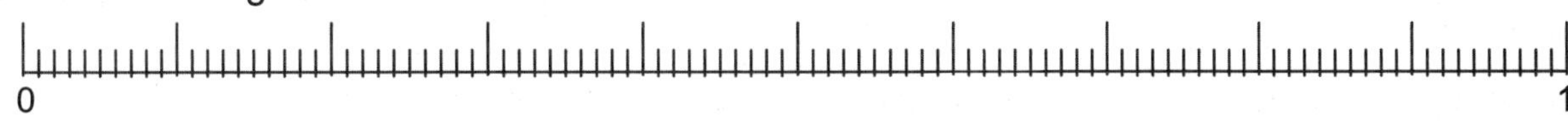


**A.** 0.76 **B.** $\frac{37}{100}$ **C.** 0.08 **D.** $\frac{37}{100}$

# NS4-58: Comparing and Ordering Fractions

1.

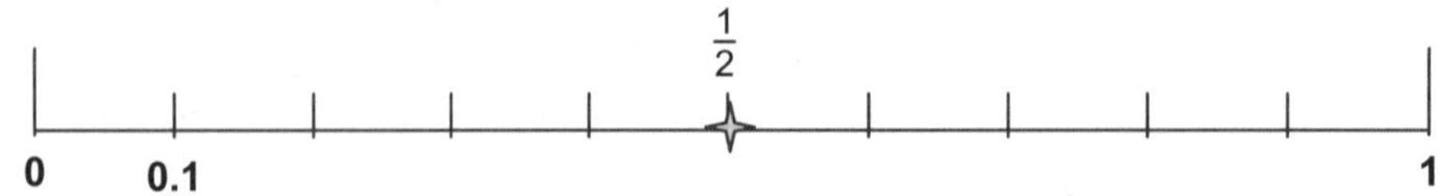


a) Write a decimal for each point marked on the number line. The first decimal is written for you.

b) Which decimal is equal to one half? $\frac{1}{2}$ =

2. Use the number line in question 1 to say whether each decimal is closer to "zero," "a half," or "one."

a) 0.2 is closer to ________  b) 0.6 is closer to ________

c) 0.9 is closer to ________  d) 0.4 is closer to ________

e) 0.8 is closer to ________  f) 0.1 is closer to ________

g) 0.7 is closer to ________  h) 0.3 is closer to ________

3.

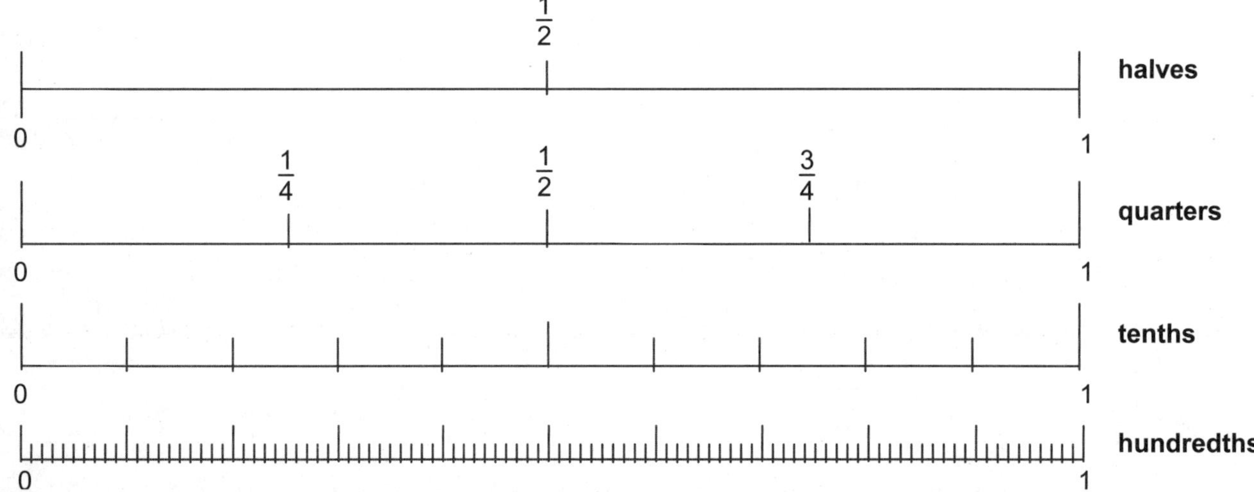


Using the number lines above to compare, write "less than" or "greater than" between each pair of numbers.

a) 0.3 is ______________________ $\frac{1}{2}$  b) 0.9 is ______________________ $\frac{3}{4}$

c) 0.6 is ______________________ $\frac{1}{4}$  d) 0.3 is ______________________ $\frac{1}{2}$

e) 0.25 is ______________________ $\frac{1}{2}$  f) 0.85 is ______________________ $\frac{3}{4}$

4. On a separate piece of paper write the numbers in order by first changing each decimal to a fraction with a denominator of 10.

a) 0.7 , 0.3 , 0.5  b) $\frac{1}{10}$ , 0.3 , 0.9  c) 0.2 , 0.6 , $\frac{1}{4}$

d) $\frac{7}{10}$ , 0.3 , $\frac{5}{10}$  e) 0.7 , 0.8 , $\frac{2}{10}$  f) 0.6 , 0.3 , $\frac{1}{2}$

5. Which whole number is each decimal or mixed fraction closest to (0, 1, 2, or 3)?

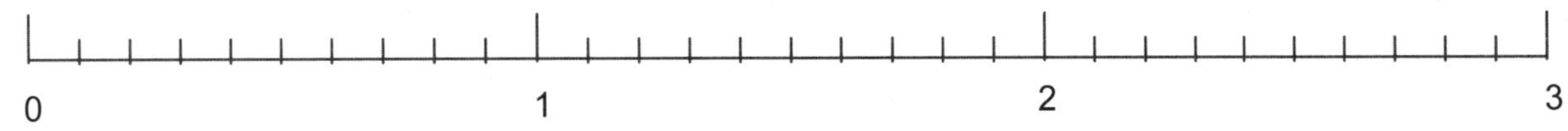


a) 1.2 is closest to __________ b) 1.7 is closest to __________

c) $2\frac{1}{10}$ is closest to __________ d) $2\frac{9}{10}$ is closest to __________

e) 0.7 is closest to __________ f) 2.7 is closest to __________

Show your work for the remaining questions on a separate piece of paper.

6. Write the numbers in order from least to greatest by first changing all of the decimals to fractions with a denominator of 10.

a) 1.2  3.5  3.1 b) 1.5  1.2  1.7 c) $1\frac{1}{10}$  0.7  3.5

d) $1\frac{3}{10}$  1.2  1.1 e) 4.5  3.2  $1\frac{7}{10}$ f) 2.3  2.9  $2\frac{1}{2}$

7. Karen says: "To compare 0.6 and 0.42, I add a zero to 0.6: 0.6 = 6 tenths = 60 hundredths = 0.60 and 60 (hundredths) is greater than 42 (hundredths). So 0.6 is greater than 0.42."

Use Karen's method to compare the decimals below (that is, add a zero to the decimal expressed in tenths). Then circle the greater number.

a) 0.7  0.52 b) 0.34  0.6 c) 0.82  0.5

8. Write each decimal as a fraction with a denominator of 100. a) 0.32 b) 0.87 c) 0.05

9. Write the numbers in order from least to greatest by first changing all of the decimals to fractions with a denominator of 100.

a) 0.2  0.8  0.35 b) $\frac{27}{100}$  0.9  0.25 c) 1.36  $1\frac{22}{100}$  $1\frac{39}{100}$

10. Fred says 0.32 is greater than 0.5 because 32 is greater than 5. Can you explain his mistake?

11. Change $\frac{23}{10}$ to a mixed fraction by shading the correct number of pieces.

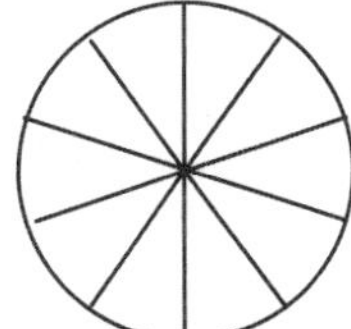
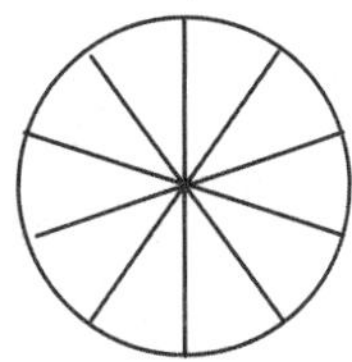
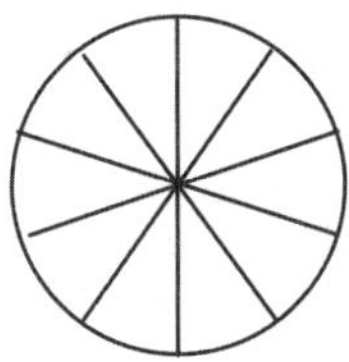

12. Which is greater, $\frac{23}{10}$ or 2.4? Explain.

# NS4-59: Adding and Subtracting Decimals

NOTE: Review the idea of "Adding Tenths."

1. Write a fraction for each shaded part. Then add the fractions together, and shade your answer. The first one is done for you.

a) 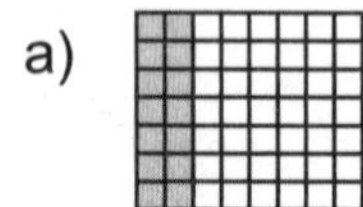 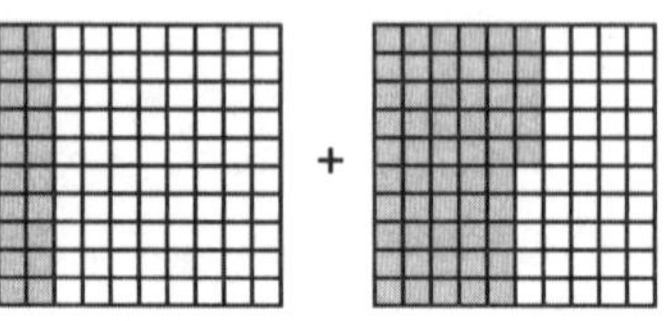 + 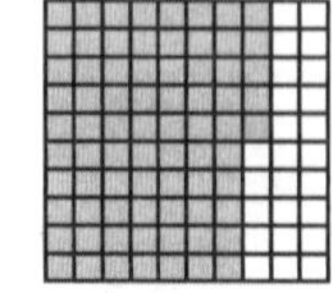 = 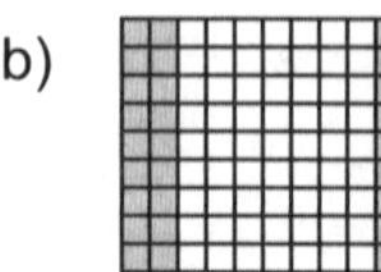

b) 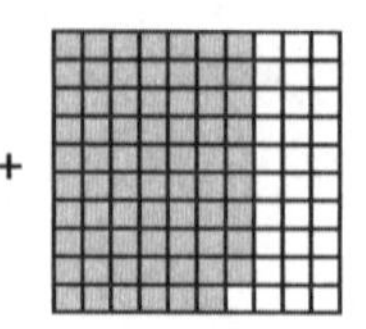 + 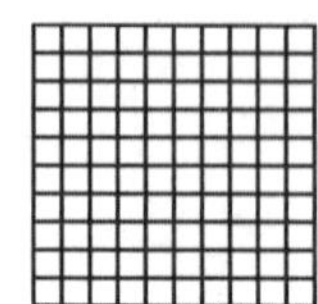 = 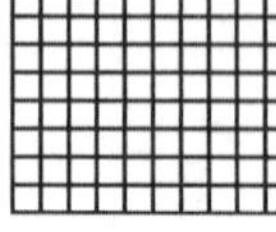

$\frac{20}{100} + \frac{55}{100} = \frac{75}{100}$      +      =

c) 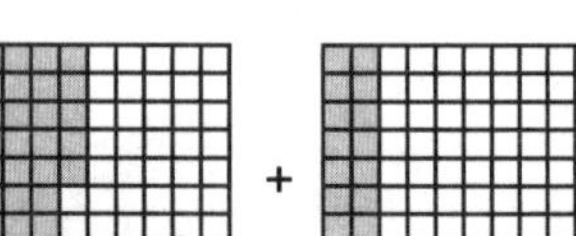 + 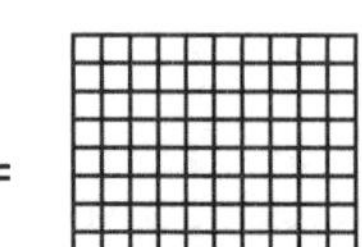 = 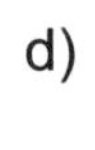

d) 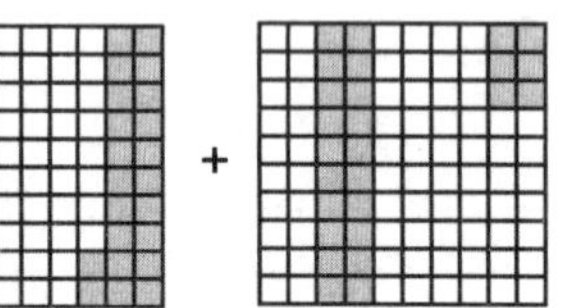 + 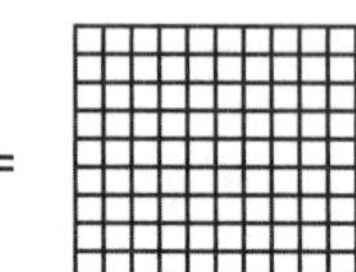 =

2. In the chart, write the decimals that correspond to the fractions in question 4 above. Then solve.

| a) 0.20 + 0.55 = 0.75 | b) |
|---|---|
| c) | d) |

3. Add or subtract the following pairs of decimals by lining the digits up one above the other. Be sure that your final answer is expressed as a decimal.

a) 0.32 + 0.57 =    b) 0.92 + 0.05 =    c) 0.54 + 0.27 =    d) 0.22 + 0.75 =

| 0 . | 3 | 2 |
|---|---|---|
| 0 . | 5 | 7 |
| 0 . | 8 | 9 |

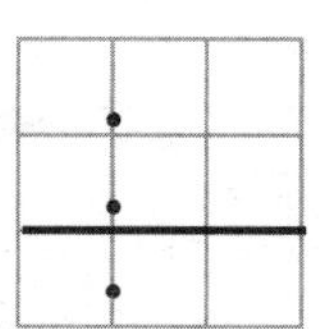

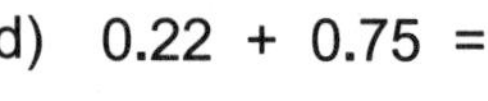

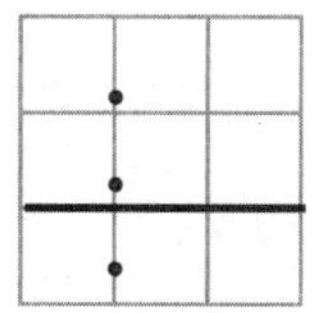

d) 0.7 + 0 .25 =    e) 0.3 + 0.87 =    f) 0.72 – 0.31 =    g) 0.38 – 0.52 =

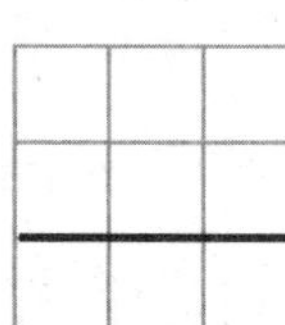

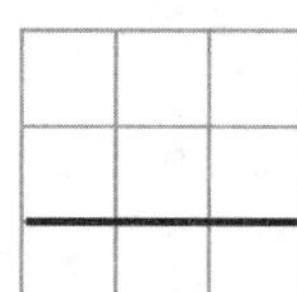

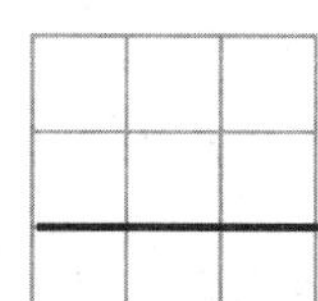

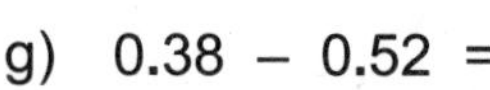

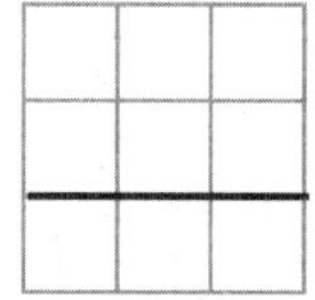

4. On a separate piece of paper, line up and add or subtract the following decimals.

a) 0.32 + 0.17 =    b) 0.64 - 0.23 =    c) 0.46 + 0.12=    d) 0.87 - 0.02 =

e) 0.94 + 0.03 =    f) 0.19 + 0.61=    g) 0.67 - 0.2 =    h) 0.48 + 0.31 =

5. A garter snake is 0.42 m long. What fraction of a metre is this? What fraction of a metre would 2 garter snakes be if they lay end to end?

6. Add by drawing a base-10 model as shown in question 6. a). Then, using the chart provided, line up the decimal points and add.
NOTE: Use a hundreds square for a whole and a tens strip for one tenth.

a) 1.23 + 1.12

| | Ones | Tenths | Hundredths |
|---|---|---|---|
| | | | |
| + | | | |
| | | | |

b) 1.14 + 1.21

| | Ones | Tenths | Hundredths |
|---|---|---|---|
| | | | |
| + | | | |
| | | | |

7. On a separate piece of paper, add each pair of numbers (i) by drawing a base-10 model and (ii) by lining up the decimal points. In question 7. c), show how you would carry by exchanging 10 tenths for 1 whole.

a) 2.15 + 1.24 b) 3.42 + 1.05 c) 2.71 + 1.42

8. Subtract by drawing a base-10 model of the greater number and then crossing out the ones, tenths, and hundredths that are in the lesser number, as shown in question 8. a).

a) 2.35 – 1.12

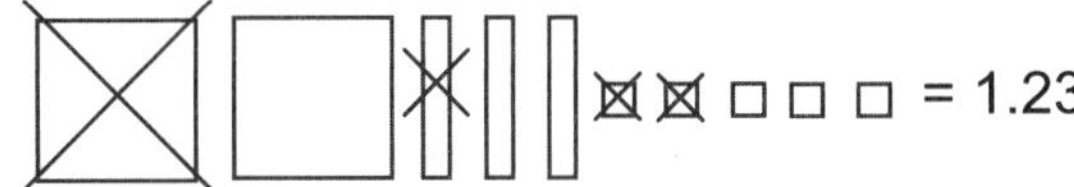


b) 3.24 – 2.11

Show your work for the remaining questions on a separate piece of paper.

9. Subtract each pair of numbers (i) by drawing a base-10 model and (ii) by lining up the decimal points. In question 9. c), borrow by exchanging 1 one for 10 tenths.

a) 3.37 – 1.24 b) 2.51 – 1.40 c) 4.25 – 1.82

10. Subtract each pair of numbers by lining up the decimal points.

a) 7.32 – 4.51 b) 9.35 – 6.99 c) 2.83 – 0.17 d) 8.91 – 1.3 e) 7.8 – 4.35

11. A banana slug is the fastest mollusk. It can crawl 0.03 km in an hour. How far could it crawl in 3 hours?

12. The largest animal heart measured belonged to a blue whale. It weighed 698.5 kg. How much would 2 hearts of that size weigh?

13. The world record for longest hair is 7.5 m. Julia's hair is 0.37 m long. How much longer is the longest hair than Julia's hair? (HINT: Estimate first—is it more than 7 m longer?)

14. Continue the patterns. a) 0.2, 0.4, 0.6, ____, ____, ____ b) 0.3, 0.6, 0.9, ____, ____, ____

# NS4-60: Concepts in Decimals

The size of a unit of measurement depends on which unit has been selected as the **whole**.

A millimetre is a **tenth** of a centimetre, but it is only a **hundredth** of a decimetre.
REMEMBER: A decimetre is 10 cm.

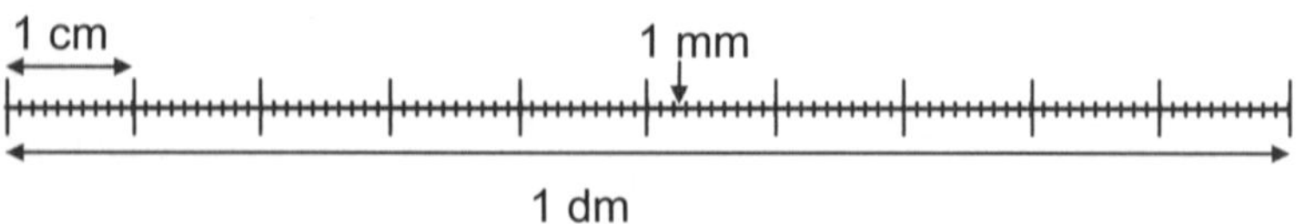


---

1. Draw a picture in the space provided to show 1 tenth of each whole.

a) 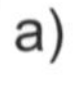 

1 whole 1 tenth

b) 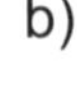 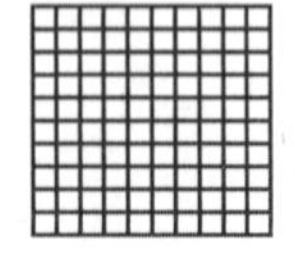

1 whole 1 tenth

c) 

1 whole 1 tenth

2. Write each measurement as a fraction and then as a decimal.
REMEMBER: 1 cm is 1 hundredth of a metre.

a) 1 cm = ________ dm ________ dm  b) 4 cm = ________ dm ________ dm

c) 1 mm = ________ cm ________ cm  d) 7 mm = ________ cm ________ cm

e) 82 mm = ________ dm ________ dm  f) 75 cm = ________ m ________ m

g) 100 cm = ________ m ________ m  h) 9 cm = ________ m ________ m

i) 7 mm = ________ dm ________ dm  j) 43 cm = ________ m ________ m

3. Add the measurements by first changing the **smaller unit** into a decimal in the **larger unit**. Then add the decimals. The first one is done for you. Show your work on a separate piece of paper.

a) 4 cm + 9.2 dm = 0.4 dm + 9.2 dm = 9.6 dm  b) 8 cm + 2.4 dm = ______

c) 6 mm + 8.2 cm = ______  d) 26 cm + 1.52 m = ______  e) 423 cm + 1.75 m = ______

4.

| Plant | Tallest plant will grow |
|---|---|
| golden rod | 1.5 m |
| field birdwell | 1 m |
| white sweet clover | 300 cm |
| yellow sorrel | 0.5 m |

Rick wants to plant a row of each type of flower, with the ones that will grow taller at the back and those that will grow shorter in the front.

a) How should he order the flowers?

b) How much taller will the clover grow than the sorrel?

5. Explain how you would change 1.72 m into centimetres. (HINT: How many centimetres are $\frac{72}{100}$ of a metre?)

6. $0.25 means 2 dimes and 5 pennies. Why do we use decimal notation for money? What is a dime a tenth of? What is a penny a hundredth of?

# NS4-61: Numbers in Careers and the Media

1. Meteorologists study the weather. The world's highest temperature in the shade was recorded in Libya in 1932. The temperature reached 58°C.

   a) How long ago was this temperature recorded?

   b) On an average summer day in Toronto, the temperature is 30°C. How much higher was the temperature recorded in Libya?

   BONUS:

   c) The lowest temperature recorded (in Antarctica) was –89°C. What is the difference between the lowest and the highest temperatures?

2. A news program recently carried the following story on the 2004 Summer Olympics:

   > The shot put was the first sporting event of the 2004 Olympic Games. The event was held at the hallowed grounds of the ancient Stadiumóthe original birthplace of the shot put in 393 B.C.E.
   >
   > Yuriy Bilonog of Ukraine won the gold medal with a toss of 21.16 m. Joachim Olsen of Denmark won the bronze with a throw of 21.07 m.

   a) How much further did Yiriy Bilonog throw the shot put than Joachim Olsen?

   b) How long ago is the date given in the story?

3. Doctors study the body. Here are some facts that a doctor might know:

   a) FACT: "The heart pumps about 0.06 L of blood with each beat." How much blood would the heart pump in 3 beats?

   b) FACT: "The heart beats about 80 times a minute." How long would it take the heart to beat 240 times? (HINT: Add 80 repeatedly until you reach 240.)

4. > "Roughly 85 percent of young Americans could not find Afghanistan, Iraq, or Israel on a map, according to a new study. Americans ages 18 to 24 came in next to last among nine countries in the National Geographic-Roper 2002 Global Geographic Literacy Survey, which quizzed more than 3000 young adults in Canada, France, Germany, Great Britain, Italy, Japan, Mexico, Sweden, and the United States. Top scorers were young adults in Sweden, Germany, and Italy. Out of 56 questions that were asked across all countries surveyed, on average young Americans answered 23 questions correctly. Young people in Canada and Great Britain fared almost as poorly as those in the U.S."

   a) In the newspaper quotation to the left, find a number that is a rounded number or an estimate.

   Then use the information in the quotation to find . . .

   b) The number of questions that young Americans answered **incorrectly**.

   c) The number of different countries that the surveyed students represented.

   d) The place that American students came in (written as an ordinal number).

5. In August 2004, Canadian newspapers carried a story about Mary Ellen Swan, a woman who was famous for helping strangers and who lived to be 112.

   a) In what year was Ms Swan born?

   b) In 1959, Ms Swan was rewarded for her charitable work with an invitation to meet Queen Elizabeth II. How old was Ms Swan when she met the Queen?

   c) When she was 92, Ms Swan made her first television commercial. In what year did she make the commercial?

# NS4-62: Word Problems

Answer the following questions on a separate piece of paper:

1. A box of 2 crayons costs 100¢. A box of 3 crayons costs 120¢. What is the cheapest way to buy 6 crayons?

2. A tray of 4 plants costs 60¢. A tray of 6 plants costs 80¢. What is the cheapest way to buy 24 plants? What strategy did you use to solve the puzzle?

3. Carol had $10.00. She spends half her money on a diary. Then she spends $1.25 for a pen. How much money does she have left?

4. Find the secret number: I am an odd number between 20 and 30. My ones digit is not 4. I am divisible by 3. My tens digit is greater than my ones digit.

5. A school has 150 students.
   a) If 80 of the students were boys, how many were girls?
   b) If each class has 25 students, how many classes are there? (HINT: Count by 25s.)
   c) Each class has one teacher. The school also has a principal, a vice-principal, and a secretary. In total, how many adults work at the school? (HINT: Use your answer from part b).)
   d) One day, 2 students from each class were sick and did not come to school. How many students were missing that day? (HINT: Use your answer from part b).)
   e) On that same day, how many students were at school? (HINT: Use your answer from part d).)

6. A clothing store has a total of 500 shirts. In one week, they sold 20 red shirts, 50 blue shirts, and 100 green shirts. How many shirts were **left** at the end of the week?

7. Fiona is having a party and needs to buy drinks for herself and her 9 guests.
   a) How many people will be at the party in total? (HINT: Count Fiona **and** her guests.)
   b) If each person has 4 drinks, how many drinks will Fiona need to have available?
   c) One bottle of juice serves 5 drinks. How many bottles of juice should Fiona buy?

8. Use the numbers 1, 2, 3, 4, 5, and 6 to fill in the boxes. NOTE: You can only use each number once.

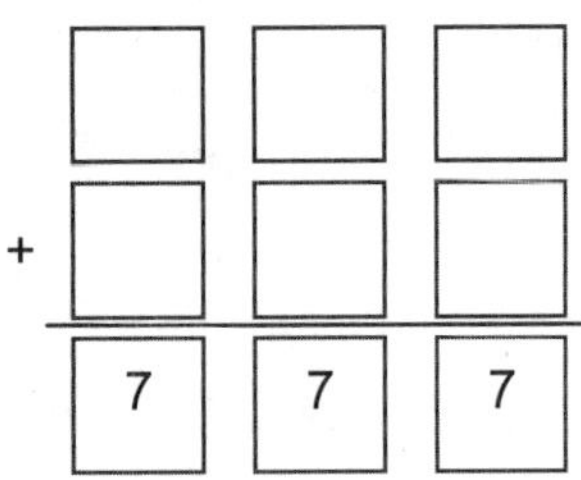


9. Use the numbers 1, 2, 3, and 4 to fill in the following boxes. NOTE: In each question, you can only use each number once.

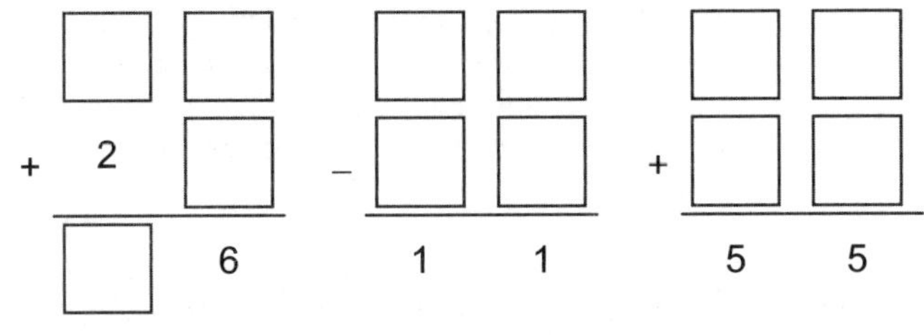


10. Henry is 4 years older than Jane. The sum of their ages is 12. How old is Henry?

11. Juan bought 2 pairs of socks and a shirt. The total cost was $18.00. The socks cost $2.50 for each pair. How much did the shirt cost?

12. Anika was born in British Columbia and lived there for 4 years. Then she moved to Nova Scotia, where she has lived for 7 years. What fraction of her life did she live in British Columbia?

# ME4-26: Telling Time—Review

1. Give the time on the following analog clocks in **two** ways: (i) in numbers; and (ii) in words. The first one is done for you.

a)

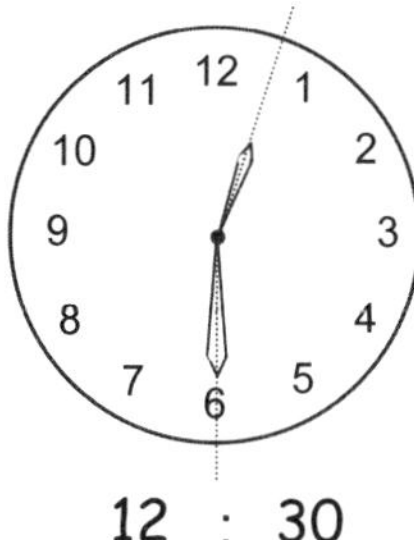

12 : 30

thirty minutes after twelve

b)

_____ : _____

______________________________

c)

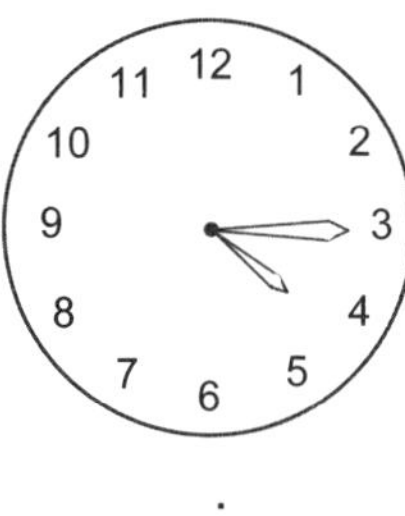

_____ : _____

______________________________

d)

_____ : _____

______________________________

2. Give the time on the following digital clocks in **two** ways: (i) in words; and (ii) as an analog clock.

a)

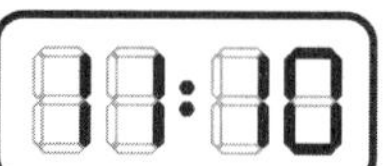


______________________________

b)

______________________________

Answer the following questions on a separate piece of paper:

3. Ria left school at 3:25 and got home at 3:45. How long did it take her to walk home?

4. Doris went on a car trip with her family. They left home at 9:00 in the morning and arrived at 11:30 that morning. How long was their trip?

5. Fuji and his brother went to the zoo for 2 hours. They arrived at 2:00. What time did they leave?

# ME4-27: Telling Time—Half and Quarter Hours

When the minute hand (the long hand) travels from the 12 around the clock until it hits the 12 again, **one hour** has passed. When the minute hand travels from the 12 to the 6, **half an hour** has passed. When the minute hand travels from the 12 to the 3, **a quarter hour** has passed.

REMEMBER:

- If the minute hand is pointing at the 6, it is **half past the hour**.
- If the minute hand is pointing at the 3, it is **quarter past the hour**.
- If the minute hand is pointing at the 9, it is **quarter to the hour**.

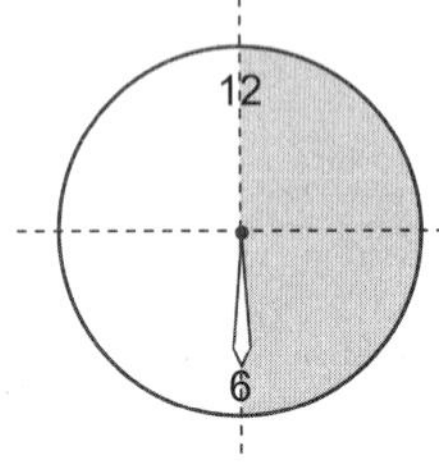

"half past"

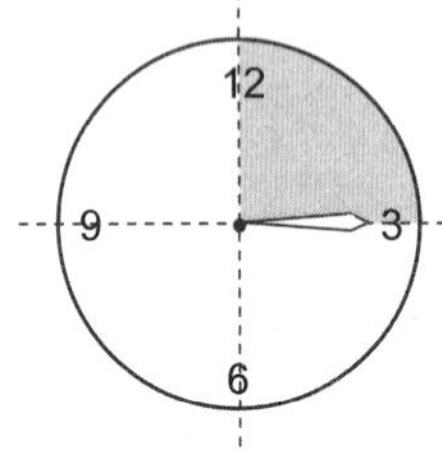

"quarter past"

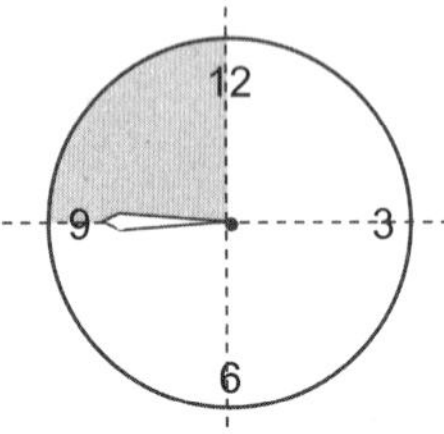

"quarter to"

---

1. In each question, shade in the space from the 12 to the minute hand as above. Then indicate whether the minute hand is "half past," "quarter past," or "quarter to" the hour.

a) 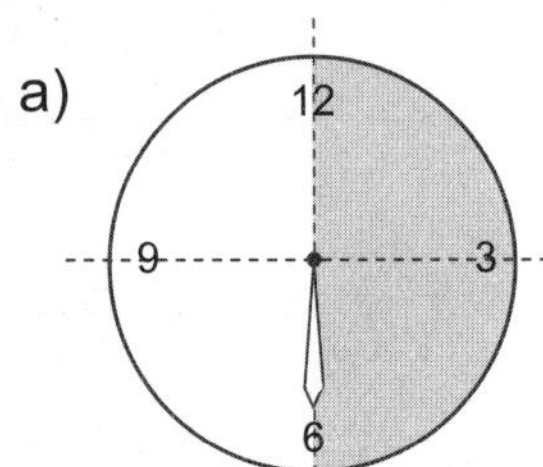

half past

b) 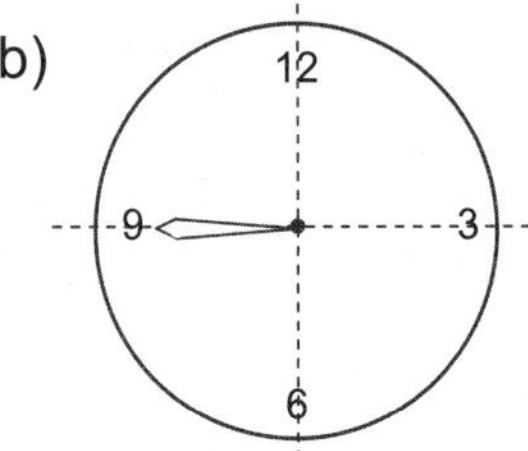

______

c) 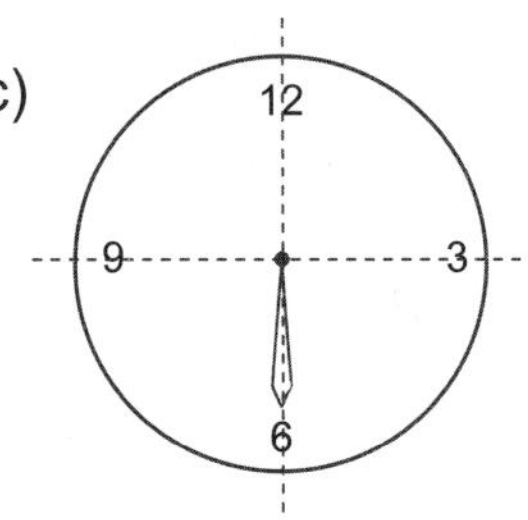

______

d) 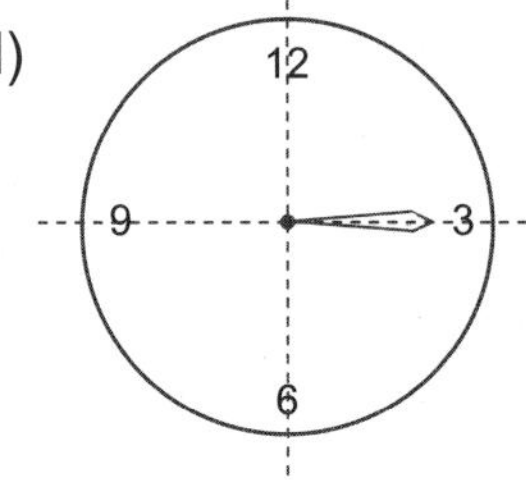

______

e) 

______

f) 

______

g) 

______

h) 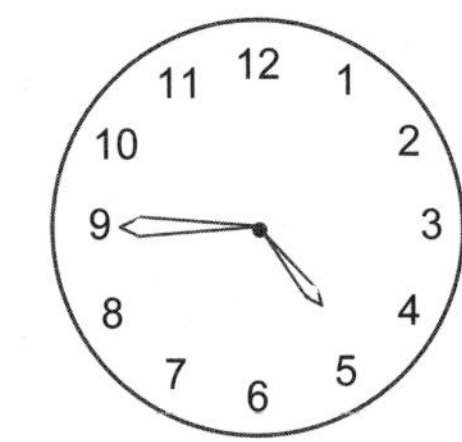

______

2. Give the time shown on each clock—including both the hour and the fraction of the hour.

a) 

quarter after seven

b) 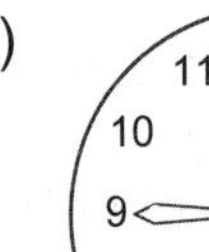
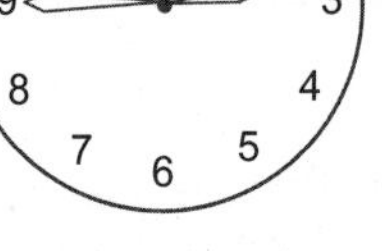

______

c) 

______

d) 

______

# ME4-28: Telling Time—One-Minute Intervals

If the (long) minute hand is exactly on the 1, we know that it is 5 minutes past the hour. But what happens when the minute hand points to the space **between** the 12 and the 1?

In this case, we divide the space between the 12 and the 1 by five (that is, a line for every individual minute) and then count the number of lines between the 12 and the spot where the minute hand points:

When we count, we can see that the minute hand is pointing 3 lines after the 12.

This means that it is **three minutes after the hour.**

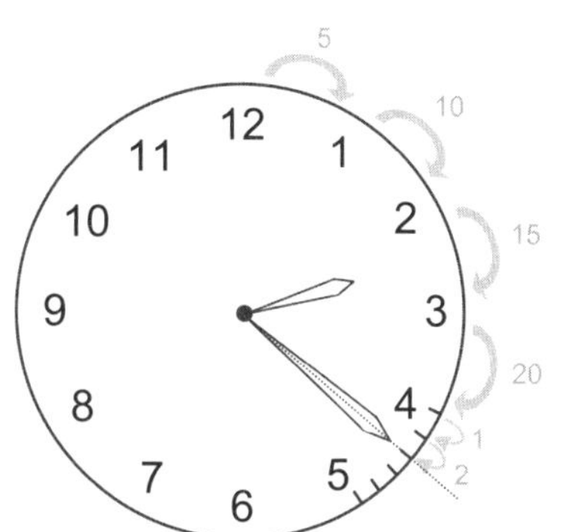

Example:
On this clock, the minute hand is pointing between the 4 and the 5.

First we count by 5s until we reach the 4. Then we count the lines between the 4 and the 5 until we reach the spot where the minute hand is pointing. To get the number of minutes after the hour, we add this second number to the number we got when first counting by 5s.

20 + 2 = 22

It is **2:22** or **twenty-two minutes after two**.

---

1. How many minutes past the hour is it? The first one is done for you.

a)

24 minutes past

b)

________ minutes past

c)

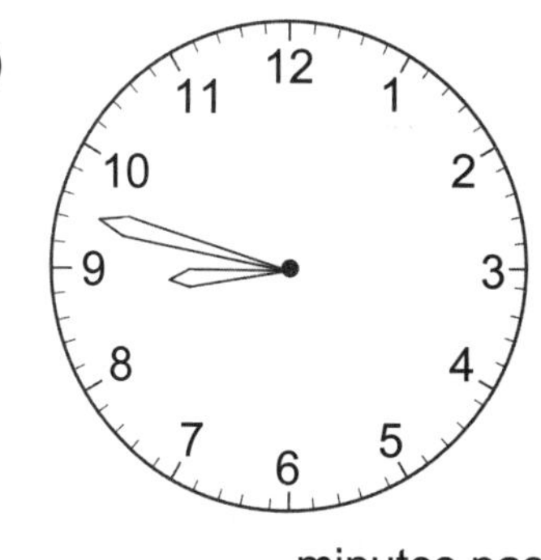

________ minutes past

d)

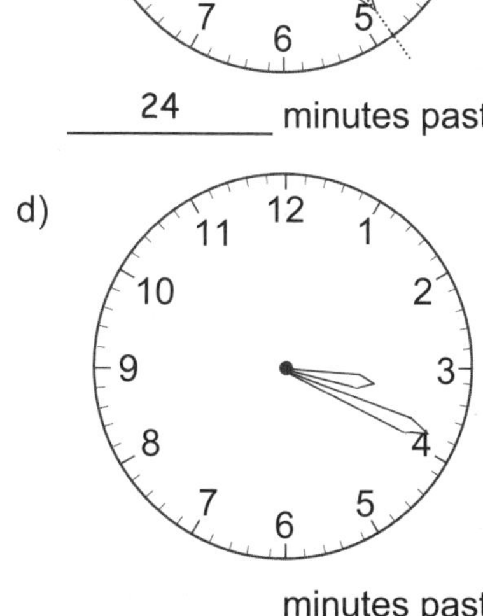

________ minutes past

e)

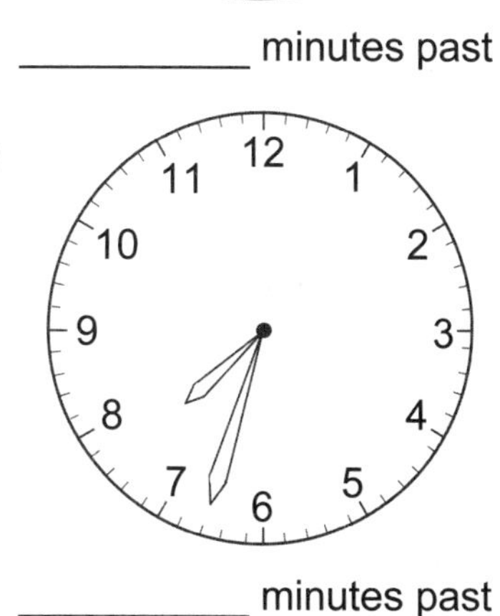

________ minutes past

f)

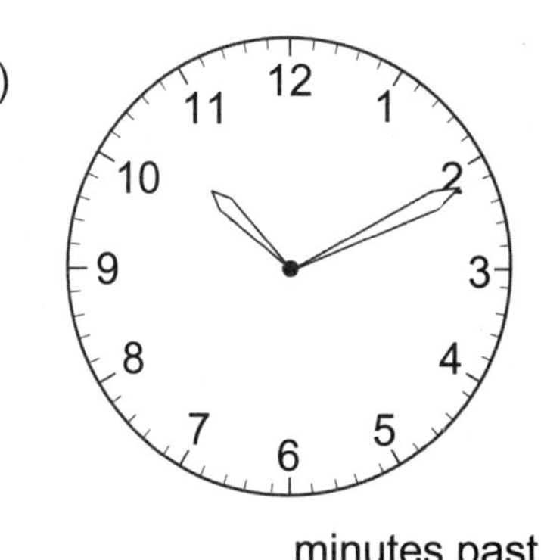

________ minutes past

2. For each clock, write the entire time—that is, the hour and the exact minute. The first one is done for you.

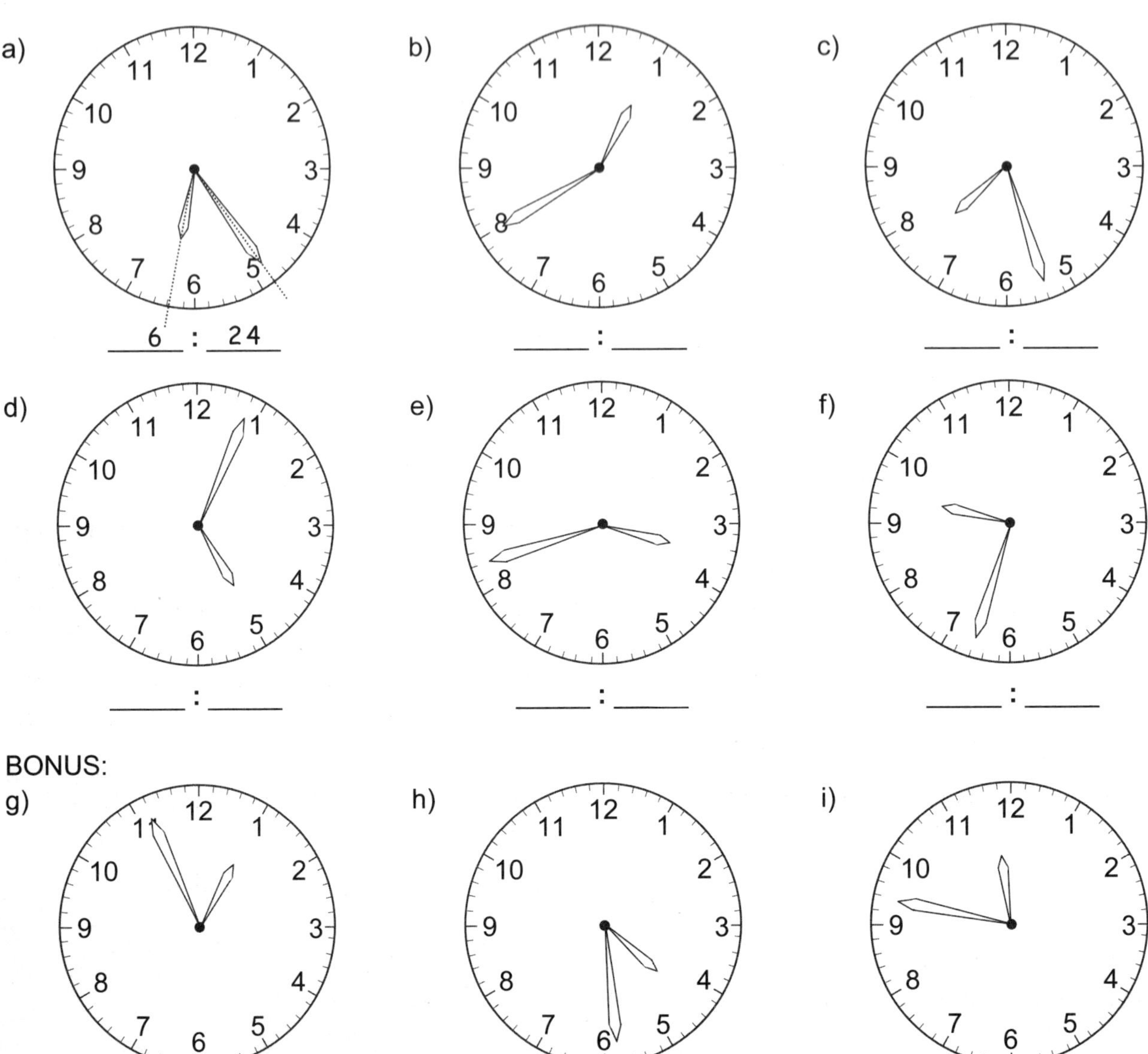


Answer these questions on a separate piece of paper.

3. Anne is baking cookies. They need to cook for 40 minutes. She puts them into the oven at 3:12. What time should she take them out?

4. Each day Mohammed is allowed to play with his friends until dinner time, which is at 5:30. Today he started playing after school at 3:45. How long is he able to play?

5. Jake is Kyla's older brother. Each night, Kyla goes to bed at 7:45. Jake's bedtime is 30 minutes later. What time does he go to bed?

# ME4-29: Days, Weeks, and Years



## DAYS

Each day is made up of **24 hours**. The day officially starts at **12 o'clock midnight** and ends just before **12 o'clock midnight** the next day.

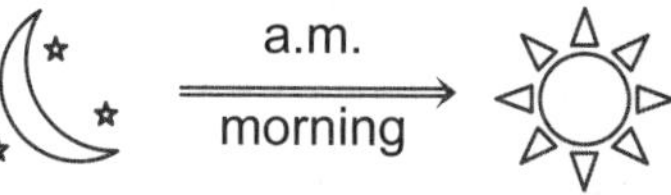


The time period from **12 o'clock midnight** to **12 o'clock noon** is called **a.m.**

Example: When you wake up at **7 o'clock in the morning**, it is called **7 a.m.**

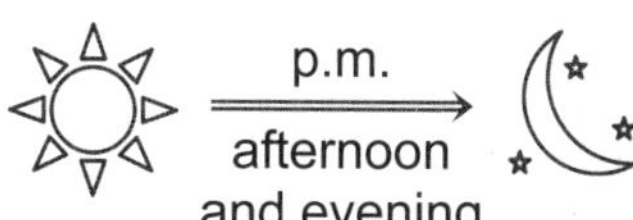


The time period from **12 o'clock noon** to **12 o'clock midnight** is called **p.m.**

Example: When you go to bed at **8 o'clock in the evening**, it is called **8 p.m.**

---

Answer the following questions on a separate piece of paper:

1. Are the following times **a.m.** or **p.m.**?

   a) 7 o'clock in the morning b) 2 o'clock in the afternoon c) 9 o'clock in the evening

   d) 10 o'clock at night e) 4 o'clock in the afternoon f) 3 o'clock in the morning

   BONUS:
   g) 2 hours **before** noon h) 3 hours **after** noon i) 1 hour **before** midnight

2. a) List 3 things you do in the a.m. b) List 3 things you do in the p.m.

---

## WEEKS

Amanda's class is learning about the relationship between days and weeks. They already know that there are seven days in a week. The days of the week are . . .

**Monday**, **Tuesday**, **Wednesday**, **Thursday**, **Friday**, **Saturday**, and **Sunday**

↑1 ↑2 ↑3 ↑4 ↑5 ↑6 ↑7

So, as a class, they write the following equals statements (or equations):

**1 week = 7 days** and **7 days = 1 week**

Example: In two weeks, it is Amanda's birthday. How many days is it until her birthday?

**Solution #1**

To solve the problem, Amanda first draws two boxes. She then draws seven lines in each:

 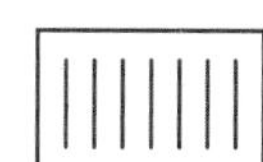

NOTE: The boxes represent weeks and the lines represent the seven days in each week.

By counting the total number of lines, Amanda knows that her birthday is in **14**
.

**Solution #2**

Amanda's teacher shows her another way to solve the problem, using multiplication:

**2 × 7**

number of weeks until Amanda's birthday → 2; number of days in one week → 7

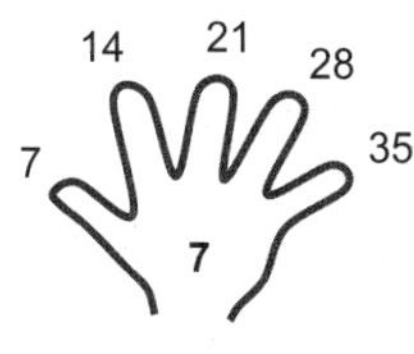


Using the numbered hand as a guide, Amanda counts by 7s until she has two fingers up. She stops at 14 so **2 × 7 = 14**.

Using her teacher's method, Amanda also knows that her birthday is in **14 days**.

3. How many days are in the following number of weeks? The first one is done for you.
NOTE: Use one of the methods from the previous page.

a) 3 weeks = __21__ days

 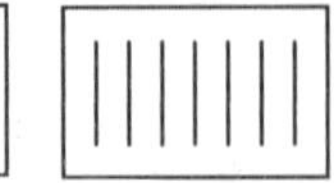 

b) 1 week = ______ days

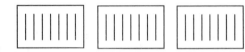

c) 2 weeks = ______ days

d) 4 weeks = ______ days

4. Janice and Jacquie are putting together a time chart to track the plant they grew together for a school project. They want to know how long it took their plant to grow a certain height **IN DAYS**.

Can you help them figure out the rest of the information and then answer the questions below? Use the "rough work" column for your calculations.

| **Height of Janice and Jacquie's plant** | **Time after planting** (in weeks and days) | **Rough work** | **Time after planting** (in days) |
|---|---|---|---|
| 2 cm | 0 weeks and 4 days | 0 × 7 = 0 0 + 4 = 4 | 4 |
| 4 cm | 0 weeks and 6 days | | |
| 6 cm | 1 week and 3 days | | |
| 8 cm | 2 weeks and 1 days | | |
| 10 cm | 2 weeks and 5 days | | |
| 12 cm | 3 week and 2 days | | |

Answer the remaining questions on a separate piece of paper.

a) Looking at the chart, how long (in days) would you guess it took for the plant to reach 7 cm?

b) How tall do you think the plant was 3 weeks after it was planted?

5. Design a time line of a typical day. This is **your** time line so be sure to include personal details such as what time you wake up, what time you eat breakfast, what time you do schoolwork, and so on. When writing the times, be sure to use a.m. and p.m. correctly. How does your typical day compare with those of your friends?

## YEARS

Minutes, hours, days, and weeks are all units of time. Sometimes, however, the time being measured is long enough that a larger unit is used—the **year**.

We use years to measure many things. In particular, years are used to measure age. Think about the question: "How old are you?" Our usual answer is: "I am ___ years old."

Although our age in years is really only an estimate (unless it is our birthday), we use it to give people a general sense of how old we are.

When we look at the relationship between **days and years**, we see that . . .

**365 days = 1 year** and **1 year = 365 days**

NOTE: There are 366 days in a leap year.

When we look at the approximate relationship between **weeks and years**, we see that . . .

**52 weeks = 1 year** and **1 year = 52 weeks**

---

6. Put the following time units in order from smallest to largest by placing the correct number in the box provided. The first one is done for you.

| day | minute | week | year | hour |
|---|---|---|---|---|
|  | 1 |  |  |  |

7. Use your knowledge of time, patterns, and multiplication to complete the following charts. Read the questions very carefully!

a)

| **Days** | 1 | 2 | 3 | 4 |
|---|---|---|---|---|
| **Hours** | 24 | 48 |  |  |

b)

| **Weeks** | 1 | 2 | 3 | 4 |
|---|---|---|---|---|
| **Days** | 7 |  |  |  |

c)

| **Years** | 1 | 2 | 3 | 4 |
|---|---|---|---|---|
| **Weeks** | 52 |  |  |  |

BONUS:

d)

| **Years** | 1 | 2 | 3 |
|---|---|---|---|
| **Days** | 365 |  |  |

**Rough work area**

$$\begin{array}{r} 24 \\ \times\ 2 \\ \hline 48 \end{array}$$

# ME4-30: Decades, Centuries, and Millennia

For this set of worksheets, it is helpful to remember our earlier lessons on Place Value.

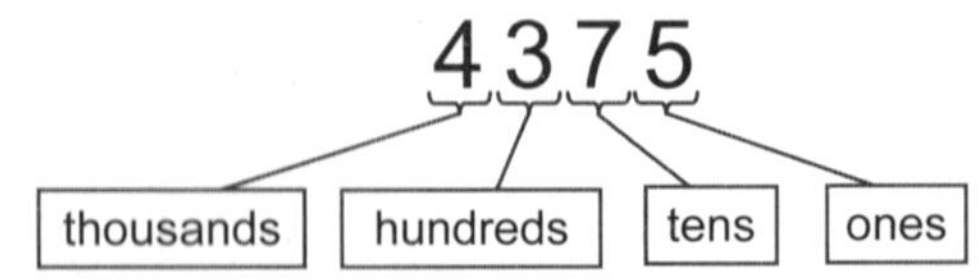


The relationship between ones, tens, hundreds, and thousands is the same as the relationship between **years**, **decades**, **centuries**, and **millennia**.

1 **decade** = 10 years; 1 **century** = 100 years; 1 **millennium** = 1000 years

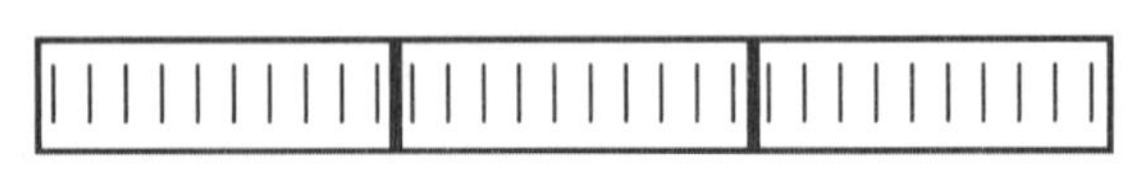

Example: Amelia's mother is 30 years old. How old is her mother in decades?

**Solution:**
We start by drawing 30 lines—one line for each year of Amelia's mother's age. From above, we know that **1 decade = 10 years**. To count the decades, we draw boxes around sets of 10 lines.

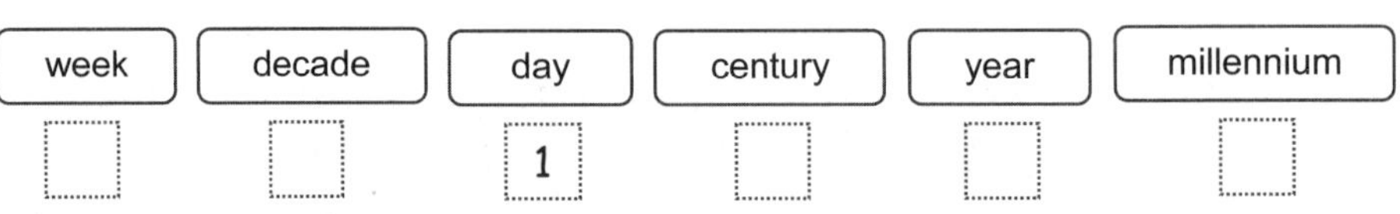

We are left with 3 sets of 10 so Amelia's mother is **3 decades old**.

**Alternate Solution:** You can also find the solution by skip counting by 10s (since 10 years = 1 decade) and stopping when you reach 30. The number of fingers you have raised (3) is the number of decades.

1. Put the following in order from smallest to largest. The first one is done for you.

| week | decade | day | century | year | millennium |
|---|---|---|---|---|---|
|  |  | 1 |  |  |  |

2. Connect a length of time in the first column to an **equal length of time** in the second column. Be sure to convert properly! The first one is done for you. NOTE: Use skip counting if you can!

| | |
|---|---|
| 1 year | 10 years |
| 100 years | 24 hours |
| 1 decade | 1 millennium |
| 20 years | 1 century |
| 1 day | 365 days |
| 4 centuries | 2 decades |
| 1 hour | 400 years |
| 1000 years | 60 minutes |

3. In each case, convert the given time into **decades**. IMPORTANT NOTE: Think about what you would count by to convert from years to decades.

a) 40 years = _____ decades  b) 60 years = _____ decades  c) 90 years = _____ decades

4. In each case, convert the given time into **centuries**. IMPORTANT NOTE: Think about what you would count by to convert from years to centuries.

a) 100 years = _____ century  b) 800 years = _____ centuries  c) 1500 years = _____ centuries

5. For each question, convert the given time into the units required. Be very careful!

a) 2 decades = _____ years  b) 2000 years = _____ millennia  c) 3 centuries = _____ years

d) 1200 years = _____ centuries  e) 40 decades = _____ centuries  f) 5 millennia = _____ centuries

# ME4-31: Estimating Time Intervals

We often estimate lengths of time.

For example, we tend to give our age in years even though it does not tell us the exact measure of time that has passed since we were born.

When estimating, it is important to use units that are appropriate to the length of time being estimated. Has anyone ever told you their age in minutes? in hours? in centuries? Probably not!

---

1. In each case, match the question with the unit of time you would use to give the answer.

| Question |
|---|
| What is your friend's age? |
| How long does it take you to walk around the block? |
| How long is a day? |
| How much time has passed since the dinosaurs lived? |
| How long does it take for your hair to grow 1 cm? |
| How long is summer? |

| Unit |
|---|
| millennia |
| years |
| weeks |
| months |
| minutes |
| hours |

2. The charts below list activities that many people do every day. Think back on your own experience—approximately how long does it take you to perform the following activities? Do not forget units!

| **Activity** | **Time Spent** |
|---|---|
| sleeping | |
| eating breakfast | |
| reading | |
| doing chores at home | |

| **Activity** | **Time Spent** |
|---|---|
| playing outside | |
| watching TV | |
| doing homework | |
| eating dinner | |

Once you have completed the chart, compare your answers with one of your friends. Did you spend the same amount of time on the different activities?

Pick **two** activities where the times are different. Complete the boxes below, being sure to include all the details requested, including a couple of reasons why your respective times may be different.

**Activity:**

My time: __________ My friend's time: __________

Reasons our times might be different:

- 
- 

**Activity:**

My time: __________ My friend's time: __________

Reasons our times might be different:

- 
- 

# ME4-32: Area in Square Centimetres

Shapes that are flat are called **two-dimensional** (2-D) shapes. The area of a two-dimensional shape is the amount of space it takes up. You can compare the area of a larger and smaller shape by counting the number of smaller shapes needed to cover the larger.

A square centimetre is a unit for measuring area. A square with sides of 1 cm has an area of one square centimetre. The short form for a square centimetre is $cm^2$.

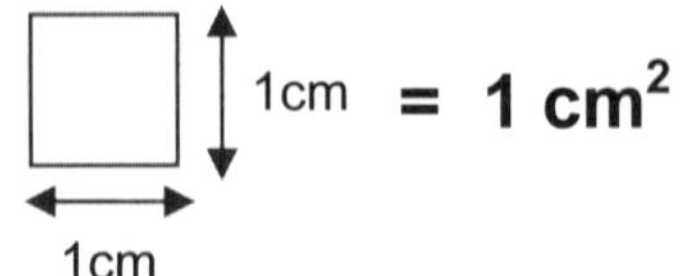


1. Find the area of these figures in square centimetres.

a) 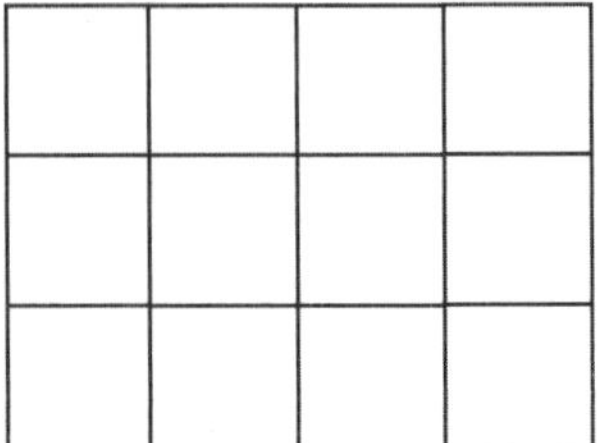

Area = _______ $cm^2$

b) 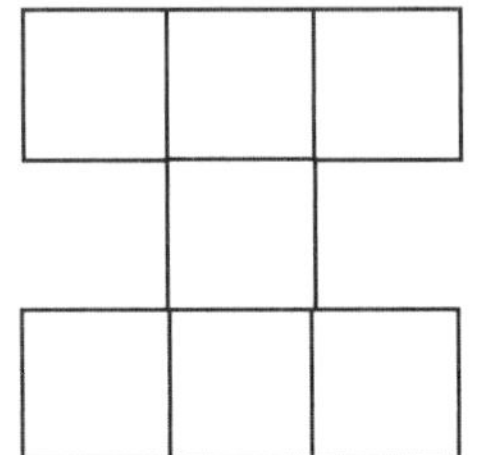

Area = _______ $cm^2$

c) 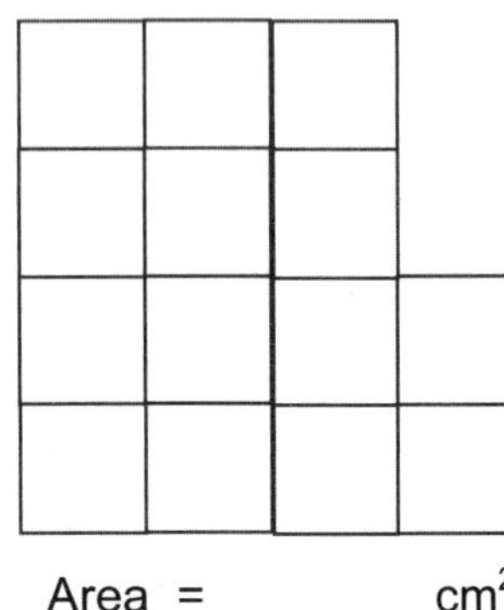

Area = _______ $cm^2$

2. The sides of the rectangles have been marked in centimetres. Using a ruler, draw lines to divide each rectangle into square centimetres.

a) 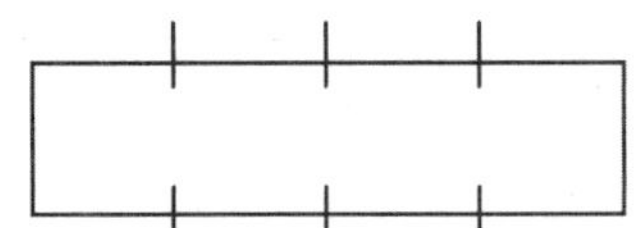

Area = _______ $cm^2$

b) 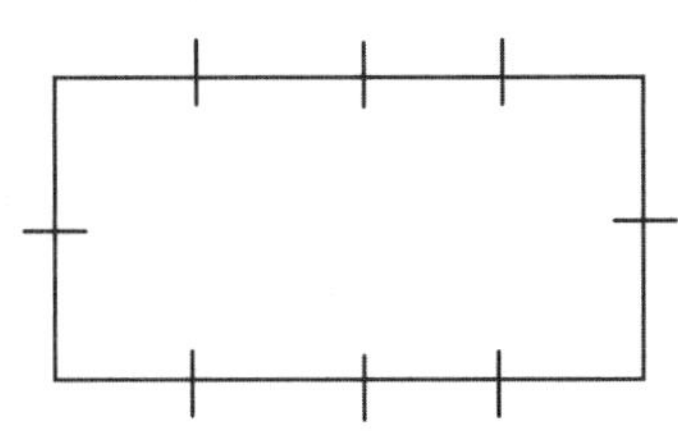

Area = _______ $cm^2$

c) 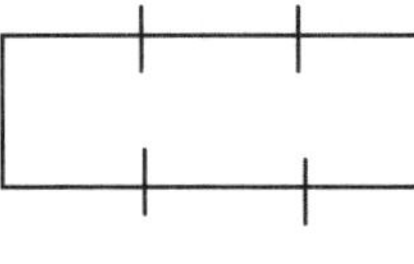

Area = _______ $cm^2$

3. How can you find the area (in square units) of each of the given shapes?

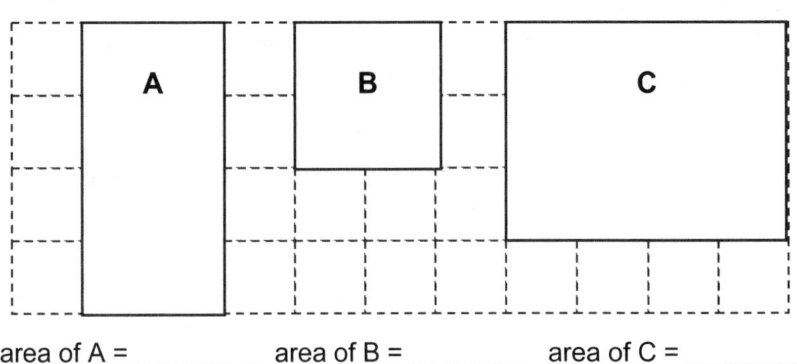


area of A = _______ area of B = _______ area of C = _______

Complete the following questions on grid paper:

4. Draw 3 different shapes that have an area of 8 $cm^2$ (the shapes do not have to be rectangles).

5. Draw several shapes and find their area and perimeter.

6. Draw a rectangle with an area of 8 $cm^2$ and perimeter of 12 cm.

# ME4-33: Area of Rectangles

1. Write a multiplication statement for each array.

a)  b)  c) 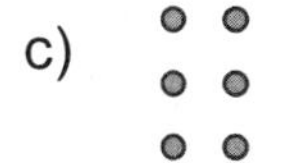 d)

_______ _______ _______ _______

2. Draw a dot in each box. Then write a multiplication statement that tells you the number of boxes in the rectangle. The first one is done for you.

a) 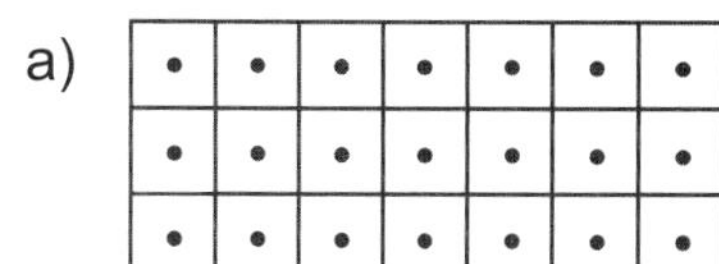 b) 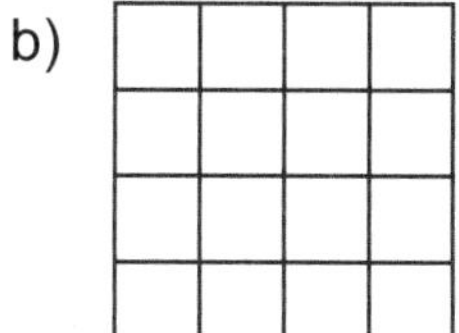 c) 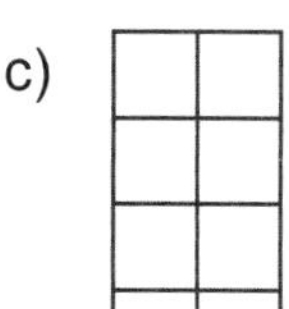 d) 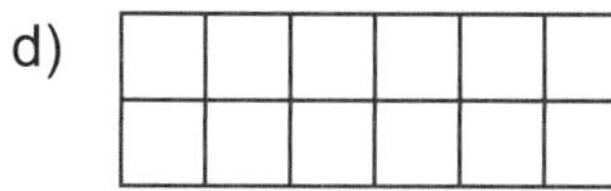

3 × 7 = 21 _______ _______ _______

3. Write the number of boxes along the width and length of each rectangle. Then write a multiplication statement for the area of the rectangle (in square units).

a) 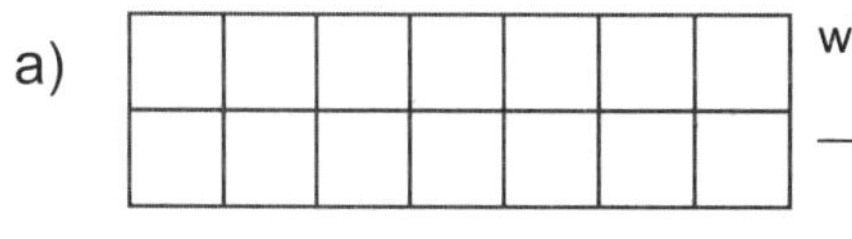 width = ____ length = ____

b) 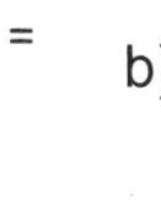 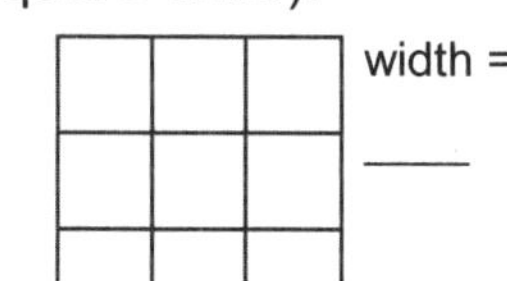 width = ____ length = ____

c)  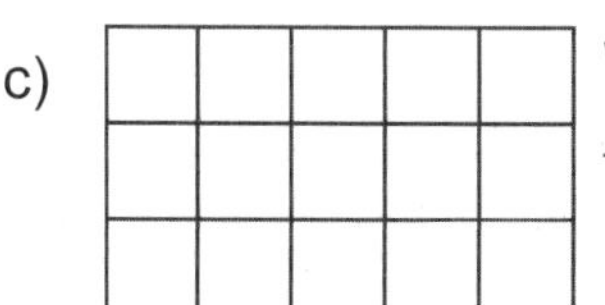 width = ____ length = ____

_______ _______ _______

4. The sides of the rectangles have been marked in centimetres. Using a ruler, draw lines to divide each rectangle into squares. On a separate piece of paper, write a multiplication statement for the area of the boxes in centimetres squared ($cm^2$). NOTE: You will have to mark the last row of boxes yourself using a ruler.

a) 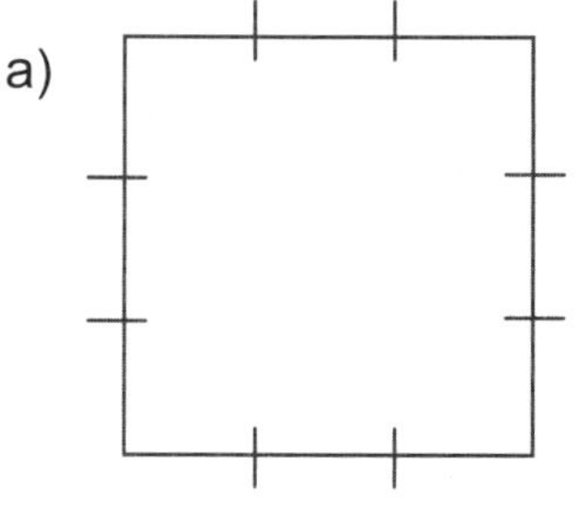 b) 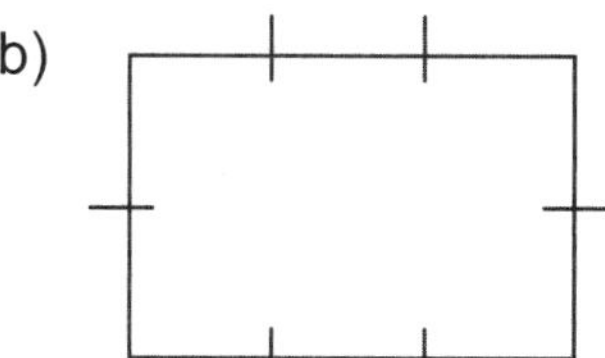 c) 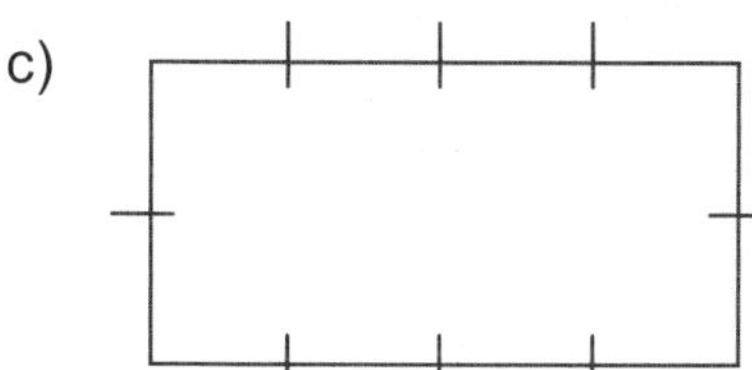

d) e) 

5. If you know the length and width of a rectangle, how can you find its area? Explain your answer on a separate piece of paper.

# ME4-34: Exploring Area

1. Measure the length and width of the figures, and then find the area.

a)

b) 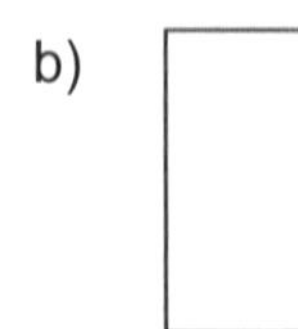

c) 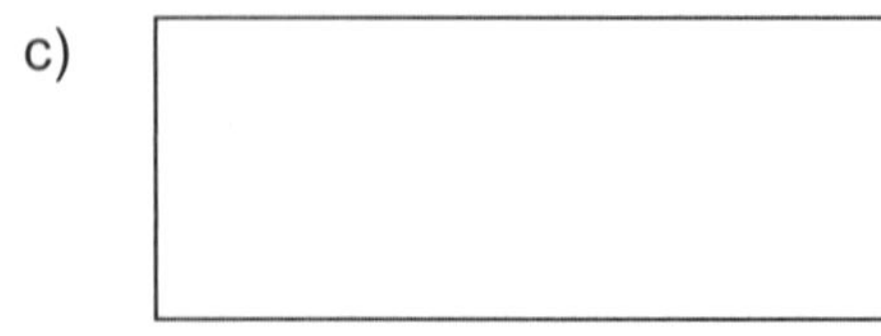

________________ ________________ ________________

Show your work for the remaining questions on a separate piece of paper.

2. Calculate the area of each rectangle (be sure to include the units). Then, by letter, create an ordered list of the rectangles from greatest to least area.

a) 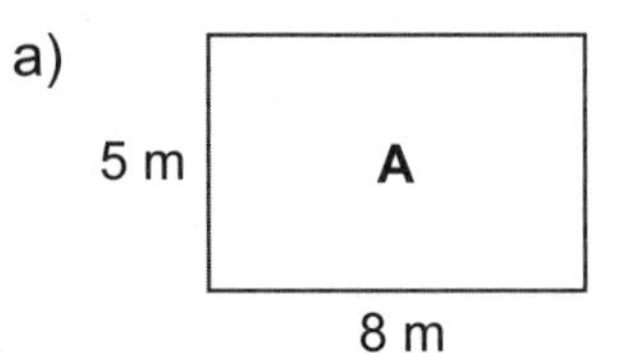


b) 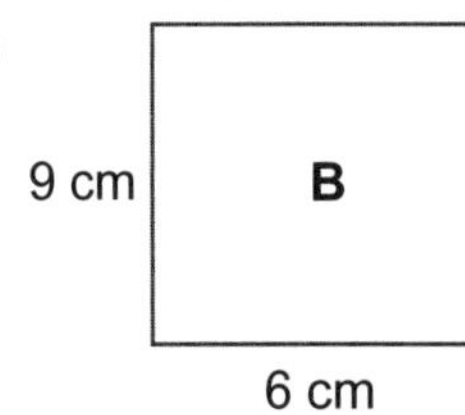


c) 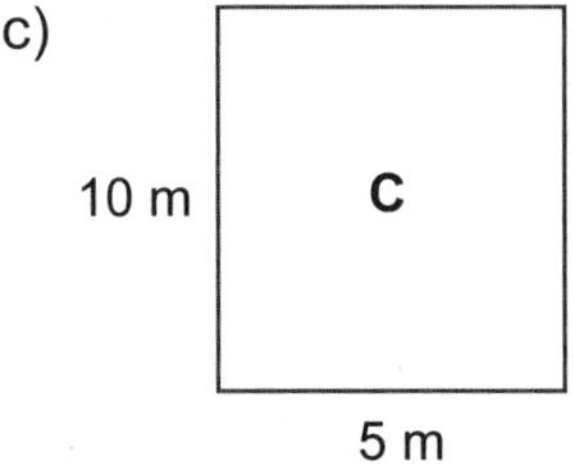


d) 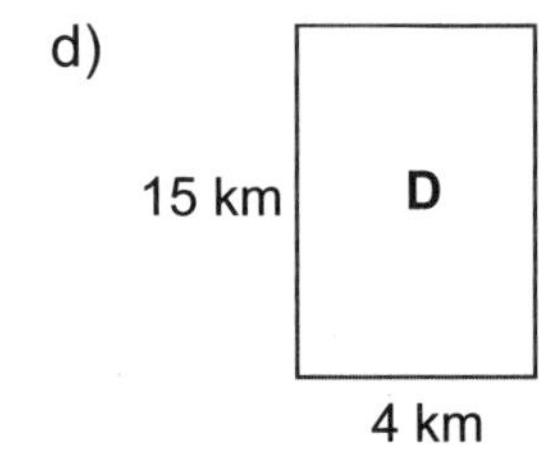


3. Find the area of the rectangle with the following dimensions:

   a) width: 5 m length: 7 m  b) width: 2 m length: 9 m  c) width: 6 cm length: 8 cm

4. A rectangle has an area of 10 $cm^2$ and a length of 5 cm. What is its width?

5. A rectangle has an area 15 $cm^2$ and a width 3 cm. What is its length?

6. A square has an area 9 $cm^2$. What is its width?

7. a) Draw 3 shapes on grid paper, each with an area of 10 square units. NOTE: The shapes do not have to be rectangles.

   b) Do shapes have to be congruent to have the same area?

8. Using grid paper or a geoboard, create 2 different rectangles with an area of 12 square units.

9. 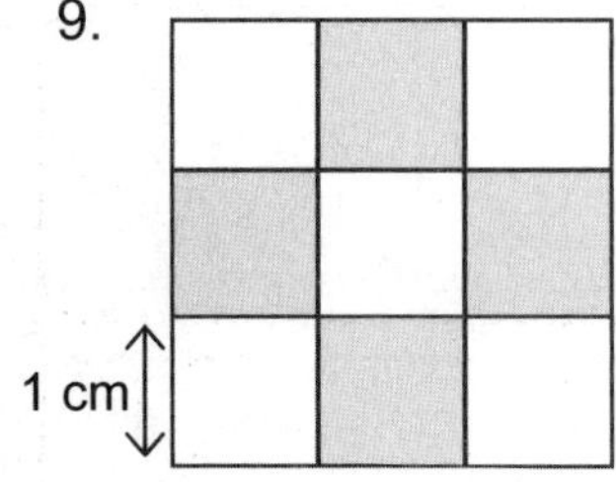


Jordan makes tiles using small black and white squares. Each small square has sides of 1 cm. Jordan arranges 4 tiles in a row.

   a) What is the area in square centimetres of the 4 tiles?

   b) What area of the 4 tiles is covered by black squares?

   c) What area of the 4 tiles is covered by white squares?

   d) How did you find your answer to part a)? Did you use a model? a list? a calculator?

# ME4-35: Area with Half Squares

1. Two half squares cover the same area as a whole square

Count each **pair** of half squares as a whole square to find the area shaded.

a) = _____ whole squares

b) = _____ whole squares

c) = _____ whole squares

d)

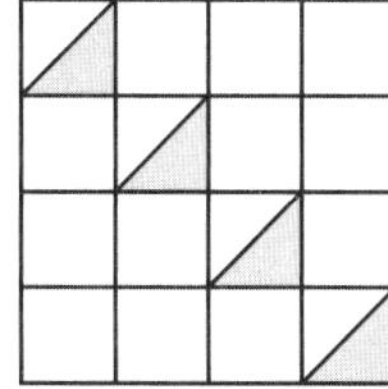

= _____ whole squares

e)

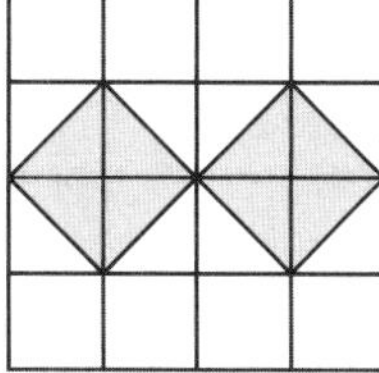

= _____ whole squares

f)

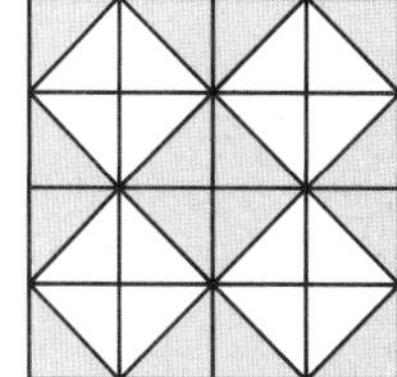

= _____ whole squares

g) = _____ whole squares

h)

= _____ whole squares

i)

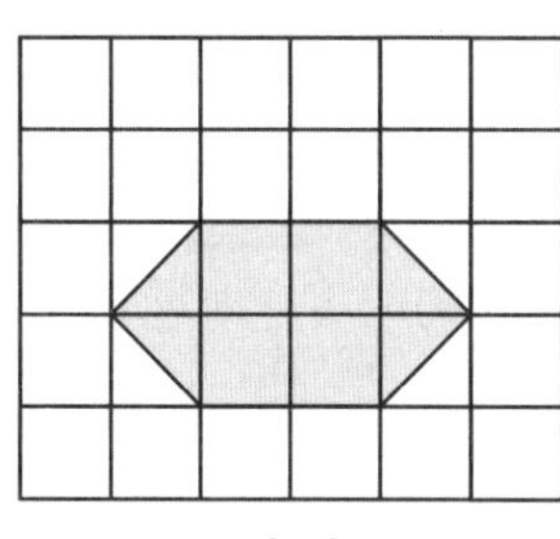

= _____ whole squares

j)

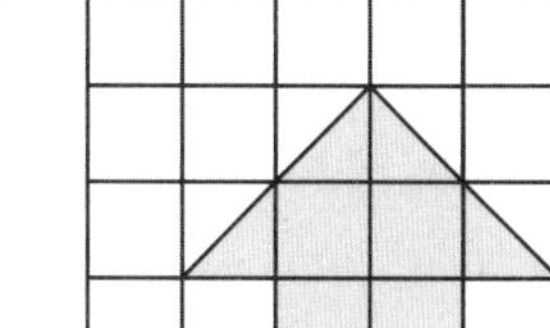

= _____ whole squares

k)

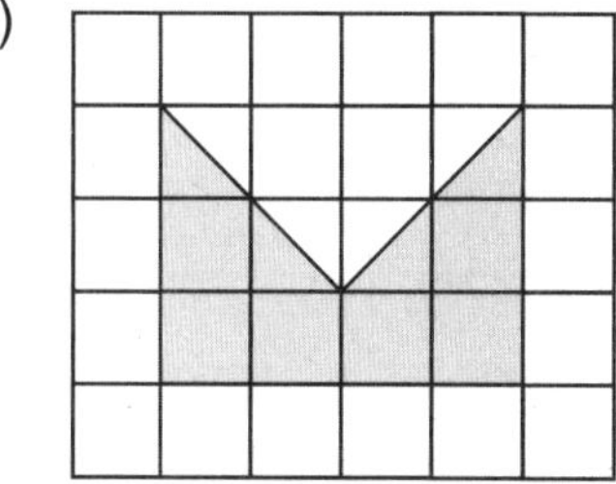

= _____ whole squares

2. Find the answer by dividing the number of half squares by 2.

a) 6 half squares = ____ whole squares

b) 8 half squares = ____ whole squares

c) 4 whole squares and 4 half squares = ____ whole squares

3. For each picture say whether the shaded area is **more** than, **less** than or **equal** to the unshaded area. Explain how you know.

a)

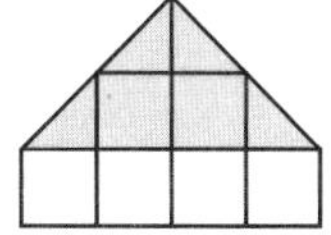

b)

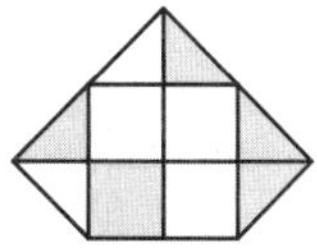

# ME4-36: Measuring the Area of Irregular Polygons

1. Each of the shaded shapes below represents ½ a square (whether divided diagonally, vertically, or horizontally). How many total squares do they add up to? REMEMBER: Two ½ squares = 1 full square.

a) 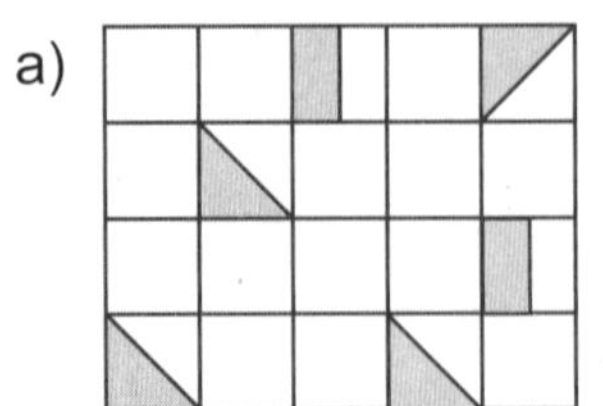

_____ half squares

_____ total squares

b) 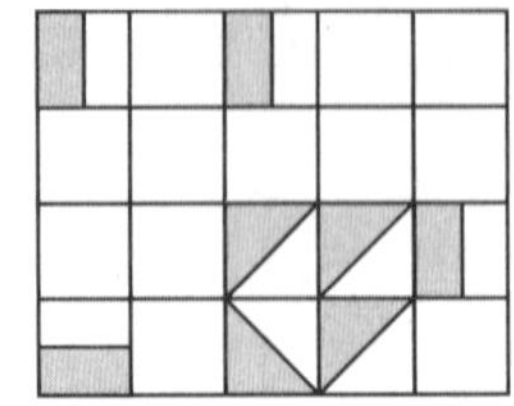

_____ half squares

_____ total squares

c) 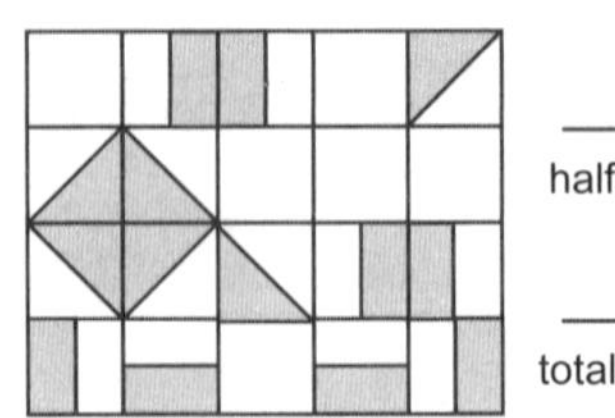

_____ half squares

_____ total squares

2. Fill in the blanks to find the total area. The first one is done for you.

a) 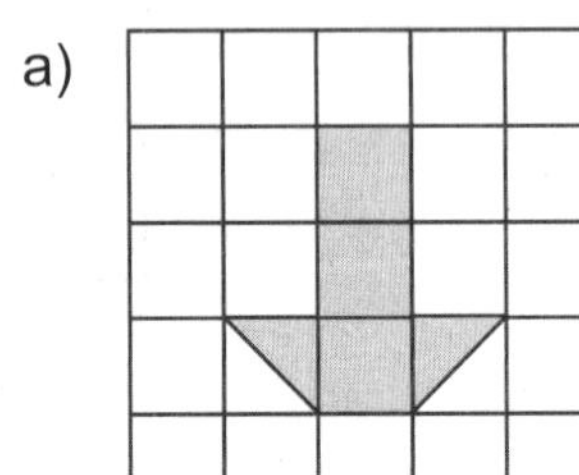

3 full squares

2 ½ squares

= 1 full squares

area = 3 + 1 = 4

b) 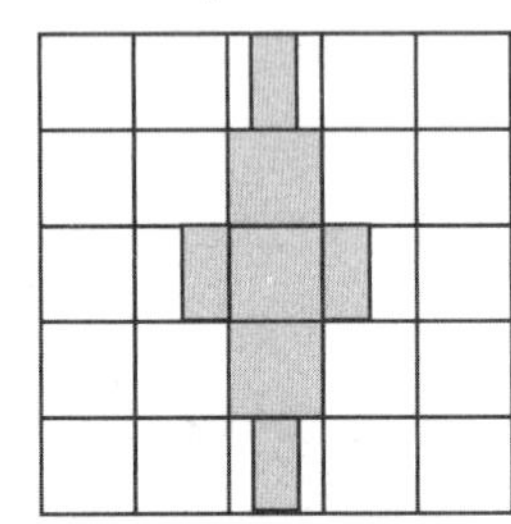

_____ full squares

_____ ½ squares

= _____ full squares

area =

c) 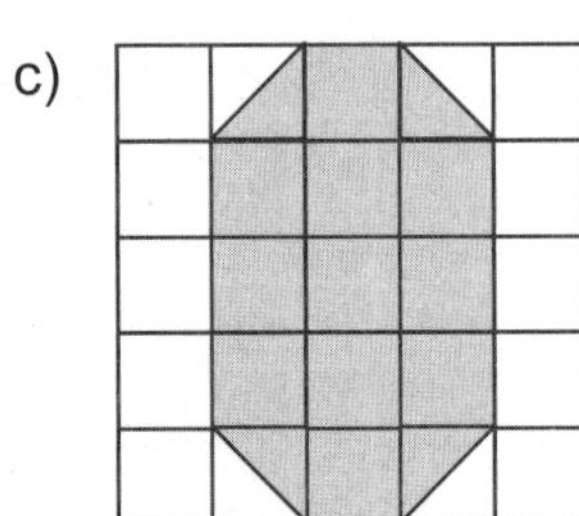

_____ full squares

_____ ½ squares

= _____ full squares

area =

d) 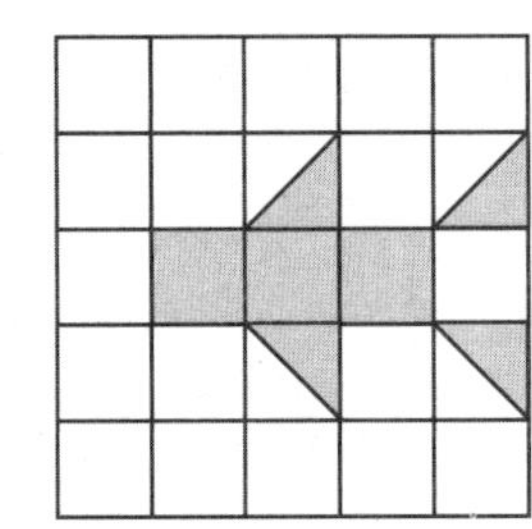

_____ full squares

_____ ½ squares

= _____ full squares

area =

3. Estimate the areas of the shaded figures below as follows:

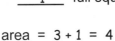

- Put a check mark in each **half** square: ✓, ✓, ✓, etc.
- Put an "X" in every **full** square **and** in every square with **more than half** shaded: × , × , × 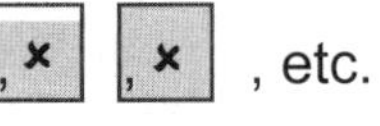, etc.
- Count all squares with an "X" as 1. Count 2 half squares (marked with a check) as 1.
- Do not count squares where **less than half** is shaded: , , etc.

a) 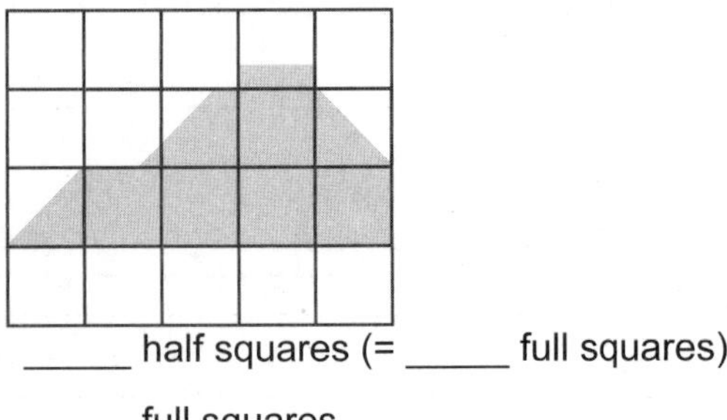

_____ half squares (= _____ full squares)

\+ _____ full squares

= _____ total squares

b) 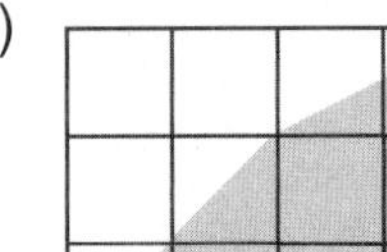 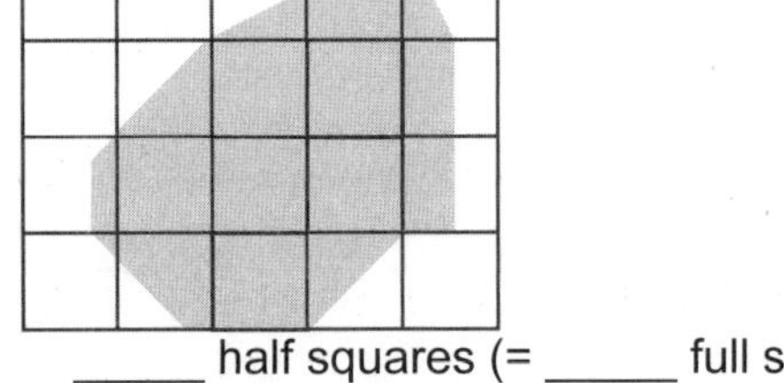

_____ half squares (= _____ full squares)

\+ _____ full squares

= _____ total squares

# ME4-37: Comparing Area and Perimeter

1. For each shape, calculate the perimeter and area of each shape, and write your answers in the chart. The first one is done for you. NOTE: Each square represents a centimetre.

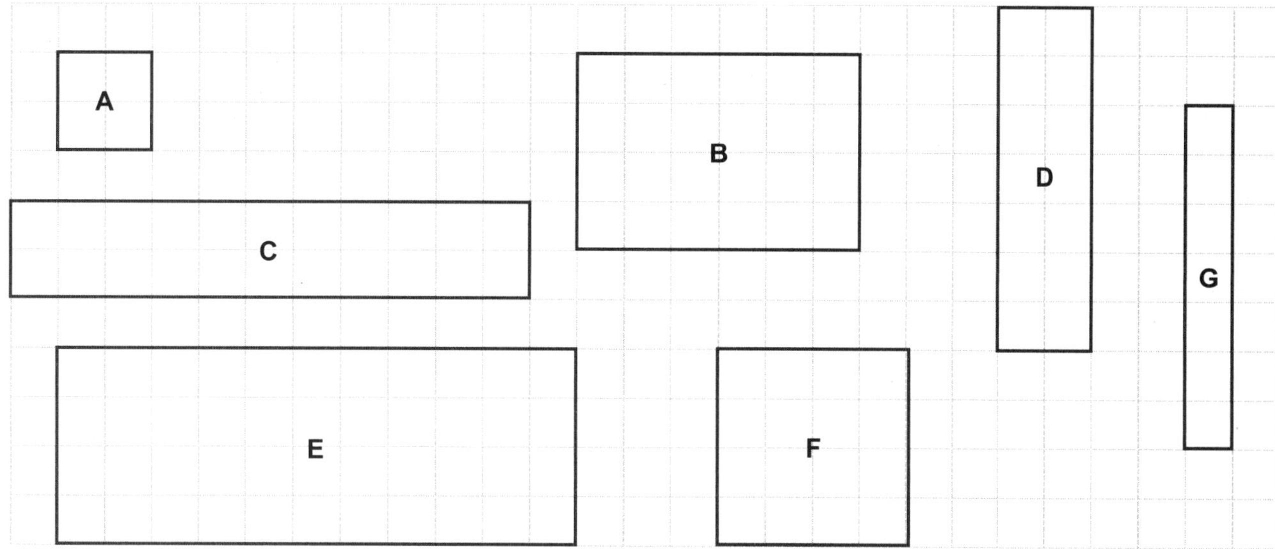


| Shape | Perimeter | Area |
|---|---|---|
| A | 2 + 2 + 2 + 2 = 8 cm | 2 x 2 = 4 $cm^2$ |
| B | | |
| C | | |
| D | | |
| E | | |
| F | | |
| G | | |

2. Shape C has greater perimeter than shape B. Does it also have greater area? ____________

3. Name two other shapes where one has a greater perimeter and the other, a greater area.

______________________________

4. Write the shapes in order from greatest to least perimeter. ______________________________

5. Write the shapes in order from greatest to least area. ______________________________

6. Are the orders in questions 4 and 5 the same? ____________________

7. What is the difference between PERIMETER and AREA? ______________________________

______________________________________________________________

______________________________________________________________

# ME4-38: Area and Perimeter

1. For each rectangle, measure the length and width and then record your answers in the chart. The first one is done for you.

5 cm

3 cm A

B

C

G

E

F

D

| Rectangle | Estimated perimeter | Estimated area | Length | Width | Actual perimeter | Actual area |
|---|---|---|---|---|---|---|
| A | cm | $cm^2$ | cm | cm | cm | $cm^2$ |
| B | | | | | | |
| C | | | | | | |
| D | | | | | | |
| E | | | | | | |
| F | | | | | | |
| G | | | | | | |

2. Measure the perimeter and find the area for each rectangle below with a ruler.

a)

Perimeter = _______ cm

Area = _______ $cm^2$

b) 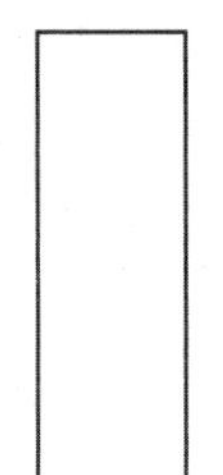

Perimeter = _______ cm

Area = _______ $cm^2$

c) 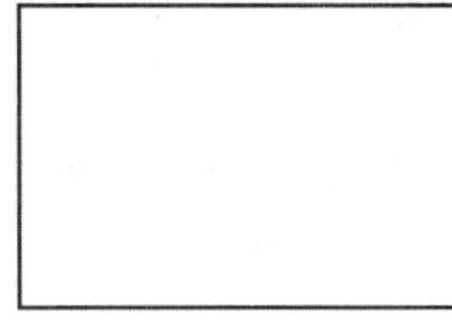

Perimeter = _______ cm

Area = _______ $cm^2$

3. Find the area of the rectangle using the clues. Show your work on a separate piece of paper.

   a) Width = 2 cm  Perimeter = 10 cm  Area = ?  b) Width = 4 cm  Perimeter = 18 cm  Area = ?

4. Draw a square on grid paper with the given perimeter. Then find the area of the square.

   a) Perimeter = 12 cm  Area = ?  b) Perimeter = 20 cm  Area = ?

# ME4-39: Mass



**Mass** measures the amount of substance in a thing. Grams (g) and kilograms (kg) are units for measuring weight or mass.

One kilogram is equal to 1000 g.

| Things that weigh about one **gram**: | Things that weigh about one **kilogram**: |
|---|---|
| ✓ a paper clip | ✓ a one-litre bottle of water |
| ✓ a dime | ✓ a bag of 200 nickels |
| ✓ a chocolate chip | ✓ a squirrel |

NOTE:
Before you answer the questions below, try to feel the weight of an object that weighs about 1 g and an object that weighs about 1 kg.

---

1. If one paper clip has a weight of approximately one gram, how much would . . .

   a) 2 paper clips weigh?   b) 8 paper clips weigh?

   Now, hold a paper clip in one hand, and your pencil in the other. How many paper clips would you need to balance the weight of the pencil?

   c) About how much does your pencil weigh?    d) About how much does your pen weigh?

2. If a dime has a weight of approximately one gram, how much would . . .

   a) 30¢ in dimes weigh?   b) 50¢ in dimes weigh?   c) 80¢ in dimes weigh?

3. Estimate the weight of the following things, in grams:

   a) a chocolate chip cookie   b) an apple   c) a shoe

4. Can you name an object that weighs about one gram?

5. If a squirrel weighs one kilogram, how much would . . .

   a) 3 squirrels weigh?   b) 7 squirrels weigh?

6. Imagine a small animal like a squirrel or a guinea pig (which weighs about 1 kg) and compare it to your own size. How many squirrels would you need to balance your weight?

   Use your answer to estimate your own weight. Then measure your weight. Was your estimate close?

7. Estimate the weight of the following things in kilograms:

   a) your math book   b) your desk   c) a bicycle

ACTIVITIES:

- Weigh your pencil and your pen, and compare their actual weights to your estimates in question 1.
- Weigh a measuring cup. Pour 10 mL of water in the cup. Calculate the mass of the water by subtracting the weight of the cup from the weight of the water with the cup. How much do 10 mL of water weigh? (How much does 1 mL of water weigh?)

8. Match the objects on the left with objects on the right that have a similar weight.

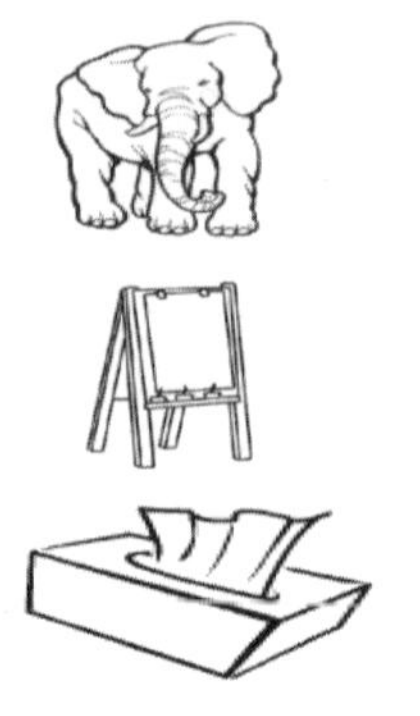

9. What unit is more appropriate to measure each item? Circle the appropriate unit.

 grams or kilograms?

 grams or kilograms?

 grams or kilograms?

ACTIVITY (using balance scales and masses):

10. Select 5 small- to medium-sized objects in your home.
    a) Estimate the mass of each object.
    b) Measure and record the mass of each object.
    c) Order the measurements from greatest to least.
    d) Compare your measurements with your estimates.

11. a) Order (by letter) the following from **least to greatest** mass:

    **A.** blue whale **B.** ant **C.** horse ______, ______, ______

    b) Order (by letter) the following from **greatest to least** mass:

    **A.** 10-year-old human **B.** house cat **C.** elephant ______, ______, ______

12. Check off the appropriate box. Would you use grams or kilograms to weigh . . .

| | | | | | |
|---|---|---|---|---|---|
| a) a moose? | ☐ **g** | ☐ **kg** | b) a desk? | ☐ **g** | ☐ **kg** |
| c) a piece of cheese? | ☐ **g** | ☐ **kg** | d) a tiny bird? | ☐ **g** | ☐ **kg** |
| e) a pencil? | ☐ **g** | ☐ **kg** | f) yourself? | ☐ **g** | ☐ **kg** |

13. Circle the weight that is more appropriate for the object in the picture. How did you know? Explain.

22 kilograms OR 222 grams

130 grams OR 13 kilograms

14. Answer the questions based on the given information on the weight of Canadian coins.
NOTE: The approximate weights of each coin are given below.

| | |
|---|---|
| **nickel** | **5 grams** |
| **dime** | **1 gram** |
| **quarter** | **6 grams** |
| **loonie** | **7 grams** |

a) How much would 15¢ in nickels weigh? ______________

b) How much would 9 dimes weigh? ______________

c) How much would $1.00 in quarters weigh? ______________

d) How much would two loonies weigh? ______________

e) How many quarters weigh as much as 6 nickels? ______________

f) Estimate how much a toonie weighs. ______________

15. Write in the missing masses to balance the scales.

a) 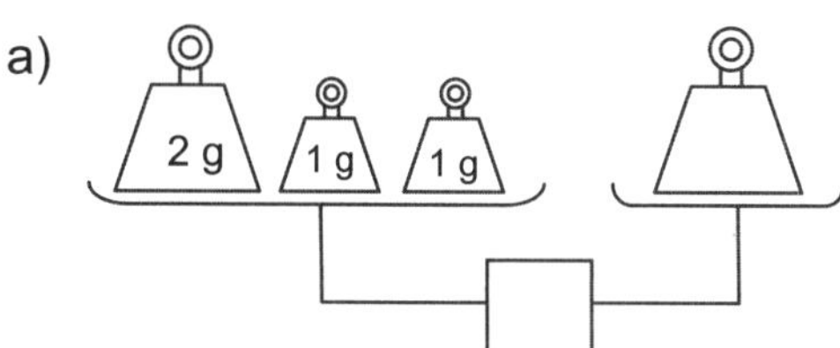


b) 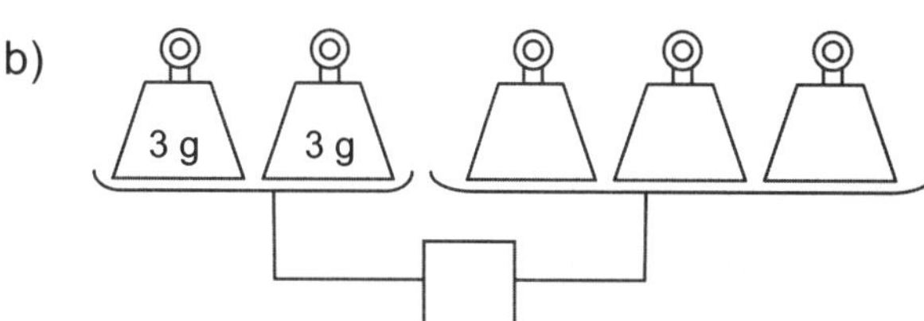


Answer the remaining problems on a separate piece of paper.

16. a) Eric's niece Jennifer weighed 5 kg when she was born. She grew at a rate of 2 kg each week. How much did Jennifer weigh when she was one month old?

b) Tomato and eggplant seeds weigh 2 g each and zucchini seeds weigh 3 g each. Daniel bought 12 tomato seeds, 8 eggplant seeds, and 5 zucchini seeds. How much did his seeds weigh altogether?

17. A male hippo weighing 1876 kg and a female hippo weighing 1347 kg are bathing in a river. How much less does the female weigh than the male?

18. A mail carrier is carrying 300 letters in her bag. Each letter has a mass of about 20 g. What is the total mass of the letters?

19. Solve the following word problems involving grams and kilograms:

a) The cost of shipping a package is $2.00 for each kilogram shipped. How much does it cost to ship a package that weighs 12 kg?

b) A spoon weighs approximately 60 g. How much would 2 spoons weigh?

c) There are 15 salmon in the pond, and each weighs approximately two kilograms. What is the total weight of all the salmon in the pond?

# ME4-40: Capacity

The **capacity** of a container is how much it can hold. For example, the capacity of a regular carton of milk is 1 L.

Litres (L) and millilitres (mL) are the basic units for measuring capacity → 1 litre (L) = 1000 millilitres (mL)

**Some sample capacities**

| | | |
|---|---|---|
| 1 teaspoon = 5 mL | 1 can of pop = 350 mL | 1 regular carton of juice = 1 L |
| 1 tube of toothpaste = 75 mL | 1 large bottle of shampoo = 750 mL | 1 large can of paint = 3 to 5 L |

NOTE:
Before you answer the questions, measure 100 mL, 500 mL, 1 L, and 5 L of water using measuring cups.

---

Answer the following questions on a separate piece of paper:

1. Clare fills a measuring cup with 40 mL of water. She pours out some water and notices there are 30 mL left. How much water did she pour out?

2. Check off the appropriate box. Would you use millilitres (mL) or litres (L) to weigh . . .

   a) a cup of tea? ☐ **mL** ☐ **L**  b) a rain drop? ☐ **mL** ☐ **L**

   c) a bath tub? ☐ **mL** ☐ **kg**  d) a bucket of ice cream? ☐ **mL** ☐ **kg**

   e) a swimming pool? ☐ **mL** ☐ **kg**  f) a medicine bottle? ☐ **mL** ☐ **kg**

3. Circle the appropriate unit to measure the capacity of each container. Is it litres (L) or millilitres (mL)?

   a)  L or mL?  b)  L or mL?

   c) 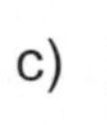  L or mL?  d)  L or mL?

4. Which set of containers has the greatest capacity? How do you know?

   a) 

   **OR**

   b) 

5. 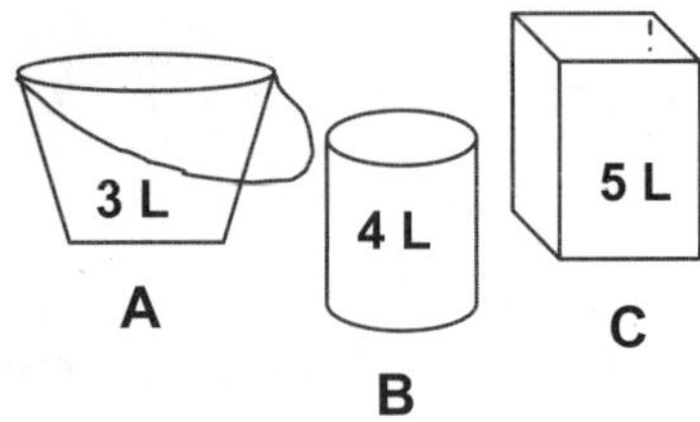


   a) How many containers of size C would hold 20 L?

   b) How many containers of size A would hold as much water as 3 containers of size B?

   c) Which will hold more, 4 containers of size B or 3 containers of size C?

6. For each of the following capacities, how many containers would be needed to make a litre? Explain how you know.

   a) 100 mL  b) 200 mL  c) 500 mL  d) 250 mL

7. Long ago, in Ninevah, an Assyrian woman filled a large clay vessel with water using a jug with a capacity of 250 mL. She filled and emptied the jug 4 times to fill the large vessel. What was the large vessel's capacity? (Can you write the capacity in 2 different ways?)

# ME4-41: Mass and Capacity

1. 1 kilogram = 1000 grams        1 kilometre = 1000 metres

   Looking at the equations above, what do you think the Latin word "kilo" means? ____________

2. What do you need to multiply a measurement in kilograms by to change it to grams? ____________

3. Change the following measurements to grams:

   a) 3 kg = ________   b) 9 kg = ________   c) 17 kg = ________   d) 25 kg = ________

4. Write an estimate of your weight in kilograms and change your estimate to grams.

5. a) A baby has a mass of 4000 g, which is the same as 4 kg. Another baby has a mass of 3000 g. What is its mass in kilograms? __________

   b) What fact did you use to change grams to kilograms?

6. A house cat weighs about 5 kg. What is its mass in grams? ____________

7. Below are masses of 1 bottle of an herb or spice. Each bottle is the same size. Order the bottles of spices and herbs by mass. Since the bottles are all the same size, why do you think the masses are different?

| | | |
|---|---|---|
| **A** ground cinnamon 50 g | **B** whole ginger 32 g | **C** tarragon leaves 9 g |
| **D** oregano leaves 13 g | **E** ground coriander 45 g | **F** whole cloves 35 g |

8. What do you need to multiply a measurement in litres by to change it to millilitres? ____________

9. Change the following measurements to millilitres:

   a) 5 L = __________   b) 2 L = __________   c) 12 L = __________   d) 47 L = __________

10. a) A bowl has a capacity of 2 L, which is the same as 2000 mL. Another bowl has a capacity of 3 L. What is its capacity in millilitres? __________

    b) A feeding trough has a capacity of 1500 mL, which is the same as 1.5 L. Another trough has a capacity of 2500 mL. What is its capacity in litres? __________

    c) What fact do you use to change millilitres to litres? ____________________________

11. a) Which will be more shampoo, four 250 mL bottles or three 300 mL bottles?_______

    b) A pitcher holds 500 mL. A tub holds 5 L. Which has a greater capacity: 10 pitchers or 2 tubs?

    ____________

12. Jenna is carrying groceries. In her bag there is a 1-L carton of milk, a 500-mL bottle of olive oil, a 500-mL bottle of vinegar, and a 700-mL jar of tomato sauce. What is the total capacity of the items in millilitres?

13. Karl has 2 watering cans with a capacity of 2 L and 5 L.
    a) How many times does he need to fill the 2-L can to give his flowers 12 L of water?
    b) How should he use the 2 watering cans to give his flowers 17 L of water with the fewest number of fill-ups?

14. For each recipe . . .
    a) circle the measurements of capacity
    b) underline the measurements of mass
    c) total the measurements of mass
    c) total the measurements of capacity

| **Ice cream** | **Tomato sauce** | **Birthday cake** |
|---|---|---|
| 1 L fresh fruit | 30 mL olive oil | 115 g butter |
| 50 mL lemon juice | 800 mL can of tomatoes | 300 g sugar |
| 250 mL heavy cream | 30 mL tomato paste | 2 eggs |
| 250 mL light cream | 5 g fresh oregano | 280 g flour |
| 150 g sugar | 2 g fresh basil | 150 mL milk |

15. Circle True or False for each question.

| | | |
|---|---|---|
| a) You would measure the weight of a car in litres. | **True** | **False** |
| b) A gram is used to measure volume. | **True** | **False** |
| c) The contents of a can of pop are usually measured in kilograms. | **True** | **False** |
| d) Grams are used to measure the weight of objects. | **True** | **False** |

16. Circle the greater measure in each pair.

| | | | | | |
|---|---|---|---|---|---|
| a) 25 g | 35 g | b) 20 g | 17 g | c) 3 L | 5 L |
| d) 50 g | 2 kg | e) 400 mL | 1 L | f) 2000 mL | 1 L |

17. Explain how you know your answers in question 16. d) and e) are correct.

18. Write a unit of measurement to make each statement reasonable.
    a) A tea cup hold about 200 _____ of tea.
    b) A chair has a mass of about 4 _______.
    c) A house cat weights over 1000 _______.
    d) A bucket holds about 2 ______ of water.

19. Use some of these masses of Antarctic birds to create a problem about mass. Solve your problem.
    **Emperor Penguin** 45 kg; **Adelie Penguin** 6.5 kg; **Giant Antarctic Petrel** 5 kg; **Cape Petrel** 550 g; **Snow Petrel** 300 g; **Storm Petrel** 34 g.

ACTIVITY (using measuring cups and scales):

20. Collect 5 containers (cups, cans, bottles, pails) of different sizes.
    a) Estimate the capacity of each container.
    b) Measure and record the capacity of each container.
    c) Order the measurements from greatest to least.
    d) Compare your measurements with your estimates.

21. a) Weigh a container that will hold 1 L of water. Record your measurement.
    b) Measure 1 L of water and pour it into the container. Weigh the container with the water in it.
    c) How can you calculate the mass of 1 L of water using the 2 measurements you made?
    d) What do you notice about the mass of the water?

# ME4-42: Volume

**Volume** is the amount of space taken up by a 3-D object. To measure volume, we use 1-cm blocks. These blocks are uniform squares with a length, width, and height of 1-cm long:

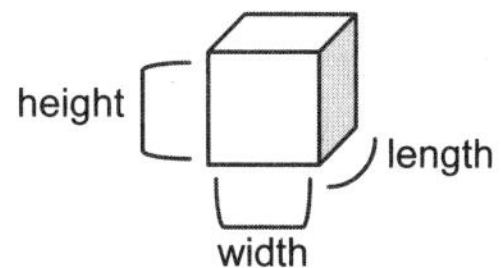


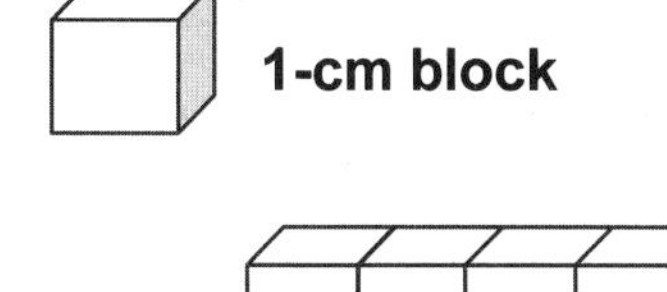

**1-cm block**

The volume of a container is based on how many of these 1-cm blocks will fit inside the container.

This object, made of centimetre cubes, has a volume 4 cubes or 4 cubic centimetres (written 4 $cm^3$).

---

Answer the written parts of the questions on a separate piece of paper.

1. Using "cubes" as your unit of measurement, write the **volume** of each object.

a) 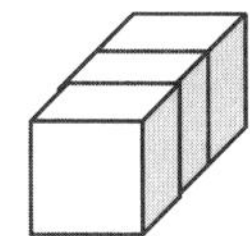

Number of cubes: _____

b)

Number of cubes: _____

c) 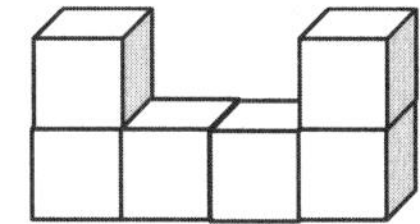

Number of cubes: _____

d) 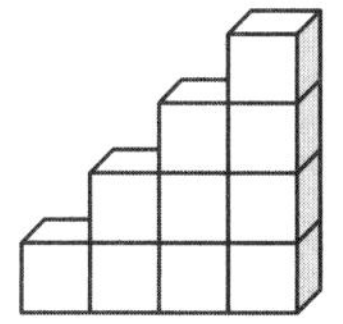

Number of cubes: _____

e) 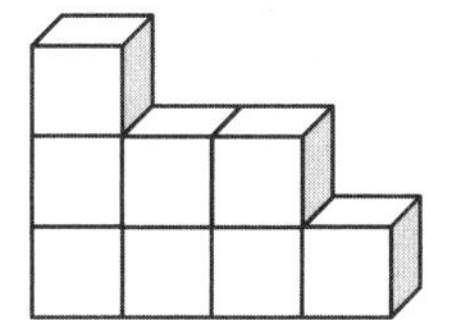

Number of cubes: _____

f) 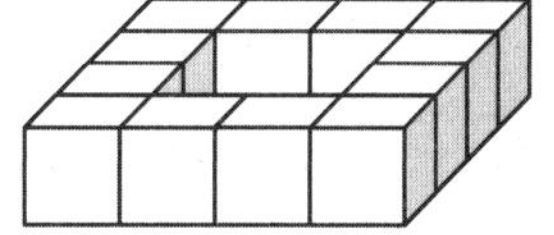

Number of cubes: _____

2. Find the volume (in cubes) of the shapes. Explain how you counted the cubes you could not see.

a) Volume: ________

b) 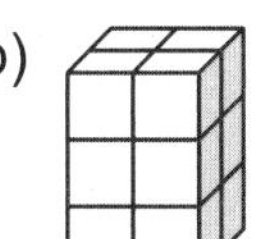 Volume: ________

c) 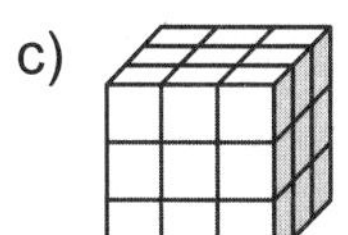 Volume: ________

3. Which object has the greatest volume? _____

How can you tell without counting the cubes?

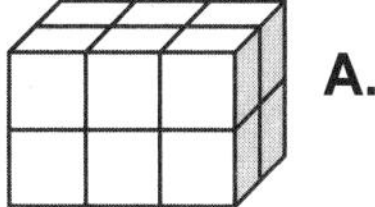 **A.**

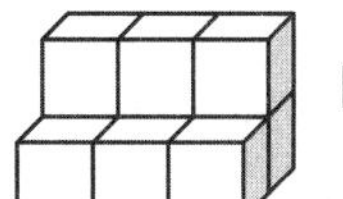 **B.**

4. Which object has the greatest volume? _____
How can you tell?

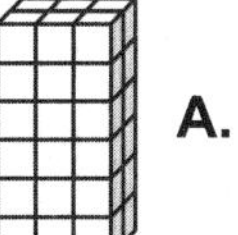 **A.**

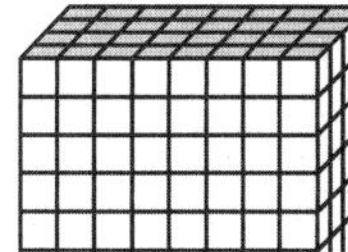 **B.**

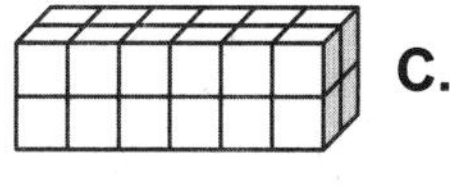 **C.**

ACTIVITY (using a rectangular box, like a cereal box):

5. Use centimetre cubes to find the volume of a rectangular prism. (Estimate the volume first.)

6. For each pair, circle the shape with the greater volume. If they have the **same** volume, circle both.

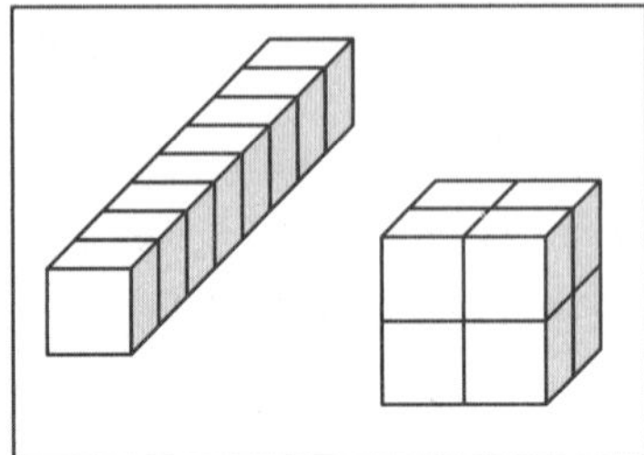
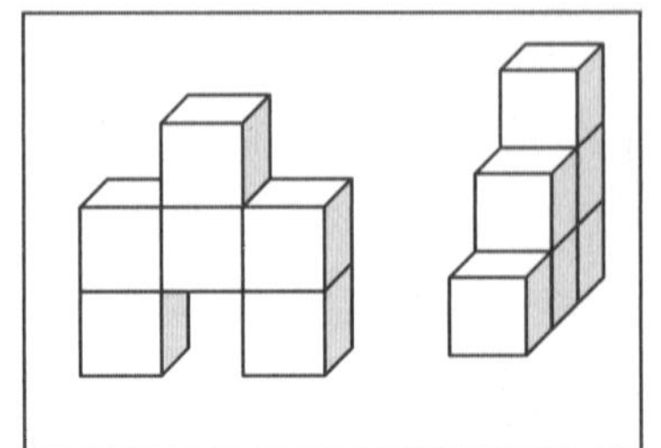
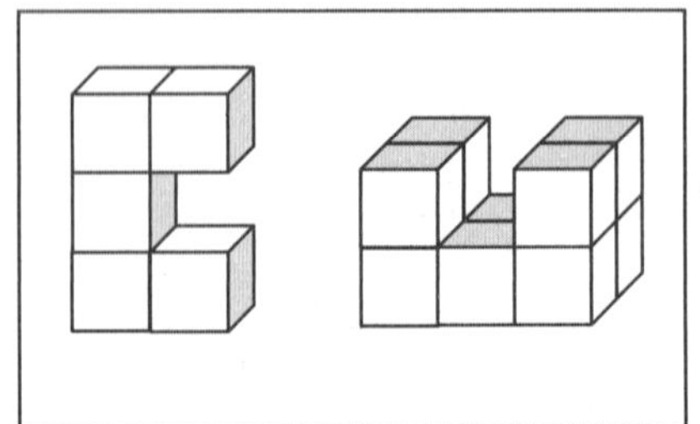

7. Find the volume. Write your answer in cubic centimetres. (How can you use skip counting to help?) (HINT: For part b), start by finding the volume of the bottom layer of cubes.)

a) 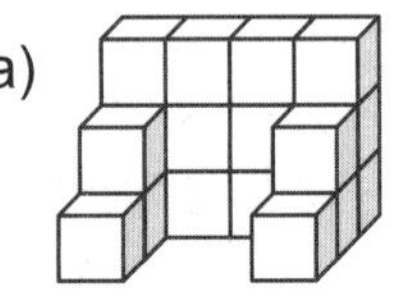

Volume of bottom layer: _______

Volume of second layer: _______

Volume of top layer: _________

b) 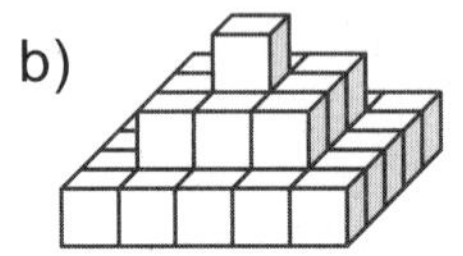

Volume of bottom layer: _______

Volume of second layer: _______

Volume of top layer: _________

8. 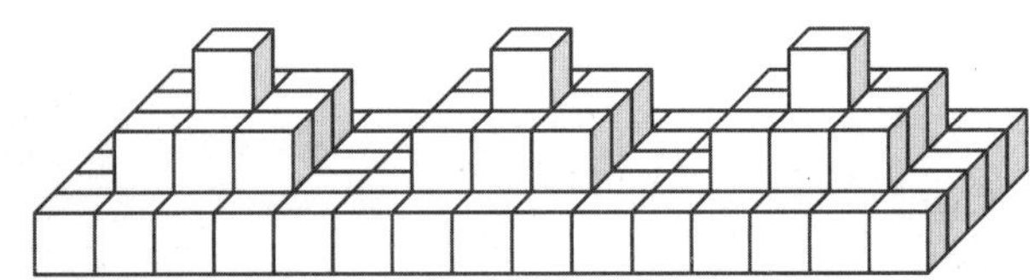

How can you calculate the volume of this structure by using your work from question 7. b)? Explain on a separate piece of paper.

9. Given a structure made of cubes, you can draw a top view as shown:

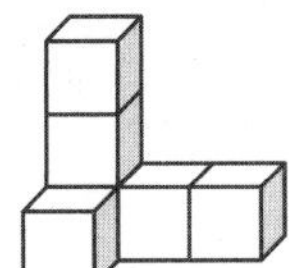
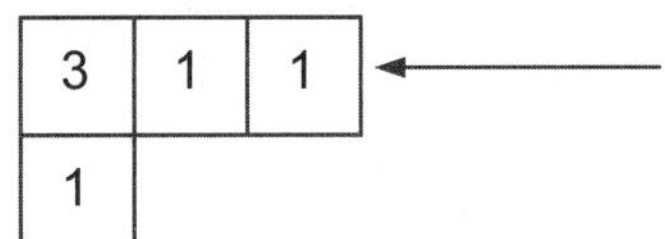


The numbers tell you how many cubes are stacked in each position.

For each figure, fill in the missing numbers in the top view.

a) 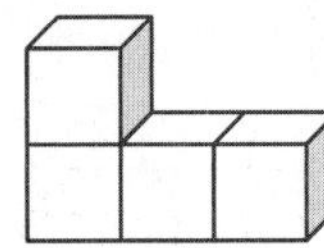 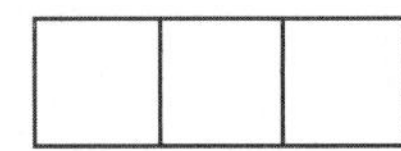

b) 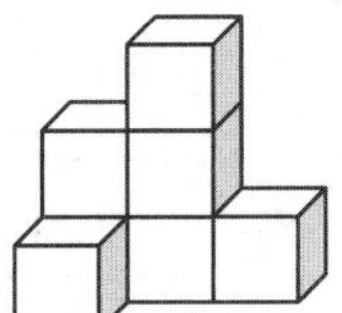 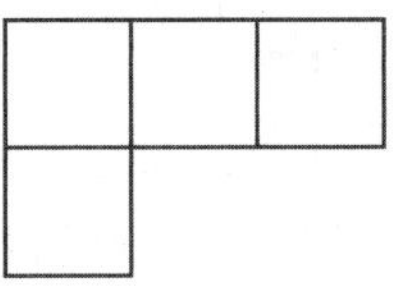

10. On grid paper, draw a top view for each of the following structures (use cubes to help):

a) 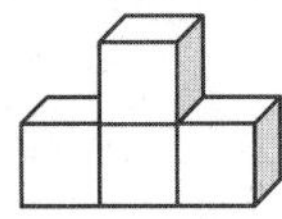

b) 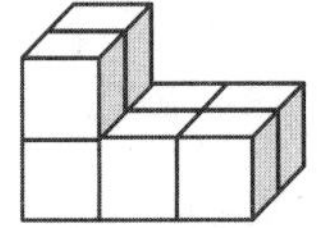

c) 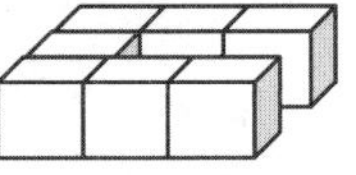

d) 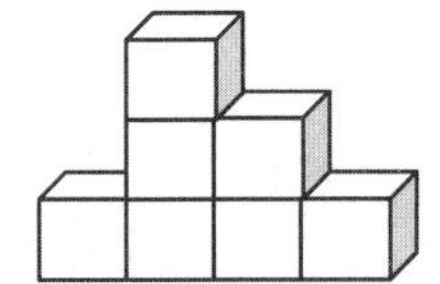

11. Using centicubes, build two different shapes that have a volume of exactly 8 cubic centimetres. Draw a top view of each of your shapes on a separate piece of paper.

12. How many different rectangular prisms can you build with 8 cubes? Draw a top view for each of your shapes on a separate piece of paper.

# ME4-43: Problems and Puzzles

1. On grid paper draw a rectangle with . . .

   a) an area of 10 squares units and a perimeter of 14 units

   b) an area of 12 square units and a perimeter of 14 units.

2. Sherry measures the area of a rhombus and a trapezoid using triangles. **Two** triangles cover a rhombus and **three** triangles cover a trapezoid. How many triangles are needed to cover . . .

   a) 5 rhombuses?  b) 6 trapezoids?  c) 3 rhombuses and 4 trapezoids?

3. 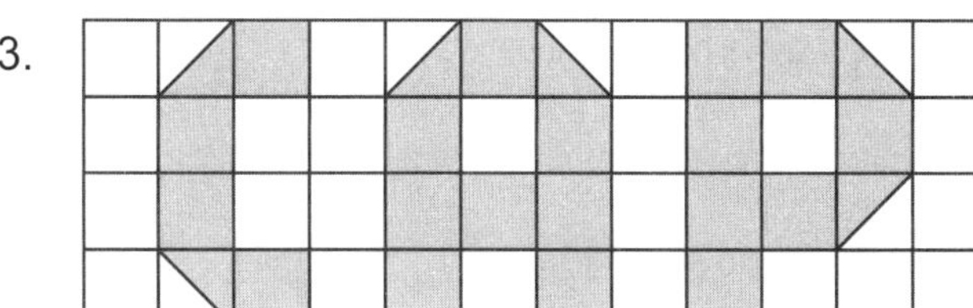

   a) Find the area of the shaded pattern block word.

   b) There are 48 squares in the grid. How can you use your answer above to find the number of **unshaded** squares (without counting them)?

4. On grid paper, shade squares to make your own letter or word. Then find its area.

5. Raj wants to build a rectangular flower bed in his garden. The width of the flower bed will be 2 m and the perimeter will be 12 m. NOTE: Each edge on the grid represents 1 m.

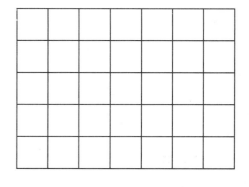

   a) Draw a sketch to show the shape of the flower bed.

   b) What is the length of the bed?

   c) Raj wants to build a fence about the bed. If fencing is $7 a metre, how much will the fencing cost?

   d) Raj will plant 14 flowers on each square metre of land. Each flower is 9¢. How much will the flowers cost?

   e) If Raj pays for the flowers with 6 toonies, how much change will he get back?

6. Find the total area of shaded and unshaded squares. Record your answers on a separate sheet of paper. Then say whether "less than half," "half," or "more than half" of the total area is shaded.

   a) 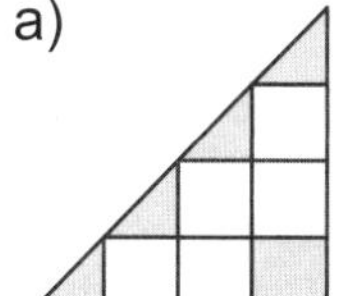

   b) 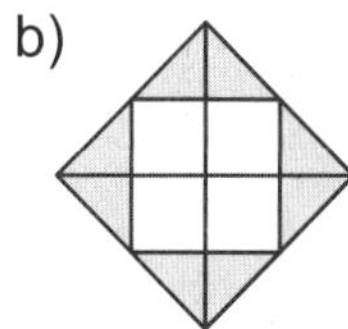

7. a) 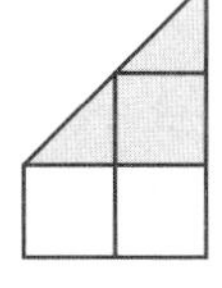

   It took George one hour to paint the part of the house that is shaded. How long will it take him to paint the rest? How do you know?

   b) 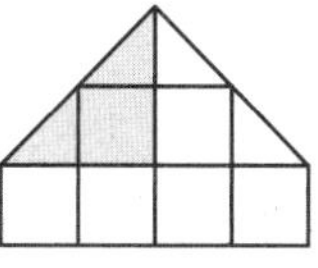

   It took Sally one hour to paint the part of the house that is shaded. How long will it take her to paint the rest? How do you know?

# PDM4-13: Outcomes

**Outcomes:** The different ways an event can turn out are called **outcomes** of the event.

When Alice plays a game of cards with a friend, there are 3 possible outcomes: Alice (1) wins, (2) loses, or (3) the game ends without a winner or a loser (this is sometimes called a **tie** or a **draw**).

REMEMBER: A coin has 2 sides, heads and tails:  A die has six sides, numbered 1 to 6: 

---

1. What are the possible outcomes when . . .

   a) you flip a coin? ______________________

   b) you roll a die (a cube with numbers from one to six on its faces)? ______________________

   c) you roll a triangular pyramid? ______________________

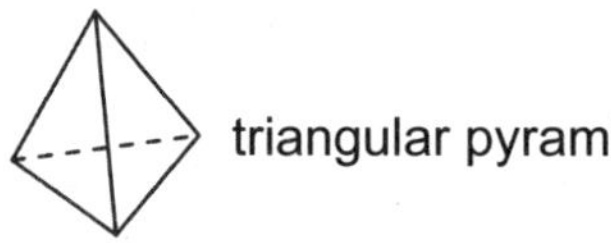


2. How many **different** outcomes are there when you . . .

   a) roll a die? _____ b) flip a coin? _____ c) play chess with a friend? _____

3. What are the possible outcomes for these spinners? The first one is done for you.

a) 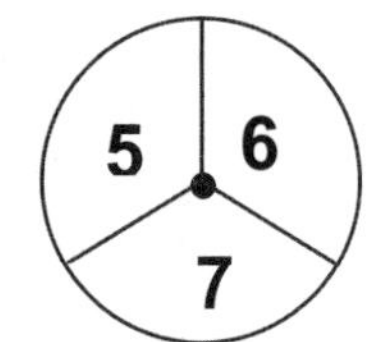


you spin a 5 or a 6 or a 7

b) 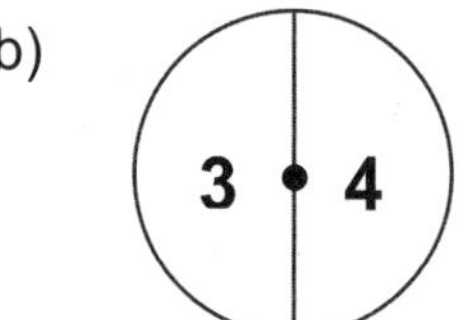


______________

c) 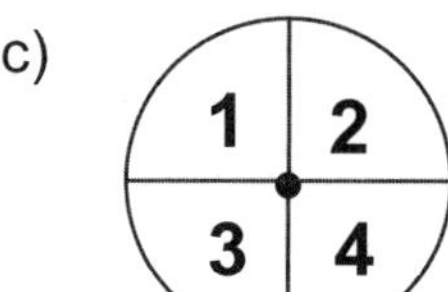


______________

d) 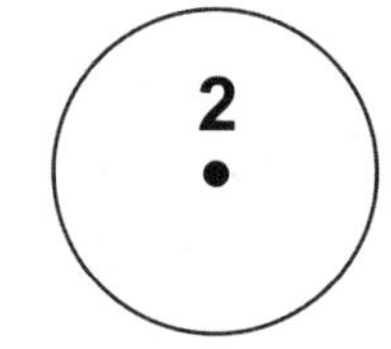


______________

4. How many outcomes are there for each spinner in question 3?

   a) _____ outcomes b) _____ outcomes c) _____ outcomes d) _____ outcome

5. You draw a ball from a box. How many different outcomes are there in each of the following cases?

a) 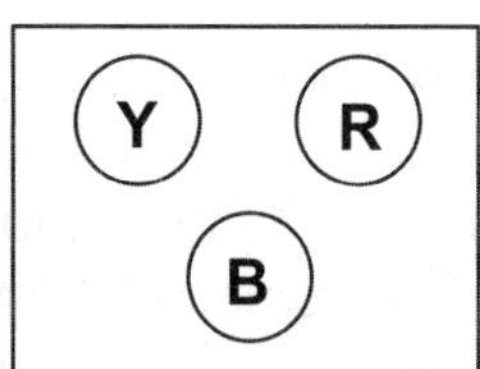


_____ outcomes

b) 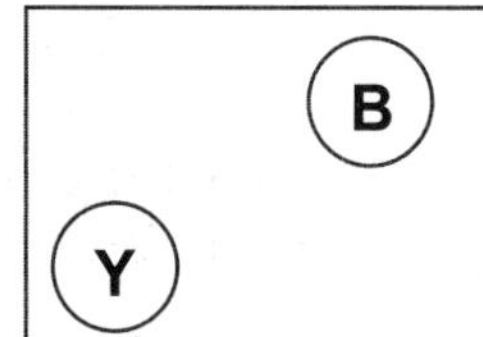


_____ outcomes

c) 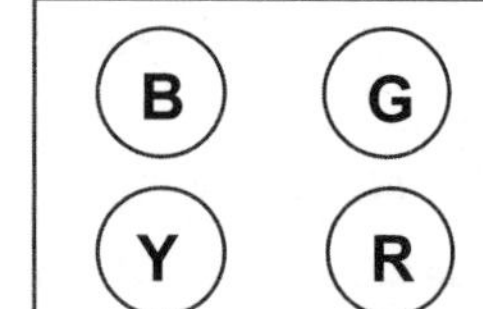


______________

d) 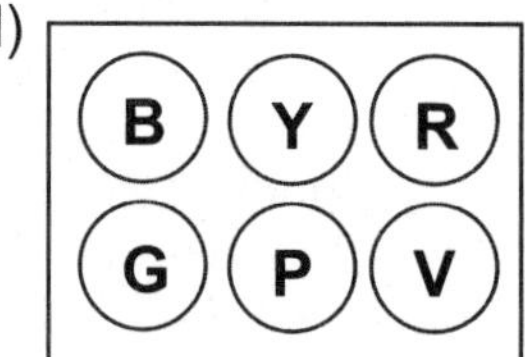


______________

# PDM4-14: Counting Combinations

Paul wants to know how many outcomes there are for a game with two spinners. He makes a list that shows all the ways he can spin a colour on the first spinner and a number on the second spinner:

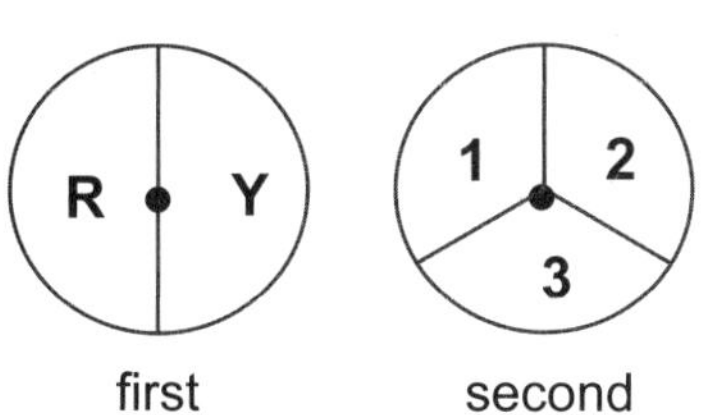


Step 1:
There are 3 **outcomes** on the second spinner. So Paul lists each colour on the first spinner **3 times**.

| First spinner | Second spinner |
|---|---|
| R | |
| R | |
| R | |
| Y | |
| Y | |
| Y | |

Step 2:
Beside each colour Paul writes the 3 possible outcomes on the second spinner.

| First spinner | Second spinner |
|---|---|
| R | 1 |
| R | 2 |
| R | 3 |
| Y | 1 |
| Y | 2 |
| Y | 3 |

The list shows that Paul could spin a red on the first spinner and a 1, 2, or 3 on the second spinner. Or Paul could spin a yellow on the first spinner and a 1, 2, or 3 on the second spinner. There are 6 outcomes for the game.

---

For each question, answer parts a) and b) first. Then complete the list of combinations to show all the ways Paul can spin a colour and a number.

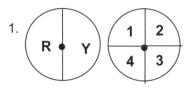

1. R Y | 1 2 4 3

| First spinner | Second spinner |
|---|---|
| | |

a) How many outcomes are there on the second spinner? ____________

b) How many times should Paul write R (for red) and Y (for yellow) on his list? ____________

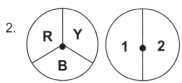

2. R Y B | 1 2

| First spinner | Second spinner |
|---|---|
| | |

a) How many outcomes are there on the second spinner? ____________

b) How many times should Paul write R (for red), B (for blue) and Y (for yellow) on his list? ____________

3. R Y | 1 2

| First spinner | Second spinner |
|---|---|
| | |

a) How many outcomes are there on the second spinner? ____________

b) How many times should Paul write R (for red) and Y (for yellow) on his list? ____________

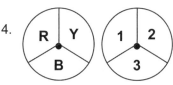

4. R Y B | 1 2 3

| First spinner | Second spinner |
|---|---|
| | |

a) How many outcomes are there on the second spinner? ____________

b) How many times should Paul write R (for red), B (for blue) and Y (for yellow) on his list? ____________

5. Say how many outcomes each game has. The game in . . .

a) question 1 has _____ outcomes.
b) question 2 has _____ outcomes.
c) question 3 has _____ outcomes.
d) question 4 has _____ outcomes.

6. If you flip a coin there are two outcomes, heads (H) and tails (T). List all the outcomes for flipping a coin and spinning the spinner.

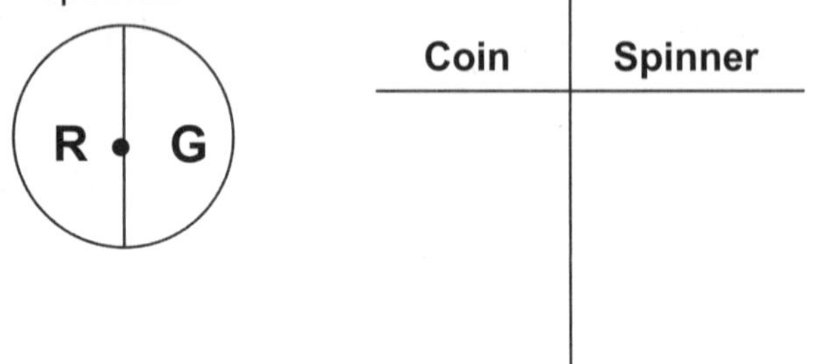


| Coin | Spinner |
|---|---|
| | |

7. Peter has a nickel and a penny in his left pocket, and a nickel and a penny in his right pocket. He pulls **one** coin from each pocket. List the combinations of coins he could pull out.

| Right pocket | Left pocket | Value of coins |
|---|---|---|
| | | |

8. Clare can choose the following activities at art camp:

**Morning:** painting or music

**Afternoon:** drama, pottery, or dance

She makes a chart so she can see all of her choice. She starts by writing each of her morning choices 3 times.

a) Why did Clare write each of her choices for the morning 3 times?

b) Complete the chart to show all of Clare's choices.

| Morning | Afternoon |
|---|---|
| painting | |
| painting | |
| painting | |
| music | |
| music | |
| music | |

9. On a separate piece of paper, make a chart to show all the activities you could choose at a camp that offered the following choices:

**Morning:** drama or music **Afternoon:** painting, drawing, or poetry

10.

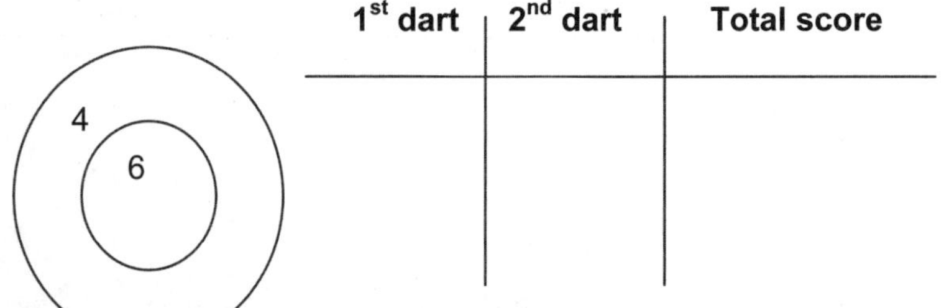


| 1st dart | 2nd dart | Total score |
|---|---|---|
| | | |

Record all scores you could get by throwing 2 darts at the dart board.

11. On a separate piece of paper list the outcomes from flipping a coin and rolling a die (a die has the numbers from 1 to 6 on its faces).

# PDM4-15: Tree Diagrams

At sports camp, Diane can choose one of two sports in the morning (tennis or swimming) and one of three in the afternoon (soccer, diving, or baseball). Diane draws a tree diagram so she can see all of her choices:

Step 1: She writes the name of her 2 morning choices at the end of 2 branches.

Step 2: Under each of her morning choices, she adds 3 branches, one for each of her 3 afternoon choices.

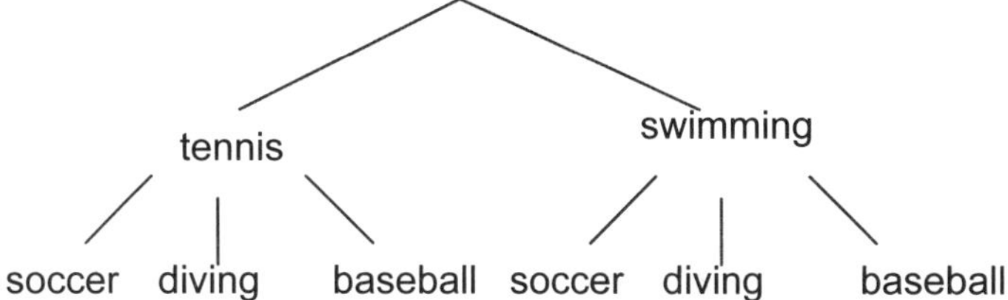


Step 3: Follow any path along the branches (from the top to the bottom of the tree) and you will find one of Diane's choices. The path highlighted by arrows shows tennis in the morning and diving in the afternoon.

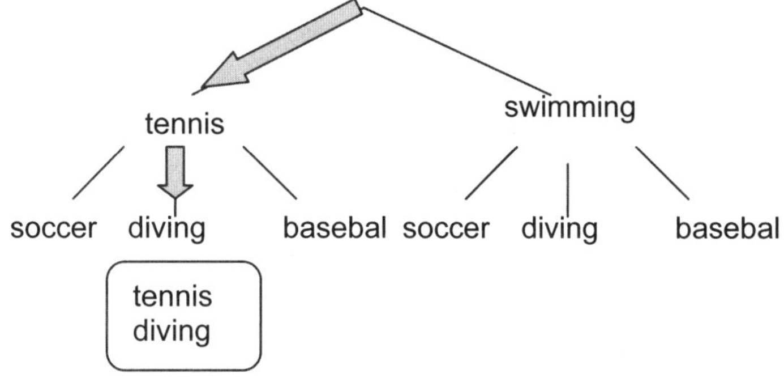


---

1. Follow a path from the top of the tree to a box at the bottom and write the sports named on the path in the box. Continue until you have filled in all the boxes.

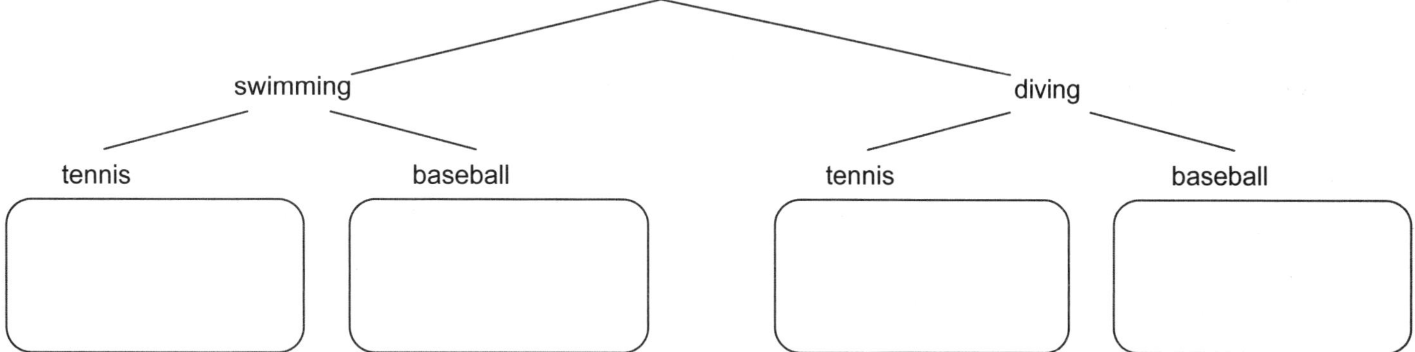


2. Daniel's camp offers the following choices of activities: **Morning**: baseball or swimming
**Afternoon**: tennis or basketball

   On a separate piece of paper, draw a tree diagram (like the one in question 1) to show all of Daniel's choices.

Emma is playing a role playing game on the computer.

R L

R L R L

Her character is lost in a maze. Emma draws a map of the maze. At each fork in the maze, she writes R (for right) or L (for left) to show which direction her character could go:

Her map shows that there are 4 different paths through the maze: RR (go right twice), RL (go right then left), LR (go left then right), and LL (go left twice).

---

3. Write U (for up) and D (for down) at each fork in the maze to show what direction Emma's character could go. List all of the paths through the maze Emma's character can take.

   How many paths are there through the maze?

   ______________________

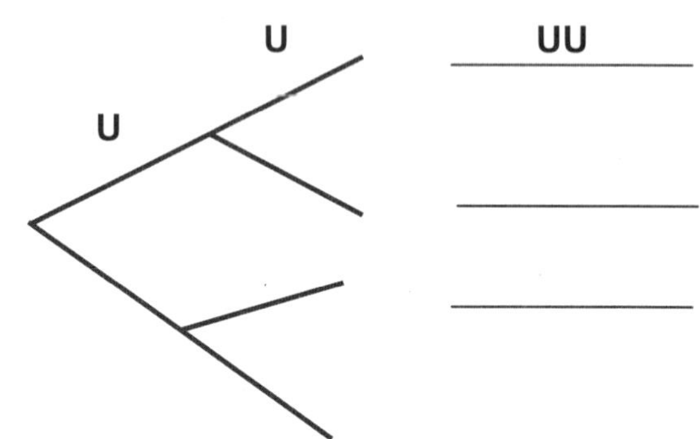


4. Complete the tree diagram to show all of the possible outcomes from flipping a coin twice (H = heads and T = tails).

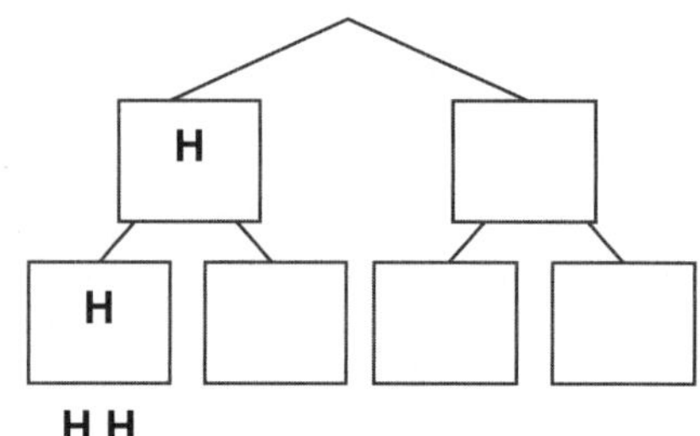


5. Complete the tree diagram to show all of the possible outcomes from flipping a coin, then spinning the spinner:

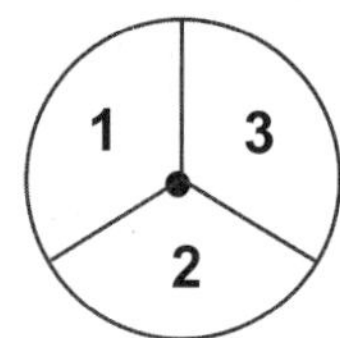


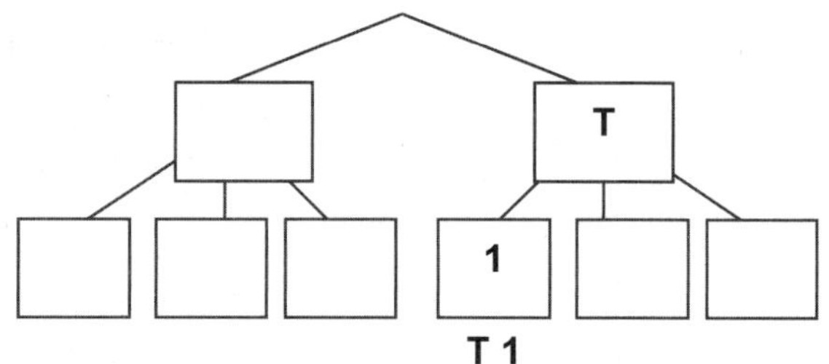


6. 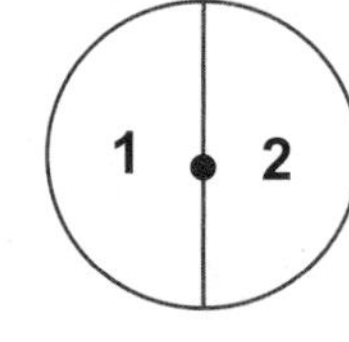


1 2

On a separate piece of paper, draw a tree diagram to show all the combinations of numbers you could spin on the two spinners. How many pairs of numbers add to four?

7. A restaurant offers the following choices for a sandwich: **Bread:** pita or bagel **Filling:** cheese, hummus, or peanut butter

   On a separate piece of paper, draw a tree diagram to show all the different sandwiches you could order at the restaurant.

# PDM4-16: Probability

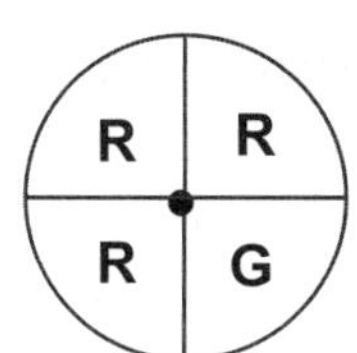


Fractions can be used to describe probability. ¾ of the spinner is red: the probability of spinning red is ¾.

(There are 3 ways of spinning red and 4 ways of spinning any colour (red or green). The fraction ¾ compared the number of chances of spinning red (the numerator) to the number of chances of spinning any colour (the denominator).

---

1. For each of the following situations, how many ways are there of . . .

a) R Y B R

drawing a red ball? ________

drawing a ball of any colour? ________

b) 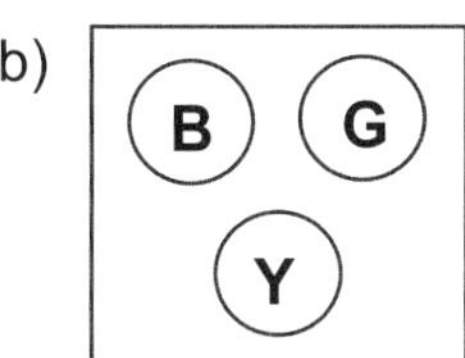


drawing a blue ball? ________

drawing a ball of any colour? ________

c) 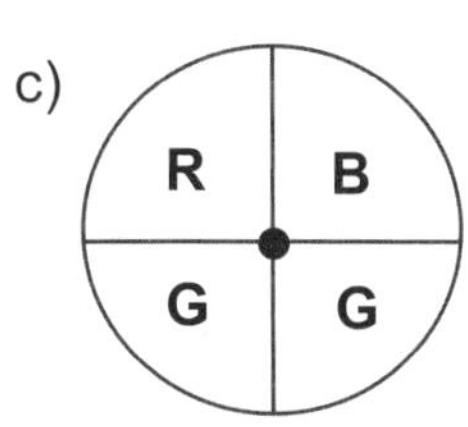


spinning green? _____

spinning any colour? _____

d) 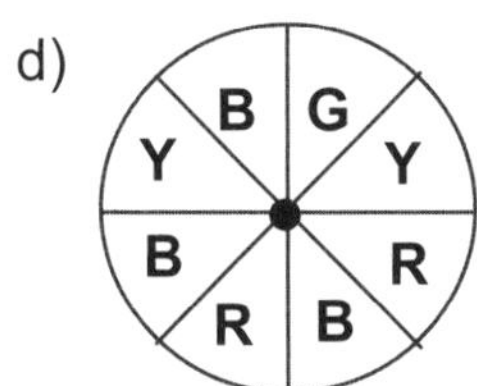


spinning blue? _____

spinning any colour? _____

2. For each spinner, what is the probability (P) of spinning red? P(Red) = $\frac{\text{\# of ways of spinning red}}{\text{\# of ways of spinning any colour}}$

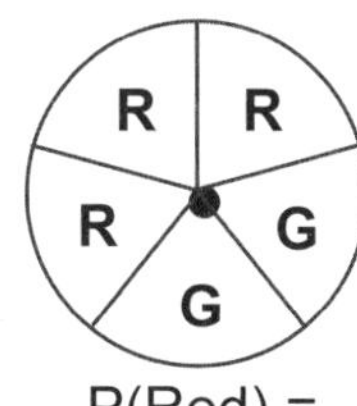

P(Red) =

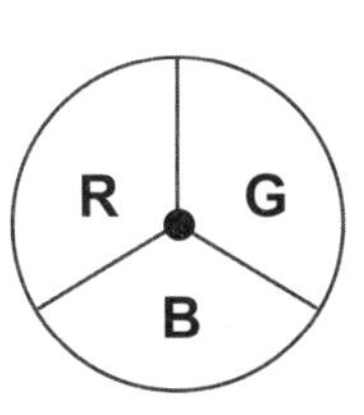

P(Red) =

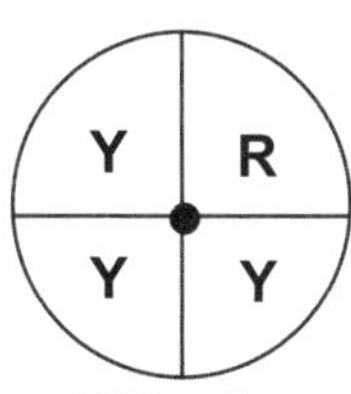

P(Red) =

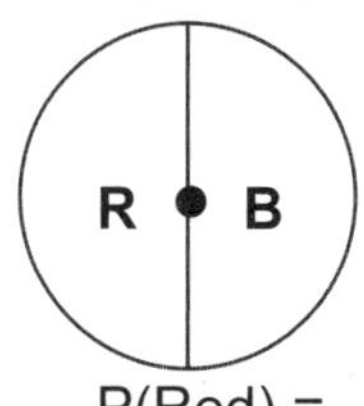

P(Red) =

3. For each spinner, write the probability of the given events. Reduce your answer if possible.

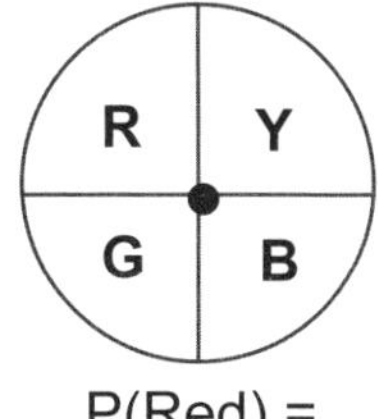

P(Red) =

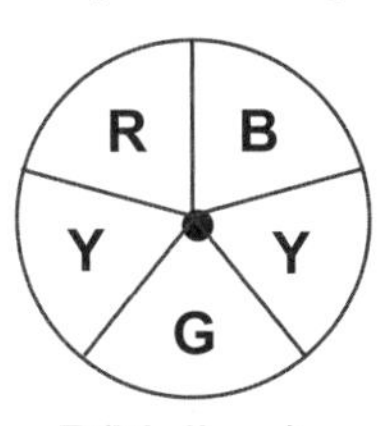

P(Yellow) =

P(Green) =

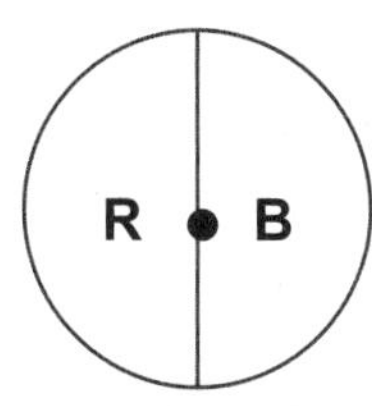

P(Blue) =

4. For each spinner, write the probability of the given events. (HINT: Cut the spinners into equal parts.)

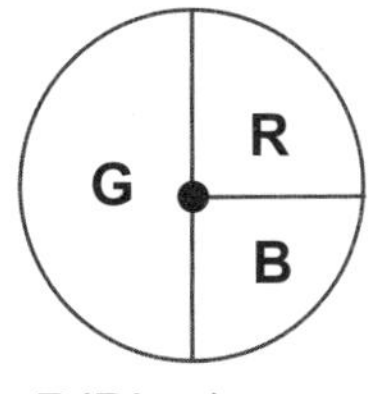

P(Blue) =

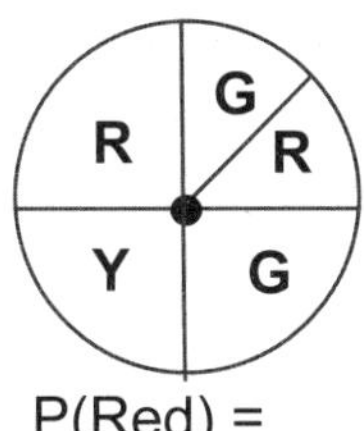

P(Red) =

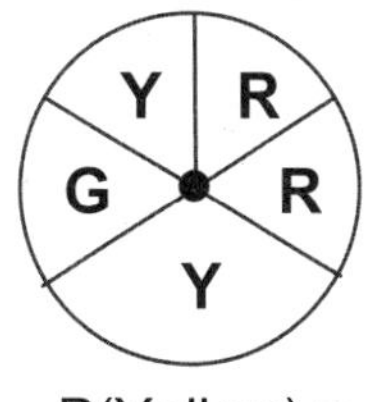

P(Yellow) =

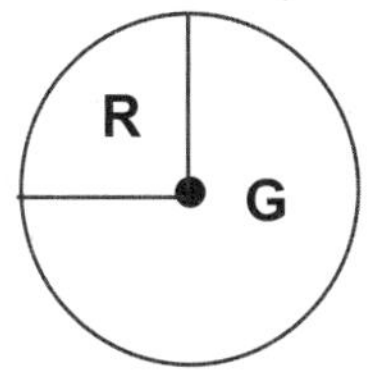

P(Green) =

5. Write a fraction for the probability of tossing heads on a coin.

6. Sketch a spinner on which the probability of spinning red is ¼.

REMEMBER: A die has the number from 1 to 6 on its faces.

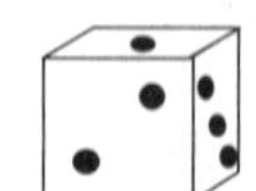

7. a) List the numbers on a die.

   ______________________

   b) How many outcomes are there when you roll a die?

   ______________________

8. a) List the numbers on a die that are odd.

   ______________

   b) How many ways can you roll an odd number on a die?

   ______________

   c) What is the probability of rolling an odd number on a die?

   ______________

9. a) List the numbers on a die that are less than 5.

   ______________

   b) How many ways can you roll an odd number less than 5?

   ______________

   c) What is the probability of rolling a number less than 5 on a die?

   ______________

10. a) i) List the numbers on a die that are greater than 2.

    ______________

    ii) What is the probability of rolling a number greater than 2 on a die?

    ______________

    b) i) List the numbers on a die that are even.

    ______________

    ii) What is the probability of rolling an even number on a die?

    ______________

    c) i) List the numbers on a die that are multiples of 3.

    ______________

    ii) What is the probability of rolling a multiple of 3 on a die?

    ______________

11. Phillip has a nickel and dime in his **right** pocket and a nickel and dime in his **left** pocket. He pulls **one** coin from each pocket.

    a) List the combinations of coins he could pull from his pocket.

    b) What is the probability that he will pull a pair of coins with a value of 15¢?

| Right pocket | Left pocket | Value of coins |
|---|---|---|
| | | |

12. What is the probability of spinning a pair of numbers that add to 3? Make a list of combinations to solve the problem.

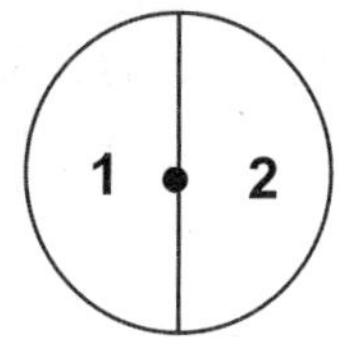


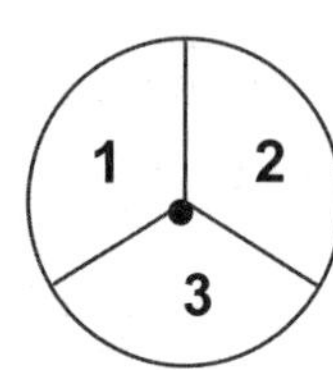


13. Clare says the probability of rolling a 5 on a die is $\frac{5}{6}$. Emma says the probability is $\frac{1}{6}$. Who is right? Explain how you know.

# PDM4-17: Expectation

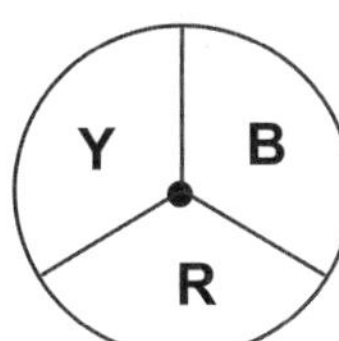


Kate plans to spin the spinner 15 times to see how many times it will land on yellow. $\frac{1}{3}$ of the spinner is yellow. Kate **expects** to spin yellow $\frac{1}{3}$ of the time. Kate finds $\frac{1}{3}$ of 15 by dividing by 3: 15 ÷ 3 = 5. She expects the spinner to land on yellow 5 times.
(The spinner may not actually land on yellow 5 times, but 5 is the **most likely** number of spins.)

---

1. Shade **half** of the pie. How many pieces are in the pie? How many pieces are in half the pie?

a) 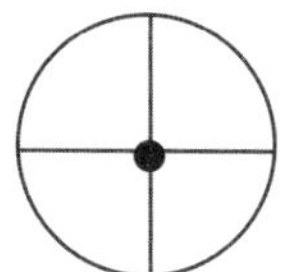

____ pieces in half the pie
____ pieces in the pie

b) 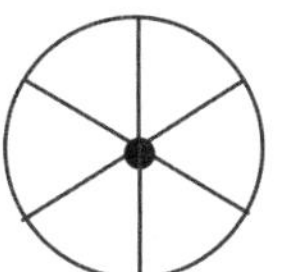

____ pieces in half the pie
____ pieces in the pie

c) 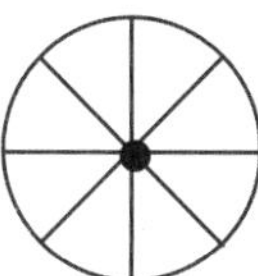

____ pieces in half the pie
____ pieces in the pie

2. a) A pie is cut into four equal pieces. How many pieces make half? _______
   b) A pie is cut into six equal pieces. How many pieces make half? _______
   c) A pie is cut into eight equal pieces. How many pieces make half? _______

3. Write the number of pieces in the pie and the number of pieces shaded. Then circle the pies where **half** the pieces are shaded.

a) 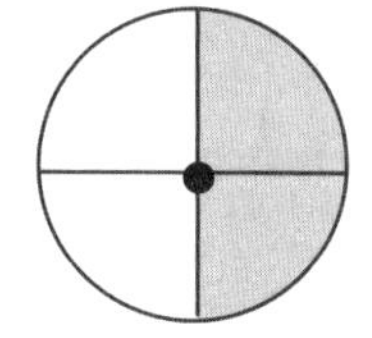

___ pieces shaded
___ pieces

b) 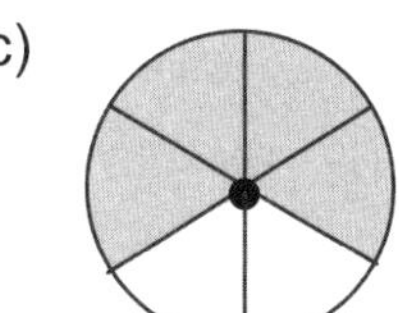

___ pieces shaded
___ pieces

c) 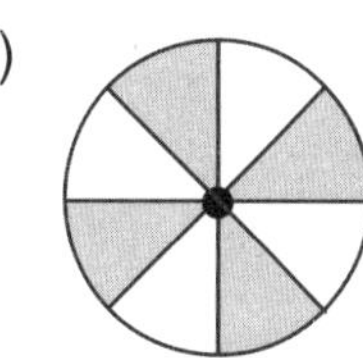

___ pieces shaded
___ pieces

d) 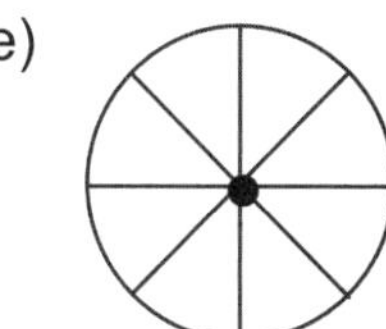

___ pieces shaded
___ pieces

e)

___ pieces shaded
___ pieces

4. Circle the pies where half the pieces are shaded. Put a large "X" through the pies where less than half the pieces are shaded. (HINT: Count the shaded and unshaded pieces first.)

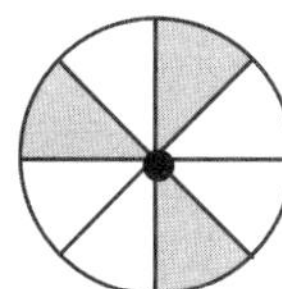 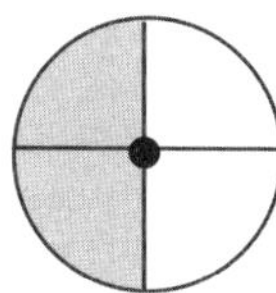 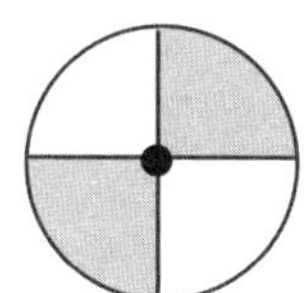 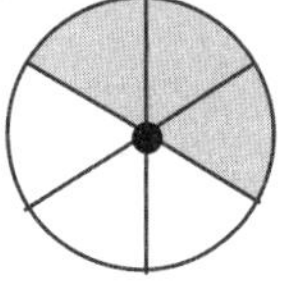 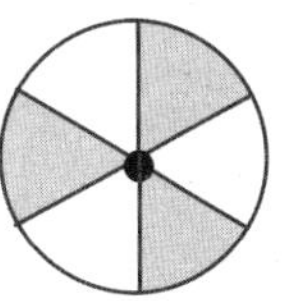 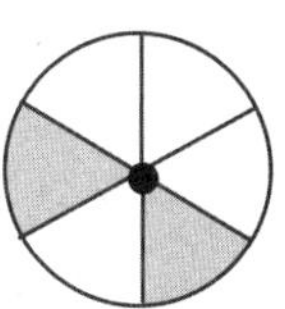

5. Divide by skip counting by 2s.

a) 10 ÷ 2 = ____ b) 12 ÷ 2 = ____ c) 18 ÷ 2 = ____ d) 20 ÷ 2 = ____ e) 16 ÷ 2 = ____

6. Write each number as a sum of two equal parts. Use skip counting by 2s to help you find the parts.

a) 10 = __5__ + __5__ b) 8 = ____ + ____ c) 14 = ____ + ____ d) 6 = ____ + ____

half of 10 is __5__ half of 8 is ____ half of 14 is ____ half of 6 is ____

7. On a separate sheet of paper find . . .

$2\overline{)10}$  $2\overline{)14}$  $2\overline{)24}$  $2\overline{)32}$  $2\overline{)56}$  $2\overline{)74}$

8. Using long division, find . . .

a) $\frac{1}{2}$ of 6  b) $\frac{1}{2}$ of 10  c) $\frac{1}{2}$ of 12  d) $\frac{1}{2}$ of 24

BONUS:

e) $\frac{1}{2}$ of 48  f) $\frac{1}{2}$ of 52  g) $\frac{1}{2}$ of 84  h) $\frac{1}{2}$ of 88

9. Sarah wants to put her coin collection into two boxes. She wants to put the same number of coins in each box. How many coins should she put in each box if she has . . .

a) 6 coins?  b) 10 coins?  c) 12 coins?

_____ coins in each box  ___________ in each box   in each box

d) 16 coins?  e) 18 coins?  f) 14 coins?

g) 22 coins?  h) 46 coins?  i) 48 coins?

j) 50 coins?  k) 62 coins?  l) 72 coins?

10. 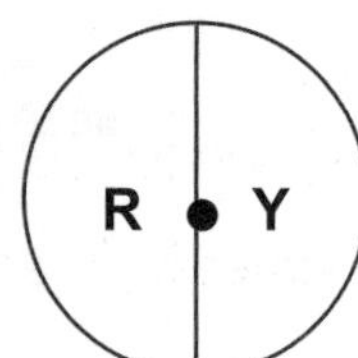


What fraction of your spins would you expect to be red?

a) I would expect ________ of the spins to be red.

b) If you spun the spinner 20 times, how many times would you expect to spin red? _______

11. If you flip a coin repeatedly, what fraction of the throws would you expect to be heads? _________

12. If you flip a coin 12 times, how many times would you expect to flip heads? Explain your answer.

13. If you flipped a coin 40 times, how many times would you expect to flip heads?

14. If you flipped a coin 60 times, how many times would you expect to flip tails?

15. On a separate sheet of paper find . . .

$3\overline{)15}$ $3\overline{)18}$ $3\overline{)27}$ $3\overline{)33}$ $3\overline{)52}$ $3\overline{)60}$

16. On a separate sheet of paper find . . .

$4\overline{)16}$ $4\overline{)24}$ $4\overline{)32}$ $4\overline{)44}$ $4\overline{)64}$ $4\overline{)92}$

17. Fill in the missing numbers.

a) $\frac{1}{3}$ of 9 is _____ b) $\frac{1}{3}$ of 12 is _____ c) $\frac{1}{3}$ of 15 is _____ d) $\frac{1}{3}$ of 18 is _____

e) $\frac{1}{3}$ of 39 is _____ f) $\frac{1}{3}$ of 42 is _____ g) $\frac{1}{3}$ of 75 is _____ h) $\frac{1}{4}$ of 8 is _____

i) $\frac{1}{4}$ of 12 is _____ j) $\frac{1}{4}$ of 36 is _____ k) $\frac{1}{4}$ of 52 is _____ l) $\frac{1}{4}$ of 84 is _____

18. For each spinner below, what fraction of your spins would you expect to be red?

a) 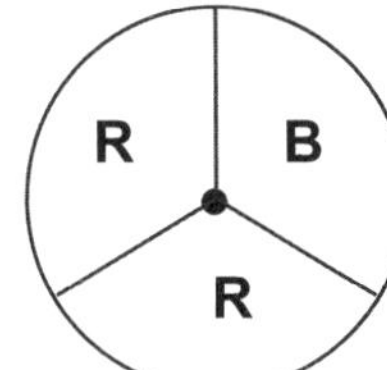


I would expect

_______________

of the spins to be red.

b) 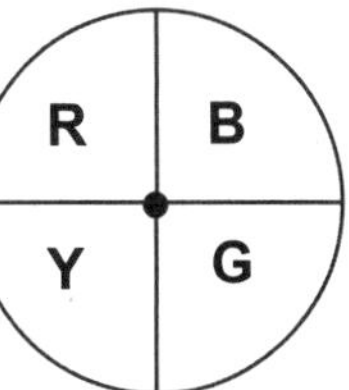


_______________

_______________

19. How many times would you expect to spin blue, if you spun the spinner . . .

a) 12 times? b) 36 times? c) 72 times?

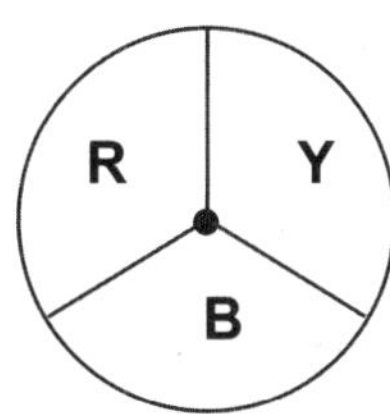


20. 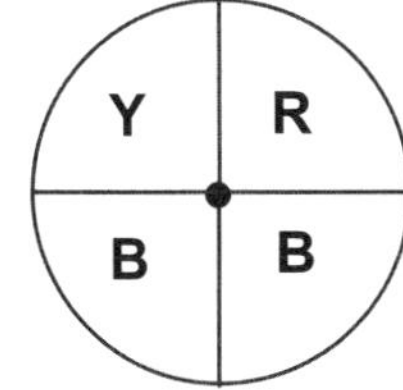


How many times would you expect to spin yellow, if you spun the spinner . . .

a) 16 times? b) 48 times? c) 92 times?

21. On a separate piece of paper, sketch a spinner on which you would expect to spin $\frac{3}{4}$ of the time.

22. On a spinner, the probability of spinning yellow is $\frac{2}{3}$. What is the probability of spinning a colour that is not yellow? Explain your answer with a picture.

23. 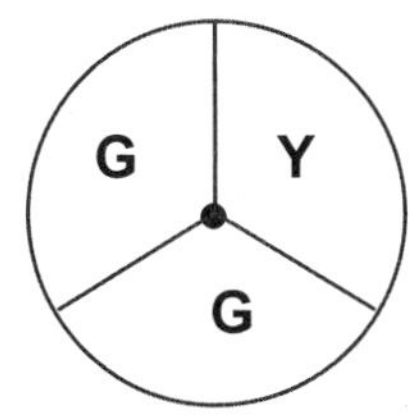


Hong wants to know how many times he is likely to spin green if he spins the spinner 24 times. He knows $\frac{1}{3}$ of 24 is 8 ($24 \div 3 = 8$). How can he use this knowledge to find how many times he is likely to spin green?

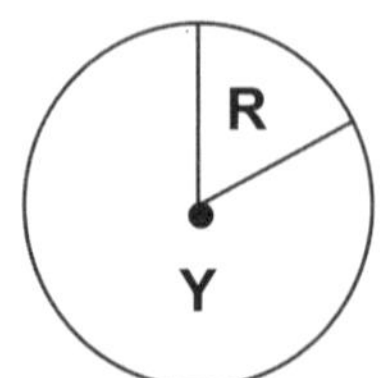


- If an event cannot happen it is **impossible**. For example: rolling the number 8 on a die is **impossible** because a die only has the numbers 1, 2, 3, 4, 5, and 6 on its faces.
- If an event **must** happen it is **certain**. For example, when you roll a die it is **certain** that you will roll a number that is less than 7.
- It is **likely** that you would spin yellow on the spinner shown (since more than half the area of the spinner is yellow).
- It is **unlikely** that you would spin red on the spinner shown (since there is only a small section of the spinner that is red).

---

1. Complete each statement by writing "more than half," "half," or "less than half."
(HINT: Start by finding half of the number by skip counting by 2s.)

a) 2 is ____________________ of 6 b) 3 is ____________________ of 8

c) 6 is ____________________ of 12 d) 7 is ____________________ of 10

e) 11 is ____________________ of 14 f) 5 is ____________________ of 10

g) 5 is ____________________ of 12 h) 11 is ____________________ of 14

**When an event is expected to occur exactly half the time, we say that there is an <u>even</u> chance of the event occurring.**

2. Write "even" where you would expect to spin red **half** the time. Write "more than half" if you would expect to spin red more than half the time, and "less than half" otherwise.

a) 

b) 

c) 

d) 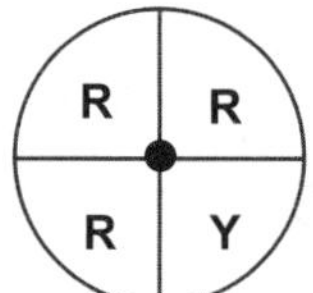


____________ ____________ ____________ ____________

3. The chances of an outcome can be described as: "unlikely" (the outcome is expected to happen **less** than half the time), "likely" (the outcome is expected to happen **more** than half the time), or "even" (exactly half the time). Describe each as "likely" or "unlikely."
(HINT: Start by finding out if the event will happen more than half the time or less than half the time.)

a) 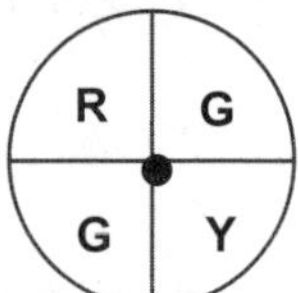


Spinning red is: ____________

b) 

Spinning blue is: ____________

c) 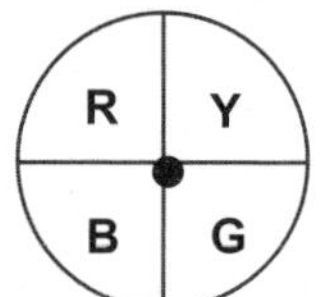


Spinning green is: ____________

d) 

Spinning red is: ____________

4. On a separate piece of paper describe the chances of each event as "unlikely" or "likely."

a) 14 marbles in a box; 7 red marbles
**Outcome**: You draw a red marble.

b) 14 marbles in a box; 5 red marbles
**Outcome**: You draw a red marble.

c) 12 socks in a drawer; 8 black socks
**Outcome**: You pull out a black sock.

d) 16 coins in a pocket; 9 pennies
**Outcome**: You pull out a penny.

BONUS:

5. If you roll a die, are your chances of rolling a number greater than 2: "unlikely," "even," or "likely." Explain your answer on a separate piece of paper.

6. Using the words "certain," "likely," "unlikely," or "impossible," describe the likelihood of . . .

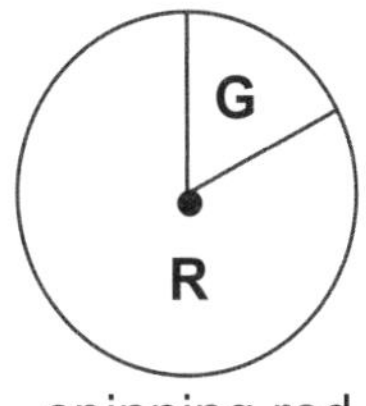


spinning red ______________

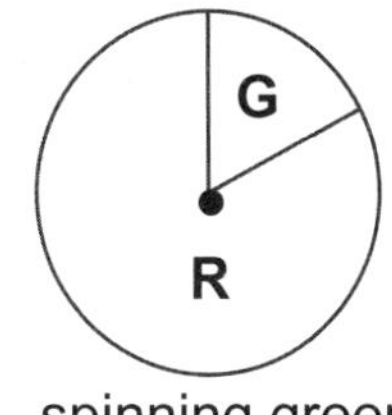


spinning green ______________

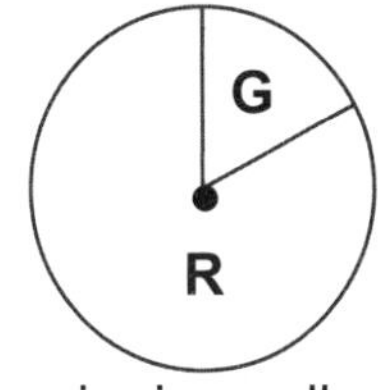


spinning yellow ______________

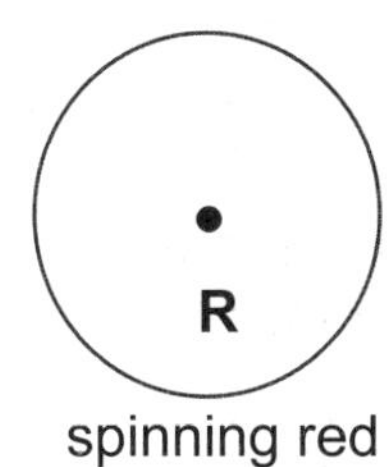


spinning red ______________

7. Describe each outcome as "impossible," "unlikely," "likely," or "certain."

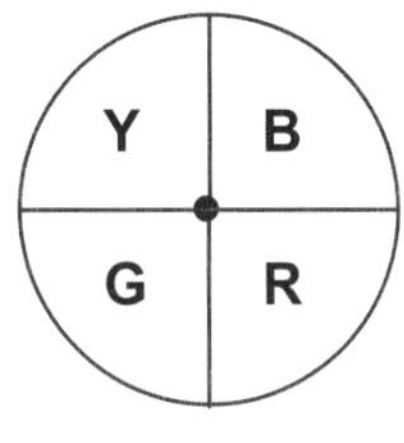


spinning green ______________

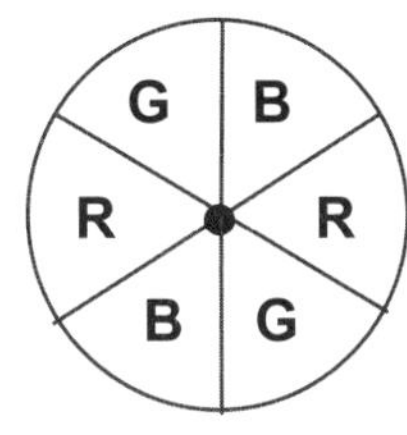


spinning red ______________

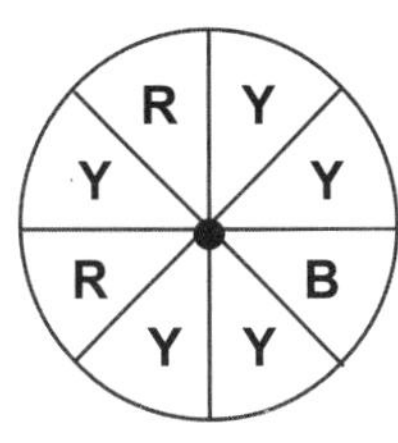


spinning yellow ______________

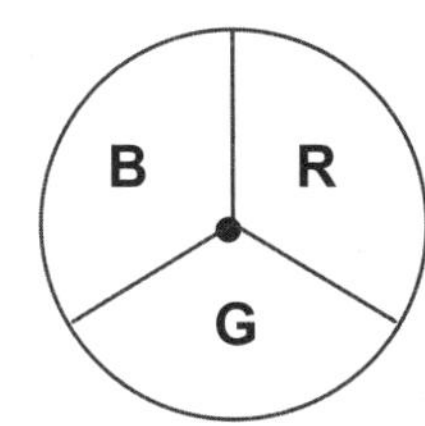


spinning yellow ______________

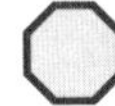

8. Count the number of balls of each colour. (Make a tally on a separate sheet of paper.) Then fill in each blank with on of the following phrases: "less probable than," "as probable as," or "more probable than." NOTE: The word probable means "likely."

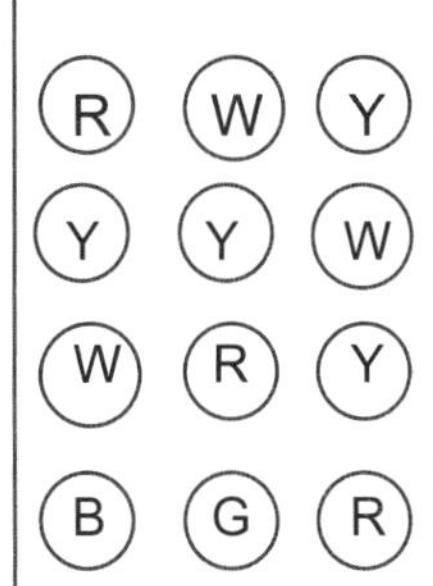


a) Drawing a red ball is ______________ drawing a green ball.

b) Drawing a yellow ball is ______________ drawing a red ball.

c) Drawing a blue ball is ______________ drawing a green ball.

d) Drawing a white ball is ______________ drawing a blue ball.

e) Drawing a red ball is ______________ drawing a white ball.

f) Drawing a blue ball is ______________ drawing a green ball.

9. Which colour of ball are you most likely to draw: red or blue? Explain your thinking.

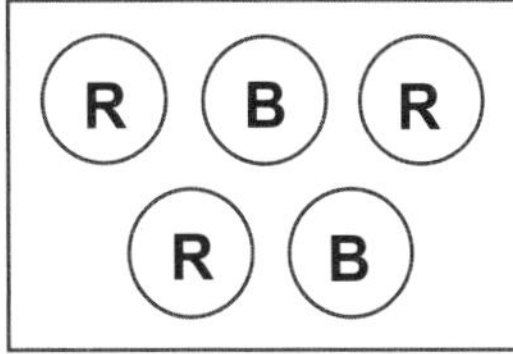


______________________________

______________________________

______________________________

10. Use the words "impossible," "likely," "unlikely," or "certain" to describe the following events. Explain your answers on a separate piece of paper.

a) If you roll a die, you will get a number greater than zero. ______________

b) If you roll a die, you will get a number greater than one. ______________

c) You will see an elephant on the street today. ______________

**When two or more events have to the same chance of occurring the events are <u>equally</u> likely.**

11. 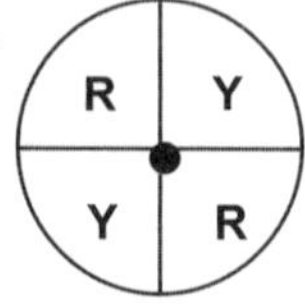

Are your chances of spinning red and yellow equally likely? Explain your answer:

12. 

Are your chances of spinning red and yellow equally likely? Explain your answer:

13. 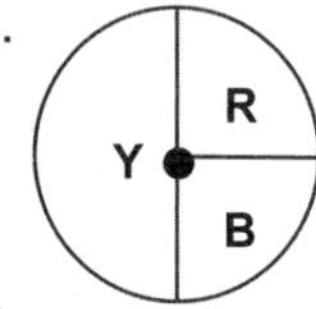

Are your chances of spinning red and yellow equally likely? Explain your answer:

14. Circle the spinners where spinning **red** and spinning **green** are equally likely.

a) 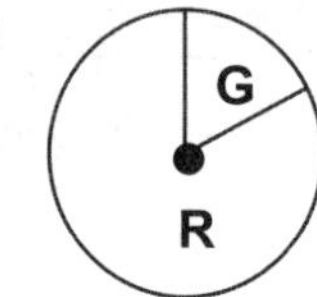

b) 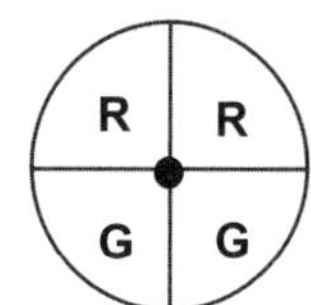

c) 

d) 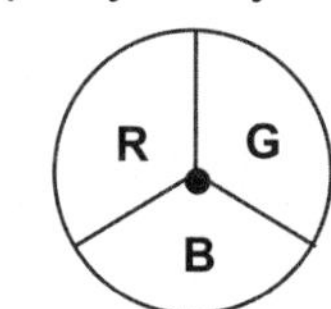

e) 

15. A game of chance is **fair** if both players have the same chance of winning. Which of the following games are fair? For the games that are not fair, who has the better chance of winning? Explain your answers on a separate piece of paper.

a) 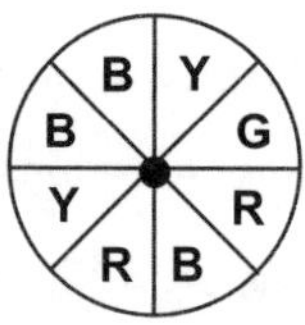

Player 1 must spin red to win.

Player 2 must spin blue to win.

Is it fair? Y N

b) 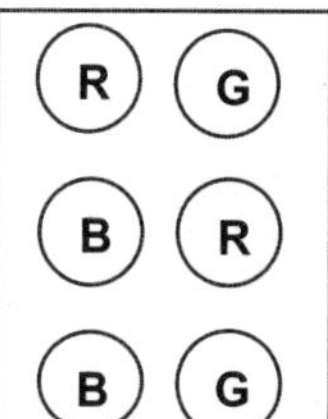

Player 1 must draw red to win.

Player 2 must draw blue to win.

Is it fair? Y N

16. Gerome's favourite colour is blue and Iman's favourite colour is yellow. Design a spinner with **at least 4 regions** so that . . .

a) Iman is most likely to win

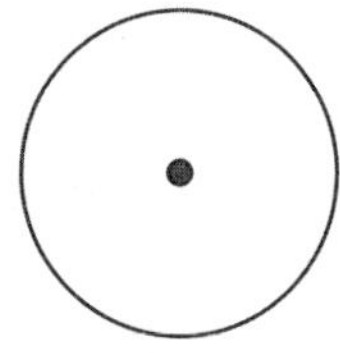

b) both players have an **equal** chance of winning

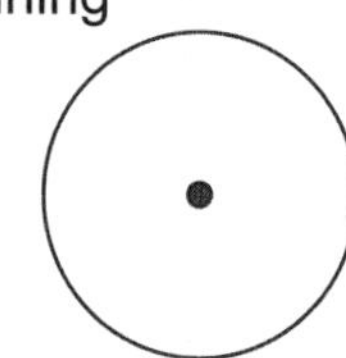

17. BONUS: Five cards numbered 1 to 5 lay face down. Player 1 must pick a number less than 4 to win. Otherwise Player 2 wins. Is the game fair? Explain your answer on a separate piece of paper.

NOTE: You can show the likelihood of events using a probability line:

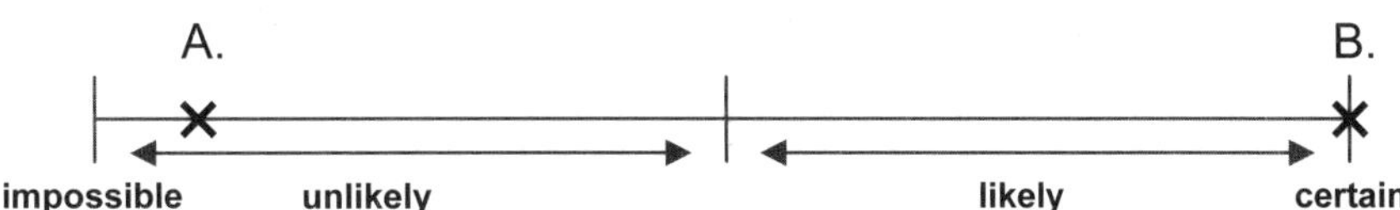


A. It could snow in Toronto in August but it is very unlikely. So you would mark that event near impossible on probability line.

B. If you roll a die, you will certainly get a number less than 19. So you would mark that even certain on the probability line.

18.

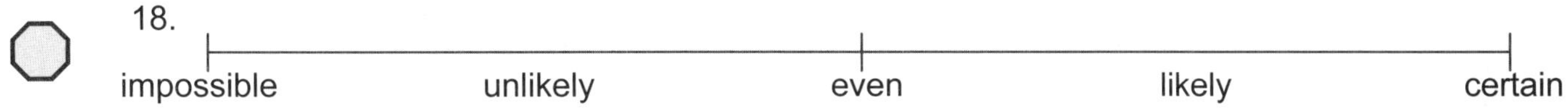


Mark a point on the above line indicating the possibility of each of the following ("even" probability means the outcome will occur half the time).

**A.** The chance of rolling a 7 on a die.

**B.** The chance of rain 20 days in a row

**C.** The chance of flipping heads on a coin.

**D.** The chance of rolling a number less than 6 on a die.

19. On a separate piece of paper, draw a probability line and mark the following events:

**A.** It will rain every day next week.

**B.** You will read a book this week.

**C.** If you roll a die you will get a number greater than 6.

**D.** From a box with 6 red balls and one blue ball, you will pick a red.

20. On a separate piece of paper, name an event that is . . .

a) impossible b) likely c) unlikely d) certain

21. On a separate piece of paper, draw a box of red balls where the probability of picking a red ball is . . .

a) impossible b) likely c) unlikely d) certain

22.

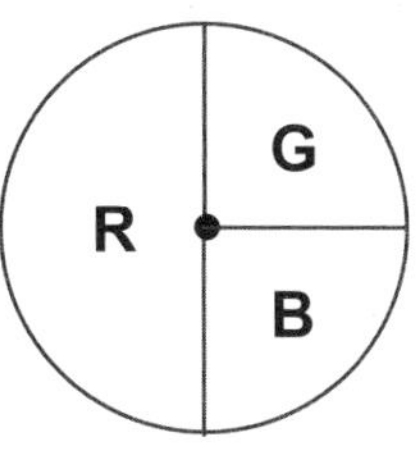


Is each outcome on the spinner equally likely? Explain.

# PDM4-19: Experiments and Expectation

Show your work for the problems on this page on a separate piece of paper.

1. If you flip a coin repeatedly, what fraction of the time would you expect to flip a head? (A half? a third? a quarter?) Explain your answer.

2. Flip a coin 10 times, making a tally of the number of heads and tails you got. Repeat the experiment five times. Did you always get approximately the same number of heads and tails each time?

3. If you toss a die repeatedly, what fraction of the time would you expect to roll the number 2? Explain.

4. Arlene and Brian play a game of chance with the spinner shown. If it lands on blue, Arlene wins. If it lands on red, Brian wins.

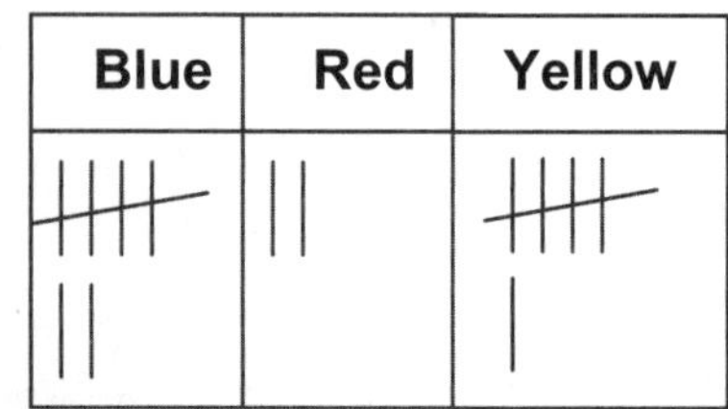

| Blue | Red | Yellow |
|---|---|---|
| 卌 \|\| | \|\| | 卌 \| |

   a) Arlene and Brian play the game sixteen times. How many times would you **predict** that the spinner would land on blue?

   b) When Arlene and Brian play the game they get the results shown in the chart. Brian says the game is not fair. Is he right?

5. Place the point of your pencil inside a paper clip in the middle of the circle. Hold the pencil still so you can spin the clip around the pencil.

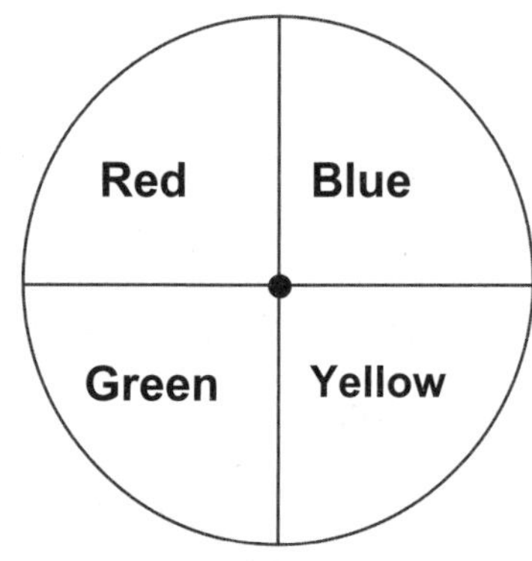


   a) If you spin the spinner 20 times, how many times would you predict spinning red? Show your work.
   (HINT: Think of dividing 20 spins into 4 equal parts.)

   b) Spin the spinner 12 times. Make a tally of your results. Did your results match your expectations?

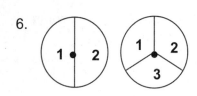

6. a) Make a T-table and list all the outcomes for spinning the 2 spinners.

   b) Circle all the outcomes that add to 3.

   c) What is the probability of spinning a pair of numbers that add to 3?

   d) If you spin the spinner 12 times, how many times would you expect to spin a pair of numbers that add to 3?

7. You have 3 coins in your pocket: a nickel (5¢), a dime (10¢), and a quarter (25¢). You reach in and pull out a pair of coins.

   a) What are all the possible combinations of two coins you could pull out?

   b) Would you expect to pull a pair of coins that add up to 30¢? Are the chances likely or unlikely?

   c) How did you solve the problem (Did you use a list? a picture? a calculation? or a combination of these things?)

# G4-15: Introduction to Coordinate Systems

1. Join the dots in the given column OR row.

Example:

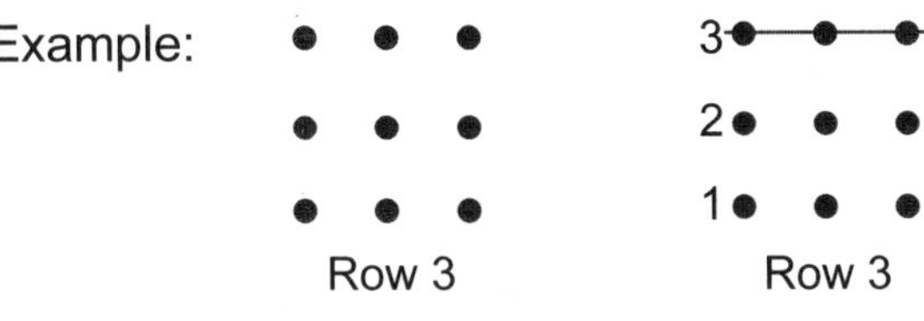

Row 3 Row 3

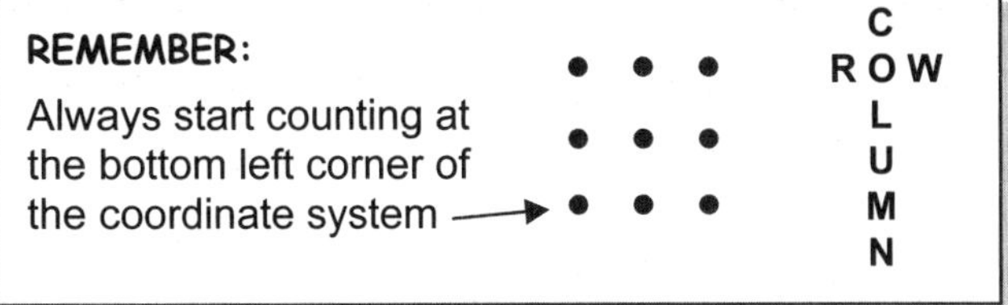

REMEMBER:
Always start counting at the bottom left corner of the coordinate system
ROW
COLUMN


a) 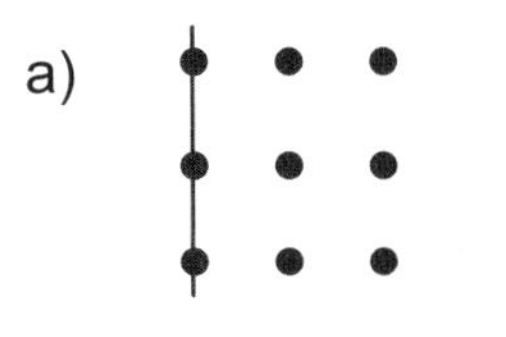
Column 1

b) 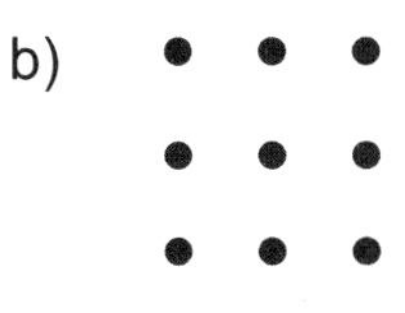
Column 2

c) 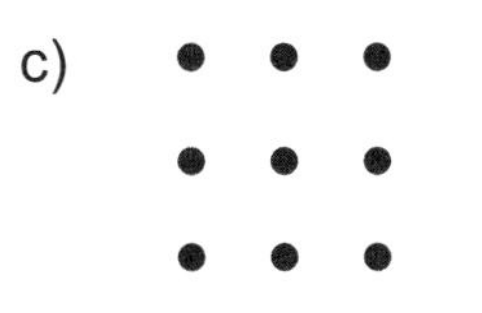
Row 3

d) 
Column 3

e) 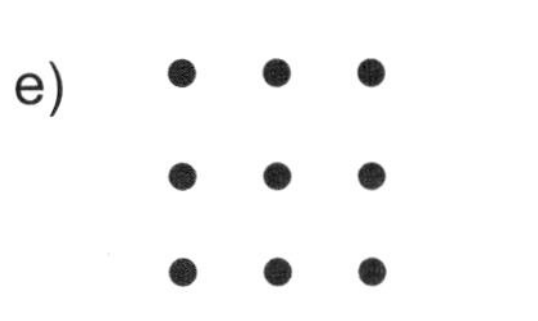
Row 2

f) 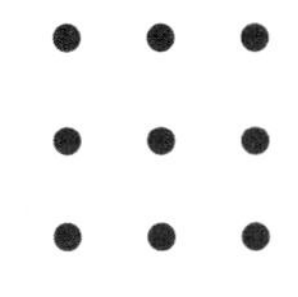
Row 1

g) 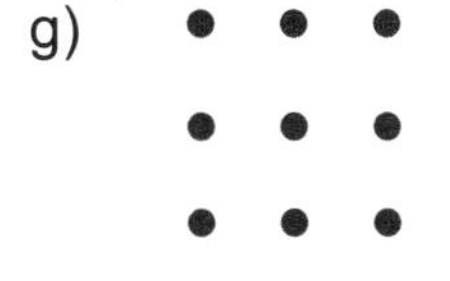
Column 1

h) 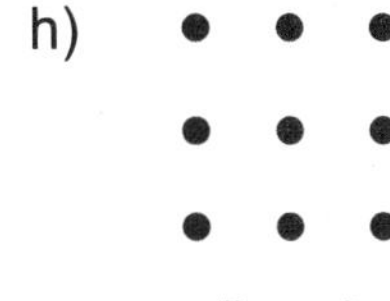
Row 3

i) 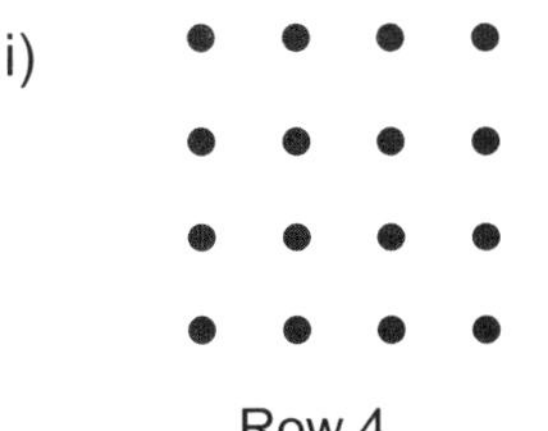
Row 4

j) 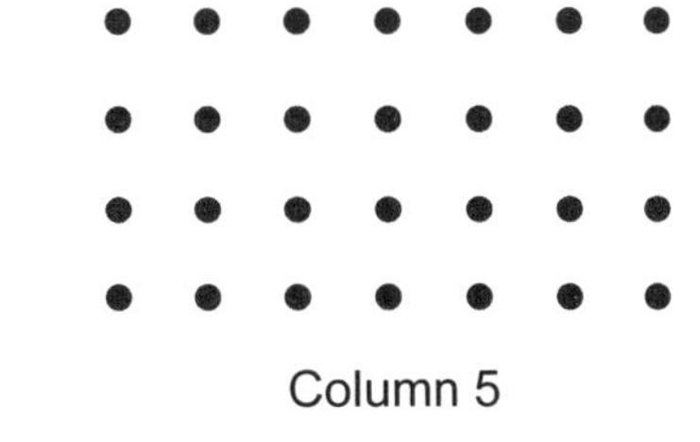
Column 5

k) 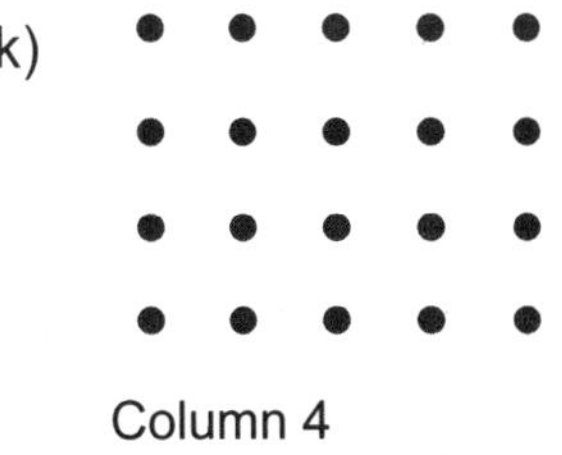
Column 4

2. Join the dots in the given column AND row.

Example:

Column 1
Row 3

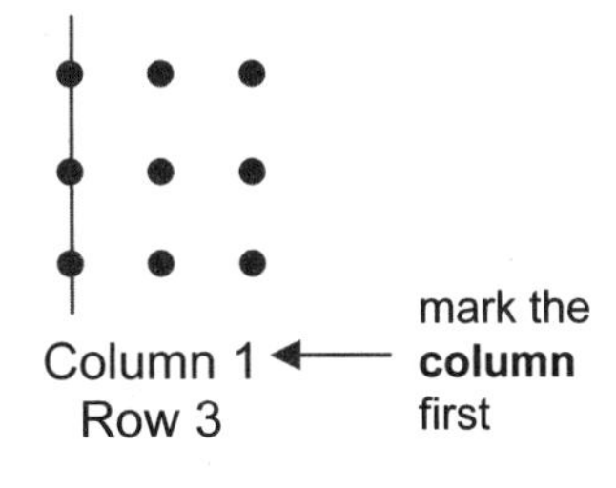
Column 1 ← mark the **column** first
Row 3

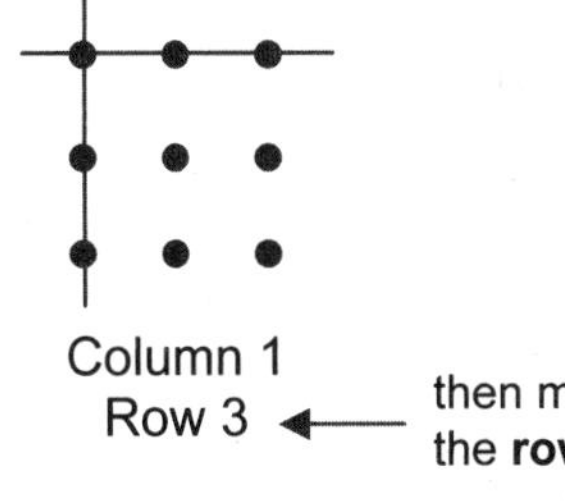
Column 1
Row 3 ← then mark the **row**

a) 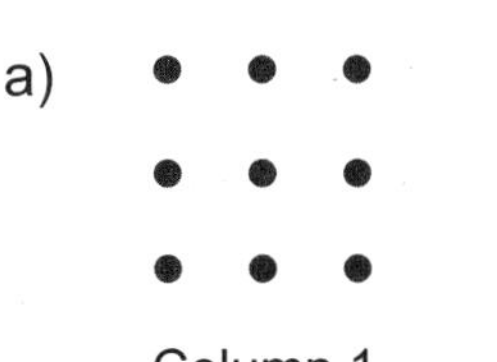
Column 1
Row 2

b) 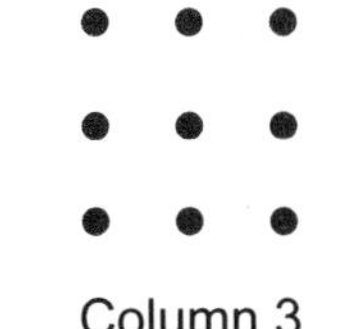
Column 3
Row 1

c) 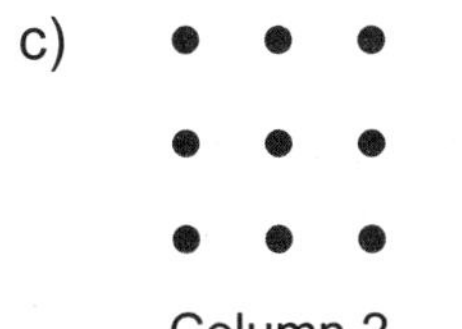
Column 2
Row 1

d) 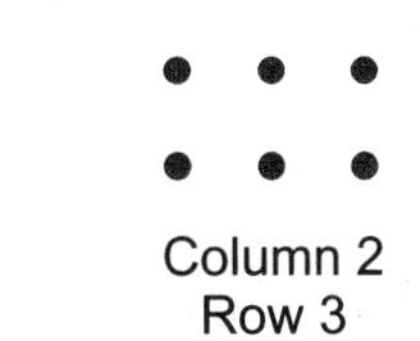
Column 2
Row 3

e) 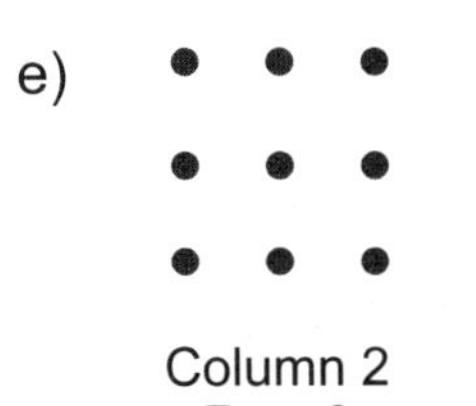
Column 2
Row 2

f)
Column 1
Row 3

g)
Column 3
Row 2

h)
Column 3
Row 3

3. Join the dots to find a hidden letter! Write each letter beside the array.

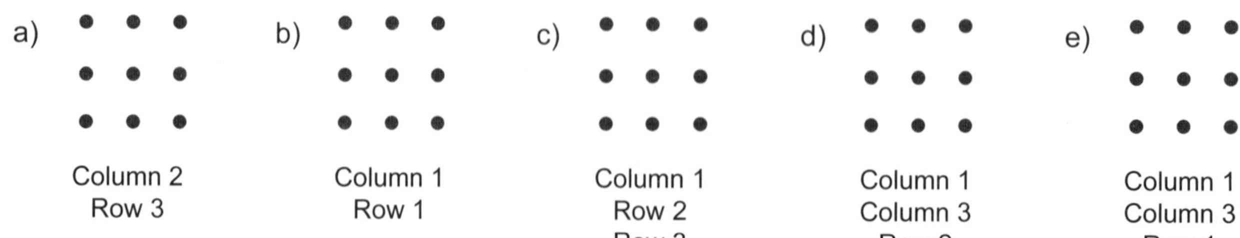


4. First, circle the dot where the two lines meet. Then identify the column and row.

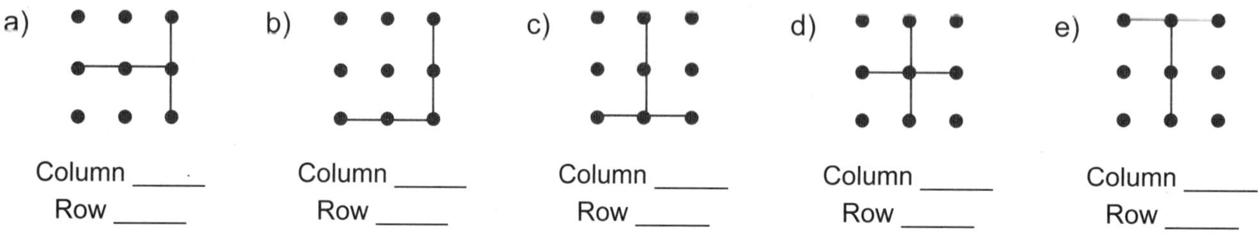


5. Circle the dot where the two lines meet.

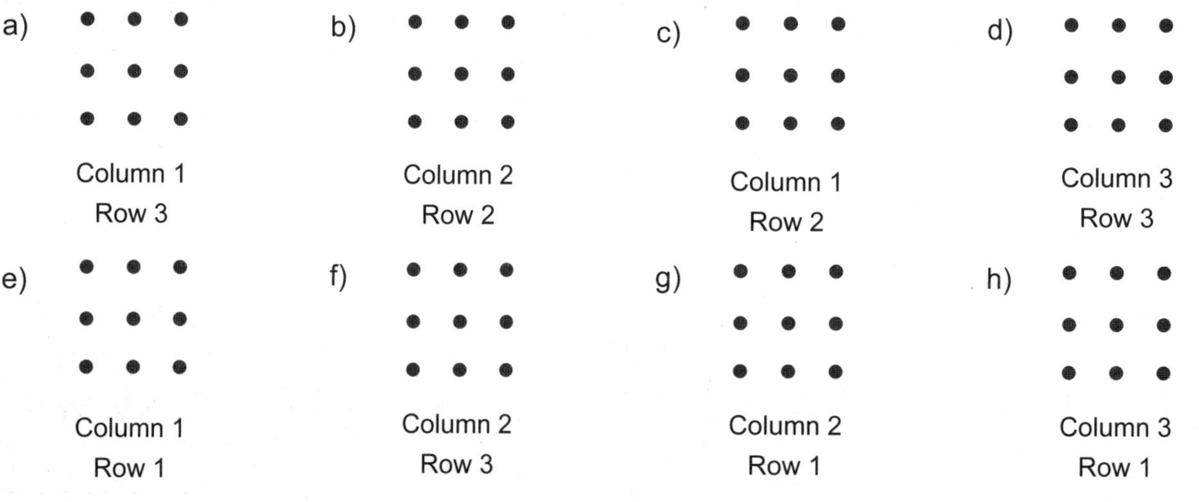


6. Identify the proper column and row for the circled dot.

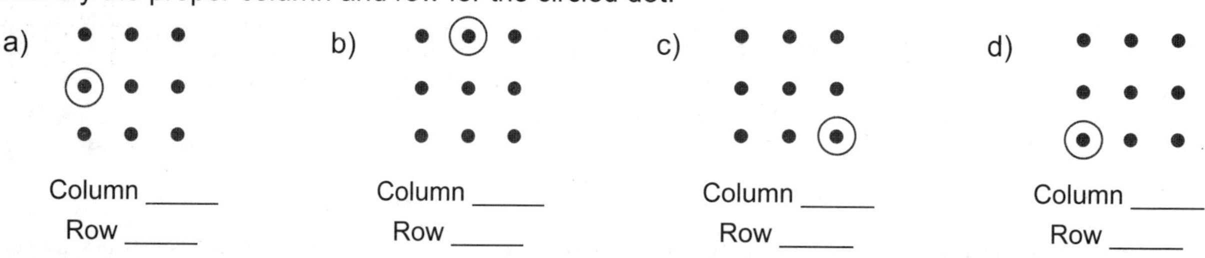


7. Draw a 4 × 4 array on grid paper and circle a dot in the array. Ask a friend to name the column and the row where the dot is.

8. Draw an array on grid paper and write a letter backwards or forwards (for example, ⊢ or ⊣ ) on the array. Then write out the column and row numbers of the lines that make up the letter.

# G4-16: Introduction to Slides

Josh slides a dot from one position to another. Slides may be described using the words "right," "left," "up," and "down."

Example:

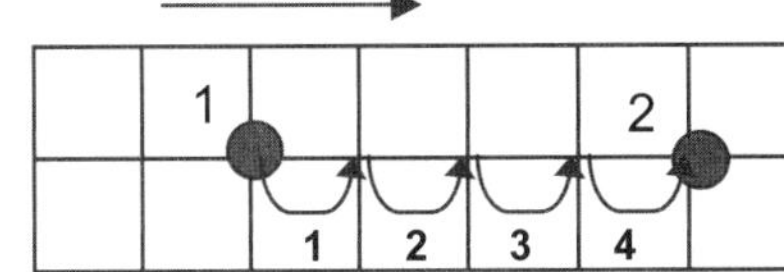


To move the dot from position 1 to position 2, Josh **slides** the dot **4 units right**.

1. How many units **right** did the dot slide from Position 1 to Position 2?

a)
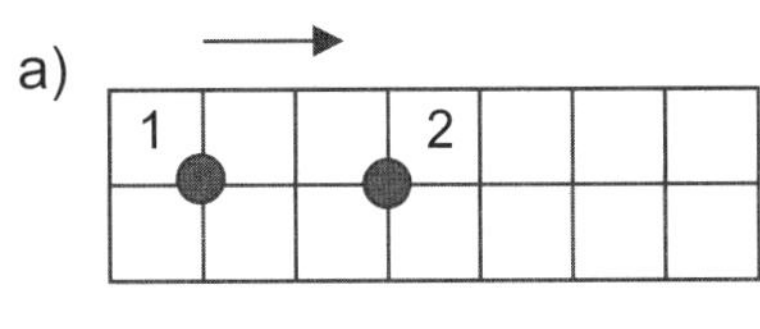


b)
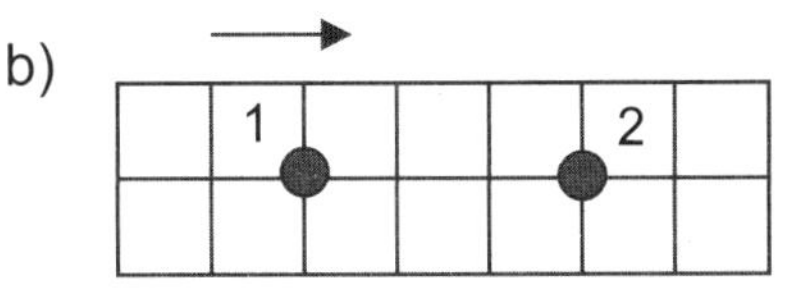


c)
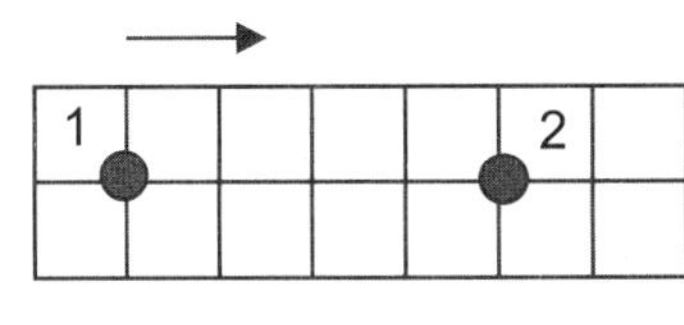


________ units right    ______________    ______________

2. How many units **left** did the dot slide from Position 1 to Position 2?

a)
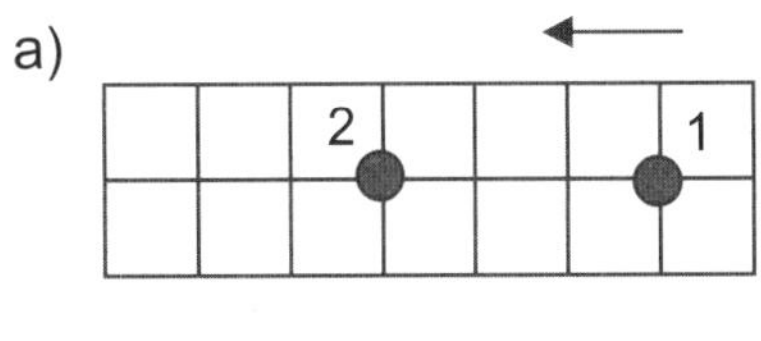


b)
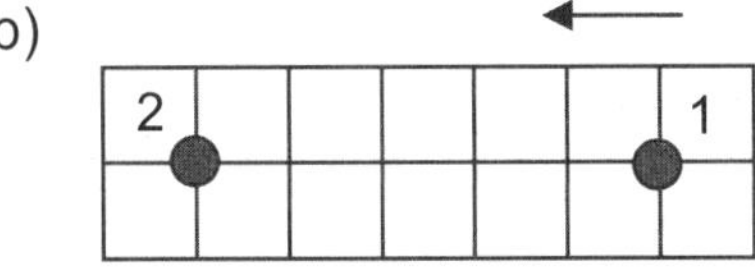


c)
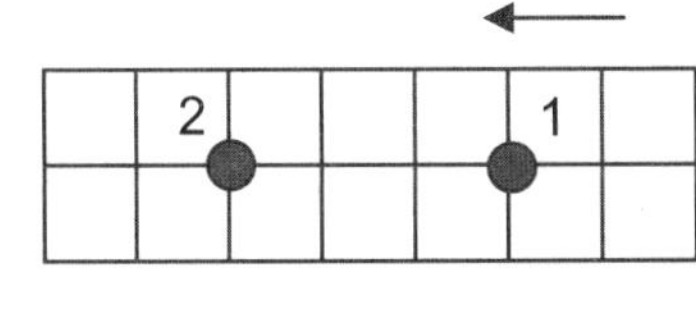


________ units left    ______________    ______________

3. Slide the dot . . .

a) 5 units right

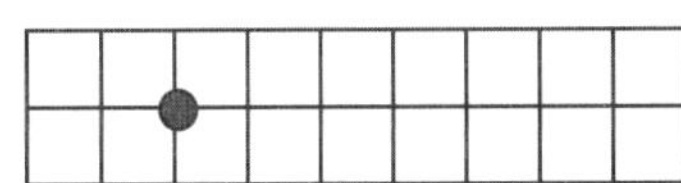

b) 4 units left

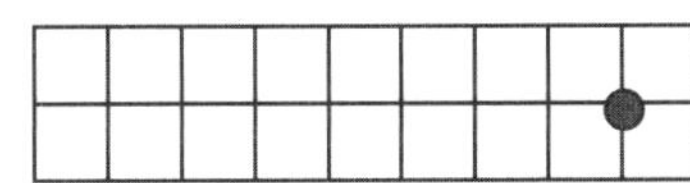

c) 7 units right

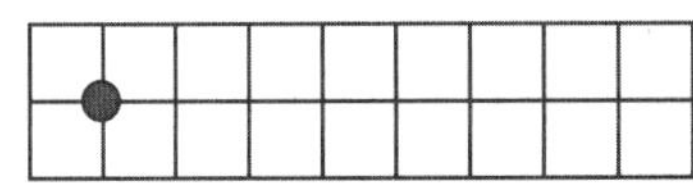

4. How many units **right** and how many units **down** did the dot slide from Position 1 to Position 2?

a)

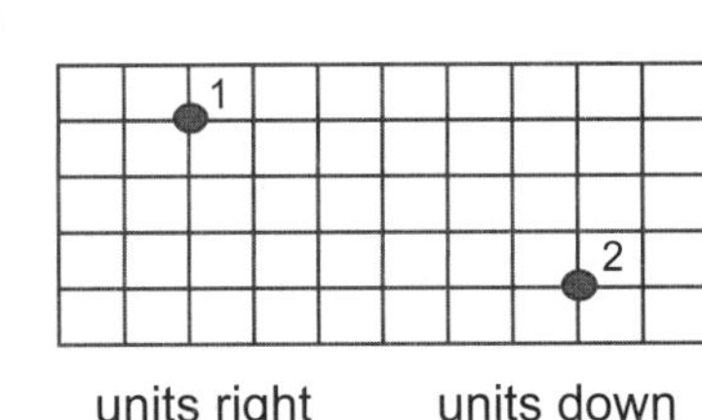


___ units right ___ units down

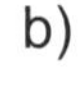
b)

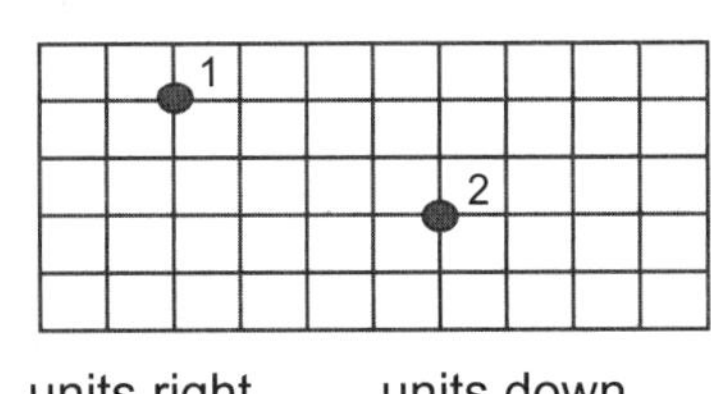


___ units right ___ units down

c)

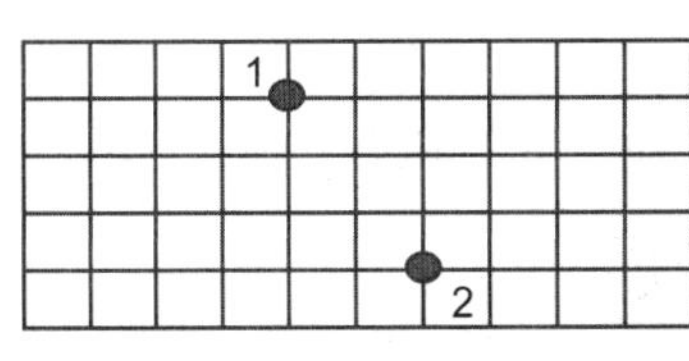


___ units right ___ units down

5. Slide the dot . . .

a) 3 units right; 3 units down

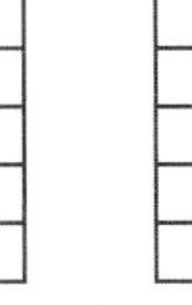

b) 5 units left; 2 units up

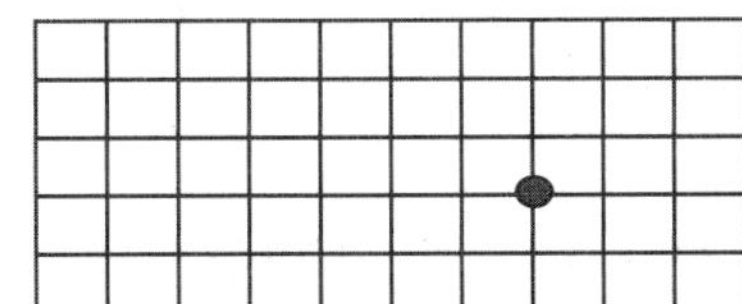

c) 6 units left; 4 units down

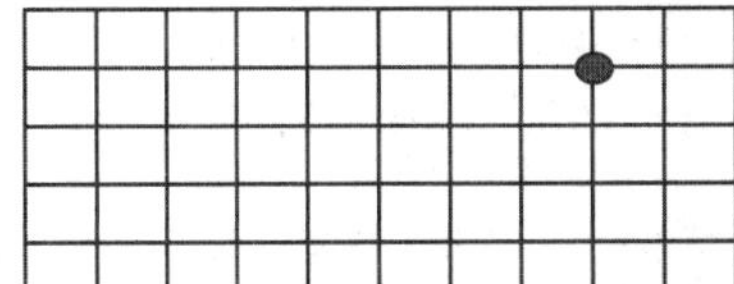

# G4-17: Slides

1. Copy the shape into the second grid. (Make sure your shape is in the same position relative to the dot.)

a) 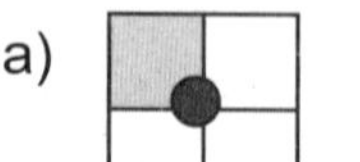 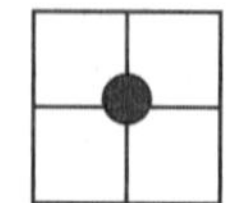
b) 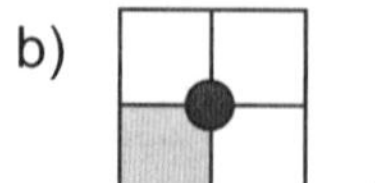 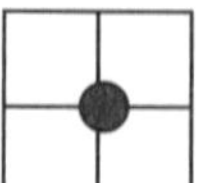
c) 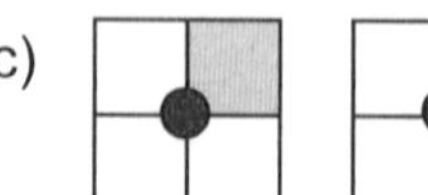 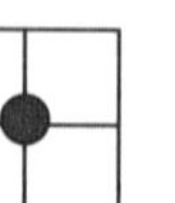
d) 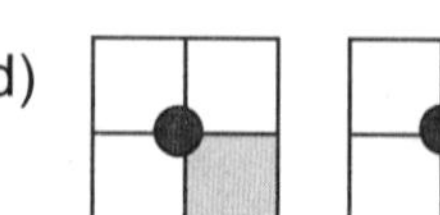

e) 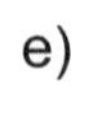 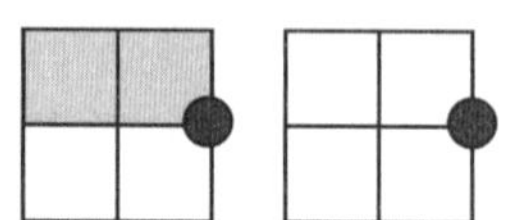
f) 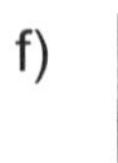 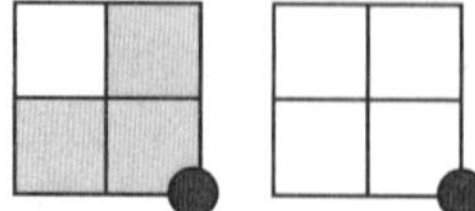
g) 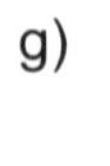 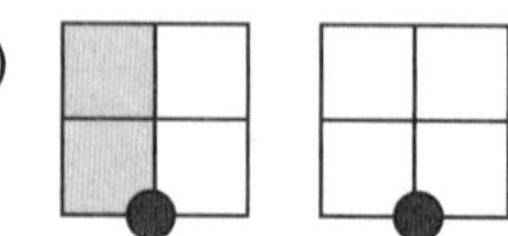
h) 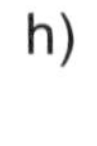 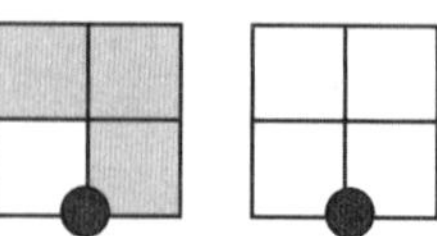

2. Copy the shape onto the second grid.

a) 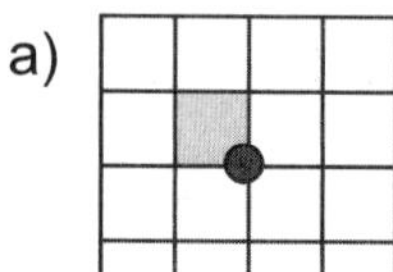 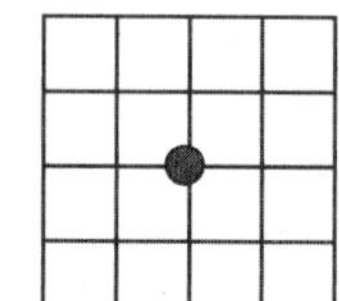
b) 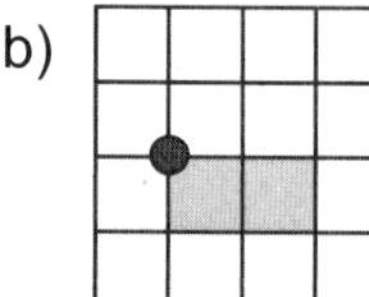 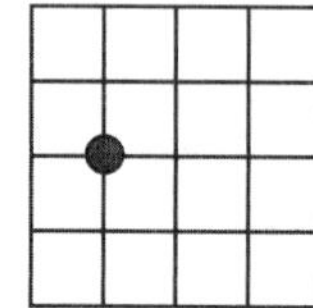
c) 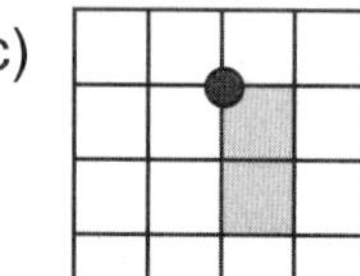 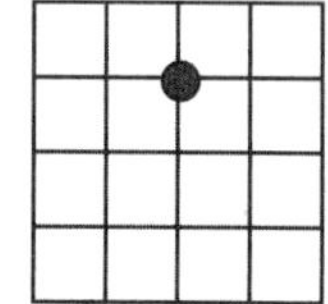

3. Slide the shapes from one end of the box to the other end. Make sure that the dot is at the bottom right hand corner of every shape you shade.

a) 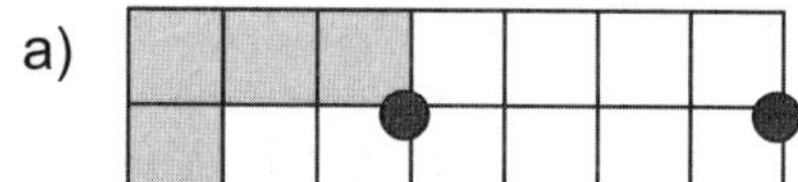
b) 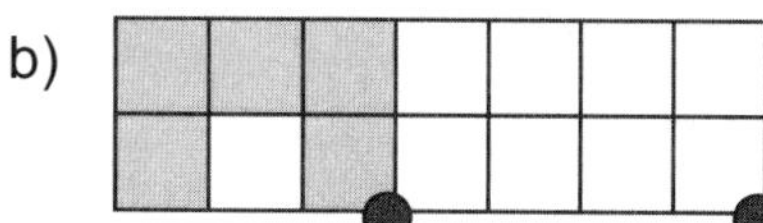
c) 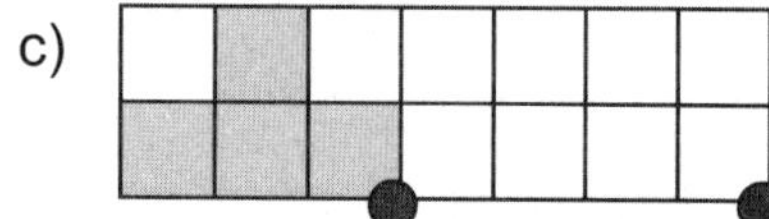

4. Slide the shapes 4 units left. First slide the dot, then copy the shape. Make sure that the dot is in the bottom left hand corner of your new shape.

a) 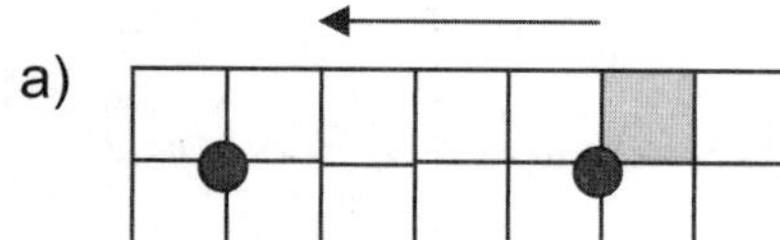
b) 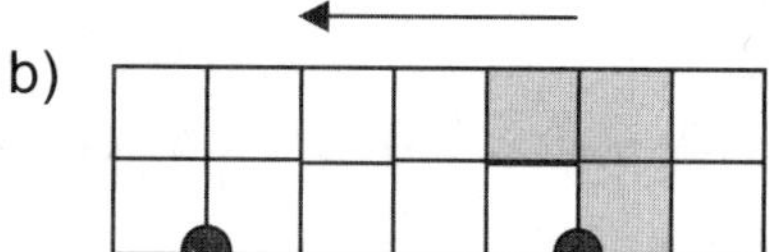
c) 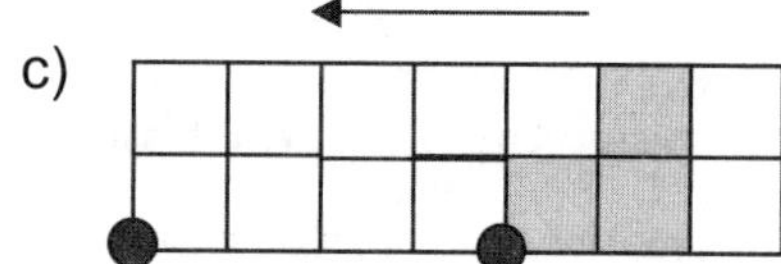

5. Slide the shapes 3 units in the direction shown. First slide the dot, then copy the shape.

a) 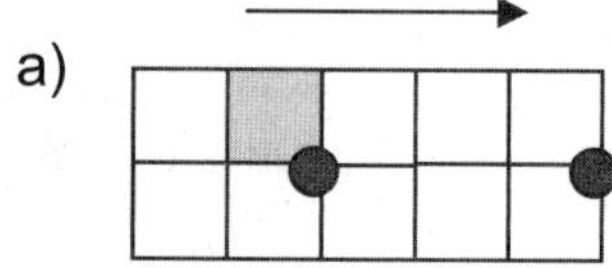
b) 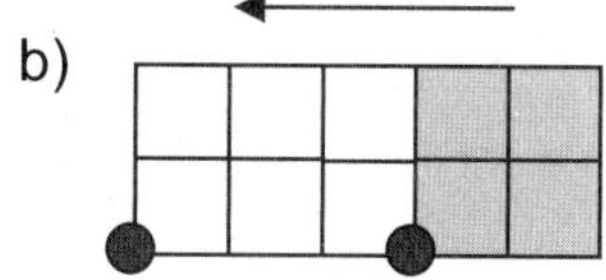
c) 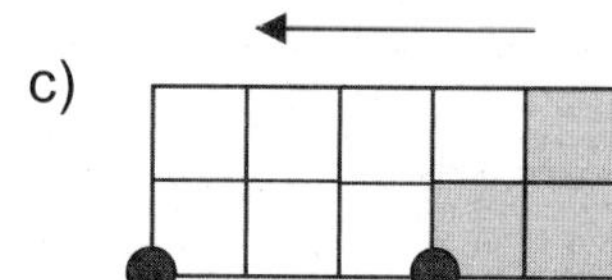

6. Slide the dot three units down, then copy the shape.

a) 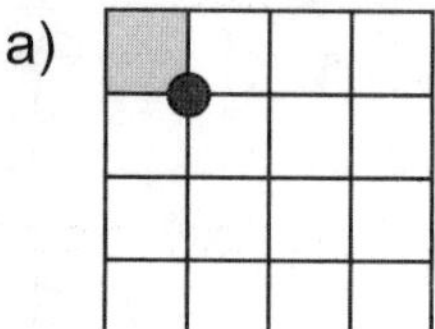
b) 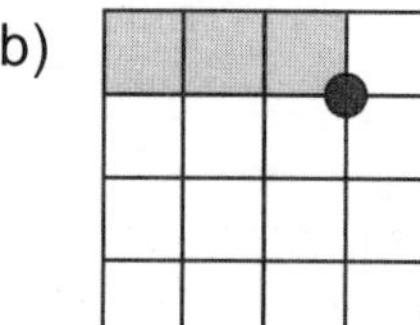
c) 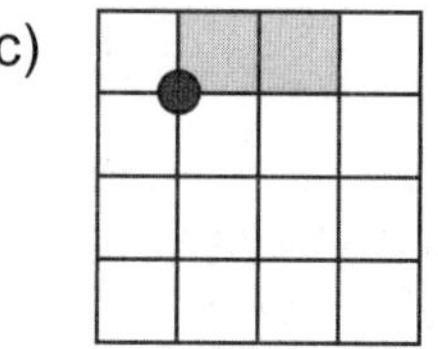
d) 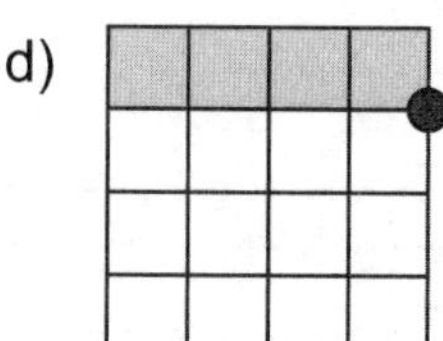

# G4-18: Slides (Advanced)

In a **slide** (or transformation), the figure moves in a straight line without turning. The image of a slide is congruent to the original figure.

Helen slides (or translates) a shape to a new position by following these steps:

1. Draw a dot in a corner of the figure.
2. Slide the dot (in this case 5 right and 2 down).
3. Draw the image of the figure.

Join the two dots with a translation arrow to show the direction of the slide.

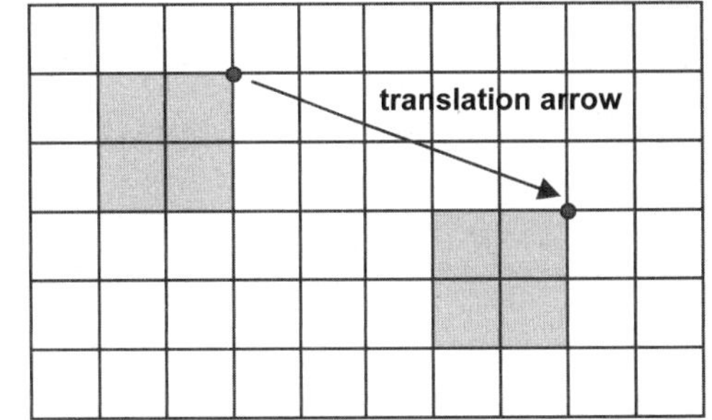

Slide the box 5 right and 2 down.

---

1. Slide each shape 4 boxes to the right. (Start by putting a dot on one of the corners of the figure. Slide the dot four boxes right, then draw the new figure.)

a) 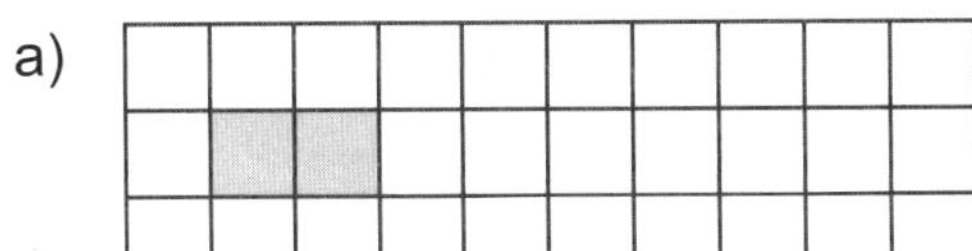

b) 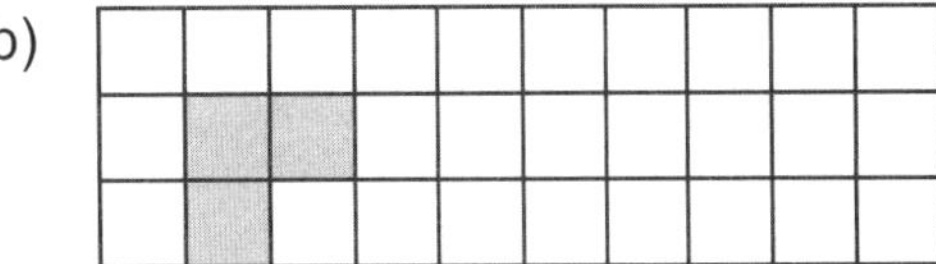

c) 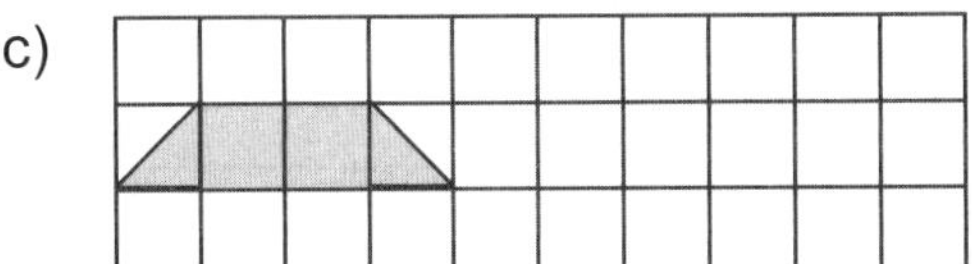

d) 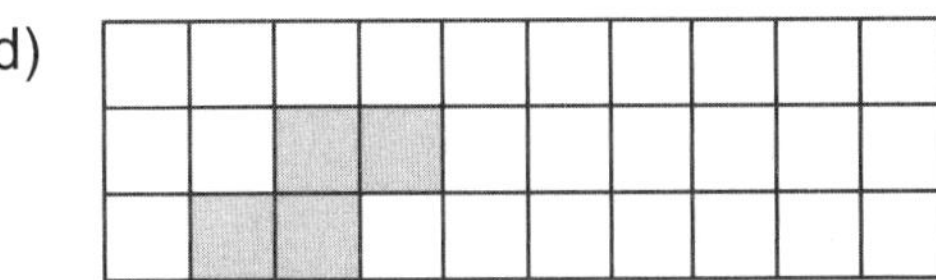

2. Slide each shape 5 boxes to the right and 2 boxes down.

a) 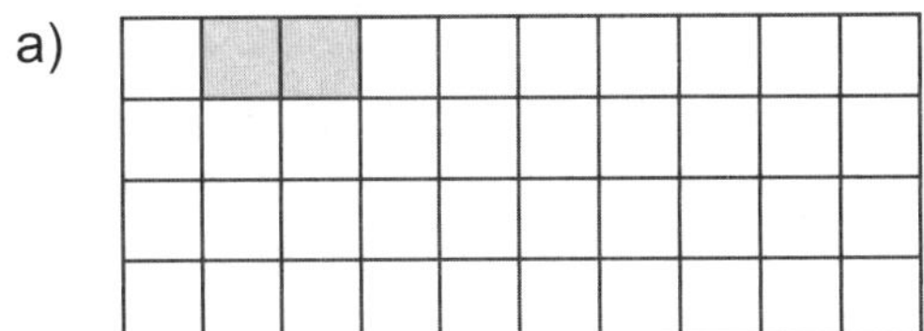

b) 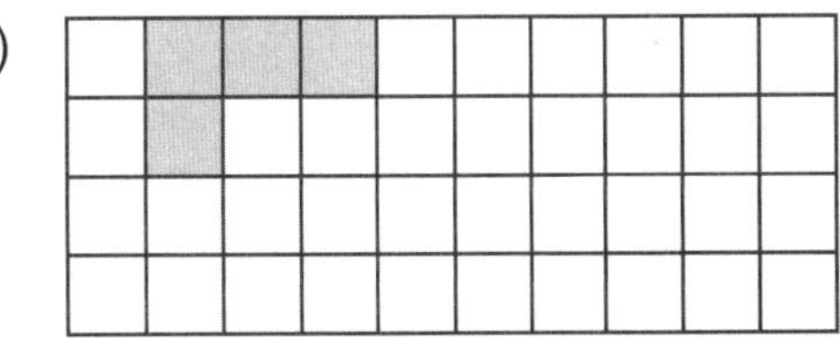

3. Slide the shapes in the grids below. Then describe the slide by writing how many boxes you moved the figure horizontally (right or left) and how many boxes you moved it vertically (up or down).

a) 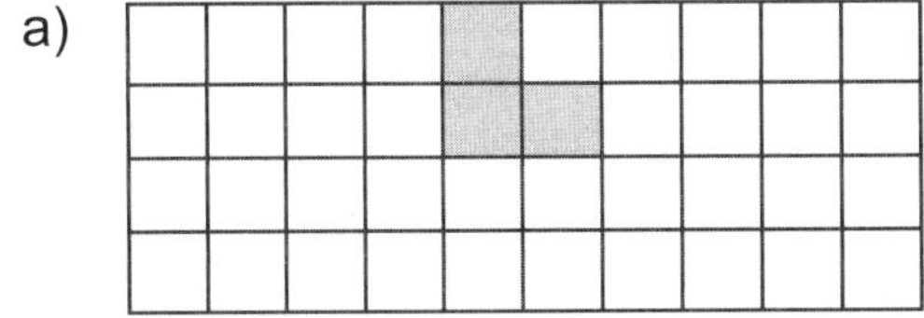

My slide: ______________________

b) 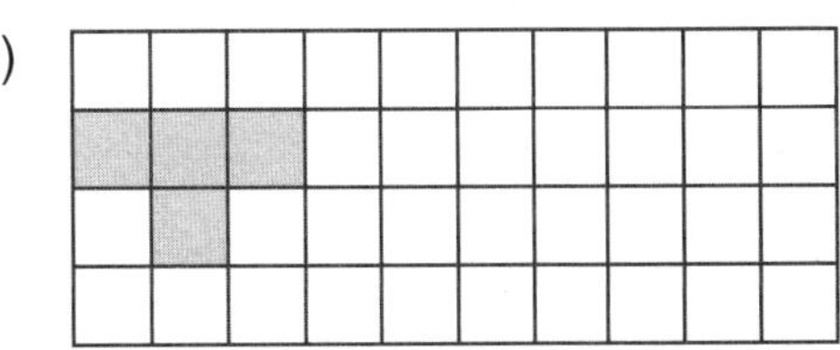

My slide: ______________________

BONUS:

4. Marco says shape B is a slide (or translation) of shape A. Is he correct? Explain your answer on a separate piece of paper.

A B

# G4-19: Coordinate Systems and Maps

1. How many units (right/left and up/down) must the star slide to reach the following points? Use the words "up" and "down," and "left" and "right" to describe how the star must move from its starting position.

A. right 3, up 1

B. ____________

C. ____________

D. ____________

E. ____________

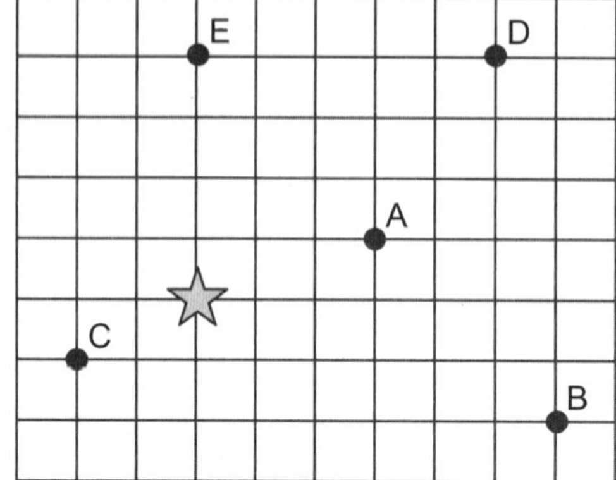


2. Using the following coordinate system, describe your path. The first one is done for you.

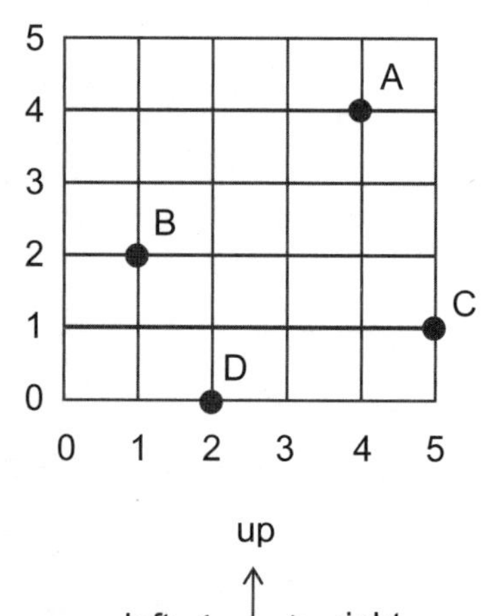


| | |
|---|---|
| a) Start at A and go to B: | 2 down and 3 left |
| b) Start at C and go to D: | |
| c) Start at B and go to C: | |
| d) Start at D and go to B: | |
| e) Start at A and go to C: | |
| f) Start at A and go to D: | |

3. Using the following coordinate system, indicate where you will **start** your journey when . . .

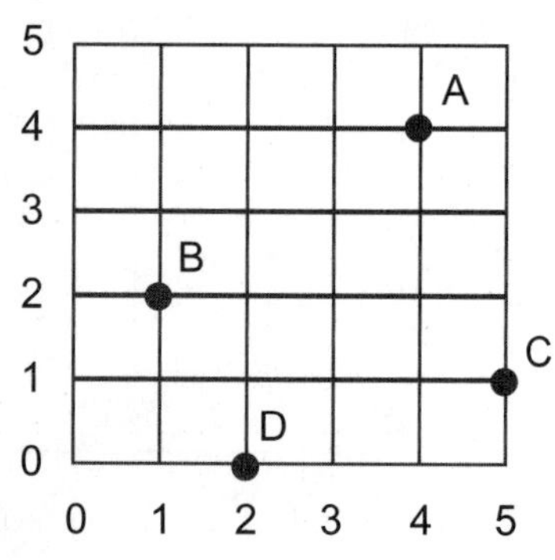


| | |
|---|---|
| a) you move from A to B: | Example: A |
| b) you move to B from C: | |
| c) you move from D to B: | |
| d) you move to D from A: | |
| e) you move to C from A: | |
| f) you move from A to C: | |

**HINT:**
Underline the word "from" in each question.

4. Answer the following questions using the coordinate system:

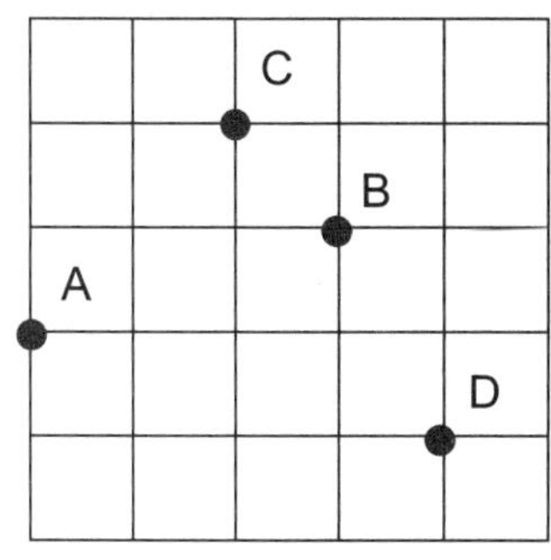


a) What point is 2 units right and 2 up from A?

b) What point is 4 units left and 1 up from D?

c) What point is 1 unit down and 1 right of C?

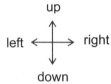

d) Describe how to get from point B to point D:

e) Describe how to go to point B from point A:

f) Describe how to get to point A from point C:

**HINT:**

Underline the word "from" in each question.

5. Answer the following questions using the coordinate system:

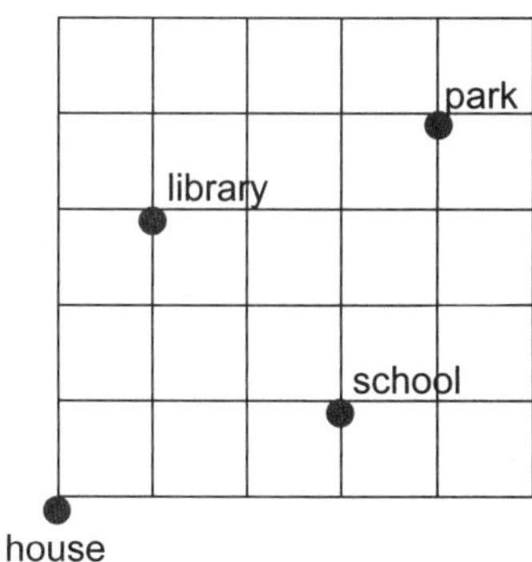


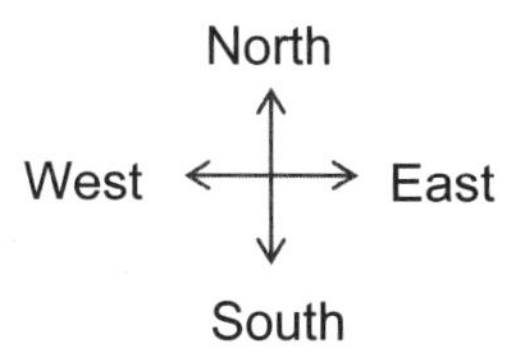


a) What building is 1 block east and 3 blocks north of the house?

b) What building is 2 blocks west and 2 blocks north of the school?

c) What building is 1 block south and 3 blocks west of the school?

d) Describe how to get from the park to the school.

e) Describe how to go to the library from the school.

f) Describe how to go to the park from the library.

6. Answer the following questions using the coordinate system:

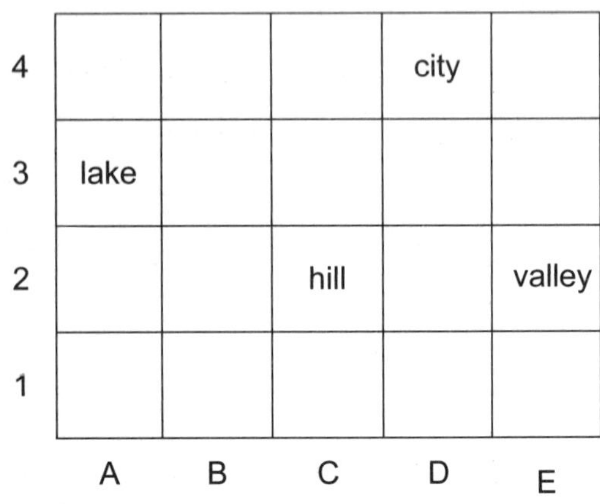


**NOTE:**
Each square represents a square km.

North
West East
South

a) What would you find in square (A,3)?

b) What would you find if you travelled 2 grid squares west of the valley?

c) Give the coordinates of the city.

d) Describe how to get from the city to the lake.

e) Describe how to get from the hill to the city.

7. Use the following clues to figure out where all the children sit:

- Walk 2 desks down and 1 desk right from Zoltan to find John's seat.
- Samir is 1 desk left of Alan.
- Sally is between Sahar and Zoltan.
- Walk 2 desks left and 1 desk up from Tom to find Mary's desk.
- Tara is 1 desk right of Zoltan.
- Noor is between Yen and Tom.

| Sahar | | Zoltan | |
|---|---|---|---|
| | Anna | | Alan |
| Yen | | Tom | |

8. Jacob is trying to cross the lake without bumping into any of the islands. Describe the path that he took to get from his start, to his finishing point.

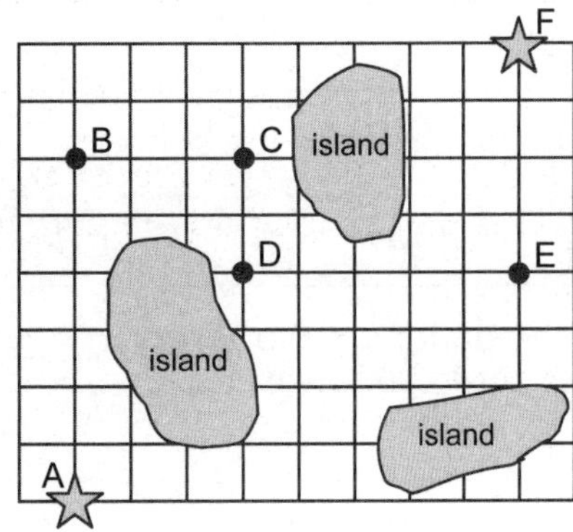


1. From A (start) to B: ________________
2. From B to C: ________________
3. From C to D: ________________
4. From D to E: ________________
5. From E to F (finish): ________________

# G4-20: Games and Activities with Maps and Grids

In this exercise, you must follow the column and then row to answer the questions. Each coordinate location should be written as (column,row) or (letter,number) for example: **(A,3)**

1. Use the given map of Canada to answer the following questions on a separate piece of paper:

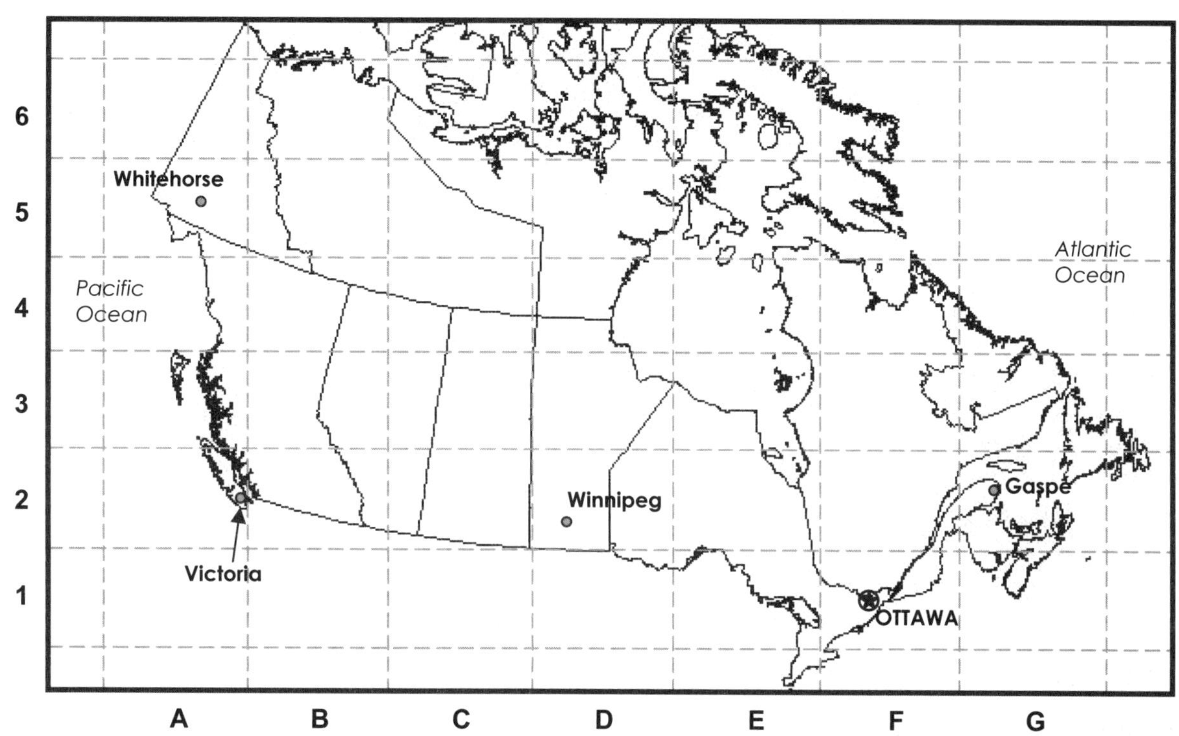


a) What are the coordinates of Ottawa (the capital city of Canada)?

b) What are the coordinates of Whitehorse, Yukon Territory?

c) What are the coordinates of Winnipeg, Manitoba?

d) What are the coordinates of Gaspé, Quebec?

e) **(A,2)** are the coordinates of which city?

f) **(G,5)** is in which body of water?

g) **(F,2)** is in which province?

2. **Secret Squares**

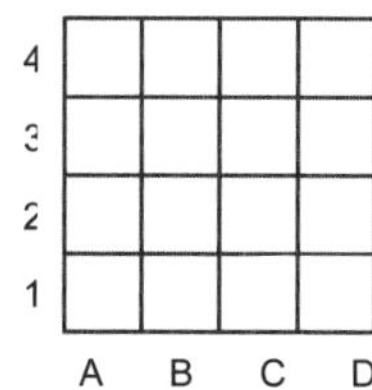


Player 1 draws a 4 x 4 grid as shown and picks a square. Player 2 tries to guess the square by giving its coordinates.

Each time Player 2 guesses, Player 1 writes the distance between the guessed square and the hidden square.

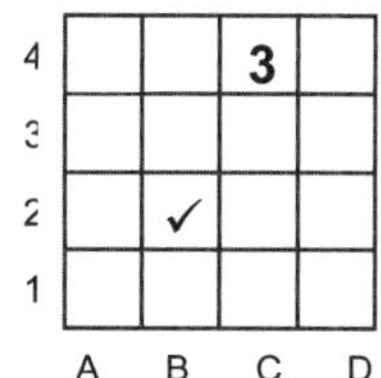


For example, if Player 1 has chosen square B2 (✓) and Player 2 guesses C4, Player 1 writes 3 in the guessed square. (Distances on the grid are counted horizontally and vertically, **never** diagonally.)

The game ends when Player 2 guesses the correct square.

As a warm-up, try to guess the locations of each hidden square from the information given in the grids. In 2 grids, not enough information is given (mark all the possible locations for the hidden square) and in one grid too much information is given (identify one piece of redundant information).

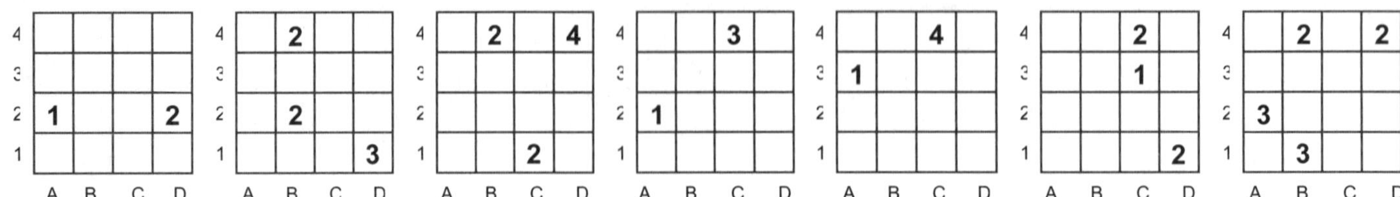

3. **Battleship**

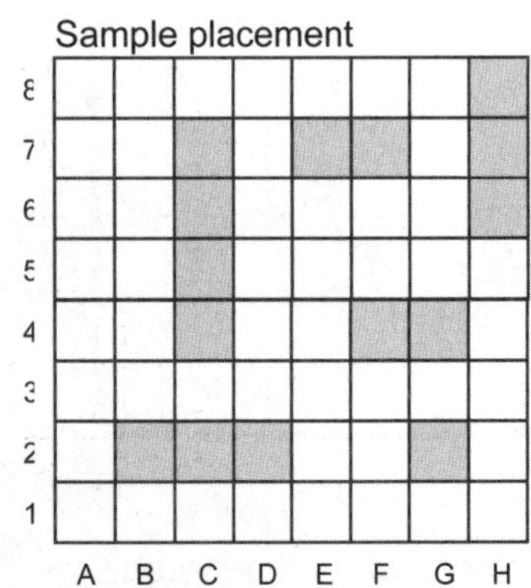

Player 1 and Player 2 each draw a grid as shown. Each player shades . . .

(See the grid for an example: no square of a ship may be adjacent to a square of another ship, including diagonally.)

Players try to sink all their partner's battleships by guessing their coordinates. If a player's ship is in a square that is called out, the player must say "hit." Otherwise they say "miss."

Each player should keep track of the squares they have guessed on a blank grid by marking hits with an ✗ and misses with a ✓. The game ends when all of one player's ships are sunk. A ship is sunk when **all** its squares are hit.

4. **Solitaire Battleship**

One cruiser, one destroyer and one submarine are hidden in each grid (see the description of Battleship for sizes). The row number tells the number of shaded squares in the row. The column number tells the number of shaded squares in that column. Find the 3 ships in each grid. (HINT: Start by putting an "X" in all the squares where you know there **cannot** be a ship.)

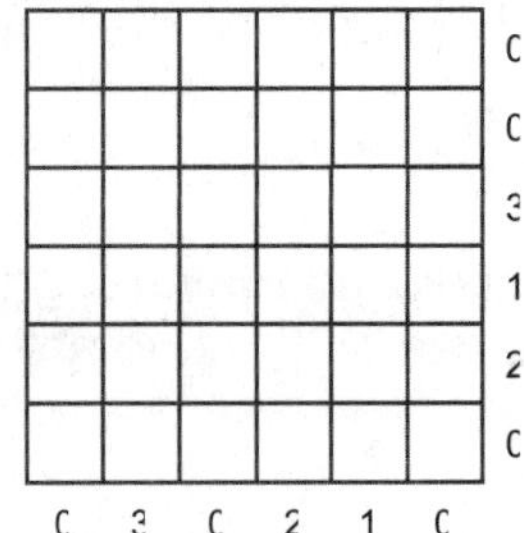

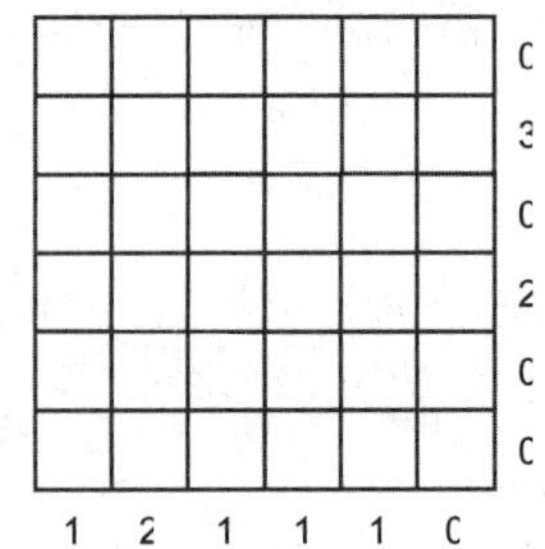

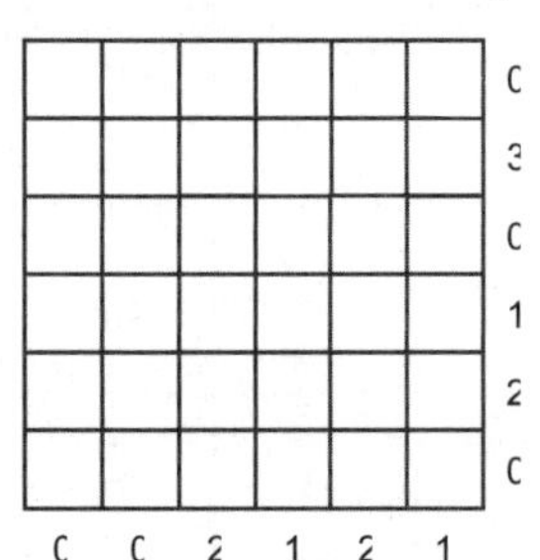

# G4-21: Reflections

O'Shane reflects the shape by flipping it over the mirror line. Each point on the figure flips to the opposite side of the mirror line, but stays the same distance from the line. O'Shane checks to see that his reflection is drawn correctly by using a mirror:

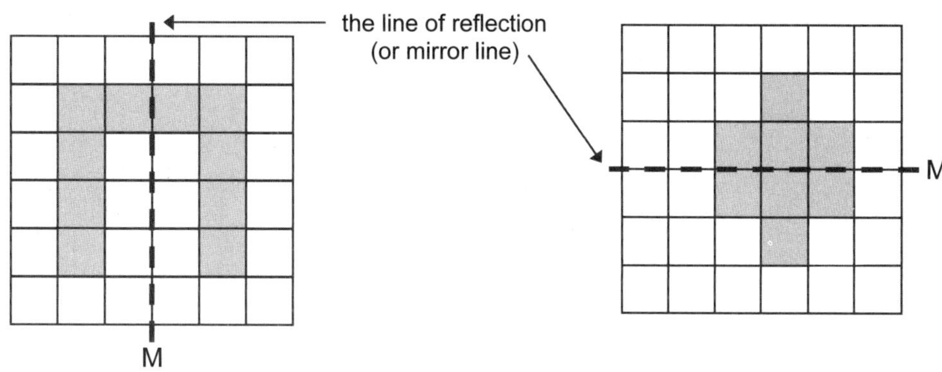


1. Draw the reflection of the shapes.

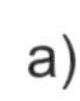

a)

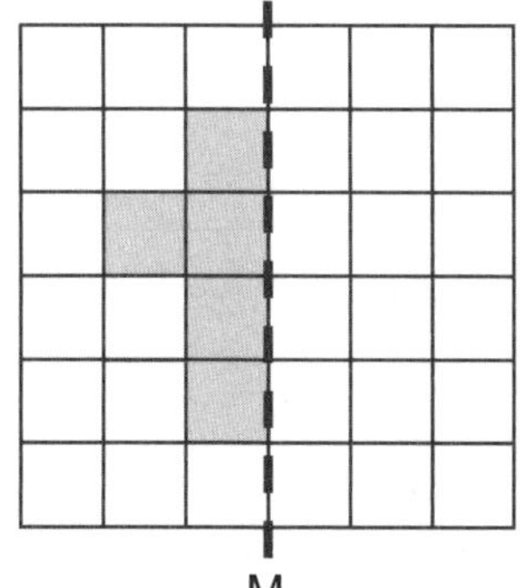


b)

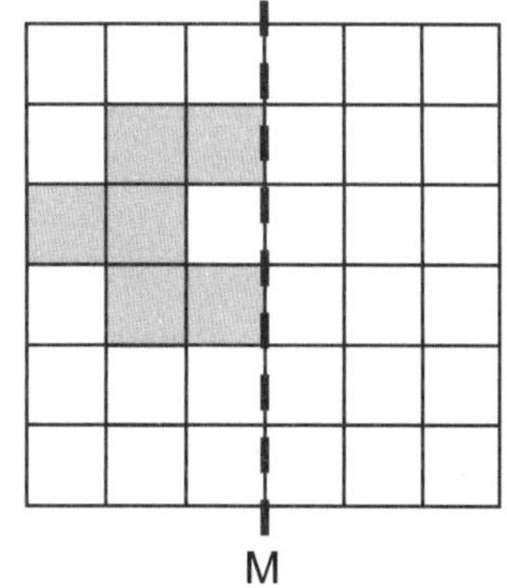


c)

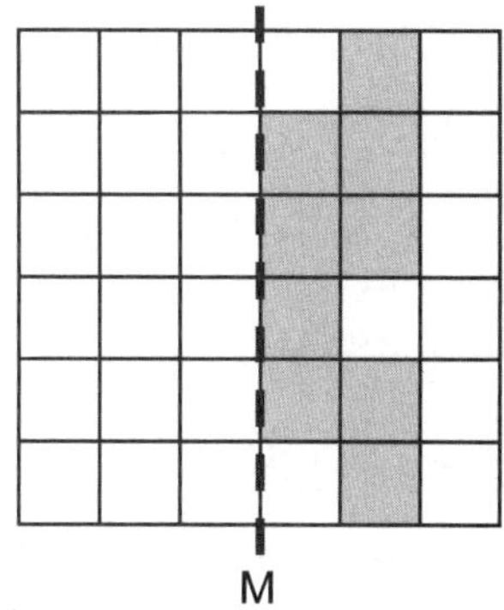


2. Draw the reflection, or flip, of the shapes.

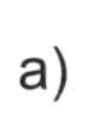

a)

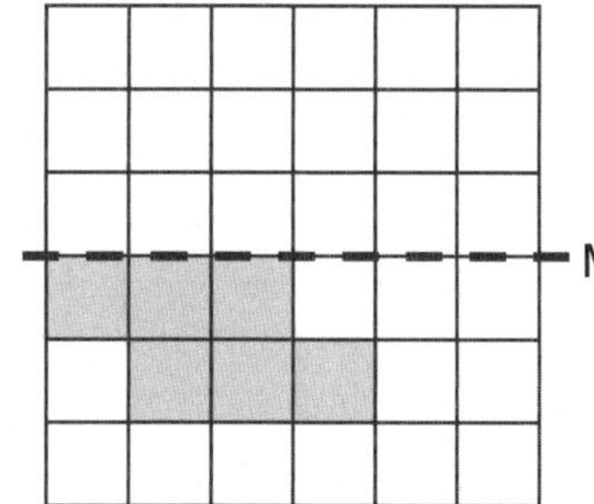


b)

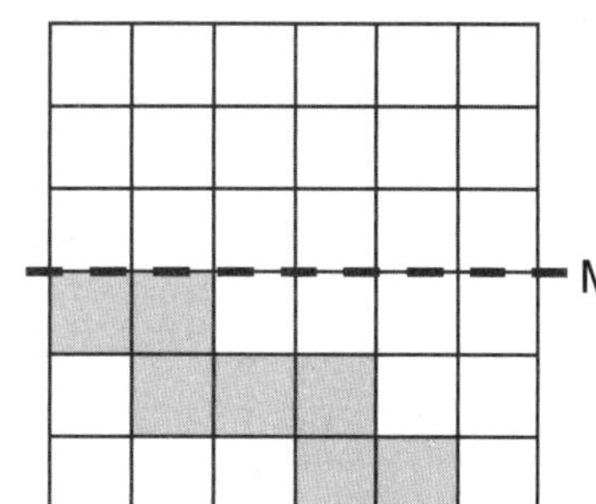


c)

M

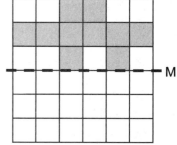

3. Draw your own shape in the box below. Now draw the flip of the shape on the other side of the mirror line.

M

BONUS: Are the shapes on either side of the mirror congruent? Explain your answer.

______________________________

______________________________

______________________________

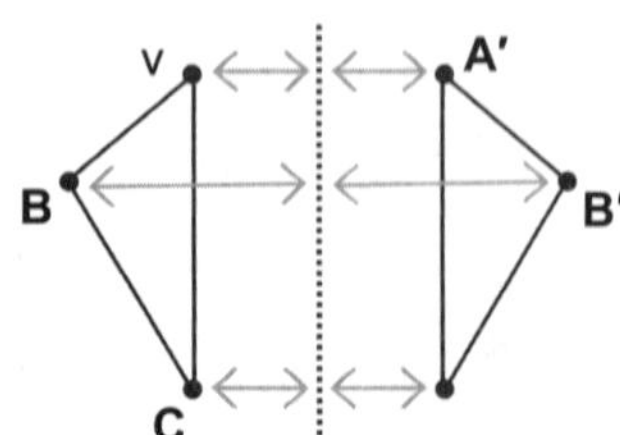


When a point is reflected in a mirror line, the point and the image of the point are the same distance from the mirror line.

A figure and its image are congruent but face in opposite directions.

4. Reflect the point P through the mirror line M.

a) 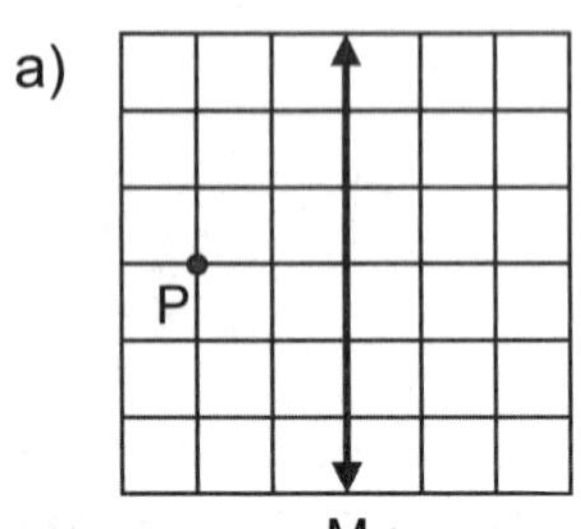


b) 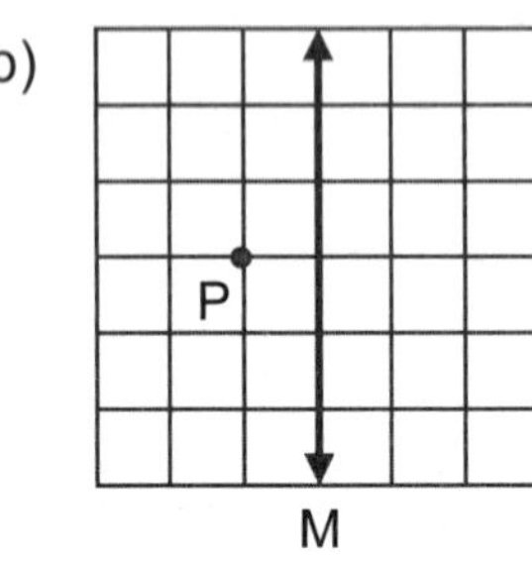


c) 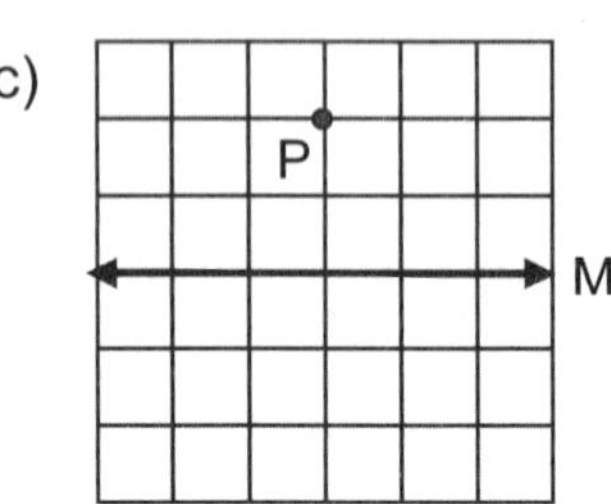


d) 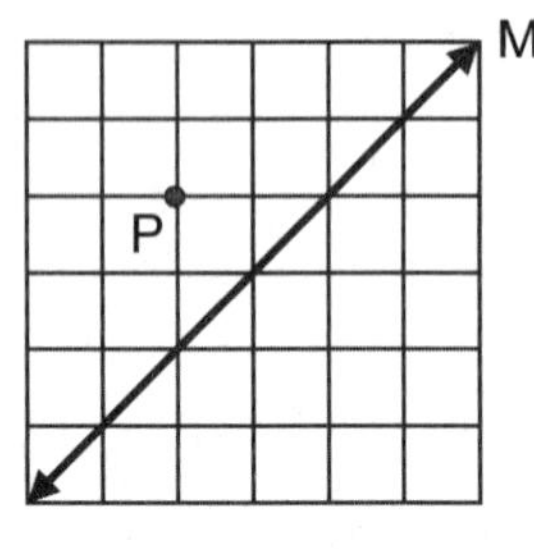


5. Reflect the set of points P, Q, and R through the mirror line.

a) 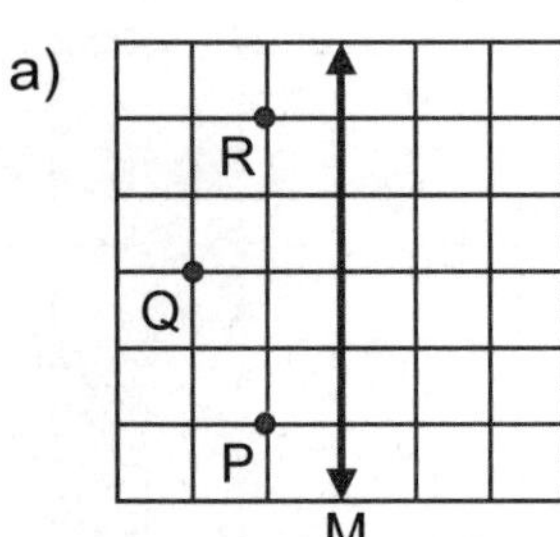


b) 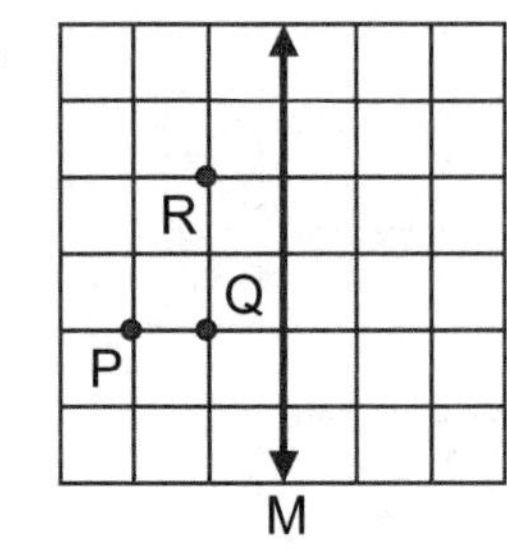


c) 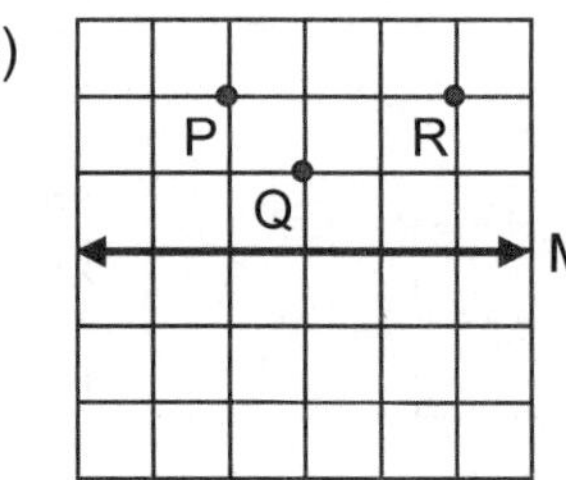


d) 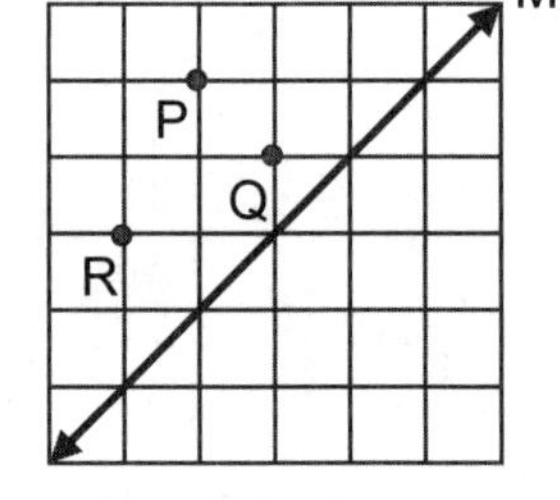


6. Reflect the figure by first reflecting the points on the figure.

a) 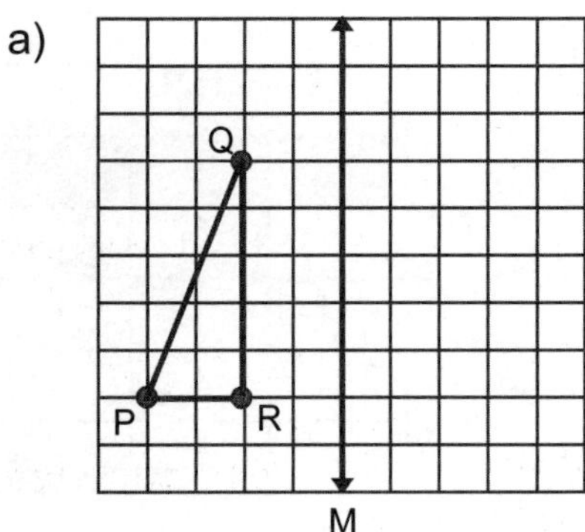


b) 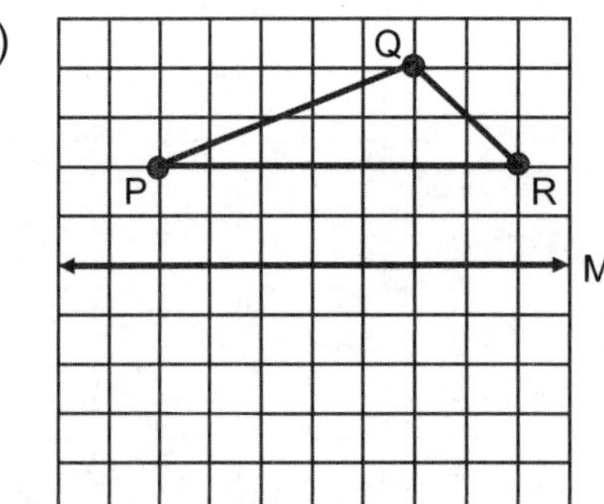


c) 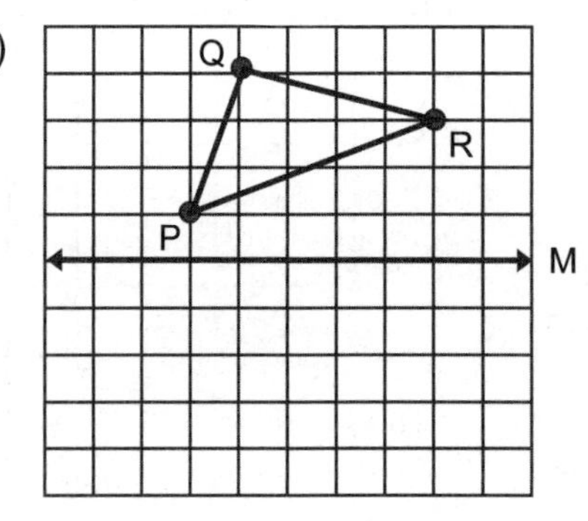


7. Sketch what each letter would look like reflected in the mirror line.
REMEMBER: The reflection must face in the opposite direction to the figure.

a) 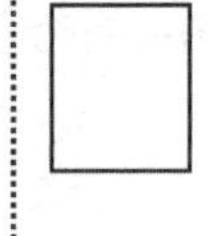


b) 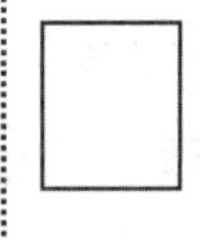


c) 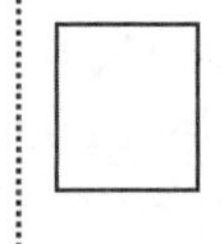


d) 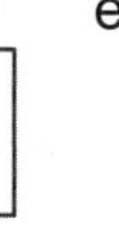


e) 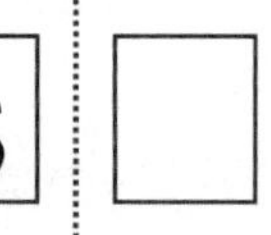

# G4-22: Rotations

NOTE:
Review the meaning of the terms “clockwise” and “counter-clockwise” before beginning this lesson.

1. Name the fraction shown by the shaded part of each shape.

a) 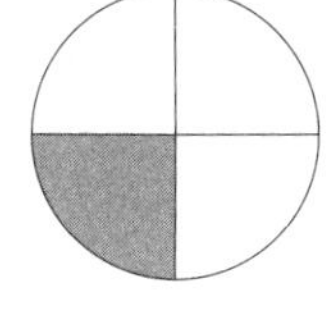
b) 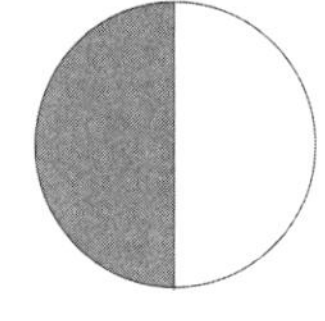
c) 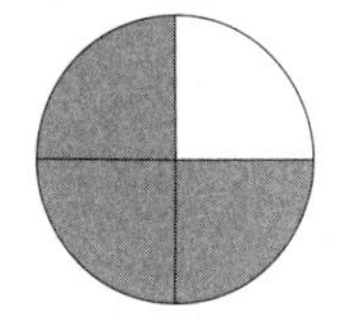
d) 

e) 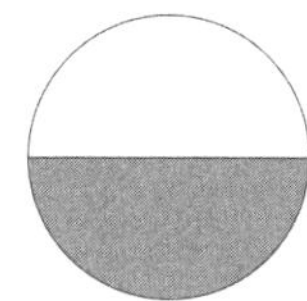
f) 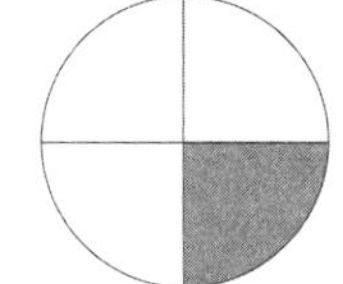
g) 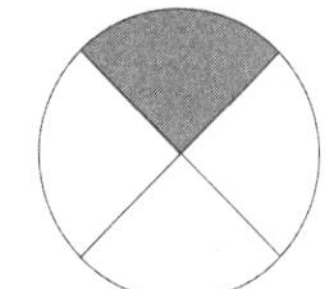
h) 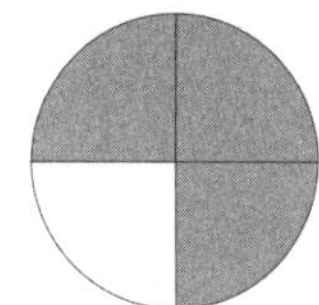

2. The picture shows how far the hand of the clock has turned. **Shade the part of the circle the hand has moved across**. Then, in the box, write what fraction of a turn the hand made. (HINT: What fraction of the circle did you shade?)

a) 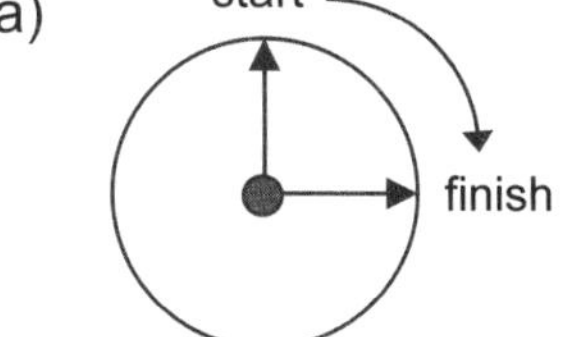


☐ turn clockwise

b) 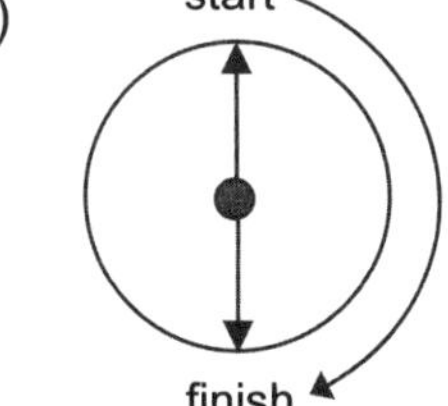


☐ turn clockwise

c) 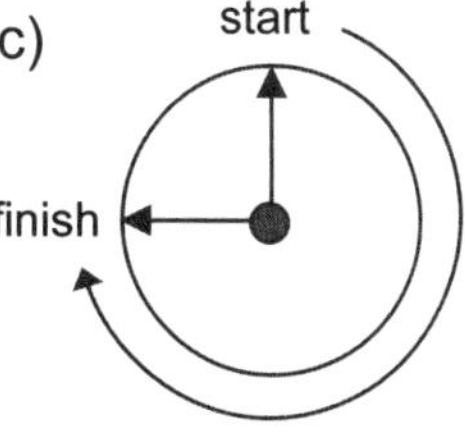


☐ turn clockwise

d) 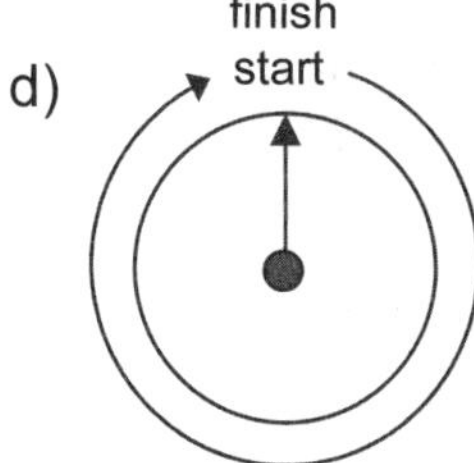


☐ turn clockwise

e) start finish

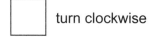

☐ turn clockwise

f) 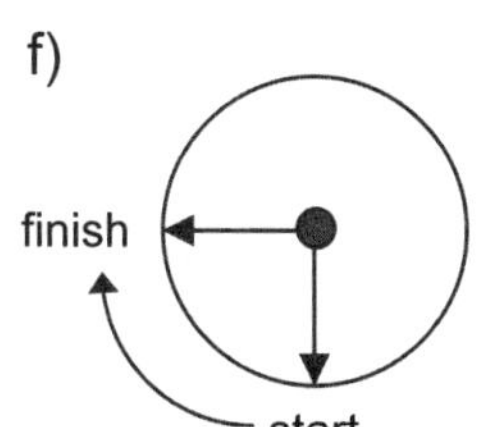


☐ turn clockwise

g) 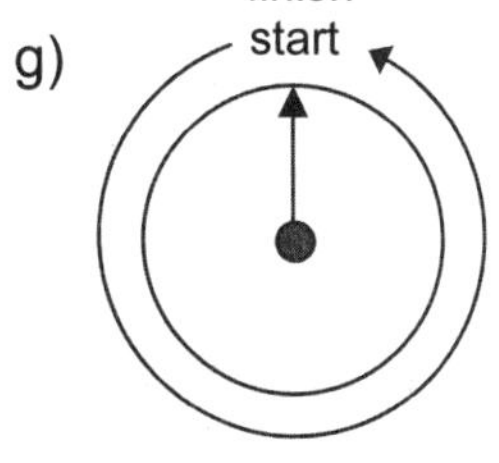

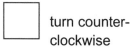

☐ turn counter-clockwise

h) 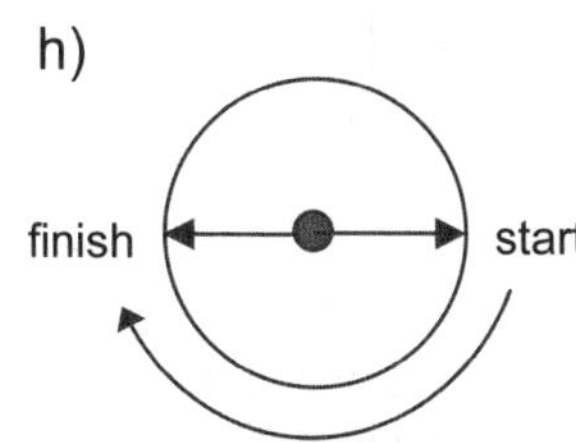

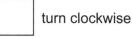

☐ turn clockwise

i) 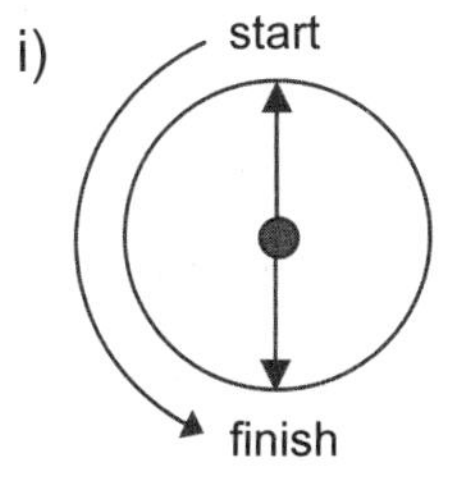


j) 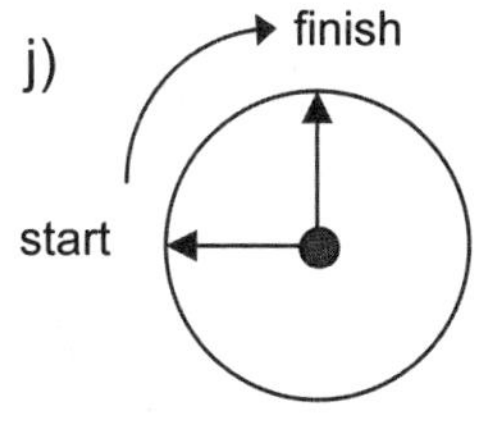


k) 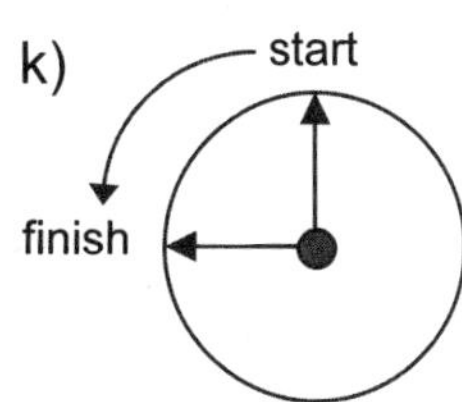


l) 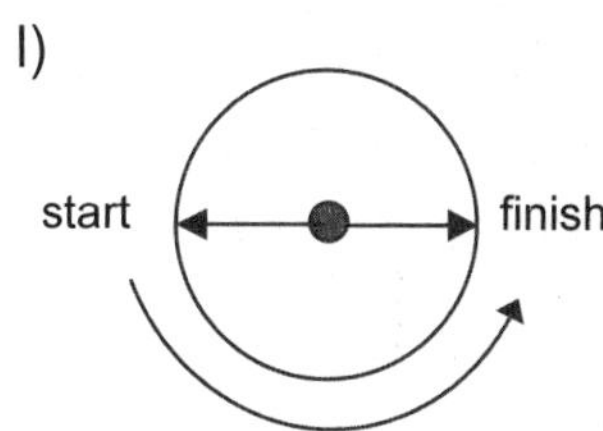

Alice wants to rotate this arrow ¼ of a turn clockwise:

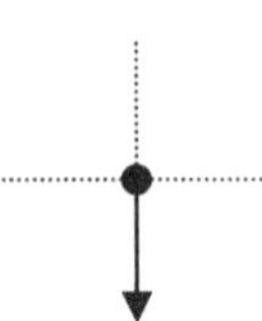

Step 1:
She draws a circular arrow to show how far the arrow should turn.

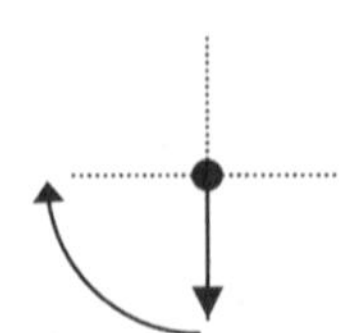

Step 2:
She draws the final position of the arrow.

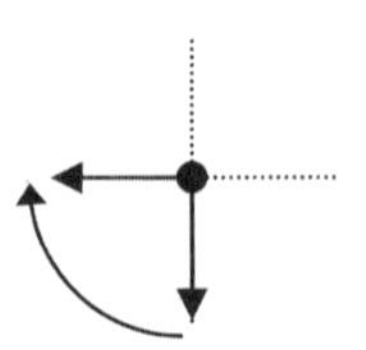

---

3. Write how far each arrow has moved from start to finish.

a) 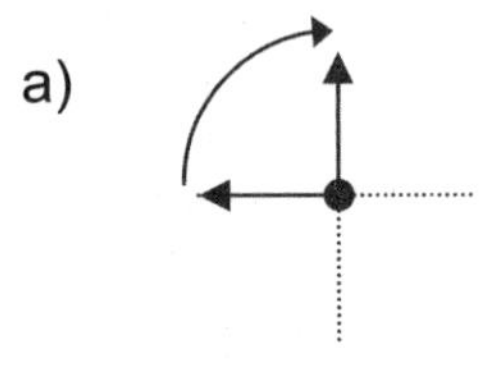

☐ turn clockwise

b) 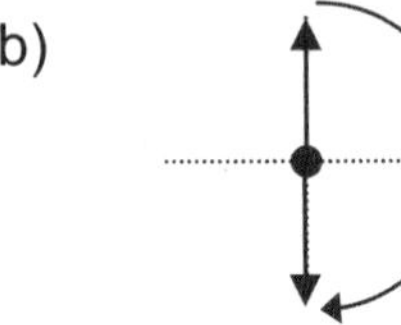

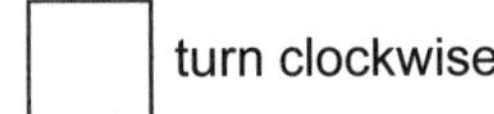

☐ turn clockwise

c) 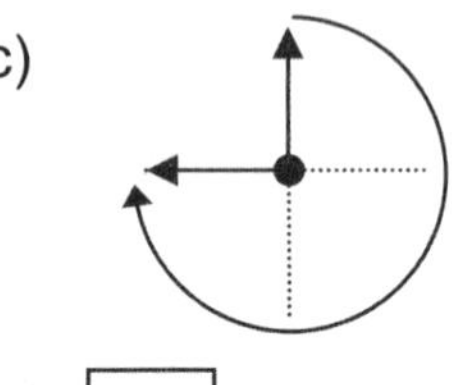

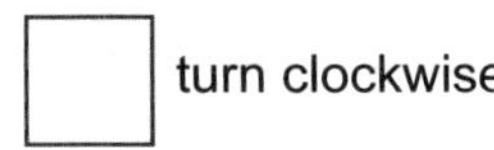

☐ turn clockwise

d) 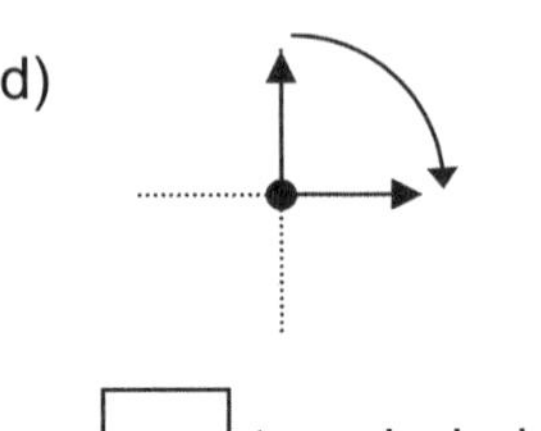

☐ turn clockwise

4. Write how far each arrow has moved counter-clockwise from start to finish.

a) 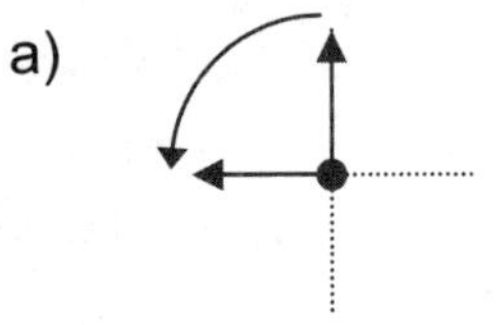

☐ turn counter-clockwise

b) 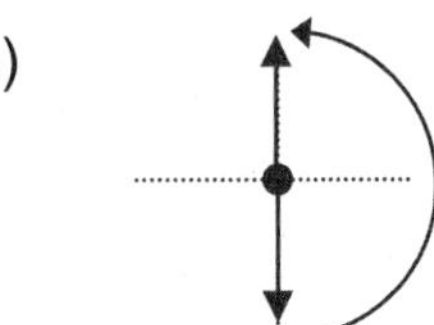

☐ turn counter-clockwise

c) 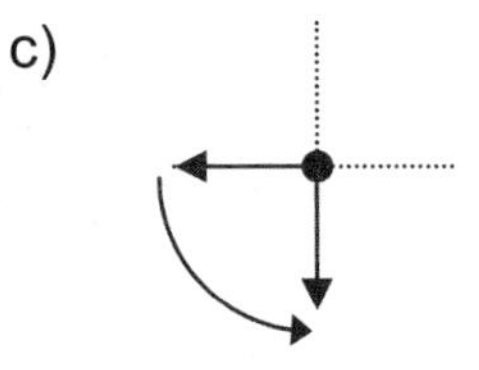

☐ turn counter-clockwise

d) 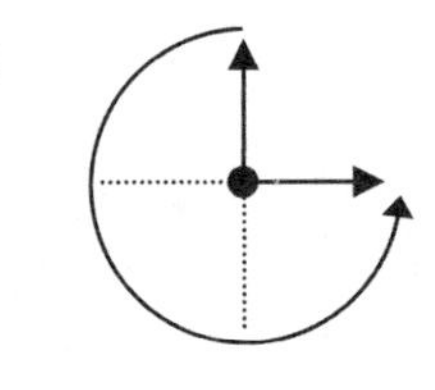

☐ turn counter-clockwise

5. Show where the arrow would be after each turn. (HINT: Use Alice's method.)

a) ¼ turn clockwise

b) 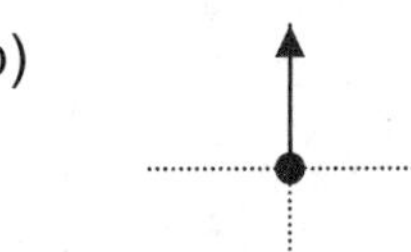

½ turn clockwise

c) 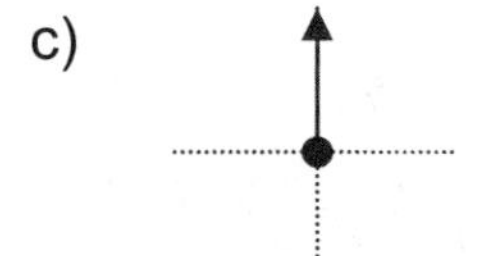

¾ turn clockwise

d) 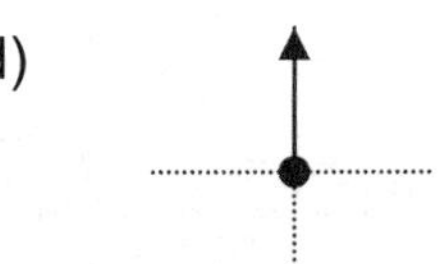

1 whole turn clockwise

e) 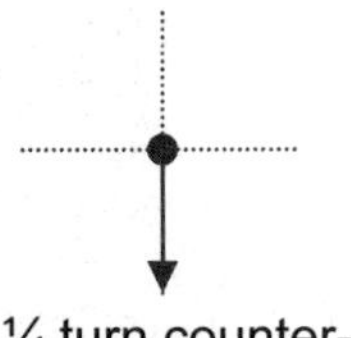

¼ turn counter-clockwise

f) 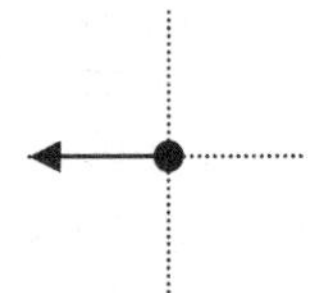

½ turn counter-clockwise

g) 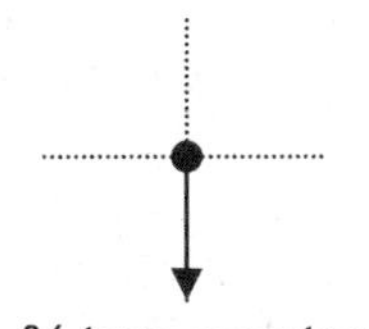

¾ turn counter-clockwise

h) 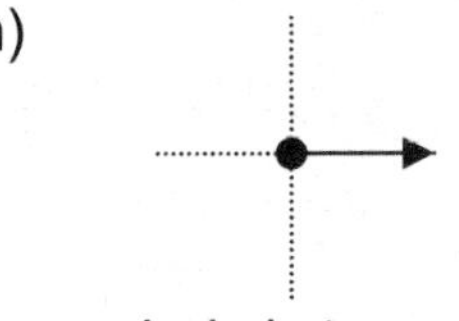

I whole turn counter-clockwise

i) ¾ turn counter-clockwise

j) 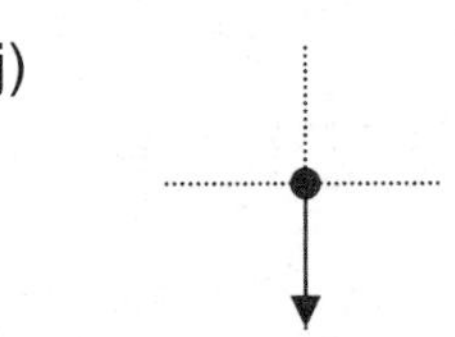

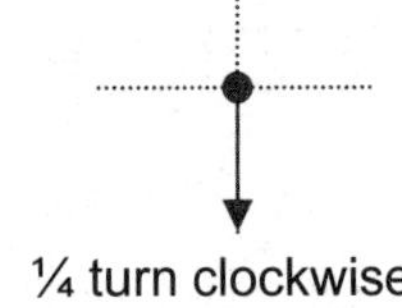

¼ turn clockwise

k) ½ turn counter-clockwise

l) 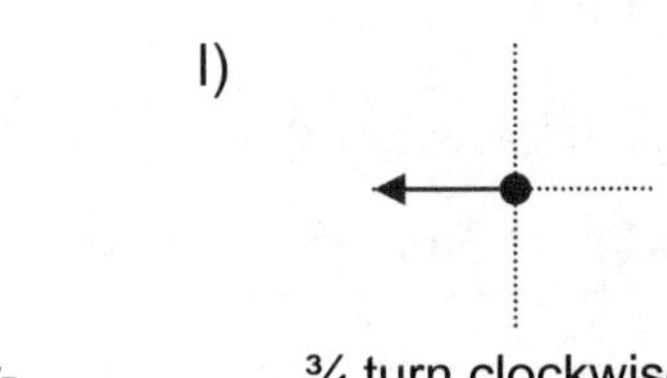

¾ turn clockwise

# G4-23: Rotations (Advanced)

1. Show what the figure would look like after the rotation. First rotate the dark line, then draw the rest of the figure.

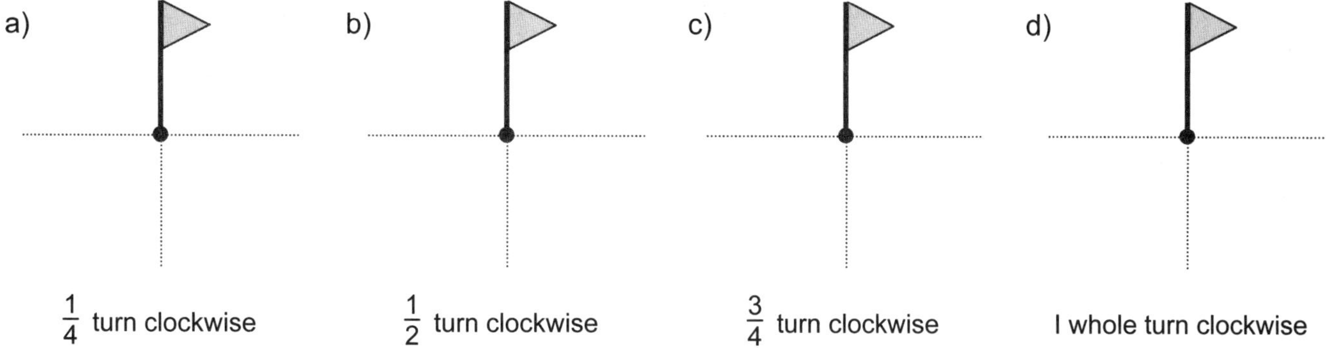


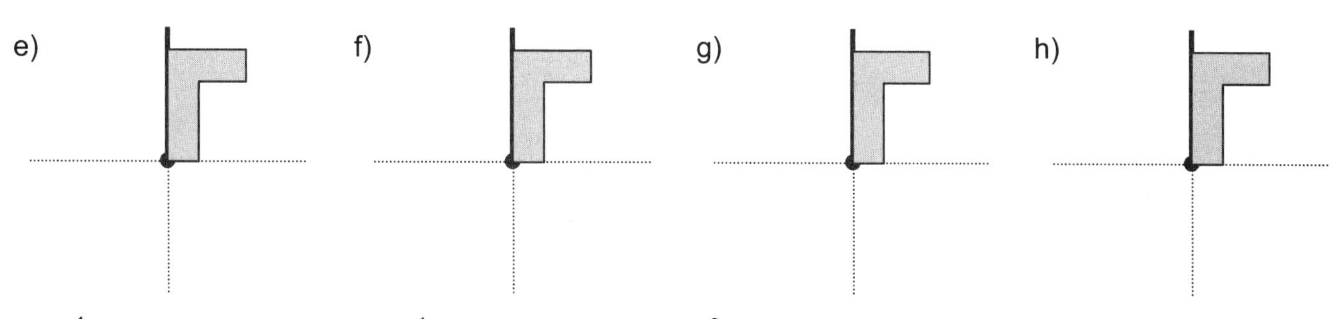


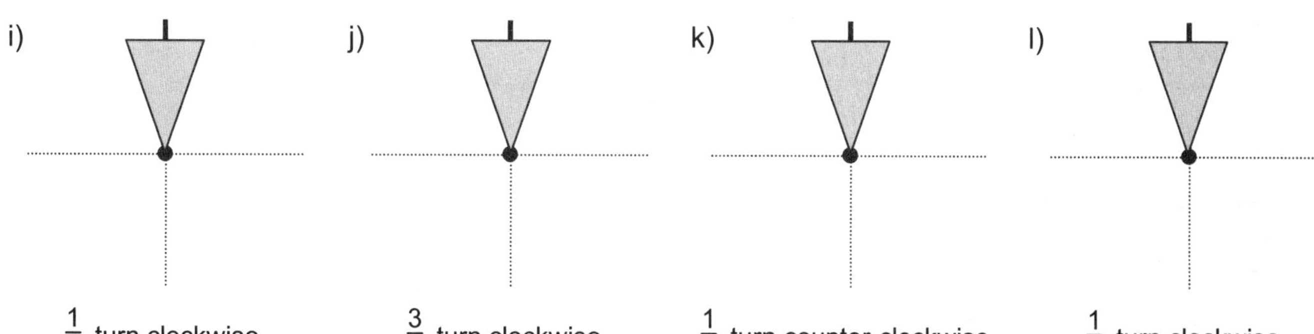


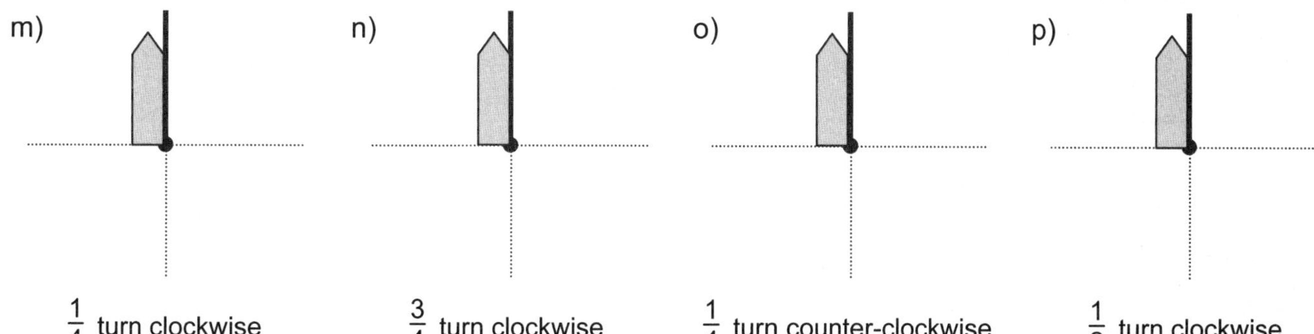

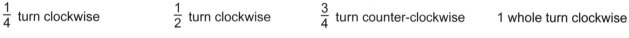

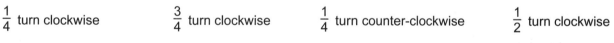

BONUS:
Draw a figure on grid paper. Draw a dot on one of its corners. Show what the figure would look like if you rotated it a quarter turn clockwise around the dot.

# G4-24: Rotations and Reflections

1. Rotate each shape 180° around centre P by showing the final position of the figure.

   Use the line to help you.

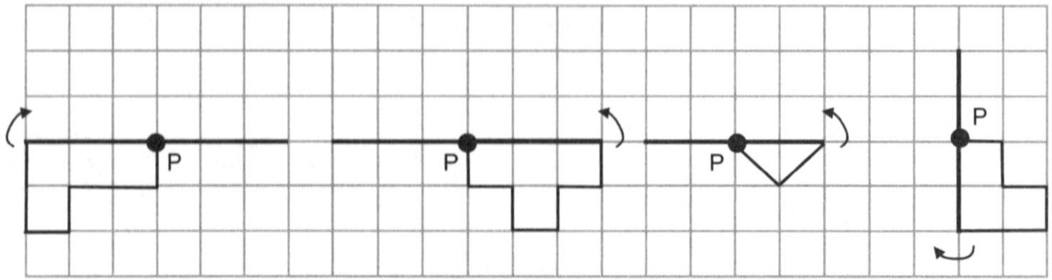


2. Rotate each shape 180° around centre P.
   (HINT: First highlight an edge of the figure and rotate the edge (as in question 1).)

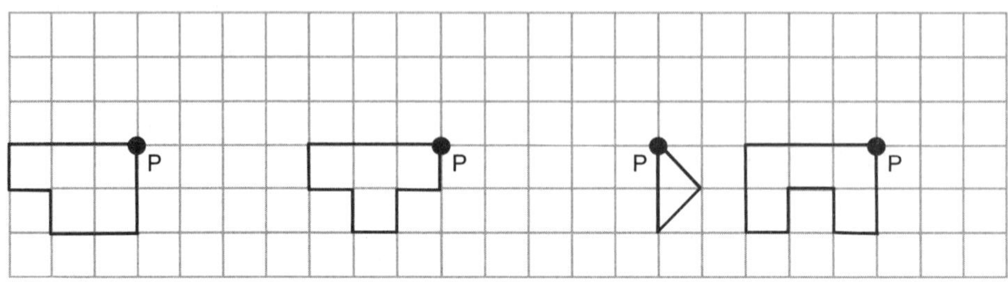


3. Rotate each shape 90° around point P in the direction shown.

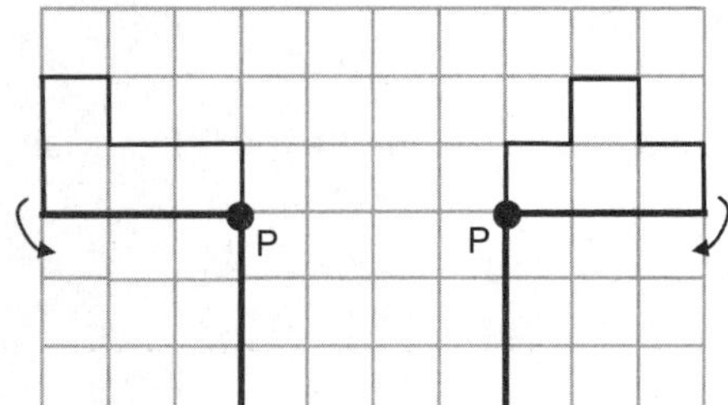


4. Rotate each shape 90° around the point in the direction shown. (HINT: First highlight a line on the figure and rotate the line 90°.)

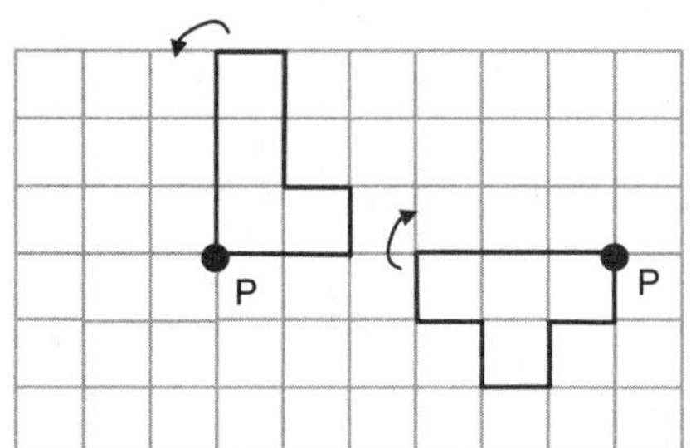


5. Identify the figure (1 or 2) that was made by rotating the original figure 90°. Write 90° beside the figure. Then identify the figure that was made by rotating the original figure 180°. Mark the centre of each rotation.

a) 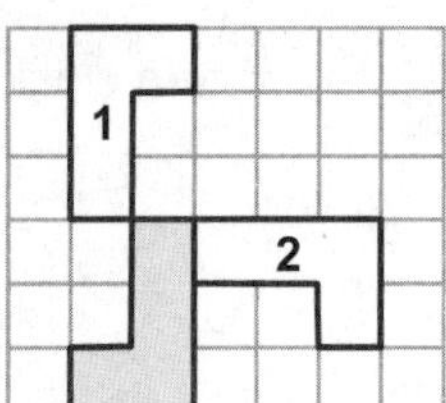


b) 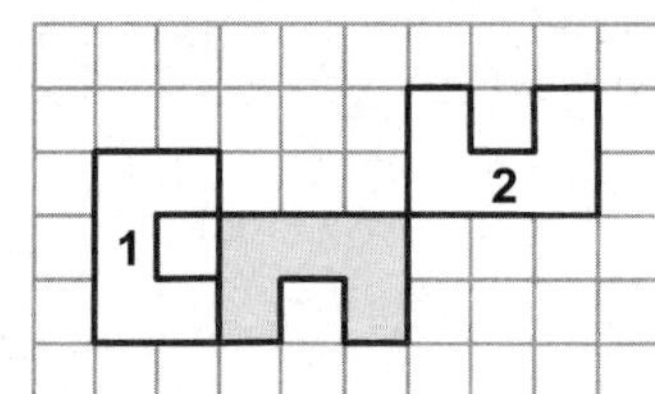


c) 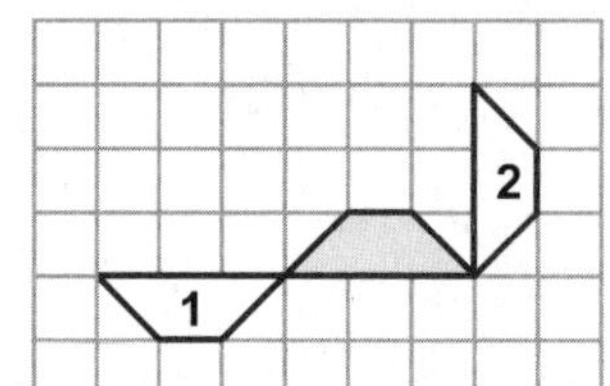


6. Identify the figure (1 or 2) that was made by rotating the original figure 180°. Write 180° beside the figure. Then write "R" for reflection on the figure that was made by a reflection. Mark the centre of the rotation and draw a mirror line for the reflection.

a) 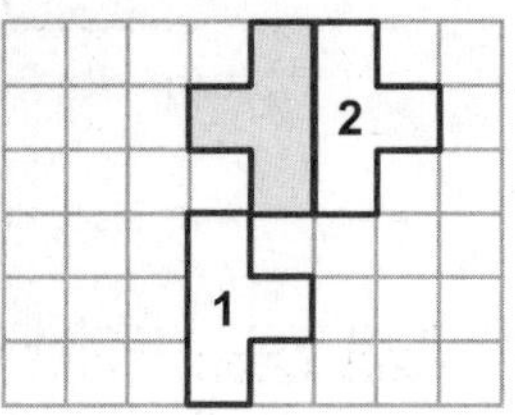


b) 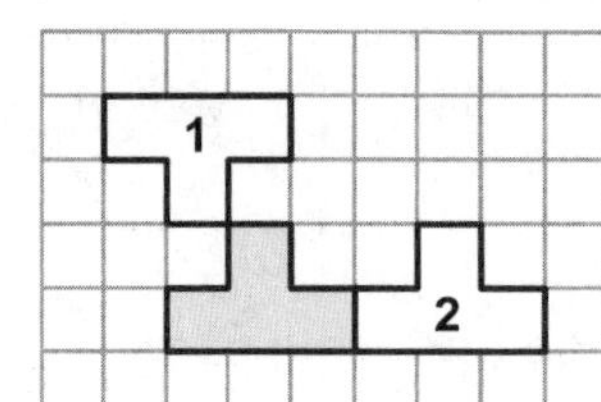


c) 1 2

# G4-25: Slides, Rotations, and Reflections



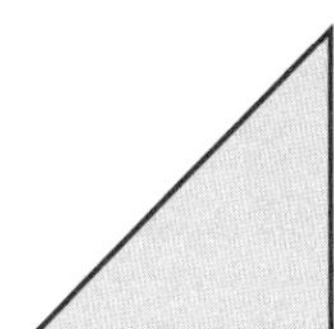

Trace and cut out the triangle. Place the triangle in Position 1 and move it to Position 2 by **one** of the transformations.

- Slide
  (1 unit right or left)
- ¼ Turn
  (clockwise/counter-clockwise around P)
- Reflection
  (in line "M")

1. Describe the transformation used.

a) 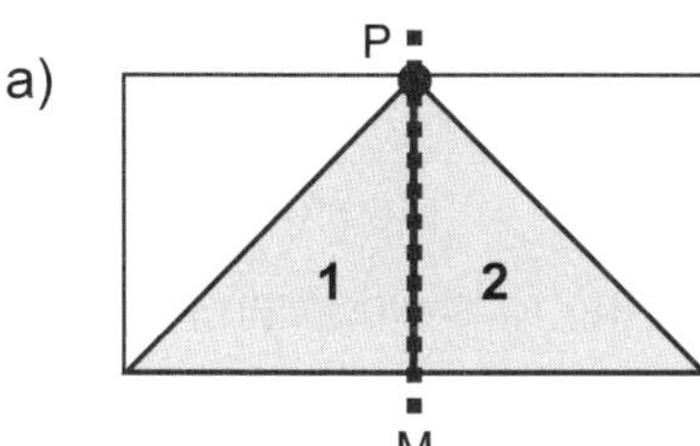


______________________

______________________

b)

P
1
2
M

______________________

______________________

c) 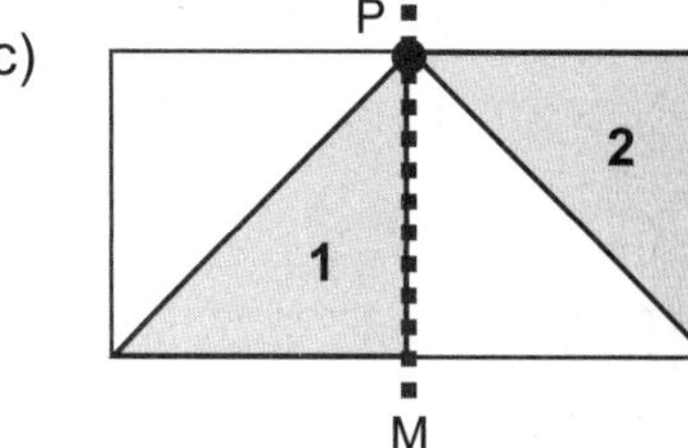


______________________

______________________

d) 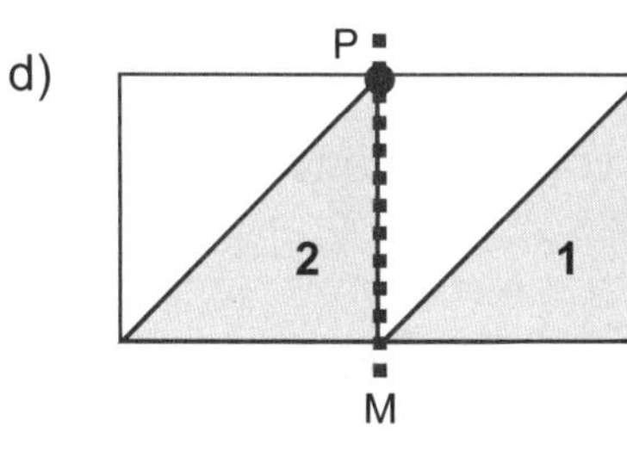


______________________

______________________

e) 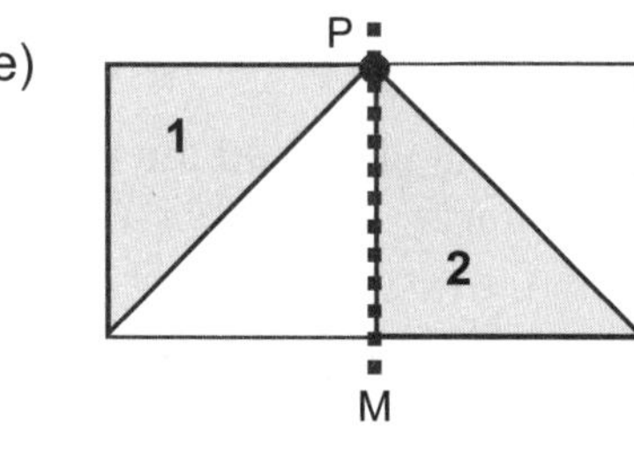


______________________

______________________

f) 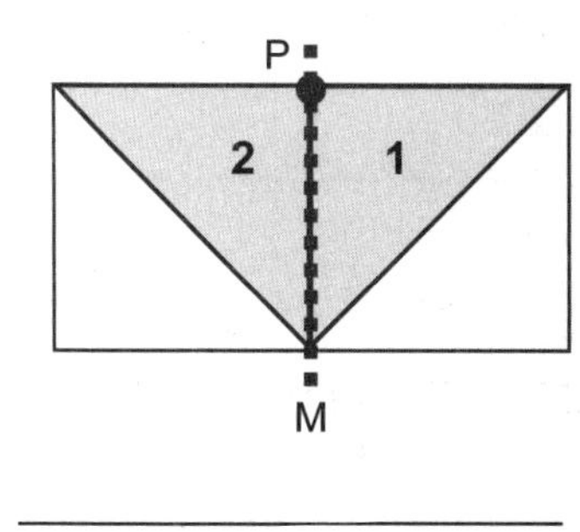


______________________

______________________

2. 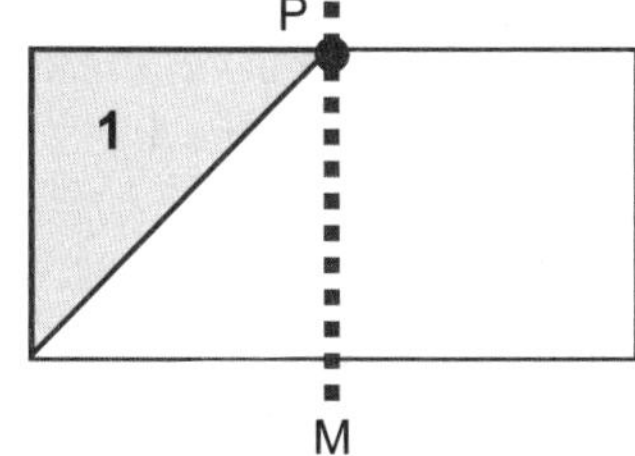


Using either a slide, a reflection, or a turn, move the triangle from Position 1 to a Position 2 of your choice. Add the second triangle to the diagram and identify the transformation you used below.

______________________________________________

3. Show the image of the figure under each transformation.

a) 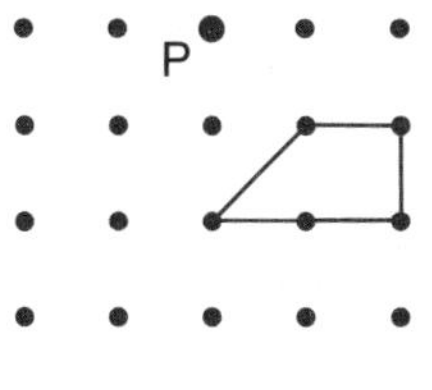


¼ turn clockwise
about point P

b) 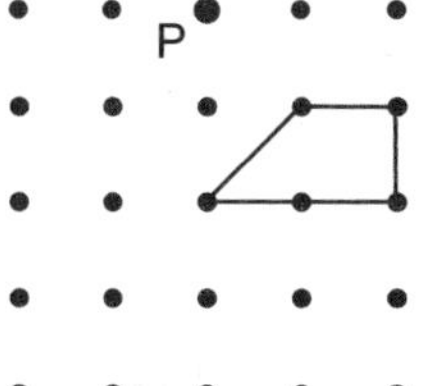


½ turn clockwise
around point P

c) 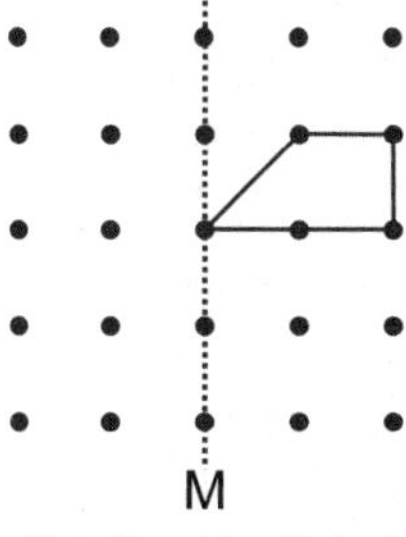


reflection in line M

d)

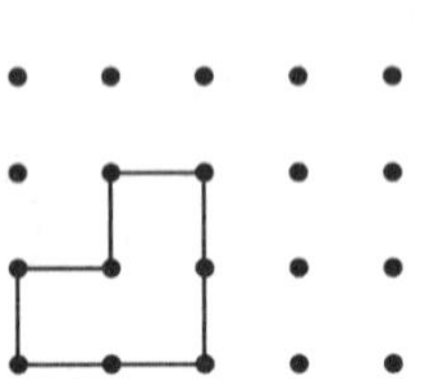

slide 2 right

e)

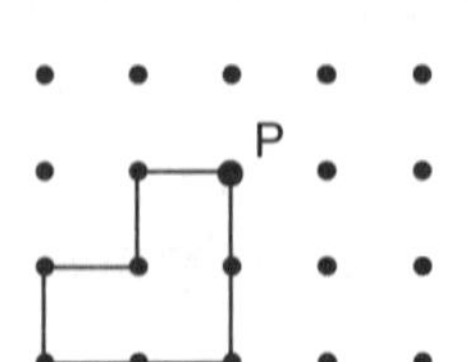


¼ turn counter-clockwise around P

f)

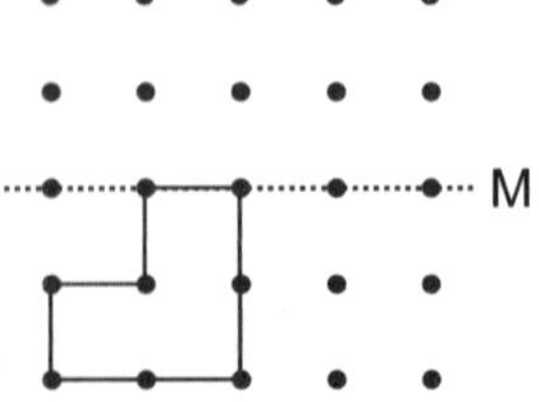


reflection in line M

**Line 2**

P

**Line 1**

In the questions below, you will use the following transformations to move the triangle in the grid:

- Slide (1 unit right/left, up/down)
- Reflection (in line 1 or line 2)
- ¼ Turn (clockwise, counter-clockwise)

NOTE:
You will still need the triangle that you traced and cut out.

4. Put the triangle (from the previous page) in Position 1 on the grid. How can you move the figure from Position 1 to Position 2 using **one** transformation?

a)

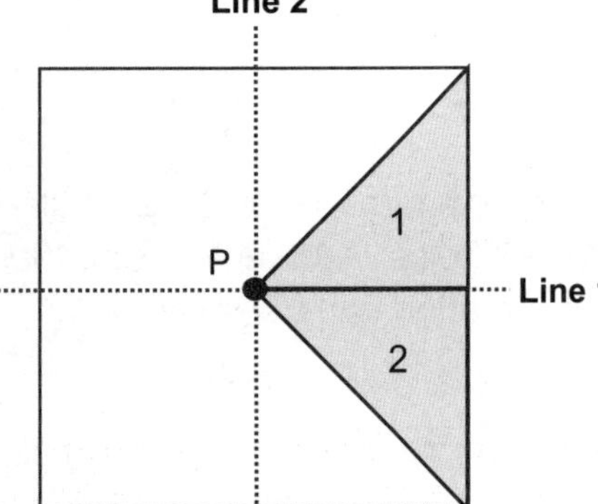


b)

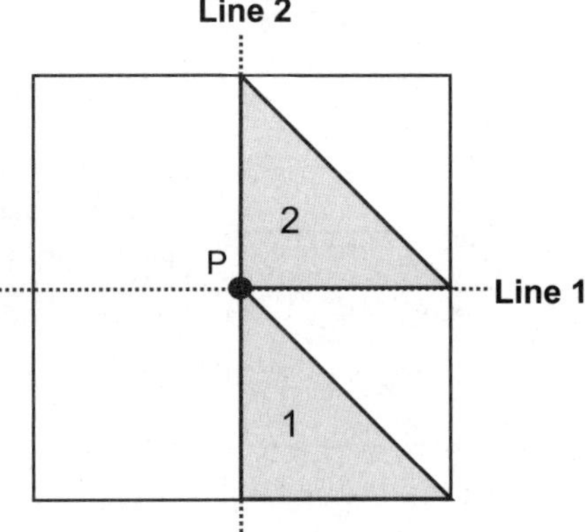


c)

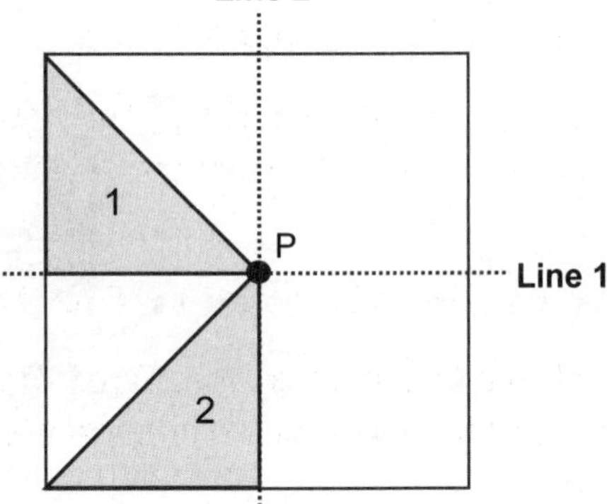


d)

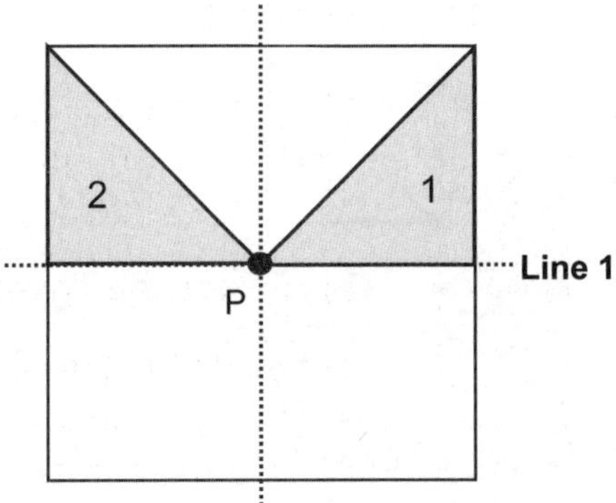

5. On a separate piece of paper, describe how the figure moved from Position 1 to Position 2 by using **two** transformations. (Some questions have more than one answer—try to find them.)

a)

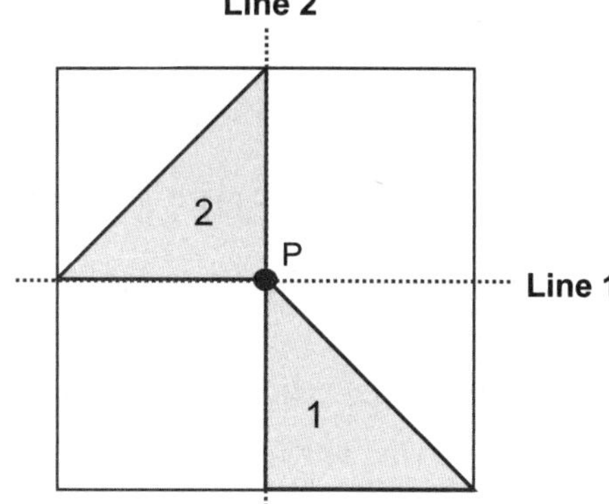


b)

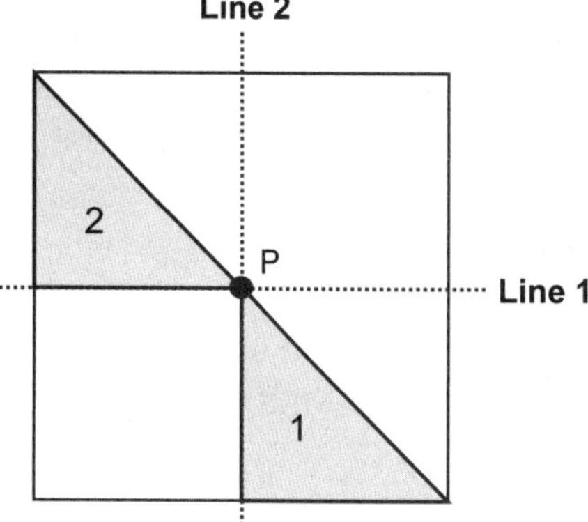


c)

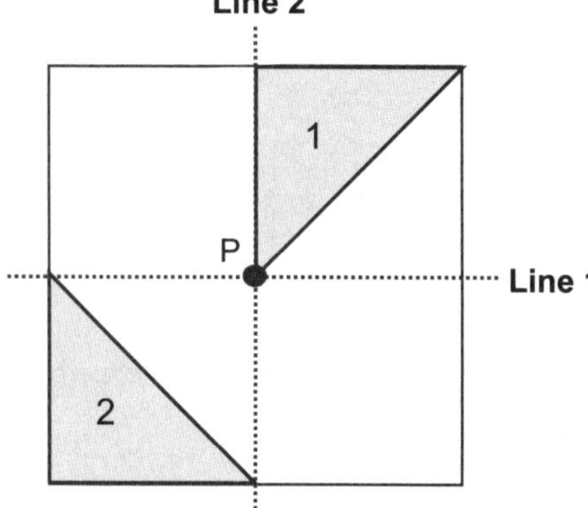


d)

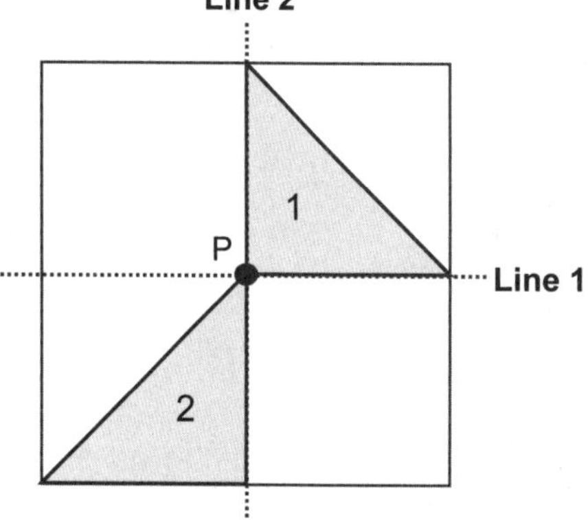


6. a)

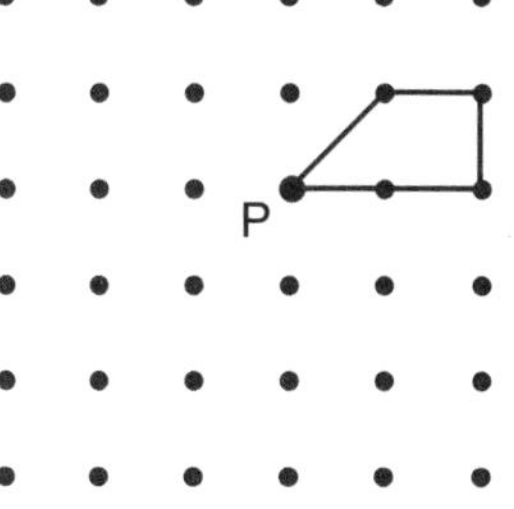


Rotate the figure ¼ turn clockwise around point P. Then slide the resulting image 2 units left.

b)

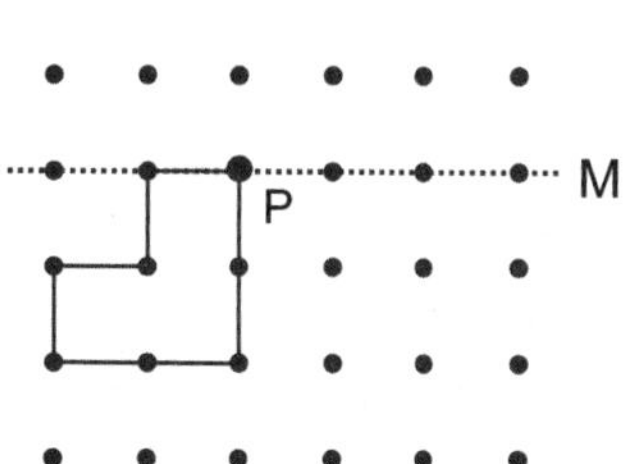


Rotate the figure ¼ turn counter-clockwise around point P. Then reflect the resulting image in the mirror line.

7. For each question below, you will need to copy the given figure onto grid paper.

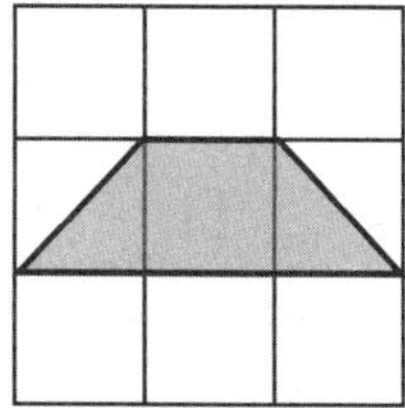

a) Pick any point on the figure as a centre of rotation and turn the figure ¼ or ½ turn around the point. Then slide the figure in any direction. Describe the transformations you used.

b) Rotate the figure around any point, then reflect it in a mirror line of your choice.

c) Move the figure by a combination of **two** transformations. Draw the initial and final positions of the figure. Ask a friend to guess which two transformations you used to move the figure.

# G4-26: Faces, Edges, and Vertices

PARENT: Your child will need copies of page xxiii: Pyramid Nets and page xxiv: Prism Nets from the Introduction for this investigation.

Solid shapes are called **3-D shapes**. Hold up examples of these 3-D shapes and point out the faces and vertices. **Faces** are the flat surfaces of the shape, **edges** are where two faces meet, and **vertices** are the points where 3 or more faces meet.

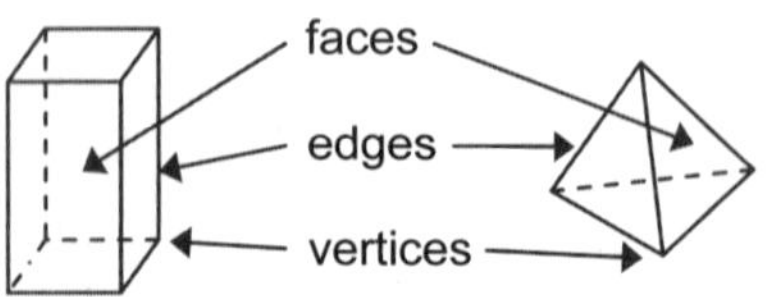


**Pyramids** have a point at one end. The base of the shape can be a triangle, quadrilateral, square, pentagon, hexagon, and so on. The base is not always at the bottom of a shape (see Section G3-32) but it is for this exercise. **Prisms** do not have a point. Their faces are the same at both ends of the shape.

| A | B | C | D | E |
|---|---|---|---|---|
| **square pyramid** | **triangular pyramid** | **rectangular prism** | **cube** | **triangular prism** |

Using a set of 3-D shapes and the chart above as reference, answer the following questions:

1. a) Describe each shape in terms of its faces, vertices and edges. The first one is done for you.

| | A | B | C | D | E |
|---|---|---|---|---|---|
| **Number of faces** | 5 | | | | |
| **Number of vertices** | 5 | | | | |
| **Number of edges** | 8 | | | | |

   b) Compare your completed chart with a friend. Did you get the same number of faces, vertices, and edges in each case? If not, double-check your answers together.

   c) Did any shapes have the same number of faces, vertices, or edges? If so, which shapes share which properties? How many faces, vertices, or edges did they have?

2. a) On a separate piece of paper, trace **each of the faces** for all the above shapes (for example, trace **all 5** of the faces on the square pyramid, even if some of them are congruent). Check your finished tracings with the numbers in your chart from question 1: Do you have the right number of faces? Be sure to organize your work neatly so you can tell which faces go with which shapes.

   b) Underneath the faces for each shape, answer the following questions:

   (i) How many different-shaped faces does this 3-D shape have? What are they?

   (ii) Circle the face (or faces) that form the base of the 3-D shape. Copy and complete this sentence: "The base of a ____(name of the 3D shape)____ is a ____(shape of the base)____."

3. Pick two 3-D shapes and say how they are similar and how they are different.

# G4-27: Nets

PARENT:
Give your child copies of page xxiii: Pyramid Nets and page xxiv: Prism Nets from the Introduction for the following 3-D shapes. Have your child cut, fold, and glue the nets into the proper shapes. Then ask him or her to fill out a chart (like the one below) on a separate piece of paper.

triangular pyramid

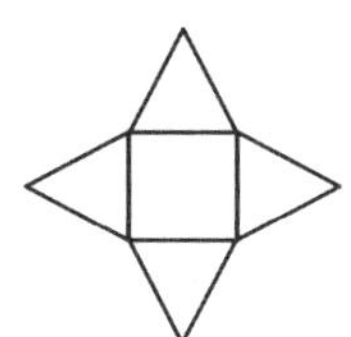
square pyramid

pentagonal pyramid

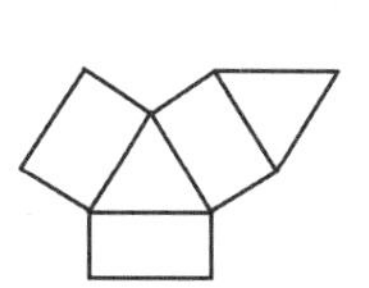
triangular prism

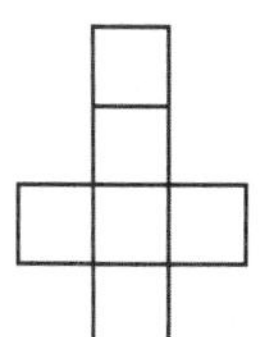
cube

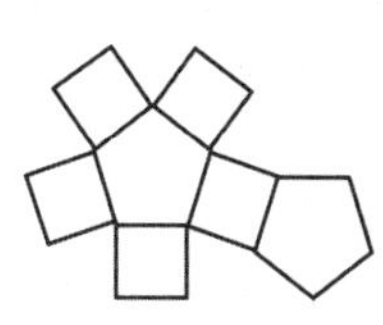
pentagonal prism

1.

| Name of figure | Shape of base | Number of faces | Number of edges |
| --- | --- | --- | --- |
| | | | |

Answer the written part of each question on a separate piece of paper.

2. Draw the missing face for each net.

i) 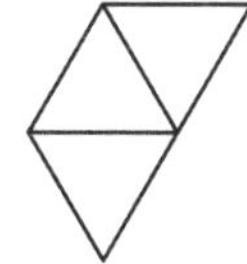

ii) 

iii) 

a) What is the shape of each missing face?

b) Are the nets pyramids or prisms? How do you know?

3. Draw the missing face for each net.

i) 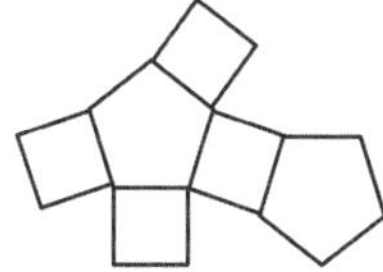

ii) 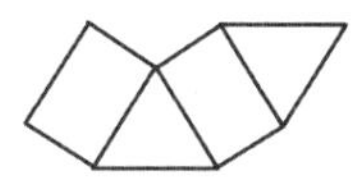

iii) 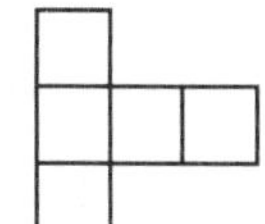

a) What is the shape of each missing face?

b) Are the nets pyramids or prisms? How do you know?

4. Copy the following nets onto centimetre grid paper (use 4 grid squares for each face). Predict which nets will make cubes. (If you predict a net will not make a cube, explain why.) Cut out each net and fold it to check your predictions.

a) 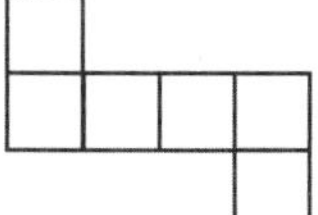

b) 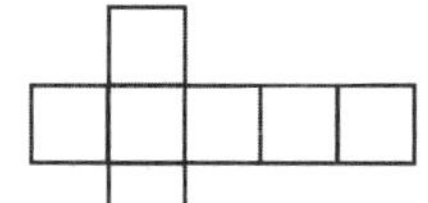

c) 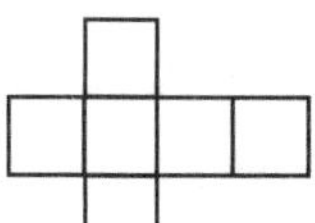

d) 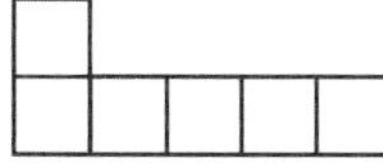

e) 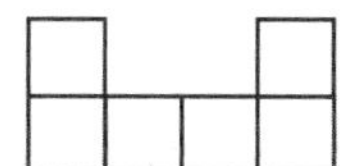

f) 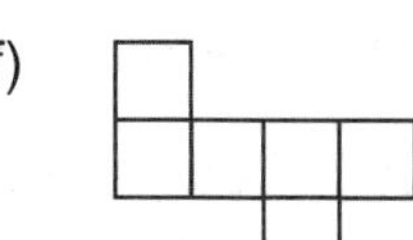

# G4-28: Building Pyramids and Prisms

NOTE: For the exercises on this page you will need modeling clay (or plasticene) and toothpicks (or straws).

To make a skeleton for a **pyramid**, start by making a base.
Your base might be a triangle, rectangle, or square:

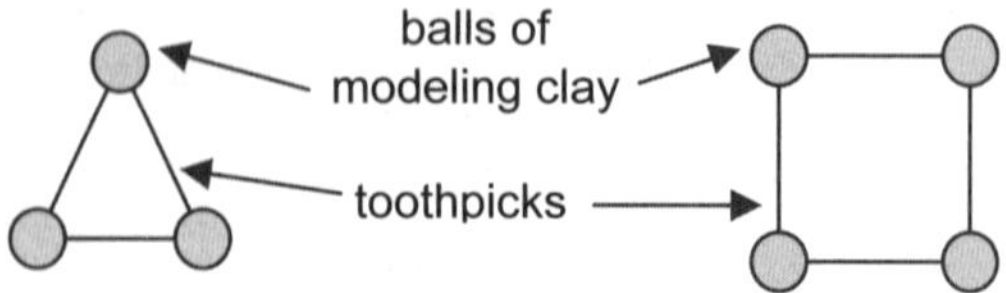


Now add an edge to each vertex on your base and join the edges at a point:

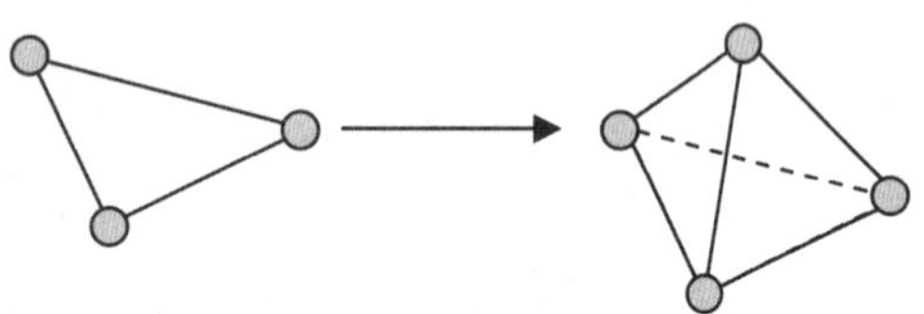

**triangular pyramid**

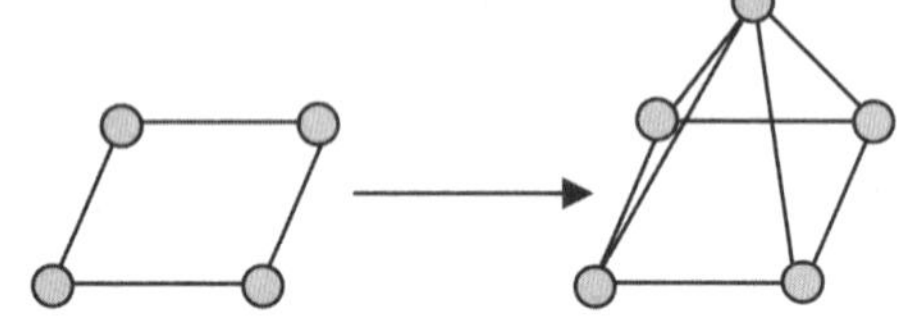

**square pyramid**

After you have made a triangular pyramid and a square pyramid, try to make one with a five-sided base (a pentagonal pyramid). Then fill in the first three rows of the chart.

1.

| | Draw shape of base | Number of sides of base | Number of edges of pyramid | Number of vertices of pyramid |
|---|---|---|---|---|
| **triangular pyramid** | | | | |
| **square pyramid** | | | | |
| **pentagonal pyramid** | | | | |
| **hexagonal pyramid** | | | | |

2. Describe the pattern in each column of your chart on a separate piece of paper.
3. Continue the patterns in the columns of your chart to find the number of edges and vertices of the hexagonal pyramid.
4. What relationship do you see between the number of sides in the **base** of a pyramid and the number of edges in the pyramid?
5. If you made an octagonal pyramid (the base would have 8 sides), how many edges and vertices would the pyramid have? (Use the patterns you discovered.)

To make a skeleton for a **prism**, start by making a base (as you did for a pyramid). However, your prism will also need a top, so you should make a copy of the base:

**base** **top** **base** **top**

Now join each vertex in the base to a vertex in the top:

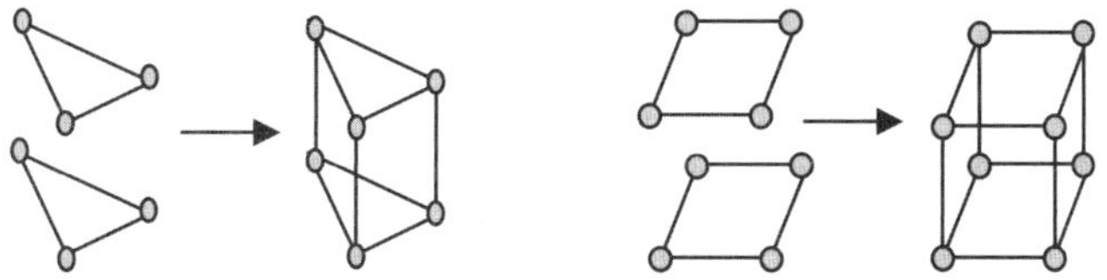

After you have made a triangular prism and a cube, try to make a prism with two five-sided bases (a pentagonal prism). Then fill in the first three rows of the chart.

| 6. | Draw shape of base | Number of sides of base | Number of edges of prism | Number of vertices of prism |
|---|---|---|---|---|
| **triangular prism** | | | | |
| **cube** | | | | |
| **pentagonal prism** | | | | |
| **hexagonal prism** | | | | |

7. Describe the pattern in each column of your chart on a separate piece of paper.

8. Continue the patterns in the columns of your chart to find the number of edges and vertices of the hexagonal prism.

9. What relationship do you see between the number of sides in the **base** of a prism and the number of edges in the prism?

10. If you made an octagonal prism (the base would have 8 sides), how many edges and vertices would the prism have? (Use the patterns you discovered.)

# G4-29: Prism and Pyramid Bases

Melissa is exploring differences between pyramids and prisms. She discovers the following:

- a **pyramid** has **one base**
  (There is one exception—a triangular pyramid with congruent faces.)

Example: 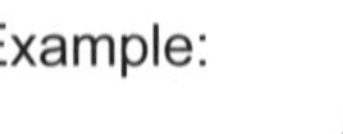

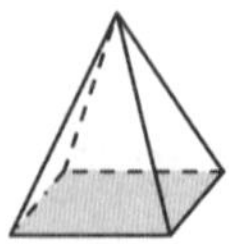

- a **prism** has **two bases**
  (There is one exception—a cube.)

Example: 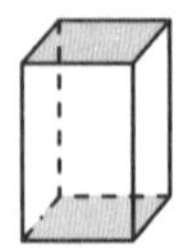

IMPORTANT NOTE:
The base(s) is not always on the "bottom" or "top" of the shape. Instead Melissa finds the base by finding the face(s) that is different from the rest. However, if all the faces of a figure are congruent, every face is a base (for example, in a cube or in a triangular pyramid).

---

1. ACTIVITY: Use the 3-D shapes you created in G4-27. Find the base of each shape and place the shape **base-down** on your table. Ask someone to check that you have found the base correctly. You should also identify the shapes whose faces are all congruent.

2. Shade the base **and** circle the point of the following pyramids:

   REMEMBER: Unless all its faces are congruent, a **pyramid** has **one base**. The base will not necessarily be on the "bottom" of the shape (but it is **always** at the end opposite the point).

a) 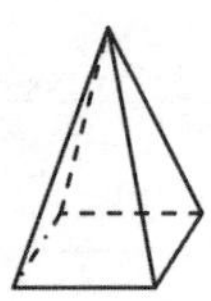

b) 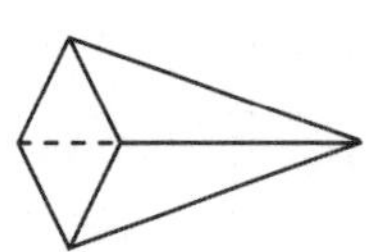

c) 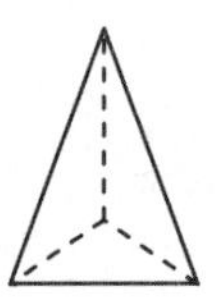

d) 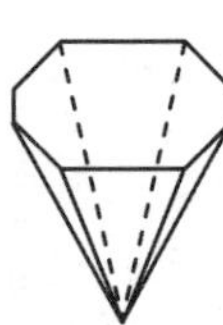

e) 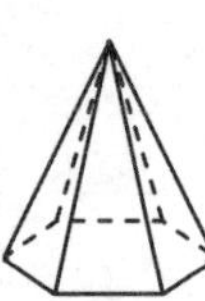

f) 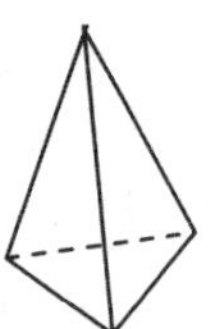

g) 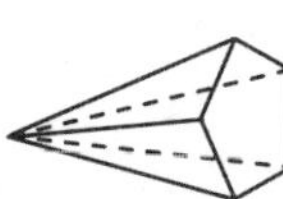

h) 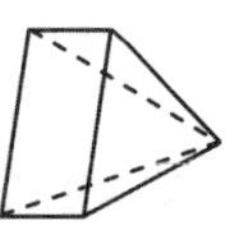

3. Now shade the bases of these prisms.

   REMEMBER: Unless all its faces are congruent, a **prism** has **two bases**. The bases will not necessarily be on the "bottom" and "top" of the shape.

a) 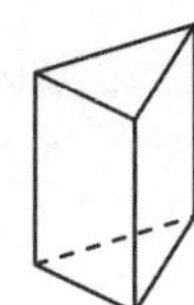

b) 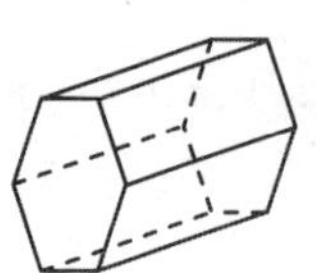

c) 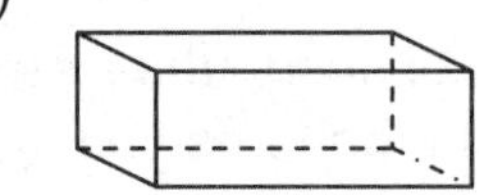

d) 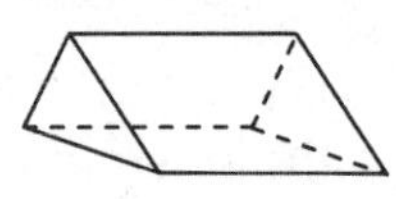

e) 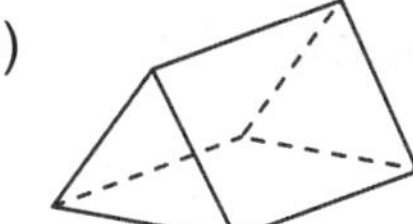 f)  g) 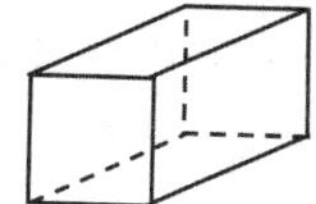 h) 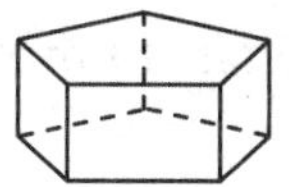

4. Melissa has many prisms and pyramids. Can you circle the ones that have **all congruent faces**?

a) 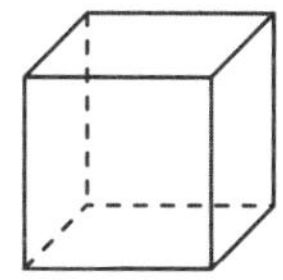 b) 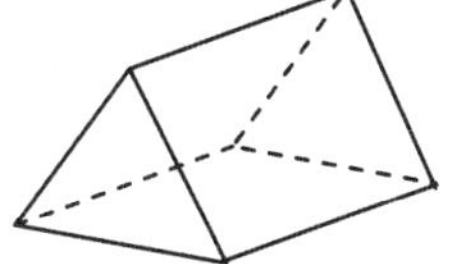 c) 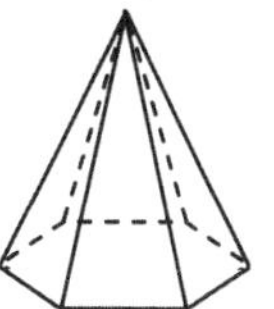 d) 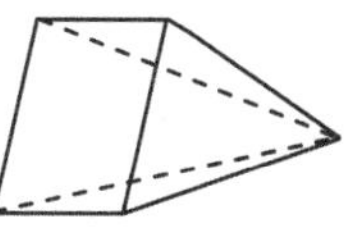

e) 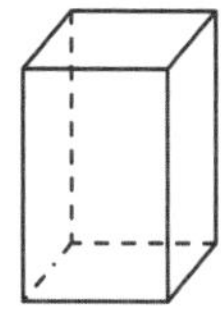 f) 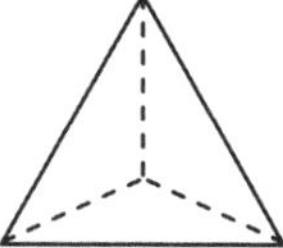 g) 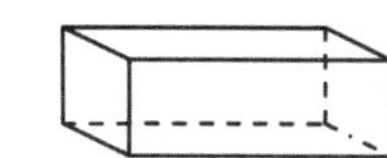 h) 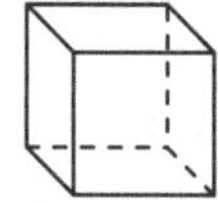

5. Shade the bases of the following figures. Be careful! Some will have two bases (the prisms) and others will have only one (the pyramids).

a) 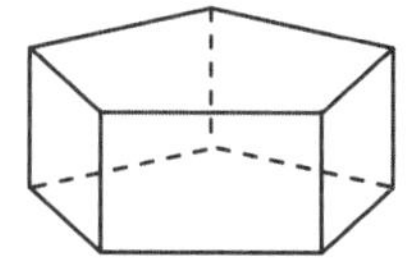 b) 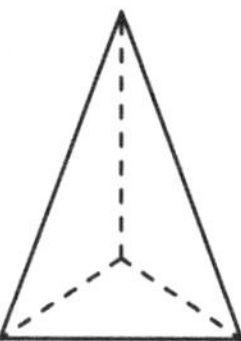 c) 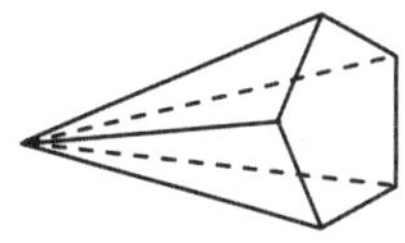 d) 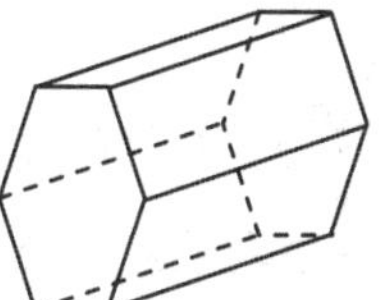

e) 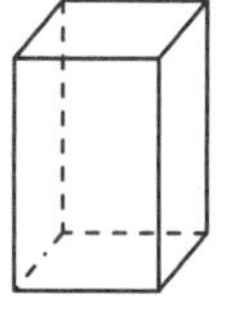 f) 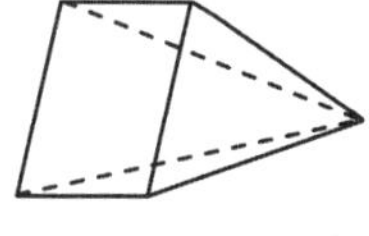 g) 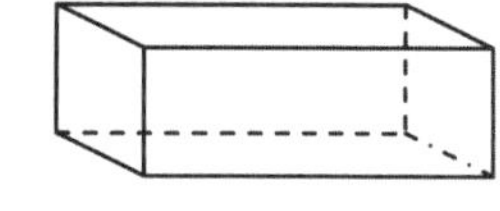 h) 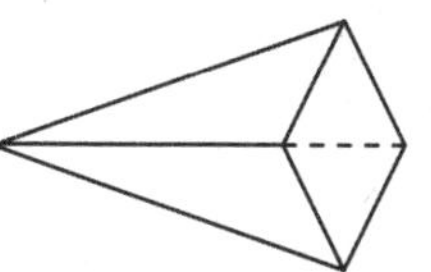

i) 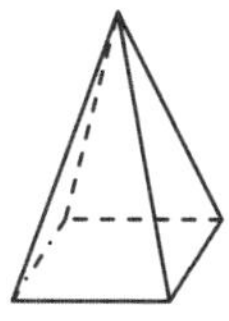 j) 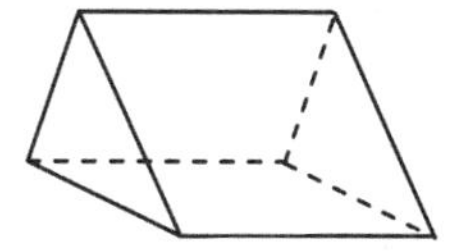 k) 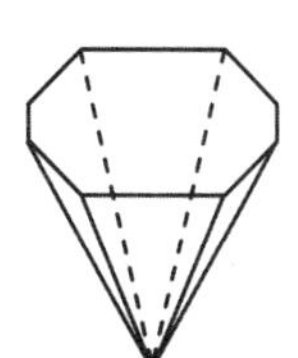 l) 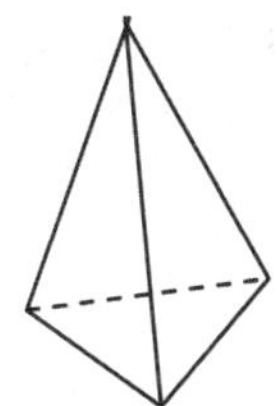

m) 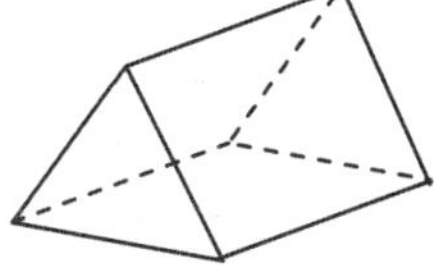 n) 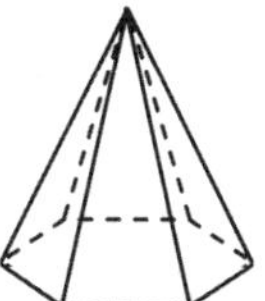 o) 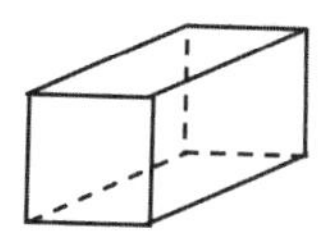 p) 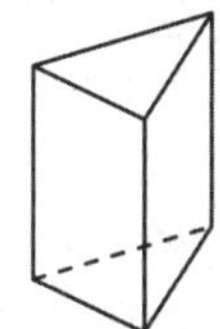

# G4-30: Drawing Pyramids and Prisms

1. Practise drawing a **triangular prism**, by drawing 2 triangles and joining the vertices as shown.

Step 1: Step 2: Step 1: Step 2:

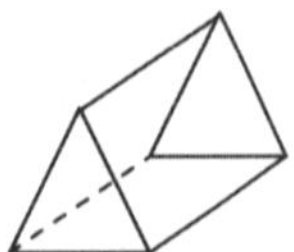

2. Practise drawing a **rectangular prism**, by drawing two rectangles and joining the vertices as shown.

Step 1: Step 2: Step 1: Step 2:

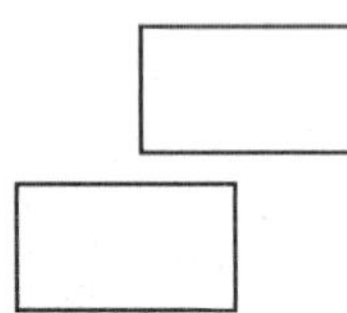
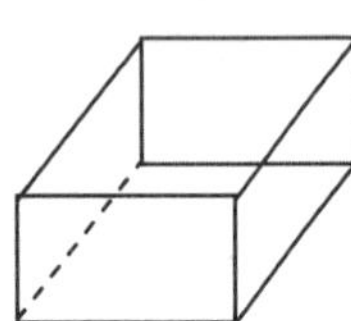

3. Practise drawing a **cube** (which is also a prism) as shown.

Step 1: Step 2: Step 1: Step 2:

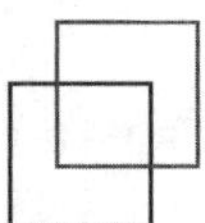
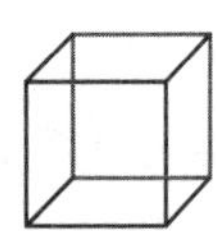

Practise drawing all three kinds of prisms on a separate piece of paper.

4. To draw a **triangular pyramid**, you draw a triangle and a point then join the vertices of the triangle to the point as shown. Use the same method to draw a **square pyramid**.

Step 1: Step 2: Step 1: Step 2:

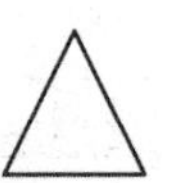
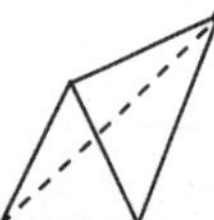

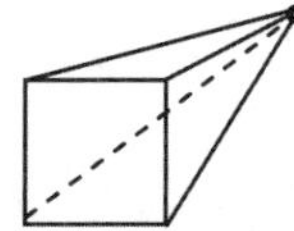

Practise drawing both kinds of pyramids on a separate piece of paper.

5. There is a different way to draw triangular and square pyramids. Try drawing these on a separate piece of paper.

Step 1: Step 2: Step 1: Step 2:

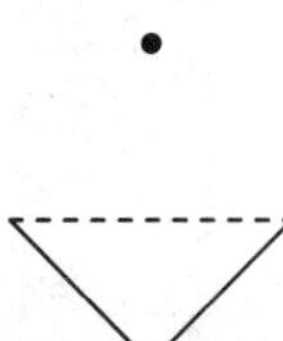
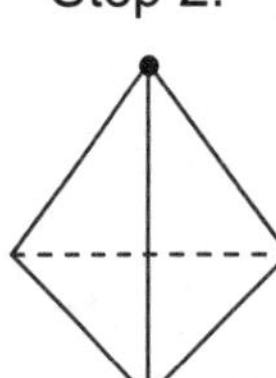
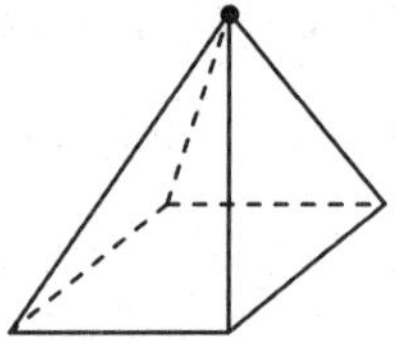

**Game for two players**:

1. Think of a 3-D shape and draw it carefully so that your partner cannot see it.
2. Describe to your partner how to draw the shape. (HINT: Describe Step 1 **then** Step 2.)
3. Look at the shape that your partner has drawn. Does it look the same as yours?

# G4-31: Properties of Pyramids and Prisms

NOTE:
Find objects in your home that are cones and cylinders before answering the questions on this page. A cone has a circular base and a curved face (like an ice cream cone), and a cylinder has two circular bases (or ends) and a curved side (like a can of pop).

1. Circle all the **pyramids**. Put an "X" through all the **prisms**.

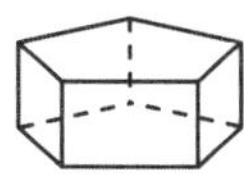 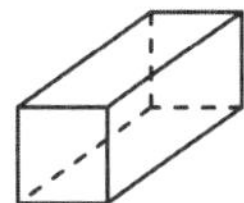 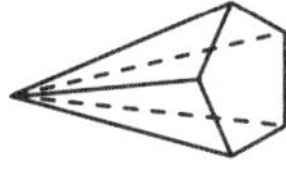 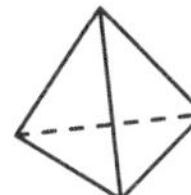 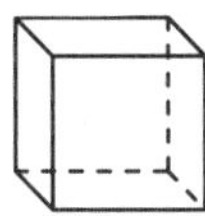  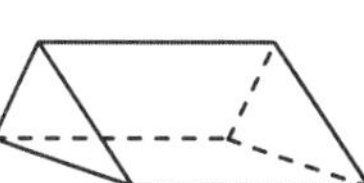 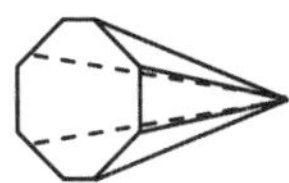

2. Match each shape to its name. The first one is done for you.

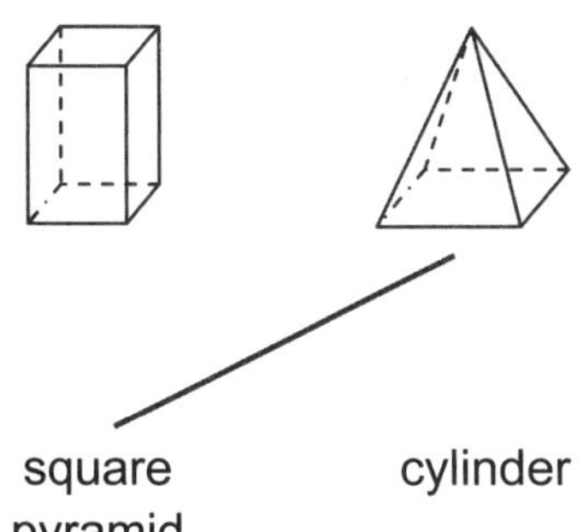  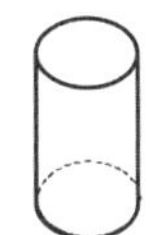 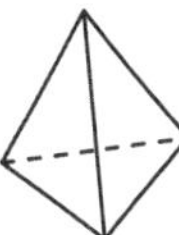 

square pyramid    cylinder    triangular prism    cone    rectangular prism    triangular pyramid

3. Compare the shapes below. Use the chart to find properties that are the **same** and **different**.

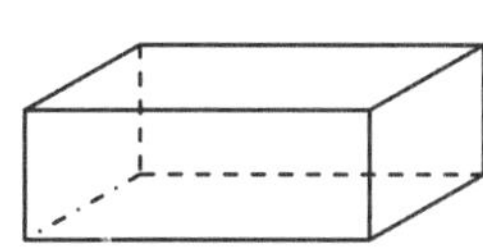 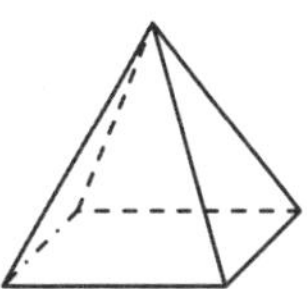

| **Property** | **Rectangular prism** | **Square pyramid** | **Same?** | **Different?** |
|---|---|---|---|---|
| number of faces | 6 | 5 | | ✓ |
| shape of base | | | | |
| number of bases | | | | |
| number of faces that are **not** bases | | | | |
| number of edges | | | | |
| number of vertices | | | | |

4. On a separate piece of paper, copy and finish writing the following sentences (using the chart above as reference).

   "A rectangular prism and a square pyramid are the **same** in these ways . . ."

   "A rectangular prism and a square pyramid are **different** in these ways . . ."

5. On a separate piece of paper, compare the sets of shapes below. For both parts a) and b), **name** the shapes first, and then write a paragraph outlining how they are the **same** and how they are **different**.

(HINT: Make and complete a chart like the one in question 3.)

a) 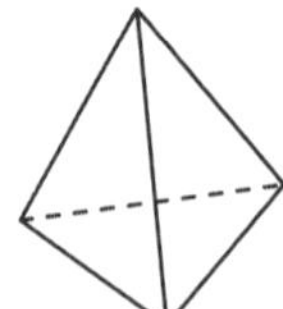 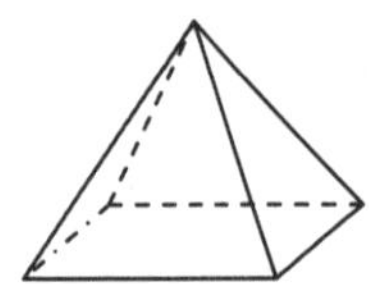

b) 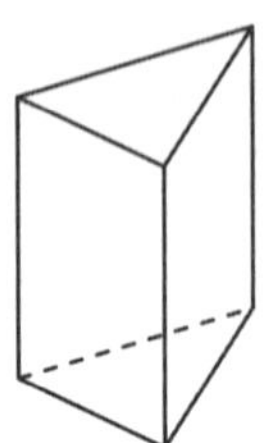 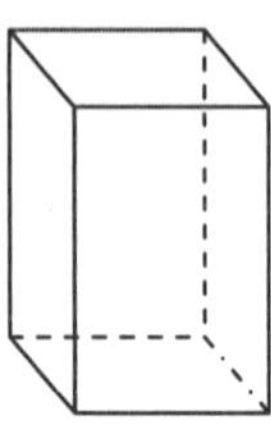

6. a) Complete the following property chart. Use the actual 3-D shapes to help you.

| Shape | Name | Number of edges | Number of vertices | Number of faces | Pictures of faces<br>* In each case, circle the base(s) |
|---|---|---|---|---|---|
| | | | | | |
| | | | | | |
| | | | | | |
| | | | | | |

b) Count the number of sides in the base of each pyramid. Compare this number with the number of vertices in each pyramid. What do you notice?

c) Count the number of sides in the base of each prism. Compare this number with the number of vertices in each prism. What do you notice?

BONUS:
On a separate piece of paper, draw rough sketches of as many everyday objects you can think of that are (or have parts that are) pyramids or prisms.

7. Sketch all the faces that make up the following 3-D shapes. The first one is done for you.

| 3-D shape | 2-D faces |
|---|---|
| a) | |
| b) | |

Show your work for parts c), d), and e) on a separate piece of paper.

c) 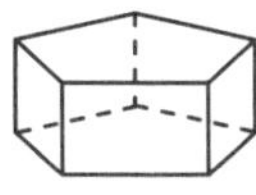

d) 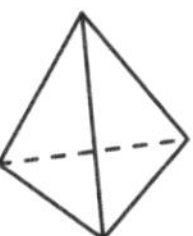

e) 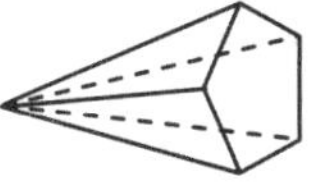

8. Match the description of the figure with its name.

| | | |
|---|---|---|
| ______ | cone | **A.** I have 6 congruent faces. |
| ______ | triangular prism | **B.** I have 5 faces: 2 triangles and 3 rectangles. |
| ______ | cube | **C.** I have 4 faces. Each face is a triangle. |
| ______ | cylinder | **D.** I have 2 circular bases and a curved face. |
| ______ | triangular pyramid | **E.** I have 1 circular base and a curved face. |

Answer the following questions on a separate piece of paper:

9. "I have a square base." Name two 3-D solids that this sentence could describe.

10. On separate paper, sketch a net for . . .

    a) a triangular pyramid b) a rectangular pyramid c) a triangular prism

11. Name the object you could make if you assembled the shapes.

    a) b) c) 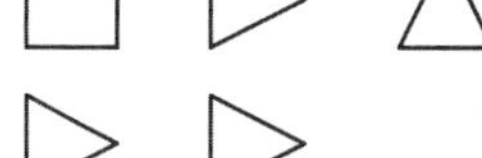

12. Sketch two views of the figure you might see and one view you could not see.

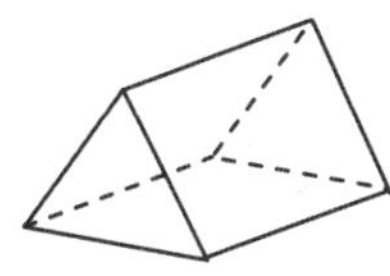

13. 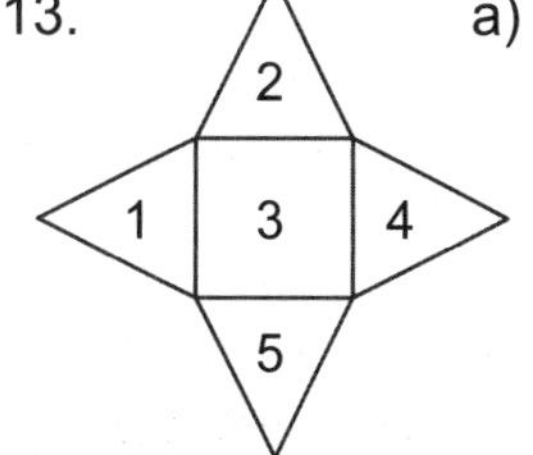


a) Which face of the net has the most vertices?

b) Which face shares a side with every other face?

# G4-32: Sorting 3-D Shapes

Eve sorts the following figures using a Venn diagram. She first decides on two properties that a figure might have (for example, "one or more square faces" and "four or more vertices") and makes a chart (see below). She then writes the letters in the chart and **checks to see which figures share both properties**.

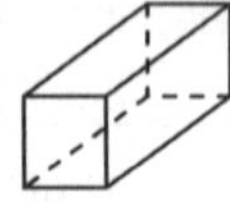
A

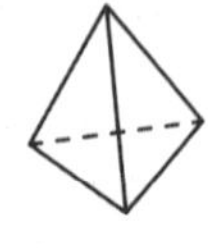
B

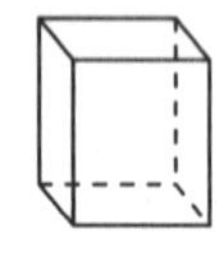
C

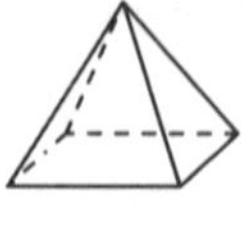
D

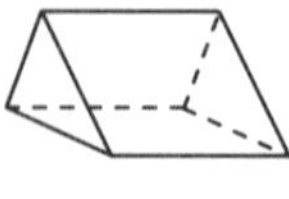
E

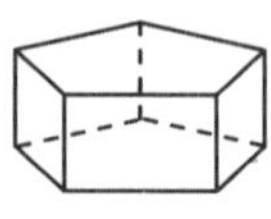
F

| Property | Figures with this property |
|---|---|
| 1. one or more triangular faces | |
| 2. five or more vertices | |

1. a) Which figure(s) share both properties? ___________

   b) Using the information in the chart above, complete the following Venn diagram. The figures that have both properties should be included in both circles so write them in the overlapping part of the diagram.

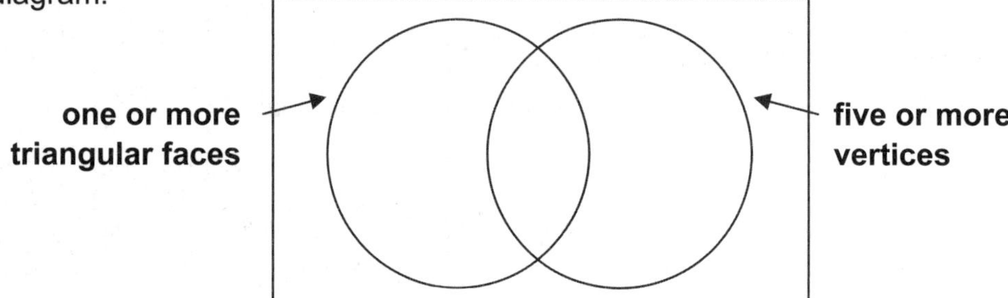


2. Complete the chart using the shapes A to F.

   a)

| Property | Figures with this property |
|---|---|
| 1. square base | |
| 2. pyramid | |

   b) Which figures share both properties? ___________

   c) Using the information in the chart above, complete the following Venn diagram:

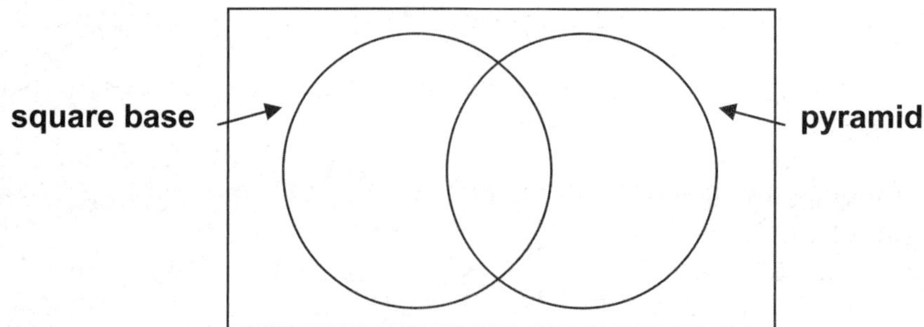


3. Pick a pair of properties and draw a Venn diagram to sort the shapes.

# G4-33: Classifying Shapes and Making Patterns

NOTE: Review these terms for polygons.

| | | | | | |
|---|---|---|---|---|---|
| **triangle:** | 3 sides | **square:** | 4 sides | **hexagon:** | 6 sides |
| **quadrilateral:** | 4 sides | **pentagon:** | 5 sides | **equilateral:** | All sides equal |
| **parallelogram** | | **trapezoid** | | **rhombus** | |

1. On a separate piece of paper, describe each shape using as many mathematical words as you can.

a) 

b) 

c) 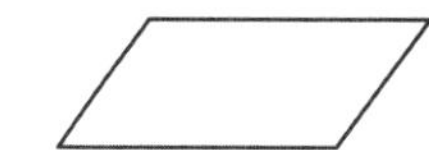

d) Does the shape in part a) have any pairs of parallel sides?

2. Sort the following set of shapes using the attributes given. If a shape does not have either of the attributes, write its letter in the box (outside of the circles).

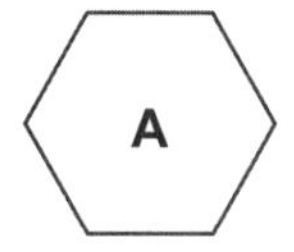

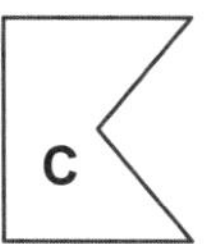

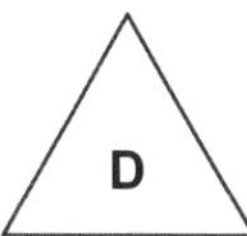

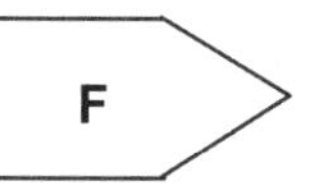

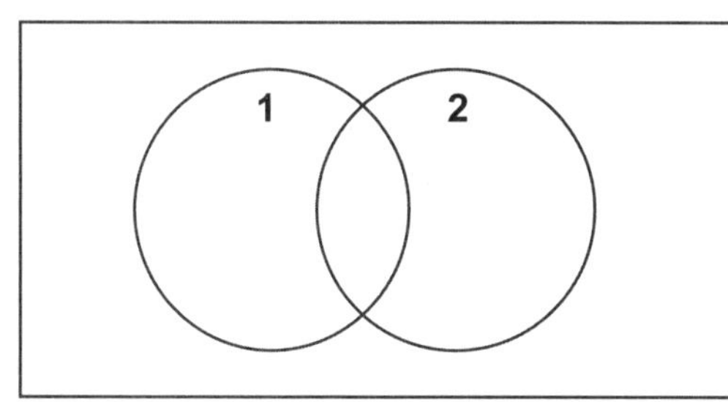


Attribute 1: equilateral

Attribute 2: 1 or more pairs of parallel sides

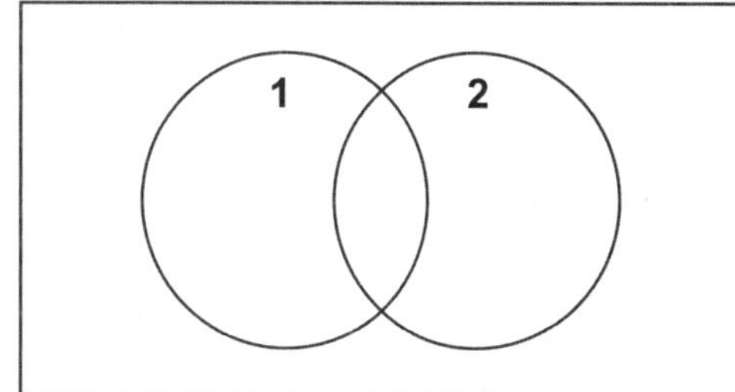


Attribute 1: 1 or more pairs of parallel sides

Attribute 2: 1 or more right angles

BONUS:

3. The chart gives the letter of the shapes that have the given attributes. Can you guess what the two attributes are?

a)

| **Shapes with attribute 1** | G, E |
|---|---|
| **Shapes with attribute 2** | G, F, C |

b)

| **Shapes with attribute 1** | B, D |
|---|---|
| **Shapes with attribute 2** | A, D, G |

4. Choose two attributes of your own. Sort the shapes. Show your work on a separate piece of paper.

5. For each pattern below, say how the attributes of shape, size, colour, number of sides, and number of pairs of parallel sides change.

Example: To describe how the colour changes in question 5. a), you could say: "colour—red, blue, then repeat."

a) 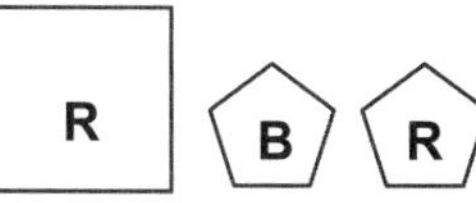

b) 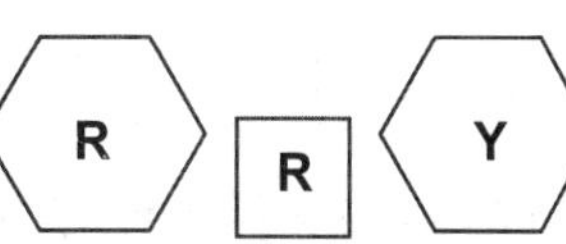

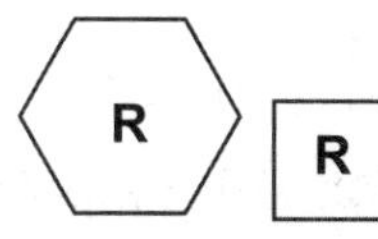

6. Say whether each letter was rotated 90° or 180°. If you identified the turn as 90°, draw an arrow to show the **direction** of the turn.

a) 
______

b) 
______

c) 
______

d) 
______

e) 
______

f) 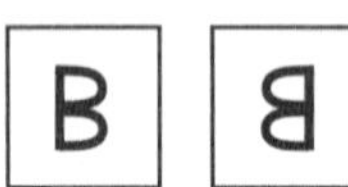
______

g) 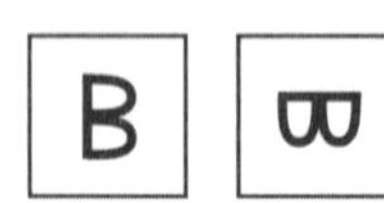
______

h) 
______

7. Draw a shape in Box 2 so it can flip, slide or turn to get to Box 3.

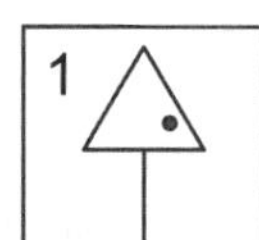

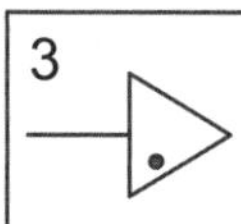

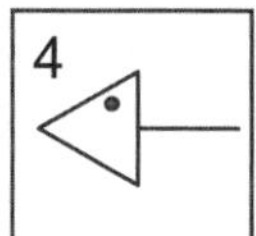


Explain the transformations made to get from . . .

a) Box 1 to Box 2 

b) Box 2 to Box 3 

c) Box 3 to Box 4

8. For each pattern below, describe how the attributes of shape, size, number of sides, and number of **parallel** sides change. Also use words that describe transformations like flip, and turn (or rotation).

a) 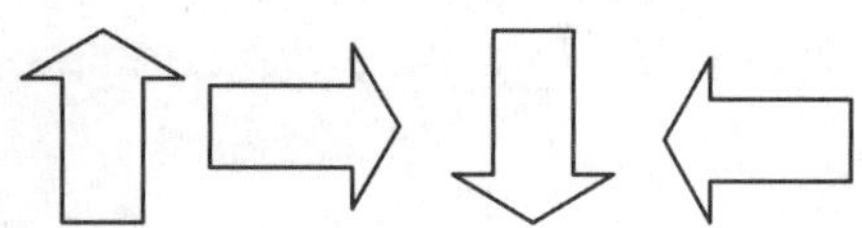

b) 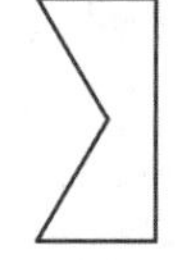   

c) 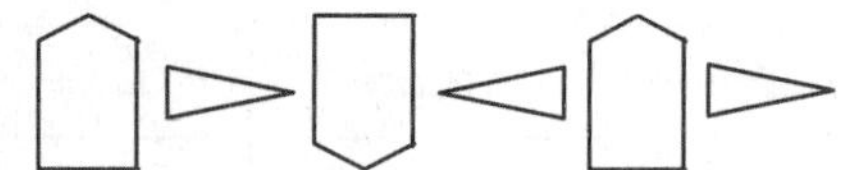

d) 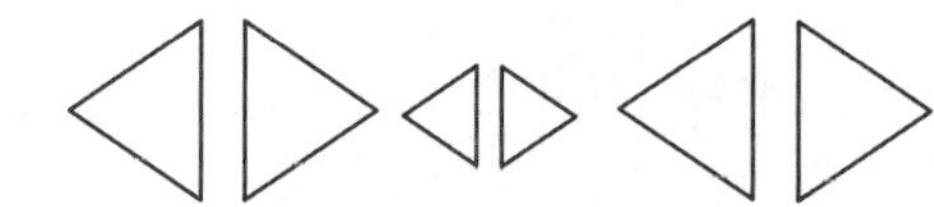

9. a) Which of these rules describes this pattern?

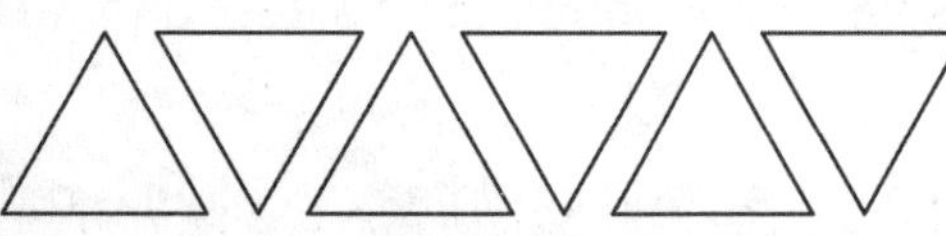

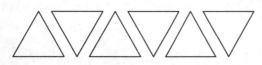

**A.** triangle pointing up, triangle pointing down, repeat
**B.** flip the triangle each time
**C.** rotate triangle 180° clockwise each time

Then answer parts b) and c) on a separate piece of paper.

b) Which rule do you think is best? Why?

c) How could you improve this rule? (HINT: Can you describe the triangle more precisely?)

10. Which design comes next in the pattern? Explain why on a separate piece of paper.

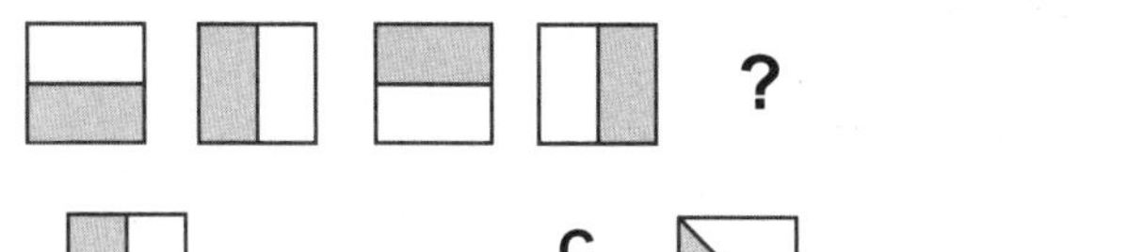


**A.** **B.** **C.** **D.**

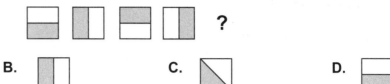

11. Trace and cut out the shape below. Make a pattern by . . .

a) sliding the shape repeatedly one unit right

b) reflecting the shape repeatedly in the mirror lines

c) rotating the shape repeatedly 180° around the dots

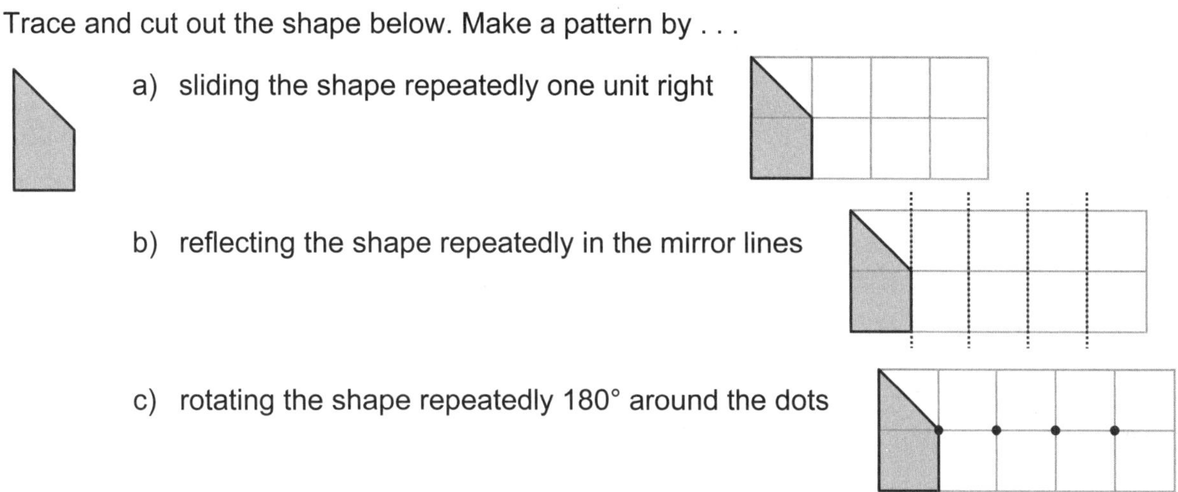

12. Each of the patterns below was made by repeating a transformation or a combination of transformations. On a separate piece of paper, use the words "slide," "rotation," or "reflection" to describe how the shape moves from . . .

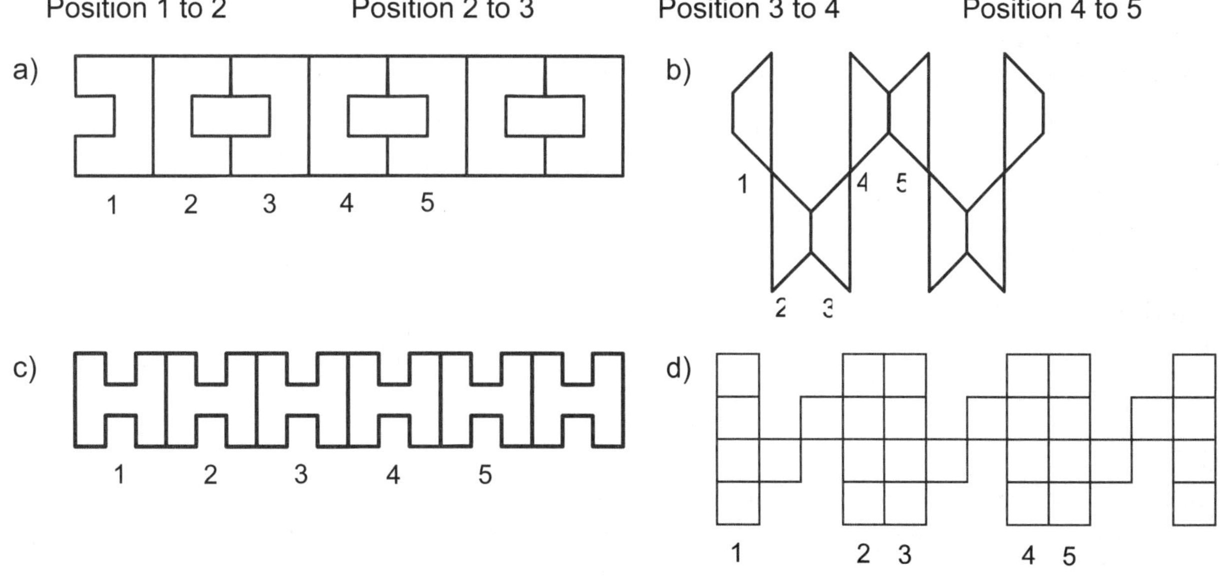


e) One of the patterns above can be described in two different ways. Which pattern is it? And which two single transformations could each produce the pattern?

13. Draw a shape on grid paper and make your own pattern by a combination of slides, rotations, and reflections. Explain which transformations you used in your pattern.

# G4-34: Tessellations

A tessellation is a pattern made up of one or more shapes that completely covers a surface (without any gaps or overlaps).

Some shapes that can be used to tessellate are:

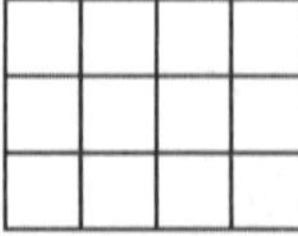
a square

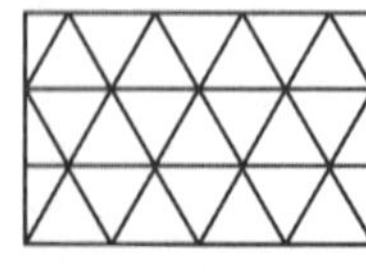
an equilateral triangle

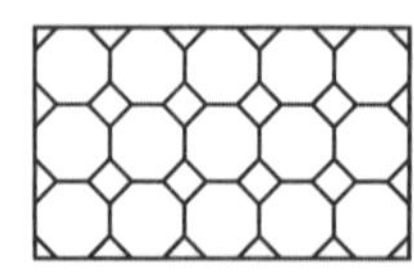
an octagon and a square

---

Show how you can tessellate a region of space by using the following shapes:

1. a) hexagons

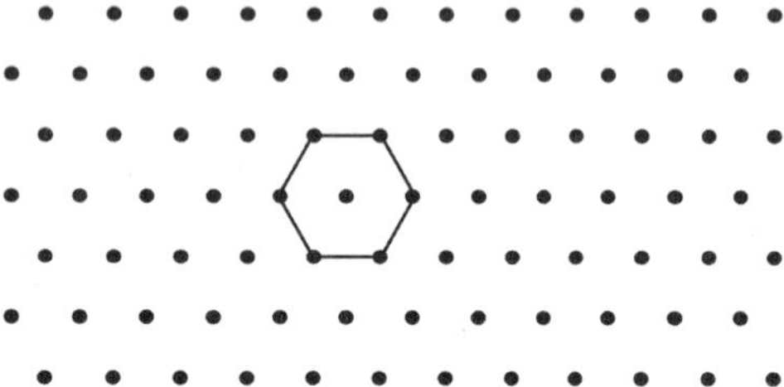

b) equilateral triangles

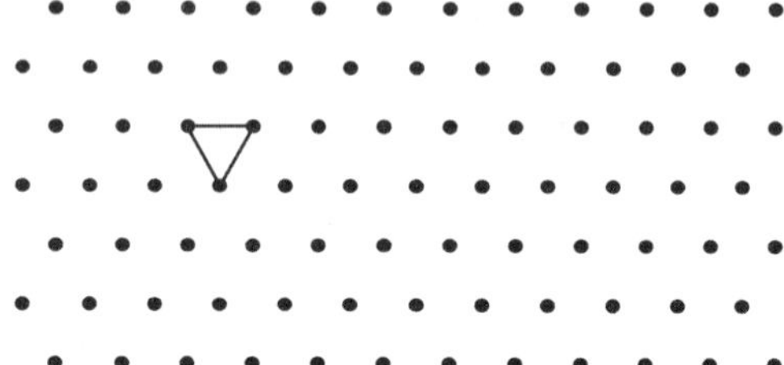

c) hexagons and triangles

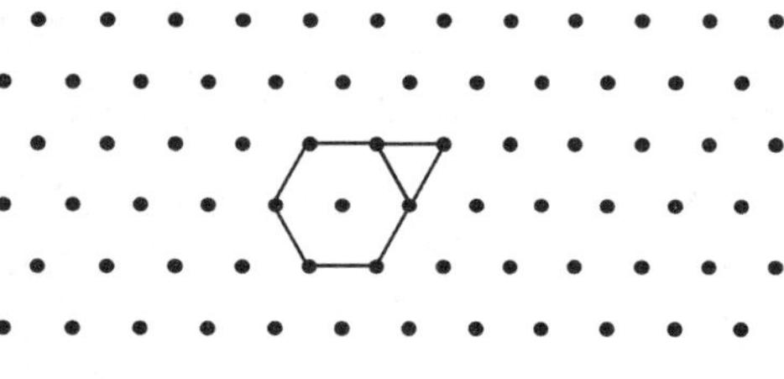

d) trapezoids

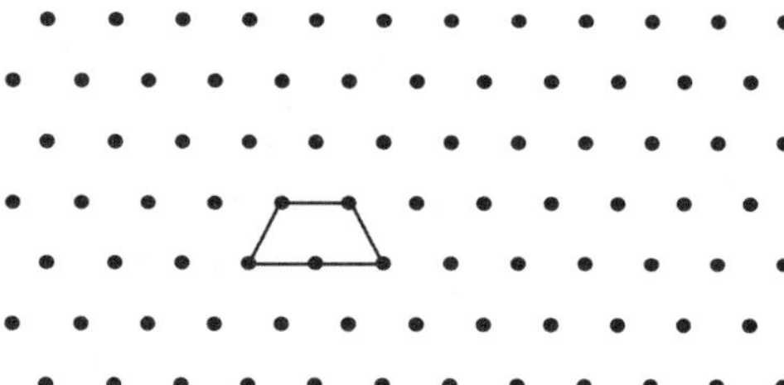

2. 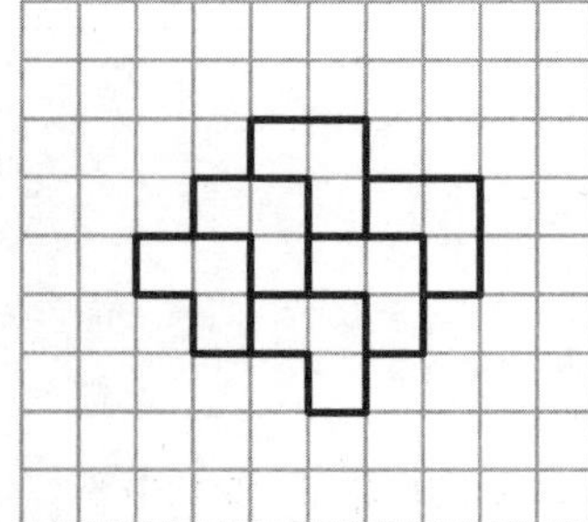

The picture shows how you can tessellate a grid using an "L" shape.

a) Add at least 6 more "L" shapes to the tessellation.

b) On grid paper, show how you could use the shapes below to tessellate the grid.

i) 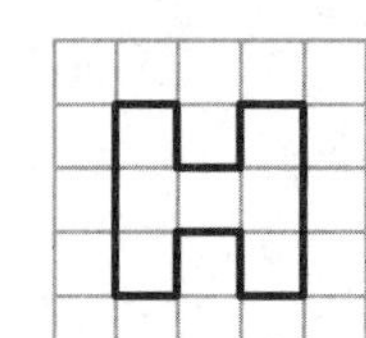

ii) 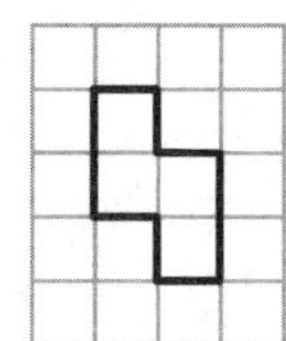

BONUS:

3. Follow the steps to create a shape that will tessellate.

cut out a grid paper rectangle and cut the shape into 2 pieces (any way you like)

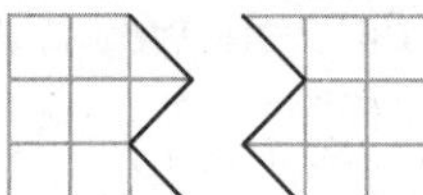

tape the two opposite ends together

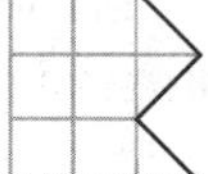

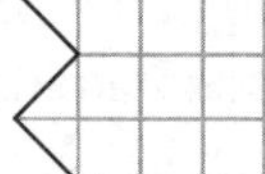

4. Find a letter of the alphabet that tessellates.

# G4-35: Problems and Puzzles



Show your work for these questions on a separate piece of paper.

1. Which picture represents . . . **A.** a slide? **B.** a rotation? **C.** a reflection?

a) 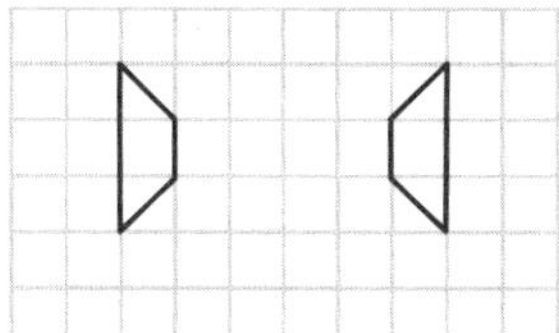

b) 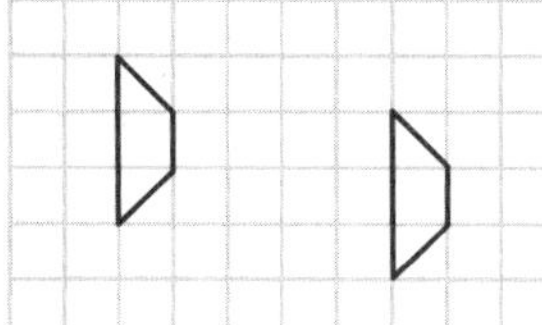

c) 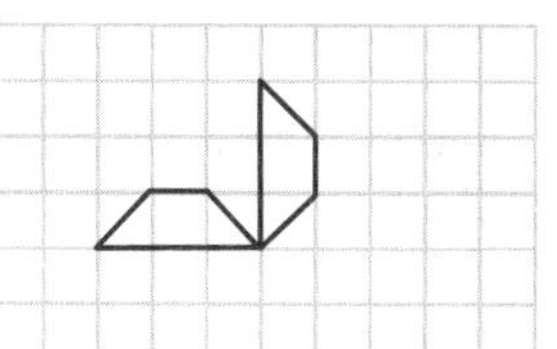

2. Circle the pictures that **do not** show reflections. Explain how you know the figures you circled are not reflections. (REMEMBER: The image must be congruent to the figure and face the opposite direction.)

a) 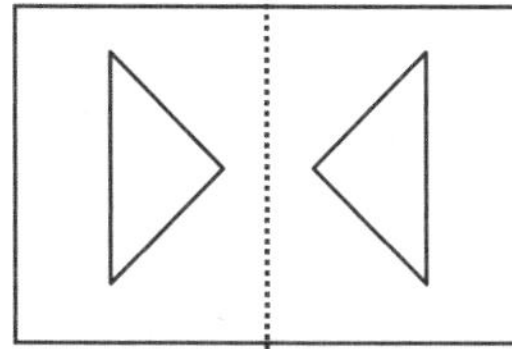

b) 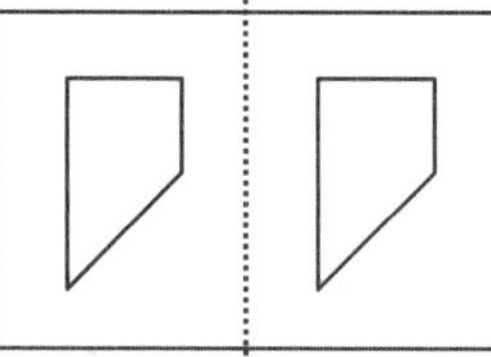

c) 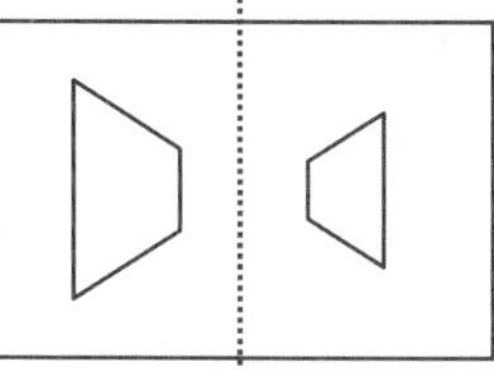

3. Draw a mirror line on grid paper. Draw a polygon with 3 or 4 sides and draw a dot at each vertex. Reflect the polygon through the mirror line by first reflecting each of the vertices.

4. 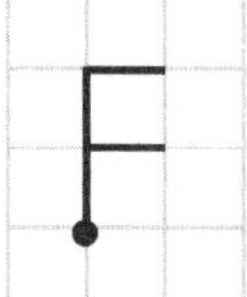

Draw the letter "F" on grid paper and put a dot in the position shown. Then:

a) Slide the letter "F" 3 units right and 2 units down by first sliding the dot.

b) Rotate the letter "F" 90° counter-clockwise around the dot.

5. Circle all the pyramids. Put an "X" through all the prisms.

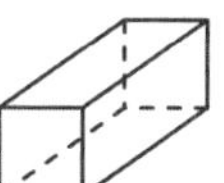 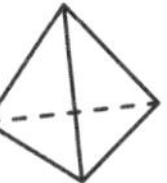 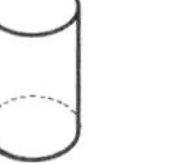  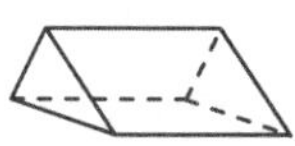 

6. 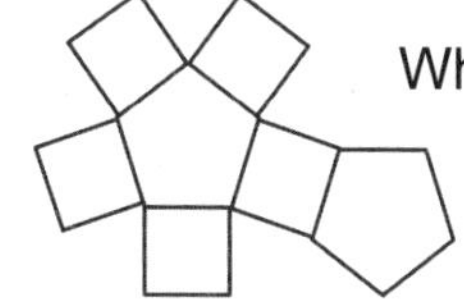

Which 3-D figure has this net? How do you know?

7. Describe the following shapes: a) a triangular prism b) a rectangular prism

8. List any 3-D shapes that have each of these properties:

a) "I have 5 faces." b) "I have 12 edges." c) "I have 6 vertices."

9. a) Colour in the sections of the left-hand square using at least 3 colours. Then create a border design by **rotating** the square.

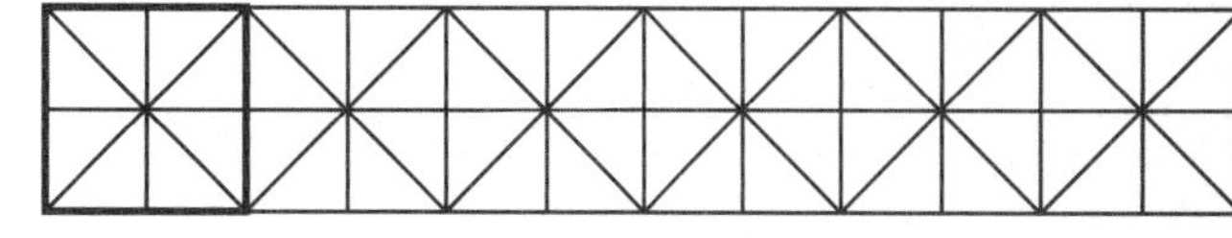

b) Choose a different set of colours and again colour in the left-hand square. Then create a border design by **reflecting** the square.

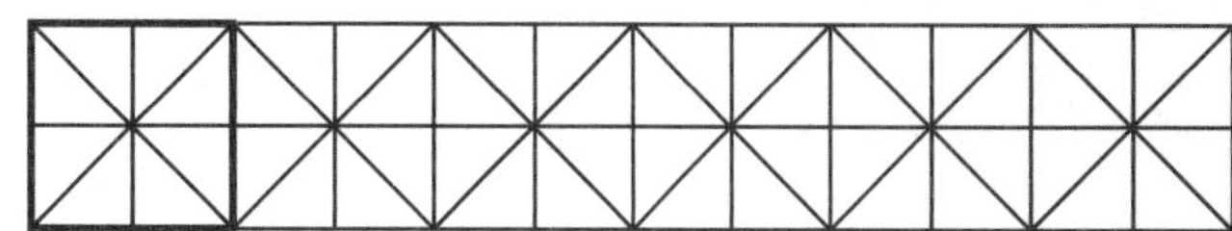

**acute angle** an angle that is less than a right angle

**add** to find the total when combining two or more numbers together

**a.m.** a time period that is in the morning, from 12 o'clock midnight until 12 o'clock noon

**angle** the amount of a turn measured in degrees

**area** the amount of space occupied by the face or surface of an object

**arms** the lines that form an angle

**array** an arrangement of things (for example, objects, symbols, or numbers) in rows and columns

**attribute** a characteristic (for example, colour, size, shape)

**bar graph** a way to display data involving four parts: a vertical and horizontal axis, a scale, labels (including a title), and data (shown in bars); the bars can be vertical or horizontal

**base** the face of a pyramid or the faces of a prism that are different from the rest

**base-10 materials** materials used to represent ones (ones squares or cubes), tens (tens strips or rods), hundreds (hundreds squares or flats), and thousands (thousands cubes)

**capacity** the amount a container can hold

**categories** a way to organize groups of data

**centimetre (cm)** a unit of measurement used to describe length, height, or thickness

**cent notation** a way to express an amount of money (for example, 40¢)

**certain** if an event must happen (for example, when you roll a die it is certain you will not roll a "7")

**circle graph** a way to display data involving a circle divided into parts

**clockwise** a circular motion of an object in the same direction to the movement of the hands of a clock

**column** things (for example, objects, symbols, numbers) that run up and down

**congruent** a term used to describe shapes if they are the same size and shape; congruent shapes can be different colours or shades

**coordinate system** a grid with labelled rows and columns, used to describe the location of a dot or object, for example the dot is at (A,3)

**core** the part of a pattern that repeats

**counter-clockwise** a circular motion opposite in direction to the movement of the hands of a clock

**cube** a block that has six equal-sided square faces

**data** facts or information

**decimal** a short form for tenths (for example, 0.2) or hundredths (for example, 0.02), and so on

**decimetre (dm)** a unit of measurement used to describe length, height, or thickness; equal to 10 cm

**decreasing sequence** a sequence where each number is less than the one before it

**degree Celsius (°C)** a unit of measurement used to describe temperature

**denominator** the number on the bottom portion of a fraction; tells you how many parts are in a whole

**diagonal** things (for example, objects, symbols, or numbers) that are in a line from one corner to another corner

**difference** the "gap" between two numbers; the remainder left after subtraction

**divide** to find how many times one number contains another number

**divisible by** containing a number a specific number of times without having a remainder (for example, 15 is divisible by 5 and 3)

**dollar notation** a way to express an amount of money (for example, $4.50)

**edge** where two faces of a shape meet; also called sides

**equally likely** when two or more events have the same chance of occurring

**equilateral** a term used to describe a polygon with sides that are all the same length

**equilateral triangle** a triangle that has all sides of equal length

**equivalent fractions** fractions that represent the same amount, but have different denominators (for example, $\frac{2}{3} = \frac{4}{6}$)

**estimate** a guess or calculation of an approximate number

**even number** the numbers you say when counting by 2s (starting at 0)

**expanded form** a way to write a number that shows the place value of each digit (for example, 27 in expanded form can be written as 2 tens + 7 ones, or 20 + 7)

**expectation** when you think a specific outcome will happen

**face** the flat surface of a 3-D shape

**fair** used to describe a game of chance if both players have the same chance of winning

**first-hand data** data you collect yourself (for example, by taking measurements, conducting experiments, or conducting surveys)

**flip** the reflection of an object or shape across a line; the image is a mirror-image of the original object or shape

**fraction** a number used to name a part of a set or a region

**gram (g)** a unit of measurement used to describe mass

**greater than** a term used to describe a number that is higher in value than another number

**group of data** similar data that are considered together, such as the colour of your hair and your friends' hair colours

**growing pattern** a pattern in which each term is greater than the previous term

**hexagon** a polygon with six sides

**horizontal** a line of things (for example, objects, symbols, or numbers) that are arranged in a row from right to left, or left to right

**hour hand** the short hand on a clock that tells what hour it is

**impossible** if an event cannot happen (for example, rolling a "7" on a die)

**improper fraction** a fraction that has a numerator that is larger than the denominator; this represents more than a whole

**increasing sequence** a sequence where each number is greater than the one before it

**key** tells what the scale of a pictograph is so you know how many each symbol represents

**kilogram (kg)** a unit of measurement used to describe mass

**kilometre (km)** a unit of measurement for length; equal to 1000 cm

**less than** a term used to describe a number that is lower in value than another number

**likely** an event that will probably happen

**litre (L)** a unit of measurement used to describe capacity

**map** a picture that represents a place (for example, Canada, or an imaginary place)

**mass** measures the amount of substance, or matter, in a thing

**metre (m)** a unit of measurement used to describe length, height, or thickness; equal to 100 cm

**millilitre (mL)** a unit of measurement used to describe capacity

**millimetre (mm)** a unit of measurement used to describe length, height, or thickness, equal to 0.1 cm

**minute hand** the long hand on a clock that tells the number of minutes past the hour

**mixed fraction** a mixture of a whole number and a fraction

**model** a physical representation (for example, using base-10 materials to represent a number)

**more than** a term used to describe a number that is higher in value than another number

**multiple of** a number that is the result of multiplying one number by another specific number (for example, the multiples of 5 are 0, 5, 10, 15, and so on)

**multiple of 2** a number that is the result of multiplying a number by 2

**multiple of 3** a number that is the result of multiplying a number by 3

**multiply** to find the total of a number times another number

**non-congruent** a term used to describe shapes if they are not the same size and shape

**number line** a line with numbers marked at intervals, used to help with skip counting

**numerator** the number on the top portion of a fraction; tells you how many parts are counted

**obtuse angle** an angle that is greater than a right angle

**odd number** the numbers you say when counting by 2s (starting at 1); numbers that are not even

**ordinal number** a word that describes the position of an object (for example, first, second, third, fourth, fifth, sixth, seventh, eighth, ninth)

**outcomes** the different ways an event can turn out

**parallel lines** lines that are straight and always the same distance apart

**parallelogram** a quadrilateral with two pairs of parallel sides

**pattern (repeating pattern)** the same repeating group of objects, numbers, or attributes

**pentagon** a polygon with five sides

**perimeter** the distance around the outside of a shape

**period** the part of a pattern that repeats; the core of the pattern

**pictograph** a way to record and count data using symbols

**piece of data** a specific item of data, such as the colour of a person's hair, or a type of fish

**pie chart** a way to display data involving a circle divided into parts

**p.m.** a time period that is in the afternoon, from 12 o'clock noon until 12 o'clock midnight

**polygon** a 2-D shape with sides that are all straight lines

**prism** a 3-D shape that has the same face at both ends

**probability** how likely it is that an outcome will happen

**product** the result from multiplying two or more numbers together

**property** an attribute or characteristic of a thing (for example, the number of edges of a shape, the number of vertices of a shape)

**protractor** a semi-circle with 180 subdivisions around its circumference; used to measure an angle

**pyramid** a shape that has a point at one end and a base at the other end

**quadrilateral** a polygon with four sides

**quotient** the result from dividing one number by another number

**rectangle** a quadrilateral with four right angles

**rectangular** having a face that is a rectangle (for example, a prism with a four-sided base)

**reflection** an object or shape that is a mirror-image of the original object

**regroup** to exchange one place value for another place value (for example, 10 ones squares for 1 tens strip)

**remainder** the number left over after dividing or subtracting (for example, 10 ÷ 3 = 3 R1)

**rhombus** a quadrilateral with equal sides

**right angle** found in many places, including the corners of squares, rectangles, and some triangles; also called a square corner

**right-angled triangle** a triangle that has one right angle, or square corner

**rotation** a circular motion of an object to a new position

**row** things (for example, objects, symbols, or numbers) that run left to right

**scale** a way to show larger numbers in a pictograph without drawing symbols for every single number

**second-hand data** data collected by someone else (for example, in books and magazines, on the Internet)

**set** a group of like objects

**side** a boundary of a shape (for example, one of the line segments that form the boundary of a polygon)

**skip counting** counting by a number (for example, 2s, 3s, 4s) by "skipping" over the numbers in between

**slide** the movement of a shape along a straight line with no turning

**square** a quadrilateral with equal sides and four right angles

**square centimetre ($cm^2$)** a unit of measurement used to describe area

**subtract** to take away one or more numbers from another number

**sum** the result from adding two or more numbers together

**symbol** an object used to represent a larger number in a pictograph (for example, 1 ✿ means 5 flowers)

**symmetrical shape** a shape that can be divided into two congruent parts (that reflect onto each other) by a line of division

**tally** a way to record and count data; each stroke represents "1" and every fifth stroke is made sideways to make counting easier (for example, ~~||||~~)

**tangram** an ancient Chinese puzzle; a square cut into seven pieces called tans

**tessellation** a pattern made up of one or more shapes that completely covers a surface (without any gaps or overlaps)

**three dimensional (3-D)** having a shape that is solid (for example, a cube, cylinder, cone, sphere)

**trapezoid** a quadrilateral with one pair of parallel sides

**tree diagram** uses branches (lines) to show all the possible choices or outcomes

**triangle** a polygon with three sides

**triangular** having a face that is a triangle (for example, a pyramid with a three-sided base)

**T-table** a chart used to compare two sequences of numbers

**turn** a circular motion of an object to a new position

**two-dimensional (2-D)** having a shape that is flat (for example, a circle, square, triangle, rectangle)

**unlikely** an event that will probably not happen

**Venn diagram** a diagram that involves two circles, used to organize things according to attributes; the areas of the circles that overlap represent items that share both attributes

**vertex** a point on a shape where two or more sides or edges meet; more than one vertex are called vertices

**vertical** a line or object that goes up and down

**volume** the amount of space taken up by a three-dimensional object

# Patterns and Algebra

**Worksheet PA4-1**

1. a) 2
   b) 4
   c) 3
   d) 2
   e) 7
   f) 3
   g) 9
   h) 8
   i) 10
2. a) 3
   b) 4
   c) 3
   d) 7
   e) 2
   f) 4
   g) 1
   h) 4
3. a) 2
   b) 3
   c) 7
   d) 3
   e) 3
   f) 1
   g) 1
   h) 4
   i) 5

**Worksheet PA4-2**

1. a) 9
   b) 10
   c) 10
   d) 7
   e) 22
   f) 22
   g) 22
   h) 25
   i) 38
   j) 36
   k) 41
   l) 37
   m) 69
   n) 90
   o) 45
   p) 72
   q) 60
   r) 68
   s) 102
   t) 101
2. a) 10
   b) 11
   c) 12
   d) 20
   e) 40
   f) 23
   g) 37
   h) 31
   i) 45

**Worksheet PA4-3**

3. 77 tonight; 82 tomorrow
4. 16 Tuesday; 20 Wednesday; 28 on Friday

**Worksheet PA4-4**

1. a) 3
   b) 3
   c) 2
   d) 4
   e) 4
   f) 5
   g) 3
   h) 1
   i) 6
2. b) –2
   c) –3
   d) –11
   e) –7
   f) –5
   g) –7
   h) –9
3. a) 3
4. b) –5
   c) –5
   d) –7
   e) –7
   f) –3
   g) –6
   h) –6
5. b) –2
   c) –5
   d) –1
   e) –4
   f) –4
   g) –7
   h) –8
6. a) –5
   b) –6
   c) –2
   d) –2
   e) –5
   f) –4
   g) –9
   h) –6
   i) –7
   j) –4
   k) –6
   l) –8

**Worksheet PA4-5**

2. a) 3
   b) 7
   c) 5
   d) 12
   e) 16
   f) 19
   g) 21
   h) 28
   i) 35

**Worksheet PA4-6**

1. a) 15, 20, 25
   b) 7, 10, 13
   c) 9, 12, 15
   d) 10, 12, 14
   e) 16, 18, 20
   f) 20, 25, 30
   g) 12, 11, 10
   h) 12, 10, 8
2. a) +3; 14, 17
   b) +2; 8, 10
   c) +4; 18, 22
   d) +2; 7, 9
   e) +3; 30, 33
   f) +5; 27, 32
   g) –2; 19, 17
   h) –5; 44, 39
3. 9 chocolates [=24-(3x5)]
4. $33 [=17+(4x4)]

**Worksheet PA4-7**

3. c) **B C A** B C
   d) **2 8 9 6** 2
   e) **3 0 0 4**
   f) **1 8 1** 1

**Worksheet PA4-8**

1. a) shape
   b) colour
   c) shape
   d) shape
   e) size
   f) colour
2. a) size
   b) shape
   c) size
   d) colour
3. a) size and colour
   b) shape and colour
   c) shape and size
   d) size and colour
4. a) size and colour
   b) shape and size
   c) shape and colour
   d) shape and colour
5. a) shape
   b) shape and colour
   c) colour
   d) shape, size, and colour
6. juice milk WATER, size and type of drink change

**Worksheet PA4-9**

1. a) **shape**: stays same; **colour**: Y Y B then repeat; **size**: big small small, then repeat
   b) **shape**: circle, pentagon, triangle, then repeat; **colour**: Y B then repeat; **size**: stays the same
   c) **shape**: pentagon, circle, square, triangle, then repeat; **colour**: B R R B, then repeat; **size**: small small bigl small, then repeat
   d) **shape**: triangle, triangle, triangle, pentagon, then repeat; **colour**: B B R, then repeat; **size**: Big small small small, then repeat
   e) **shape**: pentagon, triangle, triangle, then repeat; **colour**: B R R B, then repeat; **size**: big big small, then repeat
2. a) **shape**: ball, cube, then repeat; **colour**: B R Y, then repeat; **size**: big, big, small, small, then repeat
   b) **shape**: cylinder, cone, ball, then repeat; **colour**: R R Y Y, then repeat; **size**: small, big, then repeat

**Worksheet PA4-10**

1. a) size
   b) position
   c) shape
   d) position
   e) number
   f) colour
2. a) position and colour
   b) position and size
   c) size and shape

**Worksheet PA4-11**

1. a) 37, 40, 43
   b) 80, 85, 90
   c) 28, 30, 32
   d) 70, 80, 90
2. a) 10, 8, 6
   b) 9, 6, 3
   c) 65, 60, 55
   d) 60, 57, 54
3. a) 39, 43, 47
   b) 29, 38, 47
   c) 22, 28, 34
   d) 84, 91, 98
4. a) 38, 34, 30
   b) 35, 28, 21
   c) 85, 82, 79
   d) 109, 98, 87
6. circle c): 3, 6, 9, 12
7. Yes, because adding 4 always gets the next number.
8. Faruq, because subtracting 8 always gets the next number.

**Worksheet PA4-12**

1. a) 3
   b) 3
   c) 2
   d) 2
   e) 5
   f) 3
   g) 2
   h) 6
   i) 3
   j) 4
2. a) 2
   b) 5
   c) 1
   d) 3
   e) 3
   f) 2
   g) 10
   h) 5
   i) 2
   j) 6
   k) 5
   l) 20
3. a) Subtract 7
   b) Add 8

c) Add 4
d) Subtract 11
4. 27, 32, 37 Rule: add 5
5. a) Molly
b) Jane added the wrong number and forgot to say what to start at; Keith subtracted instead of added.

**Worksheet PA4-13**

1. a) Start at 3, add 4
b) Start at 2, add 4
c) Start at 2, add 2
d) Start at 1, add 5
e) Start at 5, add 4
f) Start at 12, add 6
g) Start at 2, add 8
h) Start at 3, add 3
i) Start at 6, add 7
2. a) 17, 22, 27; in sixth figure: 27 blocks
b) 12, 15, 18; in sixth figure: 18 blocks
c) 18, 23, 28; in sixth figure: 28 blocks.
3. a) No, she needs 15 blocks.
b) No, she needs 16 blocks.
c) Yes, she only needs 13 blocks.
4. a) 12
b) 18

**Worksheet PA4-14**

1. a) 7
b) 10
c) 8
d) 9
e) 10
f) 14
2. a) 20
b) Added 4 to the number of line segments in figure 4.
3. 15
4. a) 16
b) 19
c) 25
5. a) 13
b) 15
c) 17
6. a) 25 young
b) 20 young
c) 15 young
d) 10 young
7. a) $56
b) $48
c) $60
8. 15 triangles
9. No, she needs 10 triangles.
10. $27
11. No, she needs $30.

**Worksheet PA4-15**

1. 16 bikes
2. $50
3. 14 cm
4. 21 cm
5. 46 pages
6. 15 trees
7. 39 cm
8. 48 cans
9. a) The candle burns 3 cm every hour.
b) 18 cm
10. $14
11. $17
12. Amanda has saved $58; Jacob only $54.
13. Edith's plant is 19 cm high; Ron's only 13 cm.
14. Chloe's candle is 8 cm tall; Dora's only 6 cm.

**Worksheet PA4-16**

2. $20
3. August 16th and 28th
4. Oct. 18th
5. a) You always add 7, because there are 7 days in a week.
b) In the direction shown, you always add 8; in the other direction, you always add 6.
6. The two sums will always be the same.

**Worksheet PA4-17**

1. a) RYYRYY
b) YRYRYRY
c) RYYRRYYR
d) RYRRYRRYR
e) YYRYYYRYYRY
f) YYRYYYRYY
2. a) Yes
b) Yes
c) No
d) No
e) Yes
f) Yes
3. a) Yes
b) Yes
c) No; circle RYYR
d) No; circle YYRR
e) Yes
f) No; circle RYRYY
4. a) YRR
b) RRRY
c) YYRR
d) YRRY
e) RYRYYY
f) RY
5. yellow
6. yellow
7. red
8. red
9. red
10. Down, because all even numbered triangles point down.
11. The 45th block ends a core, so the 46th block begins a new one, which is red.
12. a) A nickel because all odd ones are nickels.
b) The 91st coin is also a nickel because 91 is odd.
13. a) A penny, because 15 ends a core.
b) There are 5 cores in 15 coins, and each core is worth 7¢, so the 15 coins are worth 7 × 5 = 35¢.

**Worksheet PA4-18**

1. 8 km [=20-(6x2)]
2. 5 km [=50-(15x3)]
3. 4 minutes [=16÷4]
4. 25 km [=250-(75x3)]
5. 200 metres[=100+(50x2)]
6. 13 m [=5+(2x4)]
7. 15 m [=3x(6-1)]
8. steps 6 and 12

**Worksheet PA4-19**

1. b) + + –
c) – – +
d) + – +
e) – + –
f) + + +
g) + – +
h) + + –
i) – – +
j) + + +
k) + – +
l) + + +
2. a) C (+ – +), A, B
b) B, C (— +), A
c) A, C (– – +), B
d) B, C (+ – +), A
3. b) +3, –1, +4, –3
c) +3, +1, +4, +2
d) –2, +4, –4, +7
e) +6, +1, –5, +8
f) –3, –4, +2, –1
g) –5, +2, +5, –3
h) +3, –7, +7, +7
4. a) A, B
b) B, A
c) A, B
d) A, B
e) C, B, A
f) C, A, D, B
5. b) start at 3, add 2
c) start at 19, subtract 3
d) start at 33, subtract 5
6. a) start at 8, add 3
b) start at 14, subtract 4
c) no rule
d) start at 61, add 4
7. a) increasing
b) repeating
c) decreasing
d) increasing
e) Repeating
f) decreasing
8. a) 6, 9, 12, 15, 18
b) 26, 22, 18, 14, 10
c) 39, 44, 49, 54, 59

**Worksheet PA4-20**

3. a) row 8, 10, 12
b) column 2, 8, 14
c) column 6, 12, 18
d) squares 2, 6, 10, 14, 18
4. a) add 2
b) add 6
c) add 6
d) start at 2, add 4
5. row: add 2
column: add 2
diagonals: add 4, stay same
6. row: add 3
column: subtract 3
diagonals: stay same, subtract 6
7. Y, O, A
8. Row: add 1
Column: add 1
Diagonals: add 2, stay same
9. B C A or C A B
C A B B C A
10. (Several answers exist.)
A A B B
A A B B
B B A A
B B A A
11. a) L R T T L
R T T L R
T T L R T
T L R T T
L R T T L
R T T L R
T T L R T
b) Row 6
12.
1, 2, 3, 4, 5, 6, 7, 8, 9, 1
2, 3, 4, 5, 6, 7, 8, 9,10, 2
3, 4, 5, 6, 7, 8, 9,10,11, 3
4, 5, 6, 7, 8, 9,10,11,12, 4
5, 6, 7, 8, 9,10,11,12,13, 5
6, 7, 8, 9,10,11,12,13,14, 6
7, 8, 9,10,11,12,13,14,15, 7
8, 9,10,11,12,13,14,15,16, 8
9,10,11,12,13,14,15,16,17, 9
10,11,12,13,14,15,16,17,18,10
[Except for tens column] Diagonal (from top right) stays same, (from top left) add 2.
13. a) 5
b) 10
c) 25
[40+40+20=100 so 10+10+5=25]
14. a) Every 3rd diagonal starting from top right to bottom left
c) 15,30,45,60,75,90
*10s:* repeating gap +2,+1, or odd-odd-even-even.
*1s:* repeating 5,0.
15. a) 9th and 18th diagonals
b) sum=9 (except 99)
c) Subtract 1
d) add 1 (except 99)
16.

| 3, 6, 9 | 12, 15, 18 |
|---|---|
| 1, 2, 4, 5, 7, 8, 10 | 13, 14, 16, 17, 19, 20 |

17. Put sum of two squares in the square above and between them.
18. a) 6
b) 8
c) 11
d) 11

e) 1
f) 3
g) 4
h) 5
i) 15
j) 5
k) 13, 5, 8
l) 17, 7, 4
m) 8, 5, 3
n) 32, 14, 18
o) 45, 26, 9
p) 123, 74, 17

**Worksheet PA4-21**

1. b) Every second column is shaded.
c) *1s:* 2, 4, 6, 8, 0
d) Look at the ones digit.
e) 82, 36, 78, 38
f) 18, 32, 76, 34, 94
g) Ones digit is not one of 2, 4, 6, 8, 0.
h) 5, 75, 37, 83
i) always even
j) always odd
k) 1, 3, 5, 7, 9, 11, 13, 15, 17, 19. All are odd.

2. b) make 2 columns
c) *1s:* 5, 0
d) Look at the ones digit.
e) 45, 60, 90, 85, 25

3. a) *Only 2s:* 6, 8, 24, 36, 86, 96
*Both 2s and 5s:* 10, 40, 50
*Only 5s:* 5, 15, 25, 65
*Not 2s nor 5s:* 17, 37, 49, 61, 79
b) 60, 70, 80, 90
c) Odd number, ones digit cannot be 5

4. b)

| | |
|---|---|
| 08 | 48 |
| 16 | 56 |
| 24 | 64 |
| 32 | 72 |
| 40 | 80 |

Repeating pattern 8, 6, 4, 2, 0
c) Repeating gap +1, +1, +1, +1, +0
d)

| | |
|---|---|
| 88 | 128 |
| 96 | 136 |
| 104 | 144 |
| 112 | 152 |
| 120 | 160 |

5. a) five-point star
b) same as 5. a)
c) pentagon
d) 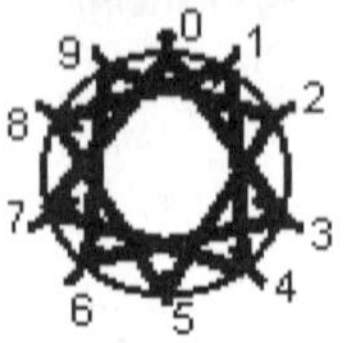
e) number 7
f) *pentagon:* numbers 2 and 8
*ten-point star:* numbers 3 and 7
*five-point star:* numbers 4 and 6

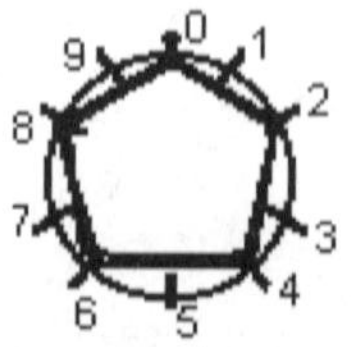

**Worksheet PA4-22**

1. a) +2, +3, +4, +5, +6; 16, 22
b) +1, +2, +3, +4, +5, +6; 18, 24
c) +3, +5, +7, +9, +11; 35, 46
d) +2, +4, +6, +8, +10, +12; 36, 48

2. a) –1, –2, –3, –4, –5; 7, 2
b) –2, –4, –6, –8, –10; 12, 2
c) –1, –3, –5, –7, –9; 15, 6
d) –5, –10, –15, –20, –25, –30; 35, 5

3. +3, +5, +7, +9, +11; 9, 16, 25, 36
4. 29 [=1+4+6+8+10]
5. 28 [=3+3+4+5+6+7]
6. 52 [=10+12+14+16]
7. a) 2
b) 32, 64, 128, 256
c) +2, +4, +8, +16, +32, +64, +128 The gap is the number.
8. 25 [=(((400÷2)÷2)÷2)÷2]
9. a) Start at 15, add 5
b) Start at 1, multiply by 2
d)

| | | |
|---|---|---|
| 5 | 16 | 35 |
| 6 | 32 | 40 |
| 7 | 64 | 45 |

Olivia saves more.
10. a) repeating: +3, –2
b) 6, 9, 7

**Worksheet PA4-23**

1. a) 120, 180, 240, 300
b) 104, 156, 208
c) 730, 1095, 1460
2. 48 months
3. 800 times
4. 2250 km; In 1 day, it flies 1500÷2=750 km, so in 3 days it flies 3x750 km.
5. $82 [=$18+($16x4)]
6. $114 [=$14+($25x4)]
7. 2062, 2138, 2214
8. a) 1998, 2997, 3996, 999x5 = 4995 9999x6 = 5994
b) 54, 594, 5994, 6x9999= 59 994 6x99 999= 599 994
c) 11, 111, 1111, 9x1234+5= 11 111

**Worksheet PA4-24**

1. a) 5
b) 3
c) 8
d) 3
e) 2
f) 6
g) 5
h) 3
i) 4
j) 6
k) 10
l) 8
m) 4
n) 5
2. a) 0,0,5 ; 1,1,3 ; 2,2,1
b) 0,0,8 ; 1,1,6 ; 2,2,4 3,3,2 ; 4,4,0
c) 0,0,4,4 ; 1,1,3,3 2,2,2,2 ; 3,3,1,1 4,4,0,0
d) Some answers are 0,1,6 ; 0,2,5 ; 0,3,4 1,1,5 ; 1,2,4 ; 1,3,3 2,2,3
3. 0,0,5 ; 1,1,3 ; 2,2,1
4. 0,0,7 ; 1,1,5 ; 2,2,3 ; 3,3,1
5. centre=3, outer=2 2+2+3=7 points
6. centre=5, outer=2 2+2+5=9 points
7. A = 3
8. c) A + 2 = B
d) A x 3 = B
e) A x 5 = B
9. 3
10. a) 3+4=7 ; 4+3=7 7–3=4 ; 7–4=3
b) 5+4=9 ; 4+5=9 9–4=5 ; 9–5=4
c) 11+2=13, 2+11=13 13–2=11, 13–11=2
d) 23+5=28, 5+23=28 28–5=23, 28–23=5
11. a) 5x2=10 ; 2x5=10 10÷2=5 ; 10÷5=2
b) 4x3=12 ; 3x4=12 12÷3=4 ; 12÷4=3
c) 8x4=32 ; 4x8=32 32÷4=8 ; 32÷8=4
d) 9x3=27 ; 3x9=27 27÷3=9 ; 27÷9=3
12. a) 1+3+5+7=16 4x4=16
b) all odd
c) 6x6=36

**Worksheet PA4-25**

1. 13 [=1+(6x2)]
2. $26 [=$17+($3x3)]
3. April 5
4. 16 triangles [=(12÷3)x4]
5. 400 m [=200 m+(50 m x4)]
6. a) rectangle, hexagon
b) 10, K, Q
c) 010, 100, 001
d) 001, 011, 111
e) 020, 030, 010
f) 060, 090, 030
g) N, N, N
h) T,2222,T,22222,T
i) AE, AF
j) 
7. square
8. a) 24
b) 32
c) 12
9. a) 3727, 3827, 3927
b) 7237, 8238, 9239
c) 4567, 5678, 6789
10. a) step 12
b) steps 6 and 12
12. a) 0: A,B,C,E,F,G
1: C,F
2: A,C,D,E,G
3: A,C,D,F,G
4: B,C,D,F
5: A,B,D,F,G
6: A,B,D,E,F,G
7: A,C,F
8: A,B,C,D,E,F,G
9: A,B,C,D,F,G
b) trapezoid F
13. $6^{th}$ and $12^{th}$ persons
14. 21 [=1+2+3+4+5+6]

# Number Sense

**Worksheet NS4-1:**

2. a) 30
b) 50
5. a) 400
b) 800
c) 1000
8. a) 3000
b) 4000
c) 5000

**Worksheet NS4-2:**

4. a) 2556
b) 5391
c) 6870
d) 8409
e) 9217
f) 9110
5. a) one thousand, two hundred and thirty-five
b) five thousand, two hundred and five
c) one thousand, six hundred and forty-nine
d) two thousand and eighty

e) nine thousand, seven hundred and one
f) two thousand, two hundred and thirty-four
g) five thousand, six hundred and five

**Worksheet NS4-3**

1. a) 252
   b) 336
   c) 185
   d) 507
5. a) 2332
   b) 3226
   c) 1239

**Worksheet NS4-4**

4. a) 100
   b) 1000
   c) 100
   d) 10
   e) 1000
   f) 100

**Worksheet NS4-5**

3. a) nine hundred and fifty-two
   b) three thousand
   c) four thousand seven hundred
   d) six thousand and forty
   e) two thousand, nine hundred and eighty-one
   f) five thousand, eight hundred and sixty-two
4. 275= 2 hundreds + 7 tens + 5 ones

   275= 200 + 70 + 5

   275= two hundred and seventy-five

   275= 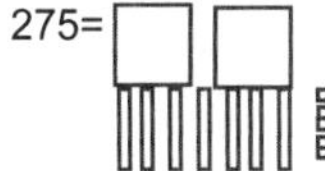

**Worksheet NS4-6**

1. a) (i) = 268
   (ii) = **354**
   b) (i) = **2362**
   (ii) = 1350
2. The group with the largest number of higher place value blocks is larger.
3. a) (i) = **424**
   (ii) = 224
   b) (i) = **1232**
   (ii) = 1230
6. Explanation should be similar to #2.
9. a) 423
   b) 770
   c) 353
10. a) 237
    b) 542
    c) 909
11. a) 432
    b) 261
    c) 754
12. a) the town library
    b) Montreal
13. a) 3603
    b) 5012
    c) 6726
    d) 3729
    e) 8175
    f) 6000
    g) 7329
    h) 4952
15. **940**, 904, 490, 409
16. a) 9641
    b) 8410
    c) 8764
17. 987

**Worksheet NS4-8**

1. a) 3 tens + 12 ones = 4 tens + 2 ones
   b) 2 tens + 15 ones = 3 tens + 5 ones
   c) 2 tens + 13 ones = 3 tens + 3 ones
   d) 4 tens + 19 ones = 5 tens + 9 ones
2. b) 8 + 12 = 9 tens, 2 ones
   c) 5 +31 = 8 tens, 1 one
   d) 7 + 17 = 8 tens, 7 ones
   e) 6 + 29 = 8 tens, 9 ones
   f) 1 + 52 = 6 tens, 2 ones
4. b) 2 + 15 = 3 hundreds, 5 tens
   c) 6 + 17 = 7 hundreds, 7 tens
   d) 6 + 12 = 7 hundreds, 2 tens
   e) 2 + 17 = 3 hundreds, 7 tens
   f) 5 + 10 = 6 hundreds, 0 tens
5. a) 4 hundreds + 3 tens + 4 ones
   b) 10 hundreds + 1 ten + 1 one
   c) 4 hundreds + 0 tens + 5 ones
   d) 4 hundreds + 4 tens + 7 ones
   e) 9 hundreds + 1 ten + 0 ones
6. b) 9 hundreds + 5 tens + 2 ones
   c) 6 hundreds + 3 tens + 6 ones
   d) 7 hundreds + 3 tens + 8 ones
   e) 7 hundreds + 6 tens + 1 one
   f) 2 hundreds + 6 tens + 3 ones
8. b) 4 thousands + 5 hundreds + 1 tens + 6 ones
   c) 7 thousands + 4 hundreds + 6 tens + 5 ones
   d) 3 thousands + 8 hundreds + 0 tens + 7 ones
   e) 9 thousands + 0 hundreds + 1 ten + 0 ones
9. b) 6 thousands + 8 hundreds + 3 tens + 5 ones
   c) 4 thousands + 1 hundred + 4 tens + 9 ones
   d) 7 thousands + 1 hundred + 1 tens+ 9 ones
   e) 7 thousands + 7 hundreds + 7 tens + 7 ones
10. Roger is unable to build the model.

**Worksheet NS4-9**

1. b) 35 + 42 = 77
   c) 31 + 27 = 58
   d) 13 + 24 = 37
2. a) 77
   b) 89
   c) 89
   d) 59
   e) 39
3. a) 37
   b) 76
   c) 92
   d) 74
   e) 89
   f) 77

**Worksheet NS4-10**

1. b) 25 + 37 = 5 tens + 12 ones = 6 tens + 2 ones =62
   c) 29 + 36 = 5 tens + 15 ones = 6 tens + 5 ones =65
   d) 17 + 35 = 4 tens + 12 ones = 5 tens + 2 ones =52
   e) 27 + 26 = 4 tens + 13 ones = 5 tens + 3 ones =53
   f) 19 + 8 = 1 ten + 17 ones = 2 tens + 7 ones =27
2. b)
```
  1
 64
+16
  0
```
   c)
```
  1
 75
+19
  4
```
   d)
```
  1
 66
+17
  3
```
   e)
```
  1
 15
+38
  3
```
3. b) 55
   c) 77
   d) 80
   e) 83
   f) 92
   g) 105
   h) 95
   i) 72
   j) 91

**Worksheet NS4-11**

1. a) **353** =3 hundreds+5 tens+3 ones
   **+164** =1 hundred +6 tens +4 ones
   =4 hundreds+11 tens+7 ones
   =5 hundreds+1 tens+7 ones
   b) **462** =4 hundreds+6 tens+2 ones
   **+375** =3 hundreds + 7 tens +5 ones
   =7 hundreds+13 tens+7 ones
   =8 hundreds+3 tens+7 ones
2. a) 819
   b) 828
   c) 836
   d) 959
   e) 879
3. a) 342
   b) 763
   c) 960
   d) 551
   e) 566
4. a) 717
   b) 672
   c) 874
   d) 836
   e) 653
   f) 990
5. a) 553
   b) 485
   c) 1361
   d) 962
   e) 419
   f) 1741
   g) 488
   h) 1757
6. a) 18
   b) 198
   c) 1998
   d) 19 998
   e) 199 998

**Worksheet NS4-12**

1. a) 6164
   b) 5478
2. a) 8177
   b) 8287
   c) 6368
   d) 4593
   e) 7597
3. a) 4817
   b) 3829
   c) 6617
   d) 9836
   e) 6387
4. a) 3561
   b) 9870
   c) 9696
   d) 7772

e) 8893
5. a) 5185
b) 6425
c) 8664
d) 8058
e) 6567
f) 8368
g) 9225
h) 9352
i) 4676
j) 6676
6. a) 7076
b) 8114
c) 8066
d) 9130

**Worksheet NS4-13**

2. b) 57=5 tens+7 ones
−34=3 tens+ 4 ones
=2 tens+3 ones
=23
c) 84=8 tens+4 ones
−63=6 tens+ 3 ones
=2 tens+1 ones
=21
d) 89=8 tens+9 ones
−56=5 tens+ 6 ones
=3 tens+3 ones
=33
e) 77=7 tens+7 ones
−44=4 tens+ 4 ones
=3 tens+3 ones
=33
f) 67=6 tens+7 ones
−45=4 tens+ 5 ones
=2 tens+2 ones
=22
3. b) 84=80+4
−52=50+2
=30+2
=32
c) 98=90+8
−37=30+7
=60+1
=61
d) 73=70+3
−12=10+2
=60+1
=61
e) 16=10+6
−14=10+4
=0+2
=2
f) 88=80+8
−33=30+3
=50+5
=55
4. a) 31
b) 13
c) 21
d) 32
e) 53
f) 49
5. a) 122
7. a) 3411
b) 21 111
c) 432 752
8. The Skylon tower is 46 m taller than the tallest tree.

**Worksheet NS4-14**

1. a) 37
b) 35
c) 23
d) 38
2. b) 38
c) 25
d) 48
e) 18
3. c) Help: 1 is less than 3
f) Help: 4 is less than 7
h) Help: 7 is less than 9
i) Help: 4 is less than 6
5. a) 153
b) 243
c) 131
d) 372
6. The Whistling Cave is 85 m longer.
7. a) 328
b) 348
c) 438
d) 718
8. a) 478
b) 489
c) 267
d) 477
9. a) 1931
b) 2722
c) 3731
d) 2913
10. b) 2982
c) 2816
d) 1949
11. a) 1912
b) 4296
c) 4223
d) 1484
e) 7274
f) 1973
g) 4293
h) 5438
12. a) 5778
b) 2888
c) 3847
d) 2579
13. a) 543
b) 25
c) 367
d) 111
14. The Canada–USA border is 2639 km longer than the Great Wall of China.

**Worksheet NS4-15**

1. 62–17 boys=45 girls
check:
17 boys+45 girls= 62
2. b) 84 m
c) 107 m
3. a) 8+3=11; 11–3=8. 11–8=3
b) 7–4=3, 3+4=7, 4+3=7
c) 19+5=24; 24–19=5, 24–5=19
4. sum: 1173;
difference: 531;
5. 2 should be the ones digit and 1 should be carried
6. a) 67 years old
b) 51 years old
7. a) 990
b) 1010
c) 900
d) 1100
8. a) 6449
b) 79
c) 858
d) 6242
e) 21216
9. cost: 45¢+49¢=94¢
Ben's 95¢ is enough to buy both pen and eraser.
10. Josh is carrying the ten from adding 5 and 7 into the tens column.

**Worksheet NS4-16**

1. b) 4 rows
4 dots in each row
4 x 4 = 16
c) 4 rows
5 dots in each row
4 x 5 = 20
2. b) 5 x 2
c) 5 x 3
d) 7 x 2
5. a) 6 x 5 = 30
b) 7 x 3 = 21
c) 8 x 4 = 32

**Worksheet NS4-17**

1. b) 8+8
c) 6+6+6+6+6
d) 2+2+2+2
e) 5+5+5
f) 3+3+3+3+3+3+3+3+3
g) 7+7+7+7+7
h) 1+1+1+1+1+1
i) 8
2. b) 3 x 5
c) 2 x 4
d) 4 x 7
e) 2 x 9
f) 3 x 8
g) 3 x 2
h) 4 x 9
i) 3 x 1
j) 5 x 6
k) 6 x 8
l) 3 x 3
3. b) 3x4; 4+4+4
c) 4x3; 3+3+3+3
d) 2x5; 5+5
4. a) 6x5; 5+5+5+5+5+5
b) 3x7; 7+7+7
c) 7x4; 4+4+4+4+4+4+4

**Worksheet NS4-19**

4. b) 3 × 5 tens=15 tens=1 hundreds + 5 tens=150
c) 5 ×5 tens=25 tens=2 hundreds + 5 tens=250
d) 4 × 6 tens=24 tens=2 hundreds + 4 tens=240

**Worksheet NS4-21**

2. a) 124
b) 106
c) 164
d) 126
e) 93
f) 142
g) 186
h) 168
i) 208
j) 44
3. a) 186
b) 148
c) 105
d) 248
e) 135

**Worksheet NS4-22**

3. a) 96
b) 60
c) 70
d) 84
e) 75
4. a) 50
b) 96
c) 140
d) 105

**Worksheet NS4-23**

1. a) 963
b) 864
3. a) 48
b) 639
c) 488
d) 969
e) 826
4. a) 492
b) 975
c) 570
d) 632
e) 672
5. a) 968
b) 755
c) 726
d) 456
e) 762
6. a) 968
b) 1560
c) 861
d) 2512
e) 2277
f) 1446

**Worksheet NS4-24**

1. 1920
2. 1056 mL
3. a) 1680 L
b) 960 L
5. No. 2×1=2; 2 +1=3
6. 1
7. 1, 2, 4, 5, 10, 20
8. a) 120
b) 240
10. 1950 m

**Worksheet NS4-28**

1. a) 20+30=50 (56)
b) 80+20=100 (93)
c) 30+60=90 (87)
2. a) 200+500=700 (699)
b) 600+100=700 (774)
c) 500 (516)
d) 1400 (1473)
4. a) 588
b) 534
c) 319

**Worksheet NS4-29**

4. $3
5. 3
6. 2

**Worksheet NS4-30**

10. 6 siblings
11. 7 envelopes
12. 3 hours

**Worksheet NS4-31**

3. a) toys; 5 sets; 4 per set

b) pencils; 7 sets; 3 per set
c) students; 4 sets; 4 per set
d) flowers; 8 sets; 3 per set
e) grapefruits; 7 sets; 6 per set
f) kids; 3 sets; 10 per set
g) cows; 3 sets; 5 per set
h) puppies; 6 sets; 6 per set

**Worksheet NS4-32**
2. a) 6 triangles per set
b) 3 triangles per set
3. 2 squares per set
4. a) 3 sets
b) 4 sets
c) 2 sets
6. c) stickers; 6 per set
d) books; 4 sets
e) kids; 5 per set
f) kids; 15 per set
g) fruit bars; 3 per set
h) chairs; 5 per set
i) kids; 4 per set
7. a) 3 dots per set
b) 3 sets
c) 3 sets
d) 2 dots per set
e) 2 dots per set
8. 3 tickets

**Worksheet NS4-33**
1. a) 12 lines; 3 sets; 4 lines in each set
12÷4=3; 12÷3=4

**Worksheet NS4-35**
2. a) 2×3=6; 3×2=6;
6÷2=3; 6÷3=2;
6 fish; 2 sets; 3 fish per set
b) 2×6=12; 6×2=12;
12÷6=2; 12÷2=6;
12 snails; 6 sets; 2 snails per set

**Worksheet NS4-36**
4. a) 18÷3=6; 6 sets
b) 5×4=20; 20 things
c) 15÷5=3; 3 things in each set
d) 8×3=24; 24 things
e) 12÷6=2; 2 sets
f) 10÷5=2; 2 things in each set
5. a) 5 people
b) 18 marbles
c) 3 flowers per pot
d) 8 chairs
e) 3 pillows per bed
f) 3 blocks

**Worksheet NS4-37**
2. a) 3 dots in each circle; 1 dot remaining
b) 2 dots in each circle; 2 dots remaining

5. 3 groups of 2 cookies or 2 groups of 3 cookies; 1 remainder in each
6. 6 or 9

**Worksheet NS4-38**
3. She can make 2 bags with 3 oranges left over.
4. a) 3 rides
b) 2 friends

**Worksheet NS4-39**
1. a) 15
b) 20
c) 10
2. a) 8
b) 4
3. a) 9
b) 6
4. a) 12
b) 20
c) 8
5. a) 3
b) 4
c) 2
6. a) 15; R-1
b) 20; R-2
7. a) 3 R-3
b) 4 R-3
8. 3 friends, 2 left over

**Worksheet NS4-40**
1. b) 4
c) 2
d) 3
e) 1
f) 4
g) 2
h) 4
2. b) 2; stop counting:10
c) 4; stop counting:20
d) 3; stop counting:15
e) 1; stop counting:5
f) 4; stop counting:12
g) 4; stop counting:20
h) 3; stop counting:6
3. b) 4 R-2
c) 5 R-2
d) 3 R-3
e) 1 R-1
f) 5 R-1
g) 1 R-2
h) 2 R-1
4. a) 4 R-3
b) 5 R-1
c) 4 R-2
d) 5 R-1
e) 8 R-1
f) 3 R-1
5. 3 per friend, R-1

**Worksheet NS4-41**
7. a) 42÷3=14
b) 65÷5=13
8. a) 2 per group, R-1
9. a) 30 per group; 82 altogether, 22 left
b) 20 per group; 77 altogether; 17 left
10. a) 23 left over
b) 21 left over
12. 20 per group, 5 left over

**Worksheet NS4-42**
5. a) 3 tens per group;
2 groups;
6 tens placed (3×2=6)
8. a) 25
b) 28
c) 46
d) 20
e) 13
f) 15
g) 17
h) 12
i) 11
j) 10
9. a) 25 R-1
b) 15
c) 27 R-1
d) 12 R-3
e) 14
f) 10 R-5
g) 45 R-1
h) 32
i) 10 R-2
j) 36 R-1
10. a) 24 R-2
b) 13 R-2
c) 13 R-1
d) 14
e) 22 R-2
f) 16 R-4
g) 16
h) 32
i) 14 R-5
j) 13 R-6
11. 2
12. 12
13. 12
14. Mike (2 apples)
15. 15 canoes (14 R-2)
16. 13 nights (12 R-3)
17. 16 with one card left
18. 11 (10 R-7)

**Worksheet NS4-43**
2. a) 144
b) 156 R-1
c) 124 R-3
d) 166
3. b) 27
c) 53 R-1
d) 37 R-1
4. a) 72 R-1
b) 135 R-3
c) 120 R-4
d) 21 R-4
e) 32 R-1
5. 155 cm
6. $153

**Worksheet NS4-44**
2. a) 28
b) 24
3. a) 35 R-2
b) $210
4. 6/6; 4/4/4; 3/3/3/3;
5. Three numbers from either sequence:
A: 4, 7, 10, 13, 16…
B: 5, 8, 11, 14, 17…
6. a) 6 eggs
b) 12 eggs
c) 360 eggs
7. 25 books
8. 53 mL
9 170 m
10. 948 m
11. 45 m
12. a) 9 eggs
b) 18 eggs

**Worksheet NS4-45**
3. a) number of pieces all together
b) number of shaded pieces
4. a) 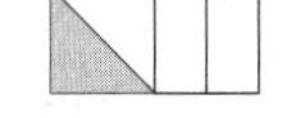
does represent $\frac{1}{4}$
10. a) $\frac{1}{3}$
b) $\frac{2}{5}$

**Worksheet NS4-46**
1. a) $\frac{3}{5}$ squares; $\frac{2}{5}$ shaded; $\frac{2}{5}$ triangles;
2. $\frac{2}{7}$ shaded; $\frac{2}{7}$ squares;
4. a) 8
b) $\frac{5}{8}$
c) yes
5. a) $\frac{7}{12}$
b) $\frac{2}{12}$
c) $\frac{3}{12}$
6. $\frac{6}{10}$
7. $\frac{2}{3}$
8. $\frac{5}{9}$

**Worksheet NS4-47**
1. $\frac{1}{8}$ (extend the lines to see the total number of pieces)
2. 6
3. a) $\frac{5}{6}$
b) $\frac{1}{6}$
c) $\frac{1}{2}$ or $\frac{3}{6}$
d) $\frac{2}{6}$
3. a) $\frac{2}{8}$
b) $\frac{1}{8}$
c) $\frac{3}{9}$ or $\frac{1}{3}$
d) $\frac{1}{12}$
5. $\frac{1}{3}$
6. $\frac{3}{6}$ or $\frac{1}{2}$
7. $\frac{2}{6}$ or $\frac{1}{3}$
8. $\frac{1}{12}$
9. $\frac{1}{6}$

**Worksheet NS4-48**

5. a) $\frac{1}{2}$
b) $\frac{1}{4}$
c) decreases
6. $\frac{1}{2}$; it has a greater denominator and therefore is a larger fraction than $\frac{1}{100}$
11. No, because the shapes and sizes are different
12. Yes. e.g.
13. a) $\frac{2}{3}$
b) $\frac{3}{4}$
c) $\frac{1}{2}$
d) $\frac{1}{3}$

**Worksheet NS4-49**
1. b) 3
c) 1
2. a) $2\frac{1}{2}$
e) $2\frac{3}{8}$
5. $3\frac{1}{2}$ (more whole pies)
6. 3

**Worksheet NS4-50**
1. a) $\frac{5}{2}$
f) $\frac{16}{6}$
4. $\frac{7}{2}$ (same denominators, and the numerator is greater )
5. $\frac{9}{4}$ and $\frac{7}{5}$ because the numerator is greater than the denominator

**Worksheet NS4-51**
1. a) $3\frac{1}{2}$ and $\frac{7}{2}$
5. Divide 13 by 4. The quotient is the whole number of pies (3).

**Worksheet NS4-52**
5. $\frac{5}{2}$ (same denominators, and the numerator is greater)
6. greater because the numerator is greater than the denominator
7. b) $\frac{5}{2}$
8. 1 and 2
9. 15
10. a) A is a whole pie, while B is only $\frac{5}{6}$ of the hexagon shape
b) This example uses pieces that are the same size, but in different configurations, which leads to his conclusion.
$\frac{5}{2}$ is always > 1

**Worksheet NS4-53**
1. a) $\frac{1}{2}$
b) $\frac{3}{4}$
c) $\frac{2}{3}$
5. the same
6. a) $\frac{1}{3}$
b) $\frac{1}{2}$
c) $\frac{1}{2}$
8. a) $\frac{4}{6}$
b) $\frac{6}{9}$
c) $\frac{2}{4}$
11. Yes.

**Worksheet NS4-54**
1. b) $\frac{4}{5}$
2. b) $\frac{1}{4}, \frac{3}{4}$
5. a) 2 plates
b) 3 plates
c) 3 plates
6. a) 2
b) 5
c) 4
d) 9
8. b) 5
c) 8
d) 10
e) 3
f) 5
g) 3
h) 3
9. a) 2 , 4
b) 3, 6, 9
c) 5, 10
14.
$\frac{1}{3} = 4$
$\therefore \frac{2}{3} = 2 \times 4 = 8$
$15 \div 3 = 5$
$5 \times 2 = 10$
15. a) less than half
b) less than half
c) half
d) more than half
16. No, because $\frac{1}{2}$ of 12 is 6, and 5 is less than 6.
18. a) less than one third
b) more than one third
c) one third
d) more than one third
20. a) 6
b) 4
21. $ 6
22. a) 6
b) Yes. Check: the answer is more than 4 (current quilt) and less than 8 (what it would be if the current size were doubled)

**Worksheet NS4-56:**
3. a) $\frac{60}{100}$; 0.60
b) $\frac{46}{100}$; 0.46
c) $\frac{18}{100}$; 0.18
d) $\frac{50}{100}$; 0.50
e) $\frac{59}{100}$; 0.59
f) $\frac{40}{100}$; 0.40
g) $\frac{70}{100}$; 0.70
h) $\frac{76}{100}$; 0.76
i) $\frac{96}{100}$; 0.96
5. 0.40; 0.06; 0.09

**Worksheet NS4-57**
1. a) 1.23
b) 1.34
c) 0.47
d) 2.3
e) 4.54
4. a) 2.35
b) 1.03
5. a) 1.5
b) 2.71
c) 8.7
7. a) $\frac{6}{10}$
b) $1\frac{3}{10}$
c) $1\frac{8}{10}$
d) $2\frac{9}{10}$
12. a) $\frac{7}{10}$
b) $1\frac{1}{10}$
c) $2\frac{4}{10}$

**Worksheet NS4-58**
1. b) 0.5
2. a) zero
b) a half
c) one
3. a) less than
b) greater than
4. a) $\frac{3}{10}, \frac{5}{10}, \frac{7}{10}$
5. a) 1
b) 2
6. a) $1\frac{2}{10}, 3\frac{1}{10}, 3\frac{5}{10},$
9. a) $\frac{20}{100}, \frac{35}{100}, \frac{80}{100}$

**Worksheet NS4-59**
1. b) $\frac{99}{100}$
c) $\frac{68}{100}$
d) $\frac{58}{100}$
3. b) 0.97
c) 0.81
d) 0.97
e) 1.17
f) 0.41
g) 0.14
0.90
4. a) 0.49
b) 0.41
c) 0.58
d) 0.85
e) 0.97
f) 0.80
g) 0.47
h) 0.79
5. $\frac{42}{100}, \frac{84}{100}$
6. a) 2.35
b) 2.35
7. a) 3.39
b) 4.47
c) 4.13
8. b) 1.13
9. a) 2.13
b) 1.11
c) 2.43
10. a) 2.81
b) 2.36
c) 2.66
d) 7.61
e) 3.45
11. 0.09 km
12. 1397 kg
13. 7.13 m

**Worksheet NS4-60**
2. a) $\frac{1}{10}$ dm; 0.1 dm
b) $\frac{4}{10}$ dm; 0.4 dm
3. b) 3.2 dm
c) 8.8 cm
d) 1.78 m
e) 5.98 m
4. a) sorrel; birdwell, golden rod; clover
b) 2.5 m

**Worksheet NS4-61**
1. b) 28°C
c) 147°C
2. a) 0.09 m
3. a) 0.18 L
b) 3 minutes
4. b) 33
c) 9
d) 8
5. a) 1892
b) 67
c) 1984

**Worksheet NS4-62**
1. 3 for 120¢
2. 6 for 80¢
3. $3.75
4. 21
5. a) 70
b) 6
c) 9
d) 12
e) 138
6. 330
7. a) 10

b) 40
c) 8
10. Henry-8, Jane-4.
11. $13
12. $\frac{4}{11}$

# Measurement

**Worksheet ME4-1**
3. a) 5
b) 10
c) 20

**Worksheet ME4-2**
1. a) 2 cm
2. a) 3 cm
3. a) 3 cm
b) 2 cm
5. a) 3 cm
b) 5 cm

**Worksheet ME4-3**
1. a) 9 cm
b) 10 cm
c) 13 cm
d) 12 cm
e) 8 cm
2. a) 3 cm
b) 2 cm
3. a) Width = 2 cm
Length = 4 cm
b) sides = 3 cm, 4 cm
hypotenuse = 5 cm

**Worksheet ME4-4**
2. a) 20
b) 30
c) 50
d) 100
3. 40¢ (4x1x10)
4. $10 (10÷2 = 5 x 2)

**Worksheet ME4-5**
1. a) 24 mm
b) 38 mm
2. a) 38 mm
b) 18 mm
6. a) 50 mm
b) 19 mm
c) 45 mm
d) 25 mm
e) 12 mm
8. a) 52 mm
b) 6 mm
c) 45 mm
d) 12 mm
9. a) 3 cm, 25 mm
b) 4 cm, 40 mm
c) 2.5 cm, 25 mm
d) 1.5 cm, 15 mm
10. a) length 5 cm
width 2.5 cm
diagonal
56 mm, 5.6 cm
b) length 5 cm
width 2 cm
diagonal
54 mm, 5.4cm

**Worksheet ME4-6**
1. 10
2. 1/10
3. 10
4. 110, 570, 50,
70, 120, 350,
1120, 1700, 2930, 80,
2570, 320
5. 10
a) 4
b) 6
c) 210
d) 9
e) 32
f) 3
g) 91
h) 65
6. 50 mm, 8 cm, 120 mm, 14 cm
190 mm, 10 mm, 18 cm, 270 cm
70 mm, 1 cm, 9.1 cm, 1102 cm
7. a) 70 mm
b) 910 mm
c) 45 cm
d) 2 cm
e) 6200 mm
f) 72 cm
8. a) width = 1 cm
length = 5 cm
9. b) width = 1 cm
length = 7 cm
16. No. 2 cm = 20 mm
20 mm > 5 mm

**Worksheet ME4-8**
1. 10, 10
2. 10, 10
7. a) 800 m
b) 1600 m
c) 4
10. 100 (100 centimetres in 1 metre)
11. 1000 (1000 millimetres in 1 metre)
12. 100, 1400, 8000
2000, 19 000, 21 000
30, 650, 1060
13 a) No. Actual lengths are the same
b) Some are more appropriate for objects of a certain size than others
16. Yes, because 4 m x 100 = 400 cm (100 cm in 1 m)

**Worksheet ME4-9**
1. b) 10
2. a) 20
b) 20
3. a) 10
b) 20
4. 100
5. a) 100
b) 200
7. 500
9. a) < 1 km
b) > 1 km
c) < 1 km
d) close
10. a) 120
b) 110
c) 210
d) 260
11. a) 330
b) 370
c) 320
d) 590

**Worksheet ME4-10**
1. a) cm
b) km
c) m
4. a) m
b) dm
c) mm
d) m
5. a) mm
b) cm
c) m
d) km
e) m
8. a) m
b) m
c) km
d) km
e) km
f) km
g) km
h) m
9. a) km
b) km
c) cm
d) cm
e) m
f) m
g) m
h) m, m
i) cm
10. d) 235 mm; b) 25 cm;
c) 3 dm; a) 327 cm
12. a) mm
b) km
c) m
d) cm
e) km

**Worksheet ME4-15**
2. a) 5
b) 10
c) 2
d) 5
e) 25
f) 2
7. a) 10, 15, 20, 25, 26, 27, 28
9. a) 25, 50, 75, 85, 95
BONUS:
25, 50, 60, 70, 80, 85, 90, 91, 92
11 b) 5, 10, 15, 25, 35, 36
BONUS:
25, 50, 75, 100, 110, 120, 125, 130, 135, 136, 137, 138, 139
13 a) 39¢
b) 120¢
c) 180¢

BONUS:
82
75
76
184
14 a) 47
b) 72
c) 76
d) 51
BONUS:
113

**Worksheet ME4-16**
1. a) 19
b) 35, 40
c) 72, 77
d) 23, 28
e) 76, 81
f) 50, 55
3. a) 1¢
b) 5¢
c) 1¢
d) 25¢
e) 5¢
f) 25¢
4. a) 5¢, 5¢
b) 5¢, 5¢
c) 5¢, 5¢
d) 5¢, 5¢
e) 5¢, 5¢, 5¢
f) 5¢, 5¢, 5¢, 5¢, 5¢, 5¢
7. a) 10¢, 1¢
b) 10¢, 10¢
c) 10¢, 5¢
d) 5¢, 1¢
e) 5¢, 1¢
f) 10¢, 5¢
10 a) 25¢, 25¢, 10¢, 10¢, 10¢
b) 25¢, 25¢, 25¢, 5¢

**Worksheet ME4-17**
1. b) 10¢, 5¢, 1¢
c) 10¢, 10¢, 1¢, 1¢
d) 25¢, 10¢, 1¢, 1¢
2. a) 10¢, 5¢
b) 10¢, 10¢
5. a) 25¢
b) 50¢
c) 75¢
d) 75¢
e) 50¢
f) 50¢
g) 25¢
h) 25¢
i) 75¢
j) 75¢
k) 25¢
l) 50¢
6. b) 50¢; 6¢
c) 25¢; 8¢
d) 75¢; 10¢
e) 75¢; 22¢
8. 25¢, 25¢, 5¢
9. a) 25¢
b) $1
c) 10¢; $2
d) 25¢; $1
e) $2; $1; 25¢
f) $2, $2, 25¢; 5¢;
10. a) $1; 25¢
b) 25¢; 25¢
c) $2; $2; $2
d) $2; $2; $2; $1; 25¢; 25¢
e) $2; $2; $2; $2; $1; 25¢; 25¢; 25¢

**Worksheet ME4-18**
2. a) 33¢; $0.33

b) 47¢; $0.47
c) 76¢; $0.76
d) 85¢; $0.85
e) 71¢; $0.71
f) 57¢; $0.57

BONUS:
88¢; $0.88

**Worksheet ME4-19**

1. b) $6.11
   c) $4.25
   d) $6.55
   e) $10.07
   f) $20.11
2. b) 96; $0.96
   c) 150; $1.50
   d) 110; $1.10
3. quarters
4. loonies
5. 2 toonies, 1 loonie, 1 quarter

**Worksheet ME4-21**

1. $25.30; $85.32; 36¢; $10.05; $0.95; $18.50; $95.99; $0.17

**Worksheet ME4-22**

1. a) 8¢
   b) 16¢
   c) 9¢
   d) 4¢
   e) 2¢
   f) 7¢
   g) 3¢
   h) 1¢
   i) 4¢
5. a) 2→70→30; 32¢
   b) 8→80→20; 28¢
   c) 7→60→40; 47¢
   d) 7→30→70; 77¢
   e) 2→50→50; 52¢
   f) 6→90→10; 16¢
6. a) 14
   b) 36
   c) 73
   d) 54
   e) 48
   f) 61
   g) 3
   h) 44
   i) 11
7. a) 13
   b) 17

**Worksheet ME4-23**

1. a) 95
   b) 77
   c) 54
   d) 89
   e) 79
2. a) 58¢
   b) 89¢
   c) 49¢
   d) 89¢
4. a) $8.68
   b) $37.49
   c) $38.48
5. a) $44.58
   b) $24.39
6. a) $39.15
   b) $71.37
   c) $51.75
   d) $60.60
   e) $34.85
   f) $48.75
7. a) $30.01
   b) $55.93
8. Meera: $12.53
   Kyle: $11.24 ∴ Meera saved more
9. Anthony- Dog F
   Mike- Dog E
   Sandor- Dog A
   Tory- Dog B
10. $16.20
11. a) Yes. She has $6.00 left over and $6.00 is more than $3.29
    b) No. She has $1.50 left over and $1.50 is less than $2.25
12. a) $3.75
    b) 3
    c) 4
    (4 x $5.25 = $21.00)
    (5 x $5.25 = $26.25)

**Worksheet ME4-24**

1. a) $1.53
   b) $3.21
   c) $5.41
   d) $2.63
   e) $2.20
2. a) $0.40
   b) $1.42
3. a) $2.55
   b) $5.74
   c) $0.09
   d) $30.69
   e) $9.00
   f) $13.82
4. $0.77
5. $2.52
6. No. $2.00 short
7. $6.75

**Worksheet ME4-25**

1. a) $15.36
   b) $30.85
   c) $27.21
   d) $22.50
3. c), e), g), i), j), k) have cent amounts less than 50¢
4. b) $13.00
   c) $23.00
   d) $7.00
   e) $37.00
   f) $12.00
   g) $48.00
   h) $412.00
   i) $4.00
   j) $35.00
   k) $30.00
   l) $46.00
5. b) $8.00
   c) $9.00
   d) $5.00
   e) $16.00
   f) $40.00
   g) $42.00
6. Actual $7.73
   Estimate $8.00
7. Actual $14.56
   Estimate $15.00
8. Actual $42.59
   Estimate $43.00
9. Actual $41.34
   Estimate $42.00
10. a) Actual $1.92
    Estimate $2.00
    b) Actual $27.06
    Estimate $27.00
11. Yes. Estimate $9.00 + $7.00 = $16.00 which is less than $16.95
12. Because both amounts round to $7.00

# Measurement: Time

**Worksheet ME4-28**

3. 3:52
4. 1 hour and 45 minutes
5. 8:15 pm

**Worksheet ME4-29**

4. a) 12 or 13 days
   b) around 11 cm
7. a) Hours: 24→48→72→96
   b) Days: 7→14→21→28
   c) Weeks: 52→104→156→208
   d) Days: 365→730→1095

**Worksheet ME4-30**

5. a) 20
   b) 2
   c) 300
   d) 12
   e) 4
   f) 50

# Measurement: Area

**Worksheet ME4-32**

1. a) 12 cm$^2$
   b) 7 cm$^2$
   c) 14 cm$^2$
2. a) 4 cm$^2$
   b) 8 cm$^2$
   c) 3 cm$^2$
3. A= 8 cm$^2$
   B= 4 cm$^2$
   C= 12 cm$^2$
6. Rectangle should be 4 cm × 2 cm

**Worksheet ME4-33**

1. a) 3 × 5
   b) 2 × 4
   c) 3 × 2
2. b) 4 cm × 4 cm = 16 cm$^2$
   c) 2 cm × 4 cm = 8 cm$^2$
   d) 6 cm × 2 cm = 12 cm$^2$
3. a) 7 cm × 2 cm = 14 cm$^2$
   b) 3 cm × 3 cm = 9 cm$^2$
   c) 3 cm × 5 cm = 15 cm$^2$
4. a) 3 cm × 3 cm = 9 cm$^2$
   b) 2 cm × 3 cm = 6 cm$^2$
   c) 2 cm × 4 cm = 8 cm$^2$
   d) 4 cm × 3 cm = 12 cm$^2$
   e) 2 cm × 5 cm = 10 cm$^2$

**Worksheet ME4-34**

1. a) 15 cm$^2$
   b) 2 cm$^2$
   c) 10 cm$^2$
2. a) 40 m$^2$
   b) 54 cm$^2$
   c) 50 m$^2$
   d) 60 km$^2$
   Order from greatest to least area: D, C, A, B.
3. a) 35 m$^2$
   b) 18 m$^2$
   c) 48 cm$^2$
4. 2 cm
5. 5 cm
6. 3 cm
9. a) 36 cm$^2$
   b) 16 cm$^2$
   c) 20 cm$^2$

**Worksheet ME4-35**

1. a) 3 whole squares
   b) 2 whole squares
   c) 3 whole squares
   d) 2 whole squares
   e) 4 whole squares
   f) 8 whole squares
   g) 5 whole squares
   h) 4 whole squares
   i) 6 whole squares
   j) 6 whole squares
   k) 8 whole squares
2. c) 6 whole squares
3. a) equal;
   shaded: 4 squares
   unshaded: 4 squares
   b) less than;
   shaded: 3 squares
   unshaded: 4 squares

**Worksheet ME4-36**

1. a) 6 half squares
   3 total squares
   b) 8 half squares
   4 total squares
   c) 14 half squares
   7 total squares
2. b) 3 full squares
   4 ½ squares
   =2 full squares
   Area = 3 + 2 = 5
   c) 11 full squares
   4 ½ squares
   =2 full squares
   Area = 11 + 2 = 13
   d) 3 full squares
   4 ½ squares
   =2 full squares
   Area = 3 + 2 = 5
3. a) 2 half-squares
   (= 1 full squares)
   + 6 full squares
   = 7 total squares
   b) 4 half-squares
   (= 2 full squares)

+ 8 full squares
= 10 total squares

**Worksheet ME4-37**

1.

| | Perimeter | Area |
|---|---|---|
| B | 20 cm | 24 cm$^2$ |
| C | 26 cm | 22 cm$^2$ |
| D | 18 cm | 14 cm$^2$ |
| E | 30 cm | 44 cm$^2$ |
| F | 16 cm | 16 cm$^2$ |
| G | 16 cm | 7 cm$^2$ |

2. No
3. D, F
4. E, C, B, D, F/G, A
5. E, B, C, F, D, G, A
6. No

**Worksheet ME4-38**

1.

| | P | A |
|---|---|---|
| B | 10 cm | 6 cm$^2$ |
| C | 14 cm | 10 cm$^2$ |
| D | 18 cm | 14 cm$^2$ |
| E | 12 cm | 8 cm$^2$ |
| F | 14 cm | 12 cm$^2$ |
| G | 16 cm | 12 cm$^2$ |

2. a) P = 14 cm; A= 10 cm$^2$
   b) P = 8 cm; A = 3 cm$^2$
   c) P = 10 cm; 6 cm$^2$
3. a) 6 cm$^2$
   b) 20 cm$^2$

# Measurement: Mass

**Worksheet ME4-39**

14. a) 15 g
    b) 9 g
    c) 24 g
    d) 14 g
    e) 5 quarters
16. a) 13 kg
    b) 55 g
17. 529 kg
18. 6 kg (6000 g)
19. a) $24
    b) 120 g
    c) 30 kg

# Measurement: Capacity

**Worksheet ME4-40**

5. a) 4 containers
   b) 4 containers
   c) 4 containers of B
6. a) 10 containers
   b) 5 containers
   c) 2 containers
   d) 4 containers
7. 1000 mL or 1 L

**Worksheet ME4-41**

11. a) 4 250 mL bottles
    b) 2 tubs
12. 2700 mL
13. a) 6 times
    b) 3 uses of the 5 L can
    1 use of the 2 L can

**Worksheet ME4-42**

2. a) 8 cubes
   b) 12 cubes
   c) 27 cubes
7. a) bottom: 8 cubes
   second: 6 cubes
   top: 4 cubes
   b) bottom: 25 cubes
   second: 9 cubes
   top: 1 cube
8. Add all the layers of cubes together and multiply by 3 (105 cubes).
9. a) 2 | 1 | 1
   b) 2 | 3 | 1
   1
10. a) 1 | 2 | 1
    b) 2 | 1 | 1
    2 | 1 | 1
    c) 1 | 1 | 1
    1
    1 | 1 | 1
    d) 1 | 3 | 2 | 1

**Worksheet ME4-43**

1. a) Rectangle should be 5 × 2.
   b) Rectangle should be 3 × 4.
2. a) 10 triangles
   b) 18 triangles
   c) 18 triangles
3. a) 22 full squares
   b) 48 – 22 = 26 squares
5. b) 4 m
   c) $84
   d) $10.08
   e) $1.92
6. a) less than half
   b) half
7. a) 1 hour because the areas are equal.
   b) 3 hours because she's painted a quarter of the total area.

# Probability and Data Management

**Worksheet PDM4-1**

1. c) House pets: 3
   Farm animals: 3
   Zoo animals: 2
2. a) Wood: 4
   Glass: 1
   Metal: 3
   b) Green: 3
   Blue: 2
   Red: 5
   (assuming the apples are red)
6. a) with pattern: A, D, F, G, H, J
   without pattern: B, C, E, I
   b) patterned: 6 shirts
   no pattern: 4 shirts
   c) dark w/pattern: 3

**Worksheet PDM4-2**

1. straight: A, C, F, J
   curved: B, E, I
   straight and curved: D, G, H
2. a) E, F, G
   b) A, B, C, D, E
   c) E
3. cat-3; gerbil-3; fish-4; lizard-2; turtle-2; dog-3

**Worksheet PDM4-3**

1. a) 5
   b) 3
   c) 6
2. a) ||||
   b) 𝍸 ||

**Worksheet PDM4-4**

1. b) July – 24 days
   May – 8 days
   c) August
   d) July
   e) 14; 30-16=14
3. blue: 12
   green: 8
   yellow: 6

**Worksheet PDM4-5**

1. a) scale of 2
   b) scale of 10
   c) scale of 3
   d) scale of 5

**Worksheet PDM4-6**

1. a) 10
   b) No
   c) 2 students
2. 4 students

**Worksheet PDM4-7**

1. a) January – March
   b) July – September
2. a) 200 cm
   b) January – March
   c) 300 cm
3. a) A=12.5; B=20
   b) B=11
   c) B=12; C=3

**Worksheet PDM4-8**

1. a) non-fiction
   b) $\frac{1}{4}$
   c) $\frac{3}{4}$
   d) 5
2. a) apple
   b) $\frac{1}{6}$
   c) $\frac{1}{6}$
   d) 6

**Worksheet PDM4-12**

1. b) 4
   c) 6
   d) Italy
   e) Canada
   f) Italy; Korea; Greece; Brazil; Canada
   g) 32
   h) 6
   i) Korea

**Worksheet PDM4-13**

1. a) heads, tails
   b) 1, 2, 3, 4, 5, 6
   c) 4 possible outcomes
2. a) 6
   b) 2
   c) 3 (win, loss, draw)
5. a) 3
   b) 2
   c) 4
   d) 6

**Worksheet PDM4-14**

1. a) 4
   b) 4 for each colour
2. a) 2
   b) 2 for each colour
3. a) 2
   b) 2 for each colour
4. a) 3
   b) 3 for each colour
5. a) 8
   b) 6
   c) 4
   d) 9
6. red and heads;
   red and tails;
   green and heads;
   green and tails
7. 5¢ & 5¢;
   5¢ & 1¢;
   1¢ & 5¢;
   1¢ & 1¢
9. drama→painting
   drama→drawing
   drama→poetry
   music→painting
   music →drawing
   music →poetry
10. 4+4=8,
    4+6=10
    6+6=12
    6+4=10
11. 12 outcomes

**Worksheet PDM4-16**

1. a) 2; 4
   b) 1; 3
   c) 2; 4
   d) 3; 8
2. $\frac{3}{5}; \frac{1}{3}; \frac{1}{4}; \frac{1}{2}$
3. $\frac{1}{4}; \frac{2}{5}; \frac{1}{4}; \frac{1}{2}$
4. $\frac{1}{4}; \frac{3}{8}; \frac{1}{2}; \frac{3}{4}$
5. $\frac{1}{2}$
8. a) 1, 3, 5
   b) 3
   c) $\frac{3}{6}$
9. a) 1, 2, 3, 4
   b) 4
   c) $\frac{4}{6}$
10. a) i) 3, 4, 5, 6
    ii) $\frac{4}{6}$
    b) i) 2, 4, 6

ii) $\frac{3}{6}$

c) i) 3, 6

ii) $\frac{2}{6}$

11. b) $\frac{2}{4}$

12. $\frac{2}{6}$

**Worksheet PDM4-17**

1. a) 2; 4
   b) 3; 6
   c) 4; 8
2. a) 2
3. a) 2; 4
   b) 3; 6
5. a) 5
   b) 6
8. e) 24
   f) 26
   g) 42
   h) 44
9. g) 11
   h) 23
   i) 24
   j) 25
   k) 31
   l) 36
10 a) $\frac{1}{2}$
   b) 10
15. 5; 6; 9; 11; 17 R1; 20
16. 4; 6; 8; 11; 16; 23
17. e) 13
    f) 14
    g) 25
    k) 13
    l) 21
18. a) $\frac{2}{3}$
    b) $\frac{1}{4}$
19. a) 4
    b) 12
    c) 24
20. a) 4
    b) 12
    c) 23

**Worksheet PDM4-18**

1. a) less than half
   b) less than half
   c) half
   d) more than half
2. a) even
   b) less than half
   c) even
   d) more than half
3. a) unlikely
   b) likely
   c) unlikely
   d) likely
4. a) likely or unlikely (equal)
   b) unlikely
   c) likely
   d) likely
5. likely
6. likely; unlikely; impossible; certain
7. a) unlikely
   b) unlikely
   c) likely
   d) impossible
8. a) more probable than
   b) more probable than
   c) as probable as
   d) more probable than
   e) as probable as
   f) as probable as
9. red
10. a) certain
    b) likely
    c) impossible
11. Yes
12. Yes
13. No
14. circled: b), d)
15. a) not fair
    b) fair
17. No
18. A: impossible
    B: unlikely
    C: even
    D: certain
19. A: unlikely
    C: impossible
    D: likely

**Worksheet PDM4-19**

1. $\frac{1}{2}$
3. $\frac{1}{6}$
4. a) 4 times
   b) No
5. a) 5 times
6. c) $\frac{2}{6}$
   d) 4
7. a) 5, 10;
   10, 25;
   5, 25
   b) unlikely

# Geometry

**Worksheet G4-1**

1. c) 8 sides/verticies
   d) 12 sides/verticies
   e) 6 sides/verticies
   h) 8 sides/verticies
   i) 8 sides/verticies
   j) 10 sides/verticies
3.

| Shapes | Letters |
|---|---|
| triangles | A |
| quadrilaterals | B, F,G, H |
| pentagons | D, C |
| hexagons | E, I |

**Worksheet G4-5**

1.

| Property | Shape w/ prop. |
|---|---|
| quadrilateral | A, C, E, G, J, L |
| non-quatrilateral | B, D, F, H, I, K |

2. a) A, B, D, E, F
   b) A, B, E
   c) C, G
   d) 5 sides
   e) quadrilaterals
   f) A (not quadrilateral)

**Worksheet G4-6**

2.

| No pair | 1 pair | 2 pairs |
|---|---|---|
| E | C, G | A, B, D, F, H |

3. a)

| Property | Shape with property |
|---|---|
| no 90° | B, G, I, K |
| 1 90° | J |
| 2 90° | D, E, F |
| 4 90° | A, C, H |

b)

| Property | Shape with property |
|---|---|
| no parallel | B, J |
| 1 pair | D, E, F, I |
| 2 pairs | A, C, G, H, K |

5. a)

| Property | Shape with property |
|---|---|
| equilateral | B, G, H, J |
| not equilateral | A, C, D, E, F, I |

b)

| Property | Shape with property |
|---|---|
| no 90° | A, B, F, H, I, J |
| 1 90° | I |
| 2 90° | D, E |
| 4 90° | C, G |

c)

| Property | Shape with property |
|---|---|
| no parallel | B, I, J |
| 1 pair | A, D, E |
| 2 pairs | C, F, G, H |

d)

| Shape | Shape with property |
|---|---|
| triangles | B, I |
| quadril-aterals | A, C, F, G, H |
| pentagons | D, E, J |

**Worksheet G4-7**

9. a) all
   b) no
   c) no
   d) some
10. rectangle, square
11. square, rhombus
15. a) rhombus
    b) rectangle
    c) trapezoid

**Worksheet G4-8**

1. 4, 6
2. 1, 2, 3, 5, 7 (congruent pairs: 1&2, 3&5)
3. 4, 6

**Worksheet G4-9**

7. 1 non-congruent shapes
   3 non-congruent shapes
8. b) 3 non-congruent shapes
   c) 4 non-congruent shapes
9. a) 3 non-congruent shapes
   b) 4 non-congruent shapes

**Worksheet G4-10**

2. a) 3 times
   b) 3 times
   c) 5 times
   d) 4 times
3. a) 6 cm
   b) 15 cm
   c) 12 cm
   d) 20 cm
6. b)

| | Original | New shape |
|---|---|---|
| A | 1 | 4 |
| B | 2 | 8 |
| C | ½ | 2 |
| D | 1 | 4 |

c) The area is multiplied by 4.

**Worksheet G4-11**

7.

| Shape | Lines of sym. |
|---|---|
| square | 4 |
| rectangle | 2 |
| rhombus | 2 |
| parallelogram | 0 |

12. Figures will all have lines of symmetry equal to the number of edges

**Worksheet G4-12**

1.

| Prop. | F.1 | F.2 | S? | D? |
|---|---|---|---|---|
| vertices | 3 | 3 | √ | |
| edges | 3 | 3 | √ | |
| par. sides | 0 | 0 | √ | |
| 90° | 0 | 1 | | √ |
| symmetry | Y | N | | √ |
| lines of symmetry | 1 | 0 | | √ |
| equilat. | N | N | √ | |

**Worksheet G4-13**

1. b) 1: D
   2: B, F
   1&2: C, H
   c) 1: A, C
   1&2: D, E, H
3.

| Shape | Quad l | Equil | 2 paral. sides | 1+ 90° angle |
|---|---|---|---|---|
| A | N | Y | N | N |
| B | N | N | N | Y |
| C | Y | N | Y | N |
| D | Y | Y | Y | Y |
| E | N | Y | N | N |

7. a) equilateral triangle
   b) rhombus
   c) rectangle, parallelogram
   d) trapezoid

**Worksheet G4-14**

1. 16
2. A: trapezoid
   B: trapezoid
   C: square
   D: square
   E: rectangle
   F: rectangle
4. 30 m
6. congruent: A and H, similar: A and F, H and F

**Worksheet G4-19**

1. B: 6 right, 2 down
   C: 1 down, 2 left
   D: 5 right, 4 up
   E: 4 up
2. b) 1 down 3 left
   c) 4 right, 1 down
   d) 2 up, 1 left
   e) 1 right, 3 down
   f) 4 down, 2 left
3. b) (1,2)
   c) (2,0)
   d) (4,4)

e) (4,4)
f) (4,4)

4. a) C
b) A
c) B
d) 2 down, 1 right
e) 3 right, 1 up
f) 2 down, 2 left

5. d) 3 south, 1 west
e) 2 west, 2 north
f) 3 east, 1 north

6. d) 1 south, 3 west
e) 1 east, 2 north

**Worksheet G4-20**

1. a) (F,1)
b) (A,5)
c) (D,2)
d) (G,2)
e) Victoria
f) Atlantic Ocean
g) Quebec

**Worksheet G4-24**

5. a) 1: 180°
2: 90°
b) 1: 90°
2: 180°
c) 1: 180°
2: 90°

6. a) 1: 180°
2: R
b) 1: 180°
2: R
c) 1: R
2: 180°

**Worksheet G4-25**

1. a) reflection
b) slide
c) ¼ turn, counter-clockwise

4. a) reflection – line 1
b) slide – 1 up
c) ¼ turn clockwise
d) reflection – line 2

5. a) reflection – line 2, slide – 1 up ( in either order)
b) slide – 1 left, slide – 1 up (in either order)
c) ¼ turn counter-clockwise, slide down (in either order)
d) reflection – line 2, slide down (in either order)

**Worksheet G4-26**

1. a)

| | B | C | D | E |
|---|---|---|---|---|
| F | 4 | 6 | 6 | 5 |
| V | 4 | 8 | 8 | 6 |
| E | 6 | 12 | 12 | 9 |

**Worksheet G4-27**

1.

| Name | Base | F | E |
|---|---|---|---|
| triang. pyramid | triangle | 4 | 6 |
| square pyramid | square | 5 | 8 |
| penta. pyramid | pentagon | 6 | 10 |
| triang. prism | triangle | 5 | 9 |
| cube | cube | 6 | 12 |
| penta. prism | pentagon | 7 | 15 |

**Worksheet G4-28**

1.

| | B. sides | E | V |
|---|---|---|---|
| triang. pyramid | 3 | 6 | 4 |
| square pyramid | 4 | 8 | 5 |
| penta. pyramid | 5 | 10 | 6 |
| hex. pyramid | 6 | 12 | 7 |

4. The number of edges is twice the number of sides of the base.

5. 16 edges, 9 vertices

6.

| | B.sides | E | V |
|---|---|---|---|
| triang. prism | 3 | 9 | 6 |
| cube | 4 | 12 | 8 |
| penta. prism | 5 | 15 | 10 |
| hex. prism | 6 | 18 | 12 |

9. The number of edges is three times the number of sides on the base.

10. 24 edges, 16 vertices

**Worksheet G4-29**

4. Circle: a), f), h)

**Worksheet G4-31**

3.

| | Rect. prism | Sq.. pyr. | S? | D? |
|---|---|---|---|---|
| Base | rect-angle | squ-are | | √ |
| # B | 2 | 1 | | √ |
| # F | 4 | 4 | √ | |
| #E | 12 | 8 | | √ |
| # V. | 8 | 5 | | √ |

6.

| Shape | E | V | F |
|---|---|---|---|
| tri. pyram. | 6 | 4 | 4 |
| rect. prism | 12 | 8 | 6 |
| tri. prism | 9 | 6 | 5 |
| squ. pyram. | 8 | 5 | 5 |

8. E Cone
B Triangular Prism
A Cube
D Cylinder
C Triangular Pyramid

**Worksheet G4-32**

1. 1: B, D, E
2: A, C, D, E, F

2. 1: A, C, D
2: B, D,

**Worksheet G4-33**

2. 1: D
2: C, E, F
1 and 2: A, G
1: A, E
2: B
1 and 2: C, F, G

3. a) 1: shapes with 4 sides
2: shapes with 2 right angles
b) 1: triangles
2: equilateral

9. a) all of them

**Worksheet G4-35**

8. a) square based pyramid triangular prism
b) cube, hexagonal pyramid
c) pentagonal pyramid, triangular prism

# Logic and Systematic Search

**Worksheet LSS4-1**

2. a) 6, 7, 8, 9
b) 5, 6, 7, 8, 9
c) 0, 1, 2, 3, 4
d) no values
e) 0, 1, 2
f) 2, 3, 4, 5, 6, 7, 8, 9
g) 0, 1, 2, 3, 4, 5, 6
h) 8, 9
i) 0, 1, 2, 3, 4, 5, 6, 7, 8
j) 0, 2, 4, 6, 8
k) 1, 3, 5, 7, 9
l) 4, 8
m) 2, 4, 6, 8
n) 3, 6, 9
o) 7

3. b) 3, 5, 7, 9
c) 1, 3, 5, 7
d) 0, 2, 4, 6, 8
e) 5, 7
f) 4, 5, 6, 7, 8, 9
g) 2, 4, 6, 8
h) 4, 8
i) 6
j) 5
k) 3, 9

**Worksheet LSS4-2**

1. a) 19; 14; 9; 4
b) 9; 7; 5; 3; 1
c) 24; 19; 14; 9; 4
d) 7, 5, 3, 1
e) 16, 11, 6, 1
f) 19, 14, 9, 4

2. Because 3 quarters or more would be greater than 55¢.

4. 0 + 9; 1 + 8; 2 + 7; 3 + 6; 4 + 5

6. a) 12; 12; 4
b) 18; 10; 8

7. a) 1 dog, 2 birds
b) 1 cat, 3 birds
c) 1 tricycle, 3 bicycles
d) 3 tricycles, 2 bicycles

8. a) 12, 21, 30
b) 15, 51, 42, 24, 33, 60
c) 11, 22, 33, 44, 55, 66, 77, 88, 99

9. 1 quarter will not work

**Worksheet LSS4-3**

1. a) 7
b) 9
c) 5
d) 3
e) 3
f) 4
g) 2

2. a) 91
b) 75
c) 40
d) 55
e) 75
f) 52

3. a) 12, 21, 30
b) 14, 41, 23, 32, 50
c) 11, 22, 33, 44, 55, 66, 77, 88, 99

4. b) 11
c) 12
d) 22

5. a) 32
b) 14
c) 55
d) 99
e) 33
f) 66

6. a) 4
b) 3
c) 6
d) 7
e) 9
f) 1

7. a) 555
b) 226
c) 923
d) 248
e) 834
f) 892
g) 333
h) 555

**Worksheet LSS4-4**

3. a) 3 and 2 or 4 and 1
b) 5 and 3 or 6 and 2

4. a) 9876
b) 1023
c) 8796
d) 4986

5. a) 2 boxes of 4
b) 2 boxes of 5
c) no combination
d) 1 box of 4 and 2 boxes of 5
e) no combination
f) 2 boxes of 4 and 2 boxes of 5
g) 1 box of 4 and 3 boxes of 5
h) 4 boxes of 4 and 1 box of 5

6. a) 4 and 2
b) 3 and 3
c) 4 and 3
d) 6 and 2